California
Real Estate Law

Fourth Edition

Walter Huber, M.S.
Professor of Business and Real Estate
Glendale College

Kim Tyler, J.D.
Professor of Law and Real Estate
Shasta College

Review Editors

Ed Culbertson
MiraCosta College

Shadrick Jefferies
San Diego Mesa College

Edwin Estes, Jr.
Palomar College

Evelyn Winkel
Rancho Santiago College

Steve Zipperman
Rancho Santiago College

COPYRIGHT© 1989, 1991, 1997, 1999, 2001, 2003

EDUCATIONAL TEXTBOOK COMPANY, INC.
P. O. Box 3597
Covina, California 91722
(626) 339-7733
FAX (626) 332-4744
www.etcbooks.com (Wholesale orders)
Call Glendale College Bookstore (For placing single orders - see form on page 564)
1-818-240-1000 ext. 3024
www.walthuber.com (Constructive suggestions are welcome)

Library of Congress Cataloging-in-Publication Data
California Real Estate Law/ Kim Tyler and Walt Huber

Summary: Covers all material in California Real Estate Law classes with special emphasis on California real estate laws. Very clear and simple language, easy-to-read format with photographs, charts and graphs. Includes glossary and index; suitable for the consumer, students and teachers seeking information about personal real estate transactions.

1. Real estate business-Law and legislation-California 2. Real estate property-California Real estate 3. Real property-California

346.79404 [347.9406437]
ISBN: 0-916772-38-1

This publication is designed to provide accurate and authoritative information in regard to the subject matter covered. It is sold with the understanding that the publisher is not engaged in rendering legal, accounting, or other professional service. If legal advice or other expert assistance is required, the services of a competent professional person should be sought.

From a Declaration of Principles jointly adopted by a Committee of the American Bar Association and a Committee of Publishers' Associations.

"Any real estate textbook that doesn't include relevant Internet information is not only incomplete, but does a disservice to students." Walt Huber

Preface

T M

In this fourth edition of **CALIFORNIA REAL ESTATE LAW**, we've not only simplified legal concepts, but we've updated the format to include Internet addresses.

In order to make navigating the Web easier, we've introduced **"Hubie the Real Estate Internet Mouse."** Hubie stands next to, and clearly marks, all Websites—making key Internet topics leap off the page and creating an easily accessible reference tool.

This unique approach makes **CALIFORNIA REAL ESTATE LAW** not only an excellent beginning Real Estate textbook, but also an essential review and reference book for buyers, sellers, and their agents. Our primary purpose is to provide the most current and comprehensive information to real estate brokers and salespersons, and to help students planning to take the California Real Estate Salesperson's or Broker's License Examination.

In addition to listing pertinent Internet Websites, this book covers all matters related to the ownership and transfer or real property. We've included all the commonly used forms, such as the CAR eight-page deposit receipt, as well as information about disclosures, such as Megan's Law and the Natural Hazard Disclosure Law. At the end of each chapter, you'll find a list of vocabulary words, as well as a multiple-choice quiz, and a case problem to test the reader's comprehension of the material. In addition, answers are listed at the end of each chapter, so students can test themselves and work at their own pace.

We want to express our appreciation to the many people who have helped make this textbook possible. Helpful suggestions have been received from the California Department of Real Estate, the California Association of Realtors®, and our statewide family of faculty advisors.

Special thanks also to the people who helped design and produce this book: Philip Dockter, art director; Melinda Winters, cover design; and Rick Lee, executive editor. Additions and revisions were made with the help of Donna Grogan, CPM from El Camino College; and Albert Ramseyer JD, Attorney, County Counsel, County of Los Angeles.

I must also offer special recognition to our legal review editors: Ed Culbertson, JD, MiraCosta College; Shadrick Jefferies, JD, San Diego Mesa College; Edwin Estes Jr., JD, Palomar College; Evelyn Winkel, JD and Steve Zipperman, JD, Santa Ana College; Robert Von Esch, Jr., JD, Fullerton College; the late, joyful Ray L. Bennigson, College of Marin; and Aaron D. Grossman, Shasta College.

We include Internet sites*, so you can get the latest information "instantly!"

TM

Our Internet ICON is "Hubie," a mouse who is placed in front of each of our LAW Websites.

Just look for "Hubie" and you'll find an Internet Address that will give you information on the subject being discussed, or a related topic.

*Educational Textbook Company does not necessarily endorse or support any Internet site. Internet sites are provided for informational purposes only.

Educational Textbook Company is not responsible for Internet sites that have been altered, upgraded, or deleted.

Table of Contents

Table of Contents

Table of Contents

Table of Contents

CHAPTER 1
An Introduction to Law

CHAPTER OVERVIEW

This chapter is a broad survey of the legal system in the United States, with a particular focus on California's system. It begins with a discussion of the nature and purposes of the law, and explains some fundamental legal categories and concepts. It goes on to discuss the sources of law: constitutions, legislatures, courts, and administrative agencies. It also examines the judicial system in detail, and describes a typical lawsuit from its outset through enforcement of the judgment.

You should come away from this chapter with a better understanding of how laws are made and how legal rights are enforced. This information serves as a backdrop for the rest of the book.

Law and the Real Estate Profession

The law has a tremendous impact on the work of a real estate agent. Hundreds of federal, state, and local laws control the use and transfer of real property. They affect property values and shape transactions. In addition, the real estate profession itself is strictly regulated. Laws prescribe the agent's qualifications and his or her duties to clients, customers, and employees.

The impact of law is growing, too. In some areas (environmental law, for example) regulations have multiplied dramatically in recent years. In other areas, legal standards of conduct are being raised: a landlord or a broker might now be held liable for conduct that would not have been the basis for a lawsuit 15 years ago.

Chapter 1

Avoiding liability is one of the most compelling reasons to learn about the law. It's a rare real estate agent that isn't at least threatened with a lawsuit from time to time. Even if you would never think of doing anything dishonest, you could end up paying for the consequences of an innocent mistake. A firm grasp of your duties toward the buyer and seller minimizes the risk that you will be sued.

Sometimes a well-informed agent can also prevent litigation between the buyer and seller. By recognizing issues that could give rise to a lawsuit, you can help the parties clarify their agreement and avoid misunderstandings.

Learning about the law is not just a matter of memorizing rules, however. It's important to understand where the rules come from and what backs them up. "The seller's agent must conduct a diligent visual inspection of the property." Who says so? What happens if that rule is ignored? How is it enforced? Can the rule be challenged or changed? Knowing how the legal system works gives the rules substance. And in learning how laws are developed, you'll see that it is sometimes possible to influence the process to advance your clients' interests or your own.

Of course, learning about the law won't enable you to give clients legal advice, or to act without legal advice yourself. But it will give you a clearer sense of when legal advice is needed. And when it is needed, you'll be better equipped to assist a client's lawyer or your own lawyer in analyzing the situation and preparing the case.

The Nature and Functions of Law

The law is a system of rights and duties established and enforced by a government. It takes the form of general rules that citizens and everyone else in the government's domain must obey.

> **Example:** The law sets out rights and duties connected with land ownership. As a landowner, A has a legal right to the exclusive possession of his property. This creates a corresponding legal duty for others to avoid entering the property without permission. If someone violates this rule, the government, through the legal system, will enforce A's rights by ejecting the trespasser.
>
> On the other hand, A has a legal duty to maintain the property so that a person entering it at his request will be reasonably safe. If A fails to live up to this duty and someone is injured as a result, the court, through the legal system, will enforce A's duty by requiring him to pay compensation to the injured person.

Functions of Law

The law serves a number of related functions:

◆ establishes order,
◆ resolves disputes,
◆ enforces promises,
◆ prevents exploitation, and
◆ promotes equality.

Most basically, law establishes order. Without law, might makes right: the strong and ruthless use violence and the threat of violence to dominate anyone who is weaker. But the law lays down rules of conduct based on other considerations besides brute force. A court or other tribunal serves as a forum for resolving disputes without violence. Thus, law makes it possible for people to live together more or less peacefully.

An important function of the law in any complex society is the enforcement of promises. Commerce depends on promises: a builder who agrees to construct a house must be able to rely on the owner's promise to pay for the house. Otherwise, the builder would have to demand payment in advance; but in that case, the owner would have to rely on the builder's promise to go through with the work. By enforcing certain promises called contracts, the law makes it possible to plan ahead and to deal with strangers.

In the United States today, the law reflects widely accepted ideas of fairness and equality. We have laws intended to protect people not merely from physical force, but from many forms of exploitation. For example, a real estate agent is not allowed to take unfair advantage of a buyer by misrepresenting or concealing facts about a property. We also have laws that promote equal treatment: a real estate agent may not refuse to show a couple a house because of their race or religion.

MORALITY AND EFFICIENCY

Laws preventing exploitation and promoting equality are examples of "sociological jurisprudence": law is used as a tool for reforming society. But law has also been used as a tool for oppression. For example, in the 1850s and 1860s, many white Californians felt their jobs were threatened by an influx of Chinese immigrants who were willing to work for low wages. The state and city governments responded to this situation by issuing tax and licensing laws designed to create social and economic hardships for the Chinese.

It's clear that a society's laws are closely connected to its ideas of justice and morality. But although the law reflects and often changes with public morality, they are by no means the same thing. There are many moral issues that the law does not address, leaving them up to the individual's conscience, to families, to churches and other organizations, and to public opinion.

Morality is not the only force that shapes the law. Efficiency, rather than justice, is the goal of many rules. When there are two ways of doing something, both may be equally effective. Yet a law (a building code, for example) may arbitrarily choose one method and require everyone to use it, because uniform procedures help society run more smoothly.

Historical Background

English Foundation. When English settlers colonized the New World, they brought English law with them. After gaining its independence, the United States retained many aspects of English law and legal institutions. These are still the foundation of the U.S. legal system.

For example, judges in the U.S. have played almost as great a role in establishing rules of law as our legislatures have (see the discussion of sources of law, below). This is based on the English model, and it contrasts with the European tradition. In France, Germany, Spain, and Italy, lawmaking has been more strictly reserved to the legislatures, and judicial decisions have not carried nearly as much weight.

Many of our basic legal concepts and rules were inherited directly from English **Common Law**, which is the body of law derived from judicial decisions rather than from statutes or constitutions.

> California Civil Code 22.2 provides that the "**common law** of England, so far as it is not repugnant to or inconsistent with the Constitution of the United States, or the Constitution or laws of this State, is the rule of decision in all the courts of this State."

Spanish Influence in California. The Spanish discovered California in 1542, and began to occupy it in 1769. California became Mexican territory in 1822, but was ceded to the U.S. in 1848 by the Treaty of Guadalupe Hidalgo. It became a state in 1850.

Under the treaty of Guadalupe Hidalgo, all public lands belonging to the Mexican government in California became public lands belonging to the U.S. government. However, the treaty provided that the U.S. would respect all private property rights established by the Mexican government.

A Board of Commissioners was appointed in 1851 to review Mexican land grants. Anyone claiming title to land in California based on a grant from the Spanish or Mexican government was required to present a claim to the commissioners for settlement. If they confirmed that the grant was valid, the claimant was issued a patent (an original deed) by the U.S. government. If the commissioners rejected the claim, the land became public.

Of course, California had been governed by Spanish and Mexican law while it was under Spanish and Mexican rule. U.S. law (with its English roots) displaced the Spanish and Mexican system.

But the Spanish left their mark in a few areas of law. For example, California's community property rules (see Chapter 4) originated in Spanish law. These rules are also used in a number of other western states, but they aren't used in eastern states, where the Spanish colonial role was very limited.

Legal Categories and Concepts

SUBSTANTIVE LAW AND PROCEDURAL LAW

In a complicated society like ours, the law covers a vast area. Mapping out some fundamental categories and concepts will make it easier to explore.

One of the most basic divisions in the law is the distinction between **substantive law** and **procedural law**. Substantive law establishes and defines rights and duties. Procedural law sets out the methods of enforcing substantive rights.

Example: The rule that an appurtenant easement runs with the land is substantive law. It gives a land purchaser a right, the right to use a previously established easement.

If the purchaser is prevented from using the easement and wants to assert her right to do so, she can start a lawsuit. There are rules prescribing how to go about it: file a complaint with the court, send a summons to the other party within a certain number of days, and so forth. These rules that set out the procedure for enforcing the easement rights are procedural law.

CRIMINAL LAW AND CIVIL LAW

Another fundamental distinction is the one between **criminal law** and **civil law**.

A person who fails to live up to a legal duty, or fails to respect another's legal right, may cause harm to another person or to property. The failure may be accidental or deliberate. The injury may be slight or serious; it may be physical, emotional, or financial.

Someone who has been injured as the result of another's act generally has the right to sue that person for compensation. The government offers a forum (the court) for resolving the dispute. When one individual sues another, it is called a civil suit, a civil action, or civil litigation.

Certain harmful or potentially harmful acts are classified as crimes. In general, crimes are those acts that are particularly dangerous to society.

Plaintiff—the person who files (starts) the lawsuit
Defendant—the person who defends against the lawsuit
Litigant—both plaintiff and defendant are called litigants

Example: Accidentally rear-ending another car causes harm, but it isn't a crime. Drunk driving is a crime (even if the driver has not caused an accident) because it has the potential to cause a great deal of harm.

Because crimes are so disruptive, the government takes a greater interest in them than it does in other harmful acts. Instead of simply offering the injured person an opportunity to sue, the government itself (represented by the public prosecutor) prosecutes the person accused of a crime. The government may start a criminal action without the victim's cooperation, or even if there was no victim. A civil suit, on the other hand, will only take place if the injured person decides to start one.

Civil cases and criminal cases have different purposes, so they offer different remedies. The goal of a civil suit is simply to compensate the injured person for the harm that was done. The remedy granted is usually a monetary award (called **damages**), paid by the person who caused the harm to the injured person. The damages award is usually limited to the financial losses that the injured person incurred. These might include lost profits or wages, money spent on repairs, or medical bills.

A criminal suit has broader goals: to punish the wrongdoer and prevent him or her from committing more crimes, and to deter others from committing similar crimes. The penalties are not based on paying for the damage done. A person convicted of a crime might have to pay a heavy fine to the government, even if the criminal act (such as drunk driving) did not result in any actual damage. He or she might also have to serve a jail sentence.

Keep in mind that the same harmful act might lead to both a criminal action and a civil action.

Example: A drunk driver causes an accident, injuring several people. The government brings a criminal action against the driver, resulting in a fine and a jail sentence. The criminal action does not compensate the victims, however. They will have to sue in civil court to force the driver to pay for their medical expenses, lost wages, and car repairs.

Real estate lawsuits are almost always civil, not criminal. The main exceptions to that rule are cases involving fraud. For example, the victim of a fraud can bring a civil suit for compensation. If the fraud was serious enough, the government will also impose criminal penalties. (See Chapter 6 for a discussion of fraud.)

Since most real estate disputes do not involve crimes, the focus of this chapter (and of the book as a whole) will be on civil law.

BASIC CIVIL LAW CONCEPTS

As our laws have grown more and more complex, it has become necessary for most lawyers to specialize in a particular area of law. Their specialties correspond to all the different areas in which disputes arise: real estate law, corporate law, family law, personal injury law, and so on. But there are three fundamental categories underlying all of these specialties:

- ◆ contracts,
- ◆ torts, and
- ◆ property

Each of these categories represents a group of basic legal concepts, relationships, and principles.

Contracts

A **contract** is a legally binding promise. When two people enter into a contractual relationship, they voluntarily take on legal (binding) duties toward on another.

Example: If A contracts to sell B his bike in exchange for $100, A has a legal duty to give B the bike, and B has a legal duty to pay A $100. Without the contract, A had no duty to give B the bike, and B had no duty to pay A $100. By entering into the contract, they voluntarily assumed these binding duties.

There is a whole body of rules that governs legal relationships based on contracts. These rules apply to real estate contracts, employment contracts, and sales contracts. They apply whether the contract concerns tomatoes, a condominium, or commercial shipping.

Various laws make special exceptions for certain kinds of contracts, but there are modifications of the basic rules that govern all contract relationships. These basic rules, as they apply to real property contracts, are discussed in detail in Chapter 7.

Torts

There are other legal duties that are not voluntarily assumed. Instead, they are imposed by law. The law requires everyone to take reasonable care to avoid injuring another person or damaging someone else's property. A failure to behave as a reasonable person would is a breach of this imposed duty; it is called a **tort**. ("Tort" is related to the French word that means "wrong". Torts are sometimes referred to as "civil wrongs," to distinguish them from criminal wrongs, or crimes.)

> **Example:** Running desperately through the depot to catch a train, A accidentally knocks B down. B's arm is broken in the fall. A has breached the legal duty to use reasonable care in passing through a public place; in other words, A has committed a tort against B.

Tort law is the body of concepts and rules concerning legally imposed duties and standards of reasonable conduct. There are rules for intentional and unintentional acts; public places and private homes; family members, business associates and total strangers. Torts connected with real estate are discussed in Chapters 6 and 15.

Property

Property law, concerns ownership of real or personal property. It includes rules about acquiring ownership and losing ownership, and about the rights and duties that ownership carries with it.

> **Example:** A gives B a deed granting B title to Blackacre, a piece of property in San Francisco. The deed confers the ownership of Blackacre onto B. The law grants B, as the owner, the right to use, encumber, will, sell, or ignore Blackacre. The law (in the form of a zoning ordinance) also places some restrictions on B's use of the property: B may build a house on Blackacre, but not a shopping mall. And the law imposes a duty on B to pay taxes on the property. These rights and duties are the automatic consequences of ownership.

Nearly every specialized area of law involves contract, tort, and property issues to some degree. A lawyer specializing in maritime law might have to deal with the legal problems surrounding a contract to ship goods to Japan, an accident at sea in which crew members were injured, and transferring ownership of a vessel.

Contract, tort, and property issues can also be presented in a single lawsuit.

Contract—a legally binding promise
Tort—breach of a duty imposed by law
Property law—laws concerning ownership of real or personal property

Example: A and B are neighbors. A has an easement over B's property for a driveway leading to his own property. A and B disagree about where the boundary between their lots is located.

A leased his house to C. A believes the lease expired at the end of the summer, but C won't give up possession, claiming the lease was supposed to last until the end of the year.

One day C slips in the driveway and breaks her collarbone. It's not clear whether she was on A's property or B's when she slipped, because of the boundary dispute.

In order to determine whether either A or B must compensate C for her injury, the lawyers will have to sort out contract issues (Had the lease expired? What evidence can be introduced to prove the contents of the agreement between A and C?), property issues (Who owned that part of the driveway? Did A have a responsibility to maintain the easement? Did C have a right to use the easement, or was she trespassing?), and tort issues (Did C slip because someone failed to make the driveway reasonably safe? Or was it because of her own carelessness?)

Sources of Law

Who makes the laws? The simple answer is that our government does. But in the United States "the government" has several facets, and all of them play a role in lawmaking.

Governmental power is divided between the federal government and the 50 independent state governments, and in each state there are regional and local governmental bodies. To complicate matters even more, there are different sources of law within the federal government and each of the state governments:

Sources of Law
1. **Constitutions**
2. **Legislatures**
3. **Courts**
4. **Administrative Agencies**

A single legal problem can involve both state and federal laws, and may be the subject of constitutional provisions, statutes, court decisions, and administrative regulations, all at the same time.

An Introduction to Law

CONSTITUTIONS

A **constitution** is a grant of power to a government. It sets out the government's basic structure and defines the limits of the government's power.

A constitution is, in effect, the fundamental law that all other laws must comply with. In issuing a new law, a government sometimes exceeds its constitutional power. Then the new law is **unconstitutional**: it is an illegal law, and cannot legally be enforced. Even a constitutional law can be applied by a government official in a way that oversteps the limits of the government's power. In that case, the law still stands, but the official's action is unconstitutional and illegal.

Constitutions are intended to be long-lasting documents that provide government stability. They can be changed (**amended**), but the procedure for amending a constitution is more difficult than the procedure for changing an ordinary law.

In the United States, there is a federal Constitution that applies to the whole country, and each of the states has its own constitution as well.

Federal Constitution

The United States Constitution was drawn up at the Constitutional Convention in 1787, approved by the states, and adopted in 1789. The Constitution declares itself to be the "supreme law of the land" (Article VI, Section 2).

www.nara.gov/exhall/charters/constitution/conmain.html
(U.S. Constitution)

POWER OF THE FEDERAL AND STATE GOVERNMENTS. The U.S. Constitution defines the relationship between the federal government and the state governments. Only the federal government may make laws concerning certain matters; these include interstate commerce, wars and the military, immigration, bankruptcy copyrights and patents, and the currency (Article 1, Section 8).

There are many other areas in which both the federal government and the state governments can and do make laws. Discrimination and environmental protection are examples.

There are also matters that are left up to the state governments. These include the ownership and transfer of real property. As a result, most of the laws affecting a piece of land are laws of whichever state the land is located in.

If there's a conflict between a federal law and a state law, the stronger rule prevails. If a federal air pollution law is tougher than a California air pollution law, a factory in California must comply with the federal standard. But if the federal law is less strict than the California law, the factory must comply with the California standard.

PROTECTION OF INDIVIDUAL RIGHTS. The first ten amendments to the U.S. Constitution are known as the Bill of Rights. They were adopted in 1791. The Thirteenth, Fourteenth, and Fifteenth Amendments were added soon after the Civil War. Together, these amendments protect the rights of individuals by limiting government power. The protections range from freedom of religion to the right to a jury trial.

Some of these amendments have a particular impact on property and the real estate profession. These include the following guarantees:

◆ due process,
◆ equal protection,
◆ just compensation, and
◆ no unreasonable searches or seizures.

Due Process. According to the Fifth and Fourteenth Amendments, no one shall be "deprived of life, liberty, or property without due process of law." This is known as the due process requirement. Due process requires a fair hearing by an impartial judge.

Example: A real estate agent is accused of grossly misrepresenting the condition of a home. The Real Estate Commissioner has the power to revoke an agent's license for this misconduct. But a real estate license is considered "property" for the purposes of the due process requirement. As a result, the Commissioner cannot deprive the agent of his license without first holding a hearing that gives the agent an opportunity to tell his side of the story.

Equal Protection. The Fourteenth Amendment also provides that the government may not deny an individual the "equal protection of the laws." The equal protection requirement prohibits governments from adopting laws that unfairly discriminate between different groups of people.

Many laws involve some sort of discrimination. For example, a law that says a person must have a real estate license to negotiate the sale of land can be said to discriminate against people who don't have licenses. But that discrimination is not considered unfair, since people with licenses are usually better qualified to negotiate land sales than people without licenses. Discrimination on the basis of race, ethnic background, or gender is considered unfair, however. That kind of discrimination generally violates the equal protection requirement.

Just Compensation. Another provision of the Fifth Amendment prevents the government from taking private property for public use "without just compensation." The government has the power to turn your land into a public garden or parking lot, but the Constitution requires the government to pay you for it. (See the discussion of eminent domain and condemnation in Chapter 10.)

Unreasonable Searches and Seizures. The Fourth Amendment prevents the government from making "unreasonable searches and seizures" of an individual's person or property. A search warrant issued by a judge is required, and a warrant may only be issued if there is "probable cause" for a search.

The Fourth Amendment is applied in criminal cases. In that context, probable cause means that the government must have reasonable grounds for believing that a search will uncover objects used in the commission of crime.

But the Fourth Amendment also applies to "administrative searches," such as a routine inspection by the fire department or health department. A search warrant is required for inspection of a residence or business, unless there is an emergency or the owner or occupant consents to the inspection.

It is not necessary to show that there is probable cause to believe the administrative search will uncover a code violation in a particular building. A legitimate government interest in conducting inspections in that neighborhood is a sufficient basis for the issuance of a search warrant. (*Camara v. Municipal Court*, 387 U.S. 523 [1967], and *See v. City of Seattle*, 387 U.S. 541[1967].)

State Action. It's important to understand that the federal Constitution's protection of individual rights is primarily protection against abuses by the government. It generally does not protect a person in relation to private individuals or entities. For the Constitution's protections to apply, there must be **state action**, which is action by a government or a government official.

> **Example:** The First Amendment protects freedom of speech. A city cannot pass a law or take action to prevent groups of protesters from gathering on city sidewalks or in city parks for political rallies. That interference with their freedom of speech would violate the First Amendment.

On the other hand, as far as the federal Constitution is concerned the owner of a shopping center may prevent the same groups from gathering in the center's mall or parking lot. Because the shopping center is private property, this policy does not involve state action, so it is not considered a violation of the First Amendment. *Hudgens v. NLRB,* 424 U.S. 507 (1967).

Due Process—the right to a fair hearing by an impartial judge

Equal Protection—the government may not adopt laws that unfairly discriminate between different groups of people

Just Compensation—if the government takes private property, it must compensate the owner

Unreasonable Search and Seizure—the government may not search you or your property without probable cause

State Action—action by a government or a government official

Yet a city or state may pass a law requiring shopping center owners to allow peaceful protests on their property. Such a law would make it a shopping center owner's interference with an orderly protest *illegal*, even though that interference would not be a violation of the federal Constitution. (*PruneYard Shopping Center v. Robins*, 447 U.S. 74 [1980]).

California State Constitution

The California state constitution was adopted in 1879. It begins with a Declaration of Rights. Among many other guarantees, Article 1, Section 1 provides: All people are by nature free and independent and have inalienable rights. Among these are enjoying and defending life and liberty, acquiring, possessing, and protecting property, and pursuing and obtaining safety, happiness, and privacy.

Many of the state constitutional rights overlap with those protected by the U.S. Constitution, such as freedom of speech and due process of law. But in some of these cases, the California constitution may offer greater protection than the U.S. Constitution. For example, the state constitution's freedom of speech provision has been interpreted to apply to shopping center owners as well as to governments, even though the federal Constitution's does not. (See *PruneYard Shopping Center v. Robins*, cited above.)

www.leginfo.ca.gov/const.html
(California State Constitution)

After its Declaration of Rights, the California constitution outlines the structure of the state government, and treats a variety of subjects (such as Education, Taxation, and Labor Relations) in detail. Articles X and XA are devoted to Water Law and Water Resources Development; Article XXXIV is called the Public Housing Project Law. Other sections of particular interest to property owners and real estate agents include Article XIV, Section 3, which provides for mechanics' liens; and Article XX, Section 1.5, which protects homesteads from forced sale. (See Chapter 3 for more information about mechanics' liens and homesteads.)

LEGISLATURES (Statutory Law)

Legislatures are the dominant source of new laws in the United States. Representatives elected to the U.S. Congress, the 50 state legislatures, and county and city councils across the country make thousands of new laws every year. The laws adopted by Congress and the state legislatures are called **acts** or **statutes**. The laws adopted by county and city councils are generally called **ordinances**.

The Legislative Process

The members of a legislative body write and adopt laws through a process of argument and compromise. Each legislative body has its own procedures. For example, here is a brief outline of the procedures used in Congress.

Congress is divided into two houses, the Senate and the House of Representatives. A proposed law (called a **bill**) is introduced in each house, often at the suggestion of a government agency (the Department of Housing and Urban Development) or a lobbying group (the National Association of Realtors®).

In each house, a legislative committee (such as the Banking Committee, or the Ways and Means Committee) analyzes and revises the bill. A Senate committee and a House committee often make different changes in a bill, so that different versions develop.

Next, the whole Senate and the whole House each consider and vote on that version of the bill. If a majority in either house votes against the bill, it dies. If a majority in each house votes in favor of the bill, the two versions must be reconciled. A conference committee of members from both houses works out a compromise version of the bill. If a majority in each house votes for version, the bill is passed.

The final stage of the legislative process involves the president. The president can express approval of the bill by signing it, or can take no action on it. Either way, the bill becomes law. But if the president **vetoes** the bill, it will not become law unless Congress votes to **override** the veto. To override a presidential veto, a two-thirds majority in each house must vote in favor of the bill. If the bill can't muster this strong support in Congress, it dies. If the veto is overridden, however, the bill becomes law in spite of the president's disapproval.

The California legislature follows a similar procedure. It is also divided into two houses, the state senate and the assembly. The state governor has the power to veto legislation.

A citizen can influence the legislative process. First, of course, you can vote for representatives who seem likely to promote your interests. You can also join or organize a lobbying group that will propose new legislation or revisions to the representatives. And when the legislature is considering a bill that you support or oppose, you can urge your representatives to vote for or against it.

Codification

Once a new statute or ordinance has been formally adopted, it is published. It is the legislature's pronouncement of what the law on a given issue will be, from the effective date forward. **Most legislation becomes effective on January 1 of the next year.**

Some statutory laws are simple and clear; many are long and complicated. Some address a very narrow issue; others cover a large area. At times a legislature will gather up all the laws on a particular subject, reconcile them and clarify them, then set them out systematically in a comprehensive statute called a **code**. This process is called **codification**.

www.romingerlegal.com/state/california.html#stat
(California State Codes)

In some states there are only a few codes, but the California legislature has codified most state law. Laws affecting property and the real estate profession are mainly found in the Civil Code and the Business and Professions Code.

CALIFORNIA STATE CODES

Business and Professions Code	Health and Safety Code
Civil Code	Insurance Code
Code of Civil Procedure	Labor Code
Commercial Code	Military and Veterans Code
Corporations Code	Penal Code
Education Code	Probate Code
Elections Code	Public Resources Code
Evidence Code	Public Utilities Code
Family Code	Revenue and Taxation Code
Financial Code	Streets and Highways Code
Fish and Game Code	Unemployment Insurance Code
Food and Agriculture Code	Vehicle Code
Government Code	Water Code
Harbors and Navigation Code	Welfare and Institutions Code

The Courts (Case Law)

Although legislatures are the main source of new law, the courts are also an important source. Courts do not issue general rules in the same way that legislatures do. A legislature can make laws on any subject it chooses (as long as it doesn't violate the federal or state constitution). A trial judge only addresses a point of law if it is at issue in a lawsuit. Then the law is developed in published written opinions of the Court of Appeal and Supreme Court in court cases that are referred to as **case law**.

CASE LAW CITATIONS

Judicial opinions are published in books called **case reports** or **reporters**. Case citations—references particular cases in the reporters—are given in a standardized form.

EXAMPLE: *Riddle v. Harmony,* **102 Cal. Apr. 3d 524 (1980)**

The citation includes the name of the case, followed by the volume (102) of the case reporter California Appellate Reports Third Series (Cal. Apr. 3d) where the opinion can be found. Then it states the page number (524) the opinion begins on. The citation ends with the year that the case was decided, in parentheses (1980).

There are separate case reporters for most state appellate courts in the country, as well as federal case reporters. In addition, there are regional reporters that compile important cases from state courts in a given region (the Pacific Reporter and the Northeastern Reporter, for example). Each reporter's title has its own abbreviation for purposes of citation. The **case reporter** abbreviations that a Californian is most likely to encounter are:

State Court Decisions
Decisions of the California Supreme Court:
 California Reports: Cal. (beginning to 1934); then Cal. 2d (1934-1969); then Cal. 3d (1969-1991); then Cal. 4th (1991-).

Decisions of the California Court of Appeal:
 California Appellate Reports: Cal. Apr (beginning to 1934); then Cal. Apr. 2d (1934-1969); then Cal. Apr. 3d (1969-1991); then Cal. Apr. 4th (1991-).

Decisions of both the California Supreme Court and Court of Appeal:
 California Reporter (began in 1960); Cal. Rptr (beginning to 1991); then Cal. Rptr. 2d (1991 -).

Decisions from state courts in California and 14 other western states:
 Pacific Reporter (dropped California Court of Appeal decisions) P., P.2d in 1930-).

 Example: *Reed v. King,* **145 Cal. Apr. 3d 261, 193 Cal. Rptr. 130 (1983).**

Federal Court Decisions
Decisions of the U.S. Supreme Court:
 United States Reports   **U.S.**
 Supreme Court Reporter   **S. Ct.**
Decisions of the U.S. Courts of Appeal (including the Ninth Circuit):
 Federal Reporter   **F., F.2d, F.3d**
Decisions of the U.S. District Courts:
 Federal Supplement   **F. Supp.**

A citation to a case from a federal court of appeals includes the circuit number in parentheses, along with the year the case was decided. So a Ninth Circuit decision would be cited like this:

 Trident Center v. Connecticut General Life Ins. Co., **847 F.2d 564 (9th Cir. 1988)**

And a citation to a case from a federal district court includes the name of the district in the parentheses. A decision from the Eastern District of California would be cited like this:

 Furey v. City of Sacramento, **592 F. Supp. 463 (E.D. Cal. 1984)**

An Introduction to Law

Historically, the courts were the primary source of law in the English common law system (in contrast to other European countries, where statutory law was dominant). As a result, case law is sometimes called common law. So the term "common law" therefore refers to judge-made case law which we inherited from England, as opposed to statutory law or constitutional law.

Dispute Resolution and Lawmaking

A judge's primary task is resolving disputes. One person accuses another of breaching a contract; the other denies it. They can't work out their disagreement, so there is a lawsuit. The judge acts as a referee and resolves disputes by applying the law to the facts of the particular dispute.

But in the course of resolving a dispute, a judge will often have to engage in a form of lawmaking. Applying the law to the facts is not a mechanical process. Nearly every case presents a new combination of circumstances, and many raise issues that have not been settled by existing law.

> **Example:** It is an established rule that a seller's real estate agent must conduct a visual inspection of the seller's house. If the agent discovers any defects, they must be disclosed to the buyer. The agent does not have to inspect areas that are not reasonably accessible to visual inspection.
>
> A's house has a small attic, really not much more than a crawlspace. It can only be reached through a trap door in the ceiling. A's broker, B, inspects the house, but she does not look at the attic. After C buys the house, extensive dry rot is discovered in the attic. C sues B because she did not discover this problem and disclose it to him.
>
> The judge must decide whether B's duty to inspect the house included looking at the attic. Was the attic "reasonably accessible to visual inspection"? The established rules do not address this particular question.

The way the judge answers this question will, of course, directly affect the parties involved in the lawsuit. If the judge says the attic was reasonably accessible, then B had a duty to inspect it. She will owe C compensation for failing to discover and disclose the dry rot problem.

But under certain circumstances, if the judge's conclusion is upheld by the Court of Appeal in a published opinion, it may affect not only the people involved in this particular lawsuit (B and C), but everyone who is in a similar situation. It may be that every broker confronted with an attic trap door will have to climb up a ladder and inspect the attic, or risk liability.

Stare Decisis and Precedent

An Appellate or Supreme courts' published decision in a specific case can become a rule of law applied to all cases because of the **doctrine of stare decisis**. The doctrine holds that once a higher court has decided a particular point of law, other courts faced with the same issue must decide it the same way. ("Stare decisis" is a Latin phrase that means, roughly, "to abide by the decision.") If the court in the previous example ruled

that the attic was reasonably accessible to visual inspection, the doctrine would require another court in a later case involving a similar attic to rule that it also was reasonably accessible. The Appellate or Supreme courts' published decision is called **precedent**, and are **binding** on lower court judges.

Stare decisis is not a law, but a policy that judges have followed for centuries (we inherited it from English common law). It tries to ensure that two people who do the same thing will be treated the same way by the law. That fits with our sense of fairness; it also makes the law more predictable. If a binding precedent holds that an attic with a trap door is reasonably accessible, real estate agents are given warning that they had better go to the trouble of climbing up into such an attic.

Not every court decision is a binding precedent for all other judges, however. It depends, for the most part, on three factors:

◆ jurisdiction,
◆ position in the court hierarchy, and
◆ a written opinion.

For a judge to be bound by the Appellate or Supreme courts' published decision, the other court must be in the same **jurisdiction**. A jurisdiction is the area under the authority of a particular court. To take a simple example, the jurisdiction of the California Supreme Court is the state of California. A decision of the California Supreme Court is not binding on a Nevada state court.

Within each jurisdiction, courts are arranged in a hierarchy, with numerous courts on the lowest level and a smaller number of courts on each higher level. There may be just one judge or several judges on a given court, depending on its function and the population of the area it serves. A judge is required to follow the precedents decided by a higher court in the same jurisdiction.

Stare decisis—doctrine requiring lower courts to follow published appellate or Supreme courts' earlier decisions

Precedent—a previously decided case concerning the same issues as a later case

Jurisdiction—an area under the authority of a particular court

---

Intermediate Court A hears a case involving an attic with a trap door and rules that such an attic is reasonably accessible. All the judges on Lower Courts A1, A2, and A3 are ordinarily required to follow that precedent if a similar case is brought before them.

When a judge on Lower Court B2 decides a similar case, he or she is also not free to hold that the attic is not reasonably accessible. That's because Lower Court B2, although not in the same jurisdiction as Intermediate Court A, is generally bound by the precedents of Intermediate Court A, since a Court of Appeal (and Supreme Court) decision must be followed by all superior courts regardless of which appellate district rendered the opinion.

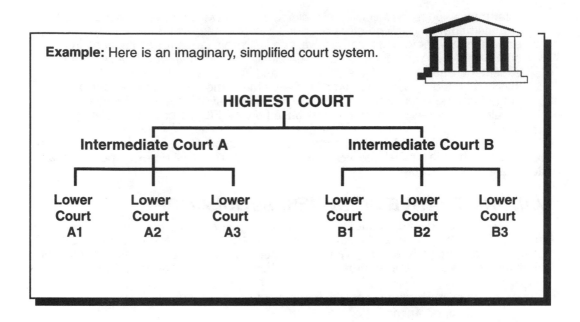

Example: Here is an imaginary, simplified court system.

HIGHEST COURT

Intermediate Court A   **Intermediate Court B**

Lower Court A1   Lower Court A2   Lower Court A3   Lower Court B1   Lower Court B2   Lower Court B3

Example: Two years later, Intermediate Court A hears another attic trap door case. The judges on Intermediate Court A would ordinarily follow their own court's precedent, but this time they reconsider the earlier decision and decide to overrule it. They hold that a broker is not required to inspect an attic if it can only be reached by climbing up a ladder and through a trap door.

If the earlier case had been decided by the Highest Court, rather than by Intermediate Court A, the precedent could not be overruled by Intermediate Court A. Judges can't overrule precedents decided by a higher court.

No decision can be a binding precedent unless a written **opinion** is published. All Supreme Court opinions are published along with many Court of Appeal opinions and, on rare occasions, a Superior Court opinion. In addition to stating the court's decision, an opinion describes the facts of the case and the court's reasoning: why it concluded that the attic was not reasonably accessible, why it did not hold the broker liable. Some courts publish an opinion for every case decided; others publish opinions only for their most important cases.

By reading the higher court's opinion, a lower court judge can determine how similar the facts of that earlier case were to the case he or she is deciding, and whether the same reasoning applies. When the facts are significantly different, the current case is **distinguished** from the earlier case. If the current case can be distinguished, the lower court judge can reach a different result than was reached in the earlier case.

Even though judges are not bound by lower court decisions or decisions from other jurisdictions, they often take those decisions into consideration. A well-reasoned opinion from another jurisdiction may be persuasive.

Example: A judge in California is deciding a case involving a very unusual type of easement. Although no other court in California has ever dealt with such an easement, courts in other states have. The California judge reads opinions from courts in New York, Florida, and Alabama. The Florida court decided the easement was valid, but the New York and Alabama courts decided it was invalid. The Florida court's reasoning makes much more sense to the California judge than the other courts' reasoning. He rules that the easement in his case is valid, and writes an opinion that is based on the Florida court's reasoning.

The relationship of different courts and the process of deciding cases are more complicated than this initial discussion might suggest. They will be examined in greater detail later in this chapter.

ADMINISTRATIVE AGENCIES: REGULATIONS

Over the past few decades, another source of law has become increasingly important in the U.S.: federal, state, and local administrative agencies. Executives (the president, governors, and mayors) and legislatures do not have the time or expertise to take care of all the details of a complex area of law, so they create administrative agencies.

http://www.lib.lsu.edu/gov/fedgov.html
(Federal Agencies)

There are agencies concerned with nearly every aspect of society. Federal agencies range from the Department of Housing and Urban Development and the Environmental Protection Agency to the Internal Revenue Service and the Federal Housing Finance Board. California state agencies include the Department of Real Estate, the Department of Housing and Community Development, and the Coastal Commission. And every county and city has a zoning authority, a building department, a planning commission, and so forth.

Rulemaking

An administrative agency is usually given broad powers within its area of authority. This includes the power to issue regulations that have the force of law. For example, the Real Estate Commissioner has issued regulations prohibiting the discriminatory sales practices called blockbusting and steering. (See Chapter 14.) An agent who violates these regulations may have his or her license revoked. The Department of Real Estate also has the power to fine agents for violations.

Before issuing a new regulation, an agency is generally required to publish a notice of its proposed action at least 45 days in advance. This gives interested parties (such as real estate agents or homeowners) the opportunity to express their ideas and concerns. In some cases the agency will hold a public hearing on the proposed new rule, and in others the agency will ask for written comments. If you file a request for notice with an agency, they'll mail you a notice of proposed rule changes.

Any new regulation must, of course, be constitutional. It also must not exceed the authority granted to the agency by the legislative body or executive that created it.

Adjudication and Enforcement

Detailed regulations give rise to many disagreements: licenses, permits, and benefits are denied or revoked, rules are violated. These disputes would overwhelm the court system, so most of them are decided by the agencies themselves.

Many of these disputes are handled through an informal process of negotiation. But when a significant liberty or property interest (such as a real estate license) is at stake, the agency usually must hold a formal administrative hearing to comply with the Constitution's due process requirement. These cases are decided by administrative law judges.

An administrative law judge is an expert in the agency's area of authority. But he or she is supposed to consider disputes impartially, rather than taking the agency's point of view.

If you're unhappy with an administrative law judge's decision, there may be a board of appeals within the agency that will review your case. If you're dissatisfied with the board of appeals' decision, you can appeal again, this time to the court system.

A court is not very likely to overturn the agency's decision, however. If the agency's record of the case contains substantial evidence to support the decision, the court will simply consider whether the agency has exceeded its grant of power or failed to follow a required procedure. If not, the court will affirm the agency's ruling.

INTERACTION OF LAWS

Constitutional provisions, statutes, case law, and administrative regulations are not isolated from one another. They are often complementary, and a judge may apply all of them in resolving a lawsuit. There is also interaction between them: a statute or a regulation can be held unconstitutional; new case law can be developed to interpret a statute; a new statute can replace old case law.

Judicial Review

The concept of unconstitutionality was introduced earlier in this chapter. If a law exceeds the limits of government power granted by the U.S. Constitution or the state constitution, it is unconstitutional.

Judges determine whether statutes, ordinances, or regulations are unconstitutional. The Constitution did not expressly assign that role to them, but in an early case the U.S. Supreme Court declared that the judiciary had that power. (See *Marbury v. Madison*, 5 U.S. [1 Cranch] 137 [1803].) **Judicial review** of legislation and regulations is established and accepted today.

Judges do not routinely review all of the statutes adopted by a legislature or all of an administrative agency's regulations. Someone who believes he or she has been harmed by an unconstitutional statute or regulation must file a lawsuit challenging the law's constitutionality before a court will review it. When a court decides that a law is unconstitutional, it cannot be enforced. The law is struck down. At that point, the legislature or administrative agency may try to revise the statute or regulation to bring it within constitutional limits.

Statutory Construction

The most common kind of interaction between different types of law occurs when a judge applies a statute in a lawsuit. This is a straightforward task when the facts of the case clearly fall inside or outside of the statute's rule. But it often isn't clear whether the statute covers a particular situation or not, so the judge must decide. This process

of interpretation is called **statutory construction**. Judges have to interpret administrative regulations in the same way.

In interpreting a statute or regulation, the judge's goal is to carry out the intention of the legislature or the administrative agency. To return to the old example, a statute may say "reasonably accessible to visual inspection," but the judge must decide whether the legislature intended that phrase to cover climbing through a trap door into an attic.

When judges interpret a statute or a regulation, case law is grafted onto the statutory or regulatory law. A whole series of cases may develop the meaning of a single statutory phrase such as "reasonably accessible to visual inspection": one case says you have to climb through a trap door into an attic, another says you don't have to go up on the roof, another says you have to crawl through a hedge to look under the back porch.

The legislature may disagree with some of the case law that develops through this process of interpretation. It can then rewrite the statute to make it clear that you don't have to climb through trap doors or hedges, or to make it clear that you do have to go up on the roof. The revised statute will supersede any case law that conflicts with it. An administrative agency can revise its regulations in the same way.

But the process of judicial interpretation will begin all over again with the revised statute or regulation. There's no such thing as a perfectly clear rule that covers all possible cases and requires no interpretation. This interaction between statutes, regulations, and court decisions is a necessary part of the law.

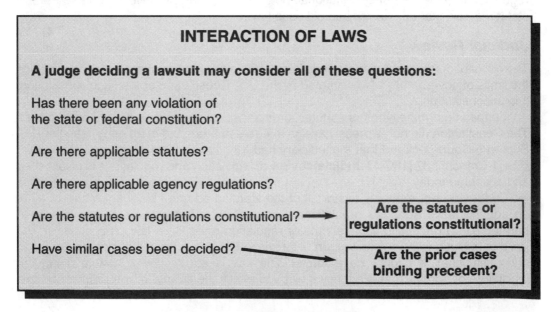

INTERACTION OF LAWS

A judge deciding a lawsuit may consider all of these questions:

Has there been any violation of
the state or federal constitution?

Are there applicable statutes?

Are there applicable agency regulations?

Are the statutes or regulations constitutional? ⟶ **Are the statutes or regulations constitutional?**

Have similar cases been decided? ⟶ **Are the prior cases binding precedent?**

The Judicial System

As you've seen, judges resolve disputes by interpreting and applying existing laws. This section of the chapter focuses on the structure of the judicial system. It explains the different functions of trial and appellate courts, and outlines the state and federal court systems. It also describes some rules that limit access to the courts.

Both the federal and state systems are overcrowded; there are too many cases and not enough judges to hear them, which often causes long delays. A number of the procedures and limitations described here were developed to help with this problem. They are intended to reserve the courts' resources for the cases where adjudication is most necessary and most likely to be effective.

TRIAL COURTS AND APPELLATE COURTS

The fundamental court proceeding in a lawsuit is the **trial**. The general outlines of a trial are no doubt familiar to you: lawyers present arguments and evidence, witnesses testify and are cross-examined, and a jury or a judge decides the case. Trials take place in a jurisdiction's lower courts, so those are often referred as **trial courts**.

If you're dissatisfied with the outcome of a trial, you generally have the opportunity to **appeal** at least once. On appeal, you are asking a higher court in the same jurisdiction to review the trial court's decision. A court that has the power to review the decisions of lower courts is called an **appellate court** and is said to have **appellate jurisdiction**. (Trial courts are said to have **original jurisdiction** because they hear cases for the first time.)

Many people expect an appeal to be just like another trial, but it is a very different proceeding. To try every appealed case all over again would be extremely expensive, both for the parties and for the court system. So the evidence is not presented again, the witnesses do not testify again, and there is no jury.

Instead, the appellate court reviews the **trial record**. The record includes a word-for-word transcript of everything that the lawyers, witnesses, and trial judge said in the courtroom. It also includes any **exhibits** that were introduced at the trial. An exhibit is documentary or physical evidence: a listing agreement, a deed, fingerprints, or an old tire. In reviewing the record, the appellate court is looking for errors committed by the trial judge. Most appellate courts will only change a trial court's decision if:

- ◆ the judge committed an error,
- ◆ the error concerned a question of law, and
- ◆ the error was prejudicial.

Questions of Fact and Questions of Law

All the issues in a trial can be classified as either questions of fact or questions of law. A **question of fact** is any question about what actually took place: Did A tell B she could lease the apartment for nine months or for a year and a half? A **question of law**, on the other hand, is any question about what the law is on a particular point: Is a lease for a year and a half valid if it isn't in writing?

Questions of fact are decided by the **trier of fact**. In a jury trial, the trier of fact is the jury; in a non-jury trial, the trier of fact is the judge. But questions of law are always decided by the judge, whether or not there is a jury.

An appellate court generally accepts the trier of fact's conclusions on questions of fact. The trier of fact had a better opportunity to assess the evidence than the appellate court. The trier of fact heard the testimony firsthand and could observe the witnesses as they were testifying, whereas the appellate judges only read a transcript of the testimony.

So if the trier of fact concluded that the plaintiff fell on the sidewalk instead of the porch, the appellate court will presume that conclusion is correct. An exception is made only if the trier of fact's findings are completely unsupported by the evidence.

In many jurisdictions, appellate courts follow this rule whether the trier of fact was a jury or the trial judge. In California, state appellate courts also follow this rule. The trial court's resolution of disputed facts issue must be affirmed so long as the finding is supported by "substantial" evidence.

But any appellate court's main focus is on the questions of law, reviewing the record to see if the trial judge decided any of those incorrectly. The trial judge may have made a mistake about an established point of law. Or the trial judge may have ruled on an issue that had never been decided before, and the appellate court might disagree with the ruling. In either case, the trial court is said to have "committed an error."

PREJUDICIAL ERROR AND HARMLESS ERROR. If the appellate court finds that the trial judge committed an error, it considers whether the error was **prejudicial** or **harmless**. A prejudicial error is one that adversely affected a substantial right of one of the litigants. This is generally interpreted to mean an error that may have made a difference in the outcome of the trial. If the trier of fact would almost certainly have reached the same final decision if the error had not been made, the error is considered harmless.

THE APPELLATE DECISION. If the appellate court does not find any error in the record, or decides that the error was harmless, it will **affirm** the trial court's decision. If it decides that there was prejudicial error, it will **modify** or **reverse** the decision.

When a trial court's decision is reversed, the appellate court may substitute its own ruling for the trial court's judgment, or it may **remand** the case back to the lower courts. If the case is remanded, the appellate court may order the original trial judge to conduct additional proceedings, or it may order a new trial.

Whereas a trial is presided over by a single judge, an appeal is heard by a panel of three or more judges. Sometimes not all of the judges on an appellate panel agree on how a case should be decided. Then the decision will be reached by majority vote.

A SECOND APPEAL (Supreme Court Review). A litigant dissatisfied with the result of an appeal may appeal again, to an even higher court. While a first appeal is generally an **appeal by right**, a second appeal is often **discretionary**. The litigant petitions the high court to hear the case, but the high court may refuse. In fact, because the courts are so crowded, the great majority of discretionary appeals are turned down.

FEDERAL COURTS AND STATE COURTS

Just as there is a federal legislature (Congress) and 50 state legislatures, there is a federal court system and 50 state court systems. But the federal court system isn't centralized in Washington, D.C.; there are federal courts in every state, along with the state courts. The jurisdictions of federal courts and state courts usually overlap.

Taking a closer look at the concept of jurisdiction will make it easier to understand the two systems and their relationship to one another. You have already seen how a court's jurisdiction can be limited to a particular geographical area: the California state courts generally don't have any authority over what takes place in Nevada. But jurisdiction can be limited in other ways as well.

A court's jurisdiction may be limited to a certain type of lawsuit, such as tax cases or patent cases. The types of cases that a court has authority to hear are called its **subject matter jurisdiction**. A court that is not limited to a specific subject is called a **court of general jurisdiction**.

There may also be monetary limits on a court's jurisdiction. For example, some courts can only hear a case if the amount of money at stake in the dispute (called the **amount in controversy**) is more than $25,000. Other courts can only hear a case if the amount in controversy is less than $5,000.

Limitations like these define the jurisdiction of the various state and federal courts. We'll look at the California state courts, then at the federal system, and then at the relationship between the two.

California Supreme Court

California Courts of Appeal
(6 Districts)

Superior Courts
(1 in each county)

Municipal Courts
(including Small Claims Divisions)

www.courtinfo.ca.gov/
(California Court System)

The California State Court System

All judges in the California state court system are elected, rather than appointed. However, the governor can appoint a judge to fill a vacancy if one occurs. Municipal, and superior court judges serve six-year terms, and court of appeals and supreme court judges serve twelve-year terms.

MUNICIPAL COURTS. The trial courts at the lowest level of the hierarchy are the municipal courts. Municipal courts try all minor criminal cases (misdemeanors), such as petty theft and drunk driving. They also hear cases involving ordinance violations: parking infractions, vagrancy, and so on.

Civil matters are tried in municipal courts when the plaintiff is seeking only money damages and the amount in controversy is $25,000 or less. For example, this would include a broker's suit against a seller for a $10,000 commission, or a buyer's suit for the return of $16,000 in earnest money.

Municipal courts also have jurisdiction in a limited range of cases where the plaintiff is asking for something other than (or in addition to) money damages. They can hear an action to foreclose a $25,000 mechanic's lien. They can also hear unlawful detainer actions (eviction suits—see Chapter 15), as long as the landlord is not suing the tenant for more than $25,000 in damages.

Small Claims Divisions. Each municipal court has a small claims division for resolving minor civil disputes quickly and inexpensively. The amount in controversy must be $5,000 or less. No one may file more than two claims for over $2,500 in one year in small claims court anywhere in California. An unlawful detainer action can no longer be heard in small claims court.

To save time and expense, the small claims process is simplified in several respects. There is no jury. Neither the plaintiff nor the defendant can be represented by a lawyer in the courtroom. (They are allowed to consult lawyers about the case, however.) The plaintiff gives up the right to an appeal. But the defendant still has the right to an appeal, since he or she was not the one who chose small claims court.

SUPERIOR COURTS. Superior courts are the trial courts for all cases that exceed the limits of municipal court jurisdiction. Thus, superior courts try serious criminal cases (felonies). They also try civil cases where the amount in controversy is more than $25,000, and most civil cases where the plaintiff is seeking a remedy other than a damages award, such as specific performance. In addition, a superior court can hear appeals in cases that were decided in municipal court, including appeals from small claims court.

There is one superior court in each county, and the number of judges on the court depends on the county's population.

Although not required to, a superior court judge will usually try to go along with the precedents decided by other judges on the same court. An Orange County Superior Court judge will follow another Orange County judge's lead. A judge on another superior court (the San Diego County Superior Court, for example) may disregard the Orange County precedent altogether.

CALIFORNIA COURTS OF APPEAL. A litigant who is unhappy with a superior court's decision has a right to a review by one of the state courts of appeal. These courts have appellate jurisdiction in all matters except criminal cases involving the death penalty. (Death penalty cases are appealed directly from superior court to the state supreme court.)

The state is divided into six appellate districts, each having jurisdiction over several counties. The First Appellate District includes San Francisco; the Second District includes Los Angeles and Santa Barbara; Sacramento is in the Third District; San Diego, San Bernardino, and Orange County are in the Fourth District; the Fifth District includes Fresno; and the Sixth District includes San Jose.

The number of judges in each district depends on the population: The larger appellate districts contain more than one division. For example, the Second Appellate District has seven divisions.

A state court of appeals opinion is published only if it involves an important new issue, or changes an established rule. A published decision from one of an appellate district's divisions is binding precedent for the other divisions in that district. In the

Fourth Appellate District, for example, if the San Bernardino Division sets a precedent, the San Diego Division must follow it.

The six districts are semi-independent. A court of appeals in one district is not bound to follow precedents decided in another district. The San Francisco Division in the First Appellate district could ignore a precedent decided by the San Bernardino Division of the Fourth Appellate District, because San Francisco is in the First Appellate District and San Bernardino is in the Fourth District. However, one district's precedents may carry weight in another district. The San Francisco Division will consider the San Bernardino Division's precedent carefully, although it doesn't have to follow it.

The published decisions of any of the courts of appeals are binding precedents for all the trial courts in the state (municipal and superior courts). This is true even when the trial court is not in the same appellate district as the court of appeal that established the precedent.

> **Example:** A San Diego County Superior Court judge is hearing a case involving breach of contract. In resolving the questions of law that the case presents, the judge looks first for precedents decided by the Fourth District Court of Appeals, because San Diego is in the Fourth District.
>
> But the judge finds that the central point of law in the case has never been addressed by the Fourth District Court of Appeals. That doesn't mean the judge gets to make up her own mind about the issue, however. Instead, she must do further research to determine whether the court of appeals in any of the five other districts has decided the question yet.
>
> It turns out that the First District Court of Appeals has established a precedent on the issue. The San Diego Superior Court judge must follow the First District precedent, even though San Diego is not in that district.

What if the judge had found two conflicting precedents, one from the First District and one from the Sixth District? She would choose between the two. That kind of conflict would eventually be cleared up by the highest court in the state system, the California Supreme Court.

THE CALIFORNIA SUPREME COURT. The state supreme court consists of a chief justice and six associate justices. A criminal defendant who has been sentenced to death has the right to appeal to the state supreme court directly from superior court. All other cases must go from superior court to a court of appeals before they can be appealed to the supreme court.

A petition for review to the California Supreme Court from a court of appeal decision is discretionary. The supreme court will grant a petition for review and hear the case if it presents a particularly important legal question, or if the courts of appeal have developed conflicting precedents.

The supreme court can resolve these conflicts because its decisions are binding on all other California state courts. One of the supreme court's most important functions is making the law uniform throughout the state. All supreme court opinions are published; they are the final word on California law.

Federal Court System

www.uscourts.gov
www.courts.net/fed/index.html
www.diviacchi.com/courts.htm

The Federal Court System

U.S. Supreme Court

U.S. Courts of Appeal
(11 Circuits + D.C. Circuit)

U.S. District Courts
(California 4 District Courts, 39 Judges)

Specialized Courts

Tax Courts   **Federal Circuit**   **Bankruptcy Courts**

All federal judges are appointed by the president and confirmed by the Senate. The Constitution provides that they hold office "during good behavior," which generally means for life or until they retire.

SPECIALIZED COURTS. There are a few specialized federal courts with narrow subject matter jurisdiction. The U.S. Tax Courts only hear cases involving the federal tax laws, the Federal Circuit Court primarily hears appeals concerning patents or foreign trade, and the U.S. Bankruptcy Courts hear nothing but bankruptcy cases.

UNITED STATES DISTRICT COURTS. The U.S. district courts are the main trial courts of the federal system. There are 91 district courts across the country, with at least one in each state. California has four district courts, with a total of 39 judges: Northern (9 judges), Eastern (3), Central (21), and Southern (6).

A federal district court judge's published decision is binding on other federal judges in the same district, but not on federal judges in other districts. So a judge in the Eastern District of California must follow Eastern District precedents, but doesn't have to follow precedents decided in the Northern District of California.

CALIFORNIA'S FOUR FEDERAL COURT DISTRICTS

California has four district courts, with a total of 39 judges:

Northern (9 judges), Eastern (3), Central 21), and Southern (6)

The U.S. district courts can hear cases that fall into one of three categories:

1. the United States government is a party.
2. a federal question is presented.
3. there is diversity of citizenship, and the amount in controversy is more than $75,000.

Cases in which the United States is a party include suits involving federal crimes: interstate car theft, racketeering, drug smuggling, and so forth. The U.S. can also be a party in a civil suit. For example, a defense contractor might sue the U.S. Army over a contract dispute. That case could be tried in a federal district court, since the army is a part of the U.S. government.

The district courts also have jurisdiction over civil cases that present a **federal question**. A federal question is any issue regarding the application or interpretation of the U.S. Constitution, a federal statute, or a U.S. treaty. if a group of political protesters sues a city for interfering with their First Amendment right to freedom of speech, the case could be heard in a federal district court.

The third category of federal district court jurisdiction covers civil cases in which there is **diversity of citizenship** and the amount in controversy is more than $75,000. There is diversity of citizenship when the plaintiff and the defendant are not citizens of the same state. if a citizen of Alabama sues a citizen of California, or if a citizen of California sues a citizen of Brazil, the case can be heard in federal district court as long as more than $75,000 is at stake. This is called **diversity jurisdiction**.

The Federal Judicial Circuits

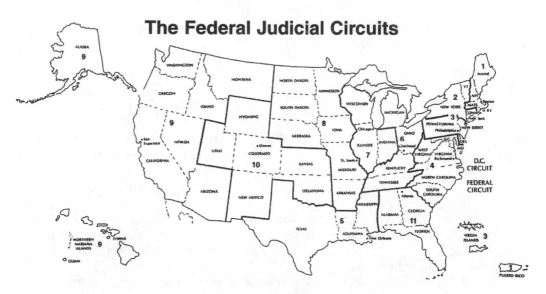

UNITED STATES COURTS OF APPEALS. The result of a trial in a U.S. district court can be appealed (by right) to one of the U.S. Courts of Appeal. There is a federal court of appeals for each of 11 numbered **circuits**; each circuit covers several states. There is an additional court of appeals in Washington, D.C., which is called the D.C. Circuit.

Chapter 1

California is in the Ninth Circuit, along with Oregon, Washington, Montana, Idaho, Nevada, Arizona, Alaska, Hawaii, and Guam. The decision of a U.S. district court sitting in any of those states—for example, the District Court for the Eastern District of California, or the Idaho District Court—could be appealed to the Ninth Circuit Court of Appeals.

There are 39 judges on the Ninth Circuit, which is the largest federal appeals court. Most appeals are heard by panels made up of three of the circuit's judges. A Ninth Circuit decision is a binding precedent for all the U.S. district courts within the circuit.

> **Example:** A judge on the U.S. District Court for the Northern District of California rules in a published decision that a broker's hiring policies violated federal employment discrimination statutes. If a case involving similar hiring policies comes before the U.S. District Court for the Eastern District of Washington, the judge does not have to follow the Northern District of California's decision. He or she may decide that the hiring policy did not violate the federal statute. However, it's a different matter if the California broker appeals to the Ninth Circuit, and a three-judge panel affirms the California district court's decision. Now a district court in Washington (or Hawaii, Arizona, or any Ninth Circuit state) is required to follow the Ninth Circuit's precedent and hold that the hiring policy violated the statute.

Other circuit courts of appeals do not have to follow the Ninth Circuit's precedent. And district courts in other circuits—the District Court for the Western District of Kentucky, or for the Southern District of New York—are also free to ignore the Ninth Circuit's decision. But a decision by one of the U.S. Courts of Appeals will usually have persuasive value for other Courts of Appeal.

Not every opinion of the U.S. Courts of Appeal is published, but all the opinions that decide new issues or change old rules are.

THE UNITED STATES SUPREME COURT. The U.S. Supreme Court is made up of a chief justice and eight associate justices. Although it is the highest and most influential court in the country, its jurisdiction is limited like the lower federal courts'.

The Supreme Court has original jurisdiction in a few special types of cases: for example, a lawsuit involving officials of a foreign government, or a lawsuit filed by a state against a citizen of a different state. However, even though the Court is empowered to conduct the trials in these cases, they will usually take place in a U.S. district court instead. The only trials that must take place in the Supreme Court are those where one state is suing another state.

The Supreme Court has appellate jurisdiction in all cases decided by the U.S. courts of appeals. Its decisions in these cases are binding precedents for all other courts. This gives the Supreme Court power to resolve conflicts between the decisions of U.S. courts of appeals in different circuits.

All appeals to the Supreme Court are discretionary. A litigant files a petition for **Writ of certiorai**, and the Supreme Court decides whether or not to grant the petition and hear the case. Petitions are filed for thousands of cases each year, but the Court hears less than 5% of them. Although "I'll take my case all the way to the Supreme Court!" is a standard threat, it can rarely be carried out. The U.S. Court Appeals is the end of the line for the overwhelming majority of federal cases.

Relationship of the Federal and State Courts

Because federal jurisdiction and state jurisdiction overlap, the relationship between the two court systems is complicated. We'll start with the simpler cases, those that must be heard in federal court and those that must be heard in state court—before moving on to the cases that can be heard in either one.

EXCLUSIVE JURISDICTION. In some federal statutes, Congress has included a requirement that lawsuits based on the statute can only be brought in federal court. For example, cases involving the Voting Rights Act of 1965 cannot be heard in state court. The same is true for suits regarding patents, copyrights, immigration, admiralty, and a number of other subjects that are controlled by federal statutes. Very few cases involving real property are in this category.

Any case that does not fall within the jurisdiction of the federal courts must be brought in state court. In other words, a case has to be state court if:

◆ the U.S. government is not a party,
◆ no federal question is presented, and
◆ there is no diversity of citizenship (or there is diversity but the amount in controversy is $75,000 or less).

For example, most real estate cases must be brought in state court rather than federal. In a typical real estate lawsuit, the plaintiff and the defendant are citizens of the same state, only questions of state law are involved, and the U.S. government is not a party.

CONCURRENT JURISDICTION. The reason state and federal jurisdictions overlap is that most cases that may be brought in federal court do not have to be. A state court can hear a diversity case, even if the amount in controversy is over $75,000. A state court can also hear a federal question case, except if it concerns those subjects (like patents) that Congress has expressly reserved for the federal courts.

When a state trial court decides a federal question case, the decision can only be appealed in the state system. In other words, the case must be taken to one of the California courts of appeal rather than to the Ninth Circuit Court of Appeals. On a second appeal, it would go to the California Supreme Court.

From that point there is the possibility of a third appeal, to the U.S. Supreme Court. The U.S. Supreme Court will review the decision of a state supreme court if (and only if) the case presents an important federal question. It will not interfere in cases that only involve questions of state law.

Choosing between federal and state court. When a case could be filed in either state or federal court, why does the plaintiff choose one over the other? The reasons aren't clear-cut.

Sometimes federal court is chosen just because the plaintiff's lawyer is accustomed to federal court, and more familiar with federal court procedures. Some lawyers believe that federal court judges tend to be better qualified or more sophisticated, since they are appointed rather than elected.

Chapter 1

At times, the federal or state courts gain a reputation for favoring plaintiffs or defendants in a particular type of case. Civil rights cases are the most prominent example. In the 1960s (and later), state courts in southern states were seen as more likely to support racial segregation than the federal courts in those states. As a result, a southern plaintiff claiming that his or her right to equal protection had been violated would almost invariably choose to bring the case in federal court.

LIMITATIONS AND ADJUDICATION

Case or Controversy Requirement

As a general rule, a lawsuit must involve an active conflict, not just a theoretical or potential conflict. Based on Article III of the U.S. Constitution, this is known as the **case** or **controversy requirement**.

> **Example:** The landlord of a large new apartment building wonders if it is necessary to go to the expense of installing various security devices. if he doesn't install them, would he be liable if one of the apartments were burglarized? Could a tenant have them installed and then deduct the cost from the rent?
>
> The landlord can consult a lawyer about these issues. The lawyer will give his or her opinion about what a court would probably decide if these cases arose.
>
> But a court would refuse to consider these hypothetical questions. A judge won't issue a binding decision on what this landlord's duty is unless one of the apartments is actually burglarized and the tenant sues the landlord, or unless a tenant actually deducts the installation costs and the landlord sues for the deducted portion of the rent.

In some situations, however, a court has discretion to grant **declaratory relief**. Instead of requiring a problem to reach a crisis, the court will let the parties know in advance what their duties under a contract are, or what their property rights are. A quiet title action is an example of declaratory relief. If there is a possible claim against a property holder's title (a boundary question, for example), he or she can ask a court to decide whether or not the claim is valid. The title holder does not have to wait for the potential claimant to sue. Without a quiet title action, the title holder might be reluctant to develop the property, since it could turn out to belong to someone else.

Statute of Limitations

A statute of limitations does not allow a court to hear a case if too much time has passed since the conflict arose. The reason for these time limits is that it becomes more and more difficult to prove or disprove a claim as years go by. Evidence is often lost, and witnesses' memories fade.

The time limits vary depending on the type of case. In California, personal injury lawsuits generally must be filed within one year after the harmful act occurred. Most contract suits must be filed within four years after the breach occurred if the contract was in writing, or within two years if the contract was oral. A suit to recover possession of real property can't be filed more than five years after the plaintiff (or whoever transferred the property to the plaintiff) was last in possession.

In certain types of cases, the statute of limitations doesn't start running until the injury or loss is *discovered*, even if the wrongful act occurred much earlier. For example, California allows an action for fraud to be filed within three years of the time the victim discovers the fraud.

And in some situations, the statute of limitations doesn't run against a minor or an incompetent person. When the minor reaches the age of majority, or if the incompetent person regains competence, the statute of limitations begins to run.

Anyone thinking about starting a lawsuit should find out the limitations period for that type of action, and keep it in mind. Once the statutory period has run out, you've lost your legal remedy for good.

Res Judicata

Res judicata is a Latin phrase meaning "the thing has been decided." The doctrine of res judicata holds that once a dispute between two parties has been tried and appealed and a final judgment has been issued, the same dispute cannot be tried again. The dissatisfied party can't start a new lawsuit on the same question, hoping to find a more sympathetic judge or a more persuasive lawyer.

The purpose of the doctrine is simple: finality. It puts the case to rest, at least as far as the court system is concerned. Without res judicata, some parties would go on suing each other over the same matter forever. That would make the courts even more crowded than they already are.

A Civil Lawsuit

Now we'll take a closer look at the litigation process. This section follows a simple civil lawsuit from its filing to the enforcement of the final judgment. The entire process would probably take at least several months; in some cases, it takes years.

THE DISPUTE

Henry Palermo has lived in the Grass River Valley in northern California for many years. The lot to the west of his property had always been vacant until Claire Mulligan bought it six months ago. Mulligan has had the lot cleared and regraded in preparation for construction of a house.

Recently there were very heavy rains, and Palermo's house was flooded. There was considerable damage to the house and yard, and many of Palermo's belongings were ruined, including expensive stereo and recording equipment and a large record collection. Palermo discovers that his homeowner's insurance policy lapsed two months earlier.

Chapter 1

Since his house was never flooded before, Palermo believes Mulligan's clearing and regrading next door changed the pattern of runoff and caused the flooding. He explains this to Mulligan, and says she should help pay for the damage.

Mulligan is furious. She tells Palermo his property flooded simply because it rained so hard. The changes she made in her property had nothing to do with it. in the course of a ten-minute conversation, the neighbors become enemies.

So Palermo consults a lawyer. The lawyer evaluates Palermo's claim by researching the law (looking up statutes and case law) about drainage onto adjoining property. He decides Palermo has a fairly strong case. California law holds that a landowner who disturbs the natural flow of surface waters may be liable for resulting damage to adjacent property.

Mulligan also hires a lawyer to look into the matter. Her lawyer concludes that it would be difficult for Palermo to prove that Mulligan's clearing caused his property to flood. Unless Palermo can prove that in court, Mulligan will not be held liable for the damage. The two lawyers discuss their clients' positions. Palermo's lawyer says that unless Mulligan pays Palermo $30,000, Palermo will sue her. Mulligan's lawyer says that Mulligan won't pay Palermo a nickel, because the damage was not her fault.

STARTING A LAWSUIT

Palermo and his lawyer decide to proceed with a lawsuit. Palermo's lawyer starts the suit (*Palermo v. Mulligan*) by filing a **complaint** in the superior court of the county where Mulligan and Palermo live. The complaint outlines the dispute, explains how the plaintiff (Palermo) believes his legal rights have been violated by the defendant (Mulligan), and asks the court to grant judgment in the plaintiff's favor. Palermo asks the court to order Mulligan to prevent any future flooding and pay him $30,000.

CHOOSING A COURT. What kind of court a lawsuit takes place in depends on the jurisdictional issues that were introduced earlier. The case must come within the court's jurisdictional limits—geographical, subject matter, and monetary limits.

Palermo's lawyer didn't have any choice about what kind of court to bring this suit in. It had to be in state court, because Mulligan and Palermo are both citizens of California, and the case does not involve any federal laws (the laws concerning drainage and flooding are state laws). And since the amount in controversy is more than $25,000, the case had to be filed in superior court rather than municipal court.

PERSONAL JURISDICTION. Even when a case is within a particular court's jurisdictional limits (geographical, subject matter, and monetary limits), that court can only hear the case if it has authority over the defendant. That authority is referred to as **personal jurisdiction**.

A court ordinarily acquires personal jurisdiction over a defendant by **service of process**. Service of process means delivery of a **summons** and a copy of the complaint to the defendant. The summons is simply a notice telling the defendant that the complaint has been filed, and that he or she must file a response with the court.

Service of process usually must take place in the state where the court sits. In most cases, the plaintiff has a process server take the summons and complaint to the defendant's home or business and hand it directly to the defendant. if the defendant tries to evade the process server, service can be accomplished by mail or publication, or through an agent of the defendant.

JURISDICTION OVER PROPERTY. A court must also have jurisdiction over any property at issue in a lawsuit. California courts have jurisdiction over all real and personal property within the state's boundaries.

THE DEFENDANT'S ANSWER. A summons and complaint was served on Mulligan at her home. Now her lawyer has 30 days to prepare an **answer** and file it with the court.

In the answer, a defendant may challenge the court's jurisdiction. The defendant may also deny the plaintiff's allegations, discuss facts that the plaintiff left out of the complaint, or make a **cross-complaint** against the plaintiff. Mulligan's answer simply denies that the clearing and regrading on her property were the cause of Palermo's flood damage.

If a defendant fails to respond to the complaint, in some cases the plaintiff can win the case by default. The court may enter a **default judgment** against the defendant.

The complaint, the answer, and any additional documents filed with the court are called **pleadings**.

A Civil Lawsuit

1. **Plaintiff files a complaint**
2. **Summons and complaint is served on defendant**
3. **Defendant files an answer**
4. **Pretrial discovery**
5. **Settlement negotiations**
6. **Trial**

Pretrial Discovery

Once a lawsuit has been started, both the plaintiff and the defendant are given an opportunity to find out more about the disputed facts through the **discovery process**. The rules of discovery require each side to provide the other with information upon request. They also enable a litigant to obtain information from reluctant witnesses.

One method of acquiring information during discovery is a **deposition**. In a deposition, one party's lawyer questions the other party or a witness about the case. The **deponent** (the person responding to the lawyer's questions) is under oath, just as if he or she were testifying in court. A word-for-word transcript of the deposition can be used as evidence in the trial.

Interrogatories are another important discovery tool. They are like a deposition conducted by mail instead of in person. One party's lawyer sends a series of questions to the other party; the other party must send back answers. Interrogatories are also answered under oath.

Palermo's lawyer sends Mulligan interrogatories asking about the clearing and grading process, and about what measures were taken regarding runoff. Mulligan's lawyer sends Palermo interrogatories asking about the extent of the water damage, and about flooding in previous years. In addition, each side deposes the other party about the facts of the dispute. If Mulligan and Palermo fail to show up for their depositions or fail to answer the interrogatories, they may be sanctioned by the court.

SETTLEMENT NEGOTIATIONS

Litigation is almost always expensive, time-consuming, and unpleasant. Both parties must weigh those costs against what they stand to gain, and how likely they are to win, if the case goes to trial.

Throughout the litigation process, Palermo's and Mulligan's lawyers negotiate to settle the case. In a settlement, the defendant pays the plaintiff a sum of money (or agrees to do something or refrain from doing something) so that the plaintiff will call off the lawsuit.

Soon after the action is filed, on the advice of her lawyer, Mulligan offers to pay Palermo $2,000 and install culvert to rechannel runoff, if he will drop the suit. On the advice of his lawyer, Palermo refuses this offer; he will take the case to trial unless Mulligan pays him $25,000 and rechannels the runoff.

As each lawyer learns more about the facts of the case through the discovery process, he reevaluates his client's claim. Palermo's lawyer may realize that it will be much more difficult than he first thought to prove that it was Mulligan's clearing and grading that caused Palermo's property to be flooded. Or Mulligan's lawyer may realize that it may be much easier to prove that than he thought.

On the basis of these reevaluations, the gap between the parties' settlement offers narrows. As the trial date approaches, Palermo is only asking $17,000 to settle, and Mulligan is offering $8,000.

It is extremely likely that Palermo and Mulligan will come to an agreement. Over 95% of civil cases settle rather than reach a judgment. Most of them settle before the trial even begins.

In some cases, however, the parties are unable to settle. It may be the facts of the case are really unclear, or that the laws governing the case are ambiguous. Or it may be that the litigants are unusually stubborn, or extremely angry with one another.

We'll assume that for some combination of these reasons, Palermo and Mulligan do not settle, and the case proceeds to trial.

JURY OR JUDGE

The U.S. Constitution and the California constitution guarantee litigants the right to trial by jury. That right applies in most civil cases, but some cases (and certain issues within some cases) cannot be tried by a jury. It depends on the remedies requested by the plaintiff.

REMEDIES AT LAW AND EQUITABLE REMEDIES. The remedies awarded in civil cases are classified either as **remedies at law** or as **equitable remedies**. A remedy at law is generally an award of money (damages). An equitable remedy, on the other hand, usually involves an **injunction**: an order to refrain from doing something or specific performance an order to do what was promised in the contract.

> **Example:** If the court ordered Mulligan to install culvert and replant protective vegetation, that would be an equitable remedy. If Mulligan were ordered to pay Palermo $30,000 in damages, that would be a remedy at law.

Equitable remedies can only be awarded when money would not adequately correct the problem. Specific performance and contract reformation (see Chapter 7), foreclosure, and quiet title are all equitable remedies.

For historical reasons, a jury is not allowed to decide equitable issues. If a plaintiff is asking only for an equitable remedy (such as foreclosure), the case cannot be heard by a jury. If a plaintiff is asking for both types of remedies (such as damages and an injunction), a jury may hear the case. The jury will decide on the remedy at law, but the judge will decide on the equitable remedy.

CHOOSING A JURY. Even when a lawsuit does not involve any equitable issues, a jury isn't automatically assigned to the case. One or both of the parties must request a jury. If neither party does, the judge will decide the questions of fact as well as the questions of law.

When should a litigant request a jury? It's an intuitive choice rather than a scientific one. Juries are supposed to be more sympathetic than judges in some cases. A jury hearing a personal injury suit may be more likely to feel compassion for the plaintiff than a judge, who might have heard dozens of similar cases. A jury may tend to side with the underdog, or favor an individual corporation.

On the other hand, if a litigant's case is based on a complicated legal argument or on detailed technical or scientific evidence, a jury might have a hard time understanding it—and jury trials take longer and are more expensive than non-jury trials.

Although Palermo's lawyer thinks that a jury would feel sorry for his client because of the property damage, he decides not to request a jury. Palermo's case depends too much on technical proof that Mulligan's changes caused the flooding. Mulligan's lawyer decides to request a jury. He hopes the jury will feel that Mulligan did nothing unreasonable, and that it is unfair to hold her responsible for Palermo's misfortune.

Jurors are taken from a pool of citizens chosen at random from the county voter registration lists. Both lawyers have an opportunity to question the potential jurors, to learn about their backgrounds and discover their personal prejudices. Those who seem biased against or in favor of one of the parties may be eliminated from the jury.

There are ordinarily 12 people on a jury in California. **In civil cases and cases involving misdemeanor crimes, the parties can agree to have fewer than 12 jurors.** Once the jury has been chosen, the trial begins.

THE TRIAL

The plaintiff's case is presented first. The plaintiff's lawyer makes an **opening statement**, telling his or her client's version of the events that gave rise to the lawsuit. This explanation helps the judge and jurors understand the point of the evidence and testimony the lawyer is about to present. The defendant's lawyer can also make an opening statement at this point, or wait until after the plaintiff's case has been fully presented.

The plaintiff's lawyer examines witnesses whose testimony supports his or her client's version of the facts. There are two types of witnesses.

A **lay (fact) witness** is someone who had an opportunity to observe events connected with the dispute. For example, Palermo's lawyer has some of his client's neighbors testify that there were even heavier rains three years earlier, yet Palermo's property wasn't flooded then. A fact witness is only supposed to describe events he or she personally observed, and is not allowed to offer opinions about the facts.

An **expert witness** is someone who has expert knowledge of a subject, either through experience or education. Litigants hire expert witnesses to evaluate their claims. if the expert's opinion supports the litigant's case, the expert is paid to testify at the trial. Palermo's lawyer calls two engineering consultants to testify about the effect of Mulligan's clearing and grading on her property's drainage. The lawyer also examines an appraiser, who testifies about how much it will cost to repair or replace the water-damaged property.

The initial questioning of witnesses by the lawyer who called them to testify is the **direct examination**. Immediately after the direct examination of a witness, the opposing lawyer has a chance to **cross-examine** that witness. In the cross-examination, the opposing lawyer tries to cast doubt on the witness's testimony and bring out any facts that are unfavorable to the other side. Then the first lawyer has a chance to repair any damage done on cross-examination by **redirect examination** of the witness. Sometimes the opposing lawyer will cross-examine the witness a second time.

Court rules provide that some testimony (or documentary or physical evidence) cannot be used in court because it is considered unreliable or unfair. Such testimony or evidence is **inadmissible**.

> **Example:** Testimony must be relevant to the issues involved in the dispute. If a neighbor testifying on behalf of Palermo says, "Mrs. Mulligan struck me as a troublemaker," Mulligan's lawyer can **object**. The witness's impression of Mulligan has no bearing on whether or not her activities caused Palermo's property to flood. The witness's comment is irrelevant and therefore inadmissible.

A lawyer can object to a witness's testimony, or to the other lawyer's questioning, on a variety of grounds. For example, a fact witness is giving an opinion; a physician is being asked to divulge confidential information about a patient; the other lawyer is leading the witness (asking yes or no questions, rather than getting the witness to describe the events in his or her own words).

If the judge agrees with the objecting lawyer that the questioning is improper, the judge will tell the witness not to answer. If the judge agrees that testimony already given is inadmissible, he or she will tell the jury to disregard the witness's remarks, and may have them stricken from the trial record.

When the plaintiff's lawyer has finished presenting evidence, it is the defense lawyer's turn. The same procedure is repeated: direct and cross examination of the defendant's witnesses, with objections from the lawyers and ruling on admissibility by the judge. The plaintiff's lawyer then has a chance to present additional evidence to rebut the defendant's case. Finally, each lawyer makes a **closing argument**, explaining how all the evidence fits together.

The Trial

1. **Opening statement**
2. **Presentation of the evidence (plaintiff goes first)**
   fact witnesses
   expert witnesses
   physical or documentary evidence
3. **Closing arguments**
4. **Jury instructions**
5. **The decision**

Example: The judge explains that California law does not hold a landowner responsible for damage caused by the natural flow of surface water from his or her property onto adjoining property. However, if the landowner changes the natural pattern of drainage, he or she is liable for resulting damage. The judge points out that this liability does not depend on whether the defendant intended to cause damage.

JURY INSTRUCTIONS. The jury instructions include an explanation of the **burden of proof**. Here, as in most cases, the plaintiff has the burden of proof. That is, it was up to Palermo to prove that Mulligan's clearing and regarding were the cause of the damage. Mulligan was not required to prove that her changes did not cause the damage.

The judge will also explain that the plaintiff must have proven his claim by a **preponderance of the evidence**. In other words, the jury doesn't have to be absolutely certain that Mulligan's changes caused the damage. It is enough if Palermo has convinced the jury that it is more likely than not that Mulligan's changes were the cause. This is the burden of proof used in nearly all civil cases.

Clear and convincing evidence requires that the evidence "be suffering strong so as to command the assent of every reasonable mind."

(In criminal cases, where the defendant has so much at stake, a stricter standard of proof is applied: the prosecution must prove its case **beyond a reasonable doubt**.)

THE DECISION. A unanimous verdict is not necessary in a civil case in California; if three-quarters of the jury agrees, that's enough. (Unanimity is required in criminal cases, however.) If there is a **hung jury**—that is, the jury cannot agree on a verdict after deliberating for a long time—the case must be tried all over again before a new jury.

The jury in *Palermo v. Mulligan* votes 10 to 2 in favor of the plaintiff. Most of the jurors found Palermo's expert witnesses more convincing than Mulligan's expert witnesses. The jurors concluded that the flooding would not have occurred if Mulligan had not cleared and regraded her lot.

The jury awards Palermo $22,000 to repair and replace his water-damaged property. This is significantly less than the $30,000 he requested. The jury wasn't willing to believe that Palermo's stereo equipment and record collection were worth as much as the appraiser testified. The lower award may also reflect some sympathy for Mulligan.

In addition to the jury's damages award, the judge issues an injunction ordering Mulligan to install culvert that will rechannel runoff. Based on the experts' testimony, the judge specifies changes that will prevent future flooding of Palermo's property, without damaging Mulligan's property.

In hindsight, Mulligan and her lawyer appear to have miscalculated. Mulligan would have been better off accepting Palermo's $17,000 settlement offer, instead of going through with the trial in the hope of avoiding liability altogether.

The Losing Party. One thing further: unless the law provides that the winner receives reasonable attorney's fees from the loser (or the parties have so provided in the contract), attorney fees are absorbed by each party. Therefore, if Palermo's attorney cost $6,000, the net is $16,000.

APPEAL

Both Mulligan and Palermo have a right to appeal the superior court decision to the California Court of Appeals for the First District. After the lower court's judgment has been entered, there is a limited period (usually 60 days) for filing a notice of appeal.

If Mulligan were to appeal, she would be the **appellant**, and Palermo would be the **appellee** or **respondent**. If Palermo were to appeal, he would be the appellant, and Mulligan would be the appellee or respondent. Both of them decide not to appeal, however. Since the jury's fact conclusions can't be challenged on appeal, neither Palermo nor Mulligan could expect to gain much, and they are both very tired of the whole business.

COLLECTING A JUDGMENT

Just because the jury has awarded Palermo $22,000, that doesn't mean Mulligan will take out her checkbook and pay him on the spot. It can take a long time to collect a judgment; some are never collected.

JUDGMENT LIENS. Mulligan (the **judgment debtor**) doesn't pay the judgment immediately, so Palermo (the **judgment creditor**) secures his interest by claiming a **lien** against Mulligan's real property. The lien attaches after Palermo obtains an **abstract of judgment** from the court clerk and files it with the county recorder. If Mulligan never pays, Palermo can foreclose on the lien, hoping to collect his $22,000 from the proceeds of a forced sale of the property. (Liens are discussed in Chapter 3.)

Judgment liens can also attach to some personal property, such as business equipment and inventory. However, many types of personal property are exempt from judgment liens, including the debtor's household furnishings and clothing.

GARNISHMENT. When a judgment debtor is a wage earner, the judgment creditor can use **wage garnishment** to collect the judgment in installments. An earnings withholding order is served on the debtor's employer, who must set aside the debtor's earnings for the creditor. An amount necessary for the support of the debtor and his or her family is exempt from garnishment.

These collection devices are cumbersome, and they aren't always successful. Some defendants turn out to be "judgment-proof": they have no wages and no assets, or their assets are either exempt from judgment liens or already heavily encumbered with other liens. Inability to collect a judgment may be a real hardship for a judgment creditor who owes his or her own lawyer a substantial fee. That can make winning a lawsuit a hollow victory.

CHAPTER SUMMARY

1. The law is a system of rights and duties established and enforced by a government. It maintains order, resolves disputes, enforces promises, and prevents exploitation.

2. Substantive law defines rights and duties, while procedural law sets out the methods for enforcing substantive rights.

The government brings a criminal action to punish a wrongdoer and protect society. In a civil action, on the other hand, an injured party sues for compensation. Some wrongful acts can lead to both criminal and civil penalties.

Contracts, torts, and property are the fundamental concepts of civil law. Contract law concerns voluntarily assumed duties; tort law concerns the duties of reasonable conduct imposed by law; property law concerns the duties inherent in ownership.

3. Federal and state constitutions, legislatures, courts, and administrative agencies are the sources of law in the United States.

Constitutions protect individual rights by limiting government power. Within those constitutional limits, legislative and administrative bodies issue general rules in the form of statutes, ordinances, and regulations.

Courts apply those rules to resolve lawsuits. In interpreting the rules, judges develop case law. The doctrine of stare decisis requires judges to follow established precedents, so that the law will be evenhanded and predictable.

4. A court system is a hierarchy of trial courts and appellate courts. An appeal is not a second trial. The appellate court reviews the trial record for prejudicial errors, focusing primarily on questions of law rather than fact.

The federal and state court systems are independent, with overlapping jurisdictions. Federal jurisdiction is limited to cases involving federal questions, diversity of citizenship, or the U.S. government. State courts can hear any case except those that Congress has reserved for the federal courts.

The case or controversy requirement, statutes of limitation, and the doctrine of res judicata limit access to the courts. But the court systems are severely overcrowded in spite of these rules.

5. A civil suit begins when the plaintiff files a complaint with the court. The pretrial discovery process gives each side access to information the other might prefer to conceal. The parties' lawyers try to negotiate a settlement, to save the expense and trouble of a trial.

Litigants have a right to trial by jury on any issue that does not involve an equitable remedy. In the trial, each side presents testimony and other evidence favorable to its case. Evidence is only admissible if it meets established standards of reliability and fairness.

If the plaintiff wins, he or she may have to resort to garnishment or lien foreclosure to collect the judgment.

CHAPTER 1 KEY TERMS	equal protection	remand
	equitable/remedy law	res judicata
	remedies	service of process
act/statute/ordinance/bill	exhibit	settlement
affirm/modify/reverse	fact witness/expert witness	specific performance
appellant/appellee	federal question	standard of proof
burden of proof	garnishment	stare decisis
case law	injunction	state action
case or controversy	judicial review	statute of limitations
codification	jurisdiction	statutory construction
common law	jury instructions	subject matter jurisdiction
criminal/civil	opinion	substantive/procedural
damages	personal jurisdiction	summons/complaint/answer
declaratory relief	plaintiff/defendant	tort
deposition/interrogatories	precedent	trial record
direct/cross examination	prejudicial error	trier of fact
diversity jurisdiction	pretrial discovery	unconstitutional
due process	question of fact/of law	veto/override

An Introduction to Law

Quiz—Chapter 1

1. The main historical influence on law in the United States was:

    a. Spanish law.
    b. feudal law.
    c. European law.
    d. English law.

2. When one individual sues another, the lawsuit is called:

    a. a civil action.
    b. an equitable suit.
    c. declaratory relief.
    d. criminal litigation.

3. The primary purpose of most civil lawsuits is to:

    a. punish a wrongdoer.
    b. compensate a person who has been harmed.
    c. protect society.
    d. deter crime.

4. A person who commits a tort:

    a. will be prosecuted by the government.
    b. will be held liable for breach of contract.
    c. has violated the standards of reasonable conduct imposed by law.
    d. must serve a jail term.

5. Which of the following would be more likely to issue an ordinance?

    a. The Pasadena City Council.
    b. The Coastal Commission.
    c. The California Assembly.
    d. The Los Angeles County Superior Court.

6. Codification refers to:

    a. reviewing statutes or regulations to determine whether they are constitutional.
    b. enforcing substantive rights.
    c. combining scattered, piecemeal laws. into a comprehensive statute.
    d. interpretation of a contract by an appellate court.

7. When the California legislature adopts a new statute, the new law:

    a. is automatically reviewed by the state supreme court to determine whether it is constitutional.
    b. may change rules that were developed in earlier court decisions.
    c. must be approved by a majority vote of state citizens.
    d. none of the above.

8. Which of these is a question of law?

    a. Was the broker required to put the earnest money in a trust account?
    b. Did the tenant inform the landlord that the railing was broken?
    c. Did the real estate agent inspect the attic?
    d. Was the buyer told that the agent was representing the seller?

9. Which of these can limit a court's jurisdiction?

    a. Geographical boundaries
    b. Subject matter of the case
    c. Amount of money at issue in the case
    d. All of the above

10. Unlike an expert witness, a fact witness:

    a. testified during the appeal.
    b. should not state his or her opinions while testifying.
    c. may not be cross-examined.
    d. all of the above.

ANSWERS: 1. d; 2. a; 3. b; 4. c; 5. a; 6. c; 7. b; 8. a; 9. d; 10. b

CHAPTER 2
Nature of Real Property

CHAPTER OVERVIEW

This chapter explains how real property is described, the distinction between real property and personal property, and the rights that go along with real property. These rules are important to everyone involved in a sale of real estate, because they determine exactly what is being sold: which piece of land, what things on that land, and what rights in regard to the land.

Land and Description

The legal description of a piece of real property determines its boundaries. Boundary disputes are one of the most common sources of real estate lawsuits. Neighbors often disagree about where one's property ends and the other's begins. Buyer often discover that the property they bought isn't the property they thought they were buying.

Sellers are usually held liable for misrepresenting the location of their property boundaries, even if the misrepresentation was innocent. Mr. and Mrs. Stone claimed they had been deceived by the man who sold the property to them, and hadn't realized there was any problem. But the court entered a judgment against the Stones for the difference between the amount the Farnells had paid for the property and the amount it was actually worth. Sellers are presumed to know the character and attributes of the property they are conveying. If they make an erroneous representation about the boundaries, they can be held liable.

Chapter 2

Case Example: The Stones sold their home in Beverly Hills to the Farnells. Before the sale agreement was signed, Mrs. Stone took the Farnells around the property and pointed out its boundaries.

Several months after the sale, the property was surveyed. The Farnells learned that the carport, the guest house, portions of the yard and driveway, and about one-third of the main house were not actually on the property described in their deed. Instead, they were on land owned by the city of Los Angeles, designated as part of Mulholland Drive. *Stone v. Farnell*, 239 F.2d 750 (9th Cir. 1956).

What if the sellers misrepresent their boundaries to a real estate agent, and the agent innocently repeats the inaccurate information to the buyers? The agent probably won't be held liable; an agent does not have to verify everything the seller says. But if there is anything to suggest that the seller could be wrong (a map or a survey marker, for example), the agent might be held liable for failing to double-check the seller's statements. California courts have expanded real estate agents' duty to inspect residential property (see Chapter 6), and that limits the agents' liability in connection with boundary problems.

Even when there is no indication that the sellers are mistaken or lying, a real estate agent should use whatever information is available to check the boundaries. Knowing how to read a legal description is an important part of that process.

METHODS OF DESCRIPTION

An accurate legal description of a property can usually be found in a recorded deed, trust deed, or lease. It's extremely important for these documents to contain accurate descriptions; an ambiguous or uncertain description is not legally adequate and may invalidate the document.

There are many methods for describing property, but the three most commonly used systems of land description are:

- ◆ metes and bounds,
- ◆ government survey, and
- ◆ lot and block.

**www.firstam.com/CFPjZaGc/faf/dimensions/metes.html
(Legal Descriptions of Property - Metes and Bounds)**

Metes and Bounds

The metes (measurements) and bounds (boundaries) system is the oldest method of describing land. British settlers used it in the thirteen colonies. The method is still frequently used in rural areas, and is especially common in eastern states.

The metes and bounds method identifies a parcel of land by describing its outline or boundaries. The boundaries are fixed by reference to three things:

1. **monuments**, which may be natural objects such as rivers or trees, or man-made objects such as roads or survey markers;
2. **courses** (directions), in the form of compass readings; and
3. **distances**, measured in any convenient unit of length.

Example

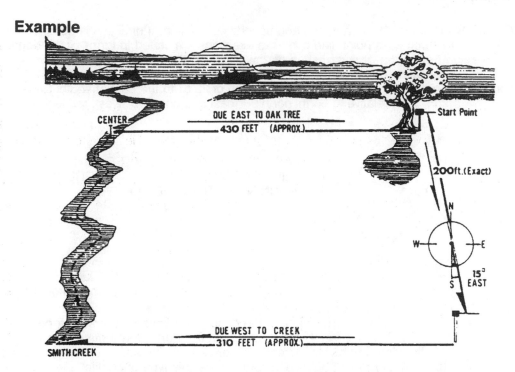

Labels in figure: CENTER · DUE EAST TO OAK TREE · 430 FEET (APPROX.) · Start Point · 200ft.(Exact) · N · W · E · S · 15° EAST · DUE WEST TO CREEK · 310 FEET (APPROX.) · SMITH CREEK

A metes and bounds description states a starting point and then proceeds around the boundary by listing a series of courses and distances. The description continues until the boundary has been described all the way around, back to the starting point.

A tract of land in Calaveras County described as follows: Beginning at the old oak tree, thence south 15° east, 200 feet, thence north 90 west, 310 feet more or less to the center line of Smith Creek, thence northwesterly along the center line of Smith Creek to a point directly west of the old oak tree, thence north 90° east, 430 feet more or less to the point of beginning.

POINT OF BEGINNING. A metes and bounds description must always start at a convenient and well-defined point that can be easily identified (such as the old oak tree in the example). The starting point is referred to as the point of beginning (or POB). The point of beginning is always described by reference to a monument.

> **Example:** "The SW corner of the intersection of 1st Ave. and Bridd St.," or "200 feet due north of the old oak tree."

Note that the point of beginning does not have to be a monument itself; it must simply be defined in relation to a monument. In the example, the oak tree is a monument and the point of beginning is 200 feet north of the tree.

Older metes and bounds descriptions often used natural monuments such as "the old oak tree." But that created some problems, since a tree can be chopped down and a boulder can be moved. So modern metes and bounds descriptions generally use government survey lines as monuments.

COMPASS BEARINGS. In a metes and bounds description, a direction is described by reference to a compass point. The compass directions are stated in terms of the degree of deviation from north or south. Thus northwest (or 315°) is written as north 45° west, since it is a deviation of 45° to the west of north. Similarly, south southeast (or 157.5°) is written as south 22.5° east, since it is a deviation of 22.5° to the east of south. East and west are both written relative to north: north 90° east and north 90° west, respectively.

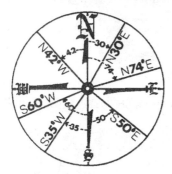

COMPASS BEARINGS IN METES AND BOUNDS DESCRIPTIONS ARE GIVEN BY REFERENCE TO A LINE RUNNING NORTH AND SOUTH.

ORDER OF PREFERENCE. Sometimes there are discrepancies between the various elements of a metes and bounds description. This is usually because the original surveyor made a mistake. For instance, if the description says "320 feet in a northerly direction to the corner of the Porter farmhouse," but the Porter farmhouse is really in a northwesterly direction, there's a discrepancy between the course (northerly) and the monument (the farmhouse). To help surveyors resolve this type of conflict, the following order of priority has been established:

1. natural monuments (Scrubfish Creek) have first priority,
2. then man-made monuments (Avondale Road),
3. then courses (south 8° east),
4. then distances (310 feet),
5. then names (the Holden Ranch),
6. then the area or amount of acreage (80 acres).

Example: A description reads "east 380 feet to the midpoint of Scrubfish Creek." It is actually 385 feet to the midpoint of Scrubfish Creek. The reference to Scrubfish Creek takes precedence over the distance. The property line extends clear to the midpoint of the creek, not just 380 feet.

Government Survey

A second method of land description is the government survey. This method was developed shortly after the American revolution when the federal government owned vast tracts of undeveloped land. Land speculators and settlers moving into the territories, and Congress was anxious to sell some of the land of in order to increase revenues and diminish the national debt. It wasn't feasible to use the metes and bounds method for all of this property, so the government survey system was created. Government survey descriptions are mainly used in states west of the Mississippi.

www.sfei.org/ecoatlas/GIS/MapInterpretation/ ProjectionsSurverySystems.html#C ™ (The Public Land Survey System)

Nature of Real Property

The government survey system is also called the **rectangular survey** method because it divides the land into a series of rectangular grids. Each grid is composed of two sets of lines, one set running north/south, and the other east/west.

NORTH/SOUTH LINES	EAST/WEST LINES
principal meridian	base line
guide meridians	correction lines
range lines	township lines
ranges	township tiers

The main north/south line in each grid is called the **principal meridian**, and the main east/west line is the **base line**. There are 35 principal meridians and 32 base lines across the country. Each principal meridian has its own name, and these are used to identify the different grids. California has three principal meridians: the Humboldt Meridian, the Mt. Diablo Meridian, and the San Bernardino Meridian.

Additional east/west lines called **correction lines** run parallel to the base lines at intervals of 24 miles. Additional north/south lines called **guide meridians** are also established at 24-mile intervals. Because of the curvature of the earth, all true north/south lines converge as they approach the North Pole. Therefore, each guide meridian only runs as far as the next correction line. Then a new interval of 24 miles is measured and a new guide meridian is run. This way the guide meridians remain approximately the same distance apart and do not converge.

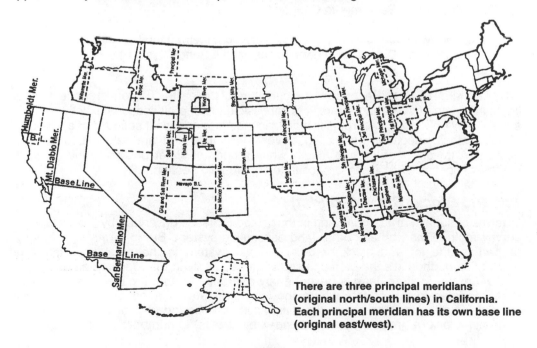

There are three principal meridians (original north/south lines) in California. Each principal meridian has its own base line (original east/west).

The large squares created by the intersection of guide meridians and correction lines are further divided into smaller tracts of land by additional north/south lines running at six-mile intervals that are called **range lines**. The range lines divide the land into columns called **ranges**. Additional east/west lines run at six-mile intervals from the correction lines and are called township lines. They divide the land into rows or tiers called **township tiers**.

The square of land located at the intersection of a range and a township tier is called a **township**. It is identified by its position relative to the principal meridian and base line.

Example: The township located in the fourth tier north of the base line and the third range east of the principal meridian is called "township north, range 3 east" or "T4N, R3E."

Each township measures 36 square miles. A township is divided into 36 sections, one square mile each. The sections are always numbered 1 through 36 in a specified sequence. (The diagram on the next page shows the numbering pattern.)

Parcels of land smaller than sections can be identified by reference to sections and partial sections.

Example: "The northwest quarter of the southwest quarter of section 12, township 4 north, range 3 east." (In abbreviated form, "the NW 1/4 of the SW 1/4 of section 12, T4N, R3E.")

Since the grid systems are identical across the country, the description has to include the name of the principal meridian to identify the particular grid. It's also a good idea to mention the county and state where the land is located.

Example: A complete description of a township would be: "T4N, R3E of the Mt. Diablo meridian, Sacramento County, California."

www.outfitters.com/genealogy/land/twprangemap.html
(Graphic Display of Federal Township and Range System)

GOVERNMENT LOTS. Because of the curvature of the earth, the convergence of range lines, and human surveying errors, it is impossible to keep all sections exactly one mile square. Any deficiency or surplus is placed in the north and west sections of a township. These irregular sections are called **government lots** and are referred to by a lot number. A government lot also results when a body of water or some other obstacle makes it impossible to survey an accurate square-mile section.

Lot and Block (Recorded Plat)

In terms of surface area, more land in the United States is described by the rectangular survey method than by any other land description system. But in terms of number of properties, the lot and block or recorded plat system is the most important land description method. It's the method used most frequently in metropolitan areas.

Under this system, land is described by reference to a map called a **subdivision plat**, recorded in the county where the land is located. Based on a survey of the subdivision, the plat map shows the dimensions and boundaries of each lot. Each lot and each block (a group of lots surrounded by streets) is numbered. After the map is recorded, reference to a lot number and block number on the specified plat is a sufficient legal description of that lot.

Example: "Lot 2, Block 4 of Hilliard's Division, in the city of Eureka, county of Humboldt, state of California, as shown on the map recorded in book 22, page 36, of Maps, in the office of the recorder of said county."

Basic Components of The Government Survey System

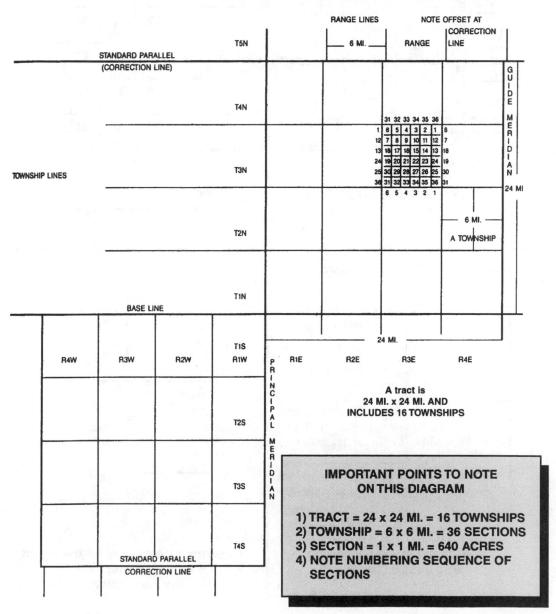

IMPORTANT POINTS TO NOTE ON THIS DIAGRAM

1) TRACT = 24 x 24 MI. = 16 TOWNSHIPS
2) TOWNSHIP = 6 x 6 MI. = 36 SECTIONS
3) SECTION = 1 x 1 MI. = 640 ACRES
4) NOTE NUMBERING SEQUENCE OF SECTIONS

A tract is
24 MI. x 24 MI. AND
INCLUDES 16 TOWNSHIPS

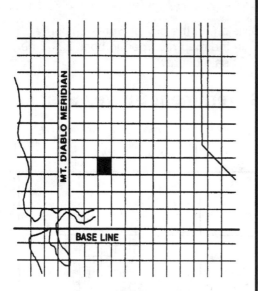

Township 4 North, Range 3 East

6	5	4	3	2	1
7	8	9	10	11	12
18	17	16	15	14	13
19	20	21	22	23	24
30	29	28	27	26	25
31	32	33	34	35	36

A Township contains 36 sections, numbered in this sequence.

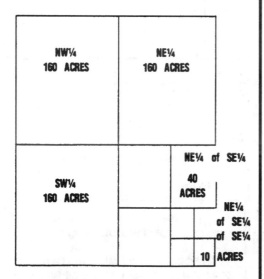

A section can be divided up into smaller parcels.

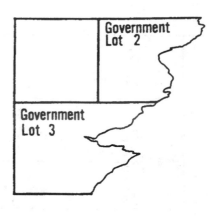

Government lots may be the result of a body of water intruding into a section.

Since a detailed description of the lot is already on file in the recorder's office, that description may be incorporated into any legal document simply by reference. To find out specific information about the lot, you look in the platbook at the county recorder's office. Plat maps frequently contain a considerable amount of information in addition to the detailed description of property boundaries. Many plat maps include this information:

◆ measurements of area,
◆ easement locations and dimensions,
◆ location of survey markers,
◆ location of sewer lines and underground wiring,
◆ subdivision restrictions,
◆ topographical details such as elevation, and
◆ school sites and recreational areas.

Keep in mind that examining a plat map isn't a substitute for a thorough title search.

Other Methods of Description

There are other ways of describing land besides the three major methods discussed above. Popular names (such as "the Bar Z Ranch") and blanket statements ("my six lots") can be legally sufficient descriptions if they make it possible to definitely determine what property is being described.

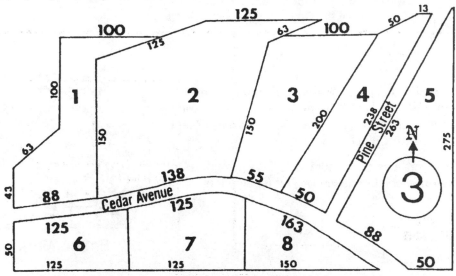

A PLAT MAP

Example: A grant of "all of my lands in San Diego County" is adequate, because it's possible to determine from the public record what property the grantor owned when the deed was executed. However, a grant of "one of my lots in San Diego County" is not acceptable; there's no way to determine which lot is being referred to.

A lazy but legally adequate way of describing property is simply by referring to the description in an earlier recorded document.

Example: "I hereby grant all the property described in that deed of trust recorded in San Luis Obispo County on March 26, 1983; under recording number 8303260002..."

AIR SPACE (Lots)

Not all real property can be described simply by reference to a position on the face of the earth. Some types of property (such as a second-story unit in a condominium) also need to be described in terms of elevation above the ground. When describing the location of a condominium unit or other air space, you can't simply measure the height from the ground, because the ground isn't a stable and precise legal marker.

The United States Geodetic Survey has established datums and bench marks as legal reference points. Most large cities have also established their own official datum and bench marks. A **datum** is an artificial horizontal plane of elevation, established in reference to sea level. At certain locations, subsidiary reference points called bench marks are established. A **bench mark** is a point whose position relative to a datum has been accurately measured. A bench mark may be a metal or concrete marker (often placed in a sidewalk or other stable position) that states the location relative to the datum.

www.lib.noaa.gov/edocs/function.html
(Functions of the Coast and Geodetic Survey)

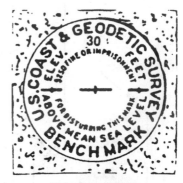

Bench Mark

Example: A metal disk in the sidewalk at the corner of Oak and Elm streets has the following words engraved on it: "Bench Mark No. 96, 17 feet above River City Datum."

Surveyors use the datum or a bench mark as a reference point in describing air (space) lots.

Example: A surveyor plotting a condominium unit on the 16th floor of a new building being built on Elm Street calculates that the floor of the unit will be 230 feet above the sidewalk. He therefore shows in his survey that the floor of the unit is 247 feet above the River City Datum as established by Bench Mark No. 96, because Bench Mark No. 96 is 17 feet above the datum.

DESCRIPTION PROBLEMS

ERRONEOUS DESCRIPTIONS. When the West was originally surveyed for the federal government, the surveyors often worked under harsh conditions, with equipment that is considered inadequate today. As a result, there are errors in the government survey, and these create errors in property descriptions that are revealed by modern surveys. A court called upon to interpret this type of erroneous description will try to carry out the original surveyor's intentions.

Other description errors are simply the result of mistakes in transcription. Often the property description on a deed is copied off of the previous deed and in the copying process, a lot of things can go wrong. A typographical error might transpose two numbers, so that "912 feet" winds up as "192 feet." Or part of the description might be left out altogether: the deed says only "Lot 3, Colvina Heights," but the subdivision has 22 blocks and there's a Lot 3 on each block.

When this kind of mistake is discovered, it may be possible to ask the person who transferred the property to execute a new deed with a corrected description. If that isn't possible, the new owner can ask a court to issue an order correcting the description. This is called **reformation** of the document.

Statutory Rules
of Land Description

- ◆ If A deeds property to B which states that a road or highway is the boundary for the property, it is presumed that the boundary goes to the center of the road unless shown to the contrary in the deed.
- ◆ If the grant describes the boundary as running a specified distance from a road, the boundary runs from the edge of the road and not from the center.
- ◆ When permanent and visible or ascertained boundaries or monuments are inconsistent with the measurement of either lines, angles, or surfaces, the boundaries or monuments are paramount.
- ◆ If in a lawsuit there is a dispute about the boundary of land patented or otherwise granted by the state or the validity of a state patent or grant dated before 1950, all parties must disclose to each other all relevant nonpriviledged written evidence known and available about the property and the boundaries.
- ◆ When the boundaries have been disturbed by earth movements such as slides, subsidence, lateral or vertical displacements or similar disasters the land is in a different location. The Culled Earthquake Act provides a procedure to equitable reestablish boundaries and quiet title to the land within those boundaries.
- ◆ Water boundaries are discussed later in this chapter.

AMBIGUOUS DESCRIPTIONS. When a deed's description is ambiguous, the deed is technically invalid. But that problem can be cured simply by possession.

> **Example:** John Alvarez owns a ranch in Merced County and a ranch in Mariposa County, and each is known locally as "the Alvarez Ranch." Alvarez conveys one of the ranches to Maria Swanson. The deed identifies the property simply as "the Alvarez Ranch," without specifying in which county the land is located.

If Swanson occupies the ranch in Merced County, the deed can be held valid. Swanson's possession of the Merced County ranch makes it clear which ranch the deed referred to.

CASE EXAMPLE: The Brandenburgers owned lot 57 of a subdivision that was surveyed in 1909 and recorded in 1910. Currently the Bryants own the west one-half of lot 57 and the Blevins own the east one-half. The Blevins believed the fence line was the boundary line. The Bryants had their property surveyed shortly after buying it. The fence that covered the property was 11 to 42 feet off the true boundary which resulted in a shortage of .4 acres. The Bryants sued to recover possession of the disputed line and the Blevins cross-complained to establish title by the doctrine of agreed boundaries.

On appeal, the California Supreme Court held that there was no evidence that the fence was erected to resolve uncertainty as to the location of the property line. More importantly, the doctrine of agreed boundary is not to be used when the true boundary can be determined from existing legal descriptions and recordings as it undermines the significance of legal descriptions and encourages litigation. It should only be used in instances in which existing legal records are inadequate to settle a boundary dispute. *Bryant v. Blevins*, 9 Cal. 4th 47, 36 Cal. Rptr. 2d 86 (1994).

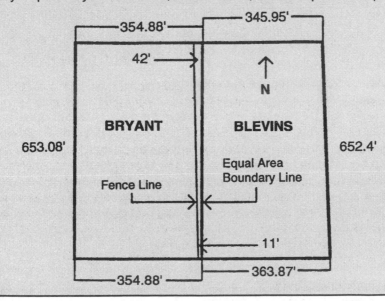

BOUNDARY DISPUTES

AGREED BOUNDARY. Often a boundary described in a deed doesn't match up with the line that has actually been treated as the boundary on the property. One neighbor may want to reassert the true legal description, while the other wants to stick with the established physical boundary.

Many of these disputes are resolved by the doctrine of agreed boundary. The doctrine applies when two adjoining landowners are uncertain as to the location of the true boundary between their property. If they agree (either expressly or implied) to treat a certain line as their common boundary, that line can become the legal boundary.

An agreed boundary must be marked or be otherwise discernible on the property, to give new owners notice of its location. Usually the agreed boundary must be accepted or acquiesced to for at least five years before it becomes the true boundary. But when one of the parties would suffer a substantial loss if the original boundary were enforced, the five year requirement does not apply.

**http://members.aol.com/e52berg/pubpage.html
(California Land Law)**

Attachments

You've decided to buy a particular property. You checked the legal description, so you have a clear idea of what piece of land is being conveyed. Of course, the legal description doesn't mention the house, but you're sure that it's included in the sale. But what about the kitchen appliances inside the house? The hot tub and the water fountain in the back yard? The poplar trees and the rose garden?

Whenever land is transferred, it's necessary to distinguish between real property and personal property. Unless otherwise agreed, all the real property is included in the transfer, but the personal property is not. Buyers and sellers, landlords and tenants, owners and foreclosing creditors often disagree about whether an item is personal property or part of the realty. These disagreements can lead to lawsuits.

Example: A homebuyer sues the seller in small claims court because the seller took the satellite dish with him and the buyer assumed it was included in the purchase price.

When there's a conflict like this, the real estate agent may end up paying for the disputed item out of his or her own pocket to keep the peace. So it's important for everyone involved in a transaction to know what things are included in the sale of the real property.

People tend to think of the actual land when they hear the term "real property." But real property is more than just rocks and dirt. Things built on the land (like houses and fences) and things growing on the land (like trees and shrubs) are called **attachments**. Attachments are considered part of the real property.

There are two main categories of attachments:

◆ natural attachments, and
◆ man-made attachments (or fixtures).

NATURAL ATTACHMENTS

Natural attachments are plants growing on the land. There are two types of natural attachments:

◆ Fructus naturales (or "fruits of nature") are all naturally occurring trees and plants.
◆ Fructus industriales (or "fruits of industry") are planted and cultivated by people.

www.iLsg.org
www.farmlandinfo.org
(Farmland Information)

Both types of natural attachments are generally considered part of the real property. But when they are severed from the land, they become personal property.

Example: A stand of timber growing on the land is part of the real property. Once the trees have been felled, however, they are personal property.

Natural attachments may be considered personal property even before they are actually severed from the land, if they are sold separately from the land.

Example: A farmer sells the timber on his east 40 acres to a lumber company. The sale contract provides that the trees are to be cut in the next year. The lumber company owns the trees as of the date of the contract. They are considered personal property from that date forward, even though they are still attached to the land.

The crops produced by fructus naturales (the berries on wild blackberry bushes, for example) are part of the realty until they are picked or sold separately from the land. But the crops produced by fructus industriales (such as the apples in a cultivated orchard) are always treated as personal property, even before they've been harvested. There's an important exception, however: between a seller and a buyer of land, crops produced by fructus industriales are part of the real property.

Example: Z lives on a small farm with an apple orchard and rampant wild blackberry bushes. The apple trees are fructus industriales, and the blackberry bushes are fructus naturales.
If Z mortgages her real property, the mortgage lien will attach to her land, the apple trees, the blackberry bushes, and the blackberries. But it won't attach to the apples, because they are personal property, not part of the realty.
However, if Z sells her farm to A, the apples will be treated as part of the realty. They will be included in the sale, unless Z specifically excludes them from it in the sale agreement.
Young plants or trees (nursery stock) temporarily placed in the soil pending sale and not intended to permanently grow in that location are personal property.

DOCTRINE OF EMBLEMENTS. A special rule called the doctrine of emblements applies to crops planted by tenant farmers. When a tenancy is for an indefinite period of time (a life estate), and the tenancy is terminated (through no fault of the tenant) before the annual crop is ready for harvest, the tenant has the right to reenter the land and harvest the crop.

> **Example:** For several years, a farmer has been renting a large field from his neighbor. They have a year-to-year lease; it is automatically renewed each June until one of the parties gives the other notice of termination.
>
> In April, the neighbor tells the farmer the lease will end in June, because she's planning to sell her land. The farmer has the right to enter the property in the autumn to harvest the crops he planted, even though the lease has ended.

To fall within this rule, the crop must be produced by the labor and industry of the farmer. For example, if the crop is wild mushrooms that grow naturally and were not planted or cultivated by the farmer, the rule does not apply. If the crops are an annual product of perennial plants, such as apples or strawberries, the right to reenter and harvest applies only to the first crop that matures after the tenancy has ended.

FIXTURES

Man-made attachments are called **fixtures**. They are items that were once personal property, but are now connected to the land in such a way that they are considered part of the real property. For instance, a pile of lumber and a batch of nails are personal property. But they become fixtures when they're used to build a barn.

Whether a particular item is a fixture or personal property is a question that real estate agents deal with constantly. Earlier, we referred to a dispute over a satellite dish. Is this a fixture? What about a tool shed? A swing set? Imported goldfish in a garden pond?

To avoid controversy over this issue, a real estate agent should discuss these kinds of items with the seller and buyer, making sure that both agree about what is and is not included in the sale. Of course, the agent must know what is ordinarily considered a fixture and what is considered personal property.

The courts have come up with a series of tests to determine when an item is a fixture.

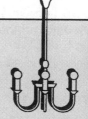

Fixture tests take into account:

- ◆ **the method of attachment,**
- ◆ **adaptation to the realty,**
- ◆ **the intention of the annexor,**
- ◆ **the relationship of the parties, and**
- ◆ **any written agreement.**

Method of Attachment

When an item is permanently attached to the land, it becomes part of the real estate. An attachment is considered permanent when the item is:

◆ permanently resting on the land (such as large buildings like houses and barns);
◆ affixed to the land by roots (as with trees and shrubs);
◆ embedded in the earth (like sewer lines or septic tanks); or
◆ attached by any enduring method (such as cement, plaster, nails, bolts, or screws).

Note that an item can be considered a fixture even when it isn't actually physically attached to the land. Attachment by the force of gravity may be sufficient, as in the case of a building without a foundation. An item may also be considered a fixture when it's enclosed within a room or building in such a way that it cannot be removed without dismantling it or tearing down part of the building. In any of these situations, there is said to be **actual annexation**.

Some completely moveable items are regarded as so strongly connected with the property that they are considered fixtures, even though they are in no way actually attached to the realty. This is called the **doctrine of constructive annexation**.

Example: A firm that manufactures widgets sells its main processing plant. The widget-making machine weighs twelve tons and is bolted to the floor. It is clearly a fixture. The key that turns on the widget maker and specialized tools for repairing the machine are also considered fixtures, although they are easily moved.

The doctrine of constructive annexation also applies to fixtures that have been temporarily removed from the real property for servicing or repair.

Example: A sells his house to B. At the time of the sale, the built-in dishwasher is at a repair shop. Even so, the dishwasher is included in the sale, and its ownership transfers to B when she takes title to the house.

Adaptation to the Realty

If an item was specially designed or adapted for use in a particular building, or is essential to the use of the building, it is probably a fixture. For example, wall-to-wall carpeting cut to fit a particular room would probably be treated as a fixture, even if it weren't tacked down.

Intention

While the method of attachment test and the adaptation test are important, courts consider the key test to be the intention of the annexor—the person who owned the item as personal property and brought it onto the real property. Did the annexor intend for the item to become part of the realty or to remain personal property?

There must be objective evidence of intent; it isn't enough for the annexor to claim that he or she always intended to remove the item. The method of attachment and the adaptation of the item to the realty are viewed as objective evidence of intent.

Example: "S" puts a bird bath in his back yard, embedding it in concrete. Two years later, he sells his house to "B". Their contract says nothing about the bird bath. When "S" moves out, he digs up the bird bath and takes it with him. "B" objects, arguing that the bird bath was a fixture, and therefore was included in the sale.

"S" protests that he never intended the bird bath to be a fixture. This claim is inadequate, since it isn't backed up by objective evidence. A court would interpret the method of attachment that "S" used (concrete) as evidence of an intent to make the bird bath a permanent part of the real property.

The California Supreme Court stated that classification of an item as a fixture "should turn on whether a reasonable person would consider the item...a permanent part of the host real property, taking into account annexation, adaptation, and other objective manifestations of permanence" (*Crocker Nat'l Bank v. San Francisco*, 49 Cal. 3d 881, 264 Cal. Rptr. 139 [1989]).

Relationships of the Parties

Another factor considered in resolving a dispute over whether an item is a fixture is the relationship of the parties: seller and buyer, borrower and secured lender, landlord and tenant.

Between a seller and a buyer of real property, the rules for determining what is a fixture are interpreted in favor of the buyer.

Example: A homeowner screws a chandelier into his dining room ceiling. Several months later, he sells his house. The chandelier is considered a fixture and is included in the sale, even though it could easily be removed.

Between a trustor (trust deed borrower) and beneficiary (trust deed lender), the rules are interpreted in favor of the beneficiary. The chandelier is part of the realty, so it is covered by the beneficiary's lien.

But between a landlord and a tenant, the rules are interpreted in favor of the tenant. If a tenant installs a chandelier (or any other ornamental or domestic item), he or she will be allowed to remove it at the end of the lease.

These rules tie in with the intention test: the law presumes that a homeowner intends to improve real property, but that a tenant intends to remove the items he or she installs.

The rule favoring the tenant extends to **trade fixtures**, equipment installed for use in the tenant's business. A tenant who operated a beauty parlor can remove the shampoo basins, lighted mirrors, and adjustable chairs, even though they are affixed to the walls or floors. The tenant is responsible for repairing any damage to the premises caused by the removal.

Allowing tenants to remove trade fixtures encourages efficiency in business. Tenants are more likely to install new equipment if they know they can take it with

them when they leave. However, if the trade fixtures have become an integral part of the building they cannot be removed. For example, a marble store front and plate glass windows become an integral part of the building and may not be removed. Trade fixtures that aren't removed when the tenant leaves automatically become the property of the landlord.

The trade fixtures rule is not always applied to items that tenants have installed for farming purposes. **Agricultural fixtures** (a silo, for example) can't necessarily be removed by tenant farmers when they leave the property.

Written Agreement

Regardless of any of the previously discussed considerations, if there is a written agreement between the parties stipulating how a particular item is to be treated, a court will enforce the agreement and it is binding on third parties with notice of it.

Case Example: Elizabeth Carpenter leased some land with a rundown old house on it. She planned to have the house repaired so that she could live there. The lease provided that the house could be taken from the land when the lease expired.

After Carpenter's death a few years later, there was a lawsuit concerning ownership of the house. The court ruled that because of the agreement in the lease, the house was personal property. *Carpenter v. Kilgour*, 46 Cal. Rptr. 115 (1965).

When a seller wants to remove things that might be considered fixtures, he or she should inform the buyer, and include a statement in the deposit receipt specifying which items are excluded from the sale. Natural attachments (shrub or rosebushes, for example) can be excluded in the same way.

Manufactured Housing

Manufactured Housing is classified as personal property until it is permanently attached to the real property by removing the wheels and mounting the unit on a foundation. As personal property, manufactured housing may be sold without a real estate license, and the sales are subject to sales tax laws.

Secured Financing and Fixtures

When personal property is purchased on credit or used as collateral, a creditor often takes a security interest in the property. What happens to that security interest if the personal property becomes attached to real property—in other words, when it becomes a fixture?

A creditor with a security interest in a fixture should record a **financing statement** in the county where the real property is located. This is called "perfecting" the security interest. The recorded financing statement gives constructive notice of the creditor's interest to prospective lienholders or purchasers of the real property. If the debtor defaults, the secured creditor will be able to repossess the fixture.

Example: Q buys a small apartment building with a loan from Vault Savings, and the loan is secured by a trust deed on the property. Q purchases a central air conditioning unit on credit, and the air conditioner company files a financing statement to give notice of its security interest in the unit. Q has the air conditioner installed in his apartment building.

Later Q defaults on the trust deed and on his air conditioner payments. Vault Savings forecloses on the trust deed and takes title to the building. Because the air conditioner is a fixture, the bank would ordinarily acquire ownership of the unit as part of the real property. However, because the air conditioner company perfected its security interest, it can repossess the unit rather than losing it to the bank.

Recorded financing statements are indexed according to the last name of the debtor. As part of a title search, a title insurance company routinely checks to determine whether there are perfected security interests in any of the fixtures on a property about to be sold or used as security for a loan.

Appurtenances

Once you know the boundaries of the real property, and what items are included in the sale, you also need to become familiar with what property rights are transferred along with the property.

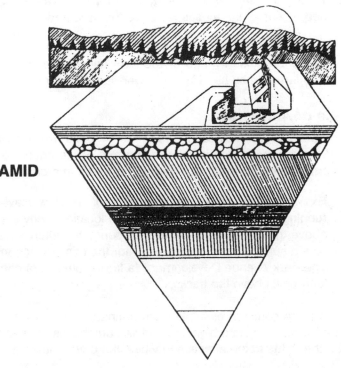

THE INVERTED PYRAMID

One of the best ways to understand the rights that accompany real property is to imagine the property as an inverted pyramid with its tip at the center of the earth and its base extending out into the sky. A property owner has rights to the surface land within the boundaries of the property, plus everything under or over the surface that falls within the pyramid. This includes rights to oil and minerals beneath the surface, plus certain air and water rights.

A right that goes along with real property is called an **appurtenance**. One basic type of appurtenance is the right to take or use something that is in or on the land, such as water, air, or minerals. When real property is transferred, appurtenant rights are ordinarily considered part of the real property and are transferred along with it. But they can be sold separately, and may be limited by past transactions.

AIR RIGHTS

According to the inverted pyramid concept, a property owner's rights extend to the upper limits of the sky. However, through the Air Commerce Act of 1926 and the Civil Aeronautics Act of 1938, Congress declared that the United States government has almost complete control over America's air space.

Use of Airspace

Although the government has restricted air rights, property owners still have the exclusive right to use the lower reaches of air space over their property, as long as they do nothing to interfere with air traffic. Property owners also have the right not to be harmed by use of the air space above their property.

> **Example:** The classic example is an airport built near a chicken farm. The noise of the airplanes flying over the farm causes the chickens to stop laying eggs. The farmer may be able to recover damages for the resulting loss of income.

Sale of Airspace

A property owner may sell rights to the airspace over the property separately from the land. As the population increases and real estate prices rise, the sale of airspace has become more common, especially in large urban areas.

> **Example:** The New York Central and the New Haven railroads had tracks running across real estate in a prime location. They sold rights to the airspace above the tracks for an enormous sum. The purchasers acquired the airspace plus a surface easement to allow for the construction and support of buildings. The Park Avenue Development (a large complex of commercial buildings) was later built above the tracks.

A more common example is an ordinary condominium sale. Someone who buys a condominium unit in a high-rise building purchases not just the physical apartment, but also the rights to the airspace in which the unit is situated.

Nature of Real Property

WATER RIGHTS

Water is vital for farming, industry, and day-to-day living. Because it is so scarce in many parts of California, water has been the source of a lot of legislation and litigation in this state. The statutes and lawsuits concern the right to use the water, ownership of the water, and ownership of lake or stream beds. Under the Water Code, the State's ownership of water is to "control and regulate use," as distinct from the common usage of the concept of "ownership." (*State of California v. Superior Court* [Underwriters at Lloyd's of London] [2000] 78 CA4th 1019, 1027-1032, 93 CR2d 276, 283-287.)

There are two main types of water rights:

◆ riparian rights and
◆ appropriative rights

http://water.wr.usgs.gov/sub/
(USGS - Land Subsidence in California)

Riparian Rights

Riparian rights are tied to land ownership. Any land that is adjacent to or crossed by water, or contains a body of water within its boundaries, is riparian land. Riparian rights attach to a natural water course not concrete aqueducts or canals used to move water from one location to another. Even the federal government has riparian rights on federal land in California. Under the riparian rights system, every riparian landowner has an equal right to use the water that touches his or her property.

All riparian owners may use the water for swimming, boating, or other recreational purposes. They all have the right to take water for domestic uses such as drinking, washing, and watering a garden. And they may use the water in any other way that is "reasonable and beneficial"—that is, not wasteful. This right is not lost by non-use. According to the California Civil Code, domestic use is the highest use of water, and irrigation is the second highest.

However the water is used, it must be used on the riparian land, the land that adjoins the body of water. A riparian landowner is not allowed to divert water for use on non-riparian land.

> **Example:** C owns two lots, one adjoining the river and another across the road, which is a landlocked. C channels irrigating water to her landlocked lot. The landlocked lot is not bordered by a stream or river and is not riparian land.

A riparian owner is also not allowed to use the water in a way that impairs other riparian owners' rights. For example, an upstream owner on a river may not diminish the water flow in quality, quantity, or velocity. In a time of water shortage, all the riparian owners must reduce their use. During a drought, a use that is ordinarily considered reasonable might be prohibited.

Landowners above an underground aquifer are said to have **overlying rights**. These are very similar to riparian rights; most of the same rules apply.

Appropriative Rights

There are vast tracts of arid land in California where the riparian system won't work. To make that land habitable and productive, water must be transported from other areas. This use of water is controlled by the **prior appropriation** system.

Chapter 2

Anyone can apply to the State Water Resources Control Board for an appropriation permit. If the application is approved, the permit holder is granted the right to take water from a particular lake, river, stream, or aquifer for a specified reasonable and beneficial use. The water does not have to be used on riparian land.

Under the prior appropriation system, if two parties both have appropriation permits for the same body of water, first in time is first in right. This means that the party who obtained a permit first can use as much water as the permit specifies, even if that leaves too little water for the people with later permits. However, appropriation for city inhabitants is first in right and does not have to be first on time.

The rights of the riparian landowners on a lake or river are taken into account when a permit to appropriate water from that lake or river is issued. Riparian rights are paramount, and appropriative rights must not interfere with them.

Example: A and B own land along the Almond River. C and D each have an appropriation permit for the river. C's permit was issued before D's.

Usually the Almond River contains enough water to serve all four individuals. But this spring, the river is very low. The riparian owners, A and B, have first claim on the water, as long as their use is reasonable under the circumstances.

C is next in line. C can take all the water allocated in the appropriation permit, even though this means there won't be enough water left over to meet D's needs. (Again, C's use must be reasonable under the circumstances.)

An appropriative right is lost if it isn't used for 5 years or it is abandoned. In the example above, if C went for a long time without taking any water from the river, C would lose the right to do so. C could obtain a new permit, but then C would have a lower priority than D and other appropriators.

A prescriptive right to water can be acquired by a user either under claim of right or color of title by taking the water for 5 years. The amount of the water acquired by prescriptive right is a fixed amount based on current beneficial use. This prescriptive right can be lost by non-use.

Navigable Waters

All navigable waterways in California are owned and controlled by the state government. When property borders on the ocean (or on a bay connected to it), the property owner only owns the land above the mean high water mark. When property borders on a navigable stream or lake, the property owner owns the land to the low water mark. Beyond those limits, coastal land and the beds of navigable lakes and rivers are owned by the government.

The government holds the state's navigable waters in trust for the public. The public has the right to use the waterways for transportation and recreation. Although landowners on a navigable lake own the land to the low water mark, their ownership of the land between the high water mark and the low water mark is subject to the public trust. They may not use that portion of their property in a way that would interfere with the public's rights. This rule significantly restricts development of many riparian properties.

Nature of Real Property

Non-Navigable Waters

A non-navigable lake is private property. if a small lake is completely within the boundaries of one landowner's property, the landowner owns the lake bed. If several different people own land around a nonnavigable lake or stream, ownership of the lake bed or stream bed is generally divided by tracing lines from each property boundary to the center of the lake or the center of a stream (thread of the stream) measured at its lowest point. Each owner has title to the parcel of the lake bed or stream bed adjoining his or her land. All owners also have the riparian right to the reasonable use of the entire surface of the lake or stream for recreational purposes.

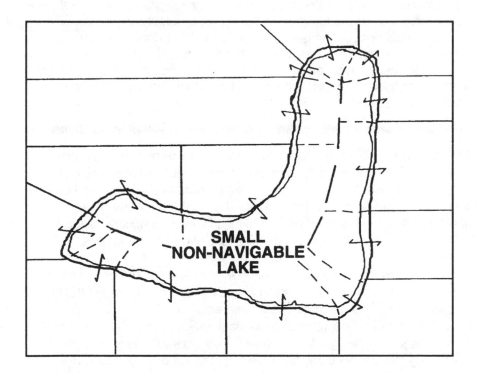

SMALL
NON-NAVIGABLE
LAKE

Mineral Rights

A landowner generally owns all minerals located in or under his or her property. Minerals are considered real property until they are extracted, when they become personal property. A landowner may sell mineral rights separately from the land. This type of sale is sometimes called a horizontal division. The right to own and use the surface property is divided from rights to the subsurface minerals.

The owner of mineral rights must give a written notice to the owner of the property (and any public utility with a recorded interest in the property if there will be a excavation of the utility interest) of an intention to explore or mine before the first entry upon the property. The notice must state the extent and location of prospecting, mining, or extraction and the approximate times of entry and exit.

Standard Methods of Dividing Mineral Rights

1. Mineral deed—a mineral deed transfers all rights to the minerals, and also grants the rights necessary to conduct mining operations to obtain the minerals. This usually includes the rights of access, development, processing, and transportation.

2. Mineral reservation—a mineral reservation is similar to a mineral deed except that the owner sells or transfers the surface property and retains the mineral rights for him or herself.

3. Mineral lease—under a mineral lease, the lessee is given the right to mine and has title to the minerals obtained, but the lessor (the property owner) will regain the mineral rights when the lease expires. The lessor is usually compensated by royalty payments based on a percentage of the value of the extracted minerals.

4. Mineral rights option—a mineral rights option grants the right to explore for the presence of minerals. After exploration, the mining company decides whether or not to exercise its option to lease or purchase the mineral rights on the terms stated in the option agreement.

It has been very common in California's past that a person selling property reserved the mineral rights to the property even though there was no foreseeable possibility that these rights would ever be used. Over time, these "dormant" mineral rights can effect the development of the land and the marketability of the property. Therefore California statutes now allow the lessor of an abandoned or expired mineral lease to demand a quitclaim deed or other document from the lessee showing abandonment. Failure of the lessee to do so may cause a lawsuit to clear the title and makes the lessee liable for the lessor's actual damages, attorneys fees, court cost and $150. The owner of a mineral right may preserve the right by recording a notice of intent to preserve the mineral right. This shows non-dormancy and non-abandonment.

An owner of property subject to a dormant mineral right can sue to terminate the right. A dormant mineral right is one which goes back 20 years from the filing of the lawsuit. During this period there have been no mining or exploration activities on the property; no separate tax assessment on the right or no taxes paid if assessed; and there is no recorded document showing the mineral right. The court must allow the recording of a notice to preserve the mineral right if the right holder pays the property owner's litigation expenses, including attorney's fees.

OIL AND GAS RIGHTS

In their natural state, oil and gas lie trapped beneath the surface of the earth under great pressure. But once an oil or gas reservoir has been tapped, the oil and gas begin to flow towards the point where the reservoir was pierced by the well, since this is the area of lowest pressure. By drilling a well, a property owner can drain an oil or gas reservoir that lies beneath his or her own property and beneath several neighbors' properties as well.

Because of their migratory nature, oil and gas are governed by the **rule of capture**. A property owner who drills a well on his or her own land owns all of the oil or gas the well produces, even though it may have migrated from under a neighbor's land. This rule stimulates oil and gas production. if the neighbors want to protect their interests in the oil or gas beneath their property, they must drill **offset wells** to keep all of the oil or gas from migrating to one well. As a result, more oil gas is produced in a shorter amount of time because more wells are drilled.

Since most landowners don't have the necessary skill, experience, or equipment to drill for oil or gas themselves, they usually enter into lease agreements with oil or gas companies to drill the wells and extract the oil or gas. There is no standard lease form (fictitious oil and gas leases may be recorded), but oil and gas leases generally involve an initial cash amount paid for granting the lease, and royalties paid to the landowner based on the amount of oil or gas actually extracted. The lease is granted for a specified period, and ordinarily provides for an extension of time if necessary. No lease can last more than 99 years after it starts.

SUPPORT RIGHTS

A piece of land is supported by the other land that surrounds it. A landowner has the right to the natural support provided by the land beside and beneath his or her property.

Lateral Support

Lateral support is support from adjacent land. A neighbor's excavations might make your land shift and settle. Traditionally, the neighbor would have been held liable for damage that resulted from the excavations, no matter how carefully they were carried out. This rule has been modified, however. Now, unless the excavations are unusually deep, the neighbor will only be held liable for damage if he or she fails to follow the procedures prescribed by statute.

Among other provisions, the statute requires a landowner planning excavations to notify neighboring landowners. This gives them the opportunity to protect their property.

> **Example:** J and K own adjacent lots. J's lot is vacant, but K's has a house and other improvements on it.
>
> J plans to build a house, so he's going to excavate for the foundation. He gives K proper notice of when, where, and how deep he's going to dig. He takes reasonable precautions to sustain the adjoining land. K does nothing to protect her property.
>
> When J carries out his excavation, K's land shifts, her foundation cracks, and the house tilts. As long as J complied with the statute and used ordinary care and skill in excavating, he is not liable for this damage. J is liable if J failed to give notice or was negligent in excavating.
>
> If the excavation is deeper than the foundations of the adjoining building and will endanger it, the owner must be given a 30-day notice to protect the property and is allowed access to the excavated property to do

so. If the excavation is deeper than 9 feet below curb level and so is the adjoining building, then the excavator must support the land and building without cost to the owner and is liable for any damage, except minor settlement cracks.

Subjacent Support

Subjacent support is support from the underlying earth. The right to subjacent support is important when a landowner transfers rights to the underlying minerals to someone else. The mineral rights owner will be held liable for surface damage caused by underground excavation, even if it was performed carefully. Liability is absolute, unless the weight of structures added on the surface contributed to the subsidence.

OTHER APPURTENANT RIGHTS

Easements and restrictive covenants also create rights that are appurtenant to real property. These types of appurtenances are discussed in Chapter 3 and Chapter 13, respectively.

CHAPTER SUMMARY

1. Knowing the correct property boundaries is important to everyone involved in a real estate transaction. A seller may be held liable for innocently misrepresenting property boundaries. A broker would probably not be held liable for an innocent misrepresentation, but should make an effort to determine if the seller's statements are accurate.

2. The three main methods of land description are metes and bounds, government (rectangular) survey, and lot and block. The lot and block method is the system used most frequently in metropolitan areas.

3. Attachments to real property are part of the real property. Unless otherwise agreed, they are transferred along with the land; personal property is not. The two types of attachments to real property are natural attachments and man-made attachments (fixtures). In deciding whether an item is a fixture, a court tries to determine the intention of the annexor. The court takes into account the method of attachment, adaptation to the realty, the relationship of the parties, and any written agreement.

4. An appurtenance is a right that goes along with or relates to real property, including air, water, oil, mineral, and support rights. These rights are ordinarily transferred with the land, but they may be severed from it and sold separately.

5. The right to use water is either a riparian right or an appropriative right. All landowners whose property adjoins a body of water have riparian rights. To acquire an appropriative right, you must obtain a permit from the government. Under the riparian system, the water must be used on riparian land. Under the prior appropriation system, the water may be used on non-riparian land.

CASE PROBLEM

M. P. Moller v. Wilson, 8 Cal. 2d 31, 63 P.2d 818 (1936)

Mr. Ferguson had a house built for himself in the San Fernando Valley. He borrowed the money for the project, and the loan was secured by a trust deed.

While the house was under construction, Ferguson ordered the plans modified to accommodate a pipe organ. The organ console (with the keyboard) was to be placed in the living room, and a chamber was constructed in the basement to house the organ chest (containing the pipes). The console and chest would be connected by a cable. Ferguson had a stairway added, leading from the living room down to the organ chamber.

Ferguson ordered an organ from the M.P. Moller Company. The organ chest was built to fit the chamber in Ferguson's basement. Ferguson agreed to pay $8,500 for the organ on an installment sales contract; the Moller Company would retain title to the organ until the contract was paid in full. The organ was installed after the house was completed.

But things didn't work out for Ferguson. Not long after moving into the house, he defaulted on the trust deed and the organ sales contract. The trust deed lender foreclosed and the home was sold at a trustee's sale. The purchaser sold it in turn to the Wilsons. When Ferguson moved out of the house, he left the organ behind. The Wilsons had the organ dismantled and placed in storage. The organ chamber became an ordinary basement room.

The Moller Company never recorded its sales contract, so the Wilsons had no notice of the company's interest in the organ. As a result, if the organ was a fixture, the Wilsons would have title to it. The Moller Company's only recourse would be to sue Ferguson for payment. But if the organ remained personal property, the company could repossess the organ unless the Wilsons paid off the sales contract.

In deciding whether or not the organ was a fixture, the court considered these additional facts: the organ console and chest stood on legs and were not fastened to the floor or walls; they were held in place by gravity, and the chest weight 1,500 pounds; to install and remove the organ's longest pipes, a hole was cut in an exterior wall and then repaired; special partitions had been built to protect the organ from vibration; the organ could not be removed without taking down these partitions, but they were not a necessary part of the structure of the house; the organ was not damaged by removal and could be used in any building that would accommodate it.

Which way did the court rule—was the organ a fixture or personal property?

Answer: The court ruled that the organ was personal property, not a fixture. The Wilsons were ordered to pay the Moller Company $4,500.

This case shows that the distinction between fixtures and personal property often isn't straightforward. A court bases its decision on all the facts in the case; some of the facts cut in one direction, and some cut the other way. Two different judges might reach two different conclusions.

In the *Moller* case, the court stated that the key issue was whether or not the organ was intended to become a permanent addition to the real property. Both the organ chest and the house had been specially modified so that the organ could be installed. But the organ could be removed without materially damaging it or the house. The organ chamber became an ordinary room after the chest and the special partitions were removed.

The court contrasted this case with an Illinois case where an organ had been installed in a church. In that case, the organ was held to be an integral part of the architectural design. The church organ was not merely a piece of furniture but an essential part of the building.

It's possible that the *Moller* case would have turned out differently if the Wilsons hadn't already removed the organ when the lawsuit was filed. They had to go to a considerable amount of trouble to remove it: taking down partitions, cutting a hole in the exterior wall of the house. But since they had already taken that trouble, the court seemed to minimize its importance. Instead, the court emphasized that the organ wasn't an essential part of the house, and that it could be used elsewhere.

CHAPTER 2
KEY TERMS

air lot	datum	plat
appurtenance	doctrine of emblements	point of beginning
attachment	financing statement	principal meridian
base line	fixture	prior appropriation
bench mark	fructus	range
common grantor	naturales/industriales	reformation
constructive annexation	government survey	riparian
correction line	government lot	rule of capture
course	guide meridian	section
	lateral/subjacent support	township
	metes and bounds	township tier
	monument	trade fixture

Nature of Real Property

Quiz—Chapter 2

1. One part of a metes and bounds description states "thence south 275 feet to the hemlock tree." A recent survey shows that it is actually 280 feet to the hemlock tree. The property:

   a. will end after 275 feet because distances take precedence over monuments.
   b. will end at the hemlock tree because monuments take precedence over distances.
   c. will have to be re-surveyed to establish a correct description.
   d. none of the above.

2. How many sections are there in township?

   a. 12
   b. 20
   c. 36
   d. 42

3. Because of the curvature of the earth:

   a. a new guide meridian is established at each correction line so that the range lines don't converge.
   b. range lines in northern states are much closer together than those in southern states.
   c. the government survey method of land description is no longer used.
   d. only lot and block descriptions are used in rural areas.

4. A government lot:

   a. is any lot owned by the federal government.
   b. is a section that isn't exactly one mile square.
   c. must be described using the lot and block system.
   d. none of the above.

5. The method of land description used most often in large metropolitan areas is:

   a. rectangular survey.
   b. lot and block.
   c. metes and bounds.
   d. government survey.

6. If a tenancy is terminated before a crop is ready to harvest, a tenant farmer has the right to re-enter the land later to harvest the crop. This rule is known as the doctrine of:

   a. fructus industriales.
   b. constructive annexation.
   c. emblements.
   d. appurtenance.

7. X is in the process of selling his house. On the closing date, the built-in dishwasher is at the repair shop. The dishwasher:

   a. is X's personal property and will not be considered part of the sale.
   b. will be considered part of the sale under the doctrine of constructive annexation.
   c. will have to be conveyed under a separate contract since it wasn't actually in the house at the sale.
   d. none of the above.

8. In determining whether or not an item is a fixture, the most important test is:

   a. relationship of the parties.
   b. adaptation to the realty.
   c. intention of the annexor.
   d. size of the item.

9. Trade fixtures:

   a. are considered real property and cannot be removed by the tenant.
   b. can't be removed unless the lease specially states that they are personal property.
   c. can be removed by the tenant before the lease expires.
   d. none of the above.

10. J owns property along a navigable river. Which of the following is true?

   a. J owns the section of the river bed adjoining her property out to the middle of the river
   b. The government owns the riverbed
   c. J is not entitled to use the water since it is owned by the government
   d. Both b) and c)

KOLL
CONSTRUCTION

WARNING!
THIS IS A CONSTRUCTION SITE

YES: **HARD HATS**
YOU MUST WEAR   **WORK BOOTS**
  SHIRTS
  LONG PANTS
NO: **DRUGS**
  ALCOHOL
  DOGS
  ·RADIOS

VIOLATORS WILL BE REMOVED FROM SITE

CHAPTER 3
Interests in Real Property

CHAPTER OVERVIEW

A person who has a property right or a claim against property is said to have an **interest** in the property. An interest might be an ownership right (such as a life estate), a right to use the property (such as an easement), or a financial claim against the title (such as a trust deed).

One of the most important steps in a real estate transaction is determining exactly what the seller's interest in the property is. You can only transfer the interest that you hold. If you're renting a house, you may be able to assign your lease to someone else, but you can't sell them the house.

A buyer also needs to know about other interests in the property. Do the neighbors have the right to swim in the pond whenever they want? Can Joe's Roofing foreclose if their bill isn't paid soon? Will ownership revert to the seller's uncle if the olive trees along the driveway are removed?

This chapter describes the various types of interests in real property. It explains how they are created and terminated, and how they affect the property.

 www.megalaw.com/top/property.php3
(Legal Specialties: Real Property Law)

Possessory Interests (Estates)

An **estate** is an interest in real property that is, will be, or may become **possessory**. In other words, a person who has an estate either has the right to possess the property now, will have that right in the future, or may have that right in the future. A right to immediate possession is called a **present interest**. A right to possession in the future is called a **future interest**. Estates are classified according to the time of enjoyment (present or future), and also according to their duration.

FREEHOLD ESTATES

Under the feudal system in medieval England, all land was essentially owned by the king. The king parceled out land to his followers in return for their services. These men then could rent portions of their property to others. The modern U.S. system of ownership interests in real property grew out of English feudal law, and many of the legal terms still used to describe estates date back to the twelfth or thirteenth century.

The term "freehold" originally referred to the holdings of a freeman under the feudal/English system. A freeman was allowed to sell his rights in the property, as long as the new owner agreed to give the same services to the lord or king, who held a higher interest in the property.

Today, a freehold estate can still be sold. A freehold is a possessory interest of uncertain duration, which means that the length of time of ownership is unspecified and indefinite. There are two main categories of freehold estates:

◆ fee simple estates, and
◆ life estates.

Fee Simple

When a person is referred to as the "owner" of property, it usually means that he or she holds a fee simple estate. A fee simple estate is the highest and largest interest that can exist in land. A fee simple estate is:

◆ inheritable,
◆ transferable, and
◆ perpetual.

An inheritable estate is, quite simply, one that can be inherited. Property held in fee simple may be left to someone in a will, or automatically passed to heirs if there is no will (by intestate succession). A fee simple estate is also freely transferable, which means that the owner can sell, divide, or even give away the property if he or she so desires. A fee simple is perpetual in that the owner has the right to possess the property for an unlimited period of time. In theory, the owner and his or her heirs could hold the fee simple estate forever.

In transferring a fee simple estate, the former owner may choose to qualify the new owner's title by including a condition or requirement in the deed. It could be a limitation on the use of the property ("on condition that the house is used as a museum"), or it might make title dependent on an event that has nothing to do with the property ("provided that the U.S. does not go to war with Mexico"). If the requirement is not met or maintained, the new owner could forfeit title to the property.

FEE SIMPLE ABSOLUTE AND FEE SIMPLE DEFEASIBLE. A fee simple estate qualified in this way is called a **fee simple defeasible**. A fee simple estate that is not qualified or subject to any conditions of this kind is called a **fee simple absolute**.

Nearly all ordinary residential property is held in fee simple absolute. And in a typical home sale, the real estate agent and the buyer probably assume the seller owns the property in fee simple absolute. But it's very important to check that assumption. Otherwise, the buyer might end up unable to use the property as planned (as a home instead of a museum), or could even lose the property because of an event beyond his or her control (war with Mexico).

Historically, certain types of defeasible fees terminated automatically if the condition stated in the deed was not met. But the California legislature abolished those in 1982 with the Marketable Record Title Act. Now the only type of defeasible fee recognized in California is a **fee simple subject to a condition subsequent** (sometimes called a **conditional fee**). If the condition in the deed isn't met, the grantor (or his or her heirs) has the right to terminate the estate and re-acquire the property. But the termination isn't automatic. The grantor or heirs must file a lawsuit if they want to get the property back. Thus, they are said to have a **power of termination**.

Example: K owned some property next door to Palabra Elementary School. In 1966, K transferred her property as a gift to the Mountain View School District. The deed granted it to the school district "provided that it is used for school purposes." For many years the property was used as a playground by the children at Palabra School.

In 1990, due to population changes and financial trouble, the Mountain View District closes down Palabra School, and K's property is no longer used for school purposes. K (or K's heirs, if she has died in the meanwhile) can take legal action to terminate the school district's interest in the property.

 www.intcounselor.com/real-property.html
(Sources of Property Law and Rights in the U.S.)

A power of termination can no longer be exercised if more than five years have passed since the deed condition was broken.

A power of termination expires 30 years after the deed granting the conditional fee was recorded, unless the power is preserved. The grantor (or grantor's heirs) can record a notice of intent to preserve the power of termination before it expires. That extends the power for another 30 years. This process can be repeated every 30 years, preserving the power of termination indefinitely. But if the power of termination is allowed to expire, the grantee's title is no longer subject to the condition. The grantee then owns the property in fee simple absolute.

The courts see forfeiture of the grantee's title as a harsh outcome that should be avoided. As a result, if the language in a deed can possibly be interpreted as a covenant rather than a condition, a court is likely to treat it as a covenant. A covenant is a legally binding promise (see Chapter 13). If a covenant in a deed is broken, the grantee may have to pay damages, but he or she will not forfeit title. This is the result courts prefer, but they are required to interpret a deed according to the language used.

Case Example: In 1908 and 1916, Elizabeth Kraft and her son Edward granted to the city of Red Bluff their property to be used as a public library. The grant provided that if the property ceased to be used as a library then it shall revert to the grantor or the heirs. In 1986, the books were removed. In 1988, Walton, the only surviving heir, sued to acquire the title. The Court of Appeal held that title reverted to Walton. Although the 1982 Marketable Record Title Act required Walton to record his notice to preserve the power of termination within 5 years of the enactment of the Act or within 30 years of the recording of the original deed, he did neither. This being the case, title should have stayed with the city. However, the attorney for Red Bluff failed to raise Walton's inaction as a defense and, therefore, Walton won. *Walton v. City of Red Bluff*, 2 Cal. App. 4th 177, 3 Cal. Rprt. 2d 275 (1991).

Thus, though it doesn't happen often, the owner of a fee simple subject to a condition subsequent may end up losing the property.

Life Estates

Unlike a fee simple estate, the duration of a life estate is not unlimited. The duration of a life estate is based on the length of someone's lifetime. For example, property formerly owned by President Lyndon Johnson and his wife, Ladybird, has been donated to the public as a National Historical Site. President Johnson died in 1969, but Ladybird Johnson has a life estate in the property. She has the right to possess and occupy the property for the rest of her life. When she dies, the life estate terminates.

Life estates are often used to simplify the division of property in a will, or to avoid the expense of probate. An owner can transfer property to another, but create a life estate in the property for him or herself. This is called **express reservation** of a life estate.

Example: To avoid probate expenses, B deeds his property to his son S, but reserves a life estate for himself. B has the right to use and occupy the property for the rest of his life, but upon his death, ownership will automatically pass to S.

An owner may also create a life estate for someone else by **express grant**.

Example: In his will H left his second wife, W, a life estate in certain property, with the remainder interest to his son, S. W has the right to use and occupy the property for the rest of her life, and when she dies the property will automatically pass to S. H has expressly granted a life estate to W.

The holder of a life estate is called the **life tenant**. In all of the previous examples, the life estate's duration is measured by the lifetime of the life tenant: the life tenant may possess the property for the rest of his or her life. But a life estate may also be based on the lifetime of someone other than the life tenant. This is called a life estate **pur autre vie** (for another's life). This type of estate is sometimes used to create security for ailing parents or disabled children who are unable to provide for themselves.

Example: A's mother, M, is afflicted with Alzheimer's disease and can't take care of herself. A's brother B has been taking care of their mother. A deeds his property to B "for the life of M, and then to S." B has a life estate based on his mother's life. B has the right to use and occupy the property only as long as his mother is still alive. When the mother dies, the property automatically passes to A's son, S.

The mother's life is the **measuring life**. The life estate lasts only as long as the mother's lifetime.

A life tenant has an ownership interest in the land that can be sold, leased, or mortgaged. Remember, however, that a person can only sell, lease, or mortgage the interest that he or she owns. If a life tenant sells his or her interest in the property, the buyers have only purchased a life estate. The buyer's interest ends at the end of the measuring life; in the example just given, it would end when M died.

Interests in Real Property

Future Interests

When a life estate is granted, another interest is created at the same time: the interest of the person who will receive the property when the life estate ends. He or she will have the right to possess the property, but not until sometime in the future (when the measuring life ends). Thus, that person has a future interest. There are two types of future interests:

◆ estates in remainder, and
◆ estates in reversion.

http://ceres.ca.gov/wetlands/introduction/remainder_interests.html
(Remainder Interests)

In the previous example, the son, S, holds an **estate in remainder**. Although he doesn't have the right to possess the property right now, he currently has an interest in the remainder of the estate (the estate left over after the life estate). S is called the **remainderman**. When B's life estate ends (on M's death), S will take title to the property in fee simple absolute.

When the property is slated to return to the original grantor at the end of the life estate, the grantor has an **estate in reversion** (or reversionary interest).

> **Example:** Q owns a house in fee simple absolute. He deeds the property to his mother for her lifetime. The deed says, "From Q to M for life, and then to Q." When M dies, Q will regain title in fee simple absolute.

The property would also revert to Q if the deed had simply said, "From Q to M for life," and nothing more. If a remainderman isn't specified in the deed, it is presumed to create an estate in reversion.

A life tenant has certain duties towards the property. He or she may not use or abuse the property in any way that would permanently damage it or reduce its market value. Such abuse is called **waste**. The term "waste" implies neglect or misconduct, and does not include the ordinary depreciation of property due to time and normal use.

A life tenant must allow for reasonable inspection of the property by the holder of the future interest (the remainderman or the grantor). If he or she discovers waste, the holder of the future interest may sue the life tenant for damages. If the waste isn't discovered until after the life tenant's death, the lawsuit can be brought against the life tenant's estate.

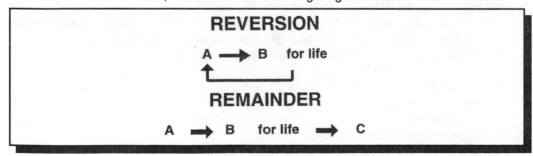

Trusts

Life estates aren't used very often anymore. A trust can provide the same benefits as a life estate, and has a number of advantages. When this kind of trust is created, a trustee is given legal title to the property for the life of the beneficiary. The beneficiary has the right to use and occupy the property under the trustee's supervision. When the beneficiary dies, the property is disposed of according to instructions in the document that created the trust. (Trusts are discussed again in Chapter 4.)

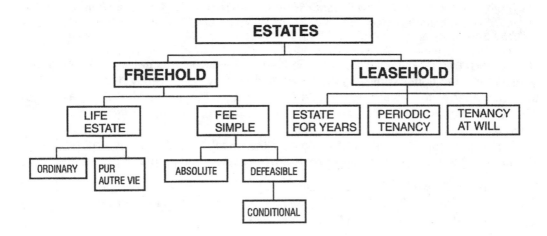

LEASEHOLD ESTATE

A leasehold estate is a more limited interest in property than a freehold estate. The holder of a leasehold estate is called the **lessee** or (a more familiar term) the **tenant**. A tenant does not own the property but merely leases or rents it. He or she has the right to exclusive possession of the property, but only for a limited time.

An owner who leases property to a tenant is called the **lessor** (or **landlord**). During the lease period, the landlord has a reversionary interest in the property, since possession will revert to the landlord when the lease ends.

The rules that govern landlord/tenant relationships are presented in Chapter 15. Here we will just describe the basic characteristics of leasehold estates.

In California, four kinds of leasehold estates are recognized:

◆ tenancy for a specific term (estate for years),
◆ periodic tenancy,
◆ tenancy at will, and
◆ tenancy at sufferance.

Term Tenancy (Lease)

A term tenancy is a leasehold estate for a fixed time period. It is sometimes called an **estate for years**, but the term doesn't have to be a year or a period of years. It may be for three months, six months and five days, two years, or any fixed rental period with a specific beginning and ending date.

> **Example:** T is a college student renting an apartment for one semester. The lease gives him the right to possess the apartment from August 20 through December 31. This is an estate for years or term tenancy.

To end a term tenancy, neither the lessor nor the lessee is required to give the other party notice. The lease terminates automatically at the end of the specified rental period. If the parties want to terminate the lease sooner, they may do so only by mutual consent. Ending a term tenancy by mutual consent is called **surrender**.

Unless expressly prohibited in the lease, a term tenancy is assignable. This means that the tenant may assign his or her interest in the property to another person. Assignment and subleasing are discussed in Chapter 15.

Periodic Tenancy (Rental Agreements)

The duration of a periodic tenancy is not limited to a specific term. It continues from period-to-period until the lessor or lessee gives the other party notice of termination. The period may be any length of time that the parties agree on. Month-to-month tenancies are the most common. A month-to-month tenancy automatically renews itself at the end of each month, unless one of the parties terminates it. (The requirements for notice of termination are explained in Chapter 15.) Like a term tenancy, a periodic tenancy is assignable unless the lease says it isn't.

Tenancy at Will

Under a tenancy at will, the tenant is in possession of the property with the owner's permission, but without any rental agreement. A tenancy at will has no specified termination date and no regular time period. Usually no rent is paid, or else rent is given in some form that has no reference to periods of time.

> **Example:** P occupies a house in return for maintaining and repairing the property. This is considered a tenancy at will because it is for an indefinite time and P is not required to pay periodic rent.

www.dca.ca.gov/legal/landlordbook/before-rent.htm
(Types of Tenancy)

To end a tenancy at will, the landlord must give the tenant at least 30 days' notice in writing.

A tenancy at will is most likely to arise at the end of a term tenancy. The term has expired, but the tenant has stayed on, and the landlord hasn't asked the tenant to leave. However, this is only a tenancy at will until the tenant starts paying rent on a regular basis. If the tenant gives the landlord a check every month, a month-to-month tenancy is established by implication.

Unlike a term tenancy or a periodic tenancy, a tenancy at will cannot be assigned to someone else. Also, a tenancy at will automatically ends upon the death of either the landlord or the tenant. The death of a month-to-month tenant usually terminates the tenancy at the end of month in which the death occurred. With an estate for years, on the other hand, the deceased tenant's heirs may take over the tenancy for the remainder of the term.

Tenancy at Sufferance

If the tenant stays without the landlord's permission the tenant is called a tenant at **sufferance**. When the landlord wants the tenant removed an eviction process must be stated.

Nonpossessory Interests (Encumbrances)

A freehold estate is a possessory interest in real property with ownership rights, and a leasehold estate is a possessory interest in real property without ownership rights. The third type of interest in real property is a nonpossessory interest. Someone who holds a nonpossessory interest has a claim or right concerning the property, but does not have the right to possess the property. Nonpossessory interests are also called **encumbrances**; they encumber or burden the title.

The two categories of nonpossessory interests discussed in this chapter are:

◆ easements, and
◆ liens.

Restrictive covenants also create nonpossessory interests. They are discussed in Chapter 13.

http://www.goodlifepublishers.com/Landowners/
(Landowner's Guide to Easements and Right of Ways)

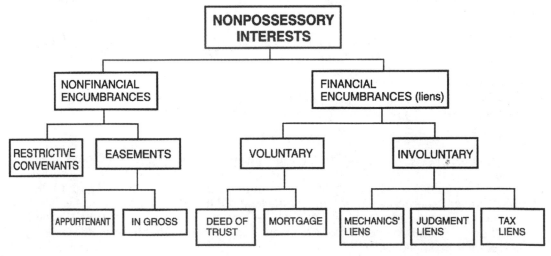

Interests in Real Property

EASEMENTS

An easement is a right held by one person to use the real property of another for a particular purpose. The California Civil Code lists a wide variety of possible easements, ranging from the right to gather wood on another's land to the right of burial on another's land or from a solar easement to gather sunlight for heating to a conservation easement to preserve natural wonders.

Types of Easements

Easements affect the use and the value of property, so real estate agents and prospective buyers should find out whether a property is subject to any easements. A standard title insurance report will list the recorded easements, but usually won't list unrecorded easements. Agents and buyers should ask the seller about easements, and should also keep an eye out for indications that the property is used by other people besides the seller (the neighbors, for instance).

POSITIVE AND NEGATIVE EASEMENTS. An easement can be either positive or negative. A **positive easement** gives someone other than the owner a right to do something on the land or take something from the land. The most common example of a positive easement is the right to cross another's land, often called a right-of-way or an access easement.

> **Example:** D has an easement that allows her to cut across the corner of her neighbor's property to reach her mailbox, instead of having to go the long way around by the road. D has a positive easement over her neighbor's land.

A **negative easement**, on the other hand, prohibits a landowner from doing something on his or her own property.

A negative easement is essentially the same thing as a restrictive covenant: both restrict the landowner's use of the property. The two terms are often used interchangeably.

Case Example: Mary Petersen and the Friedmans owned adjoining lots in San Francisco. Petersen had an easement against the Friedmans' property, entitling her to light, air, and an unobstructed view. It prohibited the Friedmans from erecting any structure on their lot that was over 28 feet high.

The Friedmans put up a TV antenna that exceeded the height limit. The court ruled that this violated Petersen's right to an unobstructed view, and ordered the Friedmans to take the antenna down. *Petersen v. Friedman*, 162 Cal. App. 2d 245, 328 P.2d 264 (1958).

In addition to being either positive or negative, an easement is either **appurtenant** or **in gross**.

www.ceres.ca.gov/search.epl
(Conservation Easements)

EASEMENT APPURTENANT. An easement is said to burden a piece of land—it is an encumbrance on the property. An easement appurtenant burdens one piece of land for the benefit of another piece of land. In the case example above, the Friedmans' property was burdened with an easement that benefited Petersen's property.

The land benefited by an easement appurtenant (like Petersen's land) is called the **dominant tenement**. ("Tenement" is an old legal term that refers to the land and all of the rights that go along with the land.) The land burdened by that easement (like the Friedmans' land) is called the **servient tenement**. The owner of the dominant tenement is called the **dominant tenant**, and the owner of the servient tenement is called the **servient tenant**. In the case example, Petersen is the dominant tenant and the Friedmans are the servient tenants.

An easement appurtenant ordinarily **runs with the land**. That means if the dominant tenement is transferred (sold, willed, or given away), the easement is also transferred. An easement appurtenant cannot be sold separately from the property. Whoever owns the dominant tenement also owns the easement.

Example: Diaz's easement allows her to drive across the west 30 feet of Sanchez property to get back and forth between her own property and the main road. The easement is appurtenant to Diaz's land (the dominant tenement). If Diaz sells her land to Chang, Chang automatically acquires the easement. Sanchez must allow Chang to cross his land (the servient tenement).

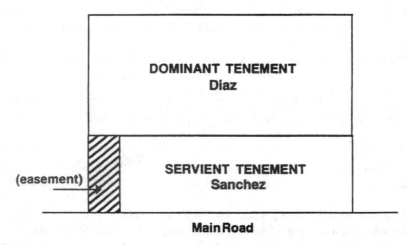

But what if the servient tenement is sold—what if Sanchez sells his land to Sullivan? Is the burden of an easement transferred to the new owner of the servient tenement? Yes, as long as the new owner has notice of the easement at the time of the transfer. Sullivan would be held to have notice of Chang's easement if someone told her about it, or if there was a recorded document that mentioned the easement, or even if an inspection of the property would have indicated that there might be an easement. Even if Sullivan didn't actually inspect the property or know about the recorded document, she would be required to let Chang use the easement. (See the discussion of actual and constructive notice in Chapter 10.)

If the dominant tenement is subdivided, the easement will usually run with all of the new lots.

Example: Continuing the previous example, suppose Chang divides the dominant tenement and sells half of it to Hernandez. Both Hernandez and Chang would have a right to use the easement over Sullivan's property. (Hernandez also has an easement over Chang's property.)

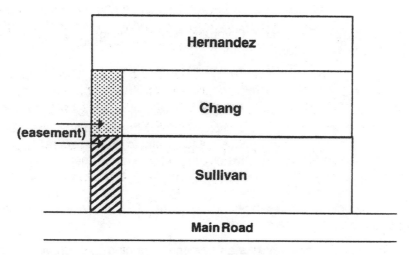

There's a limit to this rule, however: use of the easement cannot be increased so much that it increases the burden on the servient tenement. If Chang subdivided her property into 50 lots, a court would probably not permit all of the new owners to use the easement across Sullivan's land. The subdivider would have to make other arrangements for access to and from the 50 lots.

When landowners share easement rights to a right of way (for example, if A, B, C, and D use a private road crossing Z's lot to get to their lots), they must also share the cost of maintaining the easement. Unless otherwise agreed, each pays a share proportionate to how much he or she uses the road. If Z (the servient tenant—that is, the owner of the burdened property) doesn't use the road, he doesn't have an obligation to maintain or repair it for the easement holders.

EASEMENTS IN GROSS. Like an appurtenant easement, an easement in gross is a right that burdens another's land. But unlike an appurtenant easement, an easement in gross does not benefit a piece of land. There is a servient tenement (the land burdened by the easement in gross), but there is no dominant tenement.

Example: F lives five miles away from G. G grants F an easement in gross to enter G's property and fish in the small lake there.

F's easement isn't appurtenant to his land. If F sells his property, the new owner does not gain the right to fish on G's land. The easement belongs to F personally, wherever he lives. But the easement in gross does run with G's land: if G sells his land to H, F will still have the right to fish in the lake.

Chapter 3

An easement in gross that belongs to an individual (like F's right to fish) is called a personal easement in gross. In many states, a personal easement in gross cannot be transferred, and is extinguished if the easement holder dies. But in California, a personal easement in gross may be sold or inherited unless the grantor expressly limited it to a particular individual.

Most easements in gross belong to commercial enterprises (such as public utilities) rather than individuals. These are called commercial easements in gross, and they are generally freely assignable.

Example: The Greentown Electric Company has an easement in gross that allows its employees to enter C's property to install and service power lines. When MegaElectric buys the Greentown Electric Company, it also purchases the easement in gross.

Note, however, that a commercial easement for a specific purpose cannot ordinarily be sold for another purpose. The electric company could not sell its power line easement to the local sewer district so that sewer lines could be laid in the easement.

When showing property to prospective buyers, a real estate agent should be able to explain any utility easements affecting the property. A typical residence may be subject to easements for the water company, the electric company, the gas company, a cable television company, and the telephone company. Sometimes these easements have an impact on the value of the property.

Example: The electric company has an easement running through your back yard. If the company installs unsightly power lines, the value of the property could drop sharply.

Creation of Easements

An easement may be created by:

◆ express agreement,
◆ implication,
◆ estoppel, or
◆ prescription.

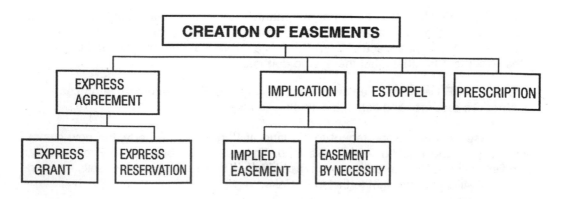

EXPRESS EASEMENTS. An easement can be expressly created in the deed that passes title to the dominant or servient property, or in a separate document that conveys only the easement. But because an easement is an interest in real property, an oral agreement isn't enough—it must be in writing. (The requirements for a valid deed are explained in Chapter 10. Most of the same rules apply to a document creating an easement.)

> **Examples:** D and S are neighbors. D asks S for an access easement allowing D to cross S's property. S agrees, but they never put it in writing. Six months later, S changes his mind and tells D to keep off his land. D can't enforce his easement right because it was only an oral agreement.
>
> But suppose S signed a document granting D the easement. Now if S changes his mind, D has an enforceable right. D should record the document to make sure that anyone who buys the servient tenement from S will have notice of his easement.

A document creating an express easement usually states the purpose of the easement and describes its boundaries. But the easement can be valid even if its exact location on the servient property isn't specified in the document.

A deed may create an easement by express grant or express reservation. An easement is created by **express grant** when the grantor states in the deed that the grantee has a right to use the grantor's property for a particular purpose.

> **Example:** A sells the west half of his property to B. In the deed, A expressly grants to B the right to use the private road located on the east half of the property (which A still owns).

A deed creates an easement by **express reservation** when the grantor reserves for him or herself (or for a third party) a right to use the grantee's property.

> **Example:** A sells the west half of his property to B. In the deed, A expressly reserves to himself the right to use the private road that is located on the west half of the property (which B now owns).

Another way that express easements are created is by plat maps. When a landowner subdivides land and sells it according to a recorded plat, anyone who buys a lot in the subdivision acquires the right to use the roads and alleys shown on the plat, even though these easements aren't mentioned in the deed.

IMPLIED EASEMENTS. An implied easement (or **easement by implication**) is not written down in a deed or other document. As a general rule, an implied easement can only arise when a tract of land was originally held by one owner and then was divided into two or more parcels. At the time of the division, the use giving rise to the easement must have been going on for a long time, and it must be apparent from a visual inspection of the property. The use must also be reasonably necessary for the enjoyment of the dominant tenement.

Case Example: Ms. Fischer owned lots 18 and 19 in a Los Angeles subdivision. The back yard of lot 18 sloped so that surface water flowed down onto lot 19. Fischer installed a drain on the boundary between the two lots.

Several years later, Fischer sold lot 18 to the Hendlers, but retained lot 19 herself. For more than two years after the sale, she continued to allow water to flow from lot 18 into the drain on the boundary. Then she closed off the drain.

With the drain closed, the Hendlers' yard and four-car garage were repeatedly flooded. They sued Fischer to establish their right to use the drain. The court ruled that the Hendlers had an easement by implication. Lot 18's use of the drain was well established and obvious at the time of the sale, and the drain was reasonably necessary for the enjoyment of the property. *Fischer v. Hendler,* 49 Cal. App. 2d 319 (1942).

An **easement by necessity** is a special type of implied easement. If a piece of property would be completely useless without an easement against another property, a court will hold that there is an easement by necessity.

Case Example: Dr. Clark owned two parcels of property. He sold one to the Sparlings. This left the other parcel landlocked, with no access to a public road.

Although nothing was said about an easement at the time of the sale, a court ruled that Dr. Clark acquired an easement by necessity across the Sparlings' parcel for access to and from his parcel. Otherwise his parcel would have been useless. *Roemer v. Pappas*, 249 Cal. Rptr. 743 (1988).

Note that for an easement by necessity, the claimant does not have to prove that the use was long-established and obvious at the time of the sale. But the claimant must prove that the easement is strictly necessary (not just reasonably necessary) for the use of the property. The easement continues only as long as the necessity.

EASEMENT BY ESTOPPEL. The term "estoppel" refers to a legal doctrine that prevents a person from asserting rights or making claims that are contrary to his or her previous acts or conduct.

Example: B owns and lives on several acres of land out in the country. Her house is connected to a large septic tank capable of serving several houses. B divides her property and sells half to C. No mention is made of the septic tank at the time of the sale.

C builds a house on his property. B watches but makes no objection when C hooks up his plumbing to the septic tank on her property.

An easement has been created by estoppel. Because of her failure to object, B cannot later claim that C has no right to use the septic tank.

EASEMENT BY PRESCRIPTION. An easement by prescription (also called a **prescriptive easement**) is created when someone makes long and continuous use of another's property, without the permission of the owner.

> **Case Example:** In 1935, Mr. Fawcett planted 75 walnut trees along a road, even though he knew he didn't own that land.
>
> For more than 20 years, Fawcett tended the trees and harvested the nuts. The landowner, Mr. Rodrigues, was aware of Fawcett's activities and did nothing to stop them. But Rodrigues sold the land to the Costas, who filed a quiet title action against Fawcett.
>
> The court held that Fawcett had acquired a prescriptive easement allowing him to enter the Costas' land to look after the trees and harvest the nuts. *Costa v. Fawcett*, 21 Cal. Rptr. 143 (1962).

For a prescriptive easement to develop, use of the other person's land must be **open and notorious**. This means that the use must be obvious and unconcealed, so that if the landowner keeps reasonably well informed about the property he or she will be aware of the use.

The use must also be **hostile** or **adverse**. This means it is without the permission of the owner and against the owner's interests. An owner may acquiesce to the use (as Mr. Rodrigues did in the case example), but may not give permission. In other words, the owner is aware of the use and does not object, but also doesn't say that it's okay. If the owner gives permission, a license has been granted (see the discussion of licenses, below), and a prescriptive easement can't develop.

In California, the use must be **continuous** and **uninterrupted** for five years. To be considered continuous, the use doesn't have to be constant, but only a regular use that is normal for the type of property in question.

> **Example:** R and G both own summer cottages on a cliff above a beach. Steps cut into the cliff on R's property lead down to the beach. Every summer for the last eight years G has used these steps to get to the beach. This is a continuous use even though G never uses the steps in winter time.

A continuous and uninterrupted use does not necessarily mean a use by only one person.

> **Example:** Drummond and Saragossa own adjoining property. For two years, Drummond drives across a corner of Saragossa's property without Saragossa's permission. Then Drummond sells his property to Digby. For another two years Digby drives across the same corner. Then Digby sells to Dillinger. Dillinger drives across Saragossa's property for another year.
>
> Dillinger may be able to claim a prescriptive easement. The time periods in which Drummond, Digby, and Dillinger drove across the property can be added together to make up the required five years. This is called **tacking**.

In California, a landowner can prevent anyone from acquiring an easement by prescription, either by posting signs on the property or recording a notice. If a recorded notice is used instead of signs, a copy of the notice must be sent by registered mail to the person who is using the property. The signs or notice must state (in language specified in the Civil Code) that use of the property is by permission and subject to the control of the owner. Since use is by permission, it can't be hostile or adverse. As a result, no prescriptive easement can develop against the property. The owner can later revoke permission and prevent the use.

Note that a prescriptive easement can never be acquired against government property.

Recorded Notice. The right of the public or any person to make any use whatsoever of the described land or any portion thereof (other than any use expressly allowed by a written or recorded map, agreement, deed or dedication) is by permission, and subject to control, of owner: Section 813, Civil Code.

Posted Notice. Right to pass by permission, and subject to control, of owner: Section 1008, Civil Code.

Termination of Easements

There are several ways in which easements may be terminated or cease to exist. These roughly correspond to the ways in which easements are created.

1. Express termination
2. Implied termination:
    through merger,
    by abandonment,
    when the necessity ends,
    when the purpose of the easement fails, or
    upon destruction of the servient tenement.
3. Termination by estoppel
4. Termination by prescription

EXPRESS TERMINATION. Most easements are granted for an indefinite period. But if the grant of the easement specifies a limited term, the easement expires automatically at the end of that period. An easement may be granted for life. This type of easement automatically terminates upon the death of the person who was the measuring life.

Even when an easement was originally granted for an indefinite period, the parties (or subsequent owners of the dominant and servient tenements) may later agree to terminate it. Then the easement holder must execute a written release, giving up his or her interest in the servient property.

Another way that an easement can be expressly terminated is by **condemnation**. That's when the state takes private property for a public use (see Chapter 10). If the state condemns either the dominant or the servient property, the easement will be terminated. The easement holder is entitled to compensation for the value of the easement.

Example: A has an easement to maintain a billboard on B's land. The state condemns B's property in order to build a new highway across it. The state has to compensate B for the value of his property, and must also compensate A for loss of the value of his easement.

IMPLIED TERMINATION. An easement may be terminated without any express agreement, either by actions of the parties or by circumstances beyond their control.

Merger or unity of title. When one person becomes the owner of both the dominant tenement and the servient tenement, the easement is extinguished by merger. You can't have an easement in your own property, since an easement is defined as an interest in another's land.

Necessity ends. If an easement was created by necessity, it terminates automatically when it is no longer necessary.

Abandonment. An easement ceases to exist if the easement holder abandons it. Failure to use the easement is not, by itself, abandonment; there usually must be an act or statement that clearly expresses an intent to abandon it.

California law presumes an easement has been abandoned, and terminates the easement holder's rights.

When during the last 20 years:

◆ the easement has not been used at any time
◆ no separate property tax was made for the easement or, if so, none was paid
◆ no instrument creating, reserving, transferring or otherwise evidencing the easement is recorded

The easement holder can prevent that by recording a notice of intent to preserve the easement, or any other document indicating the existence of the easement (a deed transferring the dominant tenement and the easement, for example). The recording will protect the easement rights for another 20 years.

There is a special rule for easements created by prescription: a court may rule that a prescriptive easement has been abandoned after only five years of non-use.

Failure of purpose. If an easement has been created for a particular purpose, it terminates when the purpose ceases or has been fulfilled. For example, a railroad's easement for train tracks across a farmer's property would terminate if the railroad discontinued that line and removed the tracks. In the walnut tree case described earlier, the court held that Fawcett's easement would end if the trees were to die. He would have no right to enter the Costas' property to plant new trees.

Destruction of servient tenement. When an easement exists in a building rather than in the land, the accidental destruction of the building terminates the easement. It won't revive automatically if the building is rebuilt.

Just as easements can be created by estoppel or prescription, they may also be terminated by estoppel or prescription.

ESTOPPEL. If the easement holder's conduct leads the servient property owner to assume that the easement holder doesn't intend to use the easement, and the property owner takes some action in reliance on this, the easement holder may be prevented from later trying to enforce the easement.

Example: D sold half of his property to S but reserved an easement for himself so he could walk across the corner of S's property to get to his mailbox. After several years, D put up a high wooden fence that blocked off the path to the mailbox.

S naturally assumed that D was no longer going to use the path, so she planted a large garden in that corner of the property, plowing up the path. D was aware of S's work and said nothing at that time. But a year later he took down the fence and told S he was going to use his easement again, even though he'd be stomping right through her vegetables.

By building the fence, D led S to believe that he didn't intend to use the easement anymore. S reasonably relied on his conduct when she planted the garden. D is now estopped from claiming the right to use the easement.

PRESCRIPTION. Actions by the owner of the servient property that interfere with the easement could extinguish the easement by prescription. There must be an open, adverse, continuous, and uninterrupted interference with the easement for five years.

Example: Consider the example just above. Now suppose it was S (the owner of the servient property) who built the fence across the easement without D's consent. The fence has been in place blocking off the path for five years. D's easement has been terminated by prescription.

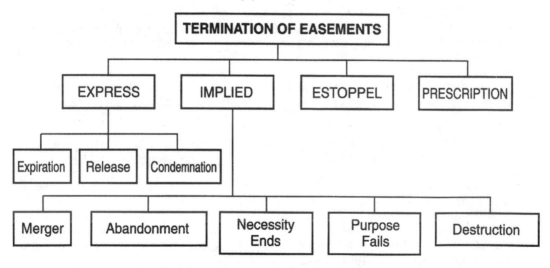

The Distinction Between Easements and Licenses

Like an easement, a license grants permission to enter another's property for a specific purpose. But a license does not create an interest in the property.

There are several differences between easements and licenses. Easements are often for an indefinite period of time, but licenses are usually temporary. Easements are created by written agreement or through action of law (implication, estoppel, or prescription), while licenses may be created by oral agreement. Appurtenant easements run with the land, and easements in gross can be assigned, but a license is a purely personal right. A license can't be sold or transferred, and becomes invalid if the licensee dies.

Perhaps the most important distinction is that an easement can't be revoked whereas a license may be revoked at any time.

Example: A owns a large pasture right next to the freeway. For $500, A agreed to allow Z to put up a billboard in one corner of the pasture. Z has a license to enter the pasture and put up the billboard.

A never asked Z what the billboard was going to say. It turns out to be an ad for an X-rated movie theater, and A strongly disapproves. A tells Z to take the billboard down immediately. Z's license is revoked; he no longer has the right to enter the property. Of course, A has to return the money Z paid for the license.

In some cases, however, a license becomes irrevocable. This can happen by estoppel, when the licensee makes a substantial financial commitment in reliance on the license. An irrevocable license is the same, for all intents and purposes, as an easement.

Case Example: The Stewarts bought Lot 11 in a new subdivision in San Pedro. Lot 12 sloped down toward Lot 11, and the boundary between the two properties was at the bottom of the slope. To make their yard more private, the Stewarts wanted to build a wall at the top of the slope (on Lot 12) instead of at the bottom.

Lot 12 was owned by Mr. Jett. The Stewarts asked Jett for an easement allowing them to build their wall at the top of the slope, and he agreed. He never got around to writing up a grant of easement, however.

The Stewarts went ahead and built their wall at the top of the slope. Afterwards, Jett sold Lot 12 to the Noronhas. Eight months later, the Noronhas demanded that the Stewarts tear down their wall.

The court held that although Jett had not fulfilled the requirements for creating an easement, he had granted the Stewarts a license. Because the Stewarts spent a considerable amount of money in reliance on the license, the Noronhas could not revoke it. *Noronha v. Stewart*, 199 Cal. App. 3d 485, 245 Cal. Rptr. 94 (1988).

LIENS (Financial Encumbrances)

A lien is a financial interest in property. It is security for a debt, giving the creditor (the **lienholder**) the right to foreclose on the debtor's property if the debt is not paid. The property is sold, and the lienholder collects the amount of the debt from the proceeds of the foreclosure sale.

A lienholder doesn't own or have a right to possess the property. Liens usually do not affect the use of the property, but they do affect the title.

The fact that there are liens against a property does not prevent its transfer or sale, but the transfer doesn't eliminate the liens. The new owner takes the property subject to the liens. It is extremely important for a buyer to know what liens are attached to the property before purchasing; otherwise, the buyer could end up forced to pay off the seller's debts to prevent foreclosure. In most real estate transactions, the seller is required to clear the title of liens before closing.

Voluntary Liens

Voluntary liens are liens that a property owner chooses to have placed against his or her property, usually to obtain a loan. There are only two kinds of voluntary liens: mortgages and deeds of trust (trust deeds).

> **Example:** A real property owner borrows money using the property as collateral. The owner voluntarily signs a trust deed, which gives the lender the right to foreclose if the money is not repaid.

Involuntary Liens

Involuntary liens (sometimes called statutory liens) arise through operation of law without the property owner's consent. Involuntary liens are created to protect those who have valid financial claims against the owner.

> **Example:** When property taxes are assessed, a tax lien arises against the property. If the taxes aren't paid, the property can be sold to satisfy the lien.

Liens are also classified as either general or specific. A **general lien** attaches to all of the debtor's property. A **specific lien** attaches only to a particular piece of property. A trust deed is an example of a specific lien. It attaches only to the particular property offered as security for the loan. The most common types of liens against real estate are:

- ◆ deeds of trust,
- ◆ mortgages,
- ◆ mechanics' liens,
- ◆ judgment liens, and
- ◆ tax liens.

DEEDS OF TRUST AND MORTGAGES. Deeds of trust and mortgages are discussed in detail in Chapter 12. For now, it's enough to know that both are voluntary, specific liens, most often used to secure a purchase money loan—a loan that enables the borrower to purchase the property the lien attaches to. The parties to a mortgage are the **mortgagor** (the borrower) and the **mortgagee** (the lender). The parties to a trust deed are the **trustor** (the borrower), the **beneficiary** (the lender), and the **trustee** (a neutral third party). The chief differences between mortgages and trust deeds have to do with the procedures for foreclosure.

MECHANICS' LIENS. When construction or improvement work is performed on real property, the property stands as security for the payment of the labor and materials costs. A worker or a materials supplier who isn't paid may obtain an involuntary, specific lien against the property. This is called a **mechanic's lien**. It gives the worker or supplier the power to force the sale of the property to collect the debt owed.

Virtually everyone connected with a construction project is entitled to a mechanic's lien: a general contractor, an architect, a landscaper, a carpenter, a plumbing supply company, and so on. The mechanic's lien law divides claimants into four groups: original contractors, subcontractors, laborers, and materialmen.

An original contractor is a licensed independent contractor who has a direct contract with the property owner (or other person who requested the work). In many cases, the original contractor is a general contractor, who has charge of the whole project and hires subcontractors. In other cases, there is no general contractor; the owner hires an electrician, a carpenter, and others directly, and then each of those workers is regarded as an original contractor.

Subcontractors are licensed independent contractors hired by an original contractor. Laborers are employees who work for wages under the control of an original contractor, a subcontractor, or the owner. A materialman is anyone who supplies construction materials or equipment for the project. Each of these groups is treated slightly differently under the mechanic's lien law.

Claiming a Lien. To claim a lien, subcontractors and materialmen are required to serve a **preliminary 20-day notice** on the property owner, their original contractor, and the construction lender. Original contractors only have to serve this notice on the construction lender, and laborers aren't required to prepare one at all. The notice warns that a lien may be claimed and provides an estimate of the cost. A copy of the notice should be filed at the county recorder's office, although it won't actually be recorded.

The preliminary notice is usually served within 20 days after the contractor or materialman begins working or supplying materials for the project. If the notice isn't sent until later, the mechanic's lien will not cover the work done or materials supplied more than 20 days before the notice was served. (The contractor or materialman is still entitled to be paid for that part of the job, but the bill for that part won't be secured by the lien.)

The next step is to have a **claim of lien** recorded. Most claims can be filed for record as soon as the claimant stops working on the project. An original contractor can't file a claim until he or she has completed the contract, however. As a general rule, no claims can be filed later than 90 days after all work (not just the individual claimant's work) on the project has stopped.

If a claim of lien isn't recorded within that 90-day period, the lien rights are lost. The claimant may still be able to sue the property owner for breach of contract, but that is a more uncertain and time-consuming process than foreclosing on a lien.

A property owner can shorten the period in which lien claims can be filed for a particular project, by recording a **notice of cessation** or a **notice of completion**. The owner can file a notice of cessation if for any reason work on the project has been stopped for at least 30 days. A notice of completion can only be recorded within 10 days after the project is completed. Once either kind of notice has been recorded, a subcontractor, laborer, or materialman has only 30 days in which to file his or her claim of lien, and an original contractor has 60 days. The county recorder will notify everyone who filed a preliminary 20-day notice that a notice of cessation or completion has been recorded.

Foreclosure. If the property owner doesn't pay, the claimant can foreclose on the lien by filing a lawsuit. The suit can be filed in municipal court if the amount in controversy is $25,000 or less; otherwise, it must be filed in superior court. In either case, the foreclosure suit ordinarily must be filed within 90 days after the claim of lien was recorded. Otherwise the lien is void.

Example: New plumbing is being installed in an apartment building. K is the materialman who supplied the new pipes. The last load of pipes was delivered on June 15th. K still had not been paid by August 1st, so he filed a claim of lien against the property.

On November 15th, K filed a legal action to foreclose on his lien. The lawsuit was dismissed, however, because it had been more than 90 days since the claim of lien was recorded.

Termination of Mechanics' Liens. A properly recorded mechanic's lien is usually terminated by payment of the debt that the lien is based on. The owner should obtain and record a release of lien after paying the claimant. But what if an owner believes that a particular claim is invalid, and intends to contest it in court? The owner can obtain a release of lien by putting up a bond for one and half times the amount of the claim. When this release is recorded, the lien is removed from the title, even though the lawsuit over the claim hasn't been resolved yet.

JUDGMENT LIENS. Judgment liens were discussed briefly in Chapter 1. At the end of a civil lawsuit, if the judge or jury determines that one of the parties owes money to the other, a judgment is entered against the losing party. The winner (the judgment creditor) may claim a lien against the loser's (the judgment debtor's) real property.

To claim a lien, the judgment creditor must obtain an abstract of judgment from the court clerk and record it in the county where the debtor's real property is located. The lien attaches to all of the debtor's real property in that county. (There is an exception if the debtor has filed a declaration of homestead. See the discussion of the homestead law, below.) Thus, a judgment lien is an involuntary, general lien.

If the debtor owns property in other counties, the judgment creditor may file an abstract of judgment in the other counties and attach those additional properties. The judgment lien also attaches to any real property in those counties that the debtor acquires during the lien period.

Example: B owns two acres of land in Shasta County. B lost a lawsuit, and a judgment was entered against him. The judgment creditor filed an abstract of judgment with the Shasta County recorder, and a lien was attached to B's two-acre property. Three months later, B's father died, leaving B a five-acre property, which is also in Shasta County. The judgment lien also attaches to this newly acquired property.

Once a judgment lien is on the real property, the debtor must pay the judgment in order to free the property from the lien. Unless the lien is paid, a transferee acquires the property subject to the lien. If it is not paid, the judgment creditor can file suit to foreclose on the debtor's property.

In California, a judgment lien is only valid for ten years after the date the judgment was entered, unless the judgment is renewed. The judgment creditor can renew the judgment for another ten years by filing an application for renewal with the court. The application can be filed at any time before the judgment expires, as long as at least five years have passed since the last time the judgment was renewed. Notice of the renewal must be served on the debtor and the debtor has an opportunity to object at a hearing. To extend the lien on real property, a certified copy of the application for renewal must be recorded in the county where the abstract was recorded.

If a transferee purchased the property subject to the lien and recorded the transfer, a judgment creditor wanting to renew the lien must serve the transferee with a copy of the application for renewal and file proof of the service within 90 days after the filing of the application for renewal. A lien can be removed by recording a satisfaction of judgment or a release of judgment lien signed by the judgment creditor.

Property Taxes in California

The annual ad valorem taxes imposed on real property are called **general property taxes**. They're described as "general" to distinguish them from special assessments. That's slightly confusing, since a property tax lien is a specific lien, attaching only to the taxed property, not a general lien attaching to everything the taxpayer owns. (See Chapter 3.)

California's first general property tax law was enacted in 1850, right after it became a state. The property tax was originally the main source of revenue for both state and local governments. In 1910, the general property tax was abandoned as a source of revenue for the state government, but it has remained local government's primary source of support. There are currently over 6,000 government entities or agencies in California that levy (impose) property taxes, or for which property taxes are levied.

These include counties, cities, school districts, irrigation districts, and other special-purpose taxing districts.

Under the state constitution, all property is subject to taxation unless it's specifically exempted. Property can be exempted from taxation by the state constitution itself, or by a California statute, or by the U.S. Constitution or a federal law.

Taxpayers and local governments often get into disputes over whether the taxpayer has a taxable property interest. And once that's settled, they argue about whether that interest is taxable as real property or personal property. Many tax questions depend on that distinction. For example, under state law banks are required to pay real property taxes, but not personal property taxes.

www.taxlawsb.com/resources/PptyTax.htm
(Resources Pertaining to California Property Taxation)

Case Example: The city classified computer components in a bank building as fixtures and taxed them as real property. The bank sued, claiming that the computers were personal property.

The city argued that the computers were an essential part of the building in question; structural changes had been made so the building could accommodate the computers and serve as the bank's data processing center. The bank argued that the computers were standard office equipment that had not been designed or modified for the building and were not permanently attached to it.

The trial court ruled in the city's favor, holding that the computer components were fixtures. The bank appealed, but the court of appeals affirmed the trial court's decision. The bank appealed again, and the state supreme court reversed the lower court's decision: the computers were not fixtures and therefore could not be taxed as real property. *Crocker National Bank v. City and County of San Francisco*, 49 Cal. 3d 881, 264 Cal. Rptr. 139 (1990).

Chapter 3

PROPOSITION 13 AND PROPERTY TAX ASSESSMENT. Proposition 13 (the Jarvis-Gann Initiative) was approved by California voters in 1978 leading to amendment of the state constitution (Article XIIIA). The amendment completely revised both the method of assessing real property and the tax rates imposed. **Assessment** is the process of determining the value of property for tax purposes.

ASSESSMENT AND TAX RATES. Before Proposition 13, property was generally assessed at 25% of its full value and property taxes were very high. In other words, the amount of tax to be paid was calculated by applying the tax rate to 25% of the property's value. Tax rates varied depending on the county and city where the property was located.

www.leginfo.ca.gov/.const/.article_13A
(California State Constitution, Article 13 - Tax Limitation)

Property is assessed at its **full cash value**. That's more or less the same thing as market value. The California Revenue and Taxation Code defines full cash value as the purchase price of the property, unless it can be shown that the property would not have been sold at that price on the open market. As a general rule, the tax rate now may not exceed one percent of the full cash value.

The Effects of Proposition 13 | *Prop. 13*

Tax rate limited to 1% of the assessed value
Assessed Value = Full Cash Value
(unless ownership hasn't changed since March 1975)
Property reassessed on change of ownership
Assessed value can't be increased more than 2% per year
(unless there's a new owner or improvements)

LIMITS ON ASSESSMENT. Proposition 13 placed certain limits on assessment to protect homeowners, who stay in the same home, from drastic tax increases when their homes appreciate in value. If there hasn't been a change in ownership since March 1, 1975, the property's 1975 value is the starting point for assessment—the **base value**. As long as the same person owns the property and no improvements are made, the assessed value can't be increased more than 2% per year. If the owner improves the property (by building a deck, for example), the assessed value may be increased by the amount the improvements add to the actual value.

The assessment is increased to the current full cash value only if there's a new owner or new construction on the property. When the property is sold or otherwise transferred, the new owner must file a **change in ownership statement** with the county recorder or assessor within 45 days. Unless the transaction is exempt from reassessment on change in ownership, the assessed value may be stepped up to the price paid or to the fair market value at the time of the transfer. That becomes the new base value.

To alleviate the harsh consequences of increased assessments following transfers of title when the property hasn't been sold or traded for profit, the law exempts several types of transfers from reassessment. These include:

◆ transfers where the method of holding title is changed but the ownership isn't.
◆ adding a joint tenant to a joint tenancy.
◆ most transfers between parents and children, grandparents and grandchildren.
◆ transfers between spouses to create or terminate community property or joint tenancy interests.
◆ transfers between spouses to create or terminate community property or joint tenancy interests.

Propositions 60 and 90. California voters approved Proposition 60 in 1987. Under Proposition 60, when a senior citizen (over 55) sells his or her home and replaces it with another home in the same county, the assessed value of the old home can be used as the assessed value of the new home. The market value of the new home must be equal to or less than the market value of the old home, and the new home must be purchased within two years after the sale of the old one.

> **Example:** M is 60 years old. She has lived in the same home in San Jose since the early 1970s. Because of Proposition 13, the assessed value of her home is only $85,000, even though it's now worth about $150,000. Her property taxes are around $850 per year.
> M would like to move to a smaller home in a quieter place. She finds a condominium in a suburb that she likes; like San Jose, it's in Santa Clara County. So M sells her old home and buys a condo unit for $135,000.
> Before Proposition 60, M's condo would have been assessed at its full cash value ($135,000). That would have made her property taxes about $1,350 per year. But because of Proposition 60, she can transfer the low assessed value of her old home ($85,000) to her condo, and save about $500 per year on her property taxes.

In 1988, the voters approved Proposition 90. It works the same way as Proposition 60, only it applies when a senior citizen buys a replacement home in a different county. The new law doesn't require all counties to allow senior citizens from other counties to keep their previous assessed value. But many counties have decided to do so, to attract new residents. If M's new condo were in some other county besides Santa Clara County, she might or might not get to use her previous assessed value there.

The benefits of Propositions 60 and 90 were extended to severely and permanently disabled homeowners in 1990.

Propositions 193. Under Proposition 193, Passed in 1996 a person who inherits property from a grandparent would receive the additional windfall of paying low property taxes based on the grandparent's old assessment.

Property Tax Exemptions and Deferments. Although the general rule is that all property is taxed at full cash value, there are many total or partial exemptions. Property owned by the federal, state, and local governments is totally exempt from taxation; so is property used for religious, scientific, educational, charitable, or welfare purposes.

Of course, there's a lot of litigation over whether particular property qualifies for an exemption or not.

Case Example: A church acquired property that had been used as a private tennis and swimming club. It included a building with meeting rooms, a sauna, a swimming pool, and five tennis courts. The church issued a statement of policy explaining that the facility was to be used for the nurture of persons within the church and to extend the gospel to other members of the community.

The church argued that the property should be exempt from taxation because the facilities were an important part of its evangelical mission. They also gave the church a way of serving the community.

The court ruled against the church. Although the property didn't have to be used exclusively for religious purposes to qualify for the exemption, that had to be its primary use. That wasn't the case here. The recreational facilities were mostly used by dues-paying members of a "boosters" club. The pool and tennis courts had been used for religious purposes only three times: two baptisms and one dramatic presentation. It appeared to the court that the church was using the property in the same way the previous owner had, as a tennis and swimming club. *Peninsula Covenant Church v. City of San Mateo*, 94 Cal. App. 3d 383, 156 Cal. Rptr. 431 (1979).

There's a partial tax exemption for homeowners. The first $7,000 of the assessed value of an owner-occupied property is exempt from taxation. (In other words $7,000 is subtracted from the assessed value, and only the remainder is taxed.) This exemption isn't automatic—the taxpayer has to apply for it. Once the exemption has been granted, it remains in effect until terminated; it isn't necessary to reapply each year.

Homeowners who are 62 or older, blind, or disabled may qualify for a property tax **deferment**. To qualify they must occupy the home, have at least a 20% equity in the property, and have an annual income of $24,000 or less. A deferment isn't the same thing as an exemption. With a deferment, the property is taxed, but the taxes don't have to be paid until the claimant no longer owns or occupies the property, or no longer qualifies for the deferment.

Appealing an Assessment. A property owner who is dissatisfied with the assessment of his or her property may appeal to the county board of equalization. The county board of supervisors either appoints a board of equalization, or plays that role itself. A board of equalization has the power to adjust the assessed value of property.

CALCULATING PROPERTY TAXES. The tax on a parcel of real estate is calculated by multiplying the tax rate by the assessed value. Because of Proposition 13, the tax rate is ordinarily close to 1%. The 1% limit may be exceeded to pay for a local government's bonded indebtedness, if the voters approved the bond issue before Proposition 13 was passed, or if the bond issue raised funds for the government's acquisition or improvement of real property.

Example: A single-family home has a market value of $95,000. Taking into account Proposition 13's limits on assessed value, the full cash value of the home is $75,000. The homeowner is entitled to a $7,000 exemption. The tax rate is 1.02% (including pre-1978 bonded indebtedness).

$75,000.00 Full cash value
  7,000.00 Homeowners exemption
$68,000.00 Taxable value

$68,000.00 x .0102 = $694.00 Annual property tax

THE LEVY AND COLLECTION PROCEDURE. Property taxes are levied annually, on or before September 1st for each tax year. The tax year runs from July 1 through June 30 of the next calendar year.

Lien date—January 1

The lien for the taxes attaches to the property on the previous **January 1**. So the lien for the July 1999 - June 2000 tax year attached January 1, 1999. Since the taxes aren't actually levied until sometime later, the specific amount of the tax lien isn't known at the time the lien attaches.

Property tax liens have priority over all other liens except special assessment liens (see Chapter 3). (Property tax liens have **parity** with special assessment liens—both types of liens have equal priority.) A property tax lien continues for 30 years, or until the taxes are paid or the property is sold for delinquent taxes.

The county assessor completes and delivers the local tax roll to the county auditor on or before July 1. Before delivering the local roll to the county auditor, the assessor must notify each property owner of the value of the property as it will appear on the tax roll. The assessor is also required to give either individual or public notice of the time and place of the board of equalization hearings where the owner may appeal the assessment.

The county board of supervisors must fix the tax rates and levy county, school, and district taxes on or before September 1. Since the equalization process often isn't complete at that time, the taxes can be adjusted if there's a change in the valuation of property. After the taxes are levied, the county auditor computes them and enters them on the assessment roll. The roll is then delivered to the county tax collector for collection.

PAYMENT OF TAXES. Property taxes may be paid in two installments. The first installment is due November 1st and is delinquent if not paid by 5:00 PM on December 10. The second installment is due February 1 and is delinquent if not paid by 5:00 PM on April 10. You can't pay the second installment until you've paid the first installment. A 10% penalty is added to any delinquent amount.

The tax collector has discretion to accept payment by electronic fund transfers. The board of supervisors can authorize payment by the use of credit card and add a fee to cover any costs related to the use of a credit card. Probably because of the nuisance of it, the tax collector can refuse payment of the tax in coins.

When property is reassessed because of a change in ownership, the new owner usually owes supplemental taxes, in addition to the taxes already billed for that year. This extra amount becomes due on the date the change of ownership occurs.

ENFORCEMENT OF THE PROPERTY TAX LAWS. When property taxes aren't paid, the tax collector forecloses on the tax liens against the property. First a notice of impending default is published, then there's a five-year redemption period, and finally the property is sold to satisfy the taxes.

Property Tax Year: July 1 - June 30

Lien attaches...................................... previous January 1
Tax rate determined................................. by September 1
Tax bill mailed... by November 1
First installment due....................................... November 1
First installment delinquent.......................... December 10
Second installment due .... February 1
Second installment delinquent............................. April 10

DEFAULT. On or before June 8, the tax collector publishes a list of properties for which the property taxes are delinquent. The notice states that these properties will be in default if the taxes aren't paid by 5:00 PM on June 30. The notice also lists the amount due, and warns that the property may be sold to satisfy the tax lien if the taxes, penalties, and fees aren't paid.

On July 1 at 12:01 AM, all properties for which the taxes have not been paid are in default by operation of law. On or before September 8th, the tax collector publishes a list of the properties for which taxes were not paid by the deadline. These are referred to as "tax defaulted" properties.

www.boe.ca.gov/coasses.htm
(Listing of County Assessors - State Board of Equalization)

REDEMPTION. Tax defaulted property may be redeemed by paying:

1. the amount of delinquent taxes,
2. the delinquency penalty and costs (a 10% delinquency penalty, and costs associated with publishing the notices),
3. the redemption penalty, and
4. the redemption fee.

Redemption fees and penalties vary depending on when the default occurred. The redemption penalty is 1.5% of the delinquent taxes for each month since the default occurred. The redemption fee covers the administrative costs of redemption; it's generally quite low (usually $15).

The total amount necessary for redemption may be paid in a lump sum or in installments. To redeem under an installment plan, the property owner must make the payments on time. Otherwise the property again becomes subject to the power of sale.

TAX SALE. If the property isn't redeemed within five years after it becomes tax defaulted, it may be sold to pay the delinquent taxes, fees, and penalties. On or before June 8, the tax collector publishes a list of the properties which have been tax defaulted for five years and will be subject to sale after June 30. This is called a **notice of power and intent to sell**. The notice is also sent by registered mail to the property owner (or other taxpayer) at his or her last known address.

If the property isn't redeemed (either by full payment or by starting an installment plan) by June 30 five years after default, the property is subject to sale. The tax collector is supposed to make a good faith effort to sell the property within two years after it becomes subject to sale. If no acceptable bids are received at the attempted sale, the tax collector may discontinue the sale and try to sell the property again later on. The tax collector is required to attempt to sell the property at least once every four years until it's sold.

At least 45 days (but not more than 60 days) before the sale, the tax collector must send a **notice of sale** by registered mail to the owner (or other taxpayer) and other persons having an interest in the property. The notice shows, among other things, the time and date set for the proposed sale and the minimum acceptable bid. If the property is the owner's residence, the tax collector must make a reasonable effort to contact the owner personally not less than 10 days (but not more than 60 days) prior to the sale date. Up to $100 can be added to the redemption amount to cover personal contact costs. The minimum bid is the amount that covers the delinquent taxes and penalties and the costs of advertising the sale.

The notice of sale must also be published in a newspaper, distributed in the county or judicial district, at least once a week for the three weeks preceding the sale. (If there isn't a newspaper, the notice has to be posted in three public places in the county or district.) If authorized by the county board of supervisors, the tax collector may advertise the sale by other means.

Tax sales are generally made to the highest bidder at public auction. (There are a few exceptions where the statute requires a sealed bid procedure.) The sale purchaser is given a **tax deed**.

Sometimes tax defaulted property can be sold to a government agency or nonprofit organization, rather than at public auction. The agency or organization must file an objection to the sale of the property. A government agency has to claim that a portion of property is needed for public use. A nonprofit organization has to agree to rehabilitate residential property and sell it to low-income persons, or to dedicate vacant land for a public use.

Sale of the property terminates the right of redemption. If the sale proceeds exceed the amount needed to pay all delinquent taxes, penalties, fees, and costs of sale, the surplus is used to pay any remaining assessments or taxes. Any remaining funds maybe claimed by the former owner, or anyone else having an interest in the property, within one year after the recording of the tax deed.

SALE WITHOUT ACTUAL NOTICE. What if the owner never actually receives notice of the default or the sale? Is the tax sale still valid? As a general rule, yes. A number of California court decisions have held that the method of notice prescribed by the tax code (by registered mail to the last known owner, and publication in a newspaper or posting in a public place) is legally sufficient notice. A property owner is expected to know that the property taxes are due every year. If the owner hasn't been paying the taxes, he or she should know that they are delinquent and that the property may be lost. However, as the following case shows, the general rule doesn't always apply.

TAX DEEDS. A tax deed conveys title to the purchaser free of almost all encumbrances that existed before the foreclosure sale. There are a few specific exceptions: certain tax and special assessment liens and easements, water rights, and restrictions of record. But aside from those, even liens or interests that were acquired or recorded before the tax lien are extinguished. As a result, a tax sale purchaser may receive better title than an ordinary buyer, who takes title subject to any earlier recorded liens or deeds.

Notice that in this respect, tax foreclosure differs from mortgage or deed of trust foreclosure. Those foreclosures eliminate only liens, encumbrances, and interests that were recorded after the lien being foreclosed. They have no effect on liens or interests recorded before the foreclosed lien.

SPECIAL ASSESSMENTS. Special assessments are taxes used to pay for a public improvement in a particular neighborhood, such as the paving of a road or installation of sewer lines. The property owners that benefit from the improvement are required to pay their share of its cost. A special assessment creates an involuntary, specific lien against those owners' properties.

> **Case Example:** Mr. and Mrs. Banas bought a home that happened to have been built partly on one lot and partly on another. Their deed only described one of the lots.
>
> After moving in, the Banases received and paid tax bills for their residence and the one lot described in their deed. The tax bills for the other lot were apparently sent to the former owners, who never paid them. Accordingly, that lot was eventually sold for tax delinquency.
>
> The Banases first learned of the problem after the tax sale, when the lot had already been transferred by tax deed. They sued to have the tax sale invalidated and the tax deed set aside, claiming that their property had been taken without due process of law.
>
> The Banases argued that the notice procedures prescribed by law weren't adequate to give them notice that the taxes were delinquent. Since they received and paid a tax bill every year, they had no reason to suspect that the taxes weren't being paid on part of the land underneath their house.
>
> The court agreed. An effective method of notification was available to the tax collector at reasonable cost: posting a notice at the property itself. Posting at the property would serve to give notice to owners who were in possession but who were not the legal owners of record. *Banas v. Transamerica Title Ins. Co.*, 133 Cal. App. 3d 845, 184 Cal. Rptr. 262 (1982).

INCOME TAX LIENS. If state or federal income taxes aren't paid, another type of tax lien arises. Income tax liens are involuntary and general. A claim of lien is recorded, attaching to all of the taxpayer's personal and real property.

STATE TAX LIEN LAW. The state tax lien law provides that any state tax liabilities create a general lien against all real property owned by the taxpayer and located in California. In other words, the lien attaches to property other than the property subject to the tax. For example, if someone fails to pay sales tax on the sale of personal property, that tax liability can create a state tax lien on that person's home.

A state tax lien doesn't have the same priority as a property tax lien. A property tax lien is senior to all other liens; but a state tax lien is junior to the interest of:

1. a subsequent purchaser without notice of the state tax lien,
2. a mortgage or trust deed lender,
3. a mechanic's lienholder, or
4. a judgment lien creditor.

In each case, the interest must have been recorded before the state tax lien was recorded.

Lien Priority

It's not at all unusual for a piece of property to have several liens against it at the same time. It may be subject to a trust deed, a mechanic's lien, and a property tax lien, for example. In some cases, the total amount of the liens is more than the property will bring at a forced sale. Then not all of the liens can be paid in full. It is therefore necessary to establish an order of priority for paying off the liens after foreclosure.

LIENS				
	Voluntary	Involuntary	General	Specific
Deed of trust	X			X
Mortgage	X			X
Mechanic's lien		X		X
Property tax lien		X		X
Special assessment		X		X
Judgment lien		X	X	
IRS lien		X	X	

As a general rule, liens are given priority according to the order in which they attached to the property. For most liens, the attachment date is the date the lien was recorded. In other words, the lien recorded first has first priority for payment.

There are important exceptions to this rule, however. Property tax liens and special assessment liens are superior to all other liens against the property. Thus, these liens have priority even over liens that attached before they did.

The priority of a mechanic's lien is determined by the date work first started on the project, rather than the date the lien was recorded. All mechanics' liens from the same project have the same priority, regardless of when the individual mechanic or materialman performed his or her work or recorded a claim of lien. If the proceeds from the foreclosure sale aren't enough to cover all the mechanics' liens, the mechanics' lienholders receive prorated shares of the money.

You've seen that once an abstract of judgment is recorded, the judgment lien automatically attaches to any real property the debtor later acquires. But if the judgment debtor took out a loan to buy the new property, the purchase money trust deed has priority over the judgment lien.

Example: D loses a lawsuit and a judgment is entered against her. The judgment creditor records an abstract of judgment to create a lien.

A year later, D buys a house. She borrows the money for the purchase and gives the lender a trust deed on the house. The trust deed is recorded on the same day D takes title to the property.

Technically, the judgment lien attached to the house at the instant D took title. But because the trust deed is for a purchase money loan, that lien has priority over the judgment lien.

Here's an example that shows how the different rules for lien priority work out after a foreclosure sale.

> **Example:** Q's property has the following liens against it: a judgment lien that attached when Q took title on October 1; a purchase money deed of trust that was recorded October 1; a second deed of trust (not for a purchase money loan) that was recorded November 12; a mechanic's lien filed January 10 (but work on the project started on October 15); a mechanic's lien filed January 14 (from the same project); and a property tax lien that attached January 1.
>
> If Q's property is sold at a foreclosure sale, the liens will be paid out of the sale proceeds in the following order: the property tax lien; the purchase money deed of trust; the judgment lien; both mechanics' liens (prorated shares, if necessary); the second deed of trust.
>
> If the sale only brings enough to pay the property tax lien, the other lienholders will receive nothing. If there's only enough to pay the tax lien and part of the trust deed, the rest will receive nothing. And so forth.

The Homestead Law

Homestead laws give owner-occupied homes limited protection from foreclosure. California's homestead law protects only against judgment lien foreclosures, giving no protection against foreclosure of a mortgage, deed of trust, tax lien, or mechanic's lien. It also doesn't protect against foreclosure of a judgment lien when the judgment is for delinquent spousal or child support payments.

A **homestead** is the dwelling of the property owner or the owner's spouse, together with its land and outbuildings. It can be a single-family home, a condo unit, or any other building, as long as the owner, or his or her spouse, lives there. The homestead law establishes an exemption, an amount of money that is exempt from judgment creditors' claims. The basic exemption is $50,000. The exemption is $75,000 if a family lives in the homestead and at least one member of the family owns no interest in it or only a community property interest in it.

> **Examples:** The judgment debtor is a single parent, living in the homestead with one child. Since the child doesn't own any interest in the property, the exemption is $75,000.
>
> Suppose the judgment debtor is married and childless, and the homestead is community property. Again, the exemption is $75,000.
>
> But now suppose the debtor and his brother own the homestead and live there by themselves. The debtor's exemption amount is only $50,000. (The brother has a separate $50,000 exemption for claims against his interest.)

The exemption is $100,000 if the debtor (or the debtor's spouse) is 65 or older, or unable to work because of a disability, or 55 or older with a low income.

Interests in Real Property

There are two types of homestead exemptions in California: a declared homestead exemption and an automatic homestead exemption. A **declared homestead exemption** is established by recording a declaration of homestead. The owner or his or her spouse must be living on the property when the declaration is recorded.

Once a declaration of homestead has been recorded, if a judgment creditor later records an abstract of judgment, the lien does not attach to the debtor's entire interest in the homestead property, as it otherwise would. Instead, the judgment lien only attaches if the value of the homestead is greater than the amount of all existing liens against it plus the amount of the homestead exemption. The amount by which the value exceeds the liens and the exemption is called the surplus of equity, and the creditor's judgment lien can attach only to that surplus. If there is no surplus—if the value of the homestead does not exceed the amount of the liens and the exemption—then the judgment lien cannot attach.

Example: Currier records a declaration of homestead, and she's entitled to a $75,000 exemption. The property is worth $165,000, but there's a deed of trust against the title, and Currier still owes $102,000 on it.

Currier loses a lawsuit and a judgment is entered against her. The judgment creditor records an abstract of judgment. But the judgment lien won't attach to Currier's homestead because there isn't a surplus of equity: the amount of the deed of trust plus the exemption is more than the value of the homestead.

$102,000 (deed of trust)
$+75,000 (exemption)
$177,000 (which is greater than $165,000, the property value)

Of course, a judgment lien will attach to a judgment debtor's home if no declaration of homestead has been filed. Yet even in that case, the debtor can claim a homestead exemption in court during a proceeding to foreclose the judgment lien. This is the **automatic homestead exemption**, sometimes called the dwelling house exemption.

Whether the debtor relies on the automatic exemption or on a declaration of homestead, the property cannot be sold unless there is a surplus of equity. The amount bid for the homestead at the foreclosure sale must be greater than the amount of all existing liens against the property (including the judgment lien) plus the amount of the homestead exemption. As a general rule, the sale bid must also be for at least 90% of the property's fair market value.

When a homestead is foreclosed, the sale proceeds are applied in the following order: first, to pay all liens not subject to the homestead exemption; second, to the homestead claimant for the exemption amount ($50,000, $75,000, or $100,000); third, to pay the costs of the sale; fourth, to pay the judgment creditor's court costs; fifth, to the judgment creditor to satisfy the debt. If there is any money left over, if goes to the homestead claimant.

After foreclosure, whatever money the claimant received as a result of the exemption (up to $50,000, $75,000, or $100,000) is still exempt for six months. This gives the claimant a chance to reinvest that money in another homestead.

One of the advantages of a declared homestead (compared to the automatic homestead exemption) is that the same six-month protection period applies to the

proceeds of a voluntary sale. If the claimant sells the homestead, the exemption amount is protected from creditors for six months after closing. Another advantage is that the protection of a declared homestead continues even when the owners have stopped living on the property, as long as they don't record a declaration of homestead for some other property.

> **Example:** Suppose after Currier recorded her declaration of homestead, she and her children moved to another city, where she rented an apartment. In the meantime, she leased her homestead property to someone else. The homestead is still protected against Currier's creditors. It would not be if Currier was relying on the automatic homestead exemption. The automatic exemption can only be claimed by an owner who is living on the homestead when the judgment lien attaches.

A declaration of homestead terminates if the homestead claimant sells the property, records a declaration of abandonment, or records a declaration of homestead for another property. The declaration does not terminate if the claimant dies, however. It continues for the benefit of family members still living on the property.

CHAPTER SUMMARY

1. An estate is an interest in property that is, will, or may become possessory. There are freehold estates and leasehold estates.

2. The highest estate is the fee simple absolute, which is of unlimited duration. The duration of a fee simple defeasible estate is also unlimited, except that title may revert to the grantor if certain events occur.

3. The duration of a life estate is measured by someone's lifetime. The measuring life is usually the life tenant's, but it may be someone else's (a life estate "pur autre vie"). During a life estate, the grantor holds an estate in reversion, or else a remainderman holds an estate in remainder. These estates are called future interests.

4. There are three types of leasehold estates: the term tenancy, the periodic tenancy, and the tenancy at will. A leasehold tenant has a temporary possessory interest in the property, but does not hold title.

5. Easements and liens are nonpossessory interests, also called encumbrances. An easement is the right to use another's property for a particular purpose. Easements are either appurtenant or in gross. They can be created or terminated expressly, by implication, by estoppel, or by prescription.

6. Local governments levy ad valorem property taxes, taxing the value of real property. Proposition 13 limits the tax rate to 1% of the property's full cash value. Assessed value can't be increased more than 2% per year, unless there's a change in ownership or improvements.

7. The property tax year runs from July 1 through June 30. A property tax lien attaches on January 1, before the tax year begins. If the current year's property taxes haven't been paid by June 30, the property is tax defaulted. Tax defaulted property may be redeemed within five years. After five years, the property may be sold.

8. The purchaser at a tax sale is given a tax deed. The tax deed conveys title free of all prior encumbrances and interests, except for some tax liens and special assessment liens, and easements, water rights, and restrictions of record.

9. Unpaid state taxes (sales taxes, use taxes, state income taxes, etc.) create a state tax lien against all of the taxpayer's real property in California.

10. A lien is a financial encumbrance. A lien gives a creditor the right to foreclose on the property and have the debt paid out of the sale proceeds. A lien is either specific or general, and either voluntary or involuntary. The most common liens are trust deeds, mechanics' liens, judgment liens, and tax liens. The homestead exemption gives a homeowner protection against judgment lien foreclosure.

CASE PROBLEM

Masin v. La Marche, 136 Cal. App. 3d 687, 186 Cal. Rptr. 619 (1982)

The Thomases owned a large tract of land in Montecito. They subdivided it, and in 1971 sold some one-acre parcels, retaining 34 acres themselves. In the deeds to the one-acre parcels, the Thomases reserved an easement to provide access to their 34 acres. The deeds were recorded. This included the deed to parcel C, which they sold to Mr. La Marche.

La Marche moved onto parcel C. In 1972 he stretched a heavy rope attached to two poles across the access easement where it entered the dominant tenement (the 34-acre tract). He hung up a sign forbidding use of the easement road, but the sign disappeared after one week. Later he erected a barrier made of a four-by-four and some two-by-fours in the middle of the road. La Marche took that barrier down in 1973, and began using the road as a storage area. From 1973 to 1979, he stored the walls of a dismantled cabin there; from 1975 to 1977, he stored a 20-foot trailer there.

Meanwhile, the Thomases sold the 34-acre dominant tenement, and after that the property changed hands a number of times. The access easement was not mentioned in any of these deeds. In 1978, the Masins purchased the 34 acres. Again, the deed did not refer to the easement.

There were other access routes onto the 34-acre property besides the easement across La Marche's lot. None of the people who owned the 34 acres before the Masins attempted to use the easement. But the Masins thought that the easement would be more convenient than the other routes. In 1979 they asked La Marche to move the cabin walls and other things that were blocking the easement road. He refused, and the Masins sued to establish their right to use the easement. Did the Masins have that right? Why or why not?

Answer: No, the Masins didn't have the right to use the easement. Although the easement was valid, La Marche terminated it by prescription.

Ordinarily, the Masins would have been entitled to use the easement even though it wasn't mentioned in their deed. Once the Thomases reserved the easement for the benefit of the 34-acre parcel, it ran with the land, belonging to whoever owned that parcel. (And since the easement was a matter of public record, it would have continued to exist even if La Marche had sold the servient tenement to someone else.) Failure to use the easement would only terminate it after 20 years of non-use, because it was created by express reservation rather than by prescription.

But La Marche actively interfered with use of the easement for more than five years, so it was terminated by prescription. Since there were other ways to reach the Masins' property, they couldn't claim an easement by necessity.

The Masins argued against La Marche's prescription claim. They pointed out that the easement could have been cleared in an afternoon just by moving La Marche's junk out of the way and cutting back the shrubbery. The road surface hadn't been harmed by La Marche's use, and he hadn't constructed anything permanent there.

But the court held that La Marche's use was sufficient to establish prescription, since it was completely inconsistent with use of the easement for access to the dominant tenement. It was open and notorious, adverse, continuous, and uninterrupted for more than five years.

CHAPTER 3 KEY TERMS

	freehold/leasehold	prescriptive easement
	full cash value	Proposition 60
	future interest	Proposition 90
abandonment	general property taxes	Proposition 13
absolute/defeasible	homestead	purchase money loan
ad valorem	implied easement	remainder/reversion
appurtenant easement	judgment lien	remainderman
assessment	levy	reservation/grant
base value	license	run with the land
board of equalization	lien priority	servient tenement
condition subsequent	lien	servient tenant
deed of trust	life estate pur autre vie	special assessment
deferment	life estate	surrender
dominant tenement	life tenant	tacking
dominant tenant	measuring life	tax lien
easement in gross	mechanic's lien	tenancy at will
easement by necessity	merger	tenant at sufferance
encumbrance	mortgage	term tenancy (estate for
estate	mortgagor/mortgagee	years)
estoppel	periodic tenancy	trust
exemption	possessory/nonpossessory	trustor/beneficiary/trustee
fee simple	power of termination	waste

Interests in Real Property

Quiz—Chapter 3

1. The highest and most complete real property ownership interest is called a:
   a. leasehold estate.
   b. fee simple absolute estate.
   c. conditional fee estate.
   d. life estate.

2. X granted A a life estate in some property. Upon A's death, the property will pass to B or his heirs. B is called the:
   a. reversionary owner.
   b. measuring life.
   c. primary owner.
   d. remainderman.

3. T rents a house. The lease gives him the right to occupy the house from September 1 through May 31. This is called a:
   a. periodic or month-to-month tenancy
   b. term tenancy or estate for years
   c. tenancy at will
   d. tenancy pur autre vie

4. A non-possessory interest in real property is also called a(n):
   a. license.
   b. leasehold estate.
   c. tenement.
   d. encumbrance.

5. L's property is landlocked, but it has an access easement that allows L to drive across her neighbor's property to the main road. This is a(n):
   a. appurtenant easement.
   b. negative easement.
   c. easement in gross.
   d. servient easement.

6. Which of these is a voluntary, specific lien?
   a. A judgment lien
   b. An easement created by express grant
   c. A trust deed
   d. A special assessment lien

7. The priority of a mechanic's lien is determined by the date that:
   a. the claim of lien was recorded.
   b. the lien claimant last performed work or delivered materials to the project.
   c. the whole project was completed
   d. work on the project started.

8. A judgment lien:
   a. expires five years after the judgment was entered.
   b. cannot be foreclosed.
   c. attaches to property acquired after the abstract of judgment was recorded.
   d. cannot be renewed.

9. In California, the homestead law only provides protection against:
   a. judgment liens.
   b. voluntary liens.
   c. mechanics' liens.
   d. tax liens.

10. Tax defaulted property may be redeemed by the owner by paying all taxes, fees and penalties within the statutory redemption period. The redemption period lasts:
    a. one year
    b. three years
    c. five years
    d. ten years

ANSWERS: 1. b; 2. d; 3. b; 4. d; 5. a; 6. c; 7. d; 8. c; 9. a; 10. c

109

CHAPTER 4
Co-Ownership of Real Property

CHAPTER OVERVIEW

Ownership of real property is frequently shared by more than one person. Two, ten, or two hundred people can be co-owners of the same piece of property at the same time (concurrently). This chapter explains the forms that concurrent ownership can take. The topic has three overlapping aspects. The first section of the chapter focuses on the various ways co-owners can hold title, such as tenancy in common. The second part of the chapter describes ownership by associations of two or more persons, such as partnerships. The third section looks briefly at condominiums and other properties specially developed for concurrent ownership.

Forms of Co-Ownership

When property is owned by one individual, he or she holds title **in severalty**. In California, when property is owned by more than one individual, they can hold title in one of five ways:

- ◆ tenancy in common,
- ◆ joint tenancy,
- ◆ community property,
- ◆ community property with right of survivorship
- ◆ in trust, or
- ◆ tenancy in partnership.

Many prospective co-owners are unaware of these various forms of co-ownership, and wind up with one or another by accident. But the way title is held is very important. It determines how control of the property is shared. It can also have dramatic consequences when co-ownership ends, whether voluntarily or through dissolution or death. Co-owners need to understand these effects and make a deliberate choice.

A real estate agent should make sure that buyers realize the importance of the form of co-ownership. But when an agent raises the subject, the buyers often ask for help in choosing how to take title. At that point, the agent must tell them to consult a lawyer. A well-intentioned agent who gives buyers friendly advice may end up charged with the unauthorized practice of law (see Chapter 6). Not only that, if buyers make the wrong choice based on the agent's advice, the agent could be liable for damages.

Even though real estate agents should avoid advising their customers about the forms of co-ownership, an agent needs a general understanding of the subject. Whenever a legal document is executed, the agent has to know whether only one co-owner may sign, or whether all the co-owners need to. For the parties, it can mean the difference between an effective sale and a void transaction. For the agent, it can mean the difference between a commission and a lawsuit.

www.south-county.org/REGuides/HoldingTitle.html
(Options for Holding Title)

TENANCY IN COMMON

Tenancy in common is the most basic form of concurrent ownership. It is the residual category: co-ownership that doesn't fit into any of the other three categories is a tenancy in common by default. If a deed transferring land to two unmarried individuals doesn't specify how they are taking title, they take title as tenants in common.

Co-owners who choose tenancy in common should make that clear in the deed, by adding "as tenants in common" after their names. If they own unequal shares in the property, that should be stated in the deed.

> **Example:** When B and C bought A's tract of land, they decided to take title as tenants in common. B came up with two-thirds of the purchase price, and C contributed one-third. Their deed reads, "B, a single woman, with an undivided 2/3 interest, and C, a single woman, with an undivided 1/3 interest, as tenants in common."

When a deed does not state each co-tenant's fraction of interest, the law presumes that the interests are equal. In a lawsuit, a tenant in common can overcome that legal presumption by submitting evidence that the parties do not own equal interest, such as the contributions to the purchase price were unequal.

> **Example:** B paid two-thirds of the purchase price and C paid one-third. But their deed simply says, "B, a single woman, and C, a single woman, as tenants in common."
>
> Later B and C have a serious disagreement, and they take each other to court over the property. Because the deed doesn't state what fractional interest each of them owns, the judge presumes that each has a 1/2 interest.
>
> But B presents evidence (her canceled check) showing that she paid two-thirds of the price. This establishes that B has a 2/3 interest in the property, and C only has a 1/3 interest.

Co-Ownership of Real Property

Unity of Possession

In principle, there's no limit to how many tenants in common can share a property. There are also no restrictions on how they divide up the ownership. One tenant in common might own a 1/2 interest in the property and 50 others might each own a 1/100 interest.

Whether tenants in common have equal interests or unequal interests, their interests are always **undivided**. That means each tenant has a right to possess and occupy the whole property, no matter how small his or her share in the ownership is. This is referred to as **unity of possession**. The concept is best illustrated by contrasting tenancy in common with ownership in severalty.

> **Example:** A owns a large tract of land. She deeds the east two-thirds of it to B, and the west third to C.
>
> B and C each own their portion of the tract in severalty. They are not co-owners; they are sole owners of two separate properties. Each has the right to exclude all others from his portion. B can exclude C from the east two-thirds, and C can exclude B from the west third.
>
> On the other hand, suppose A deeded her entire tract to B and C as tenants in common, with B taking an undivided 2/3 interest and C taking an undivided 1/3 interest. Now they are co-owners of a single property. Both have the right to possess and occupy the whole tract; neither can exclude the other from any part of it. Even though B's interest in the property is twice as great as C's, B can't fence off two-thirds of the property and tell C to keep out.

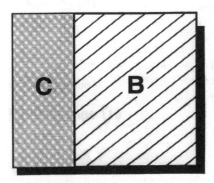

OWNERSHIP IN SEVERALTY
B owns the east 2/3
C owns the west 1/3

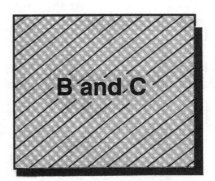

TENANCY IN COMMON
**B has an undivided 2/3 interest
in the whole property**
**C has an undivided 1/3 interest
in the whole property**

RENTS AND PROFITS. Each tenant in common has a right to a share of any products or income generated by the property. Diamonds from a mine or apples from an orchard belong to all the tenants in common. And if they lease the property to someone else, the tenants in common share the rent they collect.

Chapter 4

However, one tenant in common ordinarily doesn't have a right to charge another tenant in common rent. If tenant in common A chooses to live on the property and tenant in common B chooses not to, A is not required to pay rent to B, unless otherwise agreed. Tenant A is also not required to give tenant B a share of what the property produces as a result of A's labor.

CONTRIBUTION. All tenants in common are required to share the property's expenses: maintenance, insurance, taxes, trust deed payments, and so forth. Unless otherwise agreed, each tenant's share is proportionate to his or her ownership interest. If tenant in common A has an undivided 2/3 interest and tenant in common B has an undivided 1/3 interest, A is liable for 2/3 of the expenses, and B is liable for 1/3 of the expenses.

A co-tenant who pays more than his or her share of the expenses can demand reimbursement from the other tenants in common. This is called the **right to contribution**.

The right to contribution also applies to property improvements, but only when the other tenants in common have agreed to the improvement.

> **Example:** A, B, and C own a house as tenants in common. A and B want to add a deck, but C is opposed to the project.
>
> A pays a carpenter to build the deck. A is entitled to reimbursement from B, but not from C.

As you might guess, this rule often leads to disputes over whether a particular project (a new cedar roof, for example) was an improvement or necessary maintenance.

The right to contribution gives a paying tenant in common an **equitable lien** against a non-paying tenant's interest. But it can cost so much to enforce the lien that it may not be worth the paying tenant's while.

WASTE. A tenant in common is liable to the other tenants for any waste he or she commits on the property (just as a life tenant is liable to a remainderman). If tenant in common A drives a car through the garage wall or kills the apple orchard, he will have to compensate tenant in common B for the damage.

www.octitle.com/common.htm
(Tenancy in Common)

Transfer and Encumbrance

A tenant in common is free to sell, will, or encumber his or her undivided interest without the consent of the other tenant (s). A tenant in common's interest can also be transferred involuntarily, by foreclosure or bankruptcy. The transferee takes the interest subject to any liens or debts.

> **Example:** A. B, and C are tenants in common. A takes out a loan and gives the bank a trust deed on her undivided 1/3 interest, but that trust deed doesn't encumber B's or C's interest.
>
> A dies, leaving all her property to her friend D. Now B, C, and D are tenants in common, and D's undivided 1/3 interest is encumbered by the trust deed.

114

D can't make the trust deed payments, so eventually the bank forecloses. E purchases D's 1/3 interest at the foreclosure sale. Now B, C, and E are tenants in common.

But to transfer or encumber the whole property, all the tenants in common must sign the deed, trust deed, or other document.

Example: A, B, C, and D are tenants in common. Z offers them a great deal of money for their land. A, B, and C leap at the offer. But D (who holds an undivided 1/16 interest) turns it down, because of his sentimental attachment to the property.

A, B, and C can sell their combined undivided 15/16 interest in the property without D's consent, but they can't sell the whole. Z insists on all or nothing, since she wouldn't be able to carry out her plans for development with D still living there. The other co-owners plead with D, but he won't budge. Z withdraws her offer.

Terminating a Tenancy in Common (Partition)

A tenancy in common can be terminated by the agreement of all the tenants. They can agree to change to one of the other forms of concurrent ownership joint tenancy, community property, or tenancy in partnership) if any of those are applicable. Or they can agree to divide their property, so that each owns a portion of it in severalty. This division by agreement is called **voluntary partition**.

Example: A wills 20 acres of vacant land to B and C as tenants in common. After A's death, B and C agree that they'd each rather have half the property instead of sharing the whole.

They have the land surveyed and divided into two ten-acre parcels. B deeds her undivided 1/2 interest in the east ten acres to C, and C deeds his undivided 1/2 interest in the west ten acres to B. Now each owns a ten-acre tract in severalty.

JUDICIAL PARTITION. A tenancy in common can also be terminated by the unilateral action of one of the tenants, without the others' consent. If X wants to end the tenancy in common and the other tenants don't, X can file a **partition action** in superior court.

Everyone with a recorded interest in the property (co-tenants, lienholders) is brought into the partition suit as a defendant. The judge determines the status and priority of all the liens against the property, and what interest each party holds. Then the judge terminates the tenancy in common by partitioning the property. Each former co-tenant is granted a share proportionate to his or her ownership interest.

Whenever possible, the judge will order the property to be physically divided. But physical division often won't work. For example, if A and B own a house as tenants in common, it would not be practical to divide the house itself in two.

Any time physical partition would be impractical or inequitable, the judge can order the property sold. The sale proceeds are then divided among the former co-tenants according to their ownership interests. In some cases, a judge will order part of the property sold and part of it physically divided.

Chapter 4

A tenant in common in a partition suit may oppose a physical division of the property. He or she can present evidence (an appraisal) comparing the value of the divided property with the amount that a sale of the whole property would bring. If the divided property would be worth substantially less than the whole, the judge should order the property sold instead of physically divided.

JOINT TENANCY

As long as joint tenants are alive and well, their relationship is similar to that of tenants in common: each joint tenant has an undivided interest and shares possession of the whole property.

The distinguishing feature of joint tenancy—the **right of survivorship**— comes into play if one of the joint tenants dies. When a joint tenant dies, his or her interest in the property passes automatically to the surviving joint tenant(s).

Example: A, B, and C buy a vacation home together. Sometime later, C dies. If A, B, and C were tenants in common, C's undivided interest would go to his heir, D. Then B, C, and D would own the property as tenants in common.

But A, B, and C were joint tenants. From the moment of C's death, A and B own the whole property. As a result of the right of survivorship, D does not acquire an interest in it.

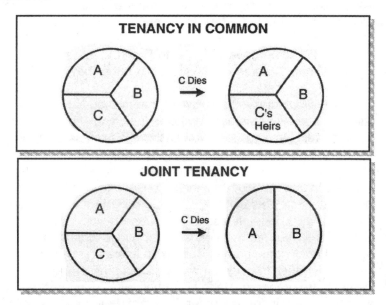

Creating a Joint Tenancy

Since joint tenancy can have such a radical effect on the disposition of property, it isn't something co-owners slip into by default. There are specific rules for creating a joint tenancy and for maintaining one. If these rules aren't followed when the property is acquired, or if they are broken during the period of ownership, the joint tenancy fails and the right of survivorship is lost. Instead of a joint tenancy, the co-owners will either have a tenancy in common or (if they're a married couple) community property.

Co-Ownership of Real Property

Four Unities (Possession, Interest, Time, and Title)

Joint tenancy requires four unities:

- ◆ unity of possession,
- ◆ unity of interest,
- ◆ unity of time, and
- ◆ unity of title.

 www.octitle.com/joint.htm
(Joint Tenancy)

Unity of possession allows all co-tenants to have the right to possess the whole property at the same time.

Unity of interest means that all the joint tenants must have an equal interest in the property. If there are two joint tenants, each must have a 1/2 interest; if there are three, each must have a 1/3 interest; if there are 20, each must have a 1/20 interest. If A has a 1/4 interest and B has a 3/4 interest, they aren't joint tenants.

Unity of time means that all of the joint tenants must acquire their interests in the property at the same moment.

Unity of title means that they all must have taken title through the same deed or will.

Example: A deeds an undivided 1/2 interest in his property to B. Two months later, A deeds an undivided 1/2 interest in the same property to C.

B and C cannot be joint tenants because they acquired title at two different times, through two different deeds. Although there is unity of interest and unity of possession, there is no unity of time and no unity of title. As a result, there is no joint tenancy.

As a general rule, when any one of the four unities is missing (at the outset or at any time during the period of co-ownership) the joint tenancy fails. In California, the legislature has created a statutory exception to the four unities rule. An owner in severalty may create a joint tenancy by deeding the property to him or herself and others.

Example: A has owned some land for many years. When her children, B and C, reach adulthood, A deeds the property "to A, B, and C, as joint tenants."

This new deed satisfies the unity of time and title requirements, even though A originally acquired the property long before and through a different deed than B and C.

The unity of possession requirement is not rigidly applied. Joint tenants may agree among themselves to give one joint tenant exclusive possession of the property. Such an agreement does not destroy the joint tenancy. The agreement can even be entered into at the same time the co-owners acquire the property, without preventing creation of a joint tenancy.

Other Requirements. A joint tenancy can only be created in writing (even in the case of personal property). The deed or will must expressly state the intention to create a joint tenancy. To be on the safe side, it should say either "as joint tenants" or "in joint tenancy." Courts have disagreed over whether any other language is sufficient evidence of intent to create a joint tenancy. The phrase "with the right of survivorship" will not create a joint tenancy by itself.

Rights and Duties of Joint Tenants

If co-owners manage to avoid all the pitfalls and establish a joint tenancy, they have basically the same rights and duties as tenants in common: the right to contribution, and to the products and rents from the property; the duty to not commit waste. A joint tenant can also encumber his or her own interest without the others' consent. However, a joint tenant in sole possession of the property does not have to share the profits of the property.

But in addition, joint tenants have a right that tenants in common don't have: the right of survivorship.

RIGHT OF SURVIVORSHIP. As explained earlier, when a joint tenant dies, his or her interest in the joint tenancy property passes directly to the surviving joint tenants.

A joint tenancy interest cannot be willed or inherited, because it no longer belongs to the joint tenant at the moment of his or her death. As a result, the joint tenancy property does not have to go through the probate process. This can spare the surviving joint tenants considerable expense and delay. (However, joint tenancy property doesn't escape federal estate taxes. The deceased joint tenant's interest is treated as part of his or her estate for tax purposes.)

Another result of the right of survivorship is that any liens against the deceased joint tenant's interest (for example, a judgment lien) are extinguished. The surviving joint tenants take the interest free and clear of the deceased joint tenant's deed of trust, judgment lien, or other debts. (Compare this to tenancy in common, where the deceased tenant's heir takes the interest subject to any liens and debts.)

Because a lien against one joint tenant's interest is so easily lost, few creditors are willing to accept such an interest as security. But a lien against the entire property—a deed of trust signed by all the joint tenants, for example—is not lost if one or more of the joint tenants dies.

Making the Title Marketable. Although surviving joint tenants acquire the deceased joint tenant's interest automatically at the moment of death, they must take steps to clear their title.

This can be accomplished by recording proof of the death, such as a court decree or a certified copy of the death certificate. When a death certificate is used instead of a court decree, the survivors should also record a sworn statement (an **affidavit**) that includes a description of the joint tenancy property, identifies the deceased as one of the joint tenants, and identifies the surviving joint tenants. It may also be necessary to record a certificate of inheritance tax release.

Until these steps have been taken, the surviving joint tenants' title is not **marketable**. That means the public record presents some question about the validity of their title.

A title company will refuse to insure a title unless it is marketable. Here again, however, a real estate agent shouldn't rely absolutely on the title company. The agent needs to know the rules and double check to make sure they've been followed. When surviving joint tenants sell property, the buyer should not go through with the transaction until the proof of death, affidavit, and tax release have been recorded.

www.callandtitle.com/title/holding.html
(Holding a Title)

Simultaneous Death. If all the joint tenants die at once, each tenant's interest in the joint tenancy property is probated separately. The heirs of each joint tenant will receive his or her interest, and all the heirs will share ownership as tenants in common.

> **Example:** A and B own property as joint tenants. They are killed at virtually the same moment when a tornado hits their house.
>
> A's undivided 1/2 interest in the property passes to his heirs, X and Y, by intestate succession. B had written a will leaving all her property to her friend Z, so Z takes B's undivided 1/2 interest in the joint tenancy property.
>
> After the probate process is completed, X, Y, and Z are tenants in common. X and Y each have an undivided 1/4 interest, and Z has an undivided 1/2 interest.

Note that although a joint tenancy interest can't usually be willed, it does pass according to will when there are no surviving joint tenants.

Terminating a Joint Tenancy

PARTITION. Just like tenants in common, joint tenants can agree to partition their property, or one joint tenant can bring suit for judicial partition. Either way, by breaking the unity of possession, partition eliminates the right of survivorship and ends the co-ownership.

But merely filing a partition action does not terminate the joint tenancy. It ends only when the court's partition judgment is entered. If one of the joint tenants dies during the trial, the right of survivorship is still effective.

There is always the problem regardless of what type of tenancy exists, that one co-tenant occupies the property exclusively and refuses to allow the other co-tenant to share occupancy. Whether such an "ouster" exists will involve a review of many facts if it is disputed. One clear and simple way to establish an ouster is to use California Civil Code Section 843. Under this section, the tenant out of possession serves a written demand on the tenant in possession for concurrent possession. If the tenant in possession does not provide unconditional concurrent possession to the requesting tenant within 60 days after service of the demand, an ouster is established. The ousted tenant may now sue for possession, partition or any other appropriate remedy. This section can not be used if the tenant out of possession is not entitled to possession or a specific remedy is provided in an existing cotenancy agreement.

SEVERANCE. A joint tenancy is also terminated when it is **severed**, which can occur in a number of different ways. Severance ends the joint tenancy and eliminates the right of survivorship, but unlike partition, it does not terminate the co-ownership. Instead, severance changes a joint tenancy into a tenancy in common.

Each joint tenant has the power to sever the joint tenancy by transferring his or her interest. Transfer severs a joint tenancy by breaking the unities of time and title.

> **Example:** A and B own some land as joint tenants. B sells her undivided 1/2 interest in the property to C. Now A and C each own an undivided 1/2 interest, but they are tenants in common, not joint tenants.

Involuntary transfer of a joint tenant's interest also severs the joint tenancy. This includes bankruptcy or foreclosure (see Chapter 12).

But transfer (either voluntary or involuntary) severs the joint tenancy only in regard to the transferred interest. When there are just two joint tenants, that ends the joint tenancy altogether. When there are more than two joint tenants, however, the co-owners who did not transfer their interests remain joint tenants in relation to one another.

Example: A, B, and C are joint tenants. C deeds her interest to her friend Z. That severs the joint tenancy as far as C's undivided 1/3 interest is concerned, so Z is not a joint tenant. Z is a tenant in common in relation to A and B. But A and B are still joint tenants in relation to one another.

If Z were to die, his interest would pass to his heirs, since the right of survivorship does not apply to him.

But if instead it's B that dies, A (rather than B's heirs) takes B's interest. The right of survivorship was still effective between A and B. After B's death, A has an undivided 2/3 interest, and Z still has an undivided 1/3 interest. A and Z are tenants in common.

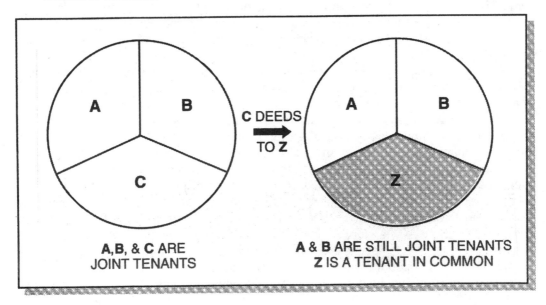

What if a joint tenant wants to sever the joint tenancy but still keep an ownership interest in the property? This problem arises when a joint tenant wants to eliminate the right of survivorship, in order to will his or her interest in the property.

Until fairly recently, the law didn't allow a person to deed property to him or herself. So the severing joint tenant had to deed his or her interest to an intermediary called a "strawman". Like any other transfer, this severed the joint tenancy. But the strawman would then deed the property back to the former joint tenant, who would take title as a tenant in common.

In California, this straw transaction is no longer necessary. A joint tenant may sever the joint tenancy simply by deeding his or her interest in the property to him or herself.

Co-Ownership of Real Property

Case Example: Mr. and Mrs. Riddle owned some real property as joint tenants. Mrs. Riddle retained a lawyer to plan her estate. The lawyer explained to her that the joint tenancy property would go to her husband upon her death.

Mrs. Riddle wanted to terminate the joint tenancy so that she could dispose of the property by will. The lawyer prepared a deed by which Mrs. Riddle granted her 1/2 interest in the property to herself. He also helped Mrs. Riddle write a will leaving her 1/2 interest to someone other than her husband. Mrs. Riddle died a few weeks after executing these documents.

When he discovered what his wife had done, Mr. Riddle sued Mrs. Riddle's estate. Following an established precedent, the trial court held that Mrs. Riddle's deed to herself had not severed the joint tenancy. By right of survivorship, Mr. Riddle now owned the entire property in severalty.

But this decision was reversed on appeal. Overruling the precedent, the appellate court held that the deed had severed the joint tenancy. Mrs. Riddle's 1/2 interest passed according to her will, not by the right of survivorship. *Riddle v. Harmon*, 102 Cal. App. 3d 524 (1980).

Transferring the property is not the only way to sever a joint tenancy. One of the co-owners can simply make a written declaration that the joint tenancy is severed. Not only that, executing any written instrument that shows an intention to sever the joint tenancy may be held to sever it.

Example: A and B own a house as joint tenants. They enter a written agreement stating that B is to have exclusive possession of the property.

This agreement suggests an intention to sever the joint tenancy, since unity of possession is one of the basic characteristics of a joint tenancy. For that reason, a court might hold that the agreement caused a severance.

However, if A and B state in their agreement that B can have exclusive possession on condition that the joint tenancy is unaffected, then it will not be severed. The joint tenants' actual intentions control in these situations.

A joint tenant's attempt to will the joint tenancy property does not automatically cause a severance. But it may be used as evidence of intent to sever.

Recording Requirement. A deed, declaration, or other document severing a joint tenancy must be recorded for the severance to be effective. If the severance document is not recorded when the severing joint tenant dies, the property will still go to the surviving joint tenants. An exception is made if the severance document was executed no more than three days before the death, and is recorded within seven days after the death.

When all joint tenants have agreed to a severance, it isn't necessary to record the agreement. Recording is also unnecessary for severance when one joint tenant deeds his or her interest to another joint tenant.

Mutual Consent Agreement. Joint tenants may agree among themselves that their joint tenancy can only be severed by mutual consent, and not by the unilateral action of one tenant. If one joint tenant later deeds his or her interest to someone else, the transfer will not be effective, and the joint tenancy won't be severed.

> **Example:** A and B agree that their joint tenancy can only be severed by mutual consent. Later A deeds his undivided 1/2 interest to C. Because of the mutual consent agreement, the deed to C is invalid, and the joint tenancy is not severed.

There's an important exception to this rule, however. If C was a good faith purchaser for value (not someone in collusion with A or receiving the deed as a gift) and was not aware of the mutual consent agreement, the deed is valid and the joint tenancy is broken.

And there's one other situation in which a mutual consent agreement does not prevent severance. If one joint tenant murders another joint tenant, the joint tenancy is severed. This prevents the murderer from gaining the victim's interest in the property through the right of survivorship. The rule applies to voluntary manslaughter (killing under extreme provocation) as well as to premeditated murder.

Advantages and Disadvantages of Joint Tenancy

Co-owners who take title as joint tenants usually choose that form of ownership so the property won't have to be probated, and so the surviving tenant can take the property free of the other's liens and debts. These are substantial advantages, if in fact one of the parties dies during the period of co-ownership.

But the right of survivorship is very easily lost through severance. Although a severance document must be recorded to be effective, a co-owner who has no reason to suspect that the joint tenancy has been severed is not likely to check the public record. He or she may be in for a shock if the other co-owner dies and wills an interest in the property to someone else.

Co-owners can prevent this kind of surprise by agreeing that their joint tenancy cannot be severed except by mutual consent. But that arrangement can create the opposite problem, by making it difficult to get out of the joint tenancy. If one of the joint tenants is unwilling to consent to a severance, the other(s) must file a partition action. Like any lawsuit, a partition action can be expensive, time-consuming, and stressful.

COMMUNITY PROPERTY

In California, all property owned by married people is classified either as the **separate property** of one spouse, or as the **community property** of both spouses. These classifications determine a couple's rights and duties in regard to the property.

Outside of California, only Arizona, Idaho, Louisiana, Nevada, New Mexico, Texas, Washington and Wisconsin have community property systems. In some other states, married couples co-own property as **tenants by the entirety**, which is similar to joint tenancy. In other states there is no special form of ownership for married couples.

Co-Ownership of Real Property

Case Example: Juan Vargas lived a double life. He married Mildred in 1929. Sixteen years later, he married Josephine. Josephine believed that Juan had previously divorced Mildred. Since Juan had not, his marriage to Josephine was invalid. When Juan died, he had been married to Mildred for 40 years, and putatively married to Josephine for 24 years. Because Josephine had believed in good faith that she was validly married, the probate court divided Juan's estate equally between the two women. *Estate of Vargas*, 36 Cal. App. 3d 714 (1974).

The concept of community property is based in Spanish law, which is how it became established in California. The treaty of Guadalupe Hidalgo (by which Mexico ceded California to the United States in 1848) required the U.S. to respect the property rights of Mexican nationals living in the ceded territory. As a result, the California state constitution (1850) included a provision recognizing the separate property rights of wives. Subsequent legislation built on the distinction between separate property and community property.

In 1970, the California legislature passed the Family Law Act, which confirmed the community property system. Amendments to the act adopted over the next few years significantly revised the respective rights of husband and wife. Earlier law had given the husband management and control of the community property, but as of January 1, 1975, husband and wife share management and control.

When Community Property Rules Apply

Community property exists only in the context of a marriage. The Family Law Property Rules Act's community property rules do not apply to non-marital relationships.

This was confirmed in the famous "palimony" case, *Marvin v. Marvin*, 18 Cal. 3d 660, 134 Cal. Rptr. 815 (1976). Lee Marvin and Michelle Triola lived together for seven years without marrying. When their relationship ended, Triola sued Marvin for support and half the property the couple had acquired. The California Supreme Court ruled that an unmarried cohabitant may have a financial claim against an ex-partner, but the claim is not based on community property rights. The plaintiff must be able to prove that there was an agreement to share property or income, or some other basis for recovery.

However, if a couple is not validly married, but one or both partners believed in good faith that they were, their property will be divided as if they had been married.

Classifying the Property

The idea behind the community property system is that a marriage is a partnership. Husband and wife each work for the good of the partnership. Any money or property acquired through the skill or labor of either spouse during marriage belongs to the marital community, not just to the individual who earned it.

In addition, anything purchased with community funds or with community credit (such as a credit card issued to both spouses) is community property. Property may belong to the community even when title is held in the name of only one spouse.

On the other hand, everything an individual owns before marriage remains his or her separate property after marriage provided it is kept separate and not mixed with community property. This includes money accumulated before marriage.

Example: W earns her living as a bus driver. While she was single, she was able to save $8,000 out of her wages. After her marriage to H, that $8,000 remains W's separate property. The wages she earns during the marriage are community property, however.

www.octitle.com/commun.htm
(Community Property)

Anything purchased with separate property funds is also separate property. So if W uses her $8,000 to buy a car during her marriage, the car is her separate property.

Property or money acquired by gift, will, or inheritance is separate property, even if it is received after marriage. It is not community property because it isn't earned by skill or labor. A gift purchased by one spouse for the other with community funds is the recipient's separate property.

But to be separate property, a gift received during marriage must be a true gift. That is, it must not have been given in exchange for services rendered, either in the past or in the future.

Example: H is a married man. H's elderly mother gives H her sailboat. It is understood between them that the sailboat is H's compensation for helping his mother with housekeeping and other chores. The sailboat is not a true gift. Because H has earned it (or will earn it), the sailboat is community property rather than separate property.

Any appreciation in separate property, and any rents or profits generated by separate property, ordinarily are also separate property. However, if the appreciation, rents, or profits are the result of a spouse's effort, skill, or labor, they are community property instead.

Example: H owns an apartment building as his separate property. If he hires a property management company and is not actively involved in managing the building himself, the rents it generates will be his separate property. But if he spends time and energy on maintaining the building and leasing the apartments, the rents may be considered community property.

The rules change when a married couple is living separately or if a decree of separation has been issued. Then the income and property each spouse acquires is his or her separate property. If a separated spouse has a minor child living with him or her, the child's earnings are also that spouse's separate property.

When a married person wins a personal injury suit, the damages award is community property if it is received while the couple is living together. But if the couple is living apart, the award is the separate property of the injured spouse. If the cause of action arose after entry of judgment of dissolution or separation, or while the parties were living separately. However, a different rule applies if the personal injury was inflicted by the other spouse rather than a third party. Then the damages award is the injured spouse's separate property even while the couple is still living together.

Co-Ownership of Real Property

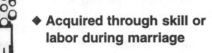

Community Property

◆ Acquired through skill or labor during marriage

◆ Purchased with community funds or community credit

Separate Property

◆ Acquired before marriage

◆ Gift or Inheritance

◆ Purchased with separate funds or separate credit

◆ Appreciation, profits, or proceeds from separate property

◆ Earnings after separation

◆ Personal injury cause of action after separation

Legal Presumptions Favor Community Property

MIXED SEPARATE AND COMMUNITY PROPERTY. Sometimes there are both separate and community interests in a single piece of property. This can occur either when the property is paid for over time, or when it is improved during the marriage.

When property is paid for over time (as with a deed of trust or an installment contract), some payments may be made with separate funds and some with community funds. This is especially likely to occur with a major purchase, such as a home.

Example: H and W purchased a residence for $150,000. They used W's separate funds to make the $30,000 downpayment. But their $120,000 deed of trust is a community obligation; that is, both H and W signed the loan documents. They also use community funds to make the monthly payments on the loan.

The home is considered community property, but W has a separate property interest in it.

Community property—either community funds, or the time, skill, and labor of one of the spouses—is often used to improve separate property. That gives the marital community an interest in the property.

Example: W inherits a house from her mother. This is her separate property. Since H and W already have a home, W decides to lease the inherited house.

In preparing the house for rental, W spends $10,000 in community funds on repairs and improvements. The house is still W's separate property, but H and W's marital community has an interest in it. Although most of the rent generated by the property will be W's separate property, a portion will be H and W's community property.

The same process works in reverse, too. Let's say W's mother left her $10,000, and she used those separate funds to improve the home she and H own as community property. Then W would have a separate interest in the home along with the community's interest.

There's a complication, however. When one spouse makes a community contribution to the other's separate property as a gift, the community does not acquire an interest in the separate property. And when one spouse makes a gift of separate property to the community, he or she does not acquire a separate interest in the community property.

Sometimes it is unclear whether or not a particular contribution was a gift. A court will apply legal presumptions to decide the question. In certain circumstances the law presumes a contribution was a gift, and in others it presumes a contribution was not a gift. For this reason, it can be difficult to tell whether there are mixed separate and community interests in a piece of property. (The presumption that a court in a dissolution proceeding will apply to separate property contributions that were used to acquire community property is discussed below.)

Consequences of Classification

Each spouse owns his or her separate property in severalty. Each has an undivided 1/2 interest in all of the couple's community property.

But the couple's rights and duties in regard to the community property are different than those they'd have if they owned the property as tenants in common or as joint tenants. For example, community property is not subject to judicial partition. It can only be divided by agreement, or when the marriage is dissolved.

MANAGEMENT AND CONTROL. Under the Family Law Act, husband and wife have equal control over community property. The only exception: when one spouse operates a business, the other spouse has no right to interfere in its management, even though the business is community property. But equal control of community property is the general rule. Equal control means that either spouse can act unilaterally, without the other's consent.

> **Example:** H and W own a car as community property. One day a passerby offers H $5,000 for the car. That strikes H as a very good price, so he accepts the offer without consulting W.
>
> When H tells W he sold the car, she's very annoyed. But it's too late to do anything about it; H's unilateral action was legally binding.

www.best.com/~marcw/cp.htm
(Community Property - Income Tax Consequences)

However, there are several important limitations on this kind of unilateral action. These are called **joinder requirements**: both husband and wife must join in the transaction. One spouse can't give away community property without the other's consent. (If H had given away the car, W could demand it back.) One spouse can't sell, lease, or encumber the couple's household furnishings without the other's consent. And one spouse can't sell the other spouse's clothing, or a minor child's clothing, even when these are community property.

For real estate agents, one joinder requirement is crucial: any transfer or encumbrance of community real property requires the signature of both husband and wife.

There are very few exceptions to this rule. It does not apply to a lease of real property that will end within one year from the date of execution. (So W can lease the couple's summer home for six months without H's consent; his signature is not necessary.) Joinder is also not required for estoppel. (If a neighbor builds a garage over the property line because H said it was okay, both H and W are estopped from objecting to the encroachment, even though W didn't give her approval.)

In any other real estate transaction—lease, encumbrance, or transfer—the consent and signatures of both husband and wife are essential.

Remedies for an Unauthorized Action. When only one spouse takes an action regarding community real property that requires the consent and signature of both, the transaction is not binding on the other spouse. The non-consenting spouse may void the transfer or encumbrance, even when the buyer or lienholder acted in good faith. Any payment received from the buyer or lienholder must be refunded.

When title is in the signing spouse's name alone and the buyer is not aware the seller is married, the non-consenting spouse must take action to void the transfer within one year after the deed or lien is recorded. If the instrument is never recorded, or the buyer knew the seller was married, this statute of limitations doesn't apply.

For real estate agents, buyers, and lenders, the rule is simple: always determine whether the grantor is married. If he or she is, the safest course is to have the spouse:

- ◆ sign a quitclaim deed transferring any interest he or she might have in the property to the grantor spouse, or
- ◆ co-sign all the documents involved in the transaction (the listing agreement, deposit receipt, and grant deed).

These steps are not legally necessary if the property is the grantor's separate property. But the grantee is taking a big risk if the grantor's spouse doesn't sign. If it turns out that the community has an interest in the property, the grantee could lose the property.

LIABILITY FOR DEBTS. Creditors' rights against a married person's property are determined by its classification as separate or community property.

One spouse's separate property is shielded from liability for the other spouse's premarital debts.

Example: At the time of H and W's marriage, W already owned a home. H owed a large judgment in connection with a car accident. Since the home is W's separate property, the judgment cannot become a lien against it.

Separate property is also protected from debts the other spouse incurs during the marriage, unless they were incurred for necessities such as food and clothing. So if H's car accident had happened during the marriage, W's separate property still could not be reached by the judgment creditor.

Community property, on the other hand, can be reached by the premarital creditor of either spouse. But the non-debtor spouse can protect his or her earnings by keeping them apart from all other community funds, in an account that the debtor spouse has no access to. This won't shield the earnings against debts the other spouse contracts during the marriage, however.

All community property is liable for the debts either spouse incurs during the marriage. Referring back to the previous example, if the home were community property, the judgment lien against H would attach to it, even though W had nothing to do with the car accident.

Chapter 4

Separate Property

	Other Spouse's Premarital Debt	Debt Incurred During Marriage
Separate Property	SAFE	SAFE unless debt is for necessities
Community Property	LIABLE unless earnings kept in a separate account	LIABLE

DIVISION OF PROPERTY ON DISSOLUTION. At the end of a marriage, the court presiding over the dissolution has the power to divide and award the couple's community property. But separate property is excluded from this process. The court cannot award one spouse's separate property to the other spouse. (However, the spouse who owns the separate property may request that the court include it in the property settlement.)

As a general rule, the community property will be divided equally. But the court can distribute it differently if that would be more equitable.

In determining whether property is separate or community property, the court relies on legal presumptions that favor community property. One important presumption is that all property acquired during marriage in joint form is presumed to be community property. That presumption is applied even if the deed states the property is held in some other way, such as tenancy in common or joint tenancy. The presumption can be rebutted if the deed or a separate written agreement states that the husband and wife hold their interests as separate property.

Case Example: Robert and Joyce Hilke held the title to their house as "husband and wife, as joint tenants." Joyce filed for divorce, judgment was entered but she died before the property was distributed by the judge who reserved the right to do so. Robert claimed the house as surviving joint tenant. Joyce's estate claims the house was community property. The California Supreme Court held that Civil Code Section 4800.1 (now Family Code Section 22580) presumes that joint tenancy property is community property and the property should be sold with the proceeds split equally between the estate and Robert. *In Re Marriage of Hilke* 4 Cal. 4th 215, 14 Cal. Rptr. 2d 371 (1992).

This presumption applies only in a dissolution, not when a married couple sells their property or when a spouse dies. Reconsidering the Hilke case, suppose the couple stayed married, but Joyce died a few years after they bought the land. In distributing her estate, the probate court would presume the land was joint tenancy property, not community property (see below).

In a dissolution, to prove that something is separate property, it is often necessary to trace the source of the funds that were used to purchase it. This can be a very complicated process, especially when separate property has changed form during the marriage (from a grand piano to cash to a motorcycle), or when separate funds have been commingled with community funds.

When there are both separate and community interests in the same piece of property, the court will order some form of reimbursement. A spouse must reimburse the community for contributions to his or her separate property, and the community must reimburse either spouse for separate contributions to community property. If the court holds that a contribution was a gift, however, reimbursement is not required.

If separate property was used to acquire community property (as when one spouse's separate funds were used to make the downpayment on the couple's home), the contribution won't be treated as a gift unless the contributing spouse signed a waiver giving up the right to reimbursement, or some other document that had the effect of a waiver. The amount reimbursed will be the amount originally contributed, without any adjustment due to a change in the property's value.

DISPOSITION OF PROPERTY AT DEATH. When a married person dies, the probate court determines what part of the estate is separate property and what part is community property. The property is then distributed according to the will, or if there is no will, according to the rules of intestate succession. (See Chapter 10 for more information about wills and intestate succession.)

A married person is free to will separate property to anyone he or she chooses. In addition, husband and wife each have the right to will an undivided 1/2 interest in any community property to someone other than the spouse.

Example: H and W own a home as community property. W wills her 1/2 interest in the property to her friend A. When W dies, H and A each own an undivided 1/2 interest in the property as tenants in common. (H and A must be tenants in common rather than joint tenants, since they don't share unity of time or title.)

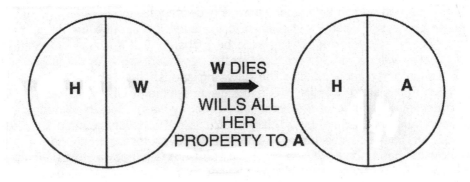

If a married person dies without having made a valid will, all the community property vests in the surviving spouse.

Example: H and W had three children. H never got around to writing a will. On his death, W takes full title to their home, car, furniture, and everything else that was community property. She now owns all of this in severalty, and the children have no rights in it.

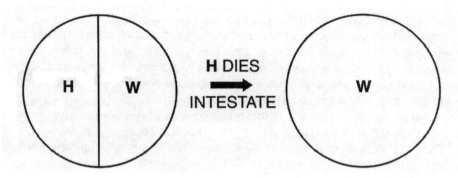

On the other hand, the intestate spouse's separate property is divided between the surviving spouse and the deceased's children. If there is one child, the spouse receives an undivided 1/2 interest and the child receives an undivided 1/2 interest. If there is more than one child, the spouse takes an undivided 1/3 interest, and the remaining 2/3 interest is apportioned equally among the children. All of these interests are, of course, held as tenants in common.

Example: W owns some land as her separate property. H and W have one daughter, D. When W dies intestate, H and D each take an undivided 1/2 interest in the land.

But suppose H and W had four children, A, B, C, and D. Then if W died intestate, H would have an undivided 1/3 interest in the land. A, B. C, and D would each have an undivided 1/6 interest in it (a 2/3 interest divided among four children).

When a married person dies, it isn't always necessary for the estate to go through the probate process. Property that passes to the surviving spouse (either by will or through intestacy) generally doesn't have to be probated. But if it isn't probated, the surviving spouse will be liable to creditors for the deceased spouse's debts (up to the value of the property acquired). So the surviving spouse may choose to have the probate court administer the entire estate and discharge the creditors' claims.

If the deceased's share of the community property was willed to someone other than the surviving spouse, that beneficiary should record a notice claiming an interest in the property. The notice must be recorded within 40 days after the death. After 40 days (unless a notice has been filed), the surviving spouse has full power to sell, lease, or encumber the community property. A buyer, lessee, or secured lender will be safe from the claims of beneficiaries and creditors.

Co-Ownership of Real Property

COMMUNITY PROPERTY WITH RIGHT OF SURVIVORSHIP

Before July 2001, a husband/and wife could hold title to jointly-owned property as: 1) community property; 2) joint tenants; or 3) tenants in common. Now, a husband and wife may enjoy both community property and joint tenancy benefits by tranferring jointly held property by deed to themselves as **community property with right of survivorship**.

If a couple held title as community property and one spouse died, there was a "stepped-up basis" for both halves of the property, which would provide a significant capital gains income tax advantage when the property was sold. That is because the income tax basis for the decedent's property is the fair market value of the property on the date of the decedent's death, not the original purchase basis. But the transfer of title was not automatic.

If a couple held title as joint tenants with a right of survivorship and one spouse died, only the decedent spouse's portion of the property received a "stepped-up" basis (on only 1/2 of the fair market value on the date of the decedent's death), because the surviving spouse already owned 1/2 of the property (1/2 of the original purchase basis). But the transfer of title was automatic. On the death of a co-owner of joint tenancy property, title automatically transfers to the surviving owners on the death of one of the owners.

Choosing a Different Form of Co-Ownership

Husband and wife may share title to property as: 1) joint tenants, 2) tenants in common, or 3) community property with right of survivorship rather than holding it as community property. Each spouse's undivided interest in a joint tenancy or tenancy in common is his or her separate property. A married couple often chooses joint tenancy because the right of survivorship will allow the surviving spouse to avoid some creditors' claims.

As you've seen, in dissolution proceedings property held in joint tenancy is presumed to be community property. The court will only treat the property as a joint tenancy if the deed or a later agreement between the spouses explicitly states not only that it is a joint tenancy, but also that it is separate property. A joint tenancy between husband and wife is not automatically severed by dissolution of the marriage. Either spouse may ask the court to partition the property during the dissolution proceedings, however.

In other types of legal proceedings involving property owned by a married couple, the court will not apply the community property presumption. On the contrary, if the deed says "as joint tenants," the court will presume the property is held in joint tenancy. Even so, the court may consider evidence that the property in question is community property, in spite of the language in the deed. Creditors, relatives, or other litigants who want the property to be treated as a community asset might argue that one or both of the spouses did not understand joint tenancy. The court will try to determine if the couple actually intended to hold the property in joint tenancy and not as community property. Unless they expressly agreed to alter the community character of the property, the court may decide that it is community property.

> **Example:** The deed to H and W's home says, "H and W, in joint tenancy." H dies, leaving a will. The will devised H's undivided 1/2 interest in the home to D, his daughter by a previous marriage.

If the home was truly owned as a joint tenancy, H's interest in it couldn't be willed. The right of survivorship would vest H's interest in W automatically. H's attempt to will his interest to D would not sever the joint tenancy.

But D wants to establish that the home was really held as community property, not in joint tenancy. In the probate court, she may argue that H and W didn't really understand what a joint tenancy was, and didn't intend to create one. D can use her father's attempt to will his interest to her as evidence that there wasn't a joint tenancy.

If D succeeds in proving that the home was community property, the court will award her H's undivided 1/2 interest, in accordance with his will. D and W would then own the home as tenants in common.

Once a couple has established a joint tenancy, they may later agree to change the property to community property. This is called a **transmutation** agreement. (A transmutation agreement may be used to change any separate property into community property, or to change community property into separate property.) Originally, such an agreement could be oral or written. That rule led to a lot of disputes over whether property was held in joint tenancy or as community property, so the legislature changed the law. Any transmutation agreement must be in writing to be valid.

	JOINT TENANCY	TENANCY IN COMMON	COMMUNITY PROPERTY	COMMUNITY PROPERTY w/RIGHT OF SURVIVORSHIP
Creation presumed		X	X	
Equal right to posession	X	X	X	X
Equal interests	X		X	X
Right of survivorship	X			X
Each co-owner can convey undivided interest	X	X		
Each co-owner can will undivided interest		X	X	

TRUSTS

An increasingly popular method of property ownership in California is in a form of trust, particularly the **revocable living (inter-vivos) trust**. The major advantages of holding title in a trust include avoiding probate, thus reducing costs, time, trouble, and public disclosure, and there are significant estate tax planning advantages.

There are many forms of trusts: revocable or irrevocable, testamentary or living, the A-B trust, A-B-C trust, family limited partnership trusts (FLIP), charitable lead trust, charitable remainder unitrust or annuity trust are some of the most frequently created forms of trusts. The determination of which type of trust is appropriate will depend on the individual circumstances of the trustor's estate.

Co-Ownership of Real Property

The most common trust for an individual with an estate under $600,000, or a couple with an estate under $1,200,000 is the revocable living (inter vivos) trust. The creator of the trust is the trustor, or settlor. The trustee administers the trust, and the beneficiary receives the trust assets, without probate, upon the death of the trustors(s), or upon the termination for the trust.

Example: Revocable inter vivos trust (living trust). Elizabeth and Robert Martin, are a married couple, and they each have two children from a former marriage. Their total estate has a value of $900,000 consisting of a home, two rental properties, and savings. Their goals are (1) to ensure that these assets will be available to both Elizabeth and Robert for life, as needed (2) to be certain the four children will equally receive the balance of the estate without the time and expense of probate, and (3) to eliminate estate taxes.

Elizabeth and Robert created the Martin family revocable living trust, dated October 1, 2XXX. They transfer title to the home, the rental units, and the savings accounts to "Elizabeth and Robert Martin, co-trustees of the Martin Revocable Trust, dated October 1, 2XXX". During Elizabeth and Robert's joint lifetime, they will manage the trust assets and will equally enjoy and benefit from the trust estate. During their joint lifetime, Elizabeth and Robert may revoke or amend the trust to correspond with their changing needs and goals.

Upon the first trustor's death, the assets will be divided 50/50, with 50% going into the A trust and 50% into the B trust. The surviving trustor will continue to have full control and benefit of the A trust, the same as he or she would have as the sole owner of these assets. The surviving trustor will also be the primary beneficiary of the assets in the B trust, if needed. The survivor will continue to administer the trust as the successor co-trustee.

Upon the survivor's death, the successor trustee(s) will distribute the remaining trust assets to the beneficiaries who were named by the trustors as the beneficiaries of the trust assets. In this example, the trust assets will pass equally to Elizabeth's two children and to Robert's two children without the time and expense of probate. There will be no estate tax due on this estate.

This method of holding title, and estate planing has the advantages of allowing the trustors to keep control, keeping the family secrets private, eliminating the time and expense of the probate, and eliminating estate taxes.

http://firms.findlaw.com/srapkin/memo1.htm
(The Pros and Cons of Revocable Living Trusts)

Living Trust

Trustor	Trustee / Successor Trustee(s)	Beneficiary
Creator(s) of the trust.	Administers the trust pursuant to trust provisions.	Named by Trustor. Usually the Trustor for life—then balance to beneficiary.
Maintain Control.		
Usually primary beneficiary for life.	Distributes balance of trust upon trustor's death, or termination.	

TENANCY IN PARTNERSHIP

The sixth type of concurrent title recognized in California is tenancy in partnership. Co-ownership takes this form when a business organized as a general or limited partnership owns property.

Partnerships are described in the next section of this chapter. The rights and duties of tenants in partnership are outlined in that discussion.

Ownership by Associations

The second aspect of co-ownership is ownership by associations—businesses, nonprofit groups, and other organizations—rather than individuals. Depending on its form, an association may be a legal entity separate from its individual members or owners. Title to property can be held in an association's name.

Ownership by associations overlaps with the different forms of co-ownership discussed in the first part of the chapter. For example, a business organization may hold property in severalty, or it may be a tenant in common with other organizations or individuals.

An association can't be a joint tenant, however, since the right of survivorship is the key trait of a joint tenancy. Artificial entities such as corporations have a potentially perpetual existence. That would prevent a co-tenant from acquiring any genuine survivorship right.

A real estate agent should understand when and how an association can hold title to real property. Most importantly, he or she needs to know who can sign and who must sign on behalf of an association to enter contracts and transfer property.

Property can be owned by:

◆ **corporations,**
◆ **general partnerships,**
◆ **limited liability companies,**
◆ **real estate investment trusts, and**
◆ **unincorporated associations.**

CORPORATIONS

The most sophisticated form of association is the corporation. The ownership interests in a corporation are divided into shares. The corporation is owned by **shareholders**, individuals who purchase shares in the company as an investment. The money invested provides the corporation with operating capital.

A corporation may have only a few shareholders, or it may have hundreds. But the corporation is legally a separate entity from its shareholders. The law treats it as an artificial individual; it can enter contracts, own property, incur debts, sue and be sued. Because of this special legal status, corporations are closely regulated by state and federal laws.

134

CREATION. To start a corporation in California, its organizers (the **incorporators**) file **articles of incorporation** with the Secretary of State's office. The articles establish the corporation's name, list the name and address of the principal agents, explain the share structure, and include a general statement of purpose. In order to sell stock, the incorporators must obtain a permit from the state Corporations Commissioner and comply with securities laws.

In California, a **domestic corporation** is one organized in compliance with California law. A **foreign corporation** is one organized under the laws of another state, or in another country. A foreign corporation involved in California real estate transactions must be certified to do business here by the California Secretary of State's office.

MANAGEMENT. A corporation's shareholders have very little direct involvement in its management. They receive an annual report and have the right to inspect the corporate records; they may attend an annual meeting and vote on some major issues (one vote per share owned).

The real power behind a corporation is its **board of directors**. The directors govern the corporation's affairs in accordance with its bylaws. They appoint corporate **officers**—the president or chief executive officer (CEO), vice presidents, the treasurer or chief financial officer, and the corporate secretary—who run the business on a day-to-day basis. In some small corporations, one person fills more than one corporate office; for example, the president and treasurer might be the same person.

The officers are not automatically authorized to convey or encumber the corporation's real property. These actions must be expressly authorized by a resolution of the board. A title company will usually require proof of the authorization before insuring a transaction, although that requirement is sometimes waived. The proof takes the form of a certificate signed by the corporate secretary, stating that the transaction is authorized.

If all (or nearly all) of a corporation's assets are being transferred, the transaction usually must be approved by the shareholders as well as the board. But as a general rule, the board may execute a trust deed on all of the corporation's assets without shareholder approval.

LIABILITY. The primary advantage of the corporate form of organization is that shareholders are protected from liability for the corporation's debts.

> **Example:** A few years ago, Z spent $3,000 on stock in the ABC Corporation. Her shares are now worth $3,600.
>
> The ABC Corporation is found liable for an injury caused by a defective product it manufactured, and a $100,000 judgment is entered against the corporation. The judgment creditor can file a lien against the corporation's assets if the judgment is not paid.
>
> However, the creditor cannot proceed against Z to collect the judgment. Her home, bank accounts, and other property are protected from liability, because the corporation is a separate legal entity.

In theory, all shareholders have this protection from liability. But in fact, creditors often require the personal guaranties of the major shareholders before they will make large loans to a corporation.

Chapter 4

TAXATION. The chief drawback to the corporate form of organization is double taxation. First the corporation must pay corporate income taxes on any profits it generates. Then if the profits are distributed to the shareholders as **dividends**, the same money is taxed again as the personal income of the shareholders.

Business investors can avoid double taxation by choosing a different form of organization, such as a partnership. But, as you'll see, other forms have disadvantages of their own.

GENERAL PARTNERSHIP

A general partnership is simply an association of two or more individuals as co-owners of a business run for profit. It doesn't have the formal structure of a corporation. Although a general partnership can own property, for most other purposes (taxation, liability) the law does not recognize a general partnership as an entity independent from its members.

General partnerships are usually created by express agreement (either oral or written). But they can be created by implied agreement, based on the actions of the parties.

Having a common interest in a business transaction doesn't automatically create a partnership, however. The parties must intend to carry on a definite, ongoing business as co-owners, sharing the management and profits. When that is their intention, they have a partnership, whether they call it that or not.

www.trustcounsel.org/tcn/articles/tcn0016.htm
(Selecting the Form of Business Organization that is Best for You)

MANAGEMENT AND PROFITS. A general partnership agreement can provide for almost any allocation of rights and duties between the partners. But if the agreement doesn't address an issue (or if it is an implied agreement), then the allocation will be according to statute. The rules outlined here are the statutory rules; most of them can be altered in the partnership agreement.

All general partners have an equal voice in the management and control of the business. The partnership is legally bound by the actions of one partner, as long as the partner is acting within the scope of his or her authority. (Each partner is an agent and a fiduciary of the partnership, so the agency rules explained in Chapter 5 apply.)

Unless otherwise agreed, the partners all share in the profits equally, even if their contributions to the business were unequal. (Some partners may only contribute skill or labor, without making any capital contribution.) Partners usually divide losses in the same way they share in the profits.

LIABILITY. General partners have unlimited liability for the acts of the partnership. Each partner can be made to pay the partnership's debts out of his or her own pocket.

> **Example:** P, Q, and R own the PQR Company, a general partnership. The PQR Company and the individual partners are sued for breach of a construction contract, and a judgment is entered against them for $95,000. The company has no assets. P, Q, and R don't pay the judgment, so the judgment creditor claims a lien against Q's home. Q ends up paying the entire $95.000 to protect his home from foreclosure.

Q can then demand reimbursement from P and R for their share of the judgment, and can sue them if they don't pay. But this personal liability is the main disadvantage of a general partnership. It contrasts sharply with the protection a corporate shareholder enjoys.

Tenancy in Partnership

All property that general partners bring into the business at the outset, and all that they later acquire for the business, is partnership property. Anything purchased with partnership funds is presumed to be partnership property.

Partners own partnership property as **tenants in partnership.** This is true whether title to the property is held in the general partnership's name or in the name of one of the partners. Unless otherwise agreed, each partner has a right to possess all partnership property for partnership purposes. A partner has no right to possess partnership property for any other purpose, except with the consent of the other partners.

It's necessary to distinguish between a partner's undivided interest in partnership property and his or her interest in the partnership itself. For example, if a partner is married, that partner's interest in the *partnership* may be treated as community property, but his or her interest in partnership *property* cannot be community property.

A partner can't transfer an interest in a piece of partnership property to someone outside the partnership, except when all of the partners assign the whole property. But (unless otherwise agreed) one partner may assign his or her interest in the partnership itself to an outsider. That gives the assignee a right to share in the partnership's profits. It does not make the assignee a partner, however, or give the assignee the right to interfere in the management of the business.

> **Example:** A and B own the A & B Company, a general partnership. They also own a building as partnership property.
>
> B is involved in a car accident, and a judgment is entered against her. The judgment creditor cannot claim a lien against the A & B Company's building. (The creditor could claim a lien if the judgment were against the partnership rather than B.)

But B's interest in the partnership itself can be reached by her judgment creditor: the creditor can garnish B's share of the profits.

When a partner dies, his or her interest in partnership property vests in the surviving partners. The deceased partner's estate has a right to an accounting and a share of the partnership profits, but it does not have an interest in the partnership property.

Title Held in the Partnership's Name. To transact business using a partnership name (rather than the names of all the individual partners), the partners must publish and record a **fictitious business name certificate** in the county where their principal place of business is located. The certificate lists the names and addresses of all the partners, and must be signed by all of them. This prevents them from concealing their identities from creditors and from the public.

Once the partners have recorded a fictitious business name certificate, title to property can be held in the partnership's name. To convey property held in the partnership's name, it is generally also necessary to record a **statement of partnership** in the county where the property is located. Title insurance companies require this before they will insure a conveyance of property held in a partnership's name. The statement lists the partnership name and the names of all the partners. It must be signed and acknowledged by at least two of the partners.

Keep in mind that neither of these steps is necessary for the creation of partnership property. Property can be partnership property if the title is held in the names of the individual partners, and even if it is held in the name of only one of the partners.

But when title is held in the partnership's name, the property can be encumbered or conveyed by the signature of any authorized partner. If any of the partners are married, their spouses' signatures are not required. When there are several partners and they live in different cities, this can save a lot of trouble.

Holding title in the partnership's name is not just a matter of convenience, however. It can also protect the partnership from a partner's unauthorized action.

Although ordinarily a partner who exceeds his or her authority can't bind the partnership, there's an important exception. If the partner conveys partnership property to a good faith purchaser who doesn't realize that the partner is not authorized to sell it, the partnership can't recover the property.

> **Example:** J, K, and L own JKL Enterprises, a general partnership. They also own some land as partnership property. Title to the land is in K's name.
>
> K sells the land to Z without his partners' consent. Because Z believes that K has authority to sell the land, the partnership will be bound by the sale. J and L can sue K for violating his duties to the partnership, but they can't get the land back from Z.

If title is in the partnership's name, the partnership can protect itself from this. Then the statement of partnership can include restrictions on the individual partners' authority to convey partnership real property. That gives everyone—including good faith purchasers like Z—constructive notice of the restrictions. If JKL Enterprises held the land in its own name and included restrictions in its statement of partnership, it could recover the land even from a good faith purchaser.

Both for convenience and protection, it is advisable for partnership property to be held in the partnership's name. Anyone purchasing partnership property should check the statement of partnership to make sure the conveyance is authorized. If there's any doubt, all the partners should be asked to join in the conveyance.

LIMITED PARTNERSHIPS

A limited partnership, like a general partnership, is an association of two or more persons as co-owners of a business. But a limited partnership has one or more general partners, plus one or more limited partners. The rights and duties of general partners in a limited partnership are the same as in a general partnership. The limited partners, however, have limited liability and a limited role in management.

Co-Ownership of Real Property

You can think of a limited partnership as a compromise between a general partnership and a corporation. Limited partners cannot participate in management of the business to the extent that general partners do, although they can have a greater role than corporate shareholders. But like corporate shareholders, limited partners are protected from the business's debts. As a result, limited partnerships are more strictly regulated than general partnerships.

But a limited partnership avoids the double taxation problem that corporations suffer from. Like general partnerships, limited partnerships do not have to pay tax on the partnership's income. The profits are taxed only once, as the personal income of the partners.

A limited partnership can only be created by a written partnership agreement. A **certificate of limited partnership** must be filed with the Secretary of State's office. The certificate should also be recorded in any county where the limited partnership owns real property.

The certificate of limited partnership authorizes the general partner(s) to sell, lease, or encumber property vested in the name of the limited partnership. As a result, the limited partners' signatures are not required on the conveyance documents. But like a statement of partnership, a certificate of limited partnership may contain restrictions on the general partners' authority to convey partnership property.

A limited partner has no ownership interest in the partnership property. The partnership property is controlled by the general partners just as in a general partnership.

www.mycorporation.com/Limpart.htm
(Limited Partnerships)

LIMITED LIABILITY COMPANIES (LLC)

The Beverly-Killea Limited Liability Company Act (Corporations Code Section 17000-17705) became effective on September 30, 1994 and California follows 45 other states which had previously enacted such legislation. A limited liability company (LLC) allows its members to enjoy the limited liability of corporate shareholders and the tax advantage of a partnership. An LLC can engage in any lawful business activity, except banking, insurance, trust company business, or profession that requires a license, registration or certification.

It is relatively simple to form an LLC since it involves completion of forms prepared by the Secretary of State. There must be two or more members which may be individuals, partnerships, corporations, or other entities. Form LLC-1 (Limited Liability Company Articles of Organization) is completed and filed with the Secretary of State along with the filing fee and at that moment the LLC begins. The name of an LLC must end with the words "LLC", "Limited Liability Company" or "Ltd. Liability Co." Each LLC must have an operating agreement dealing with the manner in which business is to be conducted, but it does not have to be filed with the Secretary of State. The LLC must also pay an annual minimum tax which is currently $800.

An ownership interest in an LLC is either a membership interest or an economic interest. The membership interest has full economic, management and voting rights but, unless otherwise provided in the article or operating agreement, may be assigned only with unanimous consent of the other members. An economic interest has no management or voting rights and is freely assignable.

Chapter 4

Unless provided otherwise the LLC is dissolved upon the death, withdrawal, explusion, bankruptcy, dissolution, or resignation of a member (unless all remaining members vote to continue the LLC within 90 days); managed by all of its members; and profits and losses are share in proportion to each members contribution as are voting rights.

The Secretary of State has provided numerous other forms for future LLC use such as an amendment of the articles; a correction of previously filed documents; certificates to dissolve, a continue, cancel or merge LLCs and an annual information statement. A foreign LLC (from another state) must file with the Secretary of State an application for registration along with a certificate of good standing from the state where the LLC was formed before transacting intrastate business in California. An unregistered LLC transacting business in California risks daily penalties for each day unauthorized business is conducted.

REAL ESTATE INVESTMENT TRUSTS (REITs)

The federal Real Estate Investment Trust Act of 1960 extended tax benefits to real estate investors who organize in accordance with its terms. The act was intended to encourage substantial investments in real estate, under strict regulation.

To obtain the act's tax benefits, a real estate investment business must be organized as a **trust**. In a trust, one or more persons (the **trustees**) manage property for the benefit of others (the **beneficiaries**). A written trust instrument vests the property in the trustees. The trustees have only those powers expressly granted to them in the trust instrument. The beneficiaries have no legal interest in the property; they only have the power to enforce performance of the trust.

A real estate investment trust (REIT) must have at least 100 investors. The investors are the trust's beneficiaries. The trustees use the money invested in the business to purchase property or real estate securities (mortgages or deeds of trust). They hold title to the property or securities, and manage them for the benefit of the investors.

The advantage of an REIT is that it has the conveniences of a corporation, but can avoid double taxation. If an REIT distributes at least 95% of its income to its investors, it only pays corporate taxes on the income it retains. So 95% (or more) of the earnings are taxed only as the investors' personal income, and not as the REIT's income. The investors, like corporate shareholders, are shielded from liability for the REIT's debts.

www.nareit.com/home.cfm
(National Association of Real Estate Investment Trusts)

UNINCORPORATED ASSOCIATIONS

The designation "unincorporated association" can be used by any group that agrees to adopt it. An unincorporated association is not a legal entity separate from its members. However, title to property can be held in the association's name, as long as the property is necessary to the association's business.

For title to be held in the association's name, its members must prepare a statement listing the names of those who are authorized to execute conveyances on behalf of the association. The statement should be recorded in any county where the association owns real property. This enables the unincorporated association to encumber and convey its property without having all the members sign every document.

Co-Ownership of Real Property

JOINT VENTURES

A joint venture is similar to a partnership, but is formed for a single transaction or a related series of transactions, not as an ongoing business. There are no formal requirements for the creation of a joint venture. The parties simply agree to work together on a project and to share the profits or losses.

A joint venture is not an entity separate from its individual members. Title to property cannot be held in the joint venture's name, unless the ventures designate their business an unincorporated association, as described above.

Syndicates

A syndicate is not a recognized legal entity. Like "company," the term "syndicate" can be used to refer to virtually any business organization. The XYZ Syndicate might be a corporation, partnership, trust, or unincorporated association, and it would hold title accordingly.

Properties Developed for Concurrent Ownership

As cities have grown more crowded, single-family homes have become harder to find and more expensive to buy and maintain. Condominiums and other multifamily housing have become popular ownership alternatives. California law refers to these as **common interest developments**. They are structured (physically and legally) to combine individual ownership with concurrent ownership. See Chapter 13 for more details about common interest developments.

CONDOMINIUMS

Office buildings and retail centers have been developed as condominiums, but most condominiums were designed for residential use. A typical condominium looks like an apartment building. But a condominium isn't owned by a landlord who rents out apartment units to tenants. Instead, it is owned by its residents.

Each resident (or family of residents) has exclusive ownership of one of the units. The other parts of the property—the grounds, the parking lot, the recreational facilities, the building's lobby, elevators, and hallways—are called the **common areas**. These are owned by all of the residents as tenants in common. Thus, each condominium owner has a separate interest in his or her unit, plus an undivided interest in the common areas.

> **Example:** J bought a unit in a 30-unit condominium. The deed describes her property as "Unit 14 in Pearl Hill, a condominium, together with an undivided 1/30 interest in the common areas of said condominium."

Unless otherwise agreed, one unit's undivided interest in the common areas is equal to the other units' undivided interests. Each unit in J's building has an undivided 1/30 interest in the common areas, even the larger and more expensive units. An undivided interest in the common areas cannot be conveyed separately from the unit it to which it attaches.

CREATION. Property can be developed as a condominium in the first place, or an existing building can be converted to a condominium. In either case, condominium status is established by recording a **condominium declaration**. The declaration describes the project and lists any restrictions on residents' use of the units and common areas.

At the same time, the developers must record a **condominium plan**, which consists of a survey map of the land, floor plans for the building, and a certificate of consent. The certificate is signed by all record owners of the property, indicating that they consent to the plan. It must also be signed by anyone holding a recorded security interest in the property.

Condominiums are considered subdivisions, so in most cases the developer will be required to comply with state and local subdivision laws (see Chapter 13). After complying with those laws and recording the declaration and plan, the condominium developer may begin selling units.

A unit's deed doesn't have to include a complete property description of the project; it may just specify the unit number and refer to the condominium plan (just as platted property can be described by its lot and block numbers). The restrictions governing use of the property must be included in the deed by reference to the condominium declaration.

MANAGEMENT. A condominium is controlled by a **community association**, made up of all the unit owners. The association's members elect a board of directors from among themselves. The board is responsible for managing the common areas of the condominium: maintenance, utility bills, repairs, taxes, insurance, and improvements. Some issues are referred back to the association as a whole for a vote. The board is required to keep the members informed about the association's finances.

The association has the power to levy regular and special assessments to pay for common area expenses. There are limits on how much can be assessed, but the limits do not apply to essential repairs. If a unit owner fails to pay his or her share of an assessment, the association may impose a fine. The association may also claim a lien against that unit by recording a notice of delinquent assessment.

ENCUMBRANCE AND TRANSFER. Each owner may give a lender a deed of trust on his or her unit and its accompanying undivided interest in the common areas. And each owner's creditors can claim a lien against his or her unit and undivided interest. If a lienholder forecloses, only that unit and its undivided interest are affected. The lienholder can't foreclose on the entire condominium. Property taxes are also levied against each unit separately, so a tax lien foreclosure won't affect the whole property.

When a condominium unit is conveyed, an undivided interest in the common areas and membership in the community association are automatically conveyed, too. The seller must provide the buyer with a copy of the condominium declaration; the association's articles of incorporation, bylaws, and most recent financial statement; and a statement concerning any unpaid assessments.

Co-Ownership of Real Property

STOCK COOPERATIVES

Like condominiums, stock cooperatives are usually residential buildings. Title to a cooperative building is held by a corporation formed for that purpose. A person who wants to live in the building buys shares of stock in the corporation, instead of renting or buying a unit. The building's residents are the corporation's shareholders. The corporation owns the building, but the residents own the corporation.

A cooperative shareholder is usually given a **proprietary lease** to a unit in the building, along with the right to use the common areas. A proprietary lease has a longer term than most ordinary leases and gives the shareholder more rights than an ordinary tenant would have.

To establish a cooperative, the developer must take the same steps required for any corporation—filing articles of incorporation, and so forth. In addition, just as with a condominium, the developer must file a declaration and plan, and comply with the subdivision laws.

A cooperative shareholder pays a pro rata share of the building's expenses. This generally includes a contribution toward payments on a **blanket trust deed**. Since each apartment isn't separately owned, they aren't separately financed. Instead, the corporation gives the lender a trust deed that covers the whole building. The expenses also include property taxes levied against the whole building. If any resident fails to pay his or her share of the expenses, the entire cooperative may be threatened with foreclosure.

To transfer an interest in a cooperative, a shareholder must convey his or her shares of stock and assign the proprietary lease to the new shareholder. Because one shareholder's financial instability can jeopardize the whole cooperative, the cooperative agreement may provide that a shareholder can't transfer an interest without the other shareholders' consent.

Consent provisions of this kind, in addition to the drawbacks of blanket trust deeds and blanket property taxes, can lead to serious conflicts among the shareholders. As a result, cooperatives have been much less popular than condominiums in California.

COMMUNITY APARTMENT PROJECTS

In a community apartment project (CAP), the residents own the whole property as tenants in common, but the deed assigns each owner an exclusive right to occupy a particular apartment unit. A recorded declaration and plan are required to establish a CAP, and in some cases it is also necessary to comply with subdivision laws. A CAP is usually governed by a community association.

PLANNED UNIT PROJECTS

In a planned unit project, each resident has separate ownership of his or her house and the lot that it's located on. How is it different from a standard subdivision of single-family homes? A planned unit project includes areas or facilities that are either owned by all the homeowners as tenants in common, or that are owned by a community association and maintained for the use of the homeowners.

Like the other forms of common interest projects, a planned unit project is established by a recorded declaration and plan.

TIMESHARES

In a timesharing arrangement, buyers purchase the exclusive right to possession of the property for specified periods each year.

> **Example:** B bought a timeshare in a condominium unit in Palm Springs. B's interest gives her the right to use the unit from December 1st through December 15th each year.

C, D, E, F, and so on have similar rights in the same unit, each for a different annual period. Of course, each timeshare costs only a fraction of what it would cost to buy the unit outright. A timesharing arrangement could be developed for any kind of housing, but it has been most commonly used for resort condominiums.

Not every timeshare project actually involves co-ownership. In some cases, individuals purchase only a license to use the property, rather than an interest in the property. This is called a **timeshare use**. When a timesharing arrangement does involve the purchase of an interest in the property, that interest is called a **timeshare estate**.

Because timesharing arrangements are complex, with many potential problems and abuses, the sale of timeshares is now strictly regulated. See the Real Estate Commissioner's Regulations, sections 2810-2813.13.

CHAPTER SUMMARY

1. A tenancy in common is the most basic form of co-ownership. Tenants in common may have unequal interests; their interests are undivided, and they share possession of the whole property. A tenant in common's interest can be freely transferred or willed. A tenancy in common may be terminated by partition, either voluntarily or by court order.

2. A joint tenancy requires the four unities (time, title, interest, and possession). The key characteristic of joint tenancy is the right of survivorship; it prevents a joint tenant from willing his or her interest, but makes probate of the property unnecessary. The transfer of a joint tenant's interest severs the joint tenancy by breaking the unities of time and title. Severance does not terminate the co-ownership, but changes it to tenancy in common.

3. Property owned by a married couple is either the separate property of one spouse or the community property of both. Husband and wife have equal control over community property. The joinder requirement prevents transfer or encumbrance of community real property without the signature of both spouses. An unauthorized transfer is voidable by the non-consenting spouse.

4. A revocable living trust may be created by an individual or a married couple who wish to maintain control, keep family secrets private, eliminate the time and expense of probate, and eliminate or reduce estate taxes.

5. Title to real property can be held by associations of individuals: corporations, general and limited partnerships, REITs, and unincorporated associations. Each form of organization has advantages and disadvantages in terms of management, taxation, regulation, and liability.

6. In a general partnership, the partners own property as tenants in partnership, whether or not title is in the partnership's name. They have equal rights of possession and control of partnership property. One partner cannot transfer or encumber his or her undivided interest in the property separately from the other partners' interests.

7. In an Limited Liability Company the members have the limited liability of a corporate shareholder and the tax advantage of a partners in a partnership.

8. The owner of a condominium unit has a separate interest in his or her unit, plus an undivided interest in the common areas. A stock cooperative is owned by a corporation; each shareholder has a proprietary lease for one of the units. The owners of a CAP own the whole property as tenants in common, but each owner has the exclusive right to occupy a particular unit. In a planned development, a homeowner has separate title to a single-family home and lot, and shares title to common areas or facilities with the neighbors.

CASE PROBLEM

Estate of Baumann, 247 Cal. Rptr. 532 (4th Dist. 1988)

When Leola Baumann purchased a condominium unit, she took title in joint tenancy with her son, John. This was done so Leola could qualify for a purchase money loan, and so the property would not have to be probated when she died.

Sometime later, John defaulted on some large business loans, and his creditors sued him. To protect the condo unit, John used a quitclaim deed to transfer his undivided 1/2 interest in it to Leola. John's creditors proceeded with their lawsuit and eventually obtained a judgment against him.

Leola died a few months later. In her will, she left the condo unit to John's two sons, Chris and Jeff (her grandsons). But John's creditors claimed a judgment lien against the unit.

The creditors argued that the quitclaim deed from John to Leola was void, because its purpose was to defraud the creditors. Therefore John and his mother still owned the unit in joint tenancy at the time of her death. As a result, the entire property vested in John by the right of survivorship.

John argued that the quitclaim had been effective, so that Leola owned the condo in severalty and had the power to will it to her two grandsons. Since John no longer owned the property, the judgment lien could not attach to it.

The court agreed with the creditors that the quitclaim deed was void and had not been effective to transfer John's interest to Leola. But the court held that the quitclaim had severed the joint tenancy. As a result of this ruling, who owns the condo unit? How is title held? Can John's judgment creditors claim a lien against the unit? How does all of this affect the other unit owners in the condominium?

Answer: John owns an undivided 1/2 interest in the property, and Chris and Jeff each own an undivided 1/4 interest in the property. All three are tenants in common.

When Leola and John held the property in joint tenancy, each had a 1/2 interest. John's quitclaim to Leola severed the joint tenancy but did not transfer his interest. Thus, John and Leola still each had an undivided 1/2 interest, but because of the severance they were tenants in common.

As a tenant in common, Leola had the power to will her undivided 1/2 interest in the condo unit to her grandsons. They each took an undivided 1/4 interest, and John still had his undivided 1/2 interest (even though he didn't want it).

John's creditors can claim a lien only against John's 1/2 interest in the condo, not against Chris and Jeff's interests. If the creditors foreclose on the lien, the purchaser at the foreclosure sale will be a tenant in common along with Chris and Jeff.

None of this affects the other unit owners in the condominium. Each unit can be transferred and encumbered separately from the rest of the condominium.

CHAPTER 4 KEY TERMS		
	living trust	severance
	marketable title	stock cooperative
	ouster	syndicate
blanket trust deed	partition	tenancy in common
common areas	partnership	tenancy in partnership
community property	(general/limited)	the four unities
condominium	partnership property	timeshare
corporation	planned unit project	trust
joinder requirements	REIT	undivided interest
joint venture	right of survivorship	unincorporated association
joint tenancy	separate property	
limited liability company	severalty	

Co-Ownership of Real Property

Quiz—Chapter 4

1. A and B own a house in San Francisco. A has an undivided 3/4 interest in the property and B has an undivided 1/4 interest. They hold the property as:

   a. a tenancy in common.
   b. a joint tenancy.
   c. a tenancy by the entirety.
   d. community property.

2. In California, a married person cannot hold title to real property as:

   a. his or her separate property.
   b. a tenant in partnership.
   c. a tenant by the entirety .
   d. a joint tenant.

3. When title to property is held in severalty:

   a. the property cannot be transferred or encumbered without the consent of a majority of the co-owners.
   b. the property is owned by one individual.
   c. none of the owners can be a corporation.
   d. the property cannot be willed.

4. The only one of the four unities required for a tenancy in common is the unity of:

   a. time.
   b. title.
   c. interest.
   d. possession.

5. When A and B took title to the house as joint tenants, they agreed that only B would live there. What effect did this agreement have on the joint tenancy?

   a. It severed the joint tenancy; unity of possession is essential.
   b. It did not sever the joint tenancy if A and B stated that they did not intend to sever it.
   c. It did not sever the joint tenancy as long as A is charging B rent.
   d. It severed the joint tenancy by partitioning the property.

6. A, B, and C own some land as joint tenants. When C dies, A and B each have a 1/2 interest, because of:

   a. the right of survivorship.
   b. unity of possession.
   c. the rules of intestate succession.
   d. the doctrine of severalty.

7. A, B, and C own a house as joint tenants. B takes out a loan, giving the lender a trust deed on her interest in the property. Which of the following is true?

   a. If B defaults on her trust deed, the lender can foreclose on the entire property
   b. The trust deed is void
   c. The trust deed severs the joint tenancy
   d. If B dies, the lender loses its lien against the property

8. H and W are a married couple; they own some land as community property. H wills all his property to A. When H dies, who owns the land?

   a. W owns the land in severalty
   b. W has an undivided 2/3 interest and A has an undivided 1/3 interest
   c. W and A each have an undivided 1/2 interest
   d. W, A, and H's minor child each have an undivided 1/3 interest

9. The ZAP Corporation owns some land in severalty. In order to sell the land, who must sign the sale documents?

   a. The CEO and at least one member of the board of directors
   b. A majority of the directors
   c. A majority of the stockholders
   d. Corporate officers authorized to sell it by a resolution of the board of directors

10. Which of these statements about condominiums is false in most cases?

   a. Each unit owner has an undivided interest in the common areas
   b. Property taxes are assessed separately for each unit
   c. A blanket trust deed covers the entire condominium property
   d. The condominium association can levy regular and special assessments to pay for maintenance of the common areas

ANSWERS: 1. a; 2. c; 3. b; 4. d; 5. b; 6. a; 7. d; 8. c; 9. d; 10. c

CHAPTER 5
Introduction to Agency Law

CHAPTER OVERVIEW

This chapter describes the agency relationships between real estate brokers and salespersons and their clients. It explains the different ways an agency relationship can be created and terminated. It also discusses the duties imposed on brokers and salespersons by the California Real Estate Law in regard to licensing, record keeping, and trust fund accounts. Other agency duties are discussed in Chapter 6.

Agency

"Real estate agent" is a very familiar term, but few people stop to think about what the word "agent" means. An **agent** is someone who is authorized to represent or act for another person (the **principal**) in dealings with third parties. Agency is a special legal relationship. The agent's authorized actions are legally binding on the principal. For example, suppose a principal authorizes her agent to negotiate and sign a contract with a third party on her behalf. The agent's signature on the contract binds the principal to the terms of the agreement, just as though the principal had signed it herself.

Another important characteristic of an agency relationship is that the knowledge of the agent can be imputed to the principal. If a third party discloses something to the agent, the principal may be held to have known it—whether or not the agent actually passed the information on to the principal.

Not only that, an agent's wrongful acts can be imputed to the principal, so that the principal is legally responsible for them. If the agent in the example above had lied to the third party to persuade him to sign the contract, the third party could sue the principal as well as the agent for fraud. The principal might be held liable even though she did not direct her agent to lie. The principal could, in turn, sue the agent, and might recover from the agent what she paid to satisfy the third party's judgment. The issue of the agent's liability to the principal generally would not affect the principal's liability to the third parties. **Third parties** are others who are involved in a contract with the principal and agent.

AGENCY—A DIFFERENT LEGAL RELATIONSHIP

AGENCY IS A SPECIAL LEGAL RELATIONSHIP

An **agent** is one who is authorized to represent or act for another person.
The **principal** is the person who hires an agent to represent him or her.
Third parties are others involved in a contract with the principal and agent.

---

www.onu.edu/user/FS/dwoods/312/agencyo.html
(Agency Law Outline - Example)

THE AGENT'S AUTHORITY

An agent's authority always comes from the principal. Authority intentionally given by the principal is called **actual authority**. Actual authority may be express or implied.

Express authority is expressly communicated by the principal to the agent either orally or in writing. **Implied authority** is inferred by the conduct of the principal indicating his or her intent to confer it or causing the agent to believe he or she possess it. For example, a seller gives a real estate agent express authority to find a buyer for the property. This is generally understood to give the agent implied authority to advertise the property, put up "For Sale" signs, show the property, and negotiate with prospective buyers.

Sometimes a person may simply *appear* to be the agent of another. This is called **ostensible (estoppel) agency**. Although the principal has not granted actual authority to the agent, a third party is led to believe by the principal not objecting, that the ostensible agent is acting as though he or she has authority. The ostensible agent is acting as though he or she is authorized, and the principal's words or conduct seem to back that up. In this situation, the principal may be bound by the acts of the ostensible agent, even though they weren't actually authorized. (See the discussion of agency created by estoppel, below.)

TYPES OF AGENTS

Agents are classified according to the scope of authority the principal has conferred on them. An agent may be universal, general, or special.

Introduction to Agency Law

A **universal agent** is authorized by the principal to do everything that can be done by a lawfully designated representative.

Example: A court-appointed guardian charged with the care of someone who is no longer competent to manage his or her own affairs is a universal agent.

A **general agent** has authority to handle all matters for the principal in a specified area.

Example: A property manager is a general agent if he or she has authority to market and maintain the property, hire and fire maintenance personnel, enter lease agreements on the owner's behalf, and take full responsibility for managing the property.

http://home.istar.ca/~c21/dualagt.html
(Agency Disclosure)

CREATING AN AGENCY RELATIONSHIP

AN AGENCY MUST BE CREATED BY:

◆ express agreement,
◆ ratification, or
◆ estoppel (ostensible)

A **special agent** has limited authority to do a specific thing or conduct a specific transaction. Most real estate brokers are special agents. Their authority is usually limited to a single transaction, such as the sale of a particular house. An agent should keep the limits of his or her authority in mind and be careful not to go beyond them. As a general rule, the principal isn't bound by or liable for the agent's acts if they exceed the scope of the authority granted.

How an Agency is Created

The principal's liability and the agent's duties arise as soon as an agency relationship is established. So it's important to understand how and when an agency is created.

EXPRESS AGREEMENT

An agency relationship can be created by oral or written agreement. In some cases the principal signs a **power of attorney**—a document that appoints another person as an agent and defines the scope of the agent's authority. An agent under a power of attorney is sometimes called an **attorney in fact**. (Don't confuse an attorney in fact with an attorney at law. Anyone can be an attorney in fact—you don't have to be a lawyer.)

An agency relationship between a real estate broker and a seller is usually created with a **written listing agreement**. The broker is the agent and the seller is the principal. The listing agreement sets forth the duties of both parties.

Chapter 5

A written listing agreement is required if the broker is to collect a commission. However, the broker is still held to the same degree of responsibility and must perform all duties owed to the principal. If the broker doesn't carry out these duties or performs them negligently, the principal may sue the broker for damages even without a written agreement.

Example: A seller orally agrees to pay a real estate broker a 5.5% commission if he finds a buyer for her house. The broker receives an offer of $152,000. But he's extremely busy, so he doesn't pass the offer on to the seller right away. The next day, before the broker has told the seller about the offer it is withdrawn.

To the broker's relief, another prospective buyer makes an offer a few days later. But this one is only for $145,000. The broker informs the seller of this offer, the seller accepts it, and the sale closes.

Afterwards, the seller refuses to pay the broker his commission. The broker can't sue for the commission because he never had a written agreement with the seller.

Later the seller finds out about the first (and higher) offer. She sues the broker for negligence and breach of duty for failing to transmit the offer to her promptly. She has a right to sue even though there was no written agency agreement.

This is a bit one-sided, but for a good reason. The law protects the public in their dealings with professionals. When an agency relationship is established, a real estate agent assumes certain responsibilities. The client's failure to pay doesn't excuse the agent from carrying out these responsibilities competently. And a real estate agent can protect him or herself very easily, by requiring the client to sign a written listing agreement.

www.cendant.com
www.remax.com
www.century21.com
www.newworldrealty.com/expect.html
(What to Expect from Your Realtor)

RATIFICATION

Sometimes one person acts on another's behalf without agency authorization. If the other person later approves these actions, he or she is said to have **ratified** them. An agency relationship is created by ratification, and the legal consequences are just the same as if the actions had been authorized beforehand.

When a certain type of agency can only be expressly created in writing, it can only be ratified in writing. For other types of agency, the ratification does not have to take a particular form. The principal simply has to say or do something that indicates an intent to adopt the agent's actions as the principal's own. If the principal accepts the benefit of the agent's actions, that's considered ratification, as long as the principal has full knowledge of the facts.

Example: X and Y are neighbors. X happens to be a real estate broker. Y casually mentions to X that he would consider selling his house if the price were right. X begins to take prospective buyers to Y's house to show them the property. She receives two offers on the property and relays them to Y. Y accepts one of the offers.

A court could rule that although Y never expressly authorized X to act as his agent, he ratified the agency relationship by accepting the benefit of her actions.

Even when a real estate broker's unauthorized actions have been ratified by the seller, the broker isn't legally entitled to a commission unless the ratification is in writing. In the example above, although an agency relationship has been established by ratification, X could not sue Y if he refused to pay her for her services.

If the seller signs a deposit receipt containing a provision stating that the seller has employed the broker and agrees to pay a commission, he or she has ratified the agency relationship in writing, and will be liable for the commission even if there was no written listing. But a seller could sign an agreement with the buyer that didn't provide for the broker's commission, and then the broker might be out of luck.

www.dre.ca.gov/homebuyers.htm
(Information for Home Buyers)

ESTOPPEL (Ostensible Agency)

An agency relationship may also be created by estoppel. (Estoppel was discussed briefly in Chapter 3.) In an estoppel situation, the principal has not authorized the agent, but the principal is now estopped (stopped) from denying the existence of an agency relationship. Because the principal intentionally and negligently causes others to believe that a particular person is his agent—he can't later argue that this particular person is not his agent. As mentioned earlier, the agent is said to have ostensible authority.

The purpose of agency by estoppel is to protect innocent third parties who have reasonably assumed that a person had authority to act for the principal. The principal is held responsible because he or she failed to advise the third party that the apparent agent was acting without authority.

> **Example:** F owns several pieces of property. In the past, his daughter, D, has handled real estate sales for him. D gives a broker an exclusive listing for one of F's properties. F doesn't protest when the broker places a "For Sale" sign on the property and shows the property to prospective purchasers. F sells the property to one of the broker's customers, but refuses to pay a commission to the broker. F claims that D was not his agent and had no authority to contract with the broker.

Since F negligently or deliberately, allowed the broker to believe in and rely on D's ostensible authority, a court would probably hold that F was estopped from denying responsibility.

Note that a third party has a duty to make a reasonable effort to discover whether or not an agent's acts are authorized. When an agent acts without actual authority, the third party can't hold the principal liable unless the principal's conduct indicated approval or acceptance of the agent's acts.

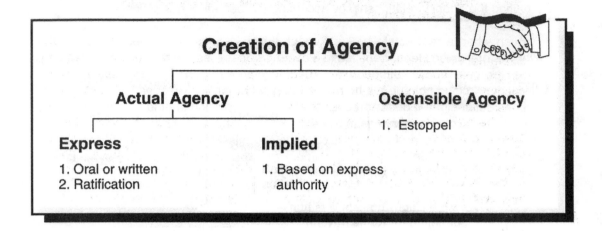

Creation of Agency

Actual Agency

Ostensible Agency

1. Estoppel

Express

1. Oral or written
2. Ratification

Implied

1. Based on express
   authority

Real Estate Agency Relationships

There is more than one agency relationship in a typical real estate transaction. In addition to the listing broker, the transaction is likely to involve at least one real estate salesperson, and it may also involve other brokers. Whose agents are they? The answer isn't simple.

SALESPERSON: THE BROKER'S AGENT

It is the standard practice for a real estate broker to hire licensed salespersons. A salesperson often handles nearly every aspect of a particular listing—advising the seller, negotiating with buyers, filling out the deposit receipt form, and so on. The seller is likely to think of the salesperson as "my real estate agent." Yet in strict legal terms, the salesperson is not the seller's agent but the broker's agent.

Under California law, a real estate salesperson is only licensed to work for a broker. Broker/Salesperson employment agreements are explained fully in Chapter 8. A salesperson cannot work directly for a member of the public in a real estate transaction. Thus, the salesperson is legally the broker's agent, not the seller's agent. The salesperson can't continue to represent the seller if the broker tells her to stop, and the salesperson can't sue the seller for a commission, except through the broker.

Liabilities to Third Parties

Even though the salesperson is not the seller's agent, the seller as well as the broker can be held liable if the salesperson does something wrong in the real estate transaction. First the salesperson's action is imputed to the salesperson's principal, the broker. Then the action is imputed to the broker's principal, the seller. The agency relationships create a chain of liability.

Introduction to Agency Law

http://libwww.cabrillo.cc.ca.us/html/depts/realestate.html
http://www.glossarist.com/glossaries/business/real-estate.asp
(Real Estate Terms)

Example: Steinberg lists his property with Borden, a real estate broker. Borden directs one of his salespersons, Markham, to handle the listing. Markham misrepresents the condition of the property to the buyers, who end up losing a considerable amount of money as a result.

The buyers sue Markham, Borden, and Steinberg. The judge decides the buyers are entitled to $36,000 in compensatory damages. A judgment for $36,000 is entered against all three defendants; the buyers can collect it from any of them. Steinberg and Borden are held liable even though they did not lie to the buyers or instruct Markham to lie to them. A principal is legally responsible to third parties for the acts of his or her agent, and for the acts of the agent's agent.

Employee or Independent Contractor

So a real estate salesperson is his or her broker's agent. For some purposes, the law also classifies the salesperson either as the broker's employee or as an independent contractor. (Any agent is either the principal's employee or an independent contractor. An employee or an independent contractor is not necessarily an agent, however. Only someone authorized to represent the principal in dealings with third parties is an agent.) All Department of Real Estate regulations of salespersons apply whether the relationship is employer and employee or independent contractor.

Certain employment laws apply only to the relationship between an employer and an employee, and do not apply when someone hires an independent contractor. For example, minimum wage laws apply only to employees. The distinction also affects liability: an employer is legally responsible for torts committed by an employee in the course of and within the scope of his or her employment. A buyer or seller who hires an independent contractor isn't liable for the contractor's torts, unless the independent contractor is also his or her agent.

Since most real estate salespeople work independently, have flexible schedules, and are paid by commission, they are independent contractors. There's a complication, however. California law requires real estate brokers to supervise the salespersons who work for them. Failure to adequately supervise a salesperson is grounds for suspension or revocation of the broker's license (see Chapter 6). In this sense, the salesperson is the broker's employee, not an independent contractor, as a matter of law. It doesn't matter how they structure their working relationship or what terms they use to describe it in their contract; the broker can't avoid the duty to supervise the salesperson's work.

In spite of that, a real estate salesperson can be treated as an independent contractor for the purposes of some employment and tax laws. The Internal Revenue Service considers a real estate salesperson to be an independent contractor if:

1. he or she is a licensed real estate agent,
2. compensation is directly related to sales rather than to hours worked, and
3. the services are performed pursuant to a written contract that states that the individual will not be treated as an employee for tax purposes.

If these three criteria are met, the broker is not required to withhold taxes and social security contributions from the salesperson's compensation. Similarly, if a salesperson is paid only by commission (with no base wage or salary), the broker is not required to pay unemployment taxes, and the salesperson is not eligible to receive unemployment compensation. A salesperson may be eligible for worker's compensation if injured on the job, however.

COOPERATING BROKERS AND SUBAGENCY

Real estate brokers in urban areas often belong to a Multiple Listing Service (MLS). Under the terms of MLS membership, when a broker obtains a listing, he or she submits it to the MLS. That permits other brokers who belong to the MLS to help find a buyer for the listed property. In relation to the listing broker, these other brokers are known as **cooperating brokers**. When a cooperating broker is the procuring cause in bringing about the sale of the property, the listing broker pays the cooperating broker a share of the commission.

Usually a cooperating broker, like the listing broker, represents the seller rather than the buyer (see Chapter 6). In some cases, the cooperating broker's agency status is the same as a salesperson's: the cooperating broker is an agent of an agent (the listing broker). But in other cases, the cooperating broker is considered a **subagent** of the seller.

 http://www.realtor.com/FindReal/default.asp?poe=realtor
(Find a Realtor®)

As you've seen, both the principal and the agent can be held liable for the actions of an agent of the agent. It's a different matter if the agent appoints a subagent to help carry out the job. Although appointed by the agent, a subagent has a direct legal relationship with the principal. A subagent (unlike an agent's agent) can sue the principal for compensation, rather than depending on the agent to do so. And if a third party sues because the subagent has done something wrong, the principal may be held liable along with the subagent, but the agent usually will not be.

A California statute provides that an agent can only delegate authority to a subagent in one of these circumstances:

1. the act to be carried out by the subagent is purely mechanical;
2. the agent can't legally perform the act and the subagent can;
3. delegating the powers in question is the standard business practice in the area; or
4. the principal has expressly authorized the delegation.

If an agent delegates authority to someone in a situation that doesn't fit into one of those four categories, then the second person is simply the agent's agent, not a subagent. In that case the agent remains liable for the second person's actions, along with the principal.

Most standard listing agreement forms authorize the listing broker to appoint subagents (see paragraph 5(g) on the listing agreement form in Chapter 8). Thus, a cooperating broker usually qualifies as a subagent under the statutory rule regarding subagency. In spite of that, courts sometimes treat a cooperating broker as an agent of the listing broker. It depends on the circumstances involved in the case.

Note that subagency is never an issue in regard to a real estate salesperson. Because the salesperson's broker is always responsible for the salesperson's actions, the salesperson cannot be considered a subagent.

Terminating an Agency

An agent's powers end when the agency ends. There are several ways in which an agency may be terminated:

- ◆ accomplishment of purpose,
- ◆ expiration of the agency term,
- ◆ operation of law,
- ◆ mutual agreement,
- ◆ renunciation by the agent, or
- ◆ revocation by the principal.

ACCOMPLISHMENT OF PURPOSE

Perhaps the most common reason for termination is that the purpose of the agency has been accomplished.

Example: An owner hires a real estate broker to help her sell some property. Once the property is sold and all of the details are taken care of, the agency relationship terminates.

EXPIRATION

When an agency agreement specifies that the agency is for a limited term, the agency ends automatically when the term expires. In California, a listing agreement must include a specific termination date. (One exception: an open listing doesn't have to have a termination date. The different types of listings are discussed at the end of this chapter.)

Example: An owner hires a real estate broker to help him sell some property. He signs an exclusive listing agreement that provides the agency will last for 90 days, until March 30th. When this date passes, the agency terminates.

OPERATION OF LAW

An agency relationship may also be terminated by operation of law. This means that the agency ends automatically, if certain events occur. An agency is terminated by operation of law if:

- ◆ either party dies or becomes incapacitated,
- ◆ either party goes bankrupt,
- ◆ the property that is the subject of the agency is destroyed or condemned, the agent loses his or her license, or
- ◆ a conflict of interest arises between the parties.

Example: A hires B (broker) to help him sell some commercial property. B happens to be part owner of a gas station located across the street from A's property. One of the potential buyers for A's property turns out to be a rival oil company that wants to build a station there.

As A's agent, B must act in his principal's best interest. It may be in A's best interest to sell the property to the rival gas station. But B has a conflict of interest, since the sale to a competing oil company could cut into B's profits from the existing gas station. B should inform A of the conflict and withdraw from the agency relationship. If B doesn't, a court might later decide the conflict of interest was so substantial that the agency terminated by operation of law.

MUTUAL AGREEMENT

An agency is a consensual relationship, which means that it is based on the written consent of both parties. If both the principal and the agent want to end the agency, they can agree to terminate it at any point. When an agency is terminated by mutual consent, neither party is liable to the other for damages.

RENUNCIATION

Because of the consensual nature of agency, each party in an agency relationship has the power to terminate it unilaterally. The agent may **renounce** his or her agency at any time. If the agency agreement was open-ended, without a specific termination date, the agent will not have any further obligation to the principal. But if there was a termination date, the agent may be liable to the principal for damages resulting from breach of contract.

An agency agreement is a personal services contract: a real estate agent (for example) agrees to provide services for a seller. A court can't force a person to perform personal services, because that would violate the constitutional prohibition against involuntary servitude (slavery). So when an agent breaches an agency contract, the principal can't demand specific performance—that is, the principal can't require the agent to provide the services as originally agreed. Instead, an award of money damages is usually the principal's only remedy. (See Chapter 7 for further discussion of specific performance and other remedies for breach of contract.)

REVOCATION

A principal can **revoke** the grant of agency powers at any time by firing the agent. If the agency agreement was open-ended, the principal may have to reimburse the agent for expenses already incurred, but will not be liable to the agent for damages. However, if the agency agreement had a specific termination date (so that the revocation is a breach of contract), the principal may be liable for any damages suffered by the agent because of the breach.

> **Example:** C is planning to sell his house. He signs a 90-day exclusive listing agreement with B, a real estate broker. Two weeks later, C starts dating a real estate salesperson who convinces him to change the listing to her brokerage. C tells B that her agency is revoked because he's changing to a different broker.
>
> C has the power to revoke, but the revocation is a breach of contract, so he's liable for the consequences. He may be required to pay B's damages, which will probably be the full amount of the commission she might have earned if C hadn't ended the agency. (C's new agent may also be in trouble. She interfered with another agent's exclusive listing, and convinced C to breach his agreement. This type of problem is discussed in Chapter 8.)

AGENCY COUPLED WITH AN INTEREST

There's an exception to the rule that a principal can revoke an agency agreement: the principal does not have the power to revoke if the agency is coupled with an interest. An agency is coupled with an interest when the agent has a financial or ownership interest in the property that is the subject of the agency. In that case, the principal can't revoke the agency, and the death, incompetency, or bankruptcy of the principal doesn't terminate the agency.

> **Example:** A broker loans funds to a contractor to complete the building of a home. In addition to agreeing to repay the loan, the contractor gives the broker an exclusive right to sell the property when the home is completed.
>
> Before the home is sold, the contractor dies. The agency is not automatically terminated by the contractor's death, because the broker has an interest in the property.

A more common example comes up when several people own property jointly and one of the owners is a real estate broker. The owners decide to sell the property and the broker/owner acts as the agent. The other owners don't have the power to revoke the agency, since the broker has an interest in the property.

Termination of Agency

Acts of the Parties	Operation of Law
1. Accomplishment of purpose	1. Death or incapacity
2. Expiration of agency term	2. Bankruptcy
3. Mutual agreement	3. Property destroyed
4. Agent renounces	4. Agent loses license
5. Principal revokes	5. Conflict of interest

Chapter 5

The California Real Estate Law

As you've seen, general agency law applies to a real estate agent's relationships with clients and customers. In addition, the California Real Estate Law governs many aspects of those relationships. The Real Estate Law can be found in the **Business and Professions Code**, starting at section 10000.

The primary purpose of the Real Estate Law is to protect the public in real estate transactions. Toward that goal, it provides detailed rules concerning licensing, record keeping, and client trust funds. These are outlined below. The law also includes rules about unethical and illegal conduct and disciplinary proceedings, and those are the focus of the next chapter.

LICENSING

In general, anyone who represents another person in a real estate transaction and is paid for those services must have a valid real estate license. But if you don't expect to be paid and in fact are not paid, a license isn't necessary.

> **Example:** As a favor, A helped her friend B sell his house. A did not expect to be paid for her services, and B did not offer her any compensation. This isn't a violation of the Real Estate Law, although A was not licensed.

Even when you are paid, it isn't necessary to be licensed if you have some other legal authorization to act for the other person—if, for example, you are a lawyer, an executor, or a trustee. And you may be allowed to represent another person without a license if he or she has recorded a power of attorney giving you authority.

However, a power of attorney can't be used on an ongoing basis to get around the licensing requirements.

Case Example: The Leins owned 23 residential and commercial properties. Mr. Lein was often out of the country because he was a commercial fisherman. Mrs. Lein was in poor health. As a result, they had a close friend, Ms. Sheetz, managed their properties for them (solicited tenants, negotiated leases and collected rents). Sheetz didn't have a real estate license, but the Leins gave her a power of attorney. The Leins paid Sheetz for her services.

After Sheetz had been managing the Leins' properties for about four years, she was charged with acting as a real estate broker without a license. The Department of Real Estate's administrative law judge found her guilty, and Sheetz appealed to the Second District Court of Appeals. The court held that the power of attorney exception to the licensing requirements was only intended to apply to isolated transactions, not to someone engaged in the real estate business. Sheetz was using the power of attorney to evade the requirements. *Sheetz v. Edmonds*, 201 Cal. App. 3d 1432, 247 Cal. Rptr. 776 (1988).

Introduction to Agency Law

A person found guilty of acting as a broker or salesperson without a license can be sentenced to up to six months in jail and fined up to $10,000.

OBTAINING AND MAINTAINING A LICENSE. To obtain a salesperson's license, you must be at least 18 years old, complete the required real estate principles course, pay application and examination fees, and pass the salesperson's exam. The salesperson must meet certain educational requirements within 18 months of issuance or the license is suspended. For a broker's license, you must have at least two years' active experience as a salesperson (or experience that the Real Estate Commissioner considers equivalent), or have a degree in real estate from a four-year college. You must also complete required courses, pay application and examination fees, and pass the broker's exam.

Real estate licenses must be renewed every four years. Ordinarily, a renewal applicant must show that he or she has completed 45 hours of continuing education courses during the previous four-year period. Of the 45 hours, there must be a three-hour course in each of the following: ethics, agency, trust funds, and fair housing. But the first time a salesperson applies for renewal, he or she is only required to have completed a three-hour ethics course and a three-hour agency course.

A broker keeps the licenses of all his or her salespersons and associate brokers. These licenses, and the broker's own license, must be available for inspection by a representative from the Commissioner's office. A licensee whose business address changes should notify the DRE and write the new address on his or her license.

A broker is required to notify the Commissioner in writing, within 5 days of hiring or 10 days terminating, whenever a salesperson joins or leaves his or her staff. A salesperson changing brokerages must transfer his or her license to the new office, writing the new address and broker's name on the face of the license.

RECORD KEEPING

The Real Estate Law requires a broker to keep a record of each transaction he or she is involved in. This should include a copy of the listing, the deposit receipt, canceled checks, trust fund records (see below), and any other documents connected with the transaction. The record must be retained for at least three years from the closing date, or if the transaction was never completed, three years from the listing date.

It's a good idea to retain the records for even longer than three years. Statutes of limitations require many lawsuits to be brought within two or three years after the wrong occurred, but suits involving an accusation of fraud can be filed up to three years after the fraud was *discovered*. That could be many years after the transaction took place. Clear records can be an important part of a defense against such charges.

TRUST FUNDS

Trust funds are money (or other things of value) that a real estate agent receives on behalf of the principal or any other person involved in a transaction. Mishandling of trust funds is probably the most common reason for suspension or revocation of a real estate agent's license.

161

When a broker receives trust funds, he or she must place them into a neutral escrow depository, the hands of the principal, or a trust fund account. This must be done no later than the next business day following receipt of the funds. If a salesperson receives trust funds, he or she must immediately turn them over to the broker, or at the broker's request, deposit them in escrow or a trust account or give them to the principal.

The trust funds that real estate brokers handle most often are earnest money deposits, tendered by prospective buyers when they make an offer to purchase property. For earnest money, there is an exception to the general rules regarding broker's trust funds. Under written instructions from the buyer, a broker may hold onto an earnest money check until the offer has been accepted, as long as the broker informs the seller (before or at the time the offer is presented) that the check is being held. Once the seller has accepted the offer, the broker must place the check in the trust account or a neutral escrow by the next business day, unless the buyer and the seller instruct the broker in writing to deliver the check to the seller, or unless the seller authorizes the broker in writing to keep holding the check.

A trust account can be opened at a bank, savings and loan, or other financial institution; the institution must be in California, with a few exceptions. The account should be in the name of the broker as trustee for the seller. It must be a demand-deposit account—one that allows withdrawal without advance notice.

Trust funds can't be withdrawn except by the broker, or (if authorized in writing by the broker) by a salesperson employed by the broker, or a bonded employee of the broker.

No matter who is authorized to make withdrawals, the broker is responsible for the funds at all times. If a salesperson or employee mishandles the funds, the broker is liable.

At the request of the owner of the trust funds or the parties to a transaction, the trust account may be a separate interest-bearing federally insured account. The account must be in the name of the broker as trustee for the owner and a full disclosure of any fees and calculations is made to the owner. But none of the interest may benefit the broker or salesperson. In their contract or in a separate agreement, the parties must specify whom the interest is to be paid or credited to.

It's always advisable to keep a separate account for each transaction (rather than putting several clients' funds into one account), and this is required if the account is interest-bearing. A broker must keep a separate trust account record for each transaction, accounting for all deposits and disbursements.

It's especially important for a broker to avoid **commingling**—mixing his or her personal money in with trust funds. Trust funds must never be placed in the broker's general account, no matter how briefly. The Real Estate Commissioner allows a broker to keep up to $100 of his or her own money in the trust account to cover the bank's service charges. But it's better to have the service charges on a trust account paid out of the broker's general account.

When a broker has earned a commission that is to be paid out of a trust account, the broker must transfer the amount of the commission to his or her own account within 30 days of the time it was earned. But this doesn't mean a broker can transfer trust funds whenever a client owes the broker money. The funds must have been earmarked for the broker (either as the commission or as reimbursement for expenses).

Example: A buyer gives a broker $10,000 as a deposit; the broker puts it in a trust account for the seller. The buyer and seller reach an agreement, and the broker has earned a $12,000 commission.

The seller later refuses to pay the broker claiming that she didn't do enough to earn that much. Although the broker is in the right about her commission, she can't transfer the $10,000 from the trust fund account to her general account without the seller's permission. The funds in a trust account are never the property of the broker.

Trust account records are subject to examination by the Commissioner, and may be audited. If the audit uncovers a violation of the trust fund rules, the broker will be charged for the cost of the audit (in addition to other penalties).

Commissions

Although many people enjoy selling real estate, nearly everyone would admit that the main reason they do it is to make money. As you've seen, to be paid for representing another person in a real estate transaction you must be properly licensed. And to be able to sue to collect a commission, you must have a written agreement with the principal.

But the written agreement between broker and principal doesn't have to be detailed to be enforceable.

If the parties never agreed on an amount, the court will determine the reasonable value of the broker's services. Of course, they should always put the terms of employment in writing, rather than having to take the matter to court. A written listing agreement should clearly set forth the amount of the commission and explain under what circumstances the broker will be entitled to receive it.

Case Example: Mr. Davinroy, a broker, represented the Thompsons in an exchange of real property. The only written agreement regarding Davinroy's employment was a provision in the exchange agreement itself. It listed Davinroy as one of the brokers involved in the transaction, and said merely, "Commissions are to be settled and paid for outside of the escrow."

The Thompsons had orally agreed to pay Davinroy $30,000, but they only paid him $1,710. Davinroy sued.

The court ruled that a broker can sue for a commission as long as there is some written memorandum showing that he or she was employed in the transaction. Evidence of an oral agreement can be used to establish the amount of the commission. *Davinroy v. Thompson*, 169 Cal. App. 2d 63, 336 P.2d 1028 (1959).

Chapter 5

COMMISSION AMOUNT

The commission rate or amount must be negotiable between the principal and the broker. It is a violation of state and federal antitrust laws for brokers to set uniform commission rates. Any discussion of commission rates among members of competing firms could give rise to a charge of price-fixing.

There's a special rule that applies to listing agreements for residential property with four units or less and for mobile homes. If the broker uses a preprinted form for the agreement, it must state, in boldface type, that the amount or rate of the commission is not fixed by law and may be negotiable. The commission rate or amount cannot be printed in the form—it must be filled in for each transaction.

EARNING A COMMISSION

Payment of a broker's commission may be made dependent on any lawful condition. A listing agreement may specify that the commission is due at the time of acceptance of an offer, on approval of financing, at closing, or out of the proceeds of the sale. When the stated conditions have been met, the broker has earned the commission.

A broker is usually hired to find a buyer who is **ready, willing,** and **able** to purchase on the terms established by the seller. A buyer is considered ready and willing if he or she makes an offer that meets the seller's terms. A buyer is considered able if he or she has the financial ability to complete the purchase. This means that the buyer must have one of the following:

1. enough cash to complete the sale;
2. a strong credit rating and enough personal assets to ensure that he or she can complete the sale; or
3. a binding commitment for a loan to finance the purchase.

EARNING A COMMISSION

◆ Agent is properly licensed
◆ Valid, written listing agreement
◆ Ready, willing, and able buyer
◆ Parties agree on essential terms of sale

In most cases, once the agent has procured a ready, willing, and able buyer, he or she has earned the commission, even if the sale is never completed. Many factors may prevent the sale from being completed without canceling the agent's right to a commission. For a seller's agent, these include:

◆ the seller's decision not to sell after all;

◆ defects in the seller's title;

◆ the seller's inability to deliver possession; or

◆ mutual agreement of the seller and buyer to cancel their agreement.

Example: K hires a broker to sell her house because she's planning to get married and move into her fiance's home. The broker finds a ready, willing, and able buyer who meets all of the terms specified in the listing agreement. Meanwhile, K has broken off her engagement, so she no longer wants to sell her house. Although she can refuse to accept the buyer's offer, she is still required to pay the broker his commission.

But if a prospective buyer's offer doesn't precisely match the terms specified by the seller in the listing, the broker isn't entitled to a commission if the seller refuses to contract.

Example: A seller lists her house for $92,500. She specifies that she wants 20% cash at closing, with the rest to be paid in monthly installments of $705 (including 11% interest).

The broker obtains an offer of $92,500 in cash. The seller refuses to accept this offer. The broker isn't entitled to a commission, since the offer didn't match the terms specified by the seller.

Types of Listing Agreements

A broker's right to a commission also depends on the type of listing agreement used. Under an **exclusive right to sell** agreement, the broker is entitled to the commission if the property is sold during the listing term, no matter who sells it. Under an **exclusive agency** agreement, the seller owes the broker the commission if the property is sold during the listing term, unless the seller finds a buyer by him or herself. The California Real Estate Commissioner requires that both types of exclusive listings (right to sell and agency) have a definite determinable termination date to be valid. But with an **open listing**, a broker is not entitled to a commission unless he or she is the **procuring cause** of the sale.

EXCLUSIVES– TERMINATION DATES

LISTING AGREEMENTS

Exclusive Right to Sell (no matter who sells)	**Exclusive Agency** (anyone except the seller sells)	**Open** (procuring cause)

To be the procuring cause, the broker must be primarily responsible for the parties' agreement, or the broker's actions must start a chain of events that results in an agreement or a signed sales contract. Sometimes two brokers contribute to a particular sale, and they agree to divide the commission.

But in some cases, brokers end up arguing over who was the procuring cause of a sale. That's one of the chief disadvantages of an open listing.

Example: A principal gave open listings to five brokers, A, B, C, D, and E. A and B both showed the property to the same buyer. A brought the buyer to the property for the first time, but it was B who successfully negotiated the offer that the principal accepted.

A claims she should receive part of the commission. But the agent who effected the sale is the procuring cause, so B is entitled to the commission.

http://websrv1.realtors.org/REALTORorg.nsf/pages/foreigncoe
(National Association of Realtors Code of Ethics)

Regardless of the type of listing used, if the buyer and seller sign an agreement before the listing expires, the broker has earned the commission even if the sale does not close until after the listing's expiration date.

And many listing agreements contain an **extender clause** (also called a protective clause, carryover clause, or safety clause). An extender clause provides that the broker is still entitled to a commission if the property is sold within a certain period after the listing expires, and the buyer is someone the broker negotiated with during the listing term. (See Chapter 8.)

CASE EXAMPLE: Irma Kellogg was interested in selling her ranch in Santa Barbara County. She orally agreed to pay her musician friend Sullivan a commission of 5% of the purchase price if he could find a buyer. Sullivan contacted an attorney friend in Denver who interested two clients, Stegall and Hopkins, in the ranch. When the attorney, Stegall and Hopkins came to Santa Barbara, Sullivan introduced them Kellogg and her attorney Crawford. Both Kellogg and her attorney Crawford assumed Sullivan was a real estate broker. Sullivan did not participate in the negotiations, but on occasion helped out by collecting information available to the public when requested by the parties. A written sales contract was entered into, selling the ranch for $1,700,000 and providing that the buyers would pay the $85,000 commission that Kellogg was originally obligated to pay. Subsequently, the buyers refused to pay the commission claiming that Sullivan had to be a licensed real estate broker to collect a commission. Sullivan claimed he was a finder and could receive a fee without being licensed.

The United States Court of Appeals stated that a finder receives a fee for bringing the parties together with no involvement in negotiating the price or any of the other terms of the transaction. Sullivan was simply obligated to bring the buyer and seller together to earn his fee. *Sullivan v. Hopkins*, 435 F.2d 1128 (1970).

Introduction to Agency Law

SALESPERSONS' COMMISSIONS

A salesperson may only receive a commission from the broker he or she is licensed under. The salesperson must not accept any compensation from any other broker or agent, or directly from the seller.

Finder's Fee (Exception to License Law)

A finder's fee is compensation paid for bringing two parties together, such as the introduction of a prospective buyer to the seller. The finder does not have to be licensed and, of course, can perform no services for which a license is required.

One who merely introduces two parties to a real estate transaction, whether or not he solicits those persons, does not need to be as knowledgeable about the real estate transactions as a licensed broker, unless of course, he or she participated in the transaction.

In general, an unlicensed individual may recover an agreed compensation where he or she merely found a buyer, seller, lender, or borrower, but if in addition to finding such a person he goes further and helps to conclude the transaction by taking part in negotiating the details of the transaction, compromising or composing differences between the parties, by way of example, he may not recover the agreed compensation."

CHAPTER SUMMARY

1. A principal authorizes an agent to act for him or her. An agent may have express or implied actual authority. A person with ostensible authority appears to be the agent of another, but doesn't have actual authority. An agent may be universal, general, or special. Most real estate agents are special agents.

2. An agency relationship can be created by express agreement, ratification, or estoppel. Most real estate agency relationships are created by express listing agreements. A real estate agent can't sue to collect a commission without a written agreement with the principal.

3. A broker must have a written employment agreement with each salesperson or broker on staff, covering duties, supervision, compensation, and termination.

4. A salesperson is his or her broker's agent, not the seller's agent. Both seller and broker can be held liable for the salesperson's wrongful acts. The broker is required to supervise the salesperson. A salesperson may be considered an independent contractor for income tax purposes.

5. An agent can delegate power to a subagent without the principal's express permission under certain circumstances. The principal is liable for the acts of a subagent. Sometimes a cooperating broker is a subagent, but not a salesperson.

6. An agency may be terminated by accomplishment of purpose, expiration of the term, operation of law, mutual agreement, renunciation, or revocation. An agent who renounces or a principal who revokes an agency may be liable to the other party for damages. An agency coupled with an interest can't be revoked, and isn't terminated by the death, incapacity, or bankruptcy of the principal.

7. The California Real Estate Law includes rules regarding licensing, record keeping, and trust funds. After receiving trust funds, a broker has until the end of the next business day to deposit them in a trust account or an escrow account, or deliver them to the principal. A broker must never commingle trust funds with his or her own money.

8. Generally, only a properly licensed real estate agent may be paid for representing another in a real estate transaction. The commission must be negotiated between the broker and the principal. A broker is ordinarily entitled to a commission after the seller and a ready, willing, and able buyer agree on the essential terms of the sale. The type of listing agreement also affects whether a broker is entitled to a commission. A salesperson may only receive a commission from his or her own broker.

CASE PROBLEM

Charles V. Webster Real Estate v. Rickard, 21 Cal. App. 3d 612, 98 Cal. Rptr. 559 (1971)

In May 1967, Dr. Moore listed his 156-acre vineyard with Watson Realty for $234,000. The exclusive right to sell agreement (which provided for a 5% commission) specified that the agency would terminate on December 31, 1968.

    Dr. Moore later gave written consent to have the listing transferred from Watson Realty to Webster Real Estate. The list price was reduced to $187,200.

    Then, in June 1968, Dr. Moore died. Without any help from the real estate agents, the executor of Dr. Moore's estate sold the vineyard in November for $152,000.

    Believing they were entitled to their commission under the exclusive right to sell agreement, Webster Real Estate filed a claim against Dr. Moore's estate for $7,600 (5% of the sale price). The executor rejected the claim, so Webster Real Estate sued the estate.

    Was Webster Real Estate entitled to its commission? Were they entitled to damages for breach of contract? Why or why not? What if Webster Real Estate had been the procuring cause of the November sale?

Answer: The court ruled that Webster Real Estate was not entitled to collect a commission. Dr. Moore's death in June automatically terminated the agency. Since the agency was terminated by operation of law, Dr. Moore's estate was not liable for breach.

    At most, Webster Real Estate could demand reimbursement for expenses it incurred before Dr. Moore's death. The court commented that it probably would have reached a different conclusion if Webster Real Estate had been the procuring cause of the sale.

CHAPTER 5 KEY TERMS	estoppel	principal
	exclusive right to sell	procuring cause
	exclusive agency	ratification
agency	extender clause	ready, willing, and able
agency coupled with an interest	finder's fee	renunciation
	implied authority	revocation
agent	independent contractor	subagent
attorney in fact	open listing	trust funds
commingling	ostensible authority	
conflict of interest	power of attorney	

Introduction to Agency Law

Quiz—Chapter 5

1. Most real estate agents are considered:
   a. general agents.
   b. universal agents.
   c. special agents.
   d. subagents.

2. An agency is terminated when:
   a. both parties agree to end it.
   b. the agent renounces it.
   c. the principal revokes it.
   d. any of the above.

3. A real estate agency is terminated by operation of law if:
   a. the principal fires the broker.
   b. the broker goes bankrupt.
   c. there is no extender clause.
   d. the broker hires a subagent without the principal's permission.

4. A real estate license must be renewed:
   a. every year.
   b. every two years.
   c. every four years.
   d. only if revoked or suspended.

5. The Real Estate Law requires brokers to keep adequate records of real estate transactions and retain these records:
   a. for one year.
   b. for three years.
   c. for ten years.
   d. until the transaction has closed.

6. All trust funds received by a broker must be deposited in a trust account or an escrow account, or given to the principal:
   a. the same day they're received
   b. no later than the first business day after receipt
   c. within three days after receipt
   d. as soon as reasonably possible

7. A broker may hold a buyer's earnest money check without depositing it in a trust account:
   a. until closing.
   b. until the buyer defaults.
   c. pursuant to written instructions from the parties.
   d. under no circumstances.

8. A real estate broker's trust account must be:
   a. interest-bearing accounts.
   b. demand-deposit accounts.
   c. uninsured accounts.
   d. all of the above.

9. A salesperson may be paid a commission:
   a. by his or her own broker.
   b. by the seller directly.
   c. by an licensed broker.
   d. any of the above.

10. The amount of the commission:
   a. is 6% of the sale price.
   b. is set by the Board of Realtors in each county.
   c. is agreed upon between the broker and the seller.
   d. must be the same for all brokers.

ANSWERS: 1. c; 2. d; 3. b; 4. c; 5. b; 6. b; 7. c; 8. b; 9. a; 10. c

CHAPTER 6
Agency Duties and Liabilities

CHAPTER OVERVIEW

The last chapter explained what an agent is, and how an agency relationship is created and terminated. This chapter describes the real estate agent's duties. It also discusses the agent's liability—the penalties for failing to carry out those duties.

A real estate agent's primary duties are owed to the principal, the person the agent is representing in a transaction. But the agent also has duties to the other parties involved in the transaction. Fulfilling both responsibilities is the agent's duty.

Buyers and sellers who understand agency law will have a better sense of what to expect from a real estate agent—and what to watch out for. For the agent, knowing what the law requires of you is the first step in avoiding liability.

Agency Disclosure

In 1988, the California legislature enacted an agency disclosure statute that applies to residential real estate transactions. Under the statute, a real estate agent has a duty to both the seller and the buyer to let them know which party the agent is representing in the transaction.

http://california.lp.findlaw.com/
(California Civil Code)

Often a salesperson shows a buyer many listings, driving the buyer from place to place, discussing the buyer's needs. In the course of a week or two, the salesperson and buyer establish a friendly relationship. When the buyer decides to make an offer on one of the listings, he or she may look to the salesperson for advice. The buyer should realize that in the eyes of the law the salesperson (through his or her broker) may be representing only the seller.

A real estate agent is required to give the buyer two agency disclosure forms before the deposit receipt is signed. The first form is called an **agency disclosure form**. This form is required of agents in sales (or leases for more than one year) on residential dwellings with from one to four units. It explains the duties of a(n): 1) seller's agent, 2) buyer's agent, and 3) agent representing both buyer and seller. The agent must ask the buyer to sign the agency disclosure form, and to also sign a receipt acknowledging that he or she received a copy of the disclosure form.

The second form is called an **agency confirmation statement**. The real estate agent checks a box on the confirmation statement to show which party or parties he or she is representing: the seller exclusively, the buyer exclusively, or both the buyer and the seller. The buyer then signs the statement, indicating that he or she understands the agent's role and accepts it.

The agent must also present these two forms to the seller. The seller should receive and sign the agency disclosure form (and a receipt) before signing a listing agreement. He or she should sign the agency confirmation statement before signing the deposit receipt.

The agency confirmation statement can be a preprinted provision in the deposit receipt rather than a separate form. But both the buyer and seller must sign the statement either before or at the same time they sign the deposit receipt.

In a transaction where the selling agent (the one who finds the buyer) is not the same person as the listing agent, the selling agent also is required to give these two forms to each of the parties. (In some cases, the selling agent is a cooperating broker from the MLS who represents the seller. Sometimes selling agents represent buyers.)

The agency disclosure statute applies only to a transaction involving a mobile home or residential property with four units or less. (And when it involves a lease rather than a sale, the statute applies only if the lease will last more than one year.) But it's a good idea to use the agency disclosure forms even in transactions where they aren't required. Clarifying agency relationships generally helps everyone involved (including the agents) and may prevent litigation in some cases.

Case Example: The 1988 Huijers retained Larson, a real estate broker, to locate suitable property in Santa Barbara County to complete a tax-deferred exchange. Larson spoke with De Marrais and had them sign a $325,000 listing which contained a 6% commission. Larson did not provide De Marrais with an agency disclosure statement. Several weeks later De Marrais told Larson to increase the price to $375,000 but Larson refused. Upon hearing this, Huijers, who was going to offer $275,000, told Larson to offer $325,000 on the exact terms of the listing. All parties met and De Marrais accepted the $325,000 offer because Huijers said they would have to pay a commission if they didn't accept since the broker had a ready, willing, and able buyer. Upon acceptance, Larson provided the agency disclosure statement showing dual agency. De Marrais wanted out of the contract. Huijers sued.

The Court of Appeal held that Larson's failure to deliver the agency disclosure at the time of the listing may be grounds to rescind the contract since De Marrais would have known of the dual agency and possible sought a different agent. The court also held that Larson was not entitled to any commission because the failure to deliver the agency disclosure. *Huijers v. De Marrais*, 11 Cal. App. 4th 676, 14 Cal. Rptr. 2d 232 (1995).

CALIFORNIA
ASSOCIATION
OF REALTORS®

**DISCLOSURE REGARDING
REAL ESTATE AGENCY RELATIONSHIPS**
(As required by the Civil Code)
(C.A.R. Form AD-11, Revised 10/01)

When you enter into a discussion with a real estate agent regarding a real estate transaction, you should from the outset understand what type of agency relationship or representation you wish to have with the agent in the transaction.

SELLER'S AGENT
A Seller's agent under a listing agreement with the Seller acts as the agent for the Seller only. A Seller's agent or a subagent of that agent has the following affirmative obligations:
To the Seller:
A Fiduciary duty of utmost care, integrity, honesty, and loyalty in dealings with the Seller.
To the Buyer and the Seller:
(a) Diligent exercise of reasonable skill and care in performance of the agent's duties.
(b) A duty of honest and fair dealing and good faith.
(c) A duty to disclose all facts known to the agent materially affecting the value or desirability of the property that are not known to, or within the diligent attention and observation of, the parties.

An agent is not obligated to reveal to either party any confidential information obtained from the other party that does not involve the affirmative duties set forth above.

BUYER'S AGENT
A selling agent can, with a Buyer's consent, agree to act as agent for the Buyer only. In these situations, the agent is not the Seller's agent, even if by agreement the agent may receive compensation for services rendered, either in full or in part from the Seller. An agent acting only for a Buyer has the following affirmative obligations:
To the Buyer:
A fiduciary duty of utmost care, integrity, honesty, and loyalty in dealings with the Buyer.
To the Buyer and the Seller:
(a) Diligent exercise of reasonable skill and care in performance of the agent's duties.
(b) A duty of honest and fair dealing and good faith.
(c) A duty to disclose all facts known to the agent materially affecting the value or desirability of the property that are not known to, or within the diligent attention and observation of, the parties.

An agent is not obligated to reveal to either party any confidential information obtained from the other party that does not involve the affirmative duties set forth above.

AGENT REPRESENTING BOTH SELLER AND BUYER
A real estate agent, either acting directly or through one or more associate licensees, can legally be the agent of both the Seller and the Buyer in a transaction, but only with the knowledge and consent of both the Seller and the Buyer.

In a dual agency situation, the agent has the following affirmative obligations to both the Seller and the Buyer:
(a) A fiduciary duty of utmost care, integrity, honesty and loyalty in the dealings with either the Seller or the Buyer.
(b) Other duties to the Seller and the Buyer as stated above in their respective sections.

In representing both Seller and Buyer, the agent may not, without the express permission of the respective party, disclose to the other party that the Seller will accept a price less than the listing price or that the Buyer will pay a price greater than the price offered.

The above duties of the agent in a real estate transaction do not relieve a Seller or Buyer from the responsibility to protect his or her own interests. You should carefully read all agreements to assure that they adequately express your understanding of the transaction. A real estate agent is a person qualified to advise about real estate. If legal or tax advice is desired, consult a competent professional.

Throughout your real property transaction you may receive more than one disclosure form, depending upon the number of agents assisting in the transaction. The law requires each agent with whom you have more than a casual relationship to present you with this disclosure form. You should read its contents each time it is presented to you, considering the relationship between you and the real estate agent in your specific transaction.

This disclosure form includes the provisions of Sections 2079.13 to 2079.24, inclusive, of the Civil Code set forth on the reverse hereof. Read it carefully.

I/WE ACKNOWLEDGE RECEIPT OF A COPY OF THIS DISCLOSURE.

BUYER/SELLER _____ Date _____ Time _____ AM/PM

BUYER/SELLER _____ Date _____ Time _____ AM/PM

AGENT _____ By _____ Date _____
        (Please Print)   (Associate-Licensee or Broker Signature)

THIS FORM SHALL BE PROVIDED AND ACKNOWLEDGED AS FOLLOWS (Civil Code §2079.14):
•When the listing brokerage company also represents the Buyer, the Listing Agent shall give one AD-11 form to the Seller and one to the Buyer.
•When Buyer and Seller are represented by different brokerage companies, then the Listing Agent shall give one AD-11 form to the Seller and the Buyer's Agent shall give one AD-11 form to the Buyer and one AD-11 form to the Seller.

SEE REVERSE SIDE FOR FURTHER INFORMATION

Published and Distributed by:
REAL ESTATE BUSINESS SERVICES, INC.
a subsidiary of the CALIFORNIA ASSOCIATION OF REALTORS®
525 South Virgil Avenue, Los Angeles, California 90020

Reviewed by _____
Broker or Designee _____ Date _____

EQUAL HOUSING
OPPORTUNITY

AD-11 REVISED 10/01 (PAGE 1 OF 1)   Print Date

DISCLOSURE REGARDING REAL ESTATE AGENCY RELATIONSHIPS (AD-11 PAGE 1 OF 1)
Reprinted with permission, CALIFORNIA ASSOCIATION OF REALTORS®. Endorsement not implied.

Chapter 6

The Agent's Duties to the Principal

The relationship between an agent and a principal is a **fiduciary** relationship. A fiduciary is someone who acts for the benefit of another in a relationship founded on trust and confidence. The law holds a fiduciary to high standards to prevent the fiduciary from disappointing or exploiting the other party's trust.

The basic fiduciary duties that an agent owes the principal are the duty to use reasonable care and skill, and the duties of obedience, utmost good faith, and loyalty. As you will see, these phrases cover a lot of responsibility. They require real estate agents to devote their energies and professional expertise to producing the best possible result for their clients.

http://ca.realtor.com
(California Living Network)

REASONABLE CARE AND SKILL

In acting for their clients, real estate agents must use reasonable care and skill. What's "reasonable"? It's the degree of care and skill ordinarily used by others competently engaged in the same business. When a court evaluates an agent's knowledge and performance, the agent will be compared with competent real estate agents, not with the average citizen.

> **Example:** X is a real estate salesperson representing B, who is buying a house from Mr. and Mrs. S. B and Mrs. S sign the deposit receipt form. B asks X if it's okay that Mr. S didn't sign. X says it isn't necessary for him to sign because one spouse's signature binds the other spouse to the agreement.
>
> The next day, Mr. S tells B they've received a better offer and are returning his deposit. B learns he can't enforce the purchase agreement because (contrary to what X told him) both spouses must sign any document transferring an interest in community real property.

Salesperson X mislead B—she just didn't realize that both spouses (in community property) have to sign the deposit receipt. Many people don't know that rule, but all competent real estate agents are expected to know it. X is required to meet the standard set by other real estate agents. Her failure to do so was a breach of her fiduciary duties to B.

A breach of duty that causes harm to another is a tort (see Chapter 1). An unintentional breach—one that results from carelessness or incompetence—is called negligence. In the previous example, X was negligent in advising B. In a civil lawsuit, X would be liable to B for any financial harm her negligence caused him.

CLAIMING EXPERTISE. All real estate agents are held to a minimum standard of competence. But an agent who claims to have expertise in a particular area—property management or appraisal, for example—is held to an even higher standard. You should never take on any special tasks beyond your ability, and never claim expertise in areas where you have no special training or skills. The claim may impress the client at first, but it might to lead to a lawsuit.

As an example, let's look at property appraisal. Helping a client decide on a listing price is one thing; claiming to perform an expert valuation is another.

Case Example: Some homeowners contacted a real estate salesperson about selling their house. They told the agent their decision to buy another house would depend on how much they could get for their current home.

The salesperson said she had the experience and professional expertise to estimate the value of the property. After inspecting the home, she told the sellers it should be listed for $168,000 and they could expect to sell it very quickly for between $162,000 and $163,000. When they expressed some doubt about the price, she assured them that she had performed many appraisals and that her representations as to market value and speed of sale were correct. To back up her opinion, she said she would have her broker take a look at the home.

After being told that the broker estimated the value at $158,000, the sellers entered an agreement to buy another home at about the same price. They listed their existing home for $167,500. Unfortunately, the home failed to sell during the three-month listing period. In fact, only five prospects saw the home and no offers were made, even though the price was reduced to $164,900. At the end of the listing term, they listed with another broker for $144,000. This was later reduced to $137,000, but at the time of trial the home still had not sold.

Independent appraisals showed that the house had originally been grossly overpriced—the price should have been at least $20,000 less than the agent had said. The sellers' inability to obtain cash from the sale of their old home forced them to sell their new home at a substantial loss.

The broker and salesperson had repeatedly claimed to have the expertise necessary to give the sellers an accurate opinion of value. They had also given the sellers a pamphlet listing reasons why they should employ a real estate agent. One of the reasons listed was that professional real estate agents knew market value and could price the property to sell quickly for full value.

Ruling that the salesperson and broker were negligent, the court stated that anyone undertaking to perform a task such as giving a professional opinion of value was required to perform that task with reasonable skill and competence. *Duhl v. Nash*, 102 ILL. App. 3d 483, 429 N.E.2d 1267 (1981).

Although that lawsuit took place in Illinois, a California court would probably reach the same result.

When an agent does not feel qualified to give accurate advice, he or she should recommend that the client seek the advice of an attorney, accountant, appraiser, or other expert. In one case, a broker was sued for failing to advise his client as to the income tax consequences of a particular transaction. He was not held liable because he had advised the client to seek professional counsel regarding the tax question. (*Santos v. Wing*, 197 Cal. App. 2d 678, 17 Cal. Rptr. 457 [1961].)

UNAUTHORIZED PRACTICE OF LAW. Many aspects of real estate transactions raise legal questions or have legal consequences. Real estate agents need to remember and to remind their clients that they are not attorneys and do not have the required license to practice law. Agents should never give legal advice or perform any acts that might amount to the unauthorized practice of law.

In California, a real estate agent is permitted to complete simple standard forms that have been approved by a lawyer or the California Bar Association. An agent may

Chapter 6

only fill out forms in connection with a real estate transaction that he or she is handling. The agent must not charge the client separately for completing the forms.

> **Example:** A broker is involved in a fairly complicated commercial real estate transaction. He is a little confused by some of the terms of the parties' agreement, so he gets another broker (a friend of his) to fill out the deposit receipt.
>
> The second broker charges the clients a separate fee for his work. The second broker's actions would be considered the unauthorized practice of law. He filled out forms for a transaction that he was not handling, and also charged a separate fee for completing the forms.

Even when filling in the blanks on standard forms in the ordinary course of business, an agent who inserts complicated clauses that require legal expertise is guilty of the unauthorized practice of law.

The unauthorized practice of law is a criminal offense, a misdemeanor. The penalty may be a fine or even a jail term. Note that a real estate agent may be convicted of the unauthorized practice of law even if he or she gave accurate legal advice. And if the advice was unsound, the clients who followed it can sue the agent for negligence to recover any damages they suffered.

OBEDIENCE, GOOD FAITH, AND LOYALTY

An agent owes the principal obedience, utmost good faith, and loyalty. The agent must faithfully carry out the principal's instructions, and may be held liable for any loss caused by failure to obey them.

DILIGENCE. An agent who acts in good faith exercises due diligence on behalf of the principal. In other words, an agent is supposed to make a reasonably diligent effort to achieve the principal's goals. As a general rule, the principal can terminate the agency without paying damages if the agent isn't trying to get the job done.

However, there are conflicting court decisions on whether a real estate broker is entitled to a commission under an exclusive listing agreement if he or she hasn't made a diligent effort to find a buyer.

Case Example: In August, Mr. Mora listed his property with Mr. Coleman. The termination date for their exclusive listing agreement was December 31.

Aside from including Mora's property in an advertisement along with several other properties, Coleman made no effort to sell it. No one even came to look at the property, much less make an offer. At the end of October, Mora entered into another listing agreement with a different brokerage. On November 25, Mora notified Coleman in writing that his agency was revoked. And on November 30, Mora accepted an offer presented by the new brokers. Coleman sued for his commission.

The court ruled that Coleman was not entitled to a commission. Coleman had a duty to make a diligent effort to find a buyer. He had failed to perform his side of the bargain, so Mora had good cause for canceling their agreement. *Coleman v. Mora*, 263 Cal. App. 2d 137, 69 Cal. Rptr. 166 (1968).

Agency Duties and Liabilities

On the other hand, in *Carlsen v. Zane*, 261 Cal. App. 2d 399, 67 Cal. Rptr. 747 (1968), the court held that the brokers were entitled to a commission even though they hadn't exercised due diligence. The Carlsen court held that requiring due diligence would blur the distinction between an exclusive listing and an open listing. The key feature of an exclusive right to sell listing is that the broker collects the commission no matter who finds the buyer. These cases were decided by two different divisions of the Fourth District Court of Appeals in 1968. Carlsen was decided by Division 2, and Coleman was decided by Division 1 just a few months later. (This shows that the doctrine of stare decisis isn't always strictly followed.) The conflict between the two decisions has never been resolved. Another California court faced with the same issue could follow either case.

CONFIDENTIALITY. The duty of loyalty means that the agent must put the principal's interests above all others, including the agent's own interests. In an agency relationship, the principal often discloses confidential information to the agent. Out of loyalty to the principal, the agent must not reveal this information to others, nor take advantage of it him or herself.

Example: S listed her house with broker X for $225,000, although she told X she'd accept as little as $200,000 for it. A prospective buyer, B, is very interested in the house, but can't afford more than $205,000.

X thinks B is a nice guy and would like him to have the house. X also needs his commission as soon as possible, so he wants S's house to sell quickly. But if X hints to B that S would be willing to accept less than the listing price, he is violating his fiduciary duties to S.

AGENT'S FIDUCIARY DUTIES TO THE PRINCIPAL

◆ Reasonable Care and Skill
◆ Obedience, Loyalty, and Utmost Good Faith
◆ Diligence
◆ Confidentiality
◆ Disclosure of material information

DISCLOSURE OF MATERIAL INFORMATION. An agent is required to disclose to his or her principal any material that affects the subject matter of the agency. Any fact that could influence the principal's judgment or decision in the transaction, is a material fact and should be brought to his or her attention. A real estate agent representing a seller should be especially careful to inform the principal of:

◆ the true value of the property, and anything that might affect its value;
◆ all offers to purchase;
◆ the identity of the purchaser;
◆ the purchaser's financial condition;
◆ any relationship between the purchaser and the broker;
◆ any commission splitting arrangements with other brokers.

Property Value. When trying to get a listing, a real estate agent may be tempted to exaggerate the market value of the property. A high value estimate might make the seller more willing to sign an exclusive listing agreement.

But that's a breach of the agent's duty to act in good faith. The agent is required to do his or her best to inform the seller of the property's true value. Anything that affects the value should be pointed out, including the condition of the title or the condition of the property itself. Sometimes inexpensive repairs or improvements could make a big difference in the value, and the agent should suggest these to the seller. And if the agent is aware of any recent or upcoming changes that may have an impact on the value (such as zoning changes, or plans to build a new school nearby), the agent should let the seller know.

This duty to inform the seller continues throughout the listing period. If the agent comes across new information (new comparable sales, for example) indicating that the original valuation was high or low, that must be passed along to the seller.

Present All Offers. Even if an offer seems totally unacceptable, the agent must present it to the principal. The principal, not the agent, decides which offer is acceptable. The agent must relay an offer to the principal even if its acceptance would mean a smaller commission, because the agent's first loyalty is to the principal.

Example: A lists his property with Z. A tells Z he would prefer a cash sale, but is willing to consider an alternative if necessary. Z receives offers from two prospective buyers. Buyer #1 offers $180,000 cash. Buyer #2 offers $195,000 if A is willing to accept a trust deed with a balloon payment in five years.

Z's commission will be $900 less if A accepts Buyer #1's offer instead of Buyer #2's. Z decides not to present Buyer #1's offer at all. Rationalizing, he tells himself that Buyer #2 has an excellent credit rating, and A will be much better off in the long run with Buyer #2's offer. Whether or not that is true, Z has violated his fiduciary duties to A. Z has the duty to disclose all offers.

What about an offer the agent receives after the seller has already accepted an earlier offer? It should also be presented to the seller. However, the agent should not try to persuade the seller to breach the agreement with the first buyer. (The first buyer might sue the agent for interfering with a contractual relationship— see Chapter 7.) If the seller wants to accept the later offer, he or she should talk to a lawyer about the legal consequences of breaching the first agreement.

Buyer's Financial Information. The seller's agent must tell the seller any material fact he or she knows about the buyer's financial position. As a general rule, a seller's agent does not lose the right to a commission simply because the buyer failed to perform under the contract. But if the agent didn't disclose detrimental financial information about the buyer, the agent may lose the right to a commission. The agent didn't actually produce a buyer who was financially ready, willing and financially able to complete the sale.

Financial information regarding the buyer is material if the seller might have refused to accept the offer if he or she had been aware of it. It could be negative information about the buyer's assets, income, or credit rating. Many cases concern the source of the downpayment (a loan from a relative rather than savings, for example), or the form of the earnest money deposit.

Self-Dealing and Secret Profits

As you've seen, in some cases an agent conceals information from the principal just to force a sale through and get the commission. But sometimes there's an extra motive behind the breach of duty: a secret profit.

A secret profit is any profit or financial benefit the agent obtains without the principal's authorization. The most common examples involve self-dealing. Self-dealing occurs, for example, when the agent has his sisters buy the property for him, and then he sells it again for a profit.

Case Example: Ms. Shannon listed her six-acre property with Mr. Rodes for $6,500. Rodes later persuaded Shannon that it would be better to sell the property quickly for $2,500 rather than trying to get more for it.

Rodes soon presented a $2,500 offer from Ms. Nelson, and Shannon accepted it. Nelson was actually an employee in Rodes's office. After the escrow was opened, Nelson assigned her interest in the property to Rodes.

Even before this first sale had closed, Rodes opened another escrow to sell the property to Mr. and Mrs. Diaz. Now Rodes himself was the seller, and the price was $6,500.

Shannon discovered what Rodes had done and cancelled the sale to Nelson. Rodes sued to enforce the sale. The court ruled that because Rodes concealed the fact that he was the buyer, Shannon did not have to go through with the sale. *Rodes v. Shannon*, 222 Cal. App. 2d 721, 35 Cal. Rptr. 339 (1963).

It isn't automatically improper for an agent to buy property from the principal. But the agent must inform the seller that he or she is the buyer. The agent must also inform the seller if the buyer is the agent's relative or close friend, or a business entity in which the agent has an interest. This alerts the seller to a possible conflict of interest, and he or she may choose to find another agent.

An agent has the duty to advise the seller of any steps that could be taken to increase the selling price of the property, such as repairs, cleanup work, or minor modifications. If the agent buys the property and then carries out these improvements, the agent has used a superior knowledge of real estate for his or her own profit instead of the principal's. This is a breach of the duty of loyalty and good faith.

Case Example: A seller owned 12 acres of rural residential property in Oregon. He was recently divorced, had custody of a small son, had been seriously ill, and was unemployed. He was forced to sell his property for financial reasons, so in February 1968 he listed the property for $15,000.

The broker advertised the property as follows:

"12 ACRES—3 bedroom furnished home (needs little work). Land is wooded and meadows. Good well. Pond. Great place for large family. $15,000. Terms."

continued

After a while, the broker told the seller that he couldn't move the property for $15,000 and asked if the seller would reduce the price. The seller mentioned $12,500, but the broker said he had other properties that were as good or better that he couldn't sell for $10,000.

In May, the broker had the seller sign an earnest money receipt (deposit receipt) agreeing to sell the property for $8,000. Three days later, the broker called the seller and told him he thought he had a buyer. When the seller arrived at the broker's office, the broker told him he was the buyer. The broker also told the seller that he had to sell the property to him because the seller had already signed the earnest money receipt. The broker bought the property for $7,520 ($8,000, less a commission of $480).

The broker spent $1,277 on the property, cleaning and painting. He then offered the property for sale in two separate parcels—one with four acres and the house for $13,500, and the other eight-acre parcel for $6,500. He ran the following advertisement:

"TAIN'T REAL FANCY—But look what $13,500 buys—Good older (large) farm home with four acres fine land. The home has been recently redecorated and painted inside and out. There are 3 or 4 bedrms. Large living room with full dining area. Big farm style kitchen with service porch. Large workshop, carport and woodshed. Livestock shelter and poultry house. Spring fed pond with year round water. Magnificent place to raise your children. Keep ponies, calves, sheep, chickens, etc. School bus at front gate. Also thrown in free of charge is some furniture which includes good heating stove; washer and dryer; dining room table and chairs; several dressers; davenport; farm and garden tractor. This charming big family farm home is located about 12 miles from town on paved road. More land available if needed. Owner will carry the paper with moderate downpayment from responsible party."

A comparison of the two ads clearly shows that the broker made a much greater effort on his own behalf than on behalf of the seller. The broker purchased the property in May for $7,520 and sold both parcels of property by the end of August for a total of $19,900. Within three months of his purchase, the broker profited by $11,103. ($19,900 - $1,277 - $7,520 = $11,103).

After learning what had happened, the seller sued the broker. The court found that the broker had breached his fiduciary duties to the seller. *Starkweather v. Shaffer*, 497 P2d 358 (1972)

This case is an example of most of the things a broker should never do. The broker abused the information that the seller was desperate to sell; he misrepresented the value of the property; he implied that he had a third-party purchaser, when in fact he was acting for himself; he coerced the seller into selling by telling him he had to sell to the broker because he had already signed the earnest money agreement; he failed to advise the seller of things that would help market the property (such as cleanup, painting, and subdividing); he failed to make his best effort in advertising the property for the seller; and he ended up self-dealing and making a secret profit for himself at the expense of the seller.

Agency Duties and Liabilities

DUAL AGENCY

A broker or salesperson who represents both the buyer and seller in a transaction is a dual agent. Although dual agency use to be controversial, it is legal as long as both parties consent to it.

A dual agent owes fiduciary duties to both buyer and seller at the same time. As a result, if one party discloses confidential information to the agent, the agent must not reveal it to the other party. This is especially important in regard to the price. The dual agent is forbidden to tell the buyer that the seller will accept anything less than the listing price, unless the seller gives written consent. And without the buyer's written permission, the agent cannot let the seller know that the buyer will pay a penny more than the amount offered.

Dual agency has drawbacks. Critics point out that there is an inherent conflict of interest in the arrangement. A seller is looking for the highest price, while the buyer is looking for the lowest price. It is difficult, if not impossible, to adequately represent these two opposing interests.

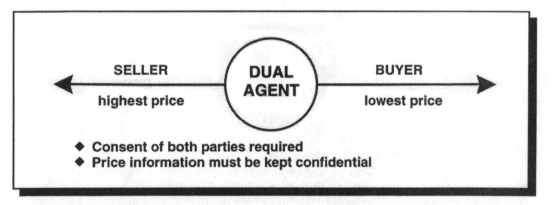

SELLER — highest price ← **DUAL AGENT** → BUYER — lowest price

◆ **Consent of both parties required**
◆ **Price information must be kept confidential**

Dual agency also gives the agent an opportunity to manipulate one client in favor of the other. This is particularly likely to occur when the agent has an ongoing relationship with one party (a friend, relative, or established client) but not the other.

Case Example: L. Bryon Culver & Associates had a history of locating property for Del Rayo (a business owned by Gene Klien), and sales agent Whiteside located 33.5 acres owned by Jaoudi Industrial and Trading Corporation. Whiteside obtained a listing from Jaoudi with a 3% commission.

Whiteside agreed on a $1,750,000 sales price. The next day Whiteside presented a $1,750,000 offer from Del Rayo with a $52,500 commission to Culver. When asked, Whiteside denied that Del Rayo and Culver were associated. Jaoudi accepted the offer but refused to pay the commission because of an undisclosed dual agency. Culver sued.

The Court of Appeal said that the failure to disclose the dual agency at the time of the transaction cost the agent a commission. The statutory agency disclosure form is not required here since this is commercial property. *L. Byron Culver & Assoc. v. Jaoudi Industrial & Trading Corporation*, 1 Cal. App. 4th 387, 1 Cal. Rptr. 2d 680, (1991).

www.bestforbuyers.com
www.realtimes.com
www.onehomebuyerplace.com
™ **(What side are you representing?)**

An agent has a strong motive for favoring an investor like the Del Rayo Company, which is likely to be a source of future commissions. Dual agency is inappropriate in this type of situation.

Inadvertent Dual Agency. Note that a dual agency may arise even though the agent doesn't intend to create one. For example, a seller's broker might behave as though she's also representing the buyer, leading the buyer to rely on her for guidance. A court could rule that there was an implied agency relationship between the broker and the buyer. Then the broker would have fiduciary duties toward the buyer as well as the seller.

The agency disclosure forms have helped prevent this kind of unintentional dual agency. But a real estate agent should make sure that both buyer and seller understand the agency relationship throughout the transaction.

The Agent's Duties to Third Parties

DISCLOSURE TO THE BUYER

In addition to an agent's duties to the principal, the agent owes third parties a duty of good faith and fair dealing. But an agent is not a fiduciary in relation to a third party. He or she is not required to advance the third party's interests; in fact, the agent's duty of loyalty to the principal will often prohibit that.

What is fair dealing? The law's view of that question has changed substantially in recent years. In the past, the rule of **caveat emptor** ("let the buyer beware") governed real estate transactions. The seller and the seller's agent had very few duties toward the buyer. It was up to the buyer to inspect the property and ask questions about it. The seller and agent were required to answer questions truthfully, but were not required to disclose information if the buyer did not ask.

That rule is no longer followed in most states, at least not in residential transactions. Especially in California, court decisions and statutes have expanded sellers' and real estate agents' duties in order to protect residential buyers. Now it's not enough to avoid misleading a buyer—there are affirmative duties to disclose certain facts and even to investigate on a buyer's behalf.

California the National Leader in Real Estate Disclosures

Consumer Protection. The following disclosures must be made in normal residential real estate transactions:

◆ **Agency disclosure:** The agent works for the seller, buyer or both with dual agency.

◆ **Transfer disclosure statement:** Facts about the property are filled out by seller and an inspection is conducted by the real estate agents. The seller and buyer each receive a copy.

If the seller and agent know anything about the property that materially affects its value or desirability, they must tell the buyer, unless it is something the buyer could easily see or determine.

> **Case Example:** A woman and her four children had been murdered in the house about ten years earlier. The seller and the real estate agent were aware of the house's history but did not mention it to the buyer. In fact, the seller asked the neighbors not to tell the buyer about the murders.
>
> But sometime after closing, one of the neighbors did tell the buyer. The buyer sued the broker, claiming that she paid much more for the property than she would have if she'd known about the murders. The court held that if the buyer could show that the fact of the murders really did affect the market value of the property, then she had a right to recover damages from the broker. *Reed v. King*, 145 Cal. App. 3d 261, 193 Cal. Rptr. 130 (1983).

As the *Reed* case suggests, there's room for argument about which facts materially affect value and desirability.

There has recently been controversy in several states over whether a seller or agent must tell a buyer that a house was occupied by someone infected with the AIDS virus. In California, the issue has been settled by the legislature. A new statute provides that there can be no cause of action against an owner or agent for failing to disclose that an occupant had AIDS or died from AIDS. If disclosure were required, it might worsen the problem of housing discrimination against people suffering from the disease.

This new statute also provides that if someone died on the property more than three years earlier, an owner or agent can't be held liable for not telling the buyer about the death. This provision applies to death from any cause. As a result, *Reed v. King* would probably be decided differently now, since the murders in that case took place ten years before the buyer bought the property. Had the deaths occurred within the last 3 years, they must be disclosed. It appears that a death from AIDS does not have to be disclosed at all. However, if a prospective buyer asks about AIDS or deaths on the property, the seller or agent can be held liable for answering falsely.

> **Case Example:** The sellers didn't tell their listing agents that there had been two landslides on the property. The agents saw various indications that there were soil problems, such as a floor that wasn't level and protective netting on a slope. But the agents did not order soil tests or investigate further, and they did not mention soil slippage to the buyer, Ms. Easton. Easton paid $170,000 for the property. After the purchase, substantial landslides reduced the value to $20,000 or less. Easton sued, and the jury found the sellers, builders, and listing agents liable.
>
> The listing agents appealed, but the court of appeals affirmed the jury's decision. The court held that a real estate broker representing a seller of residential property has a duty to conduct a reasonably competent and diligent inspection of the property. If the inspection reveals any facts that materially affect the property's value or desirability, the agent must disclose them to the buyer. *Easton v. Strassburger*, 152 Cal. App. 3d 90, 199 Cal. Rptr. 383 (1984).

DUTY TO INSPECT. Until *Easton v. Strassburger*, a seller's agent had no duty to try and find out more about the property than he or she already knew. If the seller didn't tell the agent about problems, the agent didn't have to go looking for them.

The *Easton* case decision left brokers (and their insurance companies) in doubt as to the extent of a real estate agent's duties. In 1985, the legislature passed a statute to clarify the court's ruling (the Real Estate Transfer Disclosure Statement form is required). The Real Estate Transfer Disclosure Statement applies to an agent representing a seller (or lessor) when the property includes one to four residential units, unless it is a new home in a subdivision offered for sale for the first time. The agent must conduct a reasonably competent and diligent visual inspection of the property, and disclose to the buyer (or lessee) any material information the inspection reveals. The agent is not required to inspect areas of the property that aren't reasonably accessible to visual inspection. (In the case of a condo or other common interest development, the agent is only required to inspect the unit being sold.) The statute specifically states that it does not relieve the buyer of the duty to use reasonable care to protect him or herself.

REAL ESTATE TRANSFER DISCLOSURE STATEMENT. The statute requires that the seller and real estate agent to fill out a Real Estate Transfer Disclosure Statement form for the buyer. (Again, this only applies to a transfer of property with one to four residential units, and does not apply to brand new homes in subdivisions.) The California Association of Realtors® version of the form is reprinted here.

 www.leginfo.ca.gov/cgi-bin/displaycode?section=civ&group=01001-02000&file=1102-1102.18
(California Civil Code - Transfer Disclosures)

> **Case Example:** The Court of Appeal noted that the statutory disclosure form requires disclosure of "neighborhood noise problems or other nuisances" to buyers. The case involved the McKnights whose tree trimming business, operated out of the home, uses a noisy tree chipper machine. There were late night noisy activities, too many cars on the property, a deck constructed without a building permit, and a cabana which violated the covenants, condition, and restrictions. The court held that it would be tortious not to disclose a negative fact when it is reasonably foreseeable that it has a depressing affect on the property's value. This disclosure is required even though a court has ordered abatement. *Alexander v. McKnight*, 7 Cal. App. 4th 973, 9 Cal. Rptr. 2d 453 (1992).

The form provides seller's information checklists, on which the seller is required to indicate any problems he or she is aware of. The lists cover the operating condition of a wide variety of appliances and other features (from smoke detectors to hot tubs), and defects in the interior and exterior structures (walls, plumbing, driveway, and so on). The seller is also required to check off a list of problems such as encroachments, building code or zoning violations, soil slippage, mold, and the possible presence of drug lab contamination. Easements and deed restrictions that the seller is aware of are also included.

The form also has sections to be filled out and signed by the listing agent, the selling agent and the agent who obtained the offer. (Of course, in many cases the listing agent is also the selling agent.) Each agent is required to comment on the condition of the property, as revealed by his or her own inspection. In the final section, both seller and buyer sign to acknowledge receipt of a copy.

CALIFORNIA ASSOCIATION OF REALTORS®

REAL ESTATE TRANSFER DISCLOSURE STATEMENT
(CALIFORNIA CIVIL CODE 1102, ET SEQ)
(C.A.R. Form TDS, Revised 10/01)

THIS DISCLOSURE STATEMENT CONCERNS THE REAL PROPERTY SITUATED IN THE CITY OF _____, COUNTY OF _____, STATE OF CALIFORNIA, DESCRIBED AS _____.
THIS STATEMENT IS A DISCLOSURE OF THE CONDITION OF THE ABOVE DESCRIBED PROPERTY IN COMPLIANCE WITH SECTION 1102 OF THE CIVIL CODE AS OF (date) _____. IT IS NOT A WARRANTY OF ANY KIND BY THE SELLER(S) OR ANY AGENT(S) REPRESENTING ANY PRINCIPAL(S) IN THIS TRANSACTION, AND IS NOT A SUBSTITUTE FOR ANY INSPECTIONS OR WARRANTIES THE PRINCIPAL(S) MAY WISH TO OBTAIN.

I. COORDINATION WITH OTHER DISCLOSURE FORMS

This Real Estate Transfer Disclosure Statement is made pursuant to Section 1102 of the Civil Code. Other statutes require disclosures, depending upon the details of the particular real estate transaction (for example: special study zone and purchase-money liens on residential property).

Substituted Disclosures: The following disclosures have or will be made in connection with this real estate transfer, and are intended to satisfy the disclosure obligations on this form, where the subject matter is the same:

☐ Inspection reports completed pursuant to the contract of sale or receipt for deposit.

☐ Additional inspection reports or disclosures: _____

II. SELLER'S INFORMATION

The Seller discloses the following information with the knowledge that even though this is not a warranty, prospective Buyers may rely on this information in deciding whether and on what terms to purchase the subject property. Seller hereby authorizes any agent(s) representing any principal(s) in this transaction to provide a copy of this statement to any person or entity in connection with any actual or anticipated sale of the property.

THE FOLLOWING ARE REPRESENTATIONS MADE BY THE SELLER(S) AND ARE NOT THE REPRESENTATIONS OF THE AGENT(S), IF ANY. THIS INFORMATION IS A DISCLOSURE AND IS NOT INTENDED TO BE PART OF ANY CONTRACT BETWEEN THE BUYER AND SELLER.

Seller ☐ is ☐ is not occupying the property.

A. The subject property has the items checked below (read across)

☐ Range	☐ Oven	☐ Microwave
☐ Dishwasher	☐ Trash Compactor	☐ Garbage Disposal
☐ Washer/Dryer Hookups		☐ Rain Gutters
☐ Burglar Alarms	☐ Smoke Detector(s)	☐ Fire Alarm
☐ T.V. Antenna	☐ Satellite Dish	☐ Intercom
☐ Central Heating	☐ Central Air Conditioning	☐ Evaporator Cooler(s)
☐ Wall/Window Air Conditioning	☐ Sprinklers	☐ Public Sewer System
☐ Septic Tank	☐ Sump Pump	☐ Water Softener
☐ Patio/Decking	☐ Built-in Barbecue	☐ Gazebo
☐ Sauna		
☐ Hot Tub ☐ Locking Safety Cover*	☐ Pool ☐ Child Resistant Barrier*	☐ Spa ☐ Locking Safety Cover*
☐ Security Gate(s)	☐ Automatic Garage Door Opener(s)*	☐ Number Remote Controls _____
Garage: ☐ Attached	☐ Not Attached	☐ Carport
Pool/Spa Heater: ☐ Gas	☐ Solar	☐ Electric
Water Heater: ☐ Gas	☐ Water Heater Anchored, Braced, or Strapped*	
Water Supply: ☐ City	☐ Well	☐ Private Utility or
Gas Supply: ☐ Utility	☐ Bottled	Other _____
☐ Window Screens	☐ Window Security Bars ☐ Quick Release Mechanism on Bedroom Windows*	

Exhaust Fan(s) in _____ 220 Volt Wiring in _____ Fireplace(s) in _____
☐ Gas Starter _____ ☐ Roof(s): Type: _____ Age: _____ (approx.)
☐ Other: _____
Are there, to the best of your (Seller's) knowledge, any of the above that are not in operating condition? ☐ Yes ☐ No. If yes, then describe. (Attach additional sheets if necessary): _____

(*see footnote on page 2)

TDS-11 REVISED 10/01 (PAGE 1 OF 3)   Print Date

Buyer and Seller acknowledge receipt of a copy of this page.

Buyer's Initials (_____)(_____)
Seller's Initials (_____)(_____)

EQUAL HOUSING OPPORTUNITY

Reviewed by _____
Broker or Designee _____ Date _____

REAL ESTATE TRANSFER DISCLOSURE STATEMENT (TDS-11 PAGE 1 OF 3)

Property Address: _____ Date: _____

B. Are you (Seller) aware of any significant defects/malfunctions in any of the following? ☐ Yes ☐ No. If yes, check appropriate space(s) below.

☐ Interior Walls ☐ Ceilings ☐ Floors ☐ Exterior Walls ☐ Insulation ☐ Roof(s ☐ Windows ☐ Doors ☐ Foundation ☐ Slab(s)
☐ Driveways ☐ Sidewalks ☐ Walls/Fences ☐ Electrical Systems ☐ Plumbing/Sewers/Septics ☐ Other Structural Components
(Describe:_____
_____)

If any of the above is checked, explain. (Attach additional sheets if necessary):_____
_____
_____

*This garage door opener or child resistant pool barrier may not be in compliance with the safety standards relating to automatic reversing devices as set forth in Chapter 12.5 (commencing with Section 19890) of Part 3 of Division 13 of, or with the pool safety standards of Article 2.5 (commencing with Section 115920) of Chapter 5 of Part 10 of Division 104 of, the Health and Safety Code. The water heater may not be anchored, braced, or strapped in accordance with Section 19211 of the Health and Safety Code. Window security bars may not have quick release mechanisms in compliance with the 1995 Edition of the California Building Standards Code.

C. Are you (Seller) aware of any of the following:

1. Substances, materials, or products which may be an environmental hazard such as, but not limited to, asbestos, formaldehyde, radon gas, lead-based paint, mold, fuel or chemical storage tanks, and contaminated soil or water on the subject property....☐ Yes ☐ No
2. Features of the property shared in common with adjoining landowners, such as walls, fences, and driveways, whose use or responsibility for maintenance may have an effect on the subject property ....☐ Yes ☐ No
3. Any encroachments, easements or similar matters that may affect your interest in the subject property ....☐ Yes ☐ No
4. Room additions, structural modifications, or other alterations or repairs made without necessary permits...........☐ Yes ☐ No
5. Room additions, structural modifications, or other alterations or repairs not in compliance with building codes ......☐ Yes ☐ No
6. Fill (compacted or otherwise) on the property or any portion thereof. ....☐ Yes ☐ No
7. Any settling from any cause, or slippage, sliding, or other soil problems. ....☐ Yes ☐ No
8. Flooding, drainage or grading problems. ....☐ Yes ☐ No
9. Major damage to the property or any of the structures from fire, earthquake, floods, or landslides...................☐ Yes ☐ No
10. Any zoning violations, nonconforming uses, violations of "setback" requirements. ....☐ Yes ☐ No
11. Neighborhood noise problems or other nuisances ....☐ Yes ☐ No
12. CC&R's or other deed restrictions or obligations . ...☐ Yes ☐ No
13. Homeowners' Association which has any authority over the subject property ....☐ Yes ☐ No
14. Any "common area" (facilities such as pools, tennis courts, walkways, or other areas co-owned in undivided interest with others)...☐ Yes ☐ No
15. Any notices of abatement or citations against the property ....☐ Yes ☐ No
16. Any lawsuits by or against the seller threatening to or affecting this real property, including any lawsuits alleging a defect or deficiency in this real property or "common areas" (facilities such as pools, tennis courts, walkways, or other areas, co-owned in undivided interest with others) ....☐ Yes ☐ No

If the answer to any of these is yes, explain. (Attach additional sheets if necessary): _____
_____
_____

Seller certifies that the information herein is true and correct to the best of the Seller's knowledge as of the date signed by the Seller.

Seller_____ Date _____

Seller_____ Date _____

Buyer and Seller acknowledge receipt of a copy of this page.
Buyer's Initials (_____)(_____)
Seller's Initials (_____)(_____)

EQUAL HOUSING OPPORTUNITY

Reviewed by _____
Broker or Designee _____ Date _____

REAL ESTATE TRANSFER DISCLOSURE STATEMENT (TDS-11 PAGE 2 OF 3)

Reprinted with permission, CALIFORNIA ASSOCIATION OF REALTORS®. Endorsement not implied.

Agency Duties and Liabilities

Property Address: _____ Date: _____

III. AGENT'S INSPECTION DISCLOSURE
(To be completed only if the Seller is represented by an agent in this transaction.)

THE UNDERSIGNED, BASED ON THE ABOVE INQUIRY OF THE SELLER(S) AS TO THE CONDITION OF THE PROPERTY AND BASED ON A REASONABLY COMPETENT AND DILIGENT VISUAL INSPECTION OF THE ACCESSIBLE AREAS OF THE PROPERTY IN CONJUNCTION WITH THAT INQUIRY, STATES THE FOLLOWING:

☐ Agent notes no items for disclosure.
☐ Agent notes the following items: _____
_____
_____
_____

Agent (Broker Representing Seller) _____ By _____ Date _____
(Please Print) (Associate-License or Broker Signature)

IV. AGENT'S INSPECTION DISCLOSURE
(To be completed only if the agent who has obtained the offer is other than the agent above.)

THE UNDERSIGNED, BASED ON A REASONABLY COMPETENT AND DILIGENT VISUAL INSPECTION OF THE ACCESSIBLE AREAS OF THE PROPERTY, STATES THE FOLLOWING:

☐ Agent notes no items for disclosure.
☐ Agent notes the following items: _____
_____
_____

Agent (Broker Obtaining the Offer) _____ By _____ Date _____
(Please Print) (Associate-License or Broker Signature)

V. BUYER(S) AND SELLER(S) MAY WISH TO OBTAIN PROFESSIONAL ADVICE AND/OR INSPECTIONS OF THE PROPERTY AND TO PROVIDE FOR APPROPRIATE PROVISIONS IN A CONTRACT BETWEEN BUYER AND SELLER(S) WITH RESPECT TO ANY ADVICE/INSPECTIONS/DEFECTS.

I/WE ACKNOWLEDGE RECEIPT OF A COPY OF THIS STATEMENT.

Seller _____ Date _____ Buyer _____ Date _____

Seller _____ Date _____ Buyer _____ Date _____

Agent (Broker Representing Seller) _____ By _____ Date _____
(Associate-License or Broker Signature)

Agent (Broker Obtaining the Offer) _____ By _____ Date _____
(Associate-License or Broker Signature)

SECTION 1102.3 OF THE CIVIL CODE PROVIDES A BUYER WITH THE RIGHT TO RESCIND A PURCHASE CONTRACT FOR AT LEAST THREE DAYS AFTER THE DELIVERY OF THIS DISCLOSURE IF DELIVERY OCCURS AFTER THE SIGNING OF AN OFFER TO PURCHASE. IF YOU WISH TO RESCIND THE CONTRACT, YOU MUST ACT WITHIN THE PRESCRIBED PERIOD.

A REAL ESTATE BROKER IS QUALIFIED TO ADVISE ON REAL ESTATE. IF YOU DESIRE LEGAL ADVICE, CONSULT YOUR ATTORNEY.

Reviewed by
Broker or Designee _____ Date _____

TDS-11 REVISED 10/01 (PAGE 3 OF 3)   Print Date

REAL ESTATE TRANSFER DISCLOSURE STATEMENT (TDS-11 PAGE 3 OF 3)

Reprinted with permission, CALIFORNIA ASSOCIATION OF REALTORS®. Endorsement not implied.

This Real Estate Transfer Disclosure Statement must be given to the buyer as soon as practicable before the transfer of title. If the buyer doesn't receive a copy until after making an offer to purchase, he or she has a chance to terminate the offer. The seller or seller's agent must get written notice of the termination within three days after the buyer received the disclosure statement. (If the disclosure statement was mailed rather than presented in person, the buyer has five days from the date of mailing to terminate the offer.)

Case Example: Sweat purchased the Hollister's house which was listed for sale with a Century 21 agency in Poway. The real estate transfer disclosure statement noted that the house is located in a flood plain. Sweat sued the Hollisters and their agents because the city of Poway has an ordinance which prevents altering or enlarging in a flood plain if it is destroyed by fire or other calamity and this ordinance was not disclosed. The Court of Appeal held that the factual matter leading to the alleged defect in the house—that it was in a flood plain—was revealed to Sweat. It also held that selling brokers have neither a common law nor a statutory duty to disclose the legal ramifications of facts affecting the value of the property. The existence and effect of city ordinances regulating rebuilding or improvement of a house in a flood plain constituted information that was as readily available to Sweat as to Hollister. *Sweat v. Hollister*, 37 Cal App. 4th 603, 43 Cal. Rptr. 2d 399 (1995).

Although the disclosure statement includes very specific lists of problems, the lists aren't necessarily complete. The old rule still stands: if the seller or agent is aware of anything that materially affects the value or desirability of the property, it must be disclosed to the buyer. One final thing, it is very important that the buyer realize that this statutory form is not a warranty by the seller nor is it intended to be part of the sales contract. Additionally, it can not be waived by the buyer.

The duty of care defined in the *Easton v. Strassburger* case was codified in Civil Code section 2079. Any cause of action alleging wrongful conduct by a broker/salesperson stemming from the duties imposed by that statute is subject to a two-year statute of limitations. *Loken v. Century 21-Award Properties*, 36 Cal. App. 4th 263, 274, 42 Cal. Rptr. 2d 683, 687 (App. 4 Dist. 1995).

AGENT'S DUTIES TO BUYERS

◆ good faith and fair dealing,
◆ no misrepresentation,
◆ disclosure of known material information, and
◆ residential property: inspection and real estate disclosure statement

Case Example: The buyer's agent's duty of disclosure may be more expansive than the seller's broker's inspection duty under Civil Code § 2079. A buyer's agent has "a fiduciary duty to ...[advise] the client that he is merely passing on information received from the seller without verifying its accuracy." If he makes a statement not knowing whether it is true, the statement is false. *Field v. Century 21 Klowden Forness Realty*, 63, 63 Cal. AppAth 18, 73 Cal. Rptr.2d 784 (App.4 Dist. 1998).

Agency Duties and Liabilities

Case Example: California imposes very specific disclosures on sellers of residential property in the Transfer Disclosure Statement (TDS). If the seller or his/her agent commits fraud by making intentional or negligent misrepresentations to the buyer in the TDS, the seller's disclosure duty is violated.

A seller may be liable to remote purchasers for fraudulent representations. The seller sold the property to a relocation company and knew the company would attempt immediately resell it. The seller failed to disclose a known neighborhood noise problem to the relocation company, a misrepresentation supported a fraud cause of action by the relocation company's buyer against the seller. The Court of Appeal allowed buyer to prove there was a noisy neighbor. *Shapiro v. Sutherland*, 64 Cal. App. 4th 1534, 76 Cal. Rptr. 2d 101, 107-108 (App. 2 Dist. 1998).

BUYER'S DUTY TO USE REASONABLE CARE

The agent's duty of **inspection** and **disclosure** does not relieve the buyer of the duty to exercise reasonable care to protect himself or herself, including discovery of facts known to or within the diligent attention and observation of the buyer (Civil Code § 2079.5). A buyer is also held to be aware of obvious and patent conditions.

In addition, the seller's agent may provide the buyer with a Buyer's Inspection Advisory form (See next two pages) as a substituted disclosure under Item I of the Transfer Disclosure Statement. The form clearly states in bold print that:

"YOU ARE STRONGLY ADVISED TO INVESTIGATE THE CONDITION AND SUITABILITY OF ALL ASPECTS OF THE PROPERTY. IF YOU DO NOT DO SO, YOU ARE ACTING AGAINST THE ADVICE OF BROKERS."

FRAUD

Failing to disclose information that you're required to disclose can be a form of fraud. Fraud can also take the form of actively concealing information, or making false or misleading statements (**misrepresentation**).

Actual Fraud

In California, fraud is classified as actual or constructive. **Actual fraud** includes intentional misrepresentation, concealment, and deliberate deception. It also includes negligent misrepresentation: making a false assertion without reasonable grounds for believing that it's true—even if the speaker does in fact believe that it's true. The falsehood is the result of carelessness or negligence, rather than an intention to deceive.

To sue for actual fraud, the plaintiff generally must be able to prove five elements:

1. A person makes a false statement of a material fact or fails to disclose a material fact that he or she has a legal duty to disclose.
2. In regard to a misrepresentation, the person making the statement knows (intentional) or should know that it is false (negligent).
3. Statement or concealment made with intent of inducing entry into a transaction.
4. The other person relies on the statement or lack of knowledge of the concealed information and is induced to enter the transaction.
5. The other person is harmed as a result of entering the transaction.

**CALIFORNIA
ASSOCIATION
OF REALTORS®**

BUYER'S INSPECTION ADVISORY

Property Address: _____ ("Property").

A. IMPORTANCE OF PROPERTY INSPECTION: The physical condition of the land and improvements being purchased is not guaranteed by either Seller or Brokers. For this reason, you should conduct thorough inspections of the Property personally and with professionals who should provide written reports of their inspections. A general physical inspection typically does not cover all aspects of the Property nor items affecting the Property that are not physically located on the Property. If the professionals recommend further investigation, tests or inspections, including a recommendation by a pest control operator to inspect inaccessible areas of the Property, you should contact qualified experts to conduct such additional investigations, tests or inspections.

B. BUYER RIGHTS AND DUTIES: You have an affirmative duty to exercise reasonable care to protect yourself, including discovery of the legal, practical and technical implications of disclosed facts, and the investigation and verification of information and facts that you know or are within your diligent attention and observation. The purchase agreement gives you the right to inspect the Property. If you exercise these rights, and you should, you must do so in accordance with the terms of the Agreement. This is the best way for you to protect yourself. It is extremely important for you to read all written reports provided by professionals and to discuss the results of inspections with the professional who conducted the inspection. You have the right to request that Seller make Repairs, corrections or take other action based upon items discovered in your inspections or disclosed by Seller. If Seller is unwilling or unable to satisfy your requests, and you do not want to purchase the Property in its disclosed and discovered condition, you have the right to cancel the Agreement. If you do not timely and properly cancel the Agreement and if you do not perform on the contract because of the condition of the Property, you may be in breach of contract.

C. SELLER RIGHTS AND DUTIES: Seller is required to disclose to you all material facts known to him/her that affect the value or desirability of the Property. However, Seller may not be aware of some Property defects or conditions. Seller does not have an obligation to inspect the Property for your benefit nor is Seller obligated to repair, correct or otherwise cure known defects that are disclosed to you or previously unknown defects that are discovered by you or your inspectors during escrow. The purchase agreement obligates Seller to make the Property available to you for inspections.

D. BROKER OBLIGATIONS: Brokers do not have expertise and therefore cannot advise you on many items, such as soil stability, geologic conditions, hazardous substances, structural conditions of the foundation or other improvements, or the condition of the roof, heating, air conditioning, plumbing, electrical, sewer, septic, waste disposal, or other system. The only way to accurately determine the condition of the Property is through an inspection by an appropriate professional selected by you. If Broker gives you referrals to such professionals, Broker does not guarantee their performance. You may select any professional of your choosing. In sales involving residential dwellings with no more than four units, Brokers have a duty to make a diligent visual inspection of the accessible areas of the Property, and to disclose the results of that inspection. However, as some Property defects or conditions may not be discoverable from a visual inspection, it is possible Brokers are not aware of them. If you have entered into a written agreement with a Broker, the specific terms of that agreement will determine the nature and extent of that Broker's duty to you. **YOU ARE STRONGLY ADVISED TO INVESTIGATE THE CONDITION AND SUITABILITY OF ALL ASPECTS OF THE PROPERTY. IF YOU DO NOT DO SO, YOU ARE ACTING AGAINST THE ADVICE OF BROKERS.**

E. YOU ARE ADVISED TO CONDUCT INSPECTIONS OF THE ENTIRE PROPERTY, INCLUDING, BUT NOT LIMITED TO THE FOLLOWING:

1. **GENERAL CONDITION OF THE PROPERTY, ITS SYSTEMS AND COMPONENTS:** Foundation, roof, plumbing, heating, air conditioning, electrical, mechanical, security, pool/spa, and other structural and non-structural systems and components, fixtures, built-in appliances, any personal property included in the sale, and energy efficiency of the Property. (Structural engineers are best suited to determine possible design or construction defects, and whether improvements are structurally sound.)

2. **SQUARE FOOTAGE, AGE, BOUNDARIES:** Square footage, room dimensions, lot size, age of improvements, and boundaries. Any numerical statements regarding these items are APPROXIMATIONS ONLY, and have not been and cannot be verified by Brokers. Fences, hedges, walls, retaining walls, and other natural or constructed barriers or markers do not necessarily identify true Property boundaries. (Professionals such as appraisers, architects, surveyors, or civil engineers are best suited to determine square footage, dimensions and boundaries of the Property.)

3. **PEST CONTROL:** Presence of, or conditions likely to lead to the presence of wood destroying pests and organisms and other infestation or infection. (A registered structural pest control company is best suited to perform these inspections.)

Buyer acknowledges receipt of a copy of this page.

Buyer's Initials (_____)(_____)

Reviewed by _____

Broker or Designee _____ Date _____

EQUAL HOUSING
OPPORTUNITY

BUYER'S INSPECTION ADVISORY (BIA-11 PAGE 1 OF 2)

Agency Duties and Liabilities

Property Address: _____ Date: _____

4. **SOIL STABILITY:** Existence of fill or compacted soil, expansive or contracting soil, susceptibility to slippage, settling or movement, and the adequacy of drainage. (Geotechnical engineers are best suited to determine such conditions, causes, and remedies.)

5. **ROOF:** Present condition, age, leaks, and remaining useful life. (Roofing contractors are best suited to determine these conditions.)

6. **POOL/SPA:** Cracks, leaks or operational problems. (Pool contractors are best suited to determine these conditions.)

7. **WASTE DISPOSAL:** Type, size, adequacy, capacity and condition of sewer and septic systems and components, connection to sewer, and applicable fees.

8. **WATER AND UTILITIES; WELL SYSTEMS AND COMPONENTS:** Water and utility availability, use restrictions, and costs. Water quality, adequacy, condition, and performance of well systems and components.

9. **ENVIRONMENTAL HAZARDS:** Potential environmental hazards, including asbestos, lead-based paint and other lead contamination, radon, methane, other gases, fuel, oil or chemical storage tanks, contaminated soil or water, hazardous waste, waste disposal sites, electromagnetic fields, nuclear sources, and other substances, including mold (airborne, toxic or otherwise), fungus or similar contaminant, materials, products, or conditions. (Read the booklets "Environmental Hazards: A Guide for Homeowners and Buyers," "Protect Your Family From Lead in Your Home," or consult an appropriate professional.)

10. **EARTHQUAKE AND FLOOD; HAZARD AND OTHER INSURANCE:** Susceptibility of the Property to earthquake/seismic hazards and propensity of the Property to flood. These and other conditions including age of Property may affect the availability and need for certain types of insurance. Since the time it may take to obtain certain types of insurance may vary, Buyer should not wait to explore these options. (An Insurance agent, Geologist, or Geotechnical Engineer is best suited to provide information on these conditions.)

11. **BUILDING PERMITS, ZONING AND GOVERNMENTAL REQUIREMENTS:** Permits, inspections, certificates, zoning, other governmental limitations, restrictions, and requirements affecting the current or future use of the Property, its development or size. (Such information is available through appropriate governmental agencies and private information providers. Brokers are not qualified to review, or interpret any such information.)

12. **RENTAL PROPERTY RESTRICTIONS:** Some cities and counties impose restrictions that may limit the rent, the maximum number of occupants, and the right to terminate a tenancy. Deadbolt or other locks and security systems for doors and windows, including window bars, should be examined to determine whether they satisfy legal requirements. (Local government agencies can provide information about these restrictions and other requirements.)

13. **SECURITY AND SAFETY:** State and local Law may require the installation of barriers, access alarms, self-latching mechanisms and/or other measures to decrease the risk to children and other persons of existing swimming pools and hot tubs, as well as various fire safety and other measures concerning other features of the Property. Compliance requirements differ from city to city and county to county. Unless specifically agreed, the Property will not be in compliance with these requirements. (Local government agencies can provide information about these restrictions and other requirements.)

14. **NEIGHBORHOOD, AREA, SUBDIVISION CONDITIONS; PERSONAL FACTORS:** Neighborhood or area conditions, including schools, proximity and adequacy of law enforcement, crime statistics, the proximity of registered felons or offenders, fire protection, other governmental services, availability, adequacy and cost of any speed wired, wireless internet connections or other telecommunications or other technology services and installations, proximity to commercial, industrial or agricultural activities, existing and proposed transportation, construction and development that may affect noise, view, or traffic, airport noise, noise or odor from any source, wild and domestic animals, other nuisances, hazards, or circumstances, protected species, wetland properties, historic or other governmentally protected sites or improvements, cemeteries, facilities and condition of common areas of common interest subdivisions, and possible lack of compliance with any governing documents or Homeowners' Association requirements, conditions and influences of significance to certain cultures and/or religions, and personal needs, requirements and preferences of Buyer.

> **Buyer acknowledges and agrees that Brokers: (a) do not guarantee the condition of the Property; (b) shall not be responsible for defects that are not known to Broker(s) or are not visually observable in reasonably and normally accessible areas of the Property; (c) have not verified square footage, representations made by others, or other information contained in inspection reports, Multiple Listing Service, advertisements, flyers, or other promotional material, unless otherwise agreed in writing; (d) do not guarantee the performance of others who have provided services or products to Buyer or Seller; (e) do not guarantee the adequacy or completeness of Repairs made by Seller or others; (f) cannot identify Property boundary lines; and (g) do not decide what price a buyer should pay or a seller should accept. Buyer agrees to seek desired assistance from appropriate professionals.**

By signing below, Buyer acknowledges receipt of a Copy of this document. Buyer is encouraged to read it carefully.

_____ _____   _____ _____
Buyer Signature   Date   Buyer Signature   Date

Published and Distributed by:
REAL ESTATE BUSINESS SERVICES, INC.
a subsidiary of the CALIFORNIA ASSOCIATION OF REALTORS®
525 South Virgil Avenue, Los Angeles, California 90020

Reviewed by _____
Broker or Designee _____ Date _____

REVISION DATE 10/2000   Print Date
BIA-11 (PAGE 2 OF 2)

BUYER'S INSPECTION ADVISORY (BIA-11 PAGE 2 OF 2)

Reprinted with permission, CALIFORNIA ASSOCIATION OF REALTORS®. Endorsement not implied.

Constructive Fraud

Constructive fraud consists of a breach of duty that misleads the person the duty was owed to, without an intention to deceive. If a seller or a real estate agent is aware of a hidden problem with the property and forgets to tell the buyer about it, the seller or agent may have committed constructive fraud.

Case Example: The Salahutdins retained Seigal, a real estate agent with Coldwell Banker, to locate property which could be subdivided into two lots. Seigal told them that the property had to be at least one acre and found a property listed as "1 acre+". They bought the property and discovered several years later that it was less than an acre and could not be subdivided. The Salahutdins sued the agent's employer and the Court of Appeal upheld the trial courts finding that the agent breached his fiduciary duty by not telling them he had not checked the property's size knowing it was very important to them. Salahutdins were awarded the difference between the fair market value of similar property that could be subdivided and the value of their property. The values were determined at the date the fraud was discovered. *Salahutdin v. Valley of Cal. Inc.*, 24 Cal. App. 4th 555, 29 Cal. Rptr. 2d 463 (1994).

FRAUD

◆ failure to disclose
◆ active concealment
◆ false statements
◆ misleading statements or actions

Opinion, Predictions, and Puffing

Generally, a seller or agent can't be sued for misrepresentation if his or her statements were merely opinions, predictions, or puffing.

◆ Opinion: "I think this is an excellent buy."
◆ Prediction: "That roof should last for another seven years."
◆ Puffing: "This is a dream house; it has an incredible view."

To prove fraud based on a misrepresentation, it's necessary to show that you relied on the misrepresentation. Because of their nonfactual or exaggerated nature, opinions, predictions, and puffing are not considered the type of statements a reasonable person would rely on in making a decision to buy property.

Example: The broker tells a buyer: "This is a great little house, you'll be very happy here." After purchasing the house, the buyer is not happy. He discovers several problems and decides it is not a great little house at all.

Even if it is in fact not a great house, the broker is not liable for his statement. It was just puffing—an exaggeration made to induce the purchaser to buy, but not relating any specific material fact.

Agency Duties and Liabilities

However, an agent should be very cautious about stating unsubstantiated opinions or making predictions. If it is considered a professional or expert opinion, the agent may be held liable. A court may allow recovery based on opinions given by:

◆ an expert hired to give advice,
◆ a person who has superior knowledge and is acting in a fiduciary relationship, or
◆ someone who states an opinion that he or she does not actually hold.

> **Case Example:** The real estate agents told the buyers that the condominium units were "luxurious" and had "outstanding investment potential." In fact, the agent knew the construction was substandard and violated the minimum requirements of the building code.
>
> The buyers sued the agents (along with the architects and developers). The court held that if it were shown that the agents could not reasonably have believed the opinions they expressed, they would be liable for fraud. *Cooper v. Jevne*, 56 Cal. App. 3d 860, 128 Cal. Rptr. 724 (1976).

"As is" Clause

An "as is" clause in a purchase agreement usually states that the buyer has inspected the property and agrees to accept it "as is"—in its current condition. There may be additional statements to the effect that the seller makes no warranties concerning the condition of the property. When there is an "as is" clause, the buyer takes the property subject to any defects that he or she could discover through a reasonably thorough visual inspection. This would include broken windows, cracks in walls, and other obvious flaws such as peeling paint.

However, an "as is" clause cannot relieve a seller or agent from liability for fraud. If there are hidden defects in the property that the seller and agent had a duty to disclose, a court will not enforce the "as is" clause.

> **Case Example:** Hays listed and sold her home, built in 1947, through Harry Kraft at Century 21 Great Western Realty, to Wilson through Wilson's real estate agent. The home was in poor condition and Wilson, a contractor, noticed the sloping floors and other problems stated on the disclosure statement. The house was sold AS IS with the buyer to pay for all repairs. Wilson did the termite work before escrow closed. Several months after close of escrow, Wilson learned of foundation problems from a neighbor. Wilson x-rayed the concrete floors and discovered it lacked steel reinforcement and J bolts holding the house on the foundation. Wilson sued Kraft and Century 21 for negligence and fraud regarding the disclosure statement.
>
> The Court of Appeal held that Kraft made a reasonable inspection of the property as required and was not negligent in failing to discover the defects which would take an x-ray machine and a steel prybar. The agent is not required to go beyond a reasonable visual inspection to interview neighbors or x-ray floors. *Wilson v. Century 21 Great Western Realty*, 15 Cal. App. 4th 298, 18 Cal. Rptr. 2d 779 (1993).

Penalties for Breach of Duty

When a real estate agent breaches a duty to the principal or to a third party, there are several possible consequences. These include expulsion from professional associations, disciplinary action by the Department of Real Estate, and a civil lawsuit brought by the injured party. In particularly serious cases, a breach of duty can give rise to criminal charges against the agent.

ACTION BY PROFESSIONAL ASSOCIATIONS

A **code of ethics** is a system of moral standards and rules of conduct. Many professional organizations for real estate brokers and salespersons (like NAHREP and NAREB) have adopted a code of ethics to set standards for members' conduct toward the public, clients, and other members of the profession.

The most widely recognized code is the National Association of REALTORS® Code of Ethics. The NAR's Code of Ethics is not legally binding, but all NAR members agree to follow it. A member who violates the code may be expelled from the organization. That kind of censure can be professionally disastrous, especially in a small community. **In addition, every four years REALTORS® are required to take 2fi hours of ethical training.**

In deciding cases involving real estate agents, judges sometimes refer to the NAR's Code of Ethics as evidence of prevailing industry standards for ethical and competent agents. A judge may use the code as a basis for finding negligence or incompetence on the part of an agent.

CIVIL LAWSUITS

As the case examples throughout this chapter show, a real estate agent who breaches a duty may be sued by a client or customer. These lawsuits are tort suits, since breach of a legal duty is a tort. If the plaintiff is able to prove that he or she suffered harm as the result of the breach of duty, the agent will be held liable.

Compensatory (Actual) Damages

An agent who is found liable may be required to pay **compensatory (actual) damages**, compensating the injured party for any monetary loss resulting from the breach of duty. When the plaintiff is a client, the agent may have to pay back the commission received in the transaction. In a case involving secret profits, the court may order the agent to give up the profits he or she earned unjustly.

Punitive (Exemplary) Damages

In addition to compensatory damages, a court may award **punitive damages** in some tort suits, such as fraud. While compensatory damages are intended to compensate the victim, punitive damages are intended to punish the wrongdoer and deter others from similar acts. Generally, punitive damages are only added to a compensatory damages award when the harmful act was intentional and malicious. (**Punitive damages** are also called **exemplary damages**.)

Real Estate Recovery Account

If a client or customer is awarded damages against a real estate agent, but is unable to collect the judgment from the agent, he or she may be entitled to payment out of the **Real Estate Recovery Account**. The judgment must be based on the agent's intentional fraud, misrepresentation, or deceit, or conversion of trust funds. The Recovery Account is administered by the Department of Real Estate and funded by fees charged to all agents at the time of licensing or license renewal. Payment to judgment creditors out of the Recovery Account is limited to $20,000 for liability arising from any one transaction, and to $100,000 for the misconduct of any one agent.

Case Example: Real estate agent Donald Smith had property for sale. Real estate agent Laura Onate had four offers and deposits from her clients which she presented to Smith. Smith cashed the checks and took the deposits totaling $14,000. Onate did not deposit the checks in her trust account, did not tell her clients the checks would be held by the seller, or check out whether Smith was honest. Onate paid her clients and sued Smith, recovering a judgment for $14,000 and $11,000 punitive damages. Unable to collect it, Onate filed a claim on the Real Estate Recovery Fund alleging she was subrogated to the rights of her clients. Her claim was denied because she was not an "aggrieved" person. The Court of Appeal held that the Fund is to protect consumers from fraud by agents, not agents protected from other agent's fraud. *Real Estate Commissioner v. Onate*, 2 Cal. App. 4th 549, 3 Cal. Rptr. 2d 3 (1992).

CRIMINAL PROSECUTION

A serious and intentional breach of duty may not only lead to civil liability, it may also be a crime. An agent who willfully violates or knowingly participates in a violation of the Real Estate Law is guilty of a misdemeanor. He or she may be fined up to $10,000, imprisoned for up to six months, or both. But the agent's conduct may also be the basis for a felony conviction, with more severe penalties.

ACTION BY THE REAL ESTATE COMMISSIONER

A real estate agent's breach of duty is often a violation of the Real Estate Law. An agent who violates the Real Estate Law is subject to disciplinary action by the Commissioner of Real Estate, whether or not a client or customer sues the agent. The Real Estate Law establishes specific grounds for disciplinary action, including:

 www.dre.ca.gov/regs_sub.htm
(Regulations of the Real Estate Commissioner - Title 10)

The primary grounds for professional discipline set forth in Business and Professions Code Sections 10176 and 10177 relate to fraud and other forms of dishonest dealing.

The Commissioner encourages all agents to act lawfully, but failure to do so will make an agent subject to disciplinary action.

COMMON REAL ESTATE LAW VIOLATIONS
(Sections 10176 and 10177)

Most of the common Real Estate Law violations are found in Section 10176 and Section 10177 of the Business and Professions Code. **Section 10176** is the legal guideline for the licensee engaged in the practice and performance of any of the acts within the scope of the Real Estate Law. **Section 10177** of the Real Estate Law applies to situations where the person involved was not necessarily acting as an agent or as a licensee.

Section 10176

Section 10176 of the Real Estate Law sets forth violations by those who have real estate licenses and are acting within the scope of those licenses.

Section 10177

Section 10177 applies to situations where the affected party was not necessarily acting as an agent or as a real estate licensee.

The vast majority of brokers and salespeople are honest and perform their services in a straightforward manner. Occasionally a section of the Real Estate Law may be violated inadvertently and without intent. In such cases the commissioner would most likely consider suspension of the real estate license. On the other hand, a flagrant violation would most likely cause a revocation of the license.

Performing Brokerage Activities

Section 10176
Business and Professions Code Violations

Misrepresentation—Section 10176(a)
The licensee must disclose to his principal all material facts that the principal should know. Failure to do so is cause for disciplinary action. A great majority of the complaints received by the commissioner allege misrepresentation on the part of the broker or his or her salespeople.

False Promise—Section 10176(b)
A false promise is a false statement about what the promisor is going to do in the future. Many times a false promise is proved by showing that the promise was impossible to perform, and that the person making the promise knew it was impossible.

Misrepresentation by Agents—Section 10176(c)
This section gives the commissioner the right to discipline a licensee for a continued and flagrant course of misrepresentation or making of false promises through real estate agents or salespeople.

Divided Agency—Section 10176(d)
This section requires a licensee to inform all his or her principals if he or she is acting as agent for more than one party in a transaction.

Commingling—Section 10176(e)
Commingling takes place when a broker has mixed the funds of his or her principals with his or her own money. A broker should keep all funds separate.

Definite Termination Date—Section 10176(f)
A specified termination date for all exclusive listings must be stated in writing.

Secret Profit—Section 10176(g)
Secret profit cases usually arise when the broker makes a low offer, usually through a "dummy" purchaser, when he or she already has a higher offer from another buyer. The difference is the secret profit.

Listing Option—Section 10176(h)
This section requires a licensee, when he or she has used a form which is both an option and a listing, to obtain the written consent of his or her principal approving the amount of such profit before he or she may exercise the option. This does not apply where a licensee is using an option only.

Dishonest Dealing—Section 10176(i)
Dishonest dealing is a catch-all section used when the acts of the person required a license but he or she did not have a license.

Signatures of Prospective Purchasers—Section 10176(j)
Brokers must obtain a written (business opportunities) authorization to sell from an owner before securing the signature of a prospective purchaser to the agreement. This section strikes at what was once a common practice in some areas, in the sale of business opportunities, where the prospective purchaser was forced to deal with the broker who furnished him or her with the listing.

Other Activities

Section 10177
Business and Professions Code Violations

Obtaining License by Fraud—Section 10177(a)
This section gives the Commissioner the power to take action against a licensee for misstatements of fact in an application for a license and in those instances where licenses have been procured by fraud, misrepresentation or deceit.

Convictions—Section 10177(b)
Permits proceedings against a licensee after a criminal conviction (a felony or a misdemeanor) which involves moral turpitude (contrary to justice, honesty, modesty, or good morals).

False Advertising—Section 10177(c)
This section makes licensees who are parties to false advertising subject to disciplinary action. The ban extends to subdivision sales as well as general property sales.

Violations of Other Sections—Sections 10177(d)
This section gives the Department authority to proceed against the licensee for violation of any section of the Real Estate Law, the regulations of the commissioner, and the subdivision laws.

Misuse of Trade Name—Section 10177(e)
Only active members of the national association or local associations of real estate boards are permitted to use the term "Realtor®." No advertisement as a "Realtor®." can be used without proper entitlement.

Conduct Warranting Denial—Section 10177(f)
A requirement for a license is that the applicant be honest, truthful and of good reputation. (almost any act involving crime or dishonesty will fall within it.)

Negligence or Incompetence—Section 10177(g)
Demonstrated negligence or incompetence, while acting as a licensee, is just cause for disciplinary action. The department proceeds in those cases where the licensee is so careless or unqualified that to allow him or her to handle a transaction would endanger the interests of his or her clients or customers.

Supervision of Salespeople—Section 10177(h)
A broker must exercise reasonable supervision of his or her salespeople's activities.

Violating Government Trust—Section 10177(i)
Prescribes disciplinary liability for using government employment to violate the confidential nature of records thereby made available.

Other Dishonest Conduct—Section 10177(j)
Specifies that any other conduct which constitutes fraud or dishonest dealings may subject the one so involved to license suspension or revocation.

Restricted License Violation—Section 10177(k)
Makes violation of the terms, conditions, restrictions and limitations contained in any order granting a restricted license grounds for disciplinary action.

Inducement of Panic Selling—Section 10177(l)
It is a cause for disciplinary action to solicit or induce the sale, lease, or the listing for sale or lease, of residential property on the grounds of loss of value because of entry into the neighborhood of a person or persons of another race, color, religion, ancestry or national origin.

Violation of Franchise Investment Law—Section 10177(m)
Violates the Franchise Investment Law or regulations of the Corporations Commissioner.

Violation of Securities Law—Section 10177(n)
Violates any of the provisions of the Corporations Code or any regulations of the Commissioner of Corporations relating to securities as specified.

Possible Consequences of a Real Estate Agent's Dishonesty, Disloyalty, Negligence, or Incompetence

Action by professional associations
- public censure
- expulsion

Civil lawsuit
- compensatory damages
- punitive damages

Criminal prosecution
- fines
- prison sentences

Disciplinary action by the Real Estate Commissioner
- license suspension or revocation
- fines
- desist and refrain order, injunction

Disciplinary Action by Commissioner

When an agent violates the Real Estate Law, the Commissioner may either suspend or revoke the agent's license, depending on the severity of the violation. It is also within the Commissioner's discretion to allow the agent to pay a fine instead of having his or her license suspended. The fine can be up to $250 for each day of suspension avoided, but the total can't exceed $10,000.

Disciplinary Procedure

Upon receiving a written complaint, the Commissioner must investigate the activities of a licensee. The Commissioner may also begin an investigation even if no complaint has been filed. If the investigation indicates that the licensee may have violated the Real Estate Law, an **accusation** (a written statement of the charges) must be filed, and a copy of the accusation must be served on the licensee. To request a formal hearing, the licensee must file a **notice of defense** within 15 days. The DRE will schedule a hearing and send the licensee a **notice of hearing** at least ten days before the scheduled date.

The licensee (called the **respondent** in a disciplinary proceeding) may appear at the hearing with or without a lawyer. If the respondent doesn't show up, the hearing will still take place. Witnesses testify under oath at the hearing, just as in a trial. The respondent (or the respondent's lawyer) may call and cross-examine witnesses. A hearing officer hears the case.

The hearing officer writes a proposed decision, which is submitted to the Commissioner for approval. The Commissioner rejects, accepts, or modifies the hearing officer's proposal, and issues a formal decision. If the charges against the respondent have been proven, his or her license may be suspended or revoked.

A respondent can appeal the Commissioner's decision to superior court. The respondent's license may remain in effect while the matter is under appeal. The appeal usually must be filed no later than 60 days after the Commissioner's decision was issued.

Summary Suspension

Generally, a real estate license cannot be suspended or revoked until a hearing has been held, so that the licensee has a chance to defend himself or herself. But there are a few exceptions. The main exception is if the license was obtained through fraud or misrepresentation (for example, false statements on the license application). In that case, during the first 90 days after the license was issued, the Commissioner may suspend it without a hearing.

After a summary suspension, however, the respondent may request a hearing. The order of suspension will be set aside within 30 days after the hearing, unless the Commissioner issues a formal decision revoking the fraudulently obtained license before that 30-day period expires.

Preventing Violations

If the Commissioner has evidence that a person is about to violate the Real Estate Law or is engaged in an ongoing violation, a **desist and refrain order** may be issued. The respondent is required to stop the activities in question immediately. He or she may

request a hearing. If the respondent claims that the Commissioner's order substantially interferes with his or her real estate business, the order will be rescinded unless the Commissioner obtains an injunction.

To obtain an injunction, the Commissioner must file a lawsuit in superior court. If the Commissioner proves that the respondent's activities violate the Real Estate Law, the court will enjoin the respondent from continuing those activities. If the violation jeopardizes trust funds, the court may appoint a receiver to manage the funds.

Reinstatement

When a license has been suspended or revoked, reinstatement is handled on an individual, case-by-case basis. A license suspension is temporary, and the period of suspension is specified (90 days, for example). But the license is not automatically reinstated after the suspension period ends. The respondent must apply for reinstatement. (If the license was suspended for more than one year, the respondent may apply for reinstatement after one year has passed, rather than waiting until the suspension period ends.)

Although in theory revocation is permanent (no period is specified), reinstatement is granted in some cases. The respondent may apply for reinstatement one year after the license was revoked.

The Commissioner may require an applicant for reinstatement to retake the license examination. If an applicant whose license was revoked is not ordered to retake the exam, the applicant must show that he or she has complied with the Real Estate Law's continuing education requirements.

In some cases, the Commissioner will issue the reinstated licensee a **restricted license**. The term of the license may be limited, and it may specify that the agent is only allowed to work for a particular broker. The Commissioner may also place other restrictions on the license, and require the agent to file surety bonds. An agent with a restricted license doesn't have an automatic right to renewal—that's up to the Commissioner. And a restricted license may be suspended without a hearing.

Most real estate brokers and agents are honest and hard working, and very few intentionally commit fraud. But only the very lucky get through a long career without some problems arising. Careless mistakes or misunderstandings can have drastic consequences.

The best way to avoid problems is to know the law, keep up to date on changes in the law, communicate with your clients and customers, and be careful. Competent, diligent, ethical work is the surest road to success.

National Real Estate Organizations

NAR. The National Association of REALTORS® is the national trade association for all the state associations and local boards of REALTORS® in the U.S. **www.realtor.com**

NAREB. The National Association of Real Estate Brokers, or "Realtist," is an organization of brokers with a predominance of African-American members. **www.nareb.org/index.htm**

NAHREP. The National Association of Hispanic Real Estate Professionals is a non-profit trade association made up primarily of Hispanic members. **www.nahrep.com**

Agency Duties and Liabilities

CHAPTER SUMMARY

1. The agency disclosure law requires an agent in a residential transaction to have both the buyer and the seller sign an agency disclosure form (explaining agency duties) and an agency confirmation statement (explaining which party the agent represents).

2. An agent owes fiduciary duties to the principal. These include the duty to use reasonable care and skill, and the duties of obedience, utmost good faith, and loyalty. An agent should not disclose confidential information to third parties, or conceal material information from the principal. The agent must avoid undisclosed self-dealing, secret profits, and the unauthorized practice of law.

3. Dual agency is legal as long as both the buyer and the seller agree to it, but it's difficult to adequately represent both parties at the same time.

4. An agent doesn't owe fiduciary duties to third parties, but must deal fairly with them. Both the seller and the agent are required to disclose anything they're aware of that materially affects the value or desirability of the property. An agent has to conduct a diligent visual inspection of residential property and disclose any problems he or she discovers. The seller and agent must fill out a Real Estate Transfer Disclosure Statement for the buyer.

5. Actual fraud is intentional misrepresentation or concealment, or negligent misrepresentation. Constructive fraud is a breach of duty that misleads another, without an intention to deceive. Opinions, predictions, and puffing usually aren't actionable fraud, but an expert opinion may be. An "as is" clause doesn't shield a seller or broker from liability for fraud.

6. A client or customer can sue a real estate agent for breach of duty. The agent may be required to forfeit the commission or pay compensatory and punitive damages. In cases involving intentional fraud or conversion of trust funds, a judgment creditor who is unable to collect from the agent may be paid out of the Real Estate Recovery Fund. An agent accused of a serious breach of duty may be subject to criminal prosecution as well as civil suits.

7. A breach of duty may also be a violation of the Real Estate Law. In that case, the Commissioner can suspend or revoke the agent's license or impose a fine after holding a hearing on the matter. When an agent is reinstated, he or she may be issued a restricted license.

CHAPTER 6 KEY TERMS	compensatory (actual) damages	puffing
	constructive fraud	punitive (exemplary) damages
"as is" clause	desist and refrain order	restricted license
actionable fraud	dual agency	secret profits
actual fraud	fiduciary	self-dealing
caveat emptor	misrepresentation	summary suspension
code of ethics	negligence	

Broker's Agency and Statutory Disclosures Summary

I. Seller and Real Estate Agent Required Disclosures

1. Civil Code § 1102 "Disclosures Upon the Sale of Real Property"
   a. Real Estate Transfer Disclosure Statement. The seller and his agent make disclosures. The Transfer Disclosure Statement provides details of the condition of the property. It is given to transferee as soon as practicable before transfer of title.
   1. Mold Disclosure. The Transfer Disclosure Statement prompts sellers to disclose their awareness of mold to buyers.
   2. "Drug Lab"—Illegal Controlled Substance. If a seller has actual knowledge that an illegal controlled substance has been released on the property, he/she must provide written notice to a prospective buyer.
   b. Local Option Real Estate Transfer Disclosure Statement. The seller may be required by a city or county to provide specific information about the neighborhood or community in the Transfer Disclosure Statement.
   c. Natural Hazards Disclosure. The seller or his real estate agent is required to provide prospective buyers a revised Natural Hazard Disclosure statement disclosing that the property is located within one or more of the six specified natural hazard zones.
   d. Mello-Roos Bonds and Taxes. If the property is subject to a continuing lien securing the levy of special taxes to finance designated public facilities and services under the Mello-Roos Community Facilities Act, the seller must attempt to obtain a notice from an appropriate local agency disclosing details of the tax.
   e. Ordinance Location. Seller must give written notice of any knowledge of former state or federal ordinance locations within one mile of the property.
   f. Window Security Bars. Seller must disclose existence of window security bars and safety release mechanisms on the Transfer Disclosure Statement.
2. Earthquake Guides. Seller and agent provide transferee with a copy of *Homeowner's Guide to Earthquake Safety* from the Seismic Safety Commission. <u>Important</u>: If a buyer receives a copy of the booklet, neither the seller nor agent are required to provide additional information regarding geologic and seismic hazards. Seller and agent must, however, disclose that a property is in an earthquake zone.
3. Smoke Detector Statement of Compliance. Seller must provide buyer with a written statement that the property complies with California smoke detector's law.
4. Disclosure Regarding Lead-Based Paint Hazards. Sellers must disclose the presence of lead-based paint or lead-based hazards and any known information and reports about them, e.g., location and condition of painted surfaces.
5. California's Environmental Hazards Pamphlet. The Real Estate Transfer Disclosure Statement provided to the buyer by the seller and his real estate agent must specify environmental hazards of which the seller is aware. If the buyer is given a pamphlet entitled *Environmental Hazards: A Guide for Homeowners, Buyers, Landlords, and Tenants*, neither the seller nor his real estate agent is required to furnish any more information concerning such hazards unless the seller or agent has actual knowledge of the existence of a environmental hazard on or affecting the property. ***The Environmental Hazards Pamphlet now includes a chapter on mold.***

6. Delivery of Structural Pest Control Inspection and Certification Reports. If required by contract or by the lender, the seller or his agent must deliver to the buyer before transfer of title a report and written certification by a registered structural pest control company, regarding the presence of wood-destroying organisms.

7. Foreign Investment in Real Property Tax Act. A buyer of real property must withhold and send to the IRS 10% of the gross sales price if seller is a "foreign person."

8. Notice and Disclosure to Buyer of State Tax Withholding or Disposition of California Real Property. The buyer must withhold 3 1/3% of the total sale price as state income tax in certain transactions.

9. Furnishing Controlling Documents and a Financial Statement re Common Interest Developments. Must provide a prospective buyer with the following: (a) copy of governing documents of development; (b) copy of most recent financial statement of the homeowner's association; (c) a written statement from the association specifying the amount of the current, regular, and special assessments and any unpaid assessments.

10. Notice Regarding the Advisability of Title Insurance. Where no title insurance is to be issued, the buyer must receive and sign or acknowledge a statutory notice regarding the advisability of obtaining title insurance with the close of escrow.

11. Certification Regarding Water Heater's Security Against Earthquake. A seller must certify in writing to the prospective buyer that a water heater has been braced, anchored, or strapped to resist movement due to earthquake motion.

12. Data Base Regarding Location of Registered Sex Offenders (Megan's Law.) A statutorily defined notice regarding the existence of public access to database information regarding sex offenders is required in every real property sales contract.

II. Disclosures Required of Agents in Transferring a Residence

1. Visual inspection. A listing and selling broker must each conduct a reasonably competent and diligent inspection of the property and disclose to the prospective buyer all material facts affecting the value, desirability, and intended use of the property. The real estate agent does not have to inspect; (a) areas not reasonably accessible; (b) areas off the site of the property; (c) public records or permits concerning the title or use of the property; or (d) in a common interest development and the seller or broker complies by furnishing controlling documents and a financial statement.

2. Agency Relationship Disclosure. A real estate agent must disclose in writing the duties, which arise from certain agency relationships, the broker's status as agent of the seller, agent of the buyer, or agent of both the seller and the buyer (dual agent).

3. Disclosure of the Negotiability of Real Estate Commissions. The listing or sales agreement must contain the following disclosure in not less than 10-point boldface: NOTICE: The rate of real estate commissions is not fixed by law. They are set by each broker individually and may be negotiable between the seller and the broker.

4. No Disclosure Required for Manner/Occurrence of Death; Affliction of Occupant with AIDS. Any death, which occurred within a 3-year period, should be disclosed if it is "material." If the death occurred more than 3-years before the date of

the offer to buy, there is no liability for failing to disclose the fact of death. The seller and his agent need not voluntarily disclose affliction with AIDS or death from AIDS; but cannot make any misrepresentations to a direct question about death on the property.

5. Disclosure of Sale Price Information. The broker must inform buyer and seller in writing of the selling price within one month after the close of escrow.

III. Disclosures required when financing with certain real property secured (loan) transactions and seller "carry-backs."

1. Adjustable-Rate Loan Disclosure. Lender provides information about the loan.

2. Seller Financing Disclosure Statement. Provide information about the financing.

3. Truth-in-Lending—Regulation Z. (Amount financed, finance charge, APR payments, payment schedule, and identity of the lender).

4. Real Estate Settlement Procedures Act (RESPA). Protects borrower in escrow.

5. Disclosure by Agent Receiving Compensation from a Lender.

6. Notice of Transfer of Loan Servicing. Requires notice to the borrower.

7. Disclosures to Borrower for Real Property Loans. Broker must deliver disclosure.

8. Notice of Borrower's Right to Copy of Appraisal. Applicant buys appraisal copy.

9. Broker's Disclosures to Lender or Promissory Note Purchaser.

10. Equal Credit Opportunity Act - Notice of Adverse Action. No discrimination.

11. Disclosure - Housing Financial Discrimination Act of 1977 (Holden Act). Forbids the discriminatory practice known as "red-lining."

Agency Duties and Liabilities

Quiz—Chapter 6

1. An agency confirmation statement is:

    a. a type of listing agreement.
    b. only necessary when there is no written listing agreement.
    c. filled out by the broker and given to the buyer and seller.
    d. submitted to the Real Estate Commissioner before closing.

2. Negligence is:

    a. an unintentional breach of duty.
    b. not actionable.
    c. never grounds for suspension of a real estate license.
    d. none of the above.

3. A real estate broker representing the seller is a fiduciary in relation to:

    a. the buyer.
    b. the seller.
    c. the subagent.
    d. both a) and b).

4. On Monday, the seller accepted A's offer. On Tuesday, B contacts the seller's agent and makes an offer for the same property. The agent should:

    a. encourage the seller to accept B's offer if it's higher than A's offer.
    b. only tell the seller about B's offer if it's substantially higher than A's offer.
    c. not present B's offer to the seller, because it might cause the seller to breach her contract with A.
    d. present B's offer to the seller and recommend that she consult a lawyer if she wants to accept it instead of A's offer.

5. Dual agency:

    a. was recently made illegal in California.
    b. is inappropriate when the agent has an ongoing business relationship with one party and not the other.
    c. is listed as unlawful conduct in the Commissioner's regulations.
    d. requires the agent to reveal everything one client tells him or her to the other client.

6. Which of the following information is a seller or seller's agent not required to disclose to a prospective buyer in a residential transaction?

    a. The next-door neighbors frequently have loud parties
    b. The seller's daughter died of hepatitis in the house four years ago
    c. There are cracks in the foundation
    d. There has been some soil slippage, but it hasn't damaged the house in any way

7. The legislation based on the Easton decision requires a seller's broker to:

    a. give the seller an agency disclosure form.
    b. give the buyer an agency confirmation statement.
    c. inspect a single-family home.
    d. inspect every listed property.

8. Which of the following is actual fraud?

    a. Disclosing confidential information
    b. Intentionally failing to disclose something you did not have a duty to disclose
    c. Accidentally failing to disclose something you had a duty to disclose
    d. Making a statement you should have known was false

9. A real estate agent held liable for fraud in a civil action:

    a. may be required to pay punitive damages in addition to compensatory damages.
    b. might also face criminal charges for the same transaction.
    c. will probably have his or her license suspended or revoked by the Real Estate Commissioner.
    d. all of the above

10. A buyer obtained a judgment against a real estate broker. The buyer is entitled to payment out of the Real Estate Recovery Account:

    a. unless the judgment was for more than $50,000.
    b. if the judgment was based on negligent misrepresentation.
    c. if the judgment was based on constructive fraud.
    d. only if she has tried and failed to collect from the broker.

ANSWERS: 1. c; 2. a; 3. b; 4. d; 5. b; 6. b; 7. c; 8. d; 9. a; 10. d

CHAPTER 7
Contract Law

CHAPTER OVERVIEW

A contract is an agreement, between two or more parties, to do (or not do) a certain thing which the court will enforce. It doesn't have to be a ten-page legal document; it could be a spoken promise, a bus pass, and a movie ticket. They are all examples of contracts. To be enforced by a court, an agreement must be made according to the rules of contract law. These rules are designed to protect the parties against misunderstandings and false claims.

A sale of real property often involves a number of contracts: an employment agreement between a broker and a salesperson; a listing agreement; a deposit receipt; a title insurance policy; and an escrow agreement. As a result, it's essential for a real estate agent to understand basic contract law.

This chapter describes how a valid contract is formed, and the possible remedies when a contract is not fulfilled (breach). The next chapter covers in more detail the types of contracts you're likely to encounter in real estate transactions.

Contracts Classifications

There are four fundamental ways of classifying all contracts:

- ◆ either express or implied,
- ◆ either unilateral or bilateral,
- ◆ either executory or executed, and
- ◆ either valid, voidable, void, or unenforceable.

An **express** contract is an agreement that has been expressed in words, whether spoken or written. An **implied** contract, on the other hand, hasn't been put into words. Instead, the agreement is implied by the actions of the parties. An implied contract is often based on custom, or on an established course of dealing between the parties. Some contracts are partly express and partly implied. When you order a meal in a restaurant, it's understood that you agree to pay the price on the menu, although you don't actually say that to the waiter.

A contract is **bilateral** when each party makes a binding promise to the other; the contract is formed by the exchange of promises. For example, a buyer promises to pay a seller $229,000 for his house, and the seller promises to transfer title to the buyer in exchange for the money. Both parties are legally obligated to fulfill their promises. Most contracts are bilateral.

A contract is **unilateral** when one party promises something if the other party performs a certain action, but the other party does not promise to perform it. The contract is formed only if the other party actually performs the requested action.

Example: An open listing is considered a unilateral contract. The seller promises to pay a specified commission to the broker if the broker procures a buyer for the property. The broker does not make any promise in exchange for the seller's promise. She may or may not try to find a buyer.

The listing only becomes a binding contract if the broker actually finds a buyer. At that point, the seller is obligated to pay the broker's commission. Up until that point, however, neither party was obligated to do anything.

www.bayslaw.com/contracts.htm
(What is Contract Law?)

An **executed** contract is one that has been fully performed—both parties have done what they promised to do. An executory contract has not yet been fully performed. One or all of the parties have not begun to carry out their promises, or are in the process of carrying them out. Most contracts start out executory and end up executed.

EXPRESS		IMPLIED
Written or Oral	**OR**	Conduct of the Parties
UNILATERAL		**BILATERAL**
Promise for an Act	**OR**	Two Promises for Acts
EXECUTORY		**EXECUTED**
Not Yet Fully Performed	**OR**	Fully Performed

In addition to being express or implied, unilateral or bilateral, and executory or executed, a contract is either valid, void, voidable, or unenforceable. A **valid** contract is an agreement that meets all the legal requirements for contract formation outlined in the next section of this chapter. If one of the parties doesn't fulfill his or her side of the bargain (**breaches** the contract), the other can sue to have the contract enforced.

But many agreements don't meet one or more of the requirements for contract formation. These agreements are usually considered legally **void**. In the eyes of the law, a void contract is actually not a contract at all; it can't be enforced in court.

If both parties fulfill their promises, fine. But if one breaches and the other sues, the judge will rule that no contract was formed, and will refuse to enforce the agreement.

Example: A owns a vacant lot on the eastside of town and B owns a vacant lot on the southside of town. Just before teeing off for their usual Saturday golf game, B bets his lot against A's lot that B will shoot a lower score than A. A accepts the bet. A shoots a 78 and B an 80, and A demands the deed to B's lot. B refuses to deliver and A sues B for the deed. Since gambling is illegal in California, this betting agreement is void and cannot be enforced.

Sometimes, even though an agreement doesn't comply with all the rules, it is not void. A **voidable** contract is valid on its face but one of the parties may reject it. This generally happens when one of the parties has taken advantage of the other in some way. The injured party can choose whether or not to go through with the contract. If he or she decides against it, the injured party can **disaffirm** the contract—that is, ask a court to terminate it. The situations in which a contract is voidable rather than void are explained in the next section.

Finally, some contracts are **unenforceable** even when they are not void or voidable. For example, a valid contract becomes unenforceable when the statute of limitations runs out. Or maybe all the requirements for contract formation were met, but there isn't proper evidence to prove that in court. (That problem often comes up with oral contracts.) A contract is also likely to be unenforceable if it is vaguely worded.

CONTRACT TYPE	*LEGAL EFFECT*	*EXAMPLE*
VOID	No contract at all	An agreement for which there is no consideration
VOIDABLE	Valid unless rejected by one party	A contingency in a contract, not met
UNENFORCEABLE	Neither party may sue for performance	A contract after the statute of limitations has expired
VALID or ENFORCEABLE	Binding and enforceable	An agreement that meets all requirements of a contract

Contract Formation

There are four essential elements for a valid contract:

- ◆ capacity to contract,
- ◆ mutual consent,
- ◆ consideration, and
- ◆ a lawful purpose.

These requirements apply to all contracts. In addition, certain contracts (especially real estate contracts) must be in **writing** and signed to be enforceable.

http://www.real-estate-public-records.com/
(Real Estate Public Records Search)

CAPACITY TO CONTRACT

To make a valid contract, a person must be at least **18 years old**, and must also be legally **competent**. This requirement protects minors and the mentally ill, who might enter into contracts without really understanding the consequences.

Minority

When a minor makes an agreement concerning real property, the agreement is void. Neither the minor nor the other party can sue to enforce the agreement.

> **Example:** M is only 17. He signs a deposit receipt, agreeing to buy S's house. If either M or S breaches this agreement, the other cannot enforce it, because it is void.

But most other types of contracts are *voidable* by the minor. The minor can decide whether he or she wants to go through with the transaction. If not, the minor can go to court to disaffirm the contract. But if the minor does want to go through with it, the other party is bound.

> **Example:** Suppose M bought S's car instead of her house. A week later, M decides he doesn't like the color. This contract is voidable by M, so he may ask a court to terminate it. M will return the car, and S will have to return whatever M paid her for it. This is true even if the car was destroyed in a fire and all M can return is burned, twisted metal.

A minor must **disaffirm** a voidable contract before he or she turns 18, or within a reasonable time after turning 18. What is a reasonable period of time is determined on a case by base basis. There is an additional issue called ratification. If after turning 18, the individual does something which indicates an intention to be bound by the contract entered into while a minor, the contract is binding, even though the individual acts within a reasonably amount of time. It is inconsistent to want to avoid a contract once having indicated an intention to be bound by it.

http://www.dre.ca.gov/relaw.htm
(Department of Real Estate - Real Estate Law)

> **Example:** M Bought S's car and paid $500.00 down and is paying $100.00 per month until it is paid for. Six days after turning 18, M makes another monthly payment. Seven days later M chooses to avoid the car purchase contract made while a minor. Assuming that 13 days is within a reasonable time after turning 18, M is bound by the contract. Making a monthly payment after acquiring mental capacity resulted in the ratification of the contract made while a minor, and it became a binding contract.

Even if the minor misrepresents his or her age when buying or selling something, the contract can still be disaffirmed. Consequently, verifying that the other party to a contract is 18 or older is very important. If you determine the person is under 18, consider your choices:

◆ Decline to enter into the contact because the risk is too great (having to return what you received from the minor and get back nothing if the item has been destroyed or receive it in a damaged condition with no way to recover for the damage).

◆ Enter into the contract and wait for the reasonable period after turning 18, or hope for ratification after 18.

◆ Enter into the contract but only if the minor provides a competent adult to co-sign the contract.

http://www.lawyers.com/lawyers-com/content/legalresources/useful.html#realestate (Real Estate Law Internet Sites)

There are four major areas where minors enter into valid (binding and enforceable in court) contracts.

1. Emancipation. Once a minor becomes emancipated the minor has the capacity to "Buy, sell, lease, encumber, exchange, or transfer an interest in real or personal property,..." under Family Code section 7050. An emancipated minor is a person under 18 who:

◆ is or has been married,
◆ is on active duty with armed forces, or
◆ has received a court declaration of emancipation.

To petition the superior court for a declaration of emancipation the minor:

◆ must be at least 14 years old;
◆ is willingly living separate and apart from the minor's parents or guardian with the consent or acquiescence of the minor's parents or guardian;
◆ is managing his or her own financial affairs (an income and expense declaration is required);
◆ cannot be receiving income from a criminal activity.

Once the court determines it is in the best interest of the minor, the court issues a declaration of emancipation. The court can rescind the declaration at a later time if necessary. The emancipated minor can receive a California identification card for an emancipated minor from the Department of Motor Vehicles.

2. Necessities (necessary purchases). Contracts entered into by minors for necessities (such as food or medicine) are valid. However, since most minor's necessities are provided by parents with the minor living at home, most of the minor's contracts are voidable. Additionally, what is a necessities for one minor may or may not be a necessities for another minor. Family Code section 6712 covers necessities and provides:

A contract, otherwise valid, entered into during minority, may not be disaffirmed on that ground either during the actual minority of the person entering into the contract, or at any time thereafter, if all of the following requirements are satisfied:

a. The contract is to pay the reasonable value of things necessary for the support of the minor or the minor's family.

b. These things have been actually furnished to the minor or to the minor's family.

c. The contract is entered into by the minor when not under the care of a parent or guardian able to provide for the minor or the minor's family.

3. Art, Entertainment, Sports. A minor's contract in art, entertainment, and professional sports is also valid under California law. To be binding these contracts must be approved by a superior court judge. Additionally, the judge can set aside an amount not exceeding one-half of the minor's net earnings under the contract in a trust fund for the benefit of the minor. This is important since a minor's earnings belong to the parents.

4. Medical Services. Minors were having problems getting medical treatment without parental consent. The legislature responded with a variety of situations where the minor can receive medical treatment, some without parental consent, knowledge, or liability for payment. For example, Family Code section 6926 provides:

a. A minor who is 12 years of age or older and who may have come into contact with an infectious, contagious, or communicable disease may consent to medical care related to the diagnosis or treatment of the disease, if the disease or condition is one that is required by law, or regulation adopted pursuant to law to be reported to the local health officer, or is a related sexually transmitted disease, as may be determined by the State Director of Health Services.

b. The minor's parents or guardian are not liable for payment for medical care provided pursuant to this section.

There are other sections involving consent by a minor to treatment for rape, assault, pregnancy and prevention thereof, and drug or alcohol abuse.

Incompetence

According to the Civil Code, a person who is "entirely without understanding" cannot make a contract. After a person has been declared incompetent by a court (because of mental illness, retardation, or senility), any contract he or she enters into is void. Also, if the person made a contract before the declaration of incompetence but while of unsound mind, the court-appointed guardian can ask the court to have that contract set aside.

In a few cases, if a person was under the influence of alcohol or other drugs at the time of entering into a contract, it will be voidable. To disaffirm, the person will have to prove that he or she was of unsound mind at the time of the contract or the other party had reason to know of the lack of capacity caused by drugs or alcohol.

MUTUAL CONSENT

For a contract to be a binding obligation, all the parties must consent to its terms. This mutual consent is sometimes referred to as a "meeting of the minds." It is achieved through **offer and acceptance**.

Offer

The process of forming a contract begins when one person (the **offeror**) makes an offer to another (the **offeree**). To be the basis for a contract, an offer must:

◆ express an intent to contract, and
◆ have definite terms.

Intent to Contract. The intent requirement is concerned with **objective intent** (what the offeror says and does) rather than **subjective intent** (what the offeror is actually thinking). If you say or do something a reasonable person could interpret as a serious expression of an intent to make a contract ("I'll sell you a dozen roses for $15"), it may be a legally binding offer—even if you don't have any roses and never really intended to come up with them.

On the other hand, a casual remark or a joke is not a binding offer. Because of the nature of the remark, the tone of voice, or the situation, a reasonable person would not understand the statement as a serious offer.

> **Example:** Z paid $20,000 for a sports car. After it breaks down for the second time in a week, Z tells Q, "I'm so tired of this piece of junk I'd sell it for ten bucks:" Q pulls out her wallet and hands Z a ten dollar bill.
>
> Z is not required to sell Q the car for ten dollars, because his statement was not a binding offer. A reasonable person would not have interpreted his remark as a serious expression of an intent to contract.

Note that a real estate listing is not considered a property owner's offer to sell. It is the authorization of a broker to find a buyer or renter for the owner's property. A buyer doesn't create a contract by accepting the seller's listing. Instead, a prospective buyer makes an offer to purchase, and the seller accepts or rejects the offer. (The listing agreement is an independent contract between the seller and a real estate broker, not part of the contract between the seller and buyer.)

Definite Terms. An offer must have definite terms—it isn't binding if it's too vague. It should state at least such basic terms as the subject matter, the time for performance, and the price. In some cases, a court will fill in the blanks with a reasonable time or a reasonable price. But if too many terms are left unspecified, no contract is formed. A salesperson should never make an offer without a stated price. Preliminary negotiations for a contract are not the same thing as a binding offer.

Chapter 7

> **Case Example:** Two developers needed financing for a hotel project near San Francisco. They applied for a loan from Coast Federal Savings. Coast prepared a conditional commitment letter for a $7,000,000 loan at 9% interest. But the letter did not specify the security for the loan, the payment schedule, or the disbursement procedures, among other things.
>
> After receiving the commitment letter, the developers went ahead with their project and didn't apply for financing from any other banks. But then Coast Federal decided against making the loan. The developers sued the S&L for breach of contract.
>
> The court ruled in favor of Coast Federal. The conditional commitment letter left out too many important terms; it could not be considered a binding offer, so no contract had been formed. *Laks v. Coast Federal Savings & Loan Ass'n*, 60 Cal. App. 3d 885, 131 Cal. Rptr. 836 (1976).

TERMINATION OF AN OFFER. An offer isn't legally binding until it is accepted by the offeree. It can be accepted at any time before it terminates. An offer can be terminated by one of these events:

- ◆ lapse of time,
- ◆ the death or incapacity of one of the parties,
- ◆ revocation by the offeror, or
- ◆ rejection by the offeree.

Lapse of Time. Many offers state they will expire at a certain time—"after five days" or "on March 30." And when an offer doesn't specify an expiration date, a court will generally rule that it expired after a reasonable time. But even when an offer includes an expiration date, it may end sooner, through one of the other methods of termination.

Death or Incapacity. An offer is terminated if either of the parties (the offeror or offeree) dies or becomes incompetent before it is accepted.

Revocation. If an offeror revokes the offer before the offeree accepts it, it is terminated—the offeree has lost the chance to accept the offer. This is true even if the offer stated that it was irrevocable, or that it would not expire until a particular date.

The case on the next page would have come out differently if Richardson had paid Moeller a sum of money to keep the offer open for those ten days. When a offeree pays or gives something (consideration) to the offeror in exchange for holding an offer open, the offer cannot be revoked during the specified period. (See the discussion of options at the end of this chapter.) But without such a payment, an offer can be revoked at any time before it is accepted. Once it has been accepted, however, the offeror can no longer revoke it.

Case Example: Mrs. Moeller offered to exchange her orange grove for some property owned by Mr. Richardson. Her offer stated, "Unless this offer shall be accepted in writing within 10 days of the date hereof...[it shall be void.] During said period this offer shall be irrevocable."

Moeller's real estate agent delivered the offer to Richardson on October 16. But the next day Moeller had second thoughts. She had her agent tell Richardson that nothing further should be done about the proposed exchange for the time being.

On October 20, Richardson visited the orange grove and discussed the exchange with Moeller again. On the 21, Richardson signed Moeller's offer and informed her that he had accepted it. When Moeller refused to go through with the exchange, Richardson sued her.

The court held that no contract had been formed. Richardson's acceptance was ineffective (even though it came well within the ten-day period) because Moeller revoked the offer the day after she made it. Moeller had the right to revoke the offer at any time, even though it stated that it was irrevocable. The broker however could sue Mrs. Moeller (the principal) for his or her commission. *Roth v. Moeller*, 185 Cal. 415, 197 P. 62 (1921).

A revocation is effective as soon as it is communicated to the offeree. When it isn't communicated directly (in person or over the telephone), the revocation is effective at the time it is received by the offeree. However, in California revocations are effective when sent. Thus, when a notice of revocation is mailed to the offeree, the offer is revoked the moment the revocation is mailed.

Rejection. An offer is also terminated when it is rejected by the offeree. Rejections are effective in terminating the offer when received by the offeror. If I reject your offer on Monday, I can't change my mind and call back on Tuesday to accept it. If you're still interested in the deal, we can start the process of offer and acceptance over again. But your original offer was terminated by my rejection, and if you've lost interest, I can no longer hold you to your offer.

OFFER

- ◆ intent to contract
- ◆ definite terms

TERMINATION

- ◆ lapse of time
- ◆ death or incapacity
- ◆ revocation
- ◆ rejection

NO CONTRACT

ACCEPTANCE

- ◆ by offeree
- ◆ communicated to offeror
- ◆ in specified manner
- ◆ doesn't vary terms

CONTRACT

Chapter 7

Acceptance

When an offer is accepted, a contract is formed. At that point, the parties are legally bound. Neither can back out unless the other is willing to call off the contract. There are four basic requirements for acceptance:

- ◆ an offer can only be accepted by the offeree;
- ◆ an acceptance must be communicated to the offeror;
- ◆ an acceptance must be made in the manner specified;
- ◆ an acceptance must not vary the terms of the offer.

ACCEPTED BY THE OFFEREE. The first of these requirements—that an offer can only be accepted by the offeree—may sound obvious. But it means that if A makes an offer to B and B decides not to accept it, C can't accept the offer and force A to deal with him. Of course, A may be willing to work with C, but any contract between A and C is based on a new offer, not on the offer A made to B.

COMMUNICATED TO THE OFFEROR. An acceptance must be communicated to the offeror. You may already have decided to accept my offer, but until you let me know that you've accepted it, I can still revoke it.

Case Example: Mr. Carr's agent told Mr. Lauritson that the frontage of Carr's property was 900 feet. On November 14th Lauritson signed a deposit receipt offering to buy the property, and the agent delivered it to Carr.

A few days later, however, the agent told Lauritson that the frontage was actually only 581 feet. Lauritson said he could not go through with the purchase. Carr sued.

Carr claimed that he signed the deposit receipt on November 15th, the day after he received it. But since Carr didn't send the deposit receipt back to Lauritson, or communicate his acceptance in any other way before the offer was revoked, the court ruled that no contract was formed. *Carr v. Lauritson*, 41 Cal. App. 2d 31, 106 P. 2d 19 (1940).

When an acceptance is not communicated directly (in person or over the telephone), it is effective as soon as the message is sent, even though the offeror may not receive it immediately or at all. This is called "the mailbox rule"; the acceptance creates a binding contract when the offeree drops it in the mailbox.

Manner of Acceptance. As mentioned earlier, certain types of contracts (including most contracts concerning real property) are required by law to be in writing and signed. For those, only a written, signed acceptance binds the offeree.

Example: A writes B a letter offering to sell him her house for $200,000. It's an excellent offer, so B calls A on the phone and says he's accepting it.

Two hours later, B changes his mind. He can call A back and withdraw his acceptance, because it wasn't in writing.

However, an acceptance does not necessarily have to be in writing to bind the offeror to the contract. Any reasonable method of acceptance will be effective, unless the offer specifies how it is to be accepted. If the offer does specify a particular method (such as "in writing," "by registered mail," or "by delivering a cashier's check"), the acceptance will not bind the offeror unless those instructions are followed.

Case Example: Gladstone Holmes, Inc., offered to sell 75 acres near Pomona to the Moreland Development Company. The offer took the form of a purchase agreement filled out and signed by Gladstone and delivered to Moreland.

Moreland decided to accept the offer, so it signed the agreement and sent it to Gladstone by certified mail. Moreland claimed to have mailed the document by 4:45 p.m. on March 9.

Gladstone had a messenger hand deliver a letter to Moreland's office at 5:00 p.m. on the same day. The letter stated that the offer was revoked. But since March 9 was a Friday, neither the acceptance nor the revocation was opened and read until Monday morning.

The court in this case did not decide if a contract was formed. But that question would turn on whether Moreland could prove that it mailed the acceptance before Gladstone's revocation was received. If Moreland was able to prove that, the acceptance was effective and a contract was formed—the offer was revoked too late. It doesn't matter that neither party actually learned of the other's action until Monday. *Moreland Devel. Co. v. Gladstone Holmes, Inc.*, 135 Cal. App. 3d 973, 186 Cal. Rptr. 6 (1982).

Example: A offers to sell his antique car to B. The offer states it is to be accepted by registered mail. B drops by A's office and tells him that she's accepting the offer. A can still revoke it.

http://www.dre.ca.gov/disclosures.htm
(Disclosures in Real Property Contracts)

Of course, an offeror can waive this requirement. If A chooses to treat B's spoken acceptance as effective, a contract is formed. Can silence be acceptance? Not as a general rule.

Example: X writes Z a letter offering to buy her sailboat for $2,000. The letter says, "If you have not rejected this offer by Saturday, I will consider it accepted." Z receives the letter but never replies.

X goes to Z's house with $2,000 and demands the boat. Z is not required to let him have it. Her silence in response to X's letter was not acceptance, and no contract was formed.

But if the offeree accepts the benefits of the offer, silence may be construed as acceptance. If X had enclosed a $2,000 check with his letter and Z cashed it, she would be deemed to have accepted his offer and might be required to let him have the boat.

ACCEPTANCE MUST NOT VARY THE OFFER'S TERMS. To create a contract, the offeree must accept exactly those terms that he or she was offered. The offeree can't modify the terms of the offer or add any new terms (if so, it is a counter offer).

Case Example: Mr. Brennan offered to buy Mr. Krasley's house in Chula Vista. Brennan filled out and signed a deposit receipt form and delivered it to Krasley.

A few days later, Krasley sent Brennan a signed document that stated, "The undersigned accepts the offer on the terms and conditions set forth in the [deposit receipt]...with the following changes and amendments: The terms and price are acceptable if there is included in the deed of trust an acceleration clause."

But later that same day, Krasley received a better offer from a developer, and he accepted it. Brennan sued.

The court ruled that no contract had been formed. Because Krasley's document added a term (the acceleration clause requirement) to Brennan's offer, it was technically not an acceptance. Instead, it was a **counter offer**. A counter offer is essentially a new *offer*—now Krasley is the offeror, and Brennan is the offeree. To create a binding contract, Brennan would have had to accept Krasley's counter offer (which he didn't get a chance to do). *Krasley v. Superior Court, City of San Diego*, 101 Cal. App. 3d 425, 161 Cal. Rptr. 629 (1980).

A counter offer terminates the original offer, just as a rejection would. If your counteroffer is rejected, it's too late to go back and accept the original offer. You can start again with a new offer identical to the original offer. But if the original offeror has had a change of heart, you can no longer hold him or her to the original offer. It's important to keep this in mind, since a real estate transaction often involves a series of offers and counter offers. Each counter offer terminates the previous offer.

Freedom of Consent

Offer and acceptance are the expression of mutual consent to the terms of an agreement. But to create a binding contract, consent must be freely given. It is not freely given when it is the result of one of five negative factors:

- ◆ fraud,
- ◆ undue influence,
- ◆ duress,
- ◆ menace, or
- ◆ mistake.

Any of these makes a contract voidable by the party who was victimized. The victim may choose to go ahead with the contract or disaffirm it.

To disaffirm, the victim must be able to show that consent was not freely given. For example, a victim of fraud must prove that he or she would not have entered the contract if the other party had not misrepresented the effect of the agreement or made false promises. (See Chapter 6 for a discussion of the elements of fraud.)

Undue influence refers to taking unfair advantage of another person. A contract is voidable if you persuade someone to sign it by taking advantage of his or her trust in you, or weakness of mind (due to senility, exhaustion, or stupidity, for example), or necessities or distress (drug addiction, for example). Undue influence often involves telling the victim that documents must be signed immediately, and that there's no time to consult a lawyer.

Case Example: The Channells owned a 51-acre ranch in Fresno County. Because of financial difficulties, they were no longer able to make their mortgage payments or pay their property taxes. Afraid of foreclosure, they tried to sell the property. They listed it for $60,000, but the only offer was for $40,000. That seemed too low, and the Channells did not accept it.

Then Mr. Anthony, the nephew of a neighbor, came to the Channells' rescue. Anthony said he would protect the ranch from foreclosure.

Anthony wrote up an agreement under which he would purchase the ranch by assuming the mortgage and other liens, which totaled approximately $34,700. He told the Channells that this transfer of title was "just for show," to prevent foreclosure. After the property was in escrow, the agreement would be torn up. The Channells would be able to continue living on the ranch. Anthony also said he would give Mr. Channell a job and would pay off all the Channells' bills. The Channells hesitated, but then signed the agreement.

After talking to their son and their bookkeeper, however, the Channells had second thoughts. Anthony opened an escrow, but when he asked the Channells to sign the escrow papers, they refused.

Then Anthony filed a lawsuit against the Channells to enforce the purchase agreement. The Channells were very upset; they couldn't afford to hire a lawyer. Anthony told them he'd drop the lawsuit if they signed the escrow papers. The Channells reluctantly agreed, and Anthony drove them to a notary's office.

Neither of the Channells could read without glasses. They only owned one pair, which they shared, and they forgot to bring it with them to the notary's office. When the Channells signed the escrow instructions, they didn't realize they were also signing a grant deed that Anthony had slipped in among the other papers. Anthony told the Channells that he was going to keep his promises and take care of them.

Later, the Channells learned they had signed a deed transferring the ranch to Anthony. Shortly afterwards, Anthony had the Channells evicted from the property. The Channells sued.

The jury decided that the purchase agreement was voidable by the Channells because Anthony used fraud (promises he never intended to keep) to get them to sign it. The escrow agreement was voidable because of undue influence. Anthony pressured the Channells into signing it by taking unfair advantage of their distress about being sued. *Channell v. Anthony*, 58 Cal. App. 3d 290, 129 Cal. Rptr. 704 (1976).

A person who signs a contract because he or she is being unlawfully confined (that is, forced to stay in a place against his or her will) is said to have signed under **duress**. A contract is also signed under duress if the signer's spouse, child, or close relative is being unlawfully confined, or if their property is being unlawfully detained.

Menace is the threat of duress, or the threat of violent injury to a person, or to his or her spouse, child, or close relative. The threat of injury to a person's reputation (as in blackmail) is also menace. Any contract signed as a result of duress or menace is voidable by the victim.

California courts have extended the concept of duress to include **economic duress**, also known as **business compulsion**. This refers to a situation where one person coerces another into signing a contract by threatening to take some action that will be financially disastrous for the victim—for example, threatening to withhold a payment owed to the victim, or breach a contract, or start a groundless lawsuit in bad faith.

Case Example: Rich & Whillock contracted with Ashton Development, Inc. to perform grading and excavating work. Bills were submitted for work as it was done which were regularly paid. When the final bill for $72,286.45 was submitted, Rich and Whillock were in financial difficulty and faced bankruptcy if not paid. Ashton offered to pay $50,000 on a "take it or leave it" basis making it necessary for Rich and Whilllock to bring a lawsuit to get the reminder of the money they were entitled to. After strenuously protesting Ashton's coercive tactics, the only way to avoid an economic disaster was to accept the compromise amount of $50,000, and signed a release of the balance. Later, Rich and Whilllock sued Ashton for the balance owed. Ashton defended that the claim was extinguished by the signed release. The court ruled that there is an increasing recognition of the law's role in correcting inequitable or unequal exchanges between parties of disproportionate bargaining power and a greater willingness not to enforce agreements which were entered into under coercive circumstances. Clearly Ashton acted in bad faith and are liable for the $22,286.45 due under the contract. *Rich and Whillock, Inc. v. Ashton Development, Inc.*, 157 Cal. App. 3d 1154, 204 Cal. Rptr. 86 (1984).

Unlike the other negative factors that can make a contract voidable, **mistake** usually doesn't involve any bad faith or villainy. If both parties are mistaken about some fact or law that is important to their contract, either of them may disaffirm the contract. This is known as **mutual mistake**.

Case Example: Ms. Williams leased the second floor of a building from Ms. Puccinelli. They agreed that Williams would open a restaurant in the space. Neither of them realized that under San Francisco's building code, substantial structural alterations to the whole building would be necessary before a restaurant could be operated on the second floor.

A month after signing the lease, Williams learned about the required alterations. She asked Puccinelli to have the alterations done, but Puccinelli said that wasn't her responsibility. Williams sued to disaffirm the contract.

The court ruled that the contract was voidable because it was based on a mutual mistake regarding the law. Both parties had mistakenly assumed that the second floor could be used for the designated purpose without structural changes in the rest of the building. Williams v. Puccinelli, 236 Cal. App. 2d 512, 46 Cal. Rptr. 285 (1965).

However, when only one of the parties to a contract is mistaken (**unilateral mistake**), the contract is not voidable unless the other party knew about the mistake of a material fact and did nothing to correct it.

CONSIDERATION

Even when parties who have the capacity to contract freely consent to an agreement, it isn't a valid contract unless it is supported by **consideration**. Consideration is something of value exchanged by the parties. A contract can't be a one-way street: each party must give something to the other in order to get something from the other. The exchange of consideration is what distinguishes a contractual promise from the promise of a gift.

> **Example:** If A promises B his sweater in exchange for B's wheelbarrow, they have a contract. Each has given the other some consideration: A gave B a promise, and B gave A a promise.
>
> But if A promises B his sweater and B promises A nothing in return, there is no contract. The sweater is a gift.
>
> The distinction becomes important if, after making the promise, A fails to give B the sweater. In the first case, where A received consideration for his promise (namely, B's promise to give him the wheelbarrow), B can sue A to enforce the promise.
>
> But in the second case, B can't sue A. The courts will not enforce a promise that is not supported by consideration. It wasn't very nice of A to break his promise, but since the sweater was a gift instead of a contractual obligation, the law won't get involved.

Consideration can be anything of value—a sweater, $10, or a split-level ranch house. The consideration for most contracts is a promise to give something of value, as in the example above. For this reason, the parties to a contract are sometimes referred to as the **promisor** (the one making a promise) and the **promisee** (the one who is to receive the benefit of a promise).

In a typical real estate purchase contract, the buyer promises to pay the seller money, and the seller promises to transfer title to the buyer. By exchanging promises they create an executory contract; when they fulfill their promises (when the buyer actually pays the seller and the seller actually gives the buyer the deed) the contract is executed.

To provide consideration for a contract, a promisor must either do something that benefits the promisee, or give something up. Promising to not do something can be consideration—for example, promising to stop smoking. Or if you don't smoke, promising to never start can be consideration.

But an empty promise is not consideration for a contract: if you've never smoked, promising to quit can't be consideration. And something that you've already done can't be consideration.

Example: A quit smoking, and B is very pleased. B says to A, "Because you quit smoking, I'm going to buy you a yacht." This is not a contract; since A had already quit smoking, he didn't really give B anything (or give up anything) in exchange for B's promise.

Also, promising to do something that you're already legally obligated to do (or promising to refrain from doing something that you're obligated to refrain from doing) is not consideration.

Example: A contracts to build a house for B for $200,000. When the house is more than halfway completed, A says, "You're going to have to pay me another $30,000 if you want me to finish this project." B meekly agrees. This is not an enforceable contract—A can't sue B for the additional $30,000—because A was already obligated to finish the house.

ADEQUACY. It's important to understand that the value of the consideration one party gives doesn't have to be equal to the value of what the other gives. In other words, even though one party struck a bad bargain, they still have an enforceable contract.

Example: X's house was appraised at $200,000. He's anxious to sell it very quickly, because he thinks he may have to leave the country in a hurry. When Z offers $75,000 for the house, X accepts, and they execute a written contract.

As it turns out, X won't have to leave the country. He wants to back out of the sale, but Z wants to go through with it. Although X's consideration is worth more than twice what Z is giving, their contract is binding.

Of course, when the consideration is grossly unequal, that may be a sign that there was fraud, undue influence, duress, menace, or mistake involved in the contract negotiations. But if, mutual consent is not proven, the contract is enforceable.

LAWFUL PURPOSE

The purpose of a contract (sometimes called the "object" of the contract) must be lawful when the contract is made. If one person promises to pay another for committing an illegal act, their contract is void and cannot be enforced by a court. This may seem obvious; a hit man is unlikely to take his employer to court to collect his fee. But the requirement has a considerably broader application. For example, a listing agreement hiring someone who is not a licensed real estate broker is void. Also, according to the Civil Code, even when a contract's purpose does not violate an express provision of the law, it is unlawful if it is contrary to public policy or good morals.

Many contracts have more than one purpose, and they are often severable—one part can be enforced without the other. When part of a contract is legal and part is illegal, a court may set aside the illegal part and enforce the rest. But when a contract has a single purpose, if any of the consideration given for that purpose is unlawful, the entire contract is void.

> **Example:** A agreed to sell his house to B in exchange for $100,000 and a pound of cocaine. The whole contract is void. The court can't just ignore the cocaine and enforce a sale of the house for $100,000.

THE STATUTE OF FRAUDS

The provision of the Civil Code requiring certain contracts to be in writing and signed is known as the statute of frauds. (The same name is used for similar laws in other states, too—it was adopted from common law.) As that name suggests, the writing requirement is intended to prevent fraudulent claims. The parties to an unwritten contract are likely to later disagree about exactly what each agreed to do—or whether they agreed to do anything. Putting a contract in writing helps eliminate that kind of dispute, because the document is solid evidence of the existence of an agreement and its essential terms.

www.law.cornell.edu/ucc/2A/2A-201.html
(U.C.C. Article 2A-201 - Statute of Frauds)

WHICH CONTRACTS MUST BE IN WRITING. The statute of frauds applies to any agreement that is not to be performed within one year from the time it is made, and any sale for $500 or more. It applies to any contract that is not to be performed during the lifetime of the promisor. It also applies to a promise to pay another's debt, or guarantee payment of another's debt. Most importantly for our purposes, the statute of frauds applies to these contracts concerning real property:

1. An agreement for the sale, exchange, or an interest in real property.

2. A lease of real property that will expire more than one year after it was signed.

3. An agency agreement authorizing an agent to purchase or sell real property, or lease it for more than one year. (A power of attorney, for example.)

4. An agency agreement authorizing an agent to "procure, introduce, or find" a buyer or seller (or lessee or lessor, for a lease for more than one year), if the agent will receive compensation. (A listing agreement, for example.)

5. An assumption of a mortgage or deed of trust.

To be enforceable, any of these contracts must be in writing and signed.

Although any listing agreement or finder's contract must be in writing if the agent expects to be paid (#4 on the list above), the statute of frauds doesn't apply to a commission-splitting agreement between two brokers. If a listing broker orally agrees to share a commission with another broker, they have a valid contract. The cooperating broker can sue the listing broker to collect his or her share.

The statute of frauds doesn't explicitly mention mortgages or deeds of trust, but they are considered agreements for the sale of an interest in real property (#1 on the list above). In any case, a separate provision of the Civil Code requires them to be in writing and signed.

The statute of frauds also doesn't mention employment agreements between brokers and salespersons. Nonetheless, those agreements do have to be in writing and signed—that's required by the Real Estate Commissioner's Regulations.

WHAT KIND OF WRITING SATISFIES THE STATUTE OF FRAUDS. The writing required by the statute of frauds doesn't have to be a formal legal document. A note or memorandum is enough, if it indicates there is an agreement between the parties and it is signed.

Case Example: Mr. Seck, a real estate broker, had known Mr. Foulks for a long time. Foulks asked Seck to help him sell his ranch in Sacramento County, and Seck agreed.

However, Foulks refused to give Seck a formal listing agreement. "You know dog gone well, you know me, I'm not going to cheat you out of a commission," Foulks said. But Seck took out one of his business cards and jotted down the basic terms of the listing on the back of the card. It looked like this:

310 M/L	quarterly with int
2000 per acre	keep taxes up to date
1/2 down	1/2 mineral rights
bal. 5 years	6% comm
5% int	10/1/65

Seck asked Foulks to initial and date the card. Foulks wrote, "3/24/65 GWF."

Seck found a buyer for the ranch, but Foulks refused to pay Seck a commission. When Seck sued, Foulks argued that the notes on the business card weren't enough to comply with the statute of frauds. But the court disagreed. The court said that all Seck needed was some written, signed note indicating the fact of employment. This requirement was fulfilled by "6% comm" and Foulks's initials on the business card. *Seck v. Foulks*, 25 Cal. App. 3d 556, 102 Cal. Rptr. 170 (1972).

To comply with the statute of frauds, a contract only needs to have been signed by "the party to be charged"—that is, the one who's being sued. For example, it didn't matter that Seck hadn't signed the business card, as long as Foulks had. A full signature is unnecessary; initials are enough. In fact, anything that the signer intends as a signature will do. But it may be difficult to prove that a wavy line or an "X" was someone's signature if that person later denies it.

Once you've signed a contract, you're bound by its terms, even if you claim you never read it. Before signing, an illiterate person must ask someone trustworthy to explain all the terms of a written agreement. The same is true for a person signing a document written in a foreign language. (However, California law has a special rule for certain loan contracts and residential leases: when the contract was negotiated in Spanish but is written in English, the signer must be given a written translation of the document.) Of course, if someone convinces another person to sign a document by misrepresenting its contents, that's fraud, and the contract is voidable.

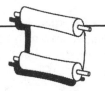

A VALID CONTRACT

CAPACITY

MUTUAL CONSENT

CONSIDERATION

LAWFUL PURPOSE

IN WRITING AND SIGNED
(for real estate contracts)

PROMISSORY ESTOPPEL

As you can see, there are many possible pitfalls in making a contract: the other party may lack capacity, the process of offer and acceptance may have gone wrong, consideration might be missing, or a signed writing might have been necessary. Many people aren't aware of these legal requirements, and they are often surprised to discover that a promise someone made them is unenforceable. The outcomes of some contract lawsuits seem very unfair.

To prevent unfairness in at least a few cases, the courts have developed the doctrine of **promissory estoppel** (also called the doctrine of **detrimental reliance**). Here's an outline of the kind of situation in which this doctrine is applied:

1. A makes a promise to B.
2. A should realize that the promise is likely to induce B to take some action.
3. B does in fact take action in reasonable reliance on A's promise.
4. If A is not required to fulfill the promise, B will suffer harm because of her reliance on it.

In such a case, a court may decide to enforce the promise, even though there was no consideration, or no signed writing, or some other contractual defect.

Example: M is S's mother. M bought a large tract of land and promised to give it to S. S cleared and fenced the land. He built a house on it and moved in with his wife.

Two years later, M and S have a fight. M tells S and his wife to get off her property, but they refuse to leave. M sues to regain possession of her land.

Originally, M's promise to S was not enforceable, since S did not give M any consideration in exchange for her promise, and there was no signed writing. But the court uses the doctrine of promissory estoppel to rule in S's favor. M should have realized that her promise would induce action by S, and she was in fact aware of all his work on the property. S's reliance on M's promise was reasonable, so the court rules that S and his wife are entitled to possession of the property.

It's important to remember that the doctrine of promissory estoppel will only be applied when the promisee's reliance on the promise was reasonable. In *Phillippe v. Shapell Industries, Inc.*, 43 Cal. 3d 1247, 241 Cal. Rptr. 22 (1987), the California Supreme Court ruled that a real estate broker without a written listing cannot use promissory estoppel to collect a commission. A broker is supposed to know that a written agreement is necessary. In effect, it is never reasonable for a broker to rely on a client's verbal promise.

However, promissory estoppel can be used in a broker's favor if the client fraudulently misled the broker into believing they had a valid written agreement.

Case Example: Mr. Owens, a broker, orally agreed to help the Foundation for Ocean Research (FOR) sell a large tract of land in San Diego. Owens began working after a lawyer representing the FOR told him a written listing agreement had been prepared and formally accepted by the board of directors. But in fact the board never accepted a written agreement, and the FOR later refused to pay a commission. Owens sued.

The court ruled that because the FOR fraudulently led Owens to believe there was a signed writing, it was estopped from using the writing requirement as a defense to his claim for a commission. *Owens v. Foundation for Ocean Research*, 107 Cal. App. 3d 179, 165 Cal. Rptr. 571 (1980).

Remember, too, that the statute of frauds only applies to an action for breach of contract. Even when a broker does not have a valid contract, he or she may be able to sue a client for fraud (which is a tort action, not a contract action).

MODIFICATION OF A CONTRACT

When both parties agree that their written contract contains an error or omission, they can simply correct it. But to make a more substantial change in the contract, they usually must exchange additional consideration. In effect, the modification is a separate contract; like any other contract, it must be supported by consideration or it is unenforceable.

Example: In March, A agrees to buy B's house for $150,000, and closing is set for April 30. A few days later, A realizes he's not going to have the money by then. He asks B if he'd be willing to modify their contract so that closing will take place on June 1. B agrees, just because he's a nice guy, and they draw up a modification.

Then B discovers he absolutely has to have the sale proceeds by May 15. He asks A if closing can be moved back to May 14, but A refuses.

B can enforce the contract as it was originally written (with an April 30 closing). The modification is unenforceable, because B did not receive any consideration for his promise to move the closing date to June 1.

If A had provided consideration for the modification—for example, by promising to pay $150,500 instead of $150,000—then it would be enforceable, and B could not demand an April 30 closing.

There are exceptions to this consideration requirement: for example, when the parties' original contract was oral, it can be modified in writing without new consideration. And once a modification is executed rather than executory—in other words, the agreement as modified has already been performed—a lack of consideration for the modification doesn't matter.

An oral contract can be modified orally if new consideration is supplied. A written contract can also be modified orally, if new consideration is supplied or if the oral agreement is executed, unless it says that it can only be modified in writing, or unless the contract as modified is subject to the statute of frauds. Thus, a modification of any deposit receipt or listing agreement must be in writing to be effective.

MODIFICATION

A modification must be supported by new consideration **unless**:

1. the original contract was oral and the modification is in writing; or
2. the modification is already executed (not executory).

A modification must be in writing **if**:

1. the original contract provides that it can only be modified in writing; or
2. the contract as modified is required to be in writing by the statute of frauds.

Otherwise, the modification may be oral, as long as it is supported by new consideration or the oral agreement has been executed.

ASSIGNMENT. When one party to a contract transfers his or her contractual rights and duties to another person, it's called an assignment. Generally, a promisor can't assign his or her duties without the promisee's consent. But as a general rule, a promisee may assign his or her rights without the promisor's consent, unless the contract states that consent is required. And in fact, many contracts do require consent to an assignment.

Example: L and T sign a two-year residential lease. It provides that T, the tenant, cannot assign her rights under the lease (the right to live in the apartment) to anyone else without L's permission.

However, the contract doesn't prevent L from assigning his rights to someone else without T's permission. L assigns the lease to C; L is the assignor and C is the assignee. Now T is required to pay rent to C.

Even without a provision prohibiting assignment, a contract for personal services can't be assigned without consent. If you hire me to play the piano at a birthday party, I can't send my sister over instead. (Listing agreements are considered personal services contracts.) A contract also can't be assigned without consent if the assignment would significantly change the other party's duties or increase his or her risks.

Chapter 7

But even when the other party consents to an assignment, the assignor isn't relieved of liability under the contract. The assignor is secondarily liable, and can be required to pay the other party if the assignee doesn't.

Example: L and T sign a two-year lease that prohibits T from assigning it without L's consent. A year later, T asks L for permission to assign the lease to X, and L agrees. T moves out and X moves in. But X doesn't pay the rent. Not only can L sue X, L can still sue T. If X turns out to be judgment-proof, L can collect the judgment from T.

NOVATION. To avoid secondary liability, a party who wants to withdraw from a contract should request a novation instead of an assignment. In a novation, a new person takes the place of one of the parties, and the withdrawing party is completely relieved of liability connected with the contract.

A novation can only be arranged with the other original party's consent. It's essentially a new contract, so it must comply with all the rules for contract formation, including the mutual consent requirement.

Note that the term "novation" doesn't necessarily refer to the substitution of a new party. It can also refer to the substitution of a new obligation in place of the original one. If the original parties tear up a two-year lease and execute a five-year lease, that's a novation.

ACCORD AND SATISFACTION. Sometimes, especially when there is a good faith dispute over contract performance, a promisee agrees to accept something different or less than what the original contract required the promisor to provide. This kind of agreement is called an **accord**; it does not have to be supported by separate consideration. To extinguish the promisor's original obligation, the promisee executes a **satisfaction**—a document expressly stating that the promisor's performance has been accepted in satisfaction of the obligation.

RELEASE. A contractual obligation can be eliminated altogether if the promisee grants the promisor a release. An oral release is valid if the promisee receives some new consideration; a written release doesn't have to be supported by new consideration. When the contract has to be in writing because of the statute of frauds, the release should also be in writing.

Performance and Breach of Contract

If one party to a contract performs his or her side of the bargain, the other party is also required to perform. If one party fails to perform (breaches the contract), the other is not required to perform. If I contract to build you a house for $250,000 and I don't build the house, you don't owe me $250,000.

www.inman.com
www.ired.com
(Indexes)

228

In most cases, each party carries out the promised performance to the other's satisfaction. In some cases, one party clearly fails to do what he or she promised.

But sometimes it's not so clear-cut. One party (A) does all of the things promised, but the other party (B) feels they were not done well. Or A does nearly everything promised, but some details aren't taken care of. Or A does everything promised, but takes longer to do it than agreed. In these cases, there is room for argument about whether or not the contract was breached. Is B required to perform his side of the bargain?

The answer to that question depends on whether there has been **substantial performance** or a **material breach**. If A hasn't fulfilled every detail of the contract but has carried out its main objectives, that may be treated as substantial performance. Although B may be able to sue for damages because of the unfulfilled details, they don't excuse B from performing his side of the bargain.

On the other hand, if A fails to perform some important part of the contract, or performs very badly, that will be treated as a material breach. If A commits a material breach, B is excused from fulfilling his promises. If B doesn't perform, he won't be liable to A for breach of their contract, because A already materially breached it. (If B has already fully performed, A will be required to pay him damages for breach of contract.)

What provisions of a contract are so important that failure to fulfill them amounts to a material breach? That depends on all the circumstances of each case. If the promisee emphasized to the promisor that a particular detail of the contract was especially important, failure to comply with that detail may be a material breach. On the other hand, if the promisee acted as though a detail was unimportant, failure to comply with it isn't a material breach.

Case Example: Because of financial problems, Mrs. Fong put her house up for sale. Mr. and Mrs. Converse wanted to buy it, so they signed a purchase contract that called for a $5,000 deposit. The Converses could only come up with $3,000, but said they'd pay the other $2,000 soon.

Then Mrs. Fong's children gave her some money so that she wouldn't have to sell the house. Fong tried to back out of her contract with the Converses, but they sued. Fong argued that their failure to pay the full deposit was a material breach, so she couldn't be required to sell them the house.

The court disagreed. Fong had requested the deposit to show the State Franchise Tax Board the house would be sold, to delay a forced tax sale of the property. The Converses' $3,000 served that purpose, and Fong said nothing to indicate that it was urgent for them to pay her the remainder. Fong did not suffer any harm as a result of the delay in payment. It was not a material breach, and Fong had to go through with the sale. *Converse v. Fong*, 159 Cal. App. 3d 86, 205 Cal. Rptr. 242 (1984).

Many standard contract forms state that **"time is of the essence."** The purpose of including that phrase is to emphasize that timely performance is crucial. That makes failure to meet a deadline a material breach. Otherwise, a delay isn't a material breach, as long as performance is completed within a reasonable time after the deadline. It is often a printed clause in a standard form, "fill-in-the-blanks" contract.

But the phrase generally doesn't have any real effect. It is often a printed clause in a standard form, "fill-in-the-blanks" contract. Unless the parties actually insist on timely performance, a court is likely to hold that the "time is of the essence" clause has been waived. So if you want to treat delay as a material breach, make sure the other party knows ahead of time that it matters to you.

CONDITIONS

Contracts often include one or more **conditions** (sometimes called **contingency clauses**). A condition makes the promisor's obligation depend on the occurrence of a particular event. If the event does not occur, the promisor can withdraw without liability for breach of contract. For example, many deposit receipts are contingent on whether the buyers qualify for financing, or on the results of an appraisal, termite inspection, or soil test.

When a contract is conditional, the promisor must make a good faith effort to fulfill the condition. He or she can't deliberately prevent its fulfillment to get out of the contract.

Case Example: The contract provided that the buyer had the right to review and approve certain reports, as a condition to the close of escrow, within 28 days of their receipt. Within that time the buyer disapproved of the reports and proposed some novel ways to keep the "deal alive." Having not heard from the seller, 60 days later the buyer wrote the seller that the objections were waived and to proceed and close escrow. The seller then canceled escrow. The buyer refused to cancel escrow and sued for specific performance.

The Court of Appeal held that the approval of the reports was a condition that had to occur before the buyer's duty to purchase arose (condition precedent). The disapproval was rejection of the reports, which therefore terminated the contract. The condition gave the buyer the option to terminate the contract, which the buyer did. Once the contract was terminated, it was impossible to revive it . The sellers were then unable to waiver the objections to the reports. *Beverly Way Associates v. Barhan*, 226 Cal. App. 3d 49, 276 Cal. Rptr. 240 (1990).

A condition can be waived by the party it was intended to benefit or protect.

Example: The purchase agreement is contingent on a satisfactory termite inspection. It states that if the results of the inspection are unsatisfactory, the buyer can withdraw from the purchase unless the seller takes action to correct the problems revealed.

The inspection shows that the house is infested with termites. The seller informs the buyer that she is not going to correct the problem, but the buyer decides to go ahead with the purchase. The buyer has a right to waive the condition, because it was included in the contract for his protection.

But when a condition is included for the benefit of both parties, neither one can waive it without the other's consent.

Example: B has interviewed for a job with a certain company, but it will be another month before he hears whether they've hired him. L agrees to loan B some money on the condition that B gets the job. This condition protects both B and L: it prevents B from taking out a loan he won't be able repay, and it prevents L from lending to someone who's very likely to default.

Suppose B doesn't get the job after all, but he still wants to borrow the money. He'd like to waive the condition. But B can't waive it unilaterally—L must also agree to waive it, or the contract is void.

TENDERING PERFORMANCE

In many cases, one party (A) has reason to believe that the other (B) is not going to fulfill the contract. The time for performance has arrived, and B hasn't taken any steps toward carrying out her side of the bargain. Before A can sue B for breach of contract, he is required to *offer* to perform his side of the bargain. This offer of performance is called a **tender offer** or simply a **tender**.

Example: B contracted to buy A's house, but A suspects B doesn't plan to go through with the purchase. On the agreed closing date, A must offer to deliver the deed to B as promised in their contract. If B refuses to pay A and accept the deed, B is in default, and A may sue.

A tender must be made in good faith. In other words, the tendering party must be willing and able to perform everything he or she promised, fully and immediately. The tender must be unconditional, unless the contract contained a condition that the other party hasn't fulfilled yet.

It is not necessary to tender performance when there has been an **anticipatory repudiation**. If B repudiates the contract by notifying A that she won't perform, A can file suit for breach without making a tender. (The tender would be a waste of time.) But an anticipatory repudiation must be a clear, unequivocal statement. A can't infer repudiation from B's behavior or from a vague remark.

Remedies for Breach of Contract

When a promisor has performed badly, or has refused to perform at all (either by anticipatory repudiation or by rejecting the tender offer), he or she has breached the contract. Then the promisee can turn to the legal system for help in enforcing the contract.

Chapter 7

ARBITRATION

As we discussed in Chapter 1, the courts are overflowing with litigation, and it can take years for a case to get to trial. Because of these long delays, more and more contracts include arbitration provisions. These provisions will be discussed in chapter 9.

Arbitration is an alternative to the court system. To save time and money, the parties to a dispute can agree to submit to arbitration instead of going to court. They hire an arbitrator to perform the functions of a judge, reviewing the evidence and resolving the dispute. When an arbitration provision is initialed in a contract, the parties agree in advance to arbitrate if a dispute arises.

Arbitration is usually much more informal than a trial; the discovery process is limited and the rules of evidence are relaxed. Unless otherwise agreed, the arbitrator's decision will be legally binding on the parties—the loser can't just shrug it off. And often they don't even have a right to appeal the decision to the court system. In their effort to save time and money, the parties agree to give that up.

As you can see, an arbitration provision in a contract has a significant effect on the parties' rights in the event of a breach. There was concern that many people involved in real estate transactions sign contracts containing arbitration provisions without understanding the legal consequences. As a result, the California legislature adopted a statute requiring real estate contracts with binding arbitration provisions to include a warning in large, boldface type. The warning states in part:

YOU ARE GIVING UP ANY RIGHTS YOU MIGHT POSSESS TO HAVE THE DISPUTE LITIGATED IN A COURT OR JURY TRIAL...YOU ARE GIVING UP YOUR JUDICIAL RIGHTS TO DISCOVERY AND APPEAL, UNLESS THOSE RIGHTS ARE SPECIFICALLY INCLUDED...IF YOU REFUSE TO SUBMIT TO ARBITRATION AFTER AGREEING TO THIS PROVISION, YOU MAY BE COMPELLED TO ARBITRATE...

This statute applies to any contract containing an arbitration clause that conveys real property or concerns a possible future conveyance of real property. That includes marketing contracts, deposit receipts, installment land contracts, and leases with options to purchase. It also applies to any agreement between a principal and an agent in a real property sale, such as a listing agreement.

www.rereader.com/alanslaw/alanslaw13.html
(Arbitration Clauses in Real Estate Contracts)

A CONTRACT LAWSUIT

STATUTE OF LIMITATIONS. In California, a lawsuit based on a written contract generally must be filed within four years after the breach occurred. For some oral contracts (such as an oral employment contract, or an oral six-month lease), suit must be filed within two years after the breach. However, suit can be filed within four years in the case of any contract (oral or written) for the sale of goods—that is, a sale of personal property, not real property.

The parties to a contract can agree to a shorter limitation period than the one prescribed by statute, but the period must not be unreasonably short. In a contract for the sale of goods, the parties can agree to shorten the limitation period to one year, but not less.

These limitation periods apply even when the suing party was not aware of the breach at the time it occurred. But there's an exception for cases involving fraud or mistake: time doesn't start to run out until the injured party discovers the fraud or mistake.

INTERPRETATION OF THE CONTRACT. To decide whether a contract has been breached (and if it has, what the plaintiff's remedy should be), the court must interpret the parties' agreement. The court tries to give effect to what the parties intended when they entered the contract.

When the contract is in writing, the court is supposed to determine the parties' intention from the written document alone, if possible. If the document is unclear or ambiguous, the judge will let the parties testify about their negotiations in drawing up the contract, to shed light on the intended meaning of the document. But when the language in the document is clear and unambiguous, the judge may refuse to admit evidence about negotiations or oral agreements that contradict the terms of the written agreement.

> **Example:** T is going to lease a townhouse from L for nine months. The written lease form clearly states that rent is due on the first of each month. Before signing the lease, T asks L if she can pay the rent on the 15th of each month instead, and L agrees. They don't change the lease form to reflect this agreement, however.
>
> Later T and L wind up in court. T wants to testify that L agreed to accept the rent on the 15th of each month. But the judge may decide to exclude this testimony, because it contradicts the written agreement between the parties.

This is known as the **parol evidence rule**. ("Parol" is a legal term that means "spoken.") Parol evidence (which can be either spoken or written) is not allowed before the court when it would modify or contradict a written contract which is a complete and final statement of the parties bargain as determined by the court, and the parol evidence was made before or at the time the written contract as executed.

This rule, like the statute of frauds, is intended to cut down on false claims and prevent promisors from weaseling out of what they agreed to do. However, parol evidence is admissible to clarify an ambiguity or show fraud, mutual mistake, duress, forgery, or illegality of the subject matter. It is advisable to show a subsequent agreement (modification) or that the parties did not intend a binding contract until a condition outside of the contract was satisfied (approval by an inspector).

Suppose that in the previous example T ask L several months after signing the lease to agree to accept rent payments on the 15th and L verbally agreed. This modification agreement comes into court because it occurred after the written contract. However, T loses because there was no consideration to support the modification. T should have gotten L to agree in writing to payments on the 15th for consideration of $10 more rent each month.

Damages

Once the court has concluded there has been a breach of contract, it must decide on a remedy. The most common remedy for breach of contract is a damages award: the

breaching party is ordered to pay a sum of money to the non-breaching party. How much? The award is supposed to be the amount that will put the non-breaching party in the position he or she would have been in if the other party had fulfilled the contract.

> **Example:** Perkins contracted to clear Hanawalt's property for $10,000, but he quit the project soon after starting. So Hanawalt hired Lopez to carry out the job. Lopez charged her $12,000.
>
> Hanawalt sues Perkins for breach of contract, and Perkins is ordered to pay her $2,000. If Perkins had not breached the contract, it would only have cost Hanawalt $10,000 (rather than $12,000) to have her property cleared. The $2,000 judgment against Perkins represents the difference between what the job actually cost Hanawalt and what it would have cost her if Perkins hadn't breached: $12,000 - $10,000 = $2,000.

However, if Lopez had charged Hanawalt only $9,000 to clear the property, Hanawalt would actually have been better off as a result of Perkins's breach. The job would have cost her $1,000 less than it would have if Perkins had fulfilled the contract. In that case, Hanawalt would not be entitled to a judgment against Perkins, because she wasn't damaged by his breach. The point of a contract lawsuit is to compensate the promisee for actual damages, not to punish the promisor for breaching. Punitive damages are generally only awarded in cases involving a tort (such as fraud), not for breach of contract. (See Chapter 6.)

CERTAINTY REQUIREMENT. To be the basis for a damages award, a loss resulting from breach of contract must be proven with certainty. Occasionally a damages award includes **lost profits**: "If Z hadn't breached the contract, I could have opened my store a month earlier, and I would have made at least $1,000 in profit during that month." But in most cases, lost profits are considered too uncertain to be included in the judgment. Who knows whether the store would have turned a profit if it had been opened that month? It might even have lost money. Unless the evidence proves that there would have been a profit, and that it definitely would have been at least a certain amount, lost profits are not awarded. Certainly a business with a lengthy profit history stands a better chance of recovering lost profits that a new business.

MITIGATION REQUIREMENT. The non-breaching party in a contract dispute is required to mitigate damages. That means the non-breaching party must do what he or she can to cut down on losses resulting from the other party's breach.

> **Example:** L leases an apartment to T for one year; T has agreed to pay $500 a month. Two months later, T decides she doesn't like the place, so she moves out and doesn't make any further rent payments. That's clearly a breach of contract.
>
> But L can't simply sue T and expect a judgment for $5,000 (the additional amount she would have received if T had honored the lease). L is required to mitigate her damages by trying to rent the apartment again.
>
> If L finds a new tenant for $500 a month, T will not be liable for any of her unpaid rent. However, T may be required to reimburse L for any expenses incurred in renting the apartment again, such as the cost of advertising.

Suppose no one will rent the apartment for $500 a month, but someone rents it for $450 a month. Then T will be liable to L for the difference between what L actually collects and what she would have collected if T hadn't breached: $50 per month, for 10 months. The damages award would be $500 ($50 x 10 = $500), plus any expenses L incurred.

LIQUIDATED DAMAGES. To lessen the possibility of expensive litigation, some contracts include a **liquidated damages** provision. The parties agree in advance that if there is a breach, the damages are set at a specified sum or calculated according to a specified formula. The non-breaching party will accept the liquidated damages instead of suing for actual damages.

Case Example: The Angells contracted to buy the Felicianos' home. To finance the purchase, the Angells executed a $30,000 deed of trust in favor of the Felicianos.

The deed of trust had a liquidated damages provision: if the transaction was not closed by November 1st, the Angells would pay the Felicianos $22 per day until it did close. That amount was intended to cover the trust deed interest that the Felicianos would lose because of the delay.

As it turned out, closing was several days late, because the Angells had some trouble selling their previous home. The Angells had to pay the Felicianos $261 in liquidated damages. *Angell v. Rowlands*, 85 Cal. App. 3d 536, 149 Cal. Rptr. 574 (1978).

As a general rule, a court will enforce a liquidated damages provision unless one of the parties proves that the amount agreed to was unreasonable at the time the contract was made.

There are restrictions on liquidated damages for certain types of contracts. In the case of a residential lease, a liquidated damages clause is void unless it would be extremely difficult to calculate the actual damages after a breach. The same rule applies to a consumer loan for the purchase of personal property. That standard is hard to meet, so a liquidated damages provision in a residential lease or a consumer loan contract is rarely enforceable.

In a contract to purchase real property, the buyer's deposit is often treated as liquidated damages. If the buyer breaches the contract, the seller keeps the deposit. However, California has some statutory limits on use of the deposit as liquidated damages. These apply in a transaction involving residential property with up to four units, if the buyer intends to occupy one of the units. If the amount paid under the contract's liquidated damages provision is 3% of the purchase price or less, the provision is presumed to be valid. The seller can keep that much of the deposit unless the buyer proves the amount is unreasonable under the circumstances. If the amount paid is more than 3% of the price, a court will regard the provision as invalid, unless the seller can prove that the amount is reasonable. In any case, the liquidated damages provision must appear in large, boldface type in the contract, and it must be separately initialed or signed by the parties.

Chapter 7

Equitable Remedies

A damages award—a sum of money intended to compensate the non-breaching party—is the standard remedy in a contract dispute. But money doesn't always do the trick. In some cases, alternative remedies are available.

INJUNCTIONS. An injunction is a court order directing a person to do something or refrain from doing something (see Chapter 1). As a general rule, a court cannot issue an injunction to keep someone from breaching a contract. The law requires payment of damages for breach, but ordinarily does not prevent the breach.

The handful of exceptions to that rule rarely apply to cases involving real estate contracts. However, an injunction can be issued to prevent the breach of a restrictive covenant (see Chapter 13), if it can be shown that the breach will cause irreparable harm. Harm is considered irreparable if it can't be adequately redressed by a damages award.

RESCISSION. If someone has done wrong to you in a contract, you may not want to go through with the contract. Instead, he or she just wants to undo the contract, erase it, go back to square one. In that case, he or she may ask a court to **rescind** the contract. When a contract is rescinded, each party returns any consideration the other has given (this is called **restitution**). All of their contractual obligations are terminated.

Rescission is available under a variety of circumstances. Whenever a voidable contract is disaffirmed—because of lack of capacity, fraud, undue influence, duress, menace, or mistake—the court will rescind it. And one party can request rescission if the other party failed to provide the promised consideration, or if that consideration turns out to be void. A court will also rescind an unlawful contract (unless the unlawfulness was clear from the contract's terms and the parties were equally at fault—then a court will refuse to become involved in any way).

A contract can also be rescinded without going to court, if both parties agree. In some situations, however, they may prefer to **cancel** their contract instead of rescinding it. When a contract is cancelled, all further obligations are terminated, but the parties aren't required to return what they've already received under the contract.

SPECIFIC PERFORMANCE. Sometimes the non-breaching party to a contract doesn't just want to be compensated for the harm that resulted from the other's breach. Instead, the non-breaching party wants to make the other party do what he or she promised to do.

Think back to a case described earlier in this chapter, Converse v. Fong. Mrs. Fong put her house up for sale to prevent foreclosure, and the Converses contracted to buy it. Then Mrs. Fong's children gave her some money so that she wouldn't have to sell her house. Mrs. Fong tried to back out of her contract with the Converses, and they sued. The Converses didn't just want to be compensated for their expenses (the appraisal, inspections, and so forth); they wanted to make Mrs. Fong sell them her house. They had their hearts set on that particular house, and finding a comparable substitute wouldn't be the same. So the court ordered Mrs. Fong to complete the sale to the Converses.

This is called **specific performance**. The court orders the breaching party to carry out the performance he or she promised in the contract. Specific performance is generally not granted when a damages award will be just as effective. For example, a car dealer won't be ordered to sell you a particular car when you could get an identical one from another dealer. (If you have to pay more at the second dealer, the first dealer is liable to you for the difference as a damages award.) If a contract is for a one of a kind item, then specific performance is an appropriate remedy. A damages award won't enable you to buy an identical one, because there isn't another just like it.

Specific performance is most often used in enforcing real estate contracts, because a piece of real property is generally unique—like Mrs. Fong's house. Under a California statute, there is a presumption that a damages award is not sufficient compensation for breach of an agreement to transfer real property. When the property in question is a single-family home that the non-breaching party intended to occupy, this presumption is conclusive: if the non-breaching party requests specific performance, the court may order it (some courts will not). When the case involves some other kind of real property, the breaching party is given an opportunity to rebut the presumption by proving that a damages award will be sufficient compensation.

When specific performance is not available. There are many circumstances in which a court cannot grant specific performance. It can never be a remedy for breach of a personal services contract: no one can be forced to work for someone, or to employ someone. Specific performance also can't be ordered for an agreement to procure the act or consent of another person—such as when a husband has agreed to persuade his wife to sign a document.

You can't be ordered to perform a contract if it wasn't just and reasonable, or if you didn't receive legally adequate consideration. For example, if you agreed to sell your $150,000 house for $75,000, the contract is enforceable even though the consideration is inadequate. But although you may be required to pay damages to the buyer ($75,000 is likely), you can't be forced to complete the sale. On the other hand, a buyer can't be ordered to complete a purchase of real property when the seller doesn't have marketable title.

You also can't be ordered to perform if the other party hasn't fulfilled all the conditions he or she agreed to. And you can't be ordered to perform if your consent to the contract was obtained by misrepresentation or unfair practices, or if your consent was given because of mistake, misapprehension, or surprise.

In spite of all these restrictions, specific performance is a common remedy when a seller breaches a deposit receipt. Note that specific performance can be ordered even when the contract includes a liquidated damages provision.

Breach of a Contract

ANTICIPATORY REPUDIATION OR REJECTION OF TENDER	*MEDIATION* OR *ARBITRATION* OR LAWSUIT	POSSIBLE REMEDIES 1. Compensatory Damages 2. Liquidated Damages 3. Rescission 4. Injunction 5. Specific Performance

INTERFERENCE WITH CONTRACT

Sometimes one of the parties to a contract is persuaded to breach it by a third party, someone outside the contractual relationship. For example, another real estate agent might convince your client to breach the listing agreement he has with you. Or a real estate agent might persuade a seller to breach a binding deposit receipt (purchase agreement) and accept a better offer.

These acts may constitute a tort called **interference with contractual relations**. In that case, the non-breaching party can file a tort lawsuit against the third party, in addition to filing a contract lawsuit against the breaching party. To win the tort suit, the plaintiff must show that the defendant (the third party) was aware of the contract and intentionally disrupted it. Because this is a tort suit instead of a contract suit, punitive damages may be awarded if the defendant's actions were malicious: if they were designed to injure the plaintiff, or were done with conscious disregard for the plaintiff's rights.

There is also a tort called **interference with prospective economic advantage**. It is similar to interference with contractual relations, but the plaintiff doesn't have to show that he or she had a binding contract with another person. It's only necessary to prove that they had an economic relationship and the defendant was aware of that relationship. In *Buckaloo v. Johnson*, 14 Cal. 3d 815, 122 Cal. Rptr. 745 (1975), the California Supreme Court ruled that a seller's broker, without a written listing agreement, could sue a buyer and another broker for interference with prospective economic advantage.

In *Aas v. Superior Court (William Lyon Company)*, 2000 Daily Journal D.A.R. 12831 (Cal., December 4, 2000), the California Supreme Court refused to permit a cause of action for interference with prospective economic advantage where homeowners and a homeowners association sought to recover damages in negligence from the developer, contractor and subcontractors who built their dwellings for construction defects that have not caused property damage. In dissent, Chief Justice George stated: "In determining that a negligently constructed home must first collapse or be gutted by fire before a homeowner may sue in tort to collect costs necessary to repair negligently constructed shear walls or fire walls, the majority today embraces a ruling that offends both established common law and basic common sense." The majority stated that adopting a rule like that proposed by the Chief Justice was for the Legislature to do.

CHAPTER SUMMARY

1. A contract is an agreement to do or not do a certain thing. Every contract is either express or implied; unilateral or bilateral; executory or executed; and valid, void, voidable, or unenforceable.

2. A person lacks capacity to contract unless he or she is competent and at least 18 years old. A contract by an incompetent person is void. A contract by a minor is void if it concerns real property; otherwise, it is generally voidable. A contract may be valid if it involves necessities; medical services; art, entertainment or professional sports; or is entered into by an emancipated minor.

3. A valid contract is based on the parties' mutual consent, achieved through offer and acceptance. An offer must express an objective intent to contract, and it must have definite terms. An offer can be revoked at any time until it has been accepted. The offeree's acceptance isn't effective until it has been communicated to the offeror in the manner specified in the offer. If the offeree changes the terms of the offer, that's a counter offer, not an acceptance.

4. When one party has obtained the other's consent through fraud, undue influence, duress, menace, or mistake, the contract is voidable by the victim.

5. A contract generally isn't valid unless it is supported by consideration: each party must give something of value to the other. But a contract is enforceable even though the consideration given by the parties is unequal.

6. A court will not enforce a contract unless its purpose is lawful.

7. The statute of frauds requires certain contracts to be in writing and signed by the party to be charged. That includes real estate purchase contracts, leases for more than one year, listing agreements, powers of attorney, and trust deed assumptions. Other laws also require mortgages, trust deeds, and broker/salesperson employment agreements to be in writing and signed.

8. A contract modification usually must be supported by new consideration. The modification may be oral, unless the original contract stated that it could only be modified in writing, or unless the statute of frauds applies to the contract as modified. Assignment, novation, and accord and satisfaction are specific types of contract modification.

9. If one party commits a material breach of contract, the other isn't required to fulfill his or her side of the bargain. But when there is substantial performance by one party, the other is also required to perform. The non-breaching party has to tender performance before he or she can sue for breach of contract, unless there has been an anticipatory repudiation.

10. When a contract is conditional, the promisor can't get out of it by preventing the condition from being fulfilled. A condition may be waived by the party it was intended to benefit.

11. The most common remedy for breach of contract is compensatory damages; punitive damages are not awarded. The non-breaching party is required to mitigate the damages. A liquidated damages provision states in advance how much one party will be entitled to collect in the event of a breach.

Other remedies for breach of contract are rescission and specific performance. Specific performance is not available in most cases, but may be ordered when a seller breaches an agreement to sell commercial real estate or lots. Most judges will not enforce it for a single-family home.

CASE PROBLEM

Hsu v. Abbara, 9 Cal, 4th 863, 39 Cal. Rptr 2d 824 (1995)

On June 5, 1987, Abbaras listed their home for sale at $299,900 with Roy Rhino of Merrill Lynch Realty. Hsus made an offer to purchase the home for $285,000 through their agent Ben Lin on June 8, 1987. The deposit receipt contained a provision for attorney's fees: "In any action between Broker, BUYER or SELLER arising out of this agreement, the prevailing party shall be entitled to reasonable attorney's fees and costs." On June 9, the Abbaras made a counter offer on a standard deposit receipt for $297,000, set to expire at 5 p.m. on June 10, and this counter offer incorporated the terms of the original offer. The Hsus viewed the property a second time and on the bottom of the counter offer wrote "All terms are accepted except price to be $292,000" and this counter offer is good until 11 a.m. on June 10.

On the evening of June 9, Lin spoke with Rhino to see if Abbaras would take a price under $297,000. Rhino said to present a new written offer. Lin called again to say that the Hsus were firm at $292,000. On June 10, Abbaras told Rhino no on $292,000 and to go back to $299,900.

The afternoon of June 10, Rhino received the Abbaras' counter offer ($297,000) with the "All terms are accepted except price to be $292,000" lined out. In it's place was handwritten "offer terms are accepted." Rhino called the Abbaras to report that Hsus agreed on $297,000. Abbaras said anything less than full price was not acceptable. Rhino was unsuccessful in finding another house for Abbaras, who then decided not to sell. Rhino prepared escrow instructions which Hsus signed but Abbaras did not. On June 22, Hsus sue the Abbaras for specific performance.

Was there a contract?

Answer: No. The Hsus' offer of $285,000 was rejected by Abbaras. Abbara's counter offer of $297,000 was rejected by Hsus when Hsus made a counter offer of $292,000. Subsequently, Hsus made a new offer at $297,000 which Abbaras rejected.

CHAPTER 7 KEY TERMS		
	economic duress	rescission
	executory/executed	right of first refusal
	express/implied	severable
acceptance	liquidated damages	specific performance
accord and satisfaction	material breach	statute of frauds
assignment	menace	substantial performance
breach	mitigation	tender offer
cancellation	mutual mistake	undue influence
capacity	novation	unenforceable
consideration	offer	unilateral/bilateral
contingency clause	offeror/offeree	valid
counteroffer	parol evidence rule	void
disaffirm	promisor/promisee	voidable
duress	promissory estoppel	

Contract Law

Quiz—Chapter 7

1. Y tells Z, "i'll pay you $15 if you promise me that you promise me that you will mow my lawn on Saturday:" Z says, "Sure, I'll do that." What type of contract is this?

   a. An implied bilateral contract
   b. An express unilateral contract
   c. An executory bilateral contract
   d. An executed unilateral contract

2. An offer can be revoked at any time before it's accepted, unless:

   a. the offer states that it's irrevocable.
   b. the offeree gives the offeror consideration for keeping the offer open.
   c. the offer has a specific termination date.
   d. any of the above.

3. On May 15, B offers to buy S's property. On May 18, S mails B a letter accepting the offer. On May 19 (before she receives S's letter), B calls S and revoked the offer. Do they have a binding contract?

   a. No, B hadn't received a letter of acceptance before revoking her offer
   b. No, because S should have accepted over the telephone instead of by mail
   c. Yes, because B waited more than three days to revoke her offer
   d. Yes, because S's acceptance became effective when he mailed it

4. S offers to sell his house to B for $200,000 if B will pay $45,000 in cash and give S a 15-year trust deed for the balance at 11 interest. B sends S a letter saying, "I accept your offer, provided that I only put $40,000 down:" This is called a:

   a. partial acceptance.
   b. unilateral acceptance.
   c. defeasible offer.
   d. counter offer.

5. B knows some dark secrets from S's past. B blackmails S into signing a contract to sell her home at half its value. This contract is:

   a. unenforceable; consideration inadequate.
   b. voidable due to menace.
   c. void due to business compulsion.
   d. severable due to unlawful purpose.

6. Which of these contracts does not have to be in writing to be enforceable?

   a. A deed of trust securing a $5,000 loan
   b. A listing agreement for a single-family home
   c. An agency agreement authorizing the agent to sell the principal's $100,000 yacht
   d. All of these contracts must be in writing

7. As a general rule, a contract modification must be:

   a. notarized and recorded.
   b. approved by a court.
   c. supported by new consideration.
   d. all of the above.

8. When a new person takes the place of one of the parties to a contract and the withdrawing party is relieved of all liability, it's called:

   a. accord and satisfaction.
   b. novation.
   c. assignment.
   d. substantial performance.

9. In which of these cases is a judge most likely to award specific performance?

   a. A seller breaches a contract to sell a single-family home to a couple for slightly more than its appraised value
   b. A real estate salesperson breaches her employment contract with her broker
   c. A lender breaches a loan commitment agreement
   d. A seller breaches a contract to sell a commercial lot for substantially less than its fair market value

10. When one sues for the completion of the contract, it is called:

   a. money damages.
   b. specific performance.
   c. rescission.
   d. liquidated damages.

ANSWERS: 1. c; 2. b; 3. d; 4. d; 5. b; 6. c; 7. c; 8. c; 9. a; 10. b

JUDICIAL COUNCIL OF CALIFORNIA

Administrative Office of the Courts

CHAPTER 8
Real Estate Contracts

CHAPTER OVERVIEW

Now that you have a general understanding of the nature of contracts and the terms involved, it is time to explore specific contracts used by people in real estate: an employment contract between a broker and a salesperson; the listing contract between the property owner and the broker; the contracts between the seller and the buyer of the property (generally referred to as the deposit receipt); and options.

A real estate agent is expected to be familiar with several different kinds of contracts. But each contract is just a particular application of the basic rules of contract law that will be outlined in the first part of this chapter.

As you've seen, the statute of frauds requires many of the contracts used in a real estate transaction to be in writing. Even when a signed written contract isn't required by law, it's always wise to have one. The parties to a contract can draft a document for themselves, but it's much safer to use standard forms or (for a complex transaction) to have lawyers do the drafting. A real estate agent preparing a contract for others must use preprinted or prepared forms, with minimal additions and changes, or risk liability for the unauthorized practice of law.

Whenever a document is executed in the course of a real estate transaction, the agent must see to it that each party receives a copy at the time of signing. That includes copies of any modifications of the agreements, too.

If a salesperson prepares documents, his or her broker is required to review, initial, and date the documents within five working days after they were prepared, or before closing, whichever occurs first. Remember: the broker must keep copies of all documents pertaining to a transaction for at least three years. This includes copies of all listings, deposit receipts, canceled checks, and trust records.

Chapter 8

Some of the contracts commonly used in real estate transactions will be discussed in this and later chapters, including title insurance policies (Chapter 10); escrow instructions (Chapter 11); deeds of trust, mortgages, and land contracts (Chapter 12); and leases (Chapter 15).

This section examines listing agreements, deposit receipts, and options. We've used the California Association of REALTORS® (CAR) forms to illustrate typical provisions, but many other forms are available. Our use of the CAR forms is not intended as an endorsement of them, nor as a criticism of any other forms. Keep in mind that the provisions discussed are not necessarily required by law; other forms may not include them, and the parties may choose to alter them.

BROKER/SALESPERSON EMPLOYMENT AGREEMENTS

The Real Estate Commissioner's Regulations require a broker to have a written employment agreement with each licensee who works for him or her. (That includes other brokers as well as salespersons.) The agreement must be signed by both parties. It should state the main terms of the employment relationship, such as duties, supervision, compensation, and termination. A copy of the California Association of Realtor's® (CAR) **Independent Contractor Agreement** form is reprinted here.

In the CAR form, the broker agrees to provide the salesperson with current listings and the use of the office facilities (paragraphs 3 and 5). The salesperson agrees to work diligently to sell or lease properties listed with the broker, and to solicit new listings (paragraph 6). But the broker's control over the salesperson's work is limited to the supervision required by law (paragraph 3). The broker does not have the right to order the salesperson to work on a particular listing, or to direct how the salesperson carries out the work.

"The salesperson licensee shall receive a share of commissions which are actually collected by the broker,..." (paragraph 9) can create a problem when the broker does not pursue collection or chooses to "let the commission go," since the transaction was for a close friend. This is emphasized further in paragraph 12. The form states that the salesperson's share of the commission is payable "immediately upon collection by Broker or as soon thereafter as practicable" (paragraph 11). This means the broker doesn't have to pay the salesperson unless the commission is collected. By law, the salesperson can only collect the commissions through the broker. Yet nothing in the contract requires the broker to sue the client for the commission or take any other steps to collect it.

The salesperson and broker agree to arbitrate any disputes through The Board of Realtor's® (paragraph 18). If the Board does not have an arbitration procedure or declines to hear the dispute, then it is arbitrated under the rules of the American Arbitration Association. This is an attempt to minimize the costs, fees, and time that would be necessary if litigation was used.

The broker does not want to have the full responsibilities associated with a salesperson classified as an employee and must make it as clear as possible that the salesperson is an independent contractor (paragraph 14). If the broker is held liable for actions of the salesperson, the contract allows the broker to pursue the salesperson for reimbursement (paragraph 20).

CALIFORNIA
ASSOCIATION
OF REALTORS®

INDEPENDENT CONTRACTOR AGREEMENT
(Between Broker and Associate-Licensee)

This Agreement, dated _____ is made between _____
_____ ("Broker") and
_____ ("Associate-Licensee").

In consideration of the covenants and representations contained in this Agreement, Broker and Associate-Licensee agree as follows:

1. **BROKER:** Broker represents that Broker is duly licensed as a real estate broker by the State of California, ☐ doing business as _____
    _____ (firm name), ☐ a sole proprietorship, ☐ a partnership, ☐ a corporation.
    Broker is a member of the _____
    Association(s) of REALTORS®, and a subscriber to the _____ multiple
    listing service(s). Broker shall keep Broker's license current during the term of this Agreement.

2. **ASSOCIATE-LICENSEE:** Associate-Licensee represents that, (a) he/she is duly licensed by the State of California as a ☐ real estate broker,
    ☐ real estate salesperson, and (b) he/she has not used any other names within the past five years, except _____
    _____. Associate-Licensee shall keep his/her license current during
    the term of this Agreement, including satisfying all applicable continuing education and provisional license requirements.

3. **INDEPENDENT CONTRACTOR RELATIONSHIP:**
    A. Broker and Associate-Licensee intend that, to the maximum extent permissible by law: (i) This Agreement does not constitute an employment
        agreement by either party; (ii) Broker and Associate-Licensee are independent contracting parties with respect to all services rendered under this
        Agreement; (iii) This Agreement shall not be construed as a partnership.
    B. Broker shall not: (i) restrict Associate-Licensee's activities to particular geographical areas or, (ii) dictate Associate-Licensee's activities with regard
        to hours, leads, open houses, opportunity or floor time, production, prospects, sales meetings, schedule, inventory, time off, vacation, or similar
        activities, except to the extent required by law.
    C. Associate-Licensee shall not be required to accept an assignment by Broker to service any particular current or prospective listing or parties.
    D. Except as required by law: (i) Associate-Licensee retains sole and absolute discretion and judgment in the methods, techniques, and procedures
        to be used in soliciting and obtaining listings, sales, exchanges, leases, rentals, or other transactions, and in carrying out Associate-Licensee's
        selling and soliciting activities, (ii) Associate-Licensee is under the control of Broker as to the results of Associate-Licensee's work only, and not
        as to the means by which those results are accomplished, (iii) Associate-Licensee has no authority to bind Broker by any promise or
        representation and (iv) Broker shall not be liable for any obligation or liability incurred by Associate-Licensee.
    E. Associate-Licensee's only remuneration shall be the compensation specified in paragraph 8.
    F. Associate-Licensee shall not be treated as an employee with respect to services performed as a real estate agent, for state and federal tax
        purposes.
    G. The fact the Broker may carry worker compensation insurance for Broker's own benefit and for the mutual benefit of Broker and licensees
        associated with Broker, including Associate-Licensee, shall not create an inference of employment.

4. **LICENSED ACTIVITY:** All listings of property, and all agreements, acts or actions for performance of licensed acts, which are taken or performed in
    connection with this Agreement, shall be taken and performed in the name of Broker. Associate-Licensee agrees to and does hereby contribute all
    right and title to such listings to Broker for the benefit and use of Broker, Associate-Licensee, and other licensees associated with Broker. Broker
    shall make available to Associate-Licensee, equally with other licensees associated with Broker, all current listings in Broker's office, except any listing
    which Broker may choose to place in the exclusive servicing of Associate-Licensee or one or more other specific licensees associated with Broker.
    Associate-Licensee shall provide and pay for all professional licenses, supplies, services, and other items required in connection with Associate-
    Licensee's activities under this Agreement, or any listing or transaction, without reimbursement from Broker except as required by law. Associate-
    Licensee shall work diligently and with his/her best efforts: **(a)** To sell, exchange, lease, or rent properties listed with Broker or other cooperating
    Brokers; **(b)** To solicit additional listings, clients, and customers; and **(c)** To otherwise promote the business of serving the public in real estate
    transactions to the end that Broker and Associate-Licensee may derive the greatest benefit possible, in accordance with law. Associate-Licensee
    shall not commit any unlawful act under federal, state or local law or regulation while conducting licensed activity. Associate-Licensee shall at all
    times be familiar, and comply, with all applicable federal, state and local laws, including, but not limited to, anti-discrimination laws and restrictions
    against the giving or accepting a fee, or other thing of value, for the referral of business to title companies, escrow companies, home inspection
    companies, pest control companies and other settlement service providers pursuant to the California Business and Professions Code and the Real
    Estate Settlement Procedures Acts (RESPA). Broker shall make available for Associate-Licensee's use, along with other licensees associated with
    Broker, the facilities of the real estate office operated by Broker at _____
    _____ and the facilities of any other office
    locations made available by Broker pursuant to this Agreement.

    Broker and Associate-Licensee acknowledge receipt of copy of this page, which constitutes Page 1 of _____ Pages.
    Broker's Initials (_____) (_____)   Associate-Licensee's Initials (_____) (_____)

Published and Distributed by:
REAL ESTATE BUSINESS SERVICES, INC.
a subsidiary of the CALIFORNIA ASSOCIATION OF REALTORS®
525 South Virgil Avenue, Los Angeles, California 90020
PRINT DATE

REVISED 10/98

OFFICE USE ONLY
Reviewed by Broker
or Designee _____
Date _____

EQUAL HOUSING
OPPORTUNITY

INDEPENDENT CONTRACTOR AGREEMENT (ICA-11 PAGE 1 OF 3)

Chapter 8

5. **PROPRIETARY INFORMATION AND FILES:** (a) All files and documents pertaining to listings, leads and transactions are the property of Broker and shall be delivered to Broker by Associate-Licensee immediately upon request or termination of their relationship under this Agreement. (b) Associate-Licensee acknowledges that Broker's method of conducting business is a protected trade secret. (c) Associate-Licensee shall not use to his/her own advantage, or the advantage of any other person, business, or entity, except as specifically agreed in writing, either during Associate-Licensee's association with Broker, or thereafter, any information gained for or from the business, or files of Broker.

6. **SUPERVISION:** Associate-Licensee, within 24 hours (or ☐ _____) after preparing, signing, or receiving same, shall submit to Broker, or Broker's designated licensee: (a) All documents which may have a material effect upon the rights and duties of principals in a transaction. (b) Any documents or other items connected with a transaction pursuant to this Agreement in the possession of or available to Associate-Licensee and, (c) All documents associated with any real estate transaction in which Associate-Licensee is a principal.

7. **TRUST FUNDS:** All trust funds shall be handled in compliance with the Business and Professions Code, and other applicable laws.

8. **COMPENSATION:**

   A. **TO BROKER:** Compensation shall be charged to parties who enter into listing or other agreements for services requiring a real estate license:
   ☐ as shown in "Exhibit A" attached, which is incorporated as a part of this Agreement by reference, or
   ☐ as follows: _____
   _____
   _____
   Any deviation which is not approved in writing in advance by Broker, shall be (1) deducted from Associate-Licensee's compensation, if lower than the amount or rate approved above; and, (2) subject to Broker approval, if higher than the amount approved above. Any permanent change in commission schedule shall be disseminated by Broker to Associate-Licensee.

   B. **TO ASSOCIATE-LICENSEE:** Associate-Licensee shall receive a share of compensation actually collected by Broker, on listings or other agreements for services requiring a real estate license, which are solicited and obtained by Associate-Licensee, and on transactions of which Associate-Licensee's activities are the procuring cause, as follows:
   ☐ as shown in "Exhibit B" attached, which is incorporated as a part of this Agreement by reference, or
   ☐ other: _____
   _____
   _____

   C. **PARTNERS, TEAMS, AND AGREEMENTS WITH OTHER ASSOCIATE-LICENSEES IN OFFICE:** If Associate-Licensee and one or more other Associate-Licensees affiliated with Broker participate on the same side (either listing or selling) of a transaction, the commission allocated to their combined activities shall be divided by Broker and paid to them according to their written agreement. Broker shall have the right to withhold total compensation if there is a dispute between associate-licensees, or if there is no written agreement, or if no written agreement has been provided to Broker.

   D. **EXPENSES AND OFFSETS:** If Broker elects to advance funds to pay expenses or liabilities of Associate-Licensee, or for an advance payment of, or draw upon, future compensation, Broker may deduct the full amount advanced from compensation payable to Associate-Licensee on any transaction without notice. If Associate-Licensee's compensation is subject to a lien, garnishment or other restriction on payment, Broker shall charge Associate-Licensee a fee for complying with such restriction.

   E. **PAYMENT:** (1) All compensation collected by Broker and due to Associate-Licensee shall be paid to Associate-Licensee, after deduction of expenses and offsets, immediately or as soon thereafter as practicable, except as otherwise provided in this Agreement, or a separate written agreement between Broker and Associate-Licensee. (2) Compensation shall not be paid to Associate-Licensee until both the transaction and file are complete. (3) Broker is under no obligation to pursue collection of compensation from any person or entity responsible for payment. Associate-Licensee does not have the independent right to pursue collection of compensation for activities which require a real estate license which were done in the name of Broker. (4) Expenses which are incurred in the attempt to collect compensation shall be paid by Broker and Associate-Licensee in the same proportion as set forth for the division of compensation (paragraph 8(B)). (5) If there is a known or pending claim against Broker or Associate-Licensee on transactions for which Associate-Licensee has not yet been paid, Broker may withhold from compensation due Associate-Licensee on that transaction amounts for which Associate-Licensee could be responsible under paragraph 14, until such claim is resolved. (6) Associate-Licensee shall not be entitled to any advance payment from Broker upon future compensation.

   F. **UPON OR AFTER TERMINATION:** If this Agreement is terminated while Associate-Licensee has listings or pending transactions that require further work normally rendered by Associate-Licensee, Broker shall make arrangements with another associate-licensee to perform the required work, or Broker shall perform the work him/herself. The licensee performing the work shall be reasonably compensated for completing work on those listings or transactions, and such reasonable compensation shall be deducted from Associate-Licensee's share of compensation. Except for such offset, Associate-Licensee shall receive the compensation due as specified above.

9. **TERMINATION OF RELATIONSHIP:** Broker or Associate-Licensee may terminate their relationship under this Agreement at any time, with or without cause. After termination, Associate-Licensee shall not solicit (a) prospective or existing clients or customers based upon company- generated leads obtained during the time Associate-Licensee was affiliated with Broker, or (b) any principal with existing contractual obligations to Broker, or (c) any principal with a contractual transactional obligation for which Broker is entitled to be compensated. Even after termination, this Agreement shall govern all disputes and claims between Broker and Associate-Licensee connected with their relationship under this Agreement, including obligations and liabilities arising from existing and completed listings, transactions, and services.

Broker and Associate-Licensee acknowledge receipt of copy of this page, which constitutes Page 2 of _____ Pages.
Broker's Initials (_____) (_____)   Associate-Licensee's Initials (_____) (_____)

REVISED 10/98

Page 2 of ____ Pages.

OFFICE USE ONLY
Reviewed by Broker
or Designee _____
Date _____

PRINT DATE

INDEPENDENT CONTRACTOR AGREEMENT (ICA-11 PAGE 2 OF 3)

Reprinted with permission, CALIFORNIA ASSOCIATION OF REALTORS®. Endorsement not implied.

10. **DISPUTE RESOLUTION:**
   A. **Mediation:** Mediation is recommended as a method of resolving disputes arising out of this Agreement between Broker and Associate-Licensee.
   B. **Arbitration:** All disputes or claims between Associate-Licensee and other licensee(s) associated with Broker, or between Associate-Licensee and Broker, arising from or connected in any way with this Agreement, which cannot be adjusted between the parties involved, shall be submitted to the Association of REALTORS® of which all such disputing parties are members for arbitration pursuant to the provisions of its Bylaws, as may be amended from time to time, which are incorporated as a part of this Agreement by reference. If the Bylaws of the Association do not cover arbitration of the dispute, or if the Association declines jurisdiction over the dispute, then arbitration shall be pursuant to the rules of California law. The Federal Arbitration Act, Title 9, U.S. Code, Section 1, et seq., shall govern this Agreement.

11. **AUTOMOBILE:** Associate-Licensee shall maintain automobile insurance coverage for liability and property damage in the following amounts $_____ /$_____. Broker shall be named as an additional insured party on Associate-Licensee's policies. A copy of the endorsement showing Broker as an additional insured shall be provided to Broker.

12. **PERSONAL ASSISTANTS:** Associate-Licensee may make use of a personal assistant, provided the following requirements are satisfied. Associate-Licensee shall have a written agreement with the personal assistant which establishes the terms and responsibilities of the parties to the employment agreement, including, but not limited to, compensation, supervision and compliance with applicable law. The agreement shall be subject to Broker's review and approval. Unless otherwise agreed, if the personal assistant has a real estate license, that license must be provided to the Broker. Both Associate-Licensee and personal assistant must sign any agreement that Broker has established for such purposes.

13. **OFFICE POLICY MANUAL:** If Broker's office policy manual, now or as modified in the future, conflicts with or differs from the terms of this Agreement, the terms of the office policy manual shall govern the relationship between Broker and Associate-Licensee.

14. **INDEMNITY AND HOLD HARMLESS:** Associate-Licensee agrees to indemnify, defend and hold Broker harmless from all claims, disputes, litigation, judgments, awards, costs and attorney's fees, arising from any action taken or omitted by Associate-Licensee, or others working through, or on behalf of Associate-Licensee in connection with services rendered. Any such claims or costs payable pursuant to this Agreement, are due as follows:
   ☐ Paid in full by Associate-Licensee, who hereby agrees to indemnify and hold harmless Broker for all such sums, or
   ☐ In the same ratio as the compensation split as it existed at the time the compensation was earned by Associate-Licensee
   ☐ Other: _____

   Payment from Associate-Licensee is due at the time Broker makes such payment and can be offset from any compensation due Associate-Licensee as above. Broker retains the authority to settle claims or disputes, whether or not Associate-Licensee consents to such settlement.

15. **ADDITIONAL PROVISIONS:** _____

16. **DEFINITIONS:** As used in this Agreement, the following terms have the meanings indicated:
   (A) "Listing" means an agreement with a property owner or other party to locate a buyer, exchange party, lessee, or other party to a transaction involving real property, a mobile home, or other property or transaction which may be brokered by a real estate licensee, or an agreement with a party to locate or negotiate for any such property or transaction.
   (B) "Compensation means compensation for acts requiring a real estate license, regardless of whether calculated as a percentage of transaction price, flat fee, hourly rate, or in any other manner.
   (C) "Transaction" means a sale, exchange, lease, or rental of real property, a business opportunity, or a manufactured home, which may lawfully be brokered by a real estate licensee.

17. **ATTORNEY FEES:** In any action, proceeding, or arbitration between Broker and Associate-Licensee arising from or related to this Agreement, the prevailing Broker or Associate-Licensee shall be entitled to reasonable attorney fees and costs.

18. **ENTIRE AGREEMENT; MODIFICATION:** All prior agreements between the parties concerning their relationship as Broker and Associate-Licensee are incorporated in this Agreement, which constitutes the entire contract. Its terms are intended by the parties as a final and complete expression of their agreement with respect to its subject matter, and may not be contradicted by evidence of any prior agreement or contemporaneous oral agreement. This Agreement may not be amended, modified, altered, or changed except by a further agreement in writing executed by Broker and Associate-Licensee.

Broker:

_____
(Brokerage firm name)

By _____
Its Broker/Office manager (circle one)

_____
(Print name)

_____
(Address)

_____
(City, State, Zip)

_____
(Telephone)   (Fax)

Associate-Licensee:

_____
(Signature)

_____
(Print name)

_____
(Address)

_____
(City, State, Zip)

_____
(Telephone)   (Fax)

REVISED 10/98

Page 3 of ___ Pages.

OFFICE USE ONLY
Reviewed by Broker or Designee ___
Date ___

INDEPENDENT CONTRACTOR AGREEMENT (ICA-11 PAGE 3 OF 3)

The contract also provides that in the event of any action, proceeding, or arbitration arising from the deposit receipt, the prevailing party is entitled to reasonable attorney fees and costs paid by the non-prevailing party (paragraph 24). If the contract did not contain such a clause, each party would pay their own attorney fees and the prevailing party would not be able to recover fees from the loser. Attorney fees are generally not recoverable unless a state law allows for recovery or there is a recovery clause in the written contract.

The California Supreme Court case of *Hsu v. Abbara*, 9 Cal. 4th 863, 39 Cal. Rptr. 2d 824 (1995), which is at the end of the contracts chapter, held that Abbara was the prevailing party in the lawsuit based on a deposit receipt offer that had an attorney fees clause in it. Abbara was entitled to attorney fees from Hsu even though there was not a binding contract providing for attorney fees. If Hsu had won and proved that a contract existed, Hsu would receive attorney fees from Abbara. Therefore, Abbara should receive attorney fees for successfully defending a lawsuit based on an alleged contract that contained an attorney fees clause.

Sometimes a party to a contract containing an attorney fees provision is motivated to bring a lawsuit since a victory will allow the recovery of reasonable attorney fees, spent on the lawsuit, from the losing defendant. However, as things progress the plaintiff may decide, for whatever reason, to dismiss the case prior to trial. Is the plaintiff entitled to attorney fees from the defendant? No, as The Court of Appeal stated in *Jue v. Patton*, 33 Cal. App. 4th 456, 39 Cal. Rptr. 2d 364 (1995), "Recovery of attorney fees based on a contract provision is not permitted when the action is voluntarily dismissed prior to trial."

The final paragraph of the CAR form states that this document is the entire contract between the parties. This is called an **integration clause**, and most standard contract forms include one. Basically, the integration clause is a way to state the parol evidence rule in the contract. When a contract contains an integration clause, neither party can rely on any oral promises or side agreements that the other makes. Any terms not included in the written document are unenforceable.

> **Example:** Z is a new salesperson. Before signing the employment contract, Z says he is concerned because his share of a commission won't be payable unless the commission is collected. The broker says, "Oh, don't worry about that. I always act fast to collect from any client who doesn't pay right away. You'll always get your money."
>
> But as it turns out, the broker doesn't always take the trouble to collect from difficult clients. On one occasion, Z ended up with nothing to show for a lot of work.

If their employment agreement did not contain an integration clause, Z might have been able to treat the broker's statement as a contractual promise to take action to collect commissions. But because the integration clause makes the written document the complete agreement between Z and the broker, the broker's statement is not an enforceable promise.

Listing Agreements

A listing agreement is another kind of employment contract, this time between a seller and a broker. As you know, a broker cannot sue for a commission unless the listing is in writing and signed by the client. The case where the broker was able to enforce a listing agreement jotted on the back of a business card (described in a previous chapter) shows that the listing doesn't have to be a formal legal document. But remember, the civil code requires that the listing agreement be in writing to be enforceable in court. It is essential for the signed writing to indicate the **fact of employment**. This requirement can be satisfied either expressly, with a statement indicating that the signer is employing the broker.

Case Example: Mr. Franklin, a broker, agreed to help Mr. Hansen sell some residential property in Newport Beach. Hansen assured Franklin a written listing was unnecessary—his word was good.

Franklin obtained an offer and called Hansen in Los Angeles. Hansen decided to accept the offer, so Franklin asked him to send a telegram as a written authorization for the sale. Hansen sent Franklin a telegram that read, "This is to confirm that I will sell 608 South Bay Front, Balboa Island for $100,000 cash... Chas. P. Hansen."

But later Hansen refused to sign the deposit receipt to complete the sale, and refused to pay Franklin's commission. Franklin sued.

The court ruled that the telegram did not fulfill the written listing requirement. Even though it was addressed to Franklin, nothing in it indicated that Hansen was employing Franklin or planning to pay him a commission. It was simply an acceptance of the buyer's offer. *Franklin v. Hansen*, 59 Cal. 2d 570, 30 Cal. Rptr. 530 (1963).

Remember that even when a broker doesn't have an enforceable listing agreement, he or she owes fiduciary duties to the client. Those duties are based on agency law, not on contract; they are in addition to, and independent of, the contractual duties the broker takes on in a listing agreement. If the client doesn't provide consideration (that is, doesn't pay the broker) the broker is not required to perform his or her contractual obligations, but can still be held liable for failing to carry out fiduciary duties. (See Chapter 6).

Also, don't forget that for a residential transaction (one to four units), a broker must provide the seller with an agency disclosure addendum before the seller signs a listing agreement. This form was discussed in Chapter 6.

Because a listing agreement is a personal services contract, it can only be assigned to another broker with the client's consent. The assignment, like the original contract, must be in writing. It should be signed by the assignor and the assignee, as well as the client.

 www.california-real-estate.cc/
California Model Homes Tour

Case Example: Hartline and Neville (Sellers) signed a standard form "Exclusive Authorization to Sell" listing agreement with Spring Valley Lake Realty (Broker) which provided, among other things, that the sellers would pay a 6% commission upon sale of the property and authorize the Broker to cooperate with subagents. The property sold for $2,310,980 and Sellers paid the commission. Pursuant to the escrow instructions, 3% was paid to the Broker and 3% to Regal Realty under the "cooperate" clause. Prior to the close of escrow, real estate broker Niebuhr demanded Regal's 3% of the commission on the grounds that he was the procuring cause (for which he made a very strong case) not Regal. Niebuhr was not paid and sued Sellers for paying the wrong person.

   The Court of Appeals held that the Sellers had no obligation to pay Niebuhr because there was no contract of employment between the Seller and Niebuhr, the cooperating broker. The listing authorized Broker to cooperate with subagents but clearly provided that payment of a commission was to be made to the Broker. Niebuhr must sue the Broker for any commission due under the cooperating broker agreement. *Colbaugh v. Hartline*, 29 Cal. App. 4th 1516, 35 Cal. Rptr. 2d 213, (1994).

Case Example: Ameri leased property in Redondo Beach and operated "Picasso's: A Bistro." Ameri listed the business for sale with Gilten for 150 days and a 10% commission on an "exclusive right to sell." Subsequently, Ameri defaulted in paying rent under the lease and the landlord filed an unlawful detainer. The lawsuit was settled by canceling the lease, Ameri vacating, and turning over possession to the landlord along with considerable personal property on site, including the liquor license, and the landlord paying cash to Ameri. Gilten claims the 10% commission because of the termination of the listing by Ameri's "sale" of the business to the landlord even though Gilten produced no offers to buy the business. And, in addition, Ameri's conduct rendered Gilten's performance impossible.

   The Court held that Ameri's litigation settlement with the landlord was not a "sale" of the business as contemplated by the listing agreement since no "sale or exchange" was entered into. Further, a settlement obligation does not constitute an act by the seller withdrawing the property from the market. *Howard Gilten & Associates, Inc. v. Ameri* 208 Cal. App. 3d 90, 256 Cal. Rptr. 36 (1989).

BASIC LISTING AGREEMENT ELEMENTS

A listing agreement should identify the property to be sold or leased. The street address is generally useful, but it may not be enough to identify the property with certainty. That usually isn't an issue, but it can become one if the client decides not to sell and tries to avoid paying a commission. It's a good practice to attach a legal description of the property to the contract as an exhibit. Any pages attached to a contract should be dated and initialed by the parties, to show that the attachments were intended to be part of the agreement.

   The exclusive right to sell agency and the exclusive agency listings (see chapter on Introduction to Agency Law) must contain a termination date.

CALIFORNIA
ASSOCIATION
OF REALTORS®

EXCLUSIVE AGENCY LISTING AGREEMENT
(And Right to Sell)
(C.A.R. Form EA, Revised 10/01)

1. **EXCLUSIVE AGENCY RIGHT TO SELL:** _____ ("Seller")
   hereby employs and grants _____ ("Broker")
   beginning (date) _____ and ending at 11:59 P.M. on (date) _____ ("Listing Period")
   the exclusive and irrevocable agency right to sell or exchange the real property in the City of _____,
   County of_____, California, described as: _____
   _____ ("Property").

2. **ITEMS EXCLUDED AND INCLUDED:** Unless otherwise specified in a real estate purchase agreement, all fixtures and fittings that are attached to the Property are included, and personal property items are excluded, from the purchase price.
   ADDITIONAL ITEMS EXCLUDED: _____.
   ADDITIONAL ITEMS INCLUDED: _____.
   Seller intends that the above items be excluded or included in offering the Property for sale, but understands that: **(i)** the purchase agreement supersedes any intention expressed above and will ultimately determine which items are excluded and included in the sale; and **(ii)** Broker is not responsible for and does not guarantee that the above exclusions and/or inclusions will be in the purchase agreement.

3. **LISTING PRICE AND TERMS:**
   A. The listing price shall be: _____
   _____ Dollars ($ _____).
   B. Additional Terms: _____
   _____.

4. **COMPENSATION TO BROKER:**
   Notice: The amount or rate of real estate commissions is not fixed by law. They are set by each Broker individually and may be negotiable between Seller and Broker (real estate commissions include all compensation and fees to Broker).
   A. Seller agrees to pay to Broker as compensation for services irrespective of agency relationship(s), either ☐ _____ percent of the listing price (or if a purchase agreement is entered into, of the purchase price), or ☐ $ _____,
   AND (if checked) ☐ an administrative/transaction fee of $_____, as follows:
      (1) If Broker or any other broker or agent procures a buyer(s) who offers to purchase the Property on the above price and terms, or on any price and terms acceptable to Seller during the Listing Period, or any extension.
      (2) If Seller, within _____ calendar days after the end of the Listing Period or any extension, enters into a contract to sell, convey, lease or otherwise transfer the Property to anyone ("Prospective Buyer") or that person's related entity: **(i)** who physically entered and was shown the Property during the Listing Period or any extension by Broker or a cooperating broker, or **(ii)** for whom Broker or any cooperating broker submitted to Seller a signed, written offer to acquire, lease, exchange or obtain an option on the Property. Seller, however, shall have no obligation to Broker under this paragraph 4A(2) unless, not later than **3 calendar days** after the end of the Listing Period or any extension, Broker has given Seller a written notice of the names of such Prospective Buyers.
      (3) If, without Broker's prior written consent, the Property is withdrawn from sale, conveyed, leased, rented, otherwise transferred, or made unmarketable by a voluntary act of Seller during the Listing Period, or any extension thereof, except as specified in paragraph 4G below.
   B. If completion of the sale is prevented by a party to the transaction other than Seller, then compensation due under paragraph 4A shall be payable only if and when Seller collects damages by suit, arbitration, settlement, or otherwise, and then in an amount equal to the lesser of one-half of the damages recovered or the above compensation, after first deducting title and escrow expenses and the expenses of collection, if any.
   C. In addition, Seller agrees to pay Broker: _____
   D. **(1)** Broker is authorized to cooperate and compensate brokers participating through the multiple listing service(s) ("MLS"): **(i)** in any manner, **OR (ii)** (if checked) shall offer MLS brokers: either ☐ _____ percent of the purchase price, or ☐ $ _____.
      (2) Broker is authorized to cooperate and compensate brokers operating outside the MLS in any manner.
   E. Seller hereby irrevocably assigns to Broker the above compensation from Seller's funds and proceeds in escrow. Broker may submit this listing agreement, as instructions to compensate Broker pursuant to paragraph 4A, to any escrow regarding the Property involving Seller and a buyer, Prospective Buyer or other transferee.
   F. **(1)** Seller represents that Seller has not previously entered into a listing agreement with another broker regarding the Property, unless specified as follows: _____
      (2) Seller warrants that Seller has no obligation to pay compensation to any other broker regarding the Property unless the Property is transferred to any of the following individuals or entities: _____
      _____
      (3) If the Property is sold to anyone listed above during the time Seller is obligated to compensate another broker: **(i)** Broker is not entitled to compensation under this agreement; and **(ii)** Broker is not obligated to represent Seller in such transaction.
   G. This is an Exclusive Agency listing. Seller reserves the right, to sell the Property directly to a purchaser without any obligation to pay compensation to Broker, unless otherwise specified in paragraph 4C above or elsewhere in writing.

Seller acknowledges receipt of a copy of this page.
Seller's Initials (_____)(_____)

EQUAL HOUSING
OPPORTUNITY

Reviewed by
Broker or Designee _____ Date _____

EXCLUSIVE AGENCY LISTING AGREEMENT (EA-11 PAGE 1 OF 3)

Chapter 8

Property Address: _____ Date: _____

5. OWNERSHIP, TITLE AND AUTHORITY: Seller warrants that: (i) Seller is the owner of the Property; (ii) no other persons or entities have title to the Property; and (iii) Seller has the authority to both execute this agreement and sell the Property. Exceptions to ownership, title and authority are as follows:_____.

6. MULTIPLE LISTING SERVICE: Information about this listing will (or ☐ will not) be provided to the MLS of Broker's selection. All terms of the transaction, including financing, if applicable, will be provided to the selected MLS for publication, dissemination and use by persons and entities on terms approved by the MLS. Seller authorizes Broker to comply with all applicable MLS rules. MLS rules allow MLS data to be made available by the MLS to additional Internet sites unless Broker gives the MLS instructions to the contrary.

7. SELLER REPRESENTATIONS: Seller represents that, unless otherwise specified in writing, Seller is unaware of: (i) any Notice of Default recorded against the Property; (ii) any delinquent amounts due under any loan secured by, or other obligation affecting, the Property; (iii) any bankruptcy, insolvency or similar proceeding affecting the Property; (iv) any litigation, arbitration, administrative action, government investigation, or other pending or threatened action that affects or may affect the Property or Seller's ability to transfer it; and (v) any current, pending or proposed special assessments affecting the Property. Seller shall promptly notify Broker in writing if Seller becomes aware of any of these items during the Listing Period or any extension thereof.

8. BROKER'S AND SELLER'S DUTIES: Broker agrees to exercise reasonable effort and due diligence to achieve the purposes of this agreement. Unless Seller gives Broker written instructions to the contrary, Broker is authorized to order reports and disclosures, as appropriate or necessary, and advertise and market the Property in any method and any medium, including the Internet, selected by Broker, and, to the extent permitted by these media, including MLS, control the dissemination of the information submitted to any medium. Seller agrees to consider offers presented by Broker, and to act in good faith to accomplish the sale of the Property by, among others things, making the Property available for showing at reasonable times and referring to Broker all inquiries of any party interested in the Property. Seller is responsible for determining at what price to list and sell the Property. **Seller further agrees to indemnify, defend and hold Broker harmless from all claims, disputes, litigation, judgments and attorney fees arising from any incorrect information supplied by Seller, or from any material facts that Seller knows but fails to disclose.**

9. DEPOSIT: Broker is authorized to accept and hold on Seller's behalf any deposits to be applied toward the sales price.

10. AGENCY RELATIONSHIPS:
    A. Disclosure: If the Property includes residential property with one-to-four dwelling units, Seller shall receive a "Disclosure Regarding Agency Relationships" form prior to entering into this agreement.
    B. Seller Representation: Broker shall represent Seller in any resulting transaction, except as specified in paragraph 4F.
    C. Possible Dual Agency With Buyer: Depending upon the circumstances, it may be necessary or appropriate for Broker to act as an agent for both Seller and buyer, exchange party, or one or more additional parties ("Buyer"). Broker shall, as soon as practicable, disclose to Seller any election to act as a dual agent representing both Seller and Buyer. If a Buyer is procured directly by Broker or an associate licensee in Broker's firm, Seller hereby consents to Broker acting as a dual agent for Seller and such Buyer. In the event of an exchange, Seller hereby consents to Broker collecting compensation from additional parties for services rendered, provided there is disclosure to all parties of such agency and compensation. Seller understands and agrees that: (i) Broker, without the prior written consent of Seller, will not disclose to Buyer that Seller is willing to sell the Property at a price less than the listing price; (ii) Broker, without the prior written consent of Buyer, will not disclose to Seller that Buyer is willing to pay a price greater than the offered price; and (iii) except for (i) and (ii) above, a dual agent is obligated to disclose known facts materially affecting the value or desirability of the Property to both parties.
    D. Other Sellers: Seller understands that Broker may have or obtain listings on other properties, and that potential buyers may consider, make offers on, or purchase through Broker, property the same as or similar to Seller's Property. Seller consents to Broker's representation of sellers and buyers of other properties before, during, and after the end of this agreement.
    E. Confirmation: If the Property includes residential property with one-to-four dwelling units, Broker shall confirm the agency relationship described above, or as modified, in writing, prior to or concurrent with Seller's execution of a purchase contract.

11. SECURITY AND INSURANCE: Broker is not responsible for loss of or damage to personal or real property or person, whether attributable to use of a keysafe/lockbox, a showing of the Property, or otherwise. Third parties, including but not limited to, appraisers, inspectors, brokers and prospective transferees, may have access to, and take videos and photographs of, the interior of the Property. Seller agrees: (i) to take reasonable precautions to safeguard and protect valuables that might be accessible during showings of the Property; and (ii) to obtain insurance to protect against these risks. Broker does not maintain insurance to protect Seller.

12. KEYSAFE/LOCKBOX: A keysafe/lockbox is designed to hold a key to the Property to permit access to the Property by Broker, cooperating brokers, MLS participants, their authorized licensees and representatives, authorized inspectors, and accompanied prospective buyers. Broker, cooperating brokers, MLS and Associations/Boards of REALTORS® are **not** insurers against injury, theft, loss, vandalism, or damage attributed to the use of a keysafe/lockbox. Seller does (or if checked ☐ does not) authorize Broker to install a keysafe/lockbox. If Seller does not occupy the Property, Seller shall be responsible for obtaining occupant(s)' written permission for use of a keysafe/lockbox.

13. SIGN: Seller does (or if checked ☐ does not) authorize Broker to install a FOR SALE/SOLD sign on the Property.

14. EQUAL HOUSING OPPORTUNITY: The Property is offered in compliance with federal, state, and local anti-discrimination laws.

15. ATTORNEY FEES: In any action, proceeding, or arbitration between Seller and Broker regarding the obligation to pay compensation under this agreement, the prevailing Seller or Broker shall be entitled to reasonable attorney fees and costs, except as provided in paragraph 19A.

16. ADDITIONAL TERMS: _____
_____
_____

17. MANAGEMENT APPROVAL: If an associate licensee in Broker's office (salesperson or broker-associate) enters into this listing agreement on Broker's behalf, and Broker or Manager does not approve of its terms, Broker or Manager has the right to cancel this listing agreement, in writing, within 5 days after its execution.

18. SUCCESSORS AND ASSIGNS: This agreement shall be binding upon Seller and Seller's successors and assigns.

EA-11 REVISED 10/01 (PAGE 2 OF 3)   Print Date

Seller acknowledges receipt of a copy of this page.

Seller's Initials (_____)(_____)

Reviewed by _____

Broker or Designee _____ Date _____

EXCLUSIVE AGENCY LISTING AGREEMENT (EA-11 PAGE 2 OF 3)

Reprinted with permission, CALIFORNIA ASSOCIATION OF REALTORS®. Endorsement not implied.

Property Address: _____ Date: _____

19. DISPUTE RESOLUTION:

    A. MEDIATION: Seller and Broker agree to mediate any dispute or claim arising between them out of this agreement, or any resulting transaction, before resorting to arbitration or court action, subject to paragraph 19B(2) below. Paragraph 19B(2) below applies whether or not the arbitration provision is initialed. Mediation fees, if any, shall be divided equally among the parties involved. If for any dispute or claim to which this paragraph applies, any party commences an action without first attempting to resolve the matter through mediation, or refuses to mediate after a request has been made, then that party shall not be entitled to recover attorney fees, even if they would otherwise be available to that party in any such action. THIS MEDIATION PROVISION APPLIES WHETHER OR NOT THE ARBITRATION PROVISION IS INITIALED.

    B. ARBITRATION OF DISPUTES: (1) Seller and Broker agree that any dispute or claim in Law or equity arising between them regarding the obligation to pay compensation under this agreement, which is not settled through mediation, shall be decided by neutral, binding arbitration, including and subject to paragraph 19B(2) below. The arbitrator shall be a retired judge or justice, or an attorney with at least five years of residential real estate law experience, unless the parties mutually agree to a different arbitrator, who shall render an award in accordance with substantive California Law. In all other respects, the arbitration shall be conducted in accordance with Part III, Title 9 of the California Code of Civil Procedure. Judgment upon the award of the arbitrator(s) may be entered in any court having jurisdiction. The parties shall have the right to discovery in accordance with Code of Civil Procedure §1283.05.

    (2) EXCLUSIONS FROM MEDIATION AND ARBITRATION: The following matters are excluded from mediation and arbitration hereunder: **(i)** a judicial or non-judicial foreclosure or other action or proceeding to enforce a deed of trust, mortgage, or installment land sale contract as defined in Civil Code §2985; **(ii)** an unlawful detainer action; **(iii)** the filing or enforcement of a mechanic's lien; **(iv)** any matter which is within the jurisdiction of a probate, small claims, or bankruptcy court; and **(v)** an action for bodily injury or wrongful death, or for any right of action to which Code of Civil Procedure §337.1 or §337.15 applies. The filing of a court action to enable the recording of a notice of pending action, for order of attachment, receivership, injunction, or other provisional remedies, shall not constitute a violation of the mediation and arbitration provisions.

        "NOTICE: BY INITIALING IN THE SPACE BELOW YOU ARE AGREEING TO HAVE ANY DISPUTE ARISING OUT OF THE MATTERS INCLUDED IN THE 'ARBITRATION OF DISPUTES' PROVISION DECIDED BY NEUTRAL ARBITRATION AS PROVIDED BY CALIFORNIA LAW AND YOU ARE GIVING UP ANY RIGHTS YOU MIGHT POSSESS TO HAVE THE DISPUTE LITIGATED IN A COURT OR JURY TRIAL. BY INITIALING IN THE SPACE BELOW YOU ARE GIVING UP YOUR JUDICIAL RIGHTS TO DISCOVERY AND APPEAL, UNLESS THOSE RIGHTS ARE SPECIFICALLY INCLUDED IN THE 'ARBITRATION OF DISPUTES' PROVISION. IF YOU REFUSE TO SUBMIT TO ARBITRATION AFTER AGREEING TO THIS PROVISION, YOU MAY BE COMPELLED TO ARBITRATE UNDER THE AUTHORITY OF THE CALIFORNIA CODE OF CIVIL PROCEDURE. YOUR AGREEMENT TO THIS ARBITRATION PROVISION IS VOLUNTARY."

        "WE HAVE READ AND UNDERSTAND THE FOREGOING AND AGREE TO SUBMIT DISPUTES ARISING OUT OF THE MATTERS INCLUDED IN THE 'ARBITRATION OF DISPUTES' PROVISION TO NEUTRAL ARBITRATION."

Seller's Initials _____ / _____	Broker's Initials _____ / _____

20. ENTIRE CONTRACT: All prior discussions, negotiations, and agreements between the parties concerning the subject matter of this agreement are superseded by this agreement, which constitutes the entire contract and a complete and exclusive expression of their agreement, and may not be contradicted by evidence of any prior agreement or contemporaneous oral agreement. If any provision of this agreement is held to be ineffective or invalid, the remaining provisions will nevertheless be given full force and effect. This agreement and any supplement, addendum, or modification, including any photocopy or facsimile, may be executed in counterparts.

By signing below, Seller acknowledges that Seller has read, understands, accepts and has received a copy of this agreement.

Seller _____ Date _____
Address _____ City _____ State _____ Zip _____
Telephone _____ Fax _____ E-mail _____

Seller _____ Date _____
Address _____ City _____ State _____ Zip _____
Telephone _____ Fax _____ E-mail _____

Real Estate Broker (Firm) _____
By (Agent) _____ Date _____
Address _____ City _____ State _____ Zip _____
Telephone _____ Fax _____ E-mail _____

| Reviewed by _____ |
| Broker or Designee _____ Date _____ |

EA-11 REVISED 10/01 (PAGE 3 OF 3) Print Date

EXCLUSIVE AGENCY LISTING AGREEMENT (EA-11 PAGE 3 OF 3)

Chapter 8

A provision stating the amount (or rate) of the broker's commission is another key part of every listing agreement. (See paragraph 5 in the CAR Exclusive Authorization and Right to Sell form). Remember that because the amount or rate is always negotiable as a matter of law, it must not be preprinted on the listing agreement form. The figure has to be filled in for each transaction. And when the listing is for a manufactured home or for residential property with one to four units, the form must include a statement in large, boldface type informing the client that the commission rate is negotiable and not fixed by law.

Other clauses of interest to the seller are:

Paragraph 12 KEYSAFE/LOCKBOX. Since there is no way of knowing how many people have access to the keybox, there is always a risk of unauthorized entry into the structure, snooping around inside, and theft of personal property, especially when the owner is away from the property. Those who have access to the property do not want to assume the risk that they bring with that access and have eliminated liability in paragraph 11. Consequently, the listing broker needs to explain that insurance may be appropriate to cover the risk (checking the sellers homeowner's insurance for coverage may be a good idea). Or the seller may wish to strike out paragraph 9 and allow access only when personally on the property or, if not on the property, allow access to others only when accompanied by the listing broker.

Paragraph 13 SIGN. Discuss with the seller when, and for how long a time period, the "Sold" sign will remain on the property.

Paragraph 19A MEDIATION OF DISPUTES. If there is a dispute between the broker and seller both agree to mediate claims before resorting to arbitration or court action. See Chapter 9 on alternatives to dispute resolution.

Paragraph 19B ARBITRATION OF DISPUTES. If initialed by broker and seller, both agree to binding arbitration of disputes and no court action is possible.

Paragraph 20 ENTIRE CONTRACT. This clause is the parol evidence rule in written form. Therefore, both parties must make sure the listing states everything agreed to. The friendly broker who says "Yeah, sure, trust me on that one, you have my word, we don't need to clutter up the contract with that stuff" is the alarm that causes everything agreed to outside the writing to now be included.

Provisions Affecting Liability For A Commission

A listing agreement ordinarily states the sales price and terms the client is willing to accept. The client can refuse any offer that doesn't meet these terms without being liable for a commission. It is, therefore, very important for the price and terms to be set forth clearly and fully in the listing. (Any personal property included in the sale should be specified, since that affects the price—see paragraph 2 of the CAR form.) Of course, if the broker presents an offer that doesn't meet the listing terms and the client accepts it anyway, he or she is liable for the commission.

Under the terms of most listing agreement forms, the broker is entitled to a commission even if the transaction never closes, as long as the client and a ready, willing, and able buyer have agreed on the essential terms of a sale (see Chapter 5). It doesn't have to work that way, however. The seller can add a condition to the listing agreement, making liability for the commission depend on the sale actually closing, or on some other event.

If the broker is not doing what he or she promised in the exclusive right to sell listing, then the seller can terminate the listing agreement. Reviewing the listing agreement, it appears that the seller is making all the promises and the broker is not making any promises. The courts fill this seeming gap by implying a term in the listing agreement that the broker use **diligence** to find a buyer. If the broker does not use diligence, the seller may terminate the listing. If the broker sues for a commission the court will decide if the broker exercised diligence or not. It may be in the best interest of the seller to impose a specific obligation on the part of the broker by including what is agreed to in the listing. This obligation could cover topics like how many open houses and how often and what kind of advertising.

A seller may spend considerable time trying to personally sell the property to two potential buyers, later decides to list the property with a broker. If he doesn't want to pay the broker a commission if the property is sold to either potential buyer, the seller could include a clause that no commission (or a reduced commission) will be paid to the broker if the property is sold to either potential buyer.

Another broker may claim a part of the commission and sue the seller if not paid.

Even under a standard listing agreement, however, if the buyer/seller contract is **conditional** (contingent on the results of an inspection, for example), the seller isn't liable for a commission unless the condition is either fulfilled or waived by the parties.

Most exclusive listing forms make the client liable for a commission if he or she withdraws the property from sale or does anything to make it unmarketable.

Extender Clauses

Exclusive listing forms usually include an **extender clause** (also called a **safety clause** or **carryover clause**). An extender clause makes the client liable for a commission during a specified period after the listing expires, if the property is sold to someone the broker dealt with during the listing term. This makes it more difficult for a buyer and seller to conspire to deprive the broker of a commission by waiting until the listing expires before signing a deposit receipt.

The extender clauses in some forms require: (1) the client to pay the commission if the broker merely introduced the buyer to the property during the listing term, or (2) that the client doesn't have to pay the commission unless the broker was the procuring cause of the sale. The CAR form extender clause makes the client liable for a commission if the property is sold to a buyer the broker negotiated with before the listing expired, provided the client received a written notice of the names of prospective purchasers before or at the time of termination of the listing. For listing purposes, is everyone the broker "had negotiations" with the same as a "prospective purchaser"?

The clause also states that if the seller signs a listing agreement with another broker during the carryover period, the seller will not be liable for a commission to the first broker. Without that provision, the seller could become liable for two commissions on the same sale, one to the first broker and one to the second broker. Some forms do not include this safeguard, so a seller should beware.

If the house isn't selling as fast as the seller thought and the seller, during the listing period, rents it out for financial reasons without the consent of the broker, the seller must pay the commission to the broker.

Deposit Receipts

The general term for a contract between a buyer and seller of real property is a "purchase and sale agreement," or something similar. But in California these contracts are usually referred to as **deposit receipts**. In most transactions, the buyers put up an earnest money deposit at the same time they make an offer to purchase. The standard form used as a written offer also serves as the buyer's receipt for the deposit. If the seller decides to accept the offer, he or she signs the form, and it becomes the parties' contract. A copy of the 8-page CAR Residential Purchase Agreement and Joint Escrow Instructions (and Receipt for Deposit) Form (RPA -11) is shown next.

ELEMENTS OF A DEPOSIT RECEIPT

The deposit receipt (Residential Purchase Agreement and Joint Escrow Instructions) is a multi-functional form and contains:

- ◆ an offer to purchase real property,
- ◆ a completed contract when accepted and signed by the buyer and seller,
- ◆ a receipt for the good faith earnest money,
- ◆ joint escrow instructions,
- ◆ the seller's agreement to pay listing broker's compensation,
- ◆ a mediation and arbitration agreement,
- ◆ a confirmation of the agency relationships, and
- ◆ an irrevocable assignment of compensation to brokers.

This CAR form is detailed enough to address most issues involving the sale of real property. While modifications may be made to insure that all of the terms of parties' agreement are accurate and clear, it should be noted that extensive modification or drafting of additional paragraphs may be considered to be the the unauthorized practice of law and should be avoided.

Escrow is open when the escrow holder signs an acknowledgment of receipt of the this completed form. Unless otherwise agreed, the parties have three days to deliver the agreement to the escrow holder - usually at the same time as the deposit is placed in escrow. However, failing to submit the agreement to escrow will not invalidate the agreement between buyer and seller.

The buyer and seller may receive additional instructions directly from the escrow holder and agree to sign reasonable forms to complete the transactions. The escrow instructions also include the compensation being paid to the broker in the agreement.

www.car.org
(Making an Offer - Things to Know About Real Estate Purchase Contracts)

CALIFORNIA ASSOCIATION OF REALTORS®

RESIDENTIAL PURCHASE AGREEMENT AND JOINT ESCROW INSTRUCTIONS
(AND RECEIPT FOR DEPOSIT)
For Use With Single Family Residential Property — Attached or Detached

Date _____, at _____, California.

1. **OFFER:**

    A. **THIS IS AN OFFER FROM** _____ ("Buyer").

    B. **THE REAL PROPERTY TO BE ACQUIRED** is described as _____
        _____, Assessor's Parcel No. _____, situated in
        _____, County of_____, California, ("Property").

    C. **THE PURCHASE PRICE** offered is _____
        _____ Dollars $ _____.

    D. **CLOSE OF ESCROW** shall occur _____ **Days** After Acceptance (or ☐ on _____ (date)).

2. FINANCING: Obtaining the loans below **is a contingency** of this Agreement unless: (i) either 2H or 2I is checked below or (ii) otherwise agreed. Buyer shall act diligently and in good faith to obtain the designated loans. Obtaining deposit, down payment and closing costs **is not a contingency**.

    A. **BUYER HAS GIVEN A DEPOSIT TO THE AGENT SUBMITTING THE OFFER** ....$_____
        (or to ☐ _____), made payable to _____by Personal
        Check, or ☐ _____, which shall be held uncashed until Acceptance and then
        deposited within **3 business days** after Acceptance or ☐ _____
        ☐ with Escrow Holder, ☐ into Broker's trust account, or ☐ _____.
        Buyer represents that funds will be good when deposited with Escrow Holder.

    B. **INCREASED DEPOSIT** shall be deposited by Buyer with Escrow Holder within _____ **Days** After Acceptance, ...$_____
        or ☐ _____.

    C. **FIRST LOAN IN THE AMOUNT OF** ....$_____
        (1) NEW First Deed of Trust in favor of LENDER, encumbering the Property, securing a note payable at maximum
            interest of _____% fixed rate, or _____% initial adjustable rate with a maximum interest rate cap of
            _____%, balance due in _____ years, amortized over _____ years. Buyer shall pay loan fees/points not to
            exceed _____. (These terms apply whether the designated loan is conventional, FHA or VA.)
        (2) ☐ FHA, ☐ VA: (The following terms only apply to the FHA or VA loan that is checked.)
            Seller shall pay (i) _____% discount points, (ii) other fees not allowed to be paid by Buyer,
            not to exceed $_____, and (iii) the cost of lender required Repairs not otherwise provided for
            in this Agreement, not to exceed $ _____
            (Actual loan amount may increase if mortgage insurance premiums, funding fees or closing costs are financed.)

    D. **ADDITIONAL FINANCING TERMS:** _____ ....$_____
        _____
        _____
        ☐ Seller financing, (C.A.R. Form SFA-11); ☐ junior financing; ☐ assumed financing (C.A.R. Form PAA-11).

    E. **BALANCE OF PURCHASE PRICE** (not including costs of obtaining loans and other closing costs) to be deposited with ....$_____
        Escrow Holder within sufficient time to close escrow.

    F. **TOTAL PURCHASE PRICE** ....$_____

    G. **LOAN CONTINGENCY** shall remain in effect until the designated loans are funded (or ☐ _____ **Days** After Acceptance, by which time Buyer shall give Seller written notice of Buyer's election to cancel this Agreement if Buyer is unable to obtain the designated loans. If Buyer does not give Seller such notice, the contingency of obtaining the designated loans shall be removed by the method specified in paragraph 14).

    H. ☐ **NO LOAN CONTINGENCY:** (If checked) Obtaining any loan in paragraphs 2C, 2D or elsewhere in this Agreement is not a contingency of this Agreement.. If Buyer does not obtain the loan, and as a result Buyer does not purchase the Property, Seller may be entitled to Buyer's deposit or other legal remedies.

    I. ☐ **ALL CASH OFFER:** (If checked) No loan is needed to purchase the Property. Buyer shall, within **5 (or** ☐ _____**) Days** After Acceptance, provide Seller written verification of sufficient funds to close this transaction. Seller may cancel this Agreement in writing within **5 Days After** (i) time to provide verification expires, if Buyer fails to provide verification or (ii) receipt of verification, if Seller reasonably disapproves it.

    J. **LOAN APPLICATIONS; PREQUALIFICATION:** Within **5 (or** ☐ _____**) Days** After Acceptance, Buyer shall provide Seller a letter from lender or mortgage loan broker stating that, based on a review of Buyer's written application and credit report, Buyer is prequalified for the NEW loan indicated above. If Buyer fails to provide such letter within that time, Seller may cancel this Agreement in writing.

    K. ☐ **APPRAISAL CONTINGENCY:** (If checked) This Agreement is contingent upon Property appraising at no less than the specified total purchase price. If there is a loan contingency, the appraisal contingency shall remain in effect until the loan contingency is removed. If there is no loan contingency, the appraisal contingency shall be removed within **10 (or** ☐ _____**) Days** After Acceptance.

Buyer and Seller acknowledge receipt of a copy of this page.
Buyer's Initials (_____)(_____)
Seller's Initials (_____)(_____)

EQUAL HOUSING OPPORTUNITY

Reviewed by
Broker or Designee _____ Date _____

REVISION DATE 10/2000   Print Date
RPA-11 (PAGE 1 OF 8)

RESIDENTIAL PURCHASE AGREEMENT (RPA-11 PAGE 1 OF 8)

Property Address: _____ Date: _____

3. CLOSING AND OCCUPANCY

A. Buyer ☐ does, ☐ does not intend to occupy Property as Buyer's primary residence.

B. Seller occupied or vacant property: Occupancy shall be delivered to Buyer at _____ AM/PM, ☐ on the date of Close Of Escrow, ☐ on _____, or ☐ no later than _____ **Days** After Close Of Escrow. (See C.A.R. Form PAA-11, paragraph 2.) If transfer of title and occupancy do not occur at the same time, Buyer and Seller are advised to (i) enter into a written occupancy agreement, and (ii) consult with their insurance advisors.

C. Tenant occupied property: At Close of Escrow, Property shall be vacant unless otherwise agreed in writing. **Seller has the responsibility to (i) comply with rent control and other Law necessary to deliver Property vacant, and (ii) determine whether timely vacancy is permitted under such Law.**

D. At Close Of Escrow, Seller assigns to Buyer any assignable warranty rights for items included in the sale and shall provide any available copies of such warranties. Brokers cannot and will not determine the assignability of any warranties.

E. At Close Of Escrow, unless otherwise agreed in writing, Seller shall provide keys and/or means to operate all locks, mailboxes, security systems, alarms and garage door openers. If Property is a unit in a condominium or other common interest subdivision, Buyer may be required to pay a deposit to the Homeowners' Association ("HOA") to obtain keys to accessible HOA facilities.

4. ALLOCATION OF COSTS (If checked): If any of the inspections or reports in 4A, B, C and D are checked, then with regard to that item, Buyer shall have approval (including approval of alternate methods of treatment, if any, recommended by the Pest Control Report), removal and cancellation rights, and obligations as specified in paragraph 14. (The rights in paragraph 14 apply whether or not Buyer and Seller agree below who is to pay for Section 1 or Section 2 recommended work.)

A. PEST CONTROL

☐ Buyer ☐ Seller shall pay for a Pest Control Report (for wood destroying pests and organisms only) ("Report"). The Report shall be prepared by _____, a registered structural pest control company, who shall separate the Report into sections for evident infestation or infection (Section 1) and for conditions likely to lead to infestation or infection (Section 2). The Report shall cover the main building and attached structures and, if checked: ☐ detached garages and carports, ☐ detached decks, ☐ the following other structures on the Property: _____ _____. The Report shall not cover roof coverings. If Property is a unit in a condominium or other common interest subdivision, the Report shall cover only the separate interest and any exclusive-use areas being transferred, and shall not cover common areas. Water tests of shower pans on upper level units may not be performed unless the owners of property below the shower consent. If Buyer requests inspection of inaccessible areas, Buyer shall pay for the cost of entry, inspection and closing for those areas, unless otherwise agreed. A written Pest Control Certification shall be issued prior to Close Of Escrow, unless otherwise agreed, and only if no infestation or infection is found or if required corrective work is completed.

(Section 1) ☐ Buyer ☐ Seller shall pay for work recommended to correct "Section 1" conditions described in the Report and the cost of inspection, entry and closing of those inaccessible areas where active infestation or infection is discovered.

(Section 2) ☐ Buyer ☐ Seller shall pay for work recommended to correct "Section 2" conditions described in the Report if requested by Buyer.

OTHER INSPECTIONS AND REPORTS

B. ☐ Buyer ☐ Seller shall pay to have septic or private sewage disposal system inspected. _____

C. ☐ Buyer ☐ Seller shall pay to have domestic wells tested for water potability and productivity. _____

D. ☐ Buyer ☐ Seller shall pay for a natural hazard zone disclosure report prepared by _____.

GOVERNMENT REQUIREMENTS AND RETROFIT

E. ☐ Buyer ☐ Seller shall pay for smoke detector installation and/or water heater bracing, if required by Law. Prior to Close Of Escrow, Seller shall provide Buyer a written statement of compliance in accordance with state and local Law, unless exempt.

F. ☐ Buyer ☐ Seller shall pay the cost of compliance with any other minimum mandatory government retrofit standards, inspections and reports if required as a condition of closing escrow under any Law.

ESCROW, TITLE AND OTHER COSTS

G. ☐ Buyer ☐ Seller shall pay escrow fee. _____
Escrow Holder shall be _____.

H. ☐ Buyer ☐ Seller shall pay for **owner's** title insurance policy specified in paragraph 12. _____
Owner's title policy to be issued by _____.
(Buyer shall pay for any title insurance policy insuring Buyer's **Lender**, unless otherwise agreed.)

I. ☐ Buyer ☐ Seller shall pay County transfer tax or transfer fee. _____

J. ☐ Buyer ☐ Seller shall pay City transfer tax or transfer fee. _____

K. ☐ Buyer ☐ Seller shall pay HOA transfer fees. _____

L. ☐ Buyer ☐ Seller shall pay HOA document preparation fees. _____

M. ☐ Buyer ☐ Seller shall pay the cost, not to exceed $ _____, of a one-year home warranty plan, issued by _____ with the following optional coverage: _____.

Buyer and Seller acknowledge receipt of a copy of this page.
Buyer's Initials (_____)(_____)
Seller's Initials (_____)(_____)

Reviewed by _____
Broker or Designee _____ Date _____

RESIDENTIAL PURCHASE AGREEMENT (RPA-11 PAGE 2 OF 8)

Reprinted with permission, CALIFORNIA ASSOCIATION OF REALTORS®. Endorsement not implied.

Real Estate Contracts

Property Address: _____ Date: _____

5. TRANSFER DISCLOSURE STATEMENT; NATURAL HAZARD DISCLOSURE STATEMENT; LEAD-BASED PAINT HAZARD DISCLOSURES; AND OTHER DISCLOSURES WITH CANCELLATION RIGHTS:

    A. Within the time specified in paragraph 14, if required by Law, a Real Estate Transfer Disclosure Statement ("TDS"), Natural Hazard Disclosure Statement ("NHD"), Federal Lead-Based Paint Disclosures and pamphlet ("Lead Disclosures"), disclosure regarding industrial use (Property is in or affected by a zone or district allowing manufacturing, commercial or airport use) and military ordnance disclosure shall be completed and delivered to Buyer, who shall return Signed Copies to Seller.

    B. In the event Seller, prior to Close Of Escrow, becomes aware of adverse conditions materially affecting the Property, or any material inaccuracy in disclosures, information, or representations previously provided to Buyer (including those made in a TDS) of which Buyer is otherwise unaware, Seller shall promptly provide a subsequent or amended disclosure, in writing, covering those items. **However, a subsequent or amended disclosure shall not be required for conditions and material inaccuracies disclosed in reports received by Buyer.**

    C. Seller shall (i) make a good faith effort to obtain a disclosure notice from any local agencies that levy a special tax on the Property pursuant to the Mello-Roos Community Facilities Act, and (ii) promptly deliver to Buyer any such notice made available by those agencies.

    D. If the TDS, the NHD, the Lead Disclosures, industrial use disclosure, military ordnance disclosure, the Mello-Roos disclosure notice, or a subsequent or amended disclosure is delivered to Buyer after the offer is Signed, Buyer shall have the right to cancel this Agreement within **3 Days** After delivery in person, or **5 Days** After delivery by deposit in the mail, by giving written notice of cancellation to Seller or Seller's agent. (Lead Disclosures sent by mail must be sent certified mail or better.)

6. DISCLOSURES: Within the time specified in paragraph 14, Seller shall: (i) disclose if Property is located in any zone identified in 6A and provide any other information required for those zones; (ii) if required by Law, provide Buyer with the disclosures and other information identified in 6B; and, (iii) if applicable, take the actions specified in 6C and 6D. Buyer, within the time specified in paragraph 14, shall then investigate the disclosures and other information provided to Buyer, and the database in 6E, and take the action specified in paragraph 14.

    A. **NATURAL HAZARD ZONE:** Special Flood Hazard Areas; Potential Flooding (Inundation) Areas; Very High Fire Hazard Zones; State Fire Responsibility Areas; Earthquake Fault Zones; Seismic Hazard Zones; or any other zone for which disclosure is required by Law.

    B. **PROPERTY DISCLOSURES AND PUBLICATIONS:** Earthquake Guides (and questionnaire) and Environmental Hazards Booklet.

    C. ☐ (If checked) **CONDOMINIUM/COMMON INTEREST SUBDIVISION:** Property is a unit in a condominium, or other common interest subdivision. Seller shall request from the HOA and, upon receipt, provide to Buyer: (i) Copies of any documents required by Law; (ii) disclosure of any pending or anticipated claims or litigation by or against the HOA; (iii) a statement containing the location and number of designated parking and storage spaces; (iv) Copies of the most recent 12 months of HOA minutes for regular and special meetings, if available; and (v) the names and contact information of all HOAs governing the Property (C.A.R. Form HOA-11).

    D. **NOTICE OF VIOLATION:** If, prior to Close Of Escrow, Seller receives notice or is made aware of any notice filed or issued against the Property for violations of any Law, Seller shall immediately notify Buyer in writing.

    E. **DATA BASE DISCLOSURE:** NOTICE: The California Department of Justice, sheriff's departments, police departments serving jurisdictions of 200,000 or more and many other local law enforcement authorities maintain for public access a data base of the locations of persons required to register pursuant to paragraph (1) of subdivision (a) of Section 290.4 of the Penal Code. The data base is updated on a quarterly basis and a source of information about the presence of these individuals in any neighborhood. The Department of Justice also maintains a Sex Offender Identification Line through which inquiries about individuals may be made. This is a "900" telephone service. Callers must have specific information about individuals they are checking. Information regarding neighborhoods is not available through the "900" telephone service.

7. CONDITION OF PROPERTY:

    A. Unless otherwise agreed, (i) **Property is sold (a) in its PRESENT physical condition on the date of Acceptance and (b) subject to Buyer inspection rights;** (ii) Property, including pool, spa, landscaping and grounds, is to be maintained in substantially the same condition as on the date of Acceptance, and (iii) all debris and personal property not included in the sale shall be removed by Close Of Escrow.

    B. **SELLER SHALL DISCLOSE KNOWN MATERIAL FACTS AND DEFECTS AND MAKE OTHER DISCLOSURES REQUIRED BY LAW.**

    C. Buyer has the right to inspect the Property and, based upon information discovered in those inspections, may reasonably request that Seller make Repairs, corrections or take other action as specified in paragraph 14.

    D. **Note to Buyer: You are strongly advised to conduct inspections of the entire Property in order to determine its present condition since Seller may not be aware of all defects affecting the Property or other factors that you consider important. Property improvements may not be built according to codes or in compliance with current Law, or have had permits issued.**

    E. **Note to Seller: Buyer may request that you make certain Repairs and, in the event you refuse or are unable to make those Repairs, Buyer may cancel this Agreement as specified in paragraph 14.**

8. A. **ITEMS INCLUDED IN SALE:** All EXISTING fixtures and fittings that are attached to the Property are INCLUDED IN THE PURCHASE PRICE (unless excluded in paragraph 8C below), and shall be transferred free of liens and without Seller warranty. Items to be transferred shall include, but are not limited to, existing electrical, mechanical, lighting, plumbing and heating fixtures, fireplace inserts, solar systems, built-in appliances, window and door screens, awnings, shutters, window coverings, attached floor coverings, television antennas, satellite dishes and related equipment, private integrated telephone systems, air coolers/conditioners, pool/spa equipment, garage door openers/remote controls, attached fireplace equipment, mailbox, in-ground landscaping, including trees/shrubs, and (if owned by Seller) water softeners, water purifiers and security systems/alarms.

    B. **ADDITIONAL ITEMS INCLUDED:** The following items of personal property, free of liens and without Seller warranty, are INCLUDED IN THE PURCHASE PRICE _____

_____

    C. **ITEMS EXCLUDED FROM SALE:** _____

Buyer and Seller acknowledge receipt of a copy of this page.

Buyer's Initials (_____)(_____)
Seller's Initials (_____)(_____)

Reviewed by _____
Broker or Designee _____ Date _____

REVISION DATE 10/2000   **Print Date**
RPA-11 (PAGE 3 OF 8)

RESIDENTIAL PURCHASE AGREEMENT (RPA-11 PAGE 3 OF 8)

Reprinted with permission, CALIFORNIA ASSOCIATION OF REALTORS®. Endorsement not implied.

Chapter 8

Property Address: _____ Date: _____

9. BUYER'S INVESTIGATION OF PROPERTY CONDITION: Buyer's Acceptance of the condition of and any other matter affecting the Property is a contingency of this Agreement, as specified in this paragraph and paragraph 14. Buyer shall have the right at Buyer's expense, unless otherwise agreed, to conduct inspections, investigations, tests, surveys, and other studies ("Inspections"), including the right to: (i) inspect for lead-based paint and other lead-based paint hazards; (ii) inspect for wood destroying pests and organisms ("Pest Control Report"); and (iii) review the registered *sex offender* database. No Inspections shall be made by any governmental building or zoning inspector, or government employee, without Seller's prior written consent, unless required by Law. Buyer shall complete these Inspections and give any written notice to Seller within the time specified in paragraph 14. At Seller's request, Buyer shall give Seller, at no cost, complete Copies of all Inspection reports supporting Buyer's written requests. Seller shall make Property available for all Inspections. Seller shall have water, gas and electricity on for Buyer's Inspections and through the date possession is made available to Buyer.

10. REPAIRS: Repairs shall be completed prior to final verification of condition unless otherwise agreed in writing. Repairs to be performed at Seller's expense may be performed by Seller or through others, provided that work complies with applicable Law, including governmental permit, inspection and approval requirements. Repairs shall be performed in a skillful manner with materials of quality and appearance comparable to existing materials. It is understood that exact restoration of appearance or cosmetic items following all Repairs may not be possible. Seller shall: (i) obtain receipts for Repairs performed by others; (ii) prepare a written statement indicating the Repairs performed by Seller and the date of such Repairs; and (iii) provide Copies of receipts and statements to Buyer prior to final verification of condition.

11. BUYER INDEMNITY AND SELLER PROTECTION FOR ENTRY UPON PROPERTY: Buyer shall: (i) keep Property free and clear of liens; (ii) indemnify and hold Seller harmless from all liability, claims, demands, damages and costs; and (iii) Repair all damages arising from Inspections. Buyer shall carry, or Buyer shall require anyone acting on Buyer's behalf to carry, policies of liability, workers' compensation, and other applicable insurance, defending and protecting Seller from liability for any injuries to persons or property occurring during any inspections or work done on the Property at Buyer's direction prior to Close Of Escrow. Seller is advised that certain protections may be afforded Seller by recording a Notice of Non-responsibility for Inspections and work done on the Property at Buyer's direction.

12. TITLE AND VESTING:
A. Within the time specified in paragraph 14, Buyer shall be provided a current preliminary (title) report, which is only an offer by the title insurer to issue a policy of title insurance, and may not contain every item affecting title. Buyer shall provide written notice to Seller in accordance with and within the time specified in paragraph 14.
B. At Close Of Escrow, Buyer shall receive a grant deed conveying title (or, for stock cooperative or long-term lease, an assignment of stock certificate or of Seller's leasehold interest), including oil, mineral and water rights if currently owned by Seller. Title shall be subject to all encumbrances, easements, covenants, conditions, restrictions, rights and other matters that are of record or disclosed to Buyer prior to Close Of Escrow, unless otherwise requested in writing by Buyer and agreed to by Seller within the time specified in paragraph 14. However, title shall not be subject to any liens against the Property, except for those specified in this Agreement. Title shall vest as designated in Buyer's supplemental escrow instructions. THE MANNER OF TAKING TITLE MAY HAVE SIGNIFICANT LEGAL AND TAX CONSEQUENCES.
C. Buyer shall receive a CLTA/ALTA Homeowner's Policy of Title Insurance, if available for the Property. If not, Buyer shall receive a standard coverage owner's policy (CLTA or ALTA-R with regional exceptions). A title company, at Buyer's request, can provide information about availability, desirability, coverage, and cost of various title insurance coverages and indorsements. If Buyer desires title coverage other than that required by this paragraph, Buyer shall instruct Escrow Holder in writing and pay any increase in costs.

13. SALE OF BUYER'S PROPERTY:
A. This Agreement is NOT contingent upon the sale of any property owned by Buyer unless paragraph 13B is checked.
OR B. ☐ (If checked) This Agreement IS CONTINGENT on the Close Of Escrow of Buyer's property, described as (address)
_____ ("Buyer's Property").
    (1) Buyer's Property is:
       (a) ☐ (if checked) not yet listed for sale.
    OR (b) ☐ (if checked) listed for sale with _____
    OR (c) ☐ (if checked) in escrow No. _____ with _____ company.
       holder, scheduled to close escrow on _____ (date). Buyer shall deliver to Seller, within **5 Days** After Seller's request, a Copy of the contract for the sale of Buyer's Property, escrow instructions, and all amendments and modifications thereto. If Buyer fails to provide the documents within that time, Seller may cancel this Agreement in writing. If Buyer's Property does not close escrow by the date specified in this paragraph for close of escrow of Buyer's Property, then either Seller or Buyer may cancel this Agreement in writing.
    (2) After Acceptance:
       (a) (Applies UNLESS B (2)(b) is checked): Seller SHALL have the right to continue to offer the Property for sale. If Seller accepts another written offer, Seller shall give Buyer written notice to: (i) remove this contingency in writing; (ii) **remove the loan contingency, if any, in writing**; and (iii) comply with the following additional requirement(s):
       _____
       If Buyer fails to complete these actions within **72 (or** ☐_____ **) hours** After receipt of such notice, Seller may cancel this Agreement in writing.
    OR (b) ☐ (if checked) Seller shall have the right to continue to offer the Property for sale for back-up offers only and shall not invoke the notice provisions in paragraph 13 B(2)(a) during the term of this Agreement.

Buyer and Seller acknowledge receipt of a copy of this page.

Buyer's Initials (_____)(_____)
Seller's Initials (_____)(_____)

REVISION DATE 10/2000   Print Date
RPA-11 (PAGE 4 OF 8)

Reviewed by _____
Broker or Designee _____ Date _____

RESIDENTIAL PURCHASE AGREEMENT (RPA-11 PAGE 4 OF 8)

Property Address: _____ Date: _____

14. TIME PERIODS;REMOVAL OF CONTINGENCIES;CANCELLATION RIGHTS: The following time periods may only be extended, altered, modified or changed by mutual written agreement.

   A. ORDERING, COMPLETING AND REVIEWING INSPECTIONS AND REPORTS:

   (1) **SELLER HAS: 5 (or ☐ _____) Days** After Acceptance to order, request or complete all reports, disclosures and information for which Seller is responsible under paragraphs 4, 5, 6A, B and C, and 12. Seller has **2 Days** After receipt (or completion) of any of these items to provide it to Buyer. **Buyer** has 5 (or ☐ _____) **Days** After receipt of **(i)** each of the above items and **(ii)** notice of code and legal violation under paragraph 6D to review the report, disclosure or other information.

   (2) **BUYER HAS: 14 (or ☐ _____) Days** After Acceptance to complete all Inspections, investigations and review of reports and other applicable information, including the sex offender database (paragraph 6E), for which Buyer is responsible.

   (3) **BUYER HAS: 10 (or ☐ _____) Days** After Buyer's receipt of Lead Disclosures pursuant to paragraph 5A, to complete Inspections for and review reports on lead-based paint and lead-based paint hazards.

   B. (1) APPROVAL OR REQUEST: Within the times specified above (or 2G for loan contingency), Buyer shall provide Seller with either **(i)** an unconditional approval and removal of the applicable contingency, or **(ii)** a reasonable written request that Seller Repair or take other action (or for loan contingency, cancellation if Buyer is unable to obtain the designated loan).

   (2) **EFFECT OF BUYER'S REQUEST:** If, pursuant to B(1), Buyer reasonably requests that Seller Repair or take other action, Buyer and Seller have 5 (or ☐ _____) **Days** After Seller's receipt of Buyer's request to reach mutual written agreement on Buyer's request. If **(i)** Seller has agreed in writing to unconditionally and completely take the action requested by Buyer,or **(ii)** Buyer and Seller have reached a mutual written agreement with respect to those items, then the transaction shall proceed on those terms. Seller has no obligation, express or implied, to satisfy Buyer's requests.

   (3) **EFFECT OF NO WRITTEN AGREEMENT ON BUYER'S REQUESTS:** If, at the expiration of the time in B(2), neither B(2)(i) nor (ii) has occurred, Buyer has 2 (or ☐ _____) **Days** to cancel this Agreement in writing.

   C. ACTIVE OR PASSIVE REMOVAL OF CONTINGENCIES AND CANCELLATION RIGHTS:

   (1) ☐ **ACTIVE METHOD** (Applies only if checked):

   (a) **(No written request or removal by Buyer)** If, within the time specified in A, a Buyer does not give Seller written notice pursuant to B(1), Seller may cancel this Agreement in writing. Notwithstanding the expiration of the time specified, Buyer retains the right to give Seller written notice under B1 at any time prior to receiving Seller's written cancellation. Once Seller receives Buyer's written request or removal, Seller may not cancel this Agreement pursuant to paragraph C(1)(a).

   (b) **(No written cancellation by Buyer)** If, within the time specified, Buyer does not give Seller written notice of cancellation pursuant to B(3), either Buyer or Seller may cancel this Agreement in writing at any time prior to Buyer and Seller reaching mutual written agreement with respect to any requests made pursuant to B(1).

   (2) **PASSIVE METHOD:** If, within the time specified, Buyer does not give Seller **(i)** a reasonable written request pursuant to B(1) (or for loan contingency, cancellation if Buyer is unable to obtain the designated loan) or **(ii)** written notice of cancellation pursuant to B(3) if no agreement is reached on Buyer's requests, then Buyer shall be deemed, as applicable, to have unconditionally approved and removed the contingency or withdrawn the request and waived any right to cancel associated with the requested item.

   D. EFFECT OF REMOVAL: If Buyer removes any contingency or cancellation right by the active or passive method, as applicable, Buyer shall conclusively be deemed to have: **(i)** completed all Inspections, investigations, and review of reports and other applicable information and disclosures pertaining to that contingency or cancellation right; **(ii)** elected to proceed with the transaction; and, **(iii)** assumed all liability, responsibility, and expense for repairs or corrections pertaining to that contingency or cancellation right, or for inability to obtain financing if the contingency pertains to financing, unless, pursuant to B(2) or elsewhere in this Agreement, Seller agrees to make Repairs or take other action.

   E. EFFECT OF CANCELLATION ON DEPOSITS: If Buyer or Seller gives written NOTICE OF CANCELLATION pursuant to rights duly exercised under the terms of this Agreement, Buyer and Seller agree to Sign mutual instructions to cancel the sale and escrow and release deposits, less fees and costs, to the party entitled to the funds. Fees and costs may be payable to service providers and vendors for services and products provided during escrow. **Release of funds will require mutual, Signed release instructions from Buyer and Seller, judicial decision or arbitration award. A party may be subject to a civil penalty of up to $1,000 for refusal to sign such instructions if no good faith dispute exists as to who is entitled to the deposited funds (Civil Code §1057.3).**

15. FINAL VERIFICATION OF CONDITION: Buyer shall have the right to make a final inspection of the Property within **5 (or _____) Days** prior to Close Of Escrow, NOT AS A CONTINGENCY OF THE SALE, but solely to confirm **(i)** Property is maintained pursuant to paragraph 7A, **(ii)** Repairs have been completed as agreed, and **(iii)** Seller has complied with Seller's other obligations.

16. LIQUIDATED DAMAGES: If Buyer fails to complete this purchase because of Buyer's default, Seller shall retain, as liquidated damages, the deposit actually paid. If the Property is a dwelling with no more than four units, one of which Buyer intends to occupy, then the amount retained shall be no more than 3% of the purchase price. Any excess shall be returned to Buyer. Release of funds will require mutual, Signed release instructions from both Buyer and Seller, judicial decision or arbitration award.
BUYER AND SELLER SHALL SIGN A SEPARATE LIQUIDATED DAMAGES PROVISION FOR ANY INCREASED DEPOSIT. (C.A.R. FORM RID-11)

Buyer's Initials _____/_____	**Seller's Initials** _____/_____

Buyer and Seller acknowledge receipt of a copy of this page.

Buyer's Initials (_____)(_____)
Seller's Initials (_____)(_____)

Reviewed by _____
Broker or Designee _____ Date _____

REVISION DATE 10/2000   Print Date
RPA-11 (PAGE 5 OF 8)

RESIDENTIAL PURCHASE AGREEMENT (RPA-11 PAGE 5 OF 8)

Property Address: _____ Date: _____

17. DISPUTE RESOLUTION:

A. MEDIATION: Buyer and Seller agree to mediate any dispute or claim arising between them out of this Agreement, or any resulting transaction, before resorting to arbitration or court action. Paragraphs 17B(2) and (3) below apply whether or not the Arbitration provision is initialed. Mediation fees, if any, shall be divided equally among the parties involved. If, for any dispute or claim to which this paragraph applies, any party commences an action without first attempting to resolve the matter through mediation, or refuses to mediate after a request has been made, then that party shall not be entitled to recover attorney fees, even if they would otherwise be available to that party in any such action. THIS MEDIATION PROVISION APPLIES WHETHER OR NOT THE ARBITRATION PROVISION IS INITIALED.

B. ARBITRATION OF DISPUTES: (1) Buyer and Seller agree that any dispute or claim in Law or equity arising between them out of this Agreement or any resulting transaction, which is not settled through mediation, shall be decided by neutral, binding arbitration, including and subject to paragraphs 17B(2) and (3) below. The arbitrator shall be a retired judge or justice, or an attorney with at least 5 years of residential real estate Law experience, unless the parties mutually agree to a different arbitrator, who shall render an award in accordance with substantive California Law. In all other respects, the arbitration shall be conducted in accordance with Part III, Title 9 of the California Code of Civil Procedure. Judgment upon the award of the arbitrator(s) may be entered in any court having jurisdiction. The parties shall have the right to discovery in accordance with Code of Civil Procedure §1283.05.

(2) EXCLUSIONS FROM MEDIATION AND ARBITRATION: The following matters are excluded from mediation and arbitration: **(i)** a judicial or non-judicial foreclosure or other action or proceeding to enforce a deed of trust, mortgage, or installment land sale contract as defined in Civil Code §2985; **(ii)** an unlawful detainer action; **(iii)** the filing or enforcement of a mechanic's lien; **(iv)** any matter that is within the jurisdiction of a probate, small claims, or bankruptcy court; and **(v)** an action for bodily injury or wrongful death, or any right of action to which Code of Civil Procedure §337.1 or §337.15 applies. The filing of a court action to enable the recording of a notice of pending action, for order of attachment, receivership, injunction, or other provisional remedies, shall not constitute a violation of the mediation and arbitration provisions.

(3) BROKERS: Buyer and Seller agree to mediate and arbitrate disputes or claims involving either or both Brokers, provided either or both Brokers shall have agreed to such mediation or arbitration prior to, or within a reasonable time after, the dispute or claim is presented to Brokers. Any election by either or both Brokers to participate in mediation or arbitration shall not result in Brokers being deemed parties to the Agreement.

"NOTICE: BY INITIALING IN THE SPACE BELOW YOU ARE AGREEING TO HAVE ANY DISPUTE ARISING OUT OF THE MATTERS INCLUDED IN THE 'ARBITRATION OF DISPUTES' PROVISION DECIDED BY NEUTRAL ARBITRATION AS PROVIDED BY CALIFORNIA LAW AND YOU ARE GIVING UP ANY RIGHTS YOU MIGHT POSSESS TO HAVE THE DISPUTE LITIGATED IN A COURT OR JURY TRIAL. BY INITIALING IN THE SPACE BELOW YOU ARE GIVING UP YOUR JUDICIAL RIGHTS TO DISCOVERY AND APPEAL, UNLESS THOSE RIGHTS ARE SPECIFICALLY INCLUDED IN THE 'ARBITRATION OF DISPUTES' PROVISION. IF YOU REFUSE TO SUBMIT TO ARBITRATION AFTER AGREEING TO THIS PROVISION, YOU MAY BE COMPELLED TO ARBITRATE UNDER THE AUTHORITY OF THE CALIFORNIA CODE OF CIVIL PROCEDURE. YOUR AGREEMENT TO THIS ARBITRATION PROVISION IS VOLUNTARY."

"WE HAVE READ AND UNDERSTAND THE FOREGOING AND AGREE TO SUBMIT DISPUTES ARISING OUT OF THE MATTERS INCLUDED IN THE 'ARBITRATION OF DISPUTES' PROVISION TO NEUTRAL ARBITRATION."

Buyer's Initials _____	Seller's Initials _____/

18. PRORATIONS OF PROPERTY TAXES AND OTHER ITEMS: Unless otherwise agreed in writing, the following items shall be PAID CURRENT and prorated between Buyer and Seller as of Close Of Escrow: real property taxes and assessments, interest, rents, HOA regular, special, and emergency dues and assessments imposed prior to Close Of Escrow, premiums on insurance assumed by Buyer, payments on bonds and assessments assumed by Buyer, and payments on Mello-Roos and other Special Assessment District bonds and assessments that are now a lien. The following items shall be assumed by Buyer WITHOUT CREDIT toward the purchase price: prorated payments on Mello-Roos and other Special Assessment District bonds and assessments and HOA special assessments that are now a lien but not yet due. Property will be reassessed upon change of ownership. Any supplemental tax bills shall be paid as follows: **(i)** for periods after Close Of Escrow, by Buyer; and, **(ii)** for periods prior to Close Of Escrow, by Seller. TAX BILLS ISSUED AFTER CLOSE OF ESCROW SHALL BE HANDLED DIRECTLY BETWEEN BUYER AND SELLER. Prorations shall be made based on a 30-day month.

19. WITHHOLDING TAXES: Seller and Buyer agree to execute any instrument, affidavit, statement or instruction reasonably necessary to comply with federal (FIRPTA) and California withholding Law, if required (C.A.R. Forms AS-11 and AB-11).

20. MULTIPLE LISTING SERVICE ("MLS"): Brokers are authorized to report the terms of this transaction to any MLS, to be published and disseminated to persons and entities authorized to use the information on terms approved by the MLS.

21. EQUAL HOUSING OPPORTUNITY: The Property is sold in compliance with federal, state and local anti-discrimination Law.

22. ATTORNEY FEES: In any action, proceeding, or arbitration between Buyer and Seller arising out of this Agreement, the prevailing Buyer or Seller shall be entitled to reasonable attorney fees and costs from the non-prevailing Buyer or Seller, except as provided in paragraph 17A.

23. SELECTION OF SERVICE PROVIDERS: If Brokers give Buyer or Seller referrals to persons, vendors, or service or product providers ("Providers"), Brokers do not guarantee the performance of any of those Providers. Buyer and Seller may select ANY Providers of their own choosing.

Buyer and Seller acknowledge receipt of a copy of this page.

Buyer's Initials (_____)(_____)
Seller's Initials (_____)(_____)

EQUAL HOUSING
OPPORTUNITY

Reviewed by _____
Broker or Designee _____ Date _____

RESIDENTIAL PURCHASE AGREEMENT (RPA-11 PAGE 6 OF 8)

Property Address: _____ Date: _____

24. TIME OF ESSENCE; ENTIRE CONTRACT; CHANGES: Time is of the essence. All understandings between the parties are incorporated in this Agreement. Its terms are intended by the parties as a final, complete and exclusive expression of their Agreement with respect to its subject matter, and may not be contradicted by evidence of any prior agreement or contemporaneous oral agreement. If any provision of this Agreement is held to be ineffective or invalid, the remaining provisions will nevertheless be given full force and effect. **Neither this Agreement nor any provision in it may be extended, amended, modified, altered or changed, except in writing Signed by Buyer and Seller.**

25. OTHER TERMS AND CONDITIONS, including ATTACHED SUPPLEMENTS:
  A. ☑ Buyer's Inspection Advisory (C.A.R. Form BIA-11)
  B. ☐ Purchase Agreement Addendum (C.A.R. Form PAA-11 paragraph numbers: _____)
  C. _____
  _____
  _____

26. DEFINITIONS: As used in this Agreement:
  A. **"Acceptance"** means the time the offer or final counter offer is accepted in writing by the other party and communicated in accordance with this Agreement or the terms of the final counter offer.
  B. **"Agreement"** means the terms and conditions of this Residential Purchase Agreement and any counter offer and addenda.
  C. **"Days"** means calendar days, unless otherwise required by Law.
  D. **"Days After"** means the specified number of calendar days after the occurrence of the event specified, not counting the calendar date on which the specified event occurs, and ending at 11:59PM on the final day.
  E. **"Close Of Escrow"** means the date the grant deed, or other evidence of transfer of title, is recorded. If scheduled close of escrow falls on a Saturday, Sunday or legal holiday, then the close of escrow date shall be the next business day after the scheduled close of escrow date.
  F. **"Copy"** means copy by any means including photocopy, NCR, facsimile and electronic.
  G. **"Law"** means any law, code, statute, ordinance, regulation, rule or order, which is adopted by a controlling city, county, state or federal legislative, judicial or executive body or agency.
  H. **"Repairs"** means any repairs (including pest control), alterations, replacements, modifications and retrofitting of the Property provided for under this Agreement.
  I. **"Signed"** means either a handwritten or electronic signature.
  J. **Singular and Plural** terms each include the other, when appropriate.
  K. **C.A.R. Form** means the specific form referenced, or another comparable form agreed to by the parties.
  L. **"Electronic Copy"** or **"Electronic Signature"** means, as applicable, an electronic copy or signature complying with California Law. Buyer and Seller agree that electronic means will not be used by either one to modify or alter the content or integrity of the Agreement without the knowledge and consent of the other.

27. AGENCY:
  A. **POTENTIALLY COMPETING BUYERS AND SELLERS:** Buyer understands that Broker representing Buyer may also represent other potential buyers, who may consider, make offers on or ultimately acquire this Property. Seller understands that Buyer may consider, make offers on or purchase other properties similar to the Property. Buyer and Seller acknowledge and consent to Broker(s)' representation of such potential buyers and sellers before, during and after Broker(s)' representation of Buyer and Seller.
  B. **CONFIRMATION:** The following agency relationships are hereby confirmed for this transaction:
  Listing Agent _____ (Print Firm Name) is the agent of (check one):
  ☐ the Seller exclusively; or ☐ both the Buyer and Seller.
  Selling Agent _____ (Print Firm Name) (if not same as Listing Agent) is the agent of (check one): ☐ the Buyer exclusively; or ☐ the Seller exclusively; or ☐ both the Buyer and Seller.
  Real Estate Brokers are not parties to the Agreement between Buyer and Seller.

28. JOINT ESCROW INSTRUCTIONS TO ESCROW HOLDER:
  A. The following paragraphs, or applicable portions thereof, of this Agreement constitute the joint escrow instructions of Buyer and Seller to Escrow Holder, which Escrow Holder is to use along with any relating counter offers and addenda, and any additional mutual instructions to close the transaction: 1, 2, 4, 12, 13B, 14E, 18, 19, 24, 25B and C, 26, 28, 30, 32A and 33. The terms and conditions of the Agreement not set forth in the specified paragraphs are additional matters for the information of Escrow Holder, but about which Escrow Holder need not be concerned. Buyer and Seller will receive Escrow Holder's general provisions directly from Escrow Holder and will execute such provisions upon Escrow Holder's request. To the extent the general provisions are inconsistent or conflict with this Agreement, the general provisions will control as to the duties and obligations of Escrow Holder only. Buyer and Seller will execute additional instructions, documents and forms provided by Escrow Holder that are reasonably necessary to complete this transaction.
  B. A Copy of this Agreement shall be delivered to Escrow Holder within 3 business days After Acceptance (or ☐ _____). **Escrow will be deemed open when Escrow Holder has Signed an acknowledgement of receipt of a Copy of this accepted Agreement.** Buyer and Seller authorize Escrow Holder to accept and rely on Copies and Signatures as defined in this Agreement as originals, to open escrow and for other purposes of escrow. The validity of this Agreement as between Buyer and Seller is not affected by whether or when Escrow Holder Signs the Agreement.
  C. Brokers are a party to the Escrow for the sole purpose of compensation pursuant to paragraphs 30 and 32A. Buyer and Seller irrevocably assign to Brokers compensation specified, respectively, in paragraphs 30 and 32A and irrevocably instruct Escrow Holder to disburse those funds to Brokers at Close Of Escrow. Compensation instructions can be amended or revoked only with the written consent of Brokers.

29. Buyer and Seller acknowledge and agree that : (a) Brokers do not decide what price Buyer should pay or Seller should accept; (b) Brokers do not guarantee the performance or Repairs of others who have provided services or products to Buyer or Seller; and (c) they will seek legal, tax, insurance, title and other desired assistance from appropriate professionals.

REVISION DATE 10/2000   Print Date
RPA-11 (PAGE 7 OF 8)

Buyer and Seller acknowledge receipt of a copy of this page.
Buyer's Initials (_____)(_____)
Seller's Initials (_____)(_____)

Reviewed by _____
Broker or Designee _____ Date _____

RESIDENTIAL PURCHASE AGREEMENT (RPA-11 PAGE 7 OF 8)

Property Address: _____ Date: _____

30. BROKER COMPENSATION FROM BUYER: Upon Close Of Escrow, **Buyer** agrees to pay compensation for services as follows:
_____ to _____, Broker.

31. TERMS AND CONDITIONS OF OFFER: This is an offer to purchase the Property on the above terms and conditions. All paragraphs with spaces for initials by Buyer and Seller are incorporated in this Agreement only if initialed by all parties. If at least one but not all parties initial, a counter offer is required until agreement is reached. Unless Acceptance of offer is Signed by Seller, and a Copy of the Signed offer is personally received by Buyer, or by _____, who is authorized to receive it, by (date) _____, at _____ AM/PM, the offer shall be deemed revoked and the deposit shall be returned. Seller has the right to continue to offer the Property for sale and to accept any other offer at any time prior to communication of Acceptance as above. Buyer has read and acknowledges receipt of a Copy of the offer and agrees to the above confirmation of agency relationships. If this offer is accepted and Buyer subsequently defaults, Buyer may be responsible for payment of Brokers' compensation. This Agreement and any supplement, addendum or modification, including any Copy, may be Signed in two or more counterparts, all of which shall constitute one and the same writing.

BUYER _____Date_____ BUYER _____Date_____

(Print name) _____ (Print name) _____

(Address) _____

32. BROKER COMPENSATION FROM SELLER:

A. Upon Close of Escrow, **Seller** agrees to pay compensation for services as follows:
_____, to _____, Broker, and
_____, to _____, Broker, and
(if checked) ☐ an administrative/transaction fee of $_____ to _____ Broker
(or, if not completed, as per listing agreement).

B. (1) If escrow does not close, compensation in 32A is payable: **(i)** upon Seller's default if completion of sale is prevented by default of Seller; or **(ii)** when and if Seller collects damages from Buyer, by suit or otherwise, if completion of sale is prevented by default of Buyer and then in an amount equal to one-half of the damages recovered, but not to exceed the above compensation, after first deducting title and escrow expenses and the expenses of collection, if any. **(2)** In any action, proceeding or arbitration relating to the payment of compensation in 32A or B, the prevailing party shall be entitled to reasonable attorney' fees and costs, except as provided in paragraph 17A.

33. ACCEPTANCE OF OFFER: Seller warrants that Seller is the owner of this Property, or has the authority to execute this Agreement. Seller accepts the above offer, agrees to sell the Property on the above terms and conditions, and agrees to the above confirmation of agency relationships. Seller has read and acknowledges receipt of a Copy of this Agreement, and authorizes Broker to deliver a Signed Copy to Buyer.

☐ (If checked) **SUBJECT TO ATTACHED COUNTER OFFER, DATED** _____.

SELLER _____Date_____ SELLER _____Date_____

(Print name) _____ (Print name) _____

(Address) _____

Agency relationships are confirmed as above. Real Estate Brokers are not parties to the Agreement between Buyer and Seller.

Agent who submitted offer for Buyer acknowledges receipt of deposit, if any, if specified in paragraph 2A.

Real Estate Broker (Selling Firm Name) _____ By _____ Date _____

Address _____ Phone/Fax/E-mail _____

Real Estate Broker (Listing Firm Name) _____ By _____ Date _____

Address _____ Phone/Fax/E-mail _____

(_____/_____) **ACKNOWLEDGMENT OF RECEIPT:** Buyer or authorized agent acknowledges receipt of Signed Acceptance on (date) _____,
(Initials)   at _____ AM/PM.

Escrow Holder Acknowledgment:

Escrow Holder acknowledges receipt of a Copy of this Agreement, (if checked, ☐ a deposit in the amount of $_____), counter offer numbers _____ and _____, and agrees to act as Escrow Holder subject to paragraph 28 of this Agreement, any supplemental escrow instructions and the terms of Escrow Holder's general provisions.

The date of communication of Acceptance of the Agreement as between Buyer and Seller is _____.

Escrow Holder _____ Escrow # _____
By _____ Date _____
Address _____ Phone/Fax/E-mail _____
Escrow Holder is licensed by the California Department of ☐ Corporations, ☐ Insurance, ☐ Real Estate. License # _____

THIS FORM HAS BEEN APPROVED BY THE CALIFORNIA ASSOCIATION OF REALTORS® (C.A.R.). NO REPRESENTATION IS MADE AS TO THE LEGAL VALIDITY OR ADEQUACY OF ANY PROVISION IN ANY SPECIFIC TRANSACTION. A REAL ESTATE BROKER IS THE PERSON QUALIFIED TO ADVISE ON REAL ESTATE TRANSACTIONS. IF YOU DESIRE LEGAL OR TAX ADVICE, CONSULT AN APPROPRIATE PROFESSIONAL.

This form is available for use by the entire real estate industry. It is not intended to identify the user as a REALTOR®. REALTOR® is a registered collective membership mark which may be used only by members of the NATIONAL ASSOCIATION OF REALTORS® who subscribe to its Code of Ethics.

Published and Distributed by:
REAL ESTATE BUSINESS SERVICES, INC.
a subsidiary of the CALIFORNIA ASSOCIATION OF REALTORS®
525 South Virgil Avenue, Los Angeles, California 90020

Reviewed by _____
Broker or Designee _____ Date _____

REVISION DATE 10/2000   Print Date
RPA-11 (PAGE 8 OF 8)

RESIDENTIAL PURCHASE AGREEMENT (RPA-11 PAGE 8 OF 8)

Real Estate Contracts

The Parties

There are two key questions to ask regarding the parties to a deposit receipt:

◆ Does everyone who is signing have the capacity to contract?
◆ Is everyone with an ownership interest signing?

If any of the parties is underage or incompetent, the contract will be void. And unless everyone with an ownership interest in the property signs, the buyer won't be able to compel conveyance of the whole property.

Conditions

Most agreements between buyers and sellers are conditional. Any conditions must be spelled out in the deposit receipt. It should state exactly what must occur to fulfill each condition. It should explain how one party is to notify the other when a condition has been fulfilled or waived. It should also state a time limit: If the condition is not fulfilled by that date, the contract will be void. Finally, it should explain the parties' rights in the event that the condition is not met or waived.

If a real estate agent believes that a contingency clause in a deposit receipt may affect the date of closing, or the time that the buyer can take possession of the property, the agent is required to explain that to the parties. Failure to do so is a violation of the Real Estate Law, and may lead to suspension or revocation of the agent's license. Here are two of the more important areas involving conditions:

Financing. Nearly all residential transactions are contingent on whether the buyer is able to obtain financing. That's why it's particularly important to describe the financing arrangements in detail. The buyer is required to make a diligent, good faith effort to obtain financing on the terms stated in the deposit receipt. If no lenders are willing to loan on those terms, the buyer can back out without forfeiting the deposit.

Sale of Buyer's Home. Many purchases are contingent on the buyer's ability to sell

---

Case Example: Mr. Fry wanted to buy the Millers' house. His written offer stated that it was "conditioned upon the buyer obtaining a $20,000 loan at 5% for 20 years." The Millers accepted the offer immediately, and Fry made a $4,250 deposit.

The Millers had previously mortgaged the house to Western Mortgage Company. Fry was advised that although most banks wouldn't be willing to make him a 20-year, $20,000 loan at 5% interest, Western Mortgage Company would be willing to refinance on those terms.

Fry applied for the loan at two banks, but both turned him down. Fry never contacted Western Mortgage, although the Millers and their broker urged him to on a number of occasions. Eventually Fry told the Millers that the deal was off, since he wasn't able to obtain the loan that their contract was conditioned on. The Millers refused to return Fry's deposit, so Fry sued.

The court held that Fry wasn't entitled to the deposit. If he had applied to Western Mortgage, they would have granted him a loan that would have fulfilled the condition. But Fry avoided contacting Western Mortgage, because in fact he had lost interest in the Millers' house. By failing to make a good faith effort to fulfill the condition, Fry breached the contract. *Fry v. George Eikins Co.*, 162 Cal. App. 2d 256, 327 P.2d 905 (1958).

his or her current home. In fact, even when that isn't an express condition, it may be a hidden condition. Often a buyer won't have enough money for a down payment unless the current home is sold. As a result, he or she can't qualify for a loan without selling the current home.

If the buyer cannot obtain financing unless his or her current home is sold, it's best to make the sale of the current home an express condition in the deposit receipt (paragraph 13). Otherwise, the seller may be misled into believing that the buyer has a much better chance of obtaining the necessary loan than he or she actually has. Note that paragraph 13 enables the seller to keep the property on the market pending fulfillment of the condition. If the seller receives another offer before the buyer's home is sold, the seller can demand that the buyer waive the condition, and verify funds to close escrow or cancel their contract.

Release of Contract. When one transaction fails because a condition is not met, the seller may want to enter into another agreement with a second buyer. In this situation, it's advisable for the seller to include an express condition in the second deposit receipt, making it contingent on the failure of the first agreement and on the first buyer's release of all claims. The seller should not proceed with the second transaction without first clearly establishing that the first agreement is terminated and the first buyer has no right to enforce it. The best way to accomplish this is by asking the first buyer to execute a release of contract form.

Deposit

The buyer's deposit is an expression of good faith and a serious intention to buy the property. Under the terms of the CAR form, the broker holds the deposit check uncashed until the seller has accepted the buyer's offer. Then if the seller rejects the offer, the check can easily be returned to the buyer.

The deposit receipt should not only acknowledge receipt of the deposit, it should explain the circumstances in which the deposit will be refunded or forfeited. The parties have the option of treating the deposit as liquidated damages. When the buyer and seller initial in the appropriate space, if the buyer defaults, the seller will keep the deposit as liquidated damages instead of suing for actual damages. For a residential transaction (where the property has up to four units and the buyer intends to occupy one of them), a liquidated damages provision must be in boldface type and initialed by the parties, as in the CAR form. The liquidated damages may not exceed 3% of the purchase price, so if the deposit was more than 3%, the seller will have to return part of it.

Be cautioned that funds deposited in escrow are not released automatically if there is a dispute. If the seller wants to retain the deposit as liquidated damages, the escrowee will usually not release that money to the seller without the buyer's consent. It may be necessary to sue or submit the matter to arbitration to establish the buyer's default and that the seller is entitled to liquidated damages.

Broker's Compensation

The final section of the CAR deposit receipt is headed "ACCEPTANCE." Here the seller accepts the buyer's offer as set forth in the rest of the document. The seller also agrees to compensate the broker. In most cases, this is merely a reaffirmation of the commission agreement in an earlier written listing. Whereas up to this point the broker has taken the risk of operating under an oral or implied listing agreement, this provision will satisfy the statute of frauds. If the deposit receipt provides for a different commission amount than the listing agreement, the deposit receipt is controlling since it was entered into at a more recent date.

Under the compensation provision of the CAR deposit receipt, if the buyer defaults the broker is entitled to half of the damages the seller receives. In practice, this generally means that the broker will take half of the forfeited deposit; if the parties initialed the liquidated damage clause. However, the broker is not allowed to receive more in damages than he or she would have received as a commission if the transaction had closed.

Counter Offers and the Deposit Receipt

Often a seller is unwilling to accept the buyer's offer as written, but would accept slightly different terms. Remember that when an offeree varies any terms in an offer, that's a counter offer instead of an acceptance. The original offeror (the buyer) is not bound unless he or she chooses to accept the seller's counter offer.

When a seller wants to make a counter offer, some agents simply cross out the appropriate terms on the buyer's deposit receipt and replace them with the seller's new terms. The seller signs the deposit receipt and initials and dates the changes. Then if the buyer is willing to accept the counter offer, he or she also initials and dates the changes. This approach may work if the changes are minor and there is enough space to indicate them clearly. But the agreement may become difficult to read (especially if the buyer makes another change). Worse, sometimes an agent fails to get every change initialed, so that it isn't clear whether the parties ever reached an agreement on all the terms.

It's clearer and more professional to write any counter offer on another form or a separate attachment. There are forms specifically designed for the purpose of making changes to the deposit receipt, such as the **CAR Counter Offer** form, shown on the next page, to change or alter the terms of the deposit receipt form, or the **CAR Addendum** form (at the end of the chapter) to incorporate additional terms that are not in the deposit receipt form.

Megan's Law Disclosure

Megan's law is federal legislation requiring law enforcement officials to make information available regarding the presence of sex offenders. California law requires real estate agents to disclose information about registered sex offenders.

Transaction documents (e.g. deposit receipts, rental agreements, etc.) will include a provision disclosing that information on registered sex offenders is available from local law enforcement. Once this is done, no additional information need be given.

CALIFORNIA
ASSOCIATION
OF REALTORS®

COUNTER OFFER   No. _____
(For use by Seller or Buyer. May be used for Multiple Counter Offer.)
(C.A.R. Form CO-11, Revised 4/01)

Date _____, at _____ California.
This is a counter offer to the: ☐ Residential Purchase Agreement, ☐ Counter Offer, ☐ Other _____ ("Offer"),
dated _____, regarding _____ ("Property"),
between _____ ("Buyer"), and _____ ("Seller").

1. **TERMS:** The terms and conditions of the above referenced document are accepted subject to the following:
   A. **Paragraphs in the Offer that require initials by all parties, but are not initialed by all parties, are excluded from the final agreement unless specifically referenced for inclusion in paragraph 1C of this or another Counter Offer.**
   B. **Unless otherwise specified in writing, down payment and loan amount(s) will be adjusted in the same proportion as in the original Offer.**
   C. _____
   _____
   _____
   _____
   _____
   _____
   _____
   _____
   _____
   _____
   _____
   _____
   _____

   D. **The following attached addenda/supplements are incorporated in this Counter Offer:** ☐ Contract Addendum No. _____
   ☐ _____ ☐ _____

2. **RIGHT TO ACCEPT OTHER OFFERS:** Seller reserves the right to continue to offer the Property for sale or for other transaction, and to accept any other offer at any time prior to communication of acceptance, as described in paragraph 3. If this is a Seller Counter Offer, Seller's acceptance of another offer prior to Buyer's acceptance and communication of acceptance of this Counter Offer, shall revoke this Counter Offer.

3. **EXPIRATION:** Unless acceptance of this Counter Offer is Signed by the Buyer or Seller to whom it is sent, and communication of acceptance is made by delivering a Signed Copy, which is personally received, to the person making this Counter Offer or to _____, by 5:00 PM on the third calendar day after this Counter Offer is written (or, if checked, ☐ date: _____, time _____ AM/PM), this Counter Offer shall be deemed revoked and the deposit shall be returned to Buyer. This Counter Offer may be executed in counterparts.

4. ☐ **(if Checked) MULTIPLE COUNTER OFFER:** Seller is making a Counter Offer(s) to another prospective buyer(s) on terms that may or may not be the same as in this Counter Offer. Acceptance of this Counter Offer by Buyer shall **not** be binding unless and until it is subsequently re-Signed by Seller in paragraph 7 below and communication of Seller's acceptance is made by delivering a Signed Copy, in person, by mail or by facsimile, which is personally received, to Buyer or to _____. Prior to the completion of all of these events, Buyer and Seller shall have no duties or obligations for the purchase or sale of the Property.

5. **OFFER: BUYER OR SELLER MAKES THIS COUNTER OFFER ON THE TERMS ABOVE AND ACKNOWLEDGES RECEIPT OF A COPY.**
   _____ Date _____
   _____ Date _____

6. **ACCEPTANCE: I/WE** accept the above Counter Offer (**If checked** ☐ **SUBJECT TO THE ATTACHED COUNTER OFFER**) and acknowledge receipt of a Copy.
   _____ Date _____ Time _____ AM/PM
   _____ Date _____ Time _____ AM/PM

7. **MULTIPLE COUNTER OFFER SIGNATURE LINE:** By signing below, Seller accepts this Multiple Counter Offer.
   NOTE TO SELLER: Do NOT sign in this box until after Buyer signs in paragraph 6.) (Paragraph 7 applies only if paragraph 4 is checked.)
   _____ Date _____ Time _____ AM/PM
   _____ Date _____ Time _____ AM/PM

8. (____/____) (Initials) **ACKNOWLEDGMENT OF RECEIPT:** The maker of the Counter Offer, or that person's authorized agent as specified in paragraph 3, (or, if this is a Multiple Counter Offer, the Buyer or Buyer's authorized agent as specified in paragraph 4) acknowledges receipt of a Signed Copy of this Counter Offer on _____ (date), at _____ AM/PM.

Published and Distributed by:
REAL ESTATE BUSINESS SERVICES, INC.
a subsidiary of the CALIFORNIA ASSOCIATION OF REALTORS®
525 South Virgil Avenue, Los Angeles, California 90020

Reviewed by _____
Broker or Designee _____ Date _____

CO-11 (PAGE 1 OF 1)   Print Date

COUNTER OFFER (CO-11 PAGE 1 OF 1)

Reprinted with permission, CALIFORNIA ASSOCIATION OF REALTORS®. Endorsement not implied.

Options

An **option** is a contract giving one party the right to do something, without obligating him or her to do it. In real estate, the most common type of option is an option to purchase. An option to purchase gives one party (the **optionee**) the right to buy the property of the other (the **optionor**) at a specified price for a limited time. Within that period, the optionee may choose to exercise the option—that is, enter into a contract to buy the property. But the optionee is under no obligation to exercise the option.

> **Example:** Sullivan is interested in buying Hubbard's house, but hasn't quite made up his mind. He asks Hubbard to grant him an option to purchase the house for $250,000. Hubbard agrees, and writes up an option agreement that will expire in two weeks.
>
> A week later, while Sullivan is still making up his mind, he hears that Pirandello i planning to offer Hubbard $275,000 for the house. Sullivan decides he does want to buy the house, so he exercises his option. Hubbard is bound to sell her house to Sullivan for $250,000, instead of selling it to Pirandello for $275,000.

Note that an option to purchase real property must be in writing and signed. The written option agreement should be as specific as possible, identifying the parties and the property, and stating all the terms of the potential sale. The option must also be exercised in writing.

CONSIDERATION FOR AN OPTION

An option does not have to be supported by consideration. That is, the optionee does not have to give the optionor anything in exchange for the option right. Without consideration, the option is a unilateral contract: the optionor is bound to perform if the optionee exercises the option. But in that case, the optionor can revoke the option at any time until it is exercised (just as if it were merely an offer to sell). In the previous example, Sullivan didn't give Hubbard any consideration for the option. If Hubbard had managed to revoke the option before Sullivan exercised it, she would have been free to sell her house to Pirandello. That's true even though she originally granted the option for two weeks.

However, if Sullivan had provided consideration for the option—for example, if he had paid Hubbard $200 to keep the option open for two weeks—then Hubbard would not have a right to revoke it during that period. To make an option irrevocable, very little consideration is necessary. But if the consideration is not legally adequate, the optionee will not be able to sue for specific performance.

> **Example:** Hubbard granted Sullivan an option to purchase her house for $250,000. Sullivan gave Hubbard $15 to keep the option open for two weeks. During that period, Pirandello offers Hubbard $275,000 for the house. Hubbard can't revoke Sullivan's option because he gave her consideration.

However, Hubbard decides to breach the option contract and sell the house to Pirandello. When Sullivan sues Hubbard for breach of contract, the court rules that $15 was not adequate consideration for a two-week option on a $250,000 house. Sullivan is entitled to damages for breach of contract (probably $25,000), but not specific performance. The court cannot order Hubbard to sell the house to Sullivan for $250,000.

The consideration paid for an option contract is not refundable. If the optionee decides not to exercise the option, he or she can't demand that the optionor return the consideration.

RELATION BACK

When an option is exercised, the interest the optionee acquires in the property relates back to the time the option was granted. In the eyes of the law, it's as though the optionee purchased the property when the option was granted, rather than when the option was exercised.

Case Example: In November 1969, the Enzlers gave C/H Realty an exclusive listing agreement that was to expire on May 15, 1970. An extender clause entitled C/H Realty to a commission if the property was sold before August 15, 1970, to anyone C/H Realty introduced to the Enzlers as a prospective buyer.

In December 1969, C/H Realty showed the property to the Armtrouts. In June 1970, the Enzlers granted the Armtrouts an option to purchase. But the Enzlers and the Armtrouts agreed that the option would not be exercised until after C/H Realty's safety period expired. That way the Enzlers wouldn't have to pay the broker's commission. So the Armtrouts did not exercise their option until September 4, 1970.

C/H Realty sued for its commission. The court ruled that the Enzlers were required to pay the broker. When the Armtrouts exercised their option, their interest in the property related back to the time the option was granted (June 1970). In effect, they were held to have purchased the property in June rather than in September. Since the safety period didn't expire until August, C/H Realty was entitled to the commission. *Anthony v. Enzler*, 61 Cal. App. 3d 872, 132 Cal. Rptr. 553 (1976).

This rule makes it particularly important for a real estate purchaser to check the public record for any options recorded against the property he or she intends to buy. When an option is exercised, any rights acquired since the option was granted are cut off, if the person who acquired the rights had actual or constructive knowledge of the option.

Example: Dunn buys Schauer's property in March. Dunn doesn't know that Nguyen has an option to purchase the property that won't expire until June. But since Nguyen recorded her option in February, Dunn is charged with constructive knowledge of the option. Without realizing it, Dunn has taken the property subject to Nguyen's option.

In May, Nguyen decides to exercise the option. She can require Dunn to convey the property to her, just as if it were still owned by Schauer.

CALIFORNIA ASSOCIATION OF REALTORS®

OPTION AGREEMENT
To be used with a purchase agreement. May also be used with a lease.

Date_____, at _____, California
_____, ("Optionor"), grants to
_____, ("Optionee"),
an option ("Agreement") to purchase the real property and improvements situated in (city) _____
_____, County of _____,
California, described as _____ ("Property") as specified in the
attached: ☐ Real Estate Purchase Agreement ☐ Other_____, which is incorporated
by this reference as a part of this Agreement, on the following terms and conditions.

1. OPTION CONSIDERATION:

    A. _____ Dollars $_____,

    ☐ (if checked) and/or (circle one), the amount specified in paragraph 6B.

    B. By ☐ cash, ☐ cashier's check, ☐ personal check, or ☐ _____
    _____.
    made payable to _____.

    C. ☐ Payable upon execution of this Agreement,

    OR ☐ Payable within _____ days after acceptance of this Agreement, by which time Optionee shall have completed a
    due diligence investigation and accepted the condition of the Property. At least 5 (or _____) days before expiration of this time
    period, Optionor shall provide to Optionee (i) any mandatory disclosures (such as those required by paragraph 7), (ii) a
    preliminary title report, and (iii) _____.

    OR ☐ _____

    D. If payment is not made by the time specified in paragraph 1C above, this Agreement shall become immediately null and void.

    E. If this Option is exercised, ☐ all, or ☐ $_____ of the Option Consideration shall be applied toward
    Optionee's down payment obligations under the terms of the attached purchase agreement, upon close of escrow of that
    agreement. Optionee is advised that the full amount of the option consideration applied toward any down payment may not be
    counted by a lender for financing purposes.

2. OPTION PERIOD: The Option shall begin on (date) _____, and shall end at 11:59 p.m.
    (or at ☐ _____), on (date) _____.

3. MANNER OF EXERCISE: Optionee may exercise the Option **only** by delivering a written unconditional notice of exercise, signed
    by Optionee, to Optionor, or _____, who is authorized to receive it, no earlier than
    _____ and no later than _____.
    A copy of the unconditional notice of exercise shall be delivered to the Brokers identified in this Agreement.

4. EFFECT OF DEFAULT ON OPTION: Optionee shall have no right to exercise this Option if Optionee has not performed any
    obligation imposed by, or is in default of, any obligation of this Agreement, any addenda, or any document incorporated by reference.

5. NON-EXERCISE: If the Option is not exercised in the manner specified, within the option period or any written extension thereof,
    or if it is terminated under any provision of this Agreement, then:

    A. The Option and all rights of Optionee to purchase the Property shall immediately terminate without notice; and

    B. All Option Consideration paid, rent paid, services rendered to Optionor, and improvements made to the Property, if any, by
    Optionee, shall be retained by Optionor in consideration of the granting of the Option; and

    C. Optionee shall execute, acknowledge, and deliver to Option or, within 5 (or ☐ _____) calendar days of Optionor's request, a
    release, quitclaim deed, or any other document reasonably required by Optionor or a title insurance company to verify the
    termination of the Option.

Optionee and Optionor acknowledge receipt of copy of this page, which constitutes Page 1 of _____ Pages.
Optionee's Initials (_____) (_____)   Optionor's Initials (_____) (_____)

Published and Distributed by:
REAL ESTATE BUSINESS SERVICES, INC.
a subsidiary of the CALIFORNIA ASSOCIATION OF REALTORS®
525 South Virgil Avenue, Los Angeles, California 90020

PRINT DATE

REVISED 10/98

OFFICE USE ONLY
Reviewed by Broker
or Designee _____
Date _____

EQUAL HOUSING
OPPORTUNITY

OPTION AGREEMENT (OA-11 PAGE 1 OF 3)

Property Address: _____   Date: _____

6. ☐ **LEASE (If checked):**
   A. The attached lease agreement, dated _____, between Optionee as Tenant and Optionor as Landlord, is incorporated by reference as part of this Agreement.
   B. $_____ per month of rent actually paid by Optionee shall be treated as Option Consideration pursuant to paragraph 1.
   C. The lease obligations shall continue until termination of the lease. If the Option is exercised, the lease shall continue until the earliest of (i) the date scheduled for close of escrow under the purchase agreement, or as extended in writing, (ii) the close of escrow of the purchase agreement, or (iii) mutual cancellation of the purchase agreement.
   D. In addition to the reason stated in paragraph 4, Optionee shall have no right to exercise this Option if Optionor, as landlord, has given to Optionee, as tenant, two or more notices to cure any default or non-performance under the terms of the lease.

7. **DISCLOSURE STATEMENTS:** Unless exempt, if the Property contains one-to-four residential dwelling units, Optionor must comply with Civil Code §1102 et seq., by providing Optionee with a Real Estate Transfer Disclosure Statement and Natural Hazard Disclosure Statement.

8. **RECORDING:** Optionor or Optionee shall, upon request, execute, acknowledge, and deliver to the other a memorandum of this Agreement for recording purposes. All resulting fees and taxes shall be paid by the party requesting recordation.

9. **DAMAGE OR DESTRUCTION:** If, prior to exercise of this Option, by no fault of Optionee, the Property is totally or partially damaged or destroyed by fire, earthquake, accident or other casualty, Optionee may cancel this Agreement by giving written notice to Optionor, and is entitled to the return of all Option Consideration paid. However, if, prior to Optionee giving notice of cancellation to Optionor, the Property has been repaired or replaced so that it is in substantially the same condition as of the date of acceptance of this Agreement, Optionee shall not have the right to cancel this Agreement.

10. **PURCHASE AGREEMENT:** All of the time limits contained in the attached purchase agreement, which begin on the date of Acceptance of the purchase agreement, shall instead begin to run on the date the Option is exercised. After exercise of this Option, if any contingency in the attached purchase agreement, including but not limited to any right of inspection or financing provision, is not satisfied or is disapproved by Optionee at any time, all option consideration paid, rent paid, services rendered to Optionor, and improvements to the Property, if any, by Optionee, shall be retained by Optionor in consideration of the granting of the Option.

11. **NOTICES:** Unless otherwise provided in this Agreement, any notice, tender, or delivery to be given by either party to the other may be performed by personal delivery or by registered or certified mail, postage prepaid, return receipt requested, and shall be deemed delivered when mailed (except for acceptance of the offer to enter into this Agreement, which must be done in the manner specified in paragraph 16). Mailed notices shall be addressed as shown below, but each party may designate a new address by giving written notice to the other.

12. **DISPUTE RESOLUTION:** Optionee and Optionor agree that any dispute or claim arising between them out of this Agreement shall be decided by the same method agreed to for resolving disputes in the attached purchase agreement.

13. **OTHER TERMS AND CONDITIONS,** including attached supplements: _____
_____
_____
_____
_____
_____
_____
_____
_____
_____
_____
_____
_____
_____
_____

14. **ATTORNEY'S FEES:** In any action, proceeding, or arbitration between Optionee and Optionor arising out of this Agreement, the prevailing Optionee or Optionor shall be entitled to reasonable attorney's fees and costs from the non-prevailing Optionee or Optionor.

Optionee and Optionor acknowledge receipt of copy of this page, which constitutes Page 2 of _____ Pages.
Optionee's Initials (_____) (_____)   Optionor's Initials (_____) (_____)

┌─────────────────────────┐
│ OFFICE USE ONLY   │
│ Reviewed by Broker   │
│ or Designee _____   │
│ Date _____   │
└─────────────────────────┘

REVISED 10/98

PRINT DATE

OPTION AGREEMENT (OA-11 PAGE 2 OF 3)

Reprinted with permission, CALIFORNIA ASSOCIATION OF REALTORS®. Endorsement not implied.

Property Address: _____ Date: _____

15. TIME OF ESSENCE; ENTIRE CONTRACT; CHANGES: Time is of the essence. All understandings between the parties are incorporated in this Agreement. Its terms are intended by the parties as a final, complete, and exclusive expression of their agreement with respect to its subject matter, and may not be contradicted by evidence of any prior agreement or contemporaneous oral agreement. **This Agreement may not be extended, amended, modified, altered, or changed, except in writing signed by Optionee and Optionor.**

16. OFFER: This is an offer for an Option to purchase Property on the above terms and conditions. Unless Acceptance of Offer is signed by Optionor, and a signed copy delivered in person, by mail, or facsimile, and personally received by Optionee, or by _____, who is authorized to receive it, by (date) _____, at _____ AM/PM, the offer shall be deemed revoked. Optionee has read and acknowledges receipt of a copy of the offer. This Agreement and any supplement, addendum, or modification, including any photocopy or facsimile, may be signed in two or more counterparts, all of which shall constitute one and the same writing.

OPTIONEE _____

OPTIONEE _____
Address _____
_____
Telephone _____ Fax _____

17. BROKER COMPENSATION: Optionor agrees to pay compensation for services as follows:
_____, to _____, Broker, and
_____, to _____, Broker,
payable upon execution of this Agreement.

18. ACCEPTANCE OF OPTION: Optionor warrants that Optionor is the owner of the Property or has the authority to execute this Agreement. Optionor accepts and agrees to grant an Option to purchase the Property on the above terms and conditions.

If checked: ☐ SUBJECT TO ATTACHED COUNTER OFFER, DATED _____.

OPTIONOR _____

OPTIONOR _____
Address _____
_____
Telephone _____ Fax _____

Real Estate Brokers are not parties to the Agreement between Optionee and Optionor.

Broker _____ By _____ Date _____
Address _____
_____
Telephone _____ Fax _____

Broker _____ By _____ Date _____
Address _____
_____
Telephone _____ Fax _____

This form is available for use by the entire real estate industry. It is not intended to identify the user as a REALTOR®. REALTOR® is a registered collective membership mark which may be used only by members of the NATIONAL ASSOCIATION OF REALTORS® who subscribe to its Code of Ethics.
PRINT DATE

Page 3 of _____ Pages.

REVISED 10/98

OFFICE USE ONLY
Reviewed by Broker
or Designee _____
Date _____

EQUAL HOUSING OPPORTUNITY

OPTION AGREEMENT (OA-11 PAGE 3 OF 3)

However, keep in mind that until an option is exercised, it is only a contract right, not an interest in the property. So an option can't be used as security for a deed of trust, and it isn't a lien.

ASSIGNMENT OF AN OPTION

An option agreement generally can be assigned, unless the contract states that assignment is prohibited. There's an exception, however, when the consideration paid by the optionee is an unsecured promissory note. In that case, the option can't be assigned without the written consent of the optionor.

An option to purchase is often included in a lease. If the lease is assigned, the option is assigned too, even when the assignment doesn't specifically mention the option.

TERMINATION

When an optionee has given consideration for the option, the death of the optionor does not terminate the option. The option contract is binding on the optionor's heirs, and the optionee can still exercise it.

An option terminates automatically if it is not exercised before its expiration date. But if the option agreement was recorded, it can still be a cloud on the title after it has expired. A title insurance company will not simply ignore a recorded option after its expiration date—they can't be sure that the optionor didn't grant an extension. So when a recorded option is no longer effective, a document canceling the option should be recorded. To make absolutely sure the optionee doesn't have any claim on the property, title insurers often require a quitclaim deed from the optionee to the optionor.

However, this precaution isn't necessary six months after the option expired. The Civil Code provides that a recorded option no longer gives constructive notice of the optionee's interest if no instrument extending or exercising it has been recorded six months after it expired. Also, if the option doesn't state an expiration date, it no longer gives constructive notice six months after it was recorded.

RIGHT OF PREEMPTION

A **right of preemption** (sometimes called a **right of first refusal**) is not the same thing as an option. Someone who holds a preemption right has the right to buy the property only if and when the owner decides to sell it. The owner can't be required sell the property against his or her will, unlike an optionor.

Preemption rights are often included in leases for office space. If adjacent space on the same floor becomes vacant, the lessor must offer the lessee the chance to expand into that space before it can be offered to a new tenant. Co-owners of property sometimes grant each other preemption rights: If one co-owner decides to sell his or her share, the other has the right to buy it instead of letting it go to a stranger.

Natural Hazard Disclosure Statement

Use of the **Natural Hazard Disclosure Statement (NHD)** form is mandatory for certain transactions. Existing law (Civil Code Section 1103) requires a seller and his/her agent to fill in the NHD form in order to disclose to a prospective buyer all material facts about the condition of the property for sale, and unless exempt, the statutory form called the "Transfer Disclosure Statement" (TDS) must be used.

The requirement to use the NHD only applies if: (1) it is a Transfer Disclosure Statement (TDS) transaction involving any transfer by sale, exchange, installment land sale contract, lease with an option to purchase, any other options to purchase, ground lease coupled with improvements of real property, or residential stock cooperative improved or consisting of not less than one or more than four residential units, or personal property manufactured homes, and (2) the property is located in one of six natural hazard zones (listed below) when there is a sale of real property.

The California Legislature cited the existence of the following six zones that a real property buyer must have knowledge of before purchasing:

1. A **special flood hazard area** (Any type Zone "A" or "V") designated by the Federal Emergency Management Agency (FEMA).

2. An area of **potential flooding shown on a dam failure inundation map** pursuant to Section 8589.5 of the Government Code.

3. A very **high fire hazard severity zone.** Government Code Sections 51178 or 51179. The owner of this property is subject to the maintenance requirements of Government Code Section 51182.

4. **Wildland area that may contain substantial forest fire risks and hazards.** Public Resources Code Section 4125. The owner of this property is subject to the maintenance requirements of Public Resources Code section 4291. Additionally, it is not the state's responsibility to provide fire protection services to any building or structure located within the wildlands unless the Department of Forestry and Fire Protection has entered into a cooperative agreement with a local agency for those purposes pursuant to Public Resources Code Section 4142.

5. An **earthquake fault zone** pursuant to Public Resources Code Section 2622.

6. A **seismic hazard zone** pursuant to Public Resources Code Section 2696. (Landslide Zone) or (Liquefaction Zone).

CALIFORNIA
ASSOCIATION
OF REALTORS®

NATURAL HAZARD DISCLOSURE STATEMENT

This statement applies to the following property: _____

The transferor and his or her agent(s) disclose the following information with the knowledge that even though this is not a warranty, prospective transferees may rely on this information in deciding whether and on what terms to purchase the subject property. Transferor hereby authorizes any agent(s) representing any principal(s) in this action to provide a copy of this statement to any person or entity in connection with any actual or anticipated sale of the property.

The following are representations made by the transferor and his or her agent(s) based on their knowledge and maps drawn by the state and federal governments. This information is a disclosure and is not intended to be part of any contract between the transferee and transferor.

THIS REAL PROPERTY LIES WITHIN THE FOLLOWING HAZARDOUS AREA(S): (Check the answer which applies.)

A SPECIAL FLOOD HAZARD AREA (Any type Zone "A" or "V") designated by the Federal Emergency Management Agency.

Yes _____   No _____   Do not know and information not available from local jurisdiction _____

AN AREA OF POTENTIAL FLOODING shown on a dam failure inundation map pursuant to Section 8589.5 of the Government Code.

Yes _____   No _____   Do not know and information not available from local jurisdiction _____

A VERY HIGH FIRE HAZARD SEVERITY ZONE pursuant to Section 51178 or 51179 of the Government Code. The owner of this property is subject to the maintenance requirements of Section 51182 of the Government Code.

Yes _____   No _____

A WILDLAND AREA THAT MAY CONTAIN SUBSTANTIAL FOREST FIRE RISKS AND HAZARDS pursuant to Section 4125 of the Public Resources Code. The owner of this property is subject to the maintenance requirements of Section 4291 of the Public Resources Code. Additionally, it is not the state's responsibility to provide fire protection services to any building or structure located within the wildlands unless the Department of Forestry and Fire Protection has entered into a cooperative agreement with a local agency for those purposes pursuant to Section 4142 of the Public Resources Code.

Yes _____   No _____

AN EARTHQUAKE FAULT ZONE pursuant to Section 2622 of the Public Resources Code.

Yes _____   No _____

A SEISMIC HAZARD ZONE pursuant to Section 2696 of the Public Resources Code.

Yes (Landslide Zone) _____
                                     No _____   Map not yet released by state _____
Yes (Liquefaction Zone) _____

THESE HAZARDS MAY LIMIT YOUR ABILITY TO DEVELOP THE REAL PROPERTY, TO OBTAIN INSURANCE, OR TO RECEIVE ASSISTANCE AFTER A DISASTER.

THE MAPS ON WHICH THESE DISCLOSURES ARE BASED ESTIMATE WHERE NATURAL HAZARDS EXIST. THEY ARE NOT DEFINITIVE INDICATORS OF WHETHER OR NOT A PROPERTY WILL BE AFFECTED BY A NATURAL DISASTER. TRANSFEREE(S) AND TRANSFEROR(S) MAY WISH TO OBTAIN PROFESSIONAL ADVICE REGARDING THOSE HAZARDS AND OTHER HAZARDS THAT MAY AFFECT THE PROPERTY.

The information in this box is not part of the statutory form.

☐ (if checked) The representations made in this form are based upon information provided by an independent third-party report provided as a substituted disclosure pursuant to California Civil Code §1102.4. Neither the seller nor the seller's agent (1) has independently verified the information contained in this form and the report or (2) is personally aware of any errors or inaccuracies in the information contained on this form.

Transferor represents that the information herein is true and correct to the best of the transferor's knowledge as of the date signed by the transferor.

Signature of Transferor _____ Date _____

Agent represents that the information herein is true and correct to the best of the agent's knowledge as of the date signed by the agent.

Signature of Agent _____ Date _____

Signature of Agent _____ Date _____

Transferee represents that he or she has read and understands this document.

Signature of Transferee _____ Date _____

Published and Distributed by:
REAL ESTATE BUSINESS SERVICES, INC.
a subsidiary of the CALIFORNIA ASSOCIATION OF REALTORS®
525 South Virgil Avenue, Los Angeles, California 90020

PRINT DATE

Page _____ of _____ Pages.
REVISED 10/99

FORM NHD-11

OFFICE USE ONLY
Reviewed by Broker
or Designee
Date _____

EQUAL HOUSING
OPPORTUNITY

Real Estate Contracts

CHAPTER SUMMARY

1. To sue for a commission, a real estate broker must have a signed writing by the client that indicates the fact of employment. A listing agreement should state the terms of sale the seller is willing to accept and should specify when the broker will be entitled to the commission. Most exclusive listing agreements include an extender clause.

2. The deposit receipt should set forth all the terms of the agreement between the buyer and seller. Most deposit receipts contain conditions, making the purchase contingent on the buyer's ability to: obtain financing, sell current home, or the results of an appraisal or inspection. A buyer's deposit may be treated as liquidated damages, but in a residential transaction, the seller may not keep more than 3% of the agreed purchase price.

3. Most contracts entered into with licensed agents are on standard preprinted forms and blanks are filled in. The preprinted forms avoid the problem of practicing law without a license.

4. The standard forms contain an attorney fee provision allowing the prevailing party to recover reasonable attorney fees from the loser. Without such a clause the winner would have to absorb the fees.

5. The standard forms also contain an integration clause which insures that the document being signed represents the final expression of the bargain and any future modification must be in writing.

6. An option to purchase gives the optionee a right to buy the property at a specified price, without requiring him or her to buy it. An option can be revoked unless it is supported by consideration. When an option is exercised, the optionee's ownership relates back to the time the option was granted. A recorded option is a cloud on the title until six months after its expiration date.

7. A right of preemption (right of first refusal) is not an option, the holder has a right to purchase the property only if the owner decides to sell.

Chapter 8

CASE PROBLEM

EPA Real Estate Partnership v. Kang, 12 Cal. App. 4th 171, 15 Cal. Rptr. 2d. 209 (1992)

EPA Real Estate Partnership and partner Jack Horton (EPA) owned Grand Security, an apartment complex in East Palo Alto. In June 1988, EPA listed Grand Security for sale with Feher Young and Associates Commercial Brokerage, Ltd. (Young) for $2.5 million. The listing expired on August 15, 1988, and provided for a 6% commission payable to Young if EPA sold or contracted to sell the property within the listing period. In July, Kang made a written offer to Horton to buy the property for $2.45 million. Horton rejected the offer because 6% of it would be payable to Young. Kang and Horton signed a written agreement selling the property to Kang if it remained unsold on August 15. To satisfy the concerns of Horton about the commission, the agreement provided that Kang would indemnify EPA if it had to pay Young a commission as a result of this sale.

After the listing expired, EPA and Kang entered into a new written sales agreement on a standard deposit receipt selling the property for $2.35 million. **Paragraph 39** of the deposit receipt stated:

> "Time is of the essence. All prior agreements between the parties are incorporated in this agreement, which constitutes the entire contract. Its terms are intended by the parties as a final, complete, and exclusive expression of their agreement with respect to its subject matter and may not be contradicted by evidence of any prior agreement or contemporaneous oral agreement. The captions in this Agreement are for convenience of reference only and are not intended as part of this Agreement. **This Agreement may not be extended, amended, modified, altered, or changed in any respect whatsoever except in writing signed by Buyer and Seller."**

Young discovered the sale and demanded arbitration, as provided in the listing agreement, for a commission and damages. EPA paid Young $249,394.33 which had been awarded in arbitration after EPA incurred $41,739.26 in litigation costs defending Young's claim. EPA then demanded that Kang indemnify it for the $291,133.59 it paid Young. Kang refused. EPA sued for breach of contract and fraud. Who wins and why?

Answer: The Court of Appeals held that "The parol evidence rule generally prohibits the introduction of extrinsic evidence-oral or written-to vary or contradict the terms of an integrated written instrument... According to this substantive rule of law, when the parties intend a written agreement to be the final and complete expression of their understanding, that writing becomes the final contract between the parties, which may not be contradicted by even the most persuasive evidence of collateral agreements. Such evidence is legally irrelevant."

EPA argued the indemnity agreement was a completely separate agreement and did not contradict any of the terms of the deposit receipt and it should stand by itself. However, the indemnity agreement deals with the same subject as the deposit receipt, and that is the sale of Grand Security. Obviously, it was important to Horton to have an indemnity agreement as part of the sale to Kang.

Paragraph 39 of the agreement for the sale of Grand Security clearly states that it is the final statement of the bargain between the parties and there are no other agreements regarding the sale. If at the time of the signing of the deposit receipt EPA had wanted an indemnity agreement for Kang, it should have included it in the deposit receipt. Judgment for Kang. **Notice how much money this parol evidence mistake cost EPA.**

CHAPTER 8 KEY TERMS	employment form (broker/salesperson)	option form optionee
	extender clause	optionor
deposit receipt	integration clause	right of preemption
counter offer form	listing agreement	

CALIFORNIA
ASSOCIATION
OF REALTORS®

ADDENDUM

(C.A.R. Form ADM, Revised 10/01)

No. _____

The following terms and conditions are hereby incorporated in and made a part of the: ☐ Residential Purchase Agreement, ☐ Manufactured Home Purchase Agreement, ☐ Business Purchase Agreement, ☐ Residential Lease or Month-to-Month Rental Agreement, ☐ Vacant Land Purchase Agreement, ☐ Residential Income Property Purchase Agreement, ☐ Commercial Property Purchase Agreement, ☐ other_____

_____,

dated _____, on property known as _____

_____,

in which _____ is referred to as ("Buyer/Tenant")
and _____ is referred to as ("Seller/Landlord").

_____
_____
_____
_____
_____
_____
_____
_____
_____
_____
_____
_____
_____
_____
_____
_____
_____
_____
_____
_____
_____
_____
_____
_____
_____
_____

The foregoing terms and conditions are hereby agreed to, and the undersigned acknowledge receipt of a copy of this document.

Date _____   Date _____

Buyer/Tenant _____   Seller/Landlord _____

Buyer/Tenant _____   Seller/Landlord _____

Published and Distributed by:
REAL ESTATE BUSINESS SERVICES, INC.
a subsidiary of the CALIFORNIA ASSOCIATION OF REALTORS®
525 South Virgil Avenue, Los Angeles, California 90020

Reviewed by _____

Broker or Designee _____ Date _____

EQUAL HOUSING OPPORTUNITY

ADM-11 REVISED 10/01 (PAGE 1 OF 1)   Print Date

ADDENDUM (ADM-11 PAGE 1 OF 1)

Reprinted with permission, CALIFORNIA ASSOCIATION OF REALTORS®. Endorsement not implied.

Real Estate Contracts

Quiz—Chapter 8

1. A contract provision which states that the written document is the entire agreement between the parties is called:

a. a liquidated provision.
b. an extender clause.
c. an integration clause.
d. such a clause is illegal in California.

2. Mark sold Mavis his house through K Realty. The listing agreement provided for payment of a 5% commission to K but the deposit receipt shows a 5.5% commission.

a. Mark must pay 5% commission since it was the first amount agreed to.
b. Mark must pay a 5.5% commission because it was the last agreement.
c. Mark must pay a 5.25% commission as the two commissions are averaged.
d. Because of the conflict between amounts, Mark pays no commission.

3. Option to purchase a specific vacant lot:

a. can never be assigned.
b. can always be assigned.
c. can be assigned if purchased for cash.
d. can be assigned unless contract prohibits.

4. An exclusive right to sell listing:

a. must contain a termination date.
b. must be in writing if broker wants to be successful in suing for a commission.
c. broker must keep for at least 3 years.
d. all of the above are correct statements.

5. Shank lists her house for sale with Rudy Realty for 6 months using a standard listing form. Shanks' found an out of town job and decided not to sell the house after 4 months into the listing. Rudy sues for the commission stated in the listing.

a. Rudy is entitle to the commission.
b. Rudy gets no commission since listing cancellation beyond Shank's control.
c. Rudy, entitled to 2/3s of the commission, since 4/6s of listing expired.
d. No commission for Rudy; seller can cancel listing any time, for any reason.

6. April offered to purchase Michelle's house, listed for $200,000, for $180,000. Michelle thought the price was too low and gave April a counter offer for $191,000. April gave Michelle a counter offer for $185,000 believing $191,000 was high. Michelle rejected April's $185,000 offer.

a. April can now accept only Michelle's $191,000 offer to form a contract.
b. April can now accept only Michelle's offer of $200,000 to form a contract.
c. there are no offers for April to accept.
d. Michelle can reconsider, accept April's $185,000 offer to form a contract.

7. In December, Andrea wants to buy Trevor's house. However, she discovers an option recorded on May 1 has no expiration date, although the option was dated April 20. No extensions recorded.

a. Andrea can safely buy the house today.
b. Andrea can safely buy the house on May 2 of the next year.
c. Andrea can safely buy the house on April 20 of next year.
d. None of the above are correct answers.

8. Most standard deposit receipts contain:

a. an attorney fee clause.
b. an arbitration clause.
c. an integration clause.
d. all of the above are correct answers.

9. Significant changes to the proposed Deposit Receipt should be made on what form?

a. Counter offer form
b. Option form
c. Listing agreement
d. None of the above are correct answers

10. A broker must retain listing agreement copies for:

a. two years.
b. three years.
c. four years.
d. six years.

ANSWERS: 1. c; 2. b; 3. d; 4. d; 5. b; 6. c; 7. b; 8. c; 9. a; 10. b

281

COURT OF APPEAL OF THE STATE OF CALIFORNIA

THIRD APPELLATE DISTRICT

SHASTA et alia,

Plaintiffs and Respondents,

FILED

SEP 1 5 1995

COURT OF APPEAL THIRD D...
ROBERT L. LISTON, C...

BY _____

CALIFORNIA
Court Directory
November 17, 1993

Judicial Transitions
United States Supreme Court
U.S. Ninth Circuit Court of Appeals
U.S. District Courts in California
U.S. Bankruptcy Courts
California Supreme Court
California State Bar Court
California Courts of Appeal

CHAPTER 9
Alternatives to Litigation

CHAPTER OVERVIEW

Today, litigation is only one of the ways used to resolve different types of controversies. Not only are contractual rights being decided outside of the courts, but also certain types of property rights.

Alternative Dispute Resolution (ADR)

Conflict between people is increasingly being resolved through the use of **Alternative Dispute Resolution (ADR)**. People and businesses dissatisfied with the time and expense of litigation are looking for alternatives to resolve their disputes. Negotiation, mediation and arbitration are three types of ADR that are being utilized to avoid litigation when controversies surrounding contracts and property rights arise. Administrative hearings are used by the Department of Real Estate to avoid the use of courts when deciding issues surrounding real estate licensees.

ADR

Alternative Dispute Resolution (ADR)

- ◆ **Negotiation**
- ◆ **Mediation**
- ◆ **Arbitration**

In fact, California has indicated its support of ADR in the real estate industry by amending the **California Arbitration Act** (Civil Procedure Code secs. 1298-1298.8) to **specifically address arbitration clauses in real estate contracts.**

NONADJUDICATIVE AND ADJUDICATIVE

These alternatives to the judicial process may be classified into two categories: nonadjudicative and adjudicative. In the **nonadjudicative alternatives**, the parties are encouraged to voluntarily enter into agreements that settle the controversy. Many times the parties will use a neutral third party to assist in reaching an agreement among themselves. The **adjudicative methods** of dispute resolution mirror the judicial process in that a third party decides the controversy much as a judge does in court. The adjudicative processes may be concerned with settling controversies among private parties or between a regulatory agency and an individual.

http://wwlia.org/~wwlia/adr1.htm
(Alternate Dispute Resolution - An Introduction)

Negotiation

Although arbitration receives much of the focus in the ADR literature, negotiation continues to serve as the primary method by which conflicts are resolved. **Negotiation** is a voluntary process where parties attempt to settle their conflicts in a peaceful manner.

> **Example:** Peters is upset that some shrubbery was damaged by his neighbor Sharon during a remodel project. Peters politely tells Sharon how upset he is over the damaged shrubbery and that it is going to cost $75 to replace it. Sharon had failed to notice she had damaged Peters' shrubs and was embarrassed she had not been more careful. Sharon offered to replace the shrubs if Peters would wait until the remodel work was completed. This was acceptable to Peters and once Sharon had finished her remodel project, she paid to replace Peter's shrubs.

To successfully negotiate, it is necessary to move beyond positions on issues and negotiate over the person's interests or needs. Looking past positions on issues can be hard for many people, yet, it is helpful to focus on underlying interests or needs if agreement is to be reached. By asking yourself "why" a person is taking a certain position, you can often determine what his or her true interests or needs are and then be better prepared to offer solutions that will lead to an agreement.

> **Example:** With only one orange between them, two sisters argue over who gets the orange. Each sister takes the position that she deserves the orange more than the other. Eventually they split the orange with each only getting one-half of what they desired. Had they known the interest behind each other's position they would have discovered that one sister wanted the orange to make juice with, while the other sister desired the peel for use in making a cake. (Adapted from Fisher, Ury and Patton's *Getting to Yes* [1991].)

Alternatives to Litigation

DISTRIBUTIVE NEGOTIATION (Win-Lose)

Negotiations may be either distributive or integrative. **Distributive negotiation** (win-lose or competitive) is where the goals of the parties are interdependent but not compatible. It occurs when one person will lose something while the other person gains what will be lost. If a seller of a house lowers the selling price, the buyer gains by paying a lower price. The seller loses and the buyer wins.

Distributive negotiators focus on their own personal situation and do not give credence to the other party's situation unless it helps to maximize the distributive negotiator's own return. To a distributive negotiator, a win occurs when the other party is defeated. A major contributor to the success of a distributive negotiator is the other party's desire to avoid the pain of litigation, i.e., time and money involved in taking the dispute through the judicial process.

INTEGRATIVE NEGOTIATION (Win-Win Attitude)

Integrative negotiation (problem-solving) occurs when the parties take a win-win attitude. The negotiators seek to achieve mutual gains and they focus on the needs and interests of both parties. This means the negotiators look past their individual positions ("their" solution to the dispute) and identify "why" those solutions are being sought by each party. This form of negotiating works best when the parties view the negotiations as part of a long-term relationship. The example with the sisters and the orange exemplifies a situation where integrative bargaining can lead to both parties' needs being met. Instead of seeing a situation where there are only limited resources, the negotiators see varied options for apportioning those resources.

BEST ALTERNATIVE TO A NEGOTIATED AGREEMENT (BATNA)

No matter which approach to negotiation is used, there are three basic stages to the negotiation process: 1) preparation; 2) actual negotiations; and 3) conclusion of negotiations. Each stage is important but the better prepared a person is, the more likely their success in negotiations. During the preparation stage, a person should attempt to determine what needs and interests are behind not only their goals, but also those of the other party. Roger Fisher, William Ury, and Bruce Patton in their original book, *Getting To Yes*: Negotiating Agreement Without Giving In (1991), suggest developing your **best alternative to a negotiated agreement (BATNA)** at this stage so you will know when to walk away from the negotiations.

A BATNA is developed by identifying what actions you could take if no agreement is reached, develop the best of those possible actions into viable alternatives, and then select the best alternative you have developed. With your BATNA you can now better judge whether to reach an agreement or to simply walk away from the negotiations. It is also important that you identify your opponent's BATNA as you prepare for the negotiations.

The case in Chapter 1 between Palermo and Mulligan illustrates how negotiation is a continual part of dispute resolution. Even though Palermo and Mulligan are litigating their dispute, there is throughout the process, opportunity for settlement discussions. These discussions on possible settlement involve the process of negotiation. They are learning that negotiation is a continuing process that evolves until either an agreement

is reached by the parties or they realize only a third party is capable of settling the dispute.

Mediation (A Neutral Third Party)

In **mediation**, a neutral third party assists the parties in voluntarily negotiating a settlement to their dispute by helping them recognize their interests involved, developing choices, and analyzing the alternatives. The goal is to overcome the problems and negotiate a mutually satisfying agreement. According to the American Arbitration Association, parties using mediation have an 80 to 95 percent success rate in settling their disputes.

Because mediation is voluntary, the parties must agree to the use of mediation in attempting to resolve the dispute. A **mediation clause** may be included in the contract the parties are executing. If there is an existing dispute but no contractually agreed to clause to mediate the dispute, the parties may stipulate to mediating the dispute. A typical mediation clause states: "The parties to this agreement hereby agree to first mediate disputes arising from this contract prior to invoking other dispute resolution mechanisms."

> **"The parties to this agreement hereby agree to first mediate disputes arising from this contract prior to invoking other dispute resolution mechanisms."**

ADVANTAGES TO MEDIATION

The most obvious advantage to mediation over adjudicative methods of resolving disputes is that the parties themselves are directly engaged in negotiating a settlement to the dispute. While the parties may utilize an attorney at their own expense, the parties will still maintain an active role in the negotiations. A second advantage is the use of a neutral third party to assist the parties to identify the real issues involved in the dispute and to develop and explore viable settlement alternatives. Third, it is likely that settlement will be quicker than litigation, thereby saving time and money. Fourth, mediation will more likely enhance longer term relations than litigation would.

MEDIATOR'S ROLE

A **mediator** facilitates the parties in reaching a voluntary agreement. He or she does this by encouraging the parties to identify obstacles that stand in the way of an agreement and assisting them to overcome these obstacles. Mediators help the parties identify alternatives for resolving the dispute by getting them to focus on their interests and needs instead of their positions. Many times the mediator will meet individually with each party to make this determination. This is called a **caucus**. It is important that the parties involved in mediation fully disclose relevant information to the mediator to enable the mediator to best perform his or her function.

http://adrr.com/adr0/links.htm
(Resolution Related Web Links)

Example: The seller of a house does not believe the buyer has made a good faith effort to obtain financing as called for in the purchase agreement. Having agreed to try mediation, both parties meet with the mediator. After meeting jointly with both parties, the mediator has a caucus with each separately and determines that the seller only wants to punish the buyer. Because the sale price of the house has actually increased during the time the seller waited for the buyer to arrange financing, the seller will not suffer any monetary losses. The seller is simply upset that the buyer did not diligently pursue adequate financing and wants to teach the buyer a lesson. Knowing the interest of the seller in only wanting to punish the buyer will assist the mediator is guiding the negotiations.

An important aspect of mediation is that the mediator facilitates resolution of the conflict instead of imposing a decision. Mediation works when the parties themselves are able to settle the dispute with the assistance of the mediator. If the parties are unwilling to voluntarily settle the dispute, mediation will not be successful.

http://wwlia.org/~wwlia/adr2.htm
(ADR - Mediation: How it Works)

MEDIATION PROCESS

First Step. In the first step, the pre-session, the parties agree to use mediation as a means of resolving the dispute. As was discussed above, the parties may use a mediation clause in their contract or may stipulate to take an existing dispute to mediation.

Second Step. A second part of this stage is for the mediator to be selected. The mediation clause should describe the procedure to be used and, if a mediation service is referenced in the clause, the procedure established by that service will determine how the mediator is to be selected. After the mediator is selected by the parties, the mediator then contacts both parties and begins the process of establishing a rapport with the parties.

Third Step. The mediation session itself is the next step in the process. The mediator begins by explaining the process to the parties and, with the agreement of the parties, guidelines are established. Throughout the actual mediation session, the mediator works to create and maintain a positive atmosphere. During the mediation session, the third stage occurs when the mediator gathers the facts behind the dispute. Once the facts have been gathered the mediator helps the parties see beyond their positions and to clarify the "real" issues. After the parties have identified their interests and needs, the mediator attempts to determine the significance of each interest and to prioritize them if possible. By asking questions of the parties, the mediator tries to get the parties to focus on the actual issues involved in the dispute. The mediator at this point starts developing a strategy to assist the parties in understanding the other party's interests and needs. The mediator will provide each party with an objective evaluation of the case in order to help each party understand how the dispute looks to a neutral third party.

Fourth Step. Once the issues have been identified, the fourth step begins. The parties will need to start creating alternatives and options to resolve the dispute. The mediator will often caucus with each of the parties to develop these alternatives and options. The information given to the mediator during these caucuses is considered confidential and the mediator should not convey this information to one party without the consent of the other party.

Fifth Step. At the fifth stage the parties either reach an agreement on an option that satisfies their needs and interests or they recognize that the dispute cannot be voluntarily resolved.

Sixth Step. If the parties have reached an agreement on an option, the final stage happens by reducing the agreement to a writing, signed by both parties.

The parties to the mediation will share the costs of mediating the dispute unless they have agreed otherwise. Organizations that supply mediation services usually charge a filing fee to set up the file and then an hourly charge for the actual mediation. The hourly fees are compensation for both the service and the mediator. Some services will apply either all or part of the filing fee to the fee charged for arbitration if the dispute is not settled in mediation and the parties continue to arbitrate the dispute.

 http://promediation.com/
(Professional Mediation Association)

Arbitration

In an **arbitration** the dispute is, by agreement of the parties, submitted to a neutral third party for a final, and unless otherwise agreed to by the parties, binding decision. The advantages of arbitration over litigation are many. It is a less formal process, it may be quicker, it may be less costly, the parties are able to have a knowledgeable expert arbitrate the dispute, and the process, including the decision, is not a public one. In an arbitration, formal pleadings are not used, discovery is normally quite limited, the rules of evidence do not apply, and should the parties so agree, the decision can be final and binding with no right to appeal the arbitrator's decision.

Because of these advantages, both the federal government and the state of California have indicated their support for arbitration. The federal government has expressed a strong preference for arbitration and has enacted the **Federal Arbitration Act (9 USCS secs. 1 et seq.).** California enacted the **California Arbitration Act (Civil Procedure secs. 1280 et seq.)** in 1961 and the courts have routinely supported its goals.

While arbitrations are meant to be less formal than litigating the dispute, the parties may agree to be represented by attorneys. In such case, each party must pay for his or her own attorney fees unless the agreement provides for recovery of the fees. If attorney fees are to be awarded by the arbitrator, it is within the arbitrator's power to determine what amount of fees should be awarded.

Court-Ordered (Mandated) Arbitrations

Arbitrations may be judicial arbitrations (court mandated arbitrations, often referred to as being court-ordered arbitrations) that are required before a case may be heard by the trial courts, or they may be private arbitrations agreed to by the parties. Court-annexed arbitrations may be ordered by the superior court when there is less than fifty thousand dollars at stake or the parties stipulate to arbitration.

Private Arbitrations

Private arbitrations create a duty to arbitrate only when the parties have contractually created this duty. This duty is created when the parties have either an agreement that calls for submitting disputes to arbitration or, if there is no existing contract with an arbitration clause, the parties must enter into an agreement to take the dispute to arbitration.

NONBINDING OR BINDING

If the arbitration may be reviewed by the courts or if the parties have agreed that it is not to be final, it is considered to be **nonbinding**. If the arbitration is **binding**, the arbitrator's award is final and, but for certain limited statutory exceptions, is not reviewable by the courts for errors of fact or law. The California Supreme Court has stated that "it is a general rule that parties to a private arbitration impliedly agree that the arbitrator's decision will be both binding and final" (*Moncharsh v. Heily & Blase et al.*, 3 Cal. 4th 1, 10 Cal. Rptr. 2d 183 [1992]).

BINDING AND NONBINDING ARBITRATION

Binding Arbitration—Not reviewable by the courts

Nonbinding Arbitration—Reviewable by the courts

Because the parties are giving up their right to use the judicial system, arbitration clauses should be knowingly executed. To help insure that a person does not unknowingly enter into a real estate contract containing an arbitration clause, California Civil Procedure Code sec. 1298 requires that contracts for the sale of real estate clearly title any clauses, calling for the binding arbitration of disputes, **"ARBITRATION OF DISPUTES."** The title must **"be set out in at least 8-point bold type or in contrasting red in at least 8-point type"** and, when part of a typed contract, the entire title must be typed in capital letters. That code section further requires specific warning language with similar typeface requirements. This warning, which must be **"in at least 10-point bold type or in contrasting red print in at least 8-point bold type"** when in a printed contract and in all capital letters when typed, states:

NOTICE: "BY INITIALING IN THE SPACE BELOW YOU ARE AGREEING TO HAVE ANY DISPUTE ARISING OUT OF THE MATTERS INCLUDED IN THE 'ARBITRATION OF DISPUTES' PROVISION DECIDED BY NEUTRAL ARBITRATION AS PROVIDED BY CALIFORNIA LAW AND YOU ARE GIVING UP ANY RIGHT YOU MIGHT POSSESS TO HAVE THE DISPUTE LITIGATED IN A COURT OR JURY TRIAL. BY INITIALING IN THE SPACE BELOW YOU ARE GIVING UP YOUR JUDICIAL RIGHTS TO DISCOVERY AND APPEAL, UNLESS THOSE RIGHTS ARE SPECIFICALLY INCLUDED IN THE 'ARBITRATION OF DISPUTES' PROVISION. IF YOU REFUSE TO SUBMIT TO ARBITRATION AFTER AGREEING TO THIS PROVISION, YOU MAY BE COMPELLED TO ARBITRATE UNDER THE AUTHORITY OF THE CALIFORNIA CODE OF CIVIL PROCEDURE, YOUR AGREEMENT TO THIS ARBITRATION PROVISION IS VOLUNTARY."

WE HAVE READ AND UNDERSTAND THE FOREGOING AND AGREE TO SUBMIT DISPUTES ARISING OUT OF THE MATTERS INCLUDED IN THE 'ARBITRATION OF DISPUTES' PROVISION TO NEUTRAL ARBITRATION.

REAL ESTATE ARBITRATION CLAUSE MUST BE INITIALED

For the arbitration clause to be valid in a real estate contract, the parties are required to initial the clause to show their willingness to arbitrate any disputes arising out of the contract. It is not necessary that both parties sign the provision, but it is possible the non-signing party may not be forced to arbitrate a dispute arising out of the contract.

Case Example: Bello entered into exclusive listing agreements with Grubb & Ellis, a real estate broker, to sell two parcels of real property. Both listing agreements contained the statutorily mandated "arbitration of disputes" and "notice" provisions immediately followed by separate spaces "for the parties to indicate their assent or non-assent to the arbitration process." Although Bello initialed each arbitration provision, Grubb failed to do so. Bello violated the agreements and Grubb sought recovery of his real estate commissions. Bello argued that there was no mutuality of obligation since Grubb did not initial the arbitration provisions and therefore the arbitration provision was not applicable to the dispute. The court held that there was no basis for adopting the mutuality of arbitration limitation advanced by Bello. Although Grubb's failure to assent in writing might have had some effect on whether Grubb could have been required to arbitrate, the statute does not purport to vitiate Bello's assent in such a situation. *Grubb & Ellis Co. v. Bello*, 19 Ca. App. 4th 231, 23 Cal. Rptr. 2d 281 (1993).

PARTIES MAY AGREES TO SUBMIT THE DISPUTE TO ARBITRATION

If an arbitration clause has not been used, it is still possible for a dispute to be taken to arbitration. If the parties have a current controversy they would like to arbitrate and there is no previous contractually created duty, the parties may execute a **submission agreement** that agrees to submit the dispute to arbitration.

Because the duty to arbitrate is contractually created, the arbitration clause (or the submission agreement), determines the scope of the arbitration and what powers the arbitrator will have. Therefore, care must be taken to insure that all possible concerns are addressed regarding how the arbitration is to be conducted. Because it is hard to insure that all contingencies are covered in the arbitration clause, it is not uncommon to find the arbitration clause refer to the procedures of an arbitration service as controlling the arbitration process. If the clause does reference an arbitration service, that service's procedures determine exactly how the arbitration is to be conducted. In fact, indicating that the arbitration will be handled by the arbitration service incorporates by reference that service's procedures. An example of an arbitration service's rules is the American Arbitration Association's (AAA) "Residential Real Estate Dispute Resolution Rules."

> **Example:** Ms. B signed a listing agreement with Broker. The listing agreement contained an arbitration clause that Ms. B initialed. The arbitration clause stated that any disputes arising out of the agreement are to be submitted to arbitration according to the rules of the American Arbitration Association. It is becoming more common to find that mere membership in a professional association may impose a duty to arbitrate disputes. As a condition of membership, some associations may require its members to submit disputes to arbitration. This requirement may be imposed by the organization's bylaws or by clauses on membership application forms. This is the type of arbitration requirement that is found in Article 14 of the **Code of Ethics and Standards of Practice** for the National Association of Realtors® (see next page).

Case Example: On July 16, 1979, the California Association of Realtors advised members Barbara Larsen and Bud Doty that member Charles R. King wanted an interboard arbitration of a controversy between the parties over a real estate sales commission. Ms. Larsen and Mr. Doty were both members of the Paso Robles Board of Realtors while Mr. King was a member of the Santa Ynez Valley Board of Realtors. Ms. Larsen and Mr. Doty objected to the jurisdiction and authority of the California Association of Realtors on the grounds they had not entered into a written agreement to arbitrate interboard disputes. When Ms. Larsen and Mr. Doty applied for membership in the Paso Robles Board of Realtors they agreed to "abide by the Code of Ethics of the National Association of Realtors, and the Constitution, Bylaws and Rules and Regulations of the Paso Robles Board of Realtors, California Association of Realtors, the State Association, and National Association of Realtors, the National Association." The Paso Robles Board of Realtors bylaws impose upon the members the duty to arbitrate according to the California Association of Realtors InterBoard Arbitration Manual.

The court ruled that the entire scheme of interboard arbitration was incorporated into the bylaws of the Paso Robles Board of Realtors. The court further held "that arbitration is purely a matter of contract...and where one contracts to abide by bylaws which contain provisions for arbitration, one is bound to arbitrate." Therefore, the court confirmed an arbitration award against Ms. Larsen and Mr. Doty. *Charles R. King v. Larsen Realty, Inc.*, 121 Cal. App. 3d 349, 175 Cal. Rptr. 226 (1981).

Controversy Between REALTORS® Shall Be Arbitrated

"In the event of a controversy between REALTORS® associated with different firms, arising out of their relationship as REALTORS®, the REALTORS® shall submit the dispute to arbitration in accordance with the regulations of their Board or Boards rather than litigate the matter.

In the event clients of REALTORS® wish to arbitrate contractual disputes arising out of real estate transactions, REALTORS® shall arbitrate those disputes in accordance with the regulations of their Boards, provided the clients agree to be bound by the decision."

Where a professional organization requires its members to arbitrate disputes among its members, the organization may discipline members refusing to arbitrate disputes.

WHO IS IN CHARGE OF SELECTING THE ARBITRATOR

Another important feature of arbitration is that the parties are able to chose who serves as the arbitrator. The method of selecting the arbitrator is up to the parties and should be part of the arbitration clause. If the parties have chosen an arbitration service, the arbitrator will be selected according to the procedures set out by that service's rules. Where the parties have failed to include how an arbitrator is to be selected and are unable to mutually agree on how to select an arbitrator, the court may be petitioned to appoint an arbitrator from a list of persons supplied jointly by the parties.

Unless the parties have by agreement provided otherwise, there will only be one arbitrator. If the parties desire more than one arbitrator, they must provide for this either in the arbitration clause or by separate agreement. Where there is more than one arbitrator, the powers and duties of the arbitrators may be exercised by a majority of the neutral arbitrators.

http://www.adrworld.com/
(Latest Developments in ADR)

ARBITRATOR'S ROLE

The arbitrator is interested in getting to the truth of the matter. To accomplish this, the arbitrator listens to the parties, their witnesses, reviews evidence offered by the parties, and then, by weighing both of these, determines what the facts of the dispute are. The arbitrator will analyze the facts and then render a decision.

It is the arbitrator's responsibility to maintain a proper decorum during the arbitration hearing. Both parties should be given the opportunity to present necessary evidence and arguments. The power to decide whether evidence is to be admitted into the hearing belongs solely to the arbitrator.

Example: In a dispute over the broker's commissions, Mr. D wanted to submit a list of expenses he had incurred during his recent European vacation. The arbitrator refused to admit the list because it was irrelevant to the dispute being arbitrated.

ARBITRATION PROCESS

If the arbitration clause is **self-executing**, the parties do not need to petition the courts to compel arbitration. On the other hand, if the arbitration clause is not self-executing, one of the parties must petition the court to compel arbitration.

A self-executing arbitration clause contains:

1. method for selection of arbitrator;
2. procedure for conducting arbitration; and
3. provision for continuing arbitration if one party refuses to proceed.

Example: The American Arbitration Association "Residential Real Estate Dispute Resolution Rules" state in section 30 under the "Arbitration Rules" that "... the arbitration may proceed in the absence of any party or representative who, after due notice, fails to be present or fails to obtain a postponement."

Where the agreement is self-executing, most arbitrations start with a written notice being sent by the claimant that indicates arbitration is being sought under the agreement. This written notice should include the nature of the dispute, the amount involved, and the remedy sought. The party receiving the demand, the respondent, may respond with a statement answering the demand.

Selection of the Arbitrator

The next step is to select the arbitrator. The method set out in the arbitration clause should be followed and if no method is stated in the clause, or if there is no arbitration clause, the parties should mutually agree on how to select the arbitrator. As was mentioned previously, if all else fails, the court will appoint an arbitrator for the parties. If an arbitration service is used, it is likely that a **"strike list"** will be utilized. A strike list is where the association sends each party a list of persons from the panel maintained by the association and each party "strikes" from the list any unacceptable names. The list is then sent back to the association where one of the acceptable names on the list is chosen to arbitrate the dispute.

Prior to the hearing, only limited discovery is permitted unless the agreement provides for extended discovery. By statute, if the dispute is over fifty thousand dollars, the parties are only entitled to demand in writing a list of witnesses the other party intends to call, with expert witnesses noted, and a list of documents the other party intends to introduce at the hearing. The party making this demand must also include a list of their witnesses and a list of documents they intend to introduce at the time they make the demand of the other party.

Power to Issue Subpoenas

The arbitrator does have the power to issue subpoenas. A **subpoena** may be issued to compel the attendance of witness and if books, records, or other documents are desired, a **subpoena duces tecum** may be issued. It is solely up to the arbitrator to make the determination as to the issuance of the subpoenas.

Rules of Judicial Procedure

Even though an arbitration hearing usually mirrors the judicial process, there is no requirement that rules of judicial procedure be followed. However, it is common for the claimant to make an opening argument, present his or her side of the dispute, offer any witnesses he or she may have, and present whatever evidence he or she want the arbitrator to use. After the claimant has finished, the respondent presents his or her side; also using any witnesses and evidence he or she may have. The parties and any witnesses that testify are subject to cross-examination. The arbitrator may ask questions of either party or witnesses. While the arbitrator has the ability to decide how the hearing will progress, the arbitrator must provide for a full and equal opportunity for each party to present relevant evidence.

After hearing all the evidence presented by the parties, the arbitrator analyzes the facts and issues the decision. If the arbitration was binding, the decision is final. Court review may only be made if there was corruption or misconduct by the arbitrator, the arbitrator improperly conducted the hearing or the arbitrator exceeded his or her powers in making the award. If the arbitration was nonbinding, either party may continue the dispute using the judicial process. Decisions rendered under binding arbitration may be enforced just as if a court had rendered the decision.

Arbitration Awards (Final Judgment)

When the arbitration clause or the procedures being followed provide that the arbitrator's decision, called the **award**, is to be rendered within a certain time period, the award must be rendered within that time period or else it is void and unenforceable. The award must be in a signed writing that states what decision the arbitrator has reached.

One aspect of binding arbitration is that the courts recognize the arbitrator's award as being a final judgment in the dispute. The courts will normally overturn an arbitrator's award only if it was obtained through corruption, fraud, or other undue means. The courts will not delve into whether the arbitrator correctly determined the facts or arrived at the award by following precedents.

Where it can be shown that an arbitrator substantially prejudiced one of the party's rights by exceeding the powers vested in him or her, refusing to postpone a hearing, or in not accepting new relevant evidence, the courts will overturn the award. The courts will also overturn the award when an arbitrator has failed to disqualify him or herself under the provisions applying to judges.

> **Case Example:** In March 1989, DiMarco entered into a real estate purchase contract to acquire property from Chaney. DiMarco changed his mind and subsequently filed an action for rescission of the purchase contract. The purchase contract contained an arbitration clause and was referred to the American Arbitration Association. Ultimately the arbitrator ruled against DiMarco but denied Chaney's request for attorney fees and costs. The purchase contract provided that the prevailing party was entitled to attorney's fees and costs if there was any action, proceeding, or arbitration arising out of the contract. **Continued**

Chaney brought suit alleging the arbitrator exceed his powers by denying Chaney's request for attorney fees and costs. The trial court held that the arbitrator had exceeded his powers by not awarding attorney fees and costs to Chaney and awarded attorney's fees with costs. The appellate court agreed that the arbitrator had exceeded his powers but ruled that the trial court should have remanded back to the arbitrator the determination of what the amount of attorney fees and costs should be. *DiMarco v. Chaney*, 31 Cal. App. 4th 1809, 37 Cal. Rptr. 2d 558 (1995).

Once the award has been rendered and the parties comply with its ruling, there is no further judicial action to be taken. If, however, one of the parties refuses to comply with the arbitration award, the other party may file with the court a **petition to confirm** the award.

Resolution Disputes
Concerning a Real Estate License

In Chapter 5 it is noted that it is unlawful to act in the capacity of a real estate broker or real estate salesperson without first obtaining a real estate license from the Department of Real Estate. Issues and disputes surrounding the issuance of a license, its revocation or suspension and hearing procedures involved are certainly areas of importance to real estate licensees. These problems are resolved through negotiation and, when that fails, then an adjudicative process takes place.

The resolution techniques become more complicated when the real estate licensee has acquired a personal property right in his or her license. A person only acquires a personal property right in his or her license when the license has been issued for more than ninety days. During the application stage and where the license has been issued less than ninety days, there is no property right acquired by the individual in his or her license. The importance of this distinction is in the manner with which the commissioner institutes action to suspend, revoke, or otherwise penalize the licensee for alleged wrongdoings.

 www.dre.ca.gov
(Frequently Asked Questions About Real Estate Licenses)

PROBLEMS ACQUIRING A LICENSE

Generally, a real estate broker license or a real estate salesperson license is acquired by written application to the commissioner, meeting certain educational requirements, passing an examination, payment of the appropriate fee, and being fingerprinted. As a result of information that may surface during the application process for a license, the commissioner may require the applicant to submit other evidence concerning his or her honesty and truthfulness. When the applicant is a corporation, the commissioner will be concerned with determining whether the officers, directors, or persons owing more than ten percent of the stock have been truthful and honest in supplying information on the application. The commissioner is authorized to hold a hearing to gather this extra evidence.

Statement of Issues

Generally, this hearing is held if the department's investigation reveals that the applicant has been convicted of a crime that is substantially related to the qualification, functions, or duties of a real estate licensee. The hearing process is initiated by the commissioner filing a **statement of issues**. The statement of issues identifies the issues being raised by the commissioner and specifies the statutes and rules that are being violated. The respondent must be served with the statement of issues and, if he or she desires, may request a hearing where evidence may be presented to counter the commissioner's allegations. The hearing process is the same as that for an accusation, which is discussed later.

RESTRICTED LICENSE

Under certain situations the commissioner may believe it necessary to issue only a restricted license to the applicant. A restricted license may be issued when the commissioner does not want to completely revoke or deny a license yet does not want to grant the unjustified retention or acquisition of a license.

> **Case Example:** Mr. Vessels and his wife wanted a property manager to collect rents for their property in Los Angeles and contacted a referral service. Mr. Vessels was contacted by Mr. Benjamin Ballinger of Apollo Estates, Inc. stating that Ballinger was to be their property manager. The Vessels agreed to let Ballinger, through Apollo Estates, Inc., manage their property, including payment of the mortgage. Ballinger only held a restricted real estate license due to past problems with his business.
>
> Ballinger took lease payments in the form of both cash and check and placed them into a file folder. The Vessels were notified that the mortgage was not being paid and upon pressing Ballinger on the issue, it was finally paid.
>
> Ballinger was terminated by the Vessels and the Vessels filed a complaint with the Department of Real Estate. Upon investigating Mr. Ballinger, the Department of Real Estate investigator was told by Mr. Ballinger that he did not maintain a trust account or a columnar journal of trust funds he received. When told that real estate law required that he maintain columnar journals showing all trust funds received, Ballinger told the investigator he believed the department was "picking on him."
>
> The Department of Real Estate revoked Ballinger's restricted licensee even though the administrative law judge had recommended a revocation of only 30 days with a right to reapply. Ballinger filed a petition for a writ of mandate seeking to set aside the commissioner's revocation of his license because he had a vested right in his license. The trial court ruled against him.
>
> The appellate court held that the tentative nature of the privileges granted by a restricted license places a licensee on notice that there is no vested right in the licensee. In fact, the very nature of a restricted license is an indication to the holder that the rights granted thereunder are neither vested nor permanent. *Apollo Estates, Inc. v. Department of Real Estate*, 174 Cal. App. 3d 625, 220 Cal. Rptr. 199 (1985).

A person acquires no property rights by the issuance of a restricted license. The holder has no right to renew the license and the commissioner may, without a hearing, issue an order suspending the restricted licensee's right to any privileges granted under a restricted license pending a final determination to be made at a formal hearing.

www.dre.ca.gov/licstats.htm
(DRE - Licensee Status Inquires)

LICENSE REVOCATION OR SUSPENSION

When a person receives an unrestricted real estate license, he or she possesses a property right in that license that requires due process if it is to be taken away. This does not mean it is impossible to revoke or suspend the license, it simply means a hearing must take place for the revocation or suspension to be legal. Where a licensee commits fraud or participates in other forms of dishonest dealings, the license may be revoked or suspended by proving these acts at a hearing.

Suspension

If the real estate license was obtained by fraud, misrepresentation, deceit, or by making any material misstatement of fact in the application for the license, the commissioner may, without a hearing, suspend that person's license. The commissioner has ninety days after the date of the license's issuance to order this suspension. The suspension remains in effect only until the effective date of the decision of the commissioner after a hearing is conducted. A statement of issues is filed and served on the respondent with the order of suspension. The respondent has thirty days after service in which to file a written request for a hearing on the statement of issues. The commissioner must hold a hearing within thirty days after a receipt of the request of a hearing from the respondent. If the hearing is not commenced within thirty days after receipt of request for the hearing or if the decision of the commissioner is not rendered within thirty days after the completion of the hearing, the order of suspension is set aside.

Investigation

The commissioner may upon his or her own motion, and shall upon a verified written complaint, investigate the actions of any licensee and may permanently revoke or temporarily suspend the license if warranted. The department's investigator will interview the parties, accumulate and review documentation, and, when necessary, have subpoenas issued to get information. If the evidence accumulated by the department's investigation does not warrant the issuance of an accusation, no further action will be taken. If the evidence is substantially in support of the complaint, the matter is turned over to the legal section for the filing of the accusation. The department may refer the matter to another agency, for example, for criminal prosecution.

After Civil Action

The commissioner, after conducting a hearing, also has the power to suspend or revoke a real estate license when a final judgment is obtained in a civil action against a licensee on the grounds of fraud, misrepresentation, or deceit with reference to any transaction for which the license is required.

The **Recovery Fund** (funded by licensee's fees) is administered by the DRE to satisfy judgments for fraud or misrepresentation against licensed real estate agents, which would otherwise go unpaid. In *Yergan v. Department of Real Estate*, 77 CA4th 959, 968-970, 92 CR2d 189, 196-197 (App.2Dist. 2000), vendors, who brought suit against a broker, were not permitted to recover from the Recovery Fund because their settlement agreement provided for entry of judgment on only the alleged negligence and breach of duty claims, but not the alleged fraud claims.

ACCUSATION

When the commissioner seeks to revoke a person's real estate license, a hearing must be held to satisfy the due process requirements. The hearing is initiated by filing an accusation and the complainant is the real estate commissioner. The **accusation** is a written statement in ordinary, concise language that sets forth the acts or omissions with which the respondent is charged and it specifies any statutes and rules which the respondent is alleged to have violated. A hearing is held before an **administrative law judge** and is conducted in the same manner as those where a statement of issues has been filed, except that with an accusation the license is considered a property right and the Department of Real Estate has the burden of proof.

STATEMENT OF ISSUES: writing identifying commissioner's concerns and specifying statutes and rules being violated; used to initiate non-property right hearings.

ACCUSATION: a clear and concise writing setting forth acts or omissions that violate specified statutes or rules; used to initiate property right hearings.

When the accusation is filed, the licensee is served with a copy of the accusation, a statement of the respondent, a notice of defense, and copies of Government Code Sections which deal with discovery procedures. The respondent is advised that unless a written request for a hearing is made within fifteen days after service of the accusation, the respondent will have waived the right to a hearing and the department may take disciplinary actions without further notice. All the respondent has to do to request a hearing is sign the enclosed "notice and defense" and mail it to the Department of Real Estate. The respondent may, but need not be, represented by an attorney at respondent's expense during the hearing proceedings. The respondent is not entitled to the appointment of a free attorney. If the notice of defense is filed by the respondent, the Department of Real Estate will schedule a hearing.

The parties may reach a settlement before the hearing and propose that it be adopted by the Commissioner in order to eliminate the need for a hearing.

Names and addresses of witnesses who may testify at the hearing and relevant documents and investigative reports may be obtained through discovery. Subpoenas for the attendance of witnesses or production of documents can be issued and served.

A hearing is presided over by an administrative law judge in a manner resembling a civil trial: oral evidence taken under oath, witnesses examined, and documents introduced into evidence as exhibits. The respondent may be called as a witness and cross-examined even if the respondent does not want to be called as a witness.

THE DECISION

The administrative law judge prepares, within thirty days after the case is concluded, a proposed decision and delivers it to the Department of Real Estate. The decision must be in writing and contain findings of fact, a determination of the issues presented and the penalty, if any. The department may act on the proposed decision by adopting it in its entirety, or reducing the proposed penalty and adopting the balance of it, or rejecting it. If the proposed decision is not adopted by the department, the department itself may decide the case upon the hearing record, including the transcript, with or without taking additional evidence or may refer the case to the administrative law judge to take additional evidence. If additional evidence is taken by the administrative law judge, a proposed decision shall again be filed. Normally, the decision is effective thirty days after it is sent to the respondent.

Additionally, a licensee who has willfully violated or knowingly participated in a violation of Business and Professions Code sections is guilty of a misdemeanor punishable by a fine not exceeding ten thousand dollars or by imprisonment in a county jail not exceeding six months, or by fine and imprisonment.

If the real estate commissioner determines that the public interest and the public welfare will be adequately served by permitting a real estate licensee to pay a monetary penalty to the department in lieu of an actual license suspension, the commissioner may stay the execution of the suspension of the license upon the condition that the licensee pay a monetary penalty and incur no other cause for disciplinary action within a stated period of time provided by the commissioner. The amount of the monetary penalty shall not exceed two hundred fifty dollars for each day of suspension stayed nor a total of ten thousand dollars per decision regardless the number of days of suspension stayed under the decision. Any monetary penalty received by the department shall be credited to the recovery account of the real estate fund.

http://secure.dre.ca.gov/publicasp/unlicenseddnr.asp
(Desist and Refrain Orders for Unlicensed Activities)

RECONSIDERATION

Reconsideration of a decision can be ordered by the Department of Real Estate on its own motion or on petition of the respondent and must be made prior to the effective day of the decision. The case may be reconsidered by the department itself, considering all pertinent parts of the record and such additional evidence and arguments as may be permitted, or it may be assigned to the administrative law judge. The proposed decision of the administrative law judge after reconsideration is subject to the same procedure as a proposed decision following a hearing on an accusation. If the reconsideration is denied, the respondent may seek judicial review by filing a petition for a writ of mandate in the superior court. Should the superior court grant the writ of mandate, it is remanded to the department. If the superior court denies the petition for a writ of mandate, the petitioner may appeal to the appellate court. The courts are unlikely to reverse a decision of the department, especially on a question involving facts.

REINSTATEMENT

A person whose license has been revoked or suspended may petition the department for reinstatement or reduction of the penalty after a period of not less than one year has lapsed from the effective date of the decision or from the date of the denial of a similar petition.

The department gives notice to the attorney general of the filing of the petition and the petitioner is afforded an opportunity to present either an oral or a written argument before the department. The department decides the petition and the decision includes reasons therefore and the terms and conditions that the department deems appropriate to impose as a condition of reinstatement, if granted. If the department's investigation shows that the petitioner has not been rehabilitated, then the petition will be denied.

CHAPTER SUMMARY

1. **Negotiation.** The use of alternative dispute resolution is increasing. Negotiation, mediation and arbitration offer alternatives to litigation as a means to resolve disputes.

2. Negotiation is still the primary method to resolve disputes. Needs and interests should be negotiated, not positions. Integrative negotiation (win-win) is preferable to distributive negotiation (win-lose).

3. Preparation is vital to good negotiating and makes the other two stages, the actual negotiations and conclusion of the negotiations, more efficient.

4. Determine your best alternative to a negotiated agreement (BATNA).

5. **Mediation.** Mediation is voluntary negotiating involving a neutral third party to facilitate the parties in reaching an agreement. The mediator does not impose an agreement but helps the parties reach their own agreement.

6. Mediation involves six steps: 1) the pre-session where parties agree to utilize mediation and select a mediator; 2) the mediation session where the mediator meets with the parties to explain processes to them and establish guidelines; 3) issues and needs are identified by the parties with the mediator's help; 4) alternatives and options are developed and analyzed; 5) agreement is either reached by the parties or the inability to reach an agreement is recognized and mediation stops; and 6) final agreement is reduced to a signed writing.

7. **Arbitration.** An arbitration is when a neutral third party resolves a dispute between parties by making a final decision to the dispute. They are normally less formal, take less time, and are less costly than litigation. They are also private proceedings as opposed to the public nature of litigation.

8. Private arbitrations require the parties to agree to arbitrate the dispute. This agreement may occur either prior to or after the dispute has arisen.

9. Arbitration clauses in real estate contracts must comply with the state mandated language. Submission agreements are used to submit an existing dispute to arbitration.

10. Associations may require its members to arbitrate disputes as a condition of membership.

11. But for limited exceptions, binding arbitrations are not reviewable by the courts.

12. Arbitrations start with a written notice being sent to the other party stating the nature of the dispute, the amount of money involved, and the remedy being sought. A response may be sent answering the demand.

13. **Resolving Disputes Concerning a Real Estate License.** A real estate license may be denied, suspended, or revoked.

14. A real estate license is obtained by a written application and all information must be truthful. The commissioner may have concerns with the application and need further information from the applicant. A hearing may be used to obtain the information.

15. A statement of issues initiates the hearing involving a licensee who has no property rights (held less than 90 days) in his or her license.

16. A restricted license may be issued by the commissioner if questions exist as to the appropriateness of the applicant receiving an unrestricted license.

17. If a licensee has held his or her license for more than 90 days and the commissioner seeks to suspend or revoke the license, an accusation must be filed and a hearing held.

18. Hearings are held by administrative law judges and are recommendations to the commissioner.

19. After the commissioner has taken action on a license, the matter may be reconsidered. If more than one year has lapsed from the date of the decision, the person may seek reinstatement.

CASE PROBLEM

Gear v. Webster, 258 Cal. App. 2d 57, 65 Cal. Rptr. 255 (1968)

Ms. Gear was a real estate salesperson and Mr. Webster, a broker, was her employer. Both were members of the Bakersfield Board of Realtors, a voluntary association and Mr. Webster was a past president of the board.

When she became a member of the Bakersfield Board of Realtors, Ms. Gear signed the following declaration: "This is to advise that I have read the Realtors' Code of Ethics and the bylaws of the above named Board and if elected to membership I agree to adhere thereto." The bylaws of the association called for disputes between members to be submitted to arbitration. The bylaws also provided that they could be amended if the board so desired. Two years after Ms. Gear joined, the bylaws were amended to require the association's members to "submit to arbitration by the Board's facilities all disputes with any other member, if either to the dispute should so request."

A dispute arose over a real estate commission between Ms. Gear and Mr. Webster. In an attempt to obtain her commission, Ms. Gear filed suit in the Kern County Superior Court to recover the share of commissions she alleged was due to her out of a sale then in escrow.

Mr. Webster petitioned the court for an order to submit the dispute to arbitration as required by the bylaws of the Bakersfield Board of Realtors. Ms. Gear objected to the petition claiming that she had not entered into an arbitration agreement with Mr. Webster and that a board of arbitrators convened according to the bylaws of the Bakersfield Board of Realtors would be prejudiced in favor of Mr. Webster since the arbitration panel would consist of two brokers and one salesperson. Ms. Gear argued that the board's bylaws governed the relationship between her and the association and that the bylaws could not control her relationship with another member of the association.

Does her membership in the Bakersfield Board of Realtors require Ms. Gear to submit this dispute to arbitration? If so, has she voluntarily agreed to submit the dispute to arbitration? Can the association's bylaws actually govern her relationship with other members of the association? Does the amendment to the bylaws apply to her?

Answer: Ms. Gear must submit this dispute to arbitration. Where people voluntarily join organizations, the organization may prescribe conditions upon which membership may be acquired. The organization may also prescribe rules of conduct, penalties for breaching those rules and establish methods for determining whether the rules have been violated. These rules become part of the contract between the member and the association and, unless they violate some public policy or other law, they are regarded as any other contract.

Ms. Gear's relationship with the other members can be governed by the association's rules of conduct. The intent of the members' controls and the intent must be determined by analyzing the manifestation of their intent. The court pointed out that public policy was in favor of arbitration and that arbitration is a matter of contract in which the parties are free to delineate the area of its application.

Because the bylaws provided that they could be amended, the amendment Ms. Gear objects to is binding upon her. Unless there was a limitation on amending the bylaws, the association is free to make changes in accordance with the bylaws.

Moral of the story? Always read what you sign and realize what you have agreed to can be used against you in a court of law!

CHAPTER 9 KEY TERMS		
	award	reconsideration
	BATNA	self-executing
	binding/nonbinding	statement of issues
accusation	caucus	strike list
administrative law judge	court-ordered	submission agreement
Alternative Dispute	distributive/integrative	subpoena duces tecum
Resolution (ADR)	mediation clause	subpoena
arbitration	mediator	
arbitrator	petition to confirm	

Alternatives to Litigation

Quiz—Chapter 9

1. Which of the following is NOT a type of alternative dispute resolution?
   a. Mediation
   b. Litigation
   c. Negotiation
   d. Arbitration

2. S disagrees with B about the conditions contained in the purchase contract between them. S calls B and explains why she believes B's interpretation is incorrect. B discusses the situation with S and they reach an agreement as to what the conditions actually mean. This is an example of:
   a. arbitration.
   b. mediation.
   c. negotiation.
   d. none of the above.

3. Z helped Y and Q settle their dispute. Z did not tell them what their agreement should be but rather guided them through a process that allowed them to reach their own agreement. This process is referred to as:
   a. mediation.
   b. negotiation.
   c. arbitration.
   d. litigation.

4. A mediator:
   a. decides the dispute for the parties
   b. assists disputing parties to voluntarily settle their dispute
   c. looks for who has the weaker position and rules in their favor
   d. none of the above

5. The role of a mediator is to:
   a. get the parties to focus on interests not positions.
   b. help find obstacles to agreement.
   c. encourage the development of alternatives and options.
   d. all of the above

6. Which of the following is NOT an advantage of arbitration?
   a. The parties are allowed a greater range of discovery than in litigation
   b. It is usually faster than litigation
   c. Normally it is less costly than litigation
   d. It is less formal that litigation

7. When X joined the Upper Valley Realtors Association she agreed to be bound by the bylaws of the association. The bylaws provided that all interboard disputes would be arbitrated. X has a complaint on how Broker, also a member of the Upper Valley Realtors Association, split the sales commission. X will:
   a. be precluded from resolving this dispute.
   b. must bring her complaint to the courts.
   c. must arbitrate her dispute with Broker.
   d. may either arbitrate the dispute with Broker or take Broker to court.

8. Binding arbitration normally:
   a. is reviewable by the courts.
   b. is not reviewable by the courts.
   c. is illegal in California.
   d. only happens when it is court mandated.

9. If the commissioner wants to suspend a restricted license, he or she must file a(n):
   a. statement of issues.
   b. accusation.
   c. petition to compel proof.
   d. hearing order.

10. If a hearing is held to revoke a licensee's unrestricted license, the hearing is conducted by:
   a. an administrative law judge.
   b. the real estate commissioner.
   c. a superior court judge.
   d. none of the above.

ANSWERS: 1. b; 2. c; 3. a; 4. b; 5. d; 6. a; 7. c; 8. b; 9. a; 10. a

303

CHAPTER 10
Title and Alienation

CHAPTER OVERVIEW

Ownership of real property is transferred from one person to another in a variety of ways. Sometimes a property owner voluntarily transfers title by deed or in a will. In other cases, property is transferred involuntarily, against the owner's wishes, as in a foreclosure sale or condemnation action. Alienation is the legal term that encompasses all the different methods of transfer, voluntary and involuntary. This chapter describes the requirements for the various types of transfers, and their effects. It also discusses the recording system and title insurance, which play an essential role in the transfer of real property.

Voluntary Alienation

There are two primary ways to voluntarily transfer property: by deed and by will. A deed can only transfer title while the owner is alive, and a will only transfers title when the owner dies.

DEEDS

A deed is a document used by an owner of real property (the **grantor**) to transfer all or part of his or her interest in the property to another party (the **grantee**). The process of alienating real property by deed is sometimes called **conveyancing**.

Chapter 10

To be valid, a deed has to contain certain elements and meet specific requirements. An invalid deed doesn't transfer title; the intended grantor still owns the property. In California, a deed is valid if it:

◆ is in writing,
◆ is signed by a competent grantor,
◆ includes words of conveyance,
◆ contains an adequate description of the property, and
◆ names an identifiable and living grantee.

Written

A deed must always be in writing. A transfer of real property cannot be accomplished orally.

Words of Conveyance

A deed has to have a granting clause; words that convey the property to the new owner. This requirement is easily satisfied: any words that express the intention to transfer an interest or ownership will do the trick.

Usually a single word—"grant" or something similar—is sufficient. However, since some lawyers like to use five or six words when one will do, some granting clauses look like this:

"The grantors do hereby give, grant, bargain, sell, and convey unto the said grantees forever . . ."

Not only are the extra technical words unnecessary, they can create confusion. It's better to keep it simple.

COMPETENT GRANTOR. A grantor must be competent—of legal age and sound mind. Minors and incompetents can own real property, but they can't convey it without their legal guardians. A deed is void if the grantor is a minor or has been declared incompetent by a court. A deed is voidable when the grantor hasn't been declared incompetent, but was not of sound mind when the deed was executed.

GRANTOR'S NAME. If the grantor took title under a different name than the one he or she is using now, the deed must state the former name as well as the current one.

> **Example:** Eileen bought a house when she was single. The name on her deed is "Eileen R. Flannigan," her maiden name. A few years after buying the house, she married and took her husband's last name, Minuscoli.
> Several years later, Eileen sells the house. On the deed to the buyer, she is identified as "Eileen R. Minuscoli, who acquired title as Eileen R. Flannigan."

If the deed had listed the grantor only under her current name, it would not be invalid. It would be effective to transfer title to the buyer, however, it would not give constructive notice of the transfer to later buyers or lienholders. That may also be true if the grantor's name is spelled differently on the two deeds, or if a nickname is used on one deed and not the other. These problems will be discussed later in the chapter, in the section on recording.

Although it isn't a legal requirement, a deed should also indicate the grantor's marital status. Marital status can affect the grantor's right to convey the property, since California is a community property state. So it's a good idea to state clearly in the deed whether the grantor is married or single.

Grantor's Signature

To be valid, a deed must be signed by the grantor. (The grantee's signature isn't required.) The grantor should sign his or her current legal name—in the example above, Eileen Minuscoli should sign her married name, not her maiden name.

If the grantor is unable to write his or her own name (because of illiteracy or a physical disability), the deed may be signed by a mark. If the grantor signs by a mark, the name should be written or typed in near the mark. Two witnesses should also sign to attest that the mark is the grantor's signature.

Power of Attorney. Sometimes a deed is executed by the grantor's agent instead of the grantor. The agent must be the grantor's attorney in fact, authorized to sign by a recorded power of attorney (see Chapter 5). The attorney in fact must sign the grantor's name, and then his or her own name beneath it.

Example: _____
Eileen R. Flannigan, Grantor

By _____ **, her Attorney in Fact**

A grantee taking title by a deed signed by an attorney in fact should make sure that the power of attorney has not expired or been revoked, and that the grantor is alive and competent.

Acknowledgment. A person signing a legal document is often required to **acknowledge** the document. That means he or she must sign it in front of a notary public and have it notarized. To get a document notarized, you have to give the notary proof of your identity and declare that you're signing voluntarily, with out coercion.

As of January 1, 1996, the person signing a grant deed, quitclaim deed or trust deed is required to place a right thumb print on the notary's sequential journal. This is because of a high rate of fraud by the use of false deeds. Additionally, a notary must immediately notify the Secretary of State if the notary's sequential journal is stolen, lost, misplaced, destroyed, damaged or otherwise rendered unusable.

Technically, a deed does not have to be acknowledged to be valid in California. But a grantee should always insist on acknowledgment. For one thing, that's usually the only way to prove the validity of the grantor's signature. Also, a deed can't be recorded in California unless it has been acknowledged by the grantor and the name and address where the tax statement is to be mailed is disclosed on the deed.

IDENTIFIABLE GRANTEE. For a deed to transfer title, it must name an existing and identifiable grantee. Note that the grantee does not have to be competent—property can be transferred to a minor or an insane person. The only requirements are that the grantee be alive and identifiable.

> **Examples:** A deed to "Zelda Higgins and her husband" is adequate to transfer ownership to Zelda and her husband. The identity of Zelda's husband can be determined, even though his name was not stated in the deed.
>
> A deed to "Zelda Higgins's brother" would be effective as long as Zelda has only one brother. But if Zelda has two brothers, the grantee is not identifiable.
>
> J executes a deed to transfer his property to M, not realizing that M was killed in an accident the day before. M's heirs try to claim the property, but in fact they don't have any legal right to it. A deed can't transfer property to a dead grantee. The deed is void, and the property still belongs to J. If he wants M's heirs to have it, he must deed it to them.
>
> If the grantee is an organization (such as a corporation or partnership) rather than a human being, it must legally exist when the deed is executed. In other words, it has to meet the requirements for incorporation, or have the proper certificates recorded, so that it's a legally recognized entity. (See Chapter 4.)

PROPERTY DESCRIPTION. A deed must contain an adequate description of the property being conveyed. A full legal description isn't required, but the property should be described well enough to identify it with reasonable certainty. (See Chapter 2.)

OTHER ELEMENTS. Many deeds contain other elements that seem to be standard, but aren't required by California law. For instance, almost all deeds are dated, but an undated deed is valid. However, a date is a good idea because, by legislation, a deed is presumed to be delivered on its date.

Another item often included is the grantee's signature. Although the grantor's signature is essential, the grantee doesn't have to sign.

Many deeds contain a recital of consideration given in exchange for the transferred property. Typically the deed doesn't state the actual purchase price, but says something like, "For $1.00 and other valuable consideration, I hereby grant..." The recital shows that the transfer was a sale rather than a gift. This is important to the grantee, because property transferred as a gift can sometimes be reached by the grantor's creditors.

Keep in mind, however, that a deed generally doesn't have to be supported by consideration. The grantor is legally bound by the deed even if the property was a gift.

> **Case Example:** Mrs. Odone owned a house as her separate property. Mr. Marzocchi, a friend of the Odones, did a lot of work on the house for free. He repaired many problems and built an addition.
>
> Mrs. Odone became seriously ill. She deeded her house to Marzocchi because he had been a good friend, and because he'd put so much work into the property. Shortly afterward, Mrs. Odone died.
>
> Mr. Odone sued Marzocchi to recover the house. He argued that the transfer was void because it wasn't supported by consideration. Something a person has already done isn't valid consideration for a contract. Since Marzocchi had already done the work on the house when Mrs. Odone decided to transfer it to him, the work was not consideration for the transfer.
>
> If Mrs. Odone had merely promised to give Marzocchi the house, that wouldn't have been an enforceable contract, because of the lack of consideration. The deed, however, was binding even without consideration. Mr. Marzocchi got to keep the house. *Odone v. Marzocchi*, 34 Cal. 2d 431, 212 P.2d 233 (1949).

There's one important exception to this rule: consideration is necessary when the deed was executed by a representative of the grantor—an attorney in fact, a guardian, or any other agent—instead of by the grantor personally.

Delivery, Donative Intent, and Acceptance

Even when a deed meets all the formal requirements, it has no legal effect until the grantor has delivered it with the intention of transferring title, and the grantee has accepted it.

DELIVERY. Generally, delivering a deed means actually placing the document in the grantee's possession. In some cases, however, a deed is considered constructively delivered when the grantor turns it over to a third person to give to the grantee. And the grantor and grantee can also agree to treat the deed as constructively delivered, as long as the grantee is unconditionally entitled to immediate possession of the deed.

> **Example:** X has decided to give some property to Z, his granddaughter. Z is out of town when X executes the deed, so he can't conveniently deliver it to her right away. But when Z calls him from New York to say hello, X tells her what he's done. "The property is yours now. The deed's all signed and waiting for you. Come by and pick it up when you get back." Z thanks him and agrees to pick up the deed on her return.

A court might consider X's deed to Z constructively delivered. This could become an important issue if X were to die before Z picked up the deed. A deed must be delivered while the grantor is alive, or it has no legal effect.

Case Example: Meta Rasmussen was old and didn't expect to live much longer. She wanted to leave some of her property to her sister, Maria Beck, and some to her friend, Robert Jansen.

But Rasmussen was concerned that if she willed her property to them, probate costs would eat up a large share of the estate. So she executed a deed for her house, granting a life estate to Beck, with the remainder interest in the property going to Jansen.

Asking another friend to act as a witness, Rasmussen sealed the deed in an envelope. On the outside of the envelope she wrote, "Signed, Sealed and Delivered in the presence of Beatrice Myers Winslow," and "This envelope and contents is the property of Maria Beck of Ferndale and Robert N. Jansen of Manteca, California. [Signed] Meta Rasmussen. Witness B. M. Winslow." But instead of giving the deed to Beck or Jansen, Rasmussen placed the envelope in her safe deposit box.

Rasmussen died a little less than a year later, and the deed was found after her death. Jansen tried to claim an interest in Rasmussen's house, but the deed was held to be ineffective. It had not been delivered to Beck and Jansen while Rasmussen was alive, in spite of the inscriptions on the envelope. *Miller v. Jansen*, 21 Cal. 2d 473, 132 P.2d 801 (1943).

DONATIVE INTENT. Even when a deed is actually given to the grantee while the grantor is alive, it isn't legally delivered unless it is given unconditionally and with the intent to transfer title. If the grantor retains any power to recall the deed, or believes the deed is invalid, it hasn't been effectively delivered and does not transfer title to the grantee. It's the grantor's intent that governs. The grantor must intend to surrender control and transfer title. This is called **donative intent**.

Case Example: Mr. Kimbro was seriously ill with pneumonia, and his doctor thought he might die. Mr. Kimbro owned several lots in Los Angeles. During his illness, Mrs. Kimbro asked her husband to deed two of his lots to her, and he agreed. Their lawyer drew up a deed. Mr. Kimbro signed it, but did not acknowledge it, before giving it to his wife.

After Mr. Kimbro recovered, he asked his wife to give him back the deed. He implied that she had taken advantage of his illness and bullied him into signing it. Outraged, Mrs. Kimbro gave him back the deed, and he destroyed it.

Several years later, the Kimbros decided to go their separate ways. In the divorce proceedings, Mrs. Kimbro claimed that she owned the two lots Mr. Kimbro had deeded to her, as her separate property.

But Mr. Kimbro testified that he believed the deed was invalid because it wasn't acknowledged. He claimed to have told his wife at the time, "Well, I will sign the deed, but it won't benefit you any for it is not acknowledged."

Of course, in California a deed does not have to be acknowledged to be valid. But the court ruled that Mr. Kimbro had not delivered the deed with donative intent, so it did not transfer title. As a result, the lots were never Mrs. Kimbro's separate property. *Kimbro v. Kimbro*, 199 Cal. 344, 249 P.180 (1926).

If Mr. Kimbro had given his wife the deed with donative intent, it wouldn't have made any difference that he destroyed it later on. Once a deed has been effectively delivered, the grantee holds title, and it can't be reconveyed just by destroying the deed or returning it to the grantor. The grantee would have to execute another deed, transferring title back to the grantor.

ACCEPTANCE. Not only is it necessary for the grantor to intend to transfer ownership, it's necessary for the grantee to accept it. And the acceptance must take place while the grantor is alive.

Case Example: In 1943, Arthur Kelly was about to have a serious operation, and there was a good chance he wouldn't survive it. He deeded his ranch to his son Everett and gave Everett the deed.

Arthur came through the operation and recuperated. He and his wife Winnie (Everett's stepmother) continued to live on the ranch. They paid the taxes and other expenses, and took out loans using the ranch as collateral. On their income tax statements, Arthur and Winnie listed the ranch as their property, reported all the income from it, and deducted its operating expenses. Everett, on the other hand, did not live or work on the ranch, pay any of the taxes or expenses, collect any of the income, or list the ranch as his property on loan applications or income tax statements.

Five years later, Arthur was dying of cancer. He asked Everett to return the deed to him, and Everett did so. Arthur made out a will, leaving all his property, including the ranch, to both Winnie and Everett. After his father's death, Everett tried to establish that he was the sole owner of the ranch. He claimed to have owned the property since 1943, when his father executed the deed. As a result, Everett contended, his father didn't have the right to leave part of the property to Winnie in his will.

The court held that Everett never owned the ranch before his father's death. The court questioned whether Arthur had delivered the deed with donative intent. But even if Arthur had, Everett hadn't accepted it (in the eyes of the law) because he didn't take on any of the rights or duties of ownership. *Kelly v. Bank of America*, 112 Cal. App. 2d 388, 246 P.2d 92 (1952).

The *Kelly* case is unusual. Problems concerning acceptance don't come up often, because most grantees are happy to acquire property and take over control of it. But occasionally a grantee may not want to accept a deed, either for personal reasons, or because the property is so encumbered with liens that it would be a liability. Without acceptance, title remains with the grantor.

A VALID DEED

I grant....................................... words of conveyance
Razorback Farm...................... description of property
to Jacob Howard .... identifiable grantee
[signed] Sylvia Peron.............. signature of competent grantor

In writing, delivered with donative intent, and accepted
Can't be recorded without grantor's acknowledgment

Types of Deeds

Only two types of deeds are frequently used in California: the grant deed and the quitclaim deed. Warranty deeds were common here at one time and are still popular in many states, but they're almost never used in California today.

www.ultranet.com/~deeds/landref.htm
(Land Record Reference)

GRANT DEEDS AND WARRANTY DEEDS. Nearly every California real estate sale involves a **grant deed**. The law treats any deed that uses "grant" in its words of conveyance as a grant deed. When that word is included, the deed carries two implied warranties (unless the deed expressly states it does not carry them). The grantor warrants to the grantee that:

1. the grantor has not previously conveyed title to anyone else, and
2. the grantor has not caused any encumbrances to attach to the property, other than those disclosed on the deed.

Warranty deeds carry additional warranties, beyond the two implied in grant deeds. A **general warranty deed** gives the grantee the broadest protection.

With a general warranty deed the grantor warrants the title even against defects arising before he or she owned the property. A **special warranty deed** isn't quite so sweeping; its warranties only extend to problems that may have arisen during the grantor's period of ownership.

The grantee has the right to sue the grantor if any of the deed warranties are breached. For example, suppose the seller gives you a grant deed and it turns out that there's a surprise tax lien against the property. If you pay off the tax lien, you can sue the seller for breach of warranty and recover the amount of the lien.

Today nearly every real estate transaction is covered by title insurance. As a result, deed warranties are no longer important. The insurance takes care of the kinds of problems that warranties were intended to address. That's why Californians use the simpler grant deed instead of bothering with general and special warranty deeds.

QUITCLAIM DEEDS. A quitclaim deed merely conveys whatever interest the grantor has. It carries no warranties of any sort. If the grantor owns no interest in the property when the quitclaim deed is executed, the deed conveys nothing to the grantee.

Example: A and B are neighbors and good friends. They're uncertain about the exact location of the boundary line between their lots. There's a fence between the properties 30 yards from B's house, but B thinks the true property line is really 32 yards from the house. A and B both want to sell their properties, but don't want to hire a surveyor. B gives A a quitclaim deed for the two yards of property on the other side of the fence.

When the properties are surveyed several years later, the survey shows that the fence is right on the true boundary line. So B's quitclaim deed didn't transfer any interest to A, since B didn't actually own the two yards on the other side of the fence.

A common reason for using a quitclaim deed is to clear up **clouds on the title**. A cloud might be a technical flaw in an earlier deed, such as a misspelling of the grantee's name, or an error in the property description. Or the cloud might be an expired option to purchase. If the optionee executes a quitclaim deed in favor of the optionor, it's absolutely clear that the optionee has no further claim against the property.

A quitclaim deed is also used when the grantor is not sure of the validity of his or her title and wants to avoid giving any warranties.

> **Example:** J's uncle left J some property in his will, but the will is being challenged in court by J's cousin. If J wants to transfer the property before the lawsuit is resolved, she should use a quitclaim deed.

www.altranet.com/~deeds/landacq.htm
(How Land in the Colonies was Acquired)

AFTER-ACQUIRED TITLE. An important difference between a grant deed and a quitclaim deed is that the grant deed conveys after-acquired title and the quitclaim deed doesn't. A quitclaim deed conveys only the interest that the grantor has when the deed is executed. If the grantor doesn't own the property at that time, the deed conveys nothing to the grantee. And if the grantor later acquires title to the property, the grantee still has nothing. With a grant deed, however, if the grantor takes title later on, it passes to the grantee automatically.

Case Example: Ms. Schwenn owned some property in Long Beach. She leased the oil and gas rights to the Atlantic-Richfield Company (ARCO). ARCO paid Schwenn royalties for the oil and gas her property produced.

In 1969, Schwenn conveyed the oil and gas rights to her daughter as a gift. ARCO began paying the royalties to Schwenn's daughter.

Five years later, Schwenn sold the property to the Kayes. The preliminary title report showed that the property was subject to ARCO's lease, but failed to show that Schwenn had conveyed the oil and gas rights to her daughter. Before closing, Schwenn agreed that the oil and gas lease would be assigned to the Kayes "if assignable." She didn't explain that she didn't have the right to assign the lease because it belonged to her daughter.

After closing, ARCO was notified of the sale and began sending the royalties to the Kayes instead of Schwenn's daughter. Schwenn protested, claiming that the royalties should still be sent to her daughter. ARCO said it would not disburse any more royalties without a court order resolving the dispute.

At this point, Schwenn asked her daughter to reconvey the oil and gas rights to her. She explained that there was going to be a lawsuit, and she didn't want her daughter to get mixed up in litigation over a gift. So the daughter deeded the rights back to Schwenn.

The court ruled that the Kayes now owned the oil and gas rights and were entitled to the royalties. Schwenn had given them a grant deed that purported to convey fee simple title to the property. She didn't own the oil and gas rights at that time, and so could not sell the rights to the Kayes. However, when Schwenn's daughter conveyed the rights back to Schwenn, they automatically belonged to the Kayes under the doctrine of after-acquired title. *Schwenn v. Kaye*, 155 Cal. App. 3d 949, 202 Cal. Rptr. 374 (1984).

Chapter 10

The case wouldn't have worked out this way if Schwenn had transferred her property to the Kayes with a quitclaim deed instead of a grant deed. Since a quitclaim deed doesn't convey after-acquired title, the Kayes would not have automatically gained title to the oil and gas rights when Schwenn's daughter transferred the rights back to Schwenn.

WILLS

The second method of voluntary alienation is by will. A will only transfers property when the owner dies. An expectation under a will (knowing that Aunt Harriet's leaving you her house) is not an interest in property. You have no legal interest in the property and no rights in regard to it until Aunt Harriet is dead.

www.mtpalermo.com/
(Crash Course in Wills and Trusts)

A person who makes out a will is called the **testator** (male) or **testatrix** (female). A testator **bequeaths** personal property to **legatees**, and **devises** real property to **devisees**. (Legatees and devisees are lumped together as the **beneficiaries** of the will.) An amendment to a will is called a **codicil**. The **executor** or **executrix** is the person appointed in the will to carry out the testator or testatrix's directions, under the supervision of the probate court. **Probate** is the legal process in which a will is proved valid and the property is distributed according to its terms. In California, probate matters are handled by the superior courts.

> **testator/testatrix:** one who makes a will
> **bequeath:** to transfer personal property by will
> **devise:** to transfer real property by will
> **codicil:** an amendment to a will
> **executor/executrix:** someone appointed in the will to carry out the testator or testatrix's directions
> **probate:** legal procedure for proving a will's validity

In the early 1980s, the California legislature substantially revised the statutes governing wills. Although many rules remained the same, many changes went into effect in 1985. As a result, a will written long ago might be treated differently depending on whether the testator or testatrix died before or after January 1, 1985. The rules outlined here, of course, are the current ones.

Any person of sound mind who is 18 years old or older may make a will. Just like a grantor, a testator or testatrix must be competent. If he or she is found to have been incompetent at the time the will was executed, it is invalid. Then the property will pass just as if the testator or testatrix had died intestate—without making a will. (The rules of intestate succession are discussed in the next section of this chapter.)

In California, a will must be in writing. Oral wills bequeathing personal property used to be recognized in very specific situations, but the legislature repealed that law. It was never possible to devise real property by an oral will.

A will must be signed by the testator or testatrix. However, as with deeds, a will may be signed with a mark or by someone else on behalf of the testator or testatrix. If the will is signed by someone else, it has to be signed in the presence of the testator or testatrix. The person signing must also sign his or her own name.

Title and Alienation

Formal, Witnessed Wills

Ordinarily, at least two witnesses must sign their names to a will. To be legitimate witnesses, they must be present either when the testator or testatrix signs the will, or when he or she acknowledges it. They must specifically understand that the document being signed is a will.

Any competent adult may witness a will. However, someone who is a beneficiary under the will should not act as a witness unless there's no alternative. That wouldn't invalidate the will, but it might cause trouble for the witness/beneficiary.

Unless there were at least two other disinterested witnesses, it would be presumed that the witness/beneficiary used fraud, duress, menace, or undue influence to make the testator or testatrix execute the will in his or her favor. If the beneficiary could prove that presumption was false, he or she would get the full bequest or devise. But if the beneficiary was unable to overcome the presumption, the beneficiary would get no more than what he or she would have inherited if the testator or testatrix had died intestate.

> **Example:** Mrs. Cox drew up a will leaving her Palm Springs condominium to her hairdresser and all the rest of her property (including her house in San Francisco) to her cook. She expressly disinherited her daughter. Mrs. Cox's signature was witnessed by the cook and the gardener.
>
> Since the cook was a beneficiary as well as a witness, there was only one disinterested witness (the gardener). In the probate proceedings after Mrs. Cox's death, the cook has to prove that he didn't use fraud or other underhanded methods to persuade Mrs. Cox to leave the bulk of her property to him. If he is able to convince the court that he did not, then he is entitled to the property.
>
> But if the cook can't convince the court, he will only be awarded what he would have received if Mrs. Cox had never made a will. Since he is not related to Mrs. Cox, that would be nothing at all. (If he were Mrs. Cox's son instead of her cook, he would receive a share of the estate according to the rules of intestate succession, outlined later in the chapter.)

If there had been a third witness to Mrs. Cox's will—also disinterested, like the gardener—then the cook would not have to defend himself against the presumption of fraud or underhandedness.

STATUTORY WILL. The law governing wills and estates is complicated, and many wills need to be drawn up by a lawyer. However, people with simple estates can use California's statutory will. This is a basic will form set out in the Probate Code. The legislature adopted the statutory will to help people with modest incomes avoid high legal fees. It's a good idea to have a statutory will reviewed by a lawyer, but that should cost considerably less than having a will drafted from scratch.

A statutory will, like any other formal will, must be witnessed by at least two people.

Chapter 10

Holographic Wills

In California, the only exception to the witnessing requirement is the holographic will. A holographic will is one that the testator or testatrix has written out by hand. As long as the signature and the main provisions are in the testator or testatrix's handwriting, the will is valid even without witnesses. It used to be that the entire will, including the date, had to be handwritten, but that rule has been relaxed. A statement of testamentary intent (such as the heading "Last Will and Testament") in a holographic will may be part of a commercially printed form. Other provisions that are typewritten or preprinted will be disregarded when a court interprets a holographic will.

A person making a will should have it witnessed whenever possible. A holographic will is much more easily challenged in court than a witnessed will.

WILLS

◆ **in writing**
◆ **signed by testator**

FORMAL

two witnesses
competent adults
disinterested if possible

statutory will may be used

HOLOGRAPHIC

in testor's handwriting
no witnesses

Foreign Wills

When someone executes a will in another state or another country in compliance with the laws of that place, California probate courts consider the will valid, even if it doesn't meet all of California's legal requirements.

> **Example:** R is vacationing in Islandia, a faraway country. While he's there, R becomes very ill and decides to execute a will in case he doesn't live. The only witness to the will is his nurse. This will is valid in Islandia, because that country's laws require only one witness for a will.
>
> R recovers and comes home to California. He never bothers to make a new will. When R dies, his Islandian will is probated in a California court. Although one witness ordinarily would not be enough in California, the court holds that the will is valid here because it was valid in the place where it was executed.

The same rule applies if a citizen of another state or country executes a will while staying in California. If the will would be valid under the laws of the state or country of citizenship, California courts will accept it.

Family Rights Under a Will

In California, when a spouse dies, half of any community property automatically belongs to the surviving spouse, regardless of the terms of the will. (See Chapter 4.) The other half of the community property and any separate property may be disposed of by will. Aside from the surviving spouse's community property rights, he or she may be disinherited. A child may be completely disinherited.

Sometimes a will makes no provision for a surviving spouse, because the testator or testatrix got married after executing the will and never wrote a new one. In that case, the omitted spouse will be awarded the community property and the share of the separate property he or she would have received if the testator or testatrix had died intestate. However, the court can't award an omitted spouse more than half the separate property.

There's a similar rule for children who aren't mentioned in a will because they were born or adopted after it was executed. These children generally receive the share of the estate they would have taken if the parent had died intestate.

Occasionally the family home is willed to someone other than the family. The surviving spouse and minor children have the right to continue living in the home for at least 60 days after the inventory of the estate property is filed with the probate court. The court may extend that grace period if necessary.

The court may also decide to treat the home as a **probate homestead**, setting it aside for the use of the spouse and children and giving it homestead protection (see Chapter 3) from some claims against the estate. A probate homestead is held for a limited period, under conditions specified by the court. The devisee the home was willed to takes title subject to the probate homestead right.

Revocation

A will is revoked if the testator or testatrix executes another will later on. The earlier will is revoked to the extent it is inconsistent with the later one, or if the later one expressly states that the earlier one is completely revoked. A will is also revoked if it is burned, torn, canceled, obliterated, or destroyed with the intent to revoke it. This destruction must either be done by the testator or testatrix, or by another person in the testator or testatrix's presence and at his or her direction.

If a will is lost or destroyed inadvertently or as a result of fraud, the court may still establish the existence of the will on the testimony of at least two witnesses. But if the will was last seen in the possession of the testator or testatrix, and he or she was competent until the time of death, the court will presume that the will was destroyed with the intention of revoking it. The survivors have to present evidence to overcome that presumption.

When a testator or testatrix gets divorced, the will provisions involving the ex-spouse are automatically revoked. If the ex-spouse was to receive property under the will, that property will go to whoever would have taken it if the ex-spouse had died before the testator or testatrix. If the ex-spouse was to act as executor or executrix, the probate court will appoint an administrator to take his or her place.

> ### REVOCATION OF A WILL
>
> ◆ **Execution of a later will**
> ◆ **Divorce**
> ◆ **Intentional destruction by the testator**

Involuntary Alienation

Involuntary alienation is any transfer of property that occurs against the owners wishes or without any action by the owner. Property is involuntarily alienated when a person dies without leaving a will, or without any heirs. And title may be involuntarily transferred by adverse possession, a court decision, or government action. Ownership also sometimes changes hands as a result of natural forces that cause geological changes in the land itself.

INTESTATE SUCCESSION

Someone who dies without leaving a will is said to have died **intestate**. The rules of intestate succession determine who is entitled to a share of the property of a person who dies intestate, or whose will is ruled invalid. (Like the statutes on wills, those governing intestate succession were changed in 1985.) The people who take property by intestate succession are called **heirs**. The probate court decides who the heirs are, and appoints an **administrator** to carry out the statutory distribution of the property.

 www.octitle.com/joint.htm
www.wwlaw.com/intest.htm
(Intestate Succession as an Estate Planning Tool)

A person's **issue** are his or her children, grandchildren, great-grandchildren, and so forth. The issue of a person's parents are that person's brothers and sisters, nieces and nephews, great-nieces, and so on. The California Probate Code provides that an intestate person's property is distributed in the following manner:

1. The **surviving spouse** is entitled to all of the community property, plus:

    a. **One-half** of the separate property if the intestate person is survived by:
       i. only one child or issue of a deceased child, or
       ii. one or both parents, or the issue of either parent.

    b. **One-third** of the separate property if the intestate person is survived by:
       i. more than one child,
       ii. one child and the issue of one or more deceased children, or
       iii. the issue of two or more deceased children.

    c. **All of the separate property** if there is no surviving issue, or parent, or brother or sister, or issue of a deceased brother or sister.

2. The portion of the separate property not going to the spouse (or the entire estate if there is no surviving spouse) is distributed to the issue of the intestate person—the children, grandchildren, and so on of the person who died.

If the issue are all of the same degree of kinship, they take equally. In other words, if the intestate person had three children and they are all still living, each of the three would get an equal share. If all three children were already dead but there were five grandchildren still living, each of those five would get an equal share.

But if the issue are not of the same degree of kinship, then those of a more remote degree divide up their deceased parent's (or grandparent's) share.

Example: Arnold and Brenda had two children, Celia and David. Celia has been dead for some time. She had two children, Eliza and Francine, who are still living. David also has a living child, Greg.

Arnold dies intestate. Brenda is entitled to all of the community property, plus 1/3 of Arnold's separate property. The other 2/3 of the separate property is divided among Arnold's issue (his children and grandchildren).

The total value of the separate property is $60,000. Brenda gets $20,000. The remaining $40,000 is divided among the issue. David, Arnold's only living child, takes $20,000 (1/2 of the $40,000). Celia would have been entitled to the other $20,000 if she were still alive. But since she is dead, her children divide her share instead. Thus, Eliza and Francine each receive $10,000. David's child, Greg, does not share in his grandfather's estate because his father is still living.

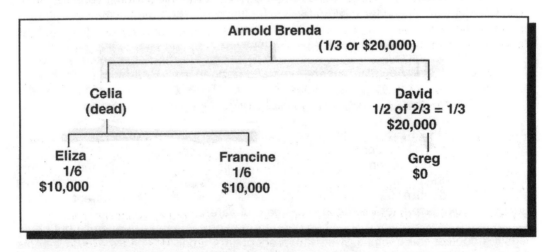

Suppose that instead of $60,000 cash, Arnold's separate property was real estate worth approximately $60,000. The shares would still be the same, but instead of money, the heirs would each take an interest in the property as tenants in common. Brenda would have a 1/3 interest, David would have a 1/3 interest, and Eliza and Francine would each have a 1/6 interest in the property.

Rather than holding a small portion of the real property as tenants in common, the heirs may want to sell the property and receive its cash value instead. In order to sell the property, all of the heirs must sign the deed to give the new owner a clear title.

Chapter 10

3. If the intestate person has no living issue (children, grandchildren, etc.), the share of separate property not taken by the surviving spouse is distributed in this order:

a. to the intestate person's parents;
b. then to the intestate person's brothers and sisters and the issue of any deceased brothers and sisters;
c. then to the intestate person's grandparents, or to their issue if they're no longer living;
d. then to issue of a predeceased spouse (someone who was married to the intestate person but died before he or she did);
e. then to the next of kin, however remote (second cousins once removed and so forth);
f. then to the parents of a predeceased spouse.

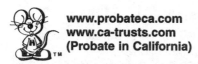

www.probateca.com
www.ca-trusts.com
(Probate in California)

Keep in mind that the members of category b only get a share if there are no living persons in category a, and the members of category c only get a share if there are no living persons in either category a or b, and so on down the list.

> **Example:** Anna, a childless widow, died intestate. She was survived by her parents (category a), her nephew (category b), her paternal grandmother (category c), her dead husband's son (category d), and six second cousins (category e).
>
> Anna's entire estate will be divided between her parents. None of her other relatives will receive a share. But if her parents were dead, the entire estate would go to her nephew. If her parents and her nephew were dead, the entire estate would go to her grandmother. And so on. The six second cousins would only receive shares if everyone else had already died before Anna died.

ADOPTED CHILDREN. Legally adopted children are treated exactly the same as a person's natural children for the purposes of intestate succession.

An adopted child ordinarily inherits only from his or her adoptive parents, not from his or her natural parents. However, the child may inherit from a natural parent (as well as from the adoptive parents) if he or she ever lived with the natural parent, or if the adoption took place after the death of the natural parent.

In some cases where a child has been treated as a member of a family but never legally adopted, the doctrine of equitable adoption is applied. Then the child inherits from an intestate parent just as if he or she had been legally adopted.

HALF-BROTHERS AND HALF-SISTERS. As far as the rules of intestate succession are concerned, half-brothers and half-sisters are the same as other brothers and sisters.

ILLEGITIMACY AND DIVORCE. Generally, inheritance by (or from) a child doesn't depend on whether the parents are still married, or whether they were ever married. An illegitimate child is entitled to share in an intestate parent's estate just like a legitimate child.

Example: Adrian was married to Becky, and they had two children (Edgar and Fred). He and Becky then divorced. Edgar and Fred live with their mother and Adrian has not seen them for 13 years.

Adrian later married Corinne. Adrian and Corinne had one child (George). During his second marriage, Adrian had an affair with Dorothy and they had an illegitimate daughter (Helen).

Adrian dies intestate. His current wife (Corinne) receives all of the community property and 1/3 of the separate property. The remaining 2/3 of the separate property is divided equally between all of Adrian's children. Edgar, Fred, George, and Helen each receive 1/6 of their father's estate.

STEPCHILDREN. Stepchildren are the only group of children that are affected by divorce. Suppose that when Adrian married Corinne, she already had a son, Ira, from an earlier marriage. As long as Corinne and Adrian are married, Ira is Adrian's stepson. If Corinne and Adrian were married when Adrian died intestate, Ira might be entitled to a share of Adrian's separate property. Corinne and Ira would have to prove to the probate court that Adrian would have adopted Ira, except that there was a legal barrier to the adoption.

But if Corinne and Adrian were divorced, Ira wouldn't be Adrian's stepson anymore. Then if Adrian died intestate, Edgar, Fred, George, and Helen would still share in Adrian's estate, but Ira would not.

ESCHEAT

When a person dies intestate and no heirs can be located, the property **escheats**. That means ownership reverts to the state. Since the state is the ultimate source of title to property, it is also the ultimate heir when there are no other claimants.

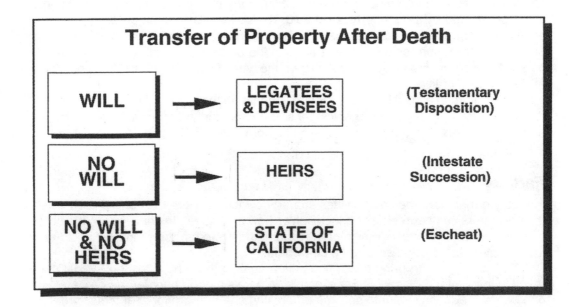

321

Chapter 10

If no heirs have come forward two years after an intestate person's death, the attorney general may bring a court action to establish the state's title to the estate property. The court will enter a judgment ordering the property to be turned over to the state treasurer. It will then be sold at public auction.

Sometimes there are very remote heirs who can't easily be located, and who aren't aware that they are entitled to inherit. In California, any heir to escheated funds or real property has five years after the Attorney General obtains a judgment in which to file a claim.

The heirs must establish their claim to the satisfaction of the court. The court then orders payment to the heirs of any escheated funds and delivery of any escheated property. When escheated property has already been sold, the heirs receive the proceeds of the sale.

If no valid claims are filed within the five-year period, the property permanently escheats. After that, the state's title to it can no longer be challenged by long-lost heirs.

Under certain circumstances, property that was left to someone in a valid will can escheat. If the beneficiary can't be located, the property goes to the state, rather than to the testator or testatrix's heirs.

COURT DECISIONS

Property can also be involuntarily alienated by court order. Aside from marital dissolutions (see Chapter 4), the most common forms of court action affecting title to property are foreclosure, partition, and quiet title actions.

Foreclosure

Creditors holding liens against a piece of real property may bring a foreclosure action if the debt secured by the property is not paid. The court will order the property sold at a public auction (sheriff's sale, tax sale, or execution sale). After a waiting period, the buyer at a foreclosure sale receives a deed to the property—usually a **sheriff's deed, trustee's deed**, or a **tax deed**, depending on the type of sale. These deeds do not carry any warranties of title.

Foreclosure is available for any type of lien that attaches to real property, including deeds of trust, mortgages, mechanics' liens, tax liens, and judgment liens. Foreclosure of trust deeds and mortgages is discussed in more detail in Chapter 12.

Partition

In a suit for partition, the court divides property owned by more than one person when the co-owners can't agree among themselves how to divide it. In some cases the court actually orders a physical division of the land, but more often the property is sold and the proceeds are divided among the co-owners.

Any co-owner can bring a partition action against the others, so the lawsuit may result in involuntary alienation. For example, if there's a good offer for the property but one co-owner doesn't want to sell, the others can sue for partition. The court-ordered sale accomplishes what persuasion could not, and the reluctant co-owner is forced to accept the money instead of keeping the property. Partition suits are discussed in more detail in Chapter 4.

Quiet Title

When there's a cloud on an owner's title, it makes the property unmarketable. As you've seen, in many cases the cloud can be cleared away with a quitclaim deed. But sometimes the owner can't get a quitclaim deed from the person who created the cloud. The person may be unknown, unavailable, or uncooperative, or may believe that he or she has a legitimate claim against the title. Then the title holder may file a quiet title action to get a judicial ruling on ownership of the property.

> **Example:** X has found a potential buyer for his property. But the title insurance company's search of the public record shows a gap in the chain of title: the recorded documents don't indicate who owned the property for a four-year period about 15 years before X bought the property.
>
> X brings a quiet title action. The defendants in the action are all the parties who have a potential interest in the land. This includes the mystery person who held title during the gap, even though this person's name is unknown.
>
> X asks the court to declare his title valid, thereby quieting title to the property. If no defendants appear to challenge X's title, the court will grant X's request. Then the buyer can go ahead with the purchase in reliance on the court's declaration.

It isn't just the record title holder who can file a quiet title action, however. The plaintiff can be anyone claiming title or an interest in the property. For example, to make title acquired by adverse possession marketable, the adverse possessor has to bring a quiet title action against the record owner. This is called **perfecting** the title. Adverse possession is discussed below.

ADVERSE POSSESSION

Adverse possession is the process by which possession and use of property can mature into title to the property. The main purpose of the adverse possession laws is to encourage the fullest and most productive use of property. The idea is that it's better to give title to someone who makes good use of the property, rather than leaving title with someone who ignores the property for a long period of time.

www.lectlaw.com/files/lat06.htm
(Tresspass, Adverse Possession, and Easements)

Owners of vacant property or land held for future sale or development should make periodic inspections of their property to check for any signs of adverse possession. Merely posting "no trespassing" signs isn't enough to prevent a claim of adverse possession.

PUBLIC LANDS. Any property can be adversely possessed except public lands. So land owned by the United States, the state of California, a county, or a city is generally secure. For example, I can't acquire title to a corner of Yosemite through adverse possession, no matter how long I camp there.

Chapter 10

Requirements

In California, title can be acquired by adverse possession if the possession is:

◆ actual, open, and notorious;
◆ hostile to the owner's interest;
◆ under claim of right or color of title; and
◆ exclusive, continuous, and uninterrupted for five years.

In addition, the adverse possessor must pay the property taxes during the five-year period of possession.

ACTUAL, OPEN, AND NOTORIOUS POSSESSION. This means that the adverse possessor must use the property openly, in a way that will put the owner on notice that his or her title is threatened. In other words, you can't sneak around on someone's property for five years and then claim adverse possession. Your use must be open enough to make the owner aware of your presence if he or she is paying reasonable attention to the property.

Case Example: Mrs. Harthan owned a large tract of land in the San Bernardino Mountains. The tract was subdivided into 1,500 unimproved lots, and these were sold off one by one. Most of the individual lot owners built vacation cabins on their properties.

In 1923 the Kleins bought one of these lots from Harthan through a real estate agent. The purchase price was $175, paid in installments on a land contract. The contract was never recorded. The Kleins paid the final installment at the end of 1924, but they never requested a deed and were never sent one.

In 1945 another real estate agent working for Harthan (not the agent who had dealt with the Kleins) accidentally sold the same lot to the Caswells that was sold to the Kleins 22 years earlier. The Caswells paid $250 in cash, recorded their deed, and built a cabin on the lot.

While the Caswells were putting up their cabin, the Kleins learned that their lot had been sold out from under them. They contacted Harthan to object. She explained that it was a mistake and pointed out that they had never asked for a deed. She offered to refund everything the Kleins had paid, including the taxes, or to give them another equally desirable lot.

However, the Kleins wanted the lot the Caswells had, so they sued to quiet title. Since they had no deed to the property, the Kleins' claim against the Caswells was based on adverse possession rather than record title.

But the court ruled that the Kleins' adverse possession claim failed. They had not made enough "ordinary use" of the property to put Harthan on notice. The Kleins occasionally had picnics on the lot and Mr. Klein once camped out there for a week. But they never built on the lot (ordinary use) or used it very regularly during the 22 years since they bought it. Harthan and almost all of the neighbors had never seen anyone using the Kleins' lot, and assumed it was unsold. *Klein v. Caswell*, 88 Cal. App. 2d 774, 199 P.2d 689 (1948).

The degree of use and occupancy required for adverse possession depends on the type of property involved. The Kleins wouldn't have had to live on the lot year-round to establish adverse possession. More frequent and conspicuous summer use would probably have been enough. An adverse possessor is simply required to occupy and use the property as it would ordinarily be occupied and used. For example, farmland can be adversely possessed by a person who only plants and harvests there, while living somewhere else.

HOSTILITY AND CLAIM OF RIGHT. Possession of the property must also be hostile. That doesn't mean the adverse possessor has to hate the owner, or even be embroiled in a dispute over the title. It simply means that the nature of the possession must conflict with the owner's interest. If the owner has given someone else permission to use the property, that use is not hostile and can never develop into adverse possession.

The requirement that the possession be under a claim of right is virtually identical to the hostility requirement. The adverse possessor must be claiming the property as his or her own. In many cases, the adverse possessor's claim is simply a mistake, rather than a deliberate plan to take over someone else's property. When the adverse possessor's claim to the property is based on a defective deed or some other invalid written document, he or she is said to have **color of title**.

California Civil Code section 323 states when a person has possession under color of title:

For the purpose of constituting an adverse possession by any person claiming a title founded upon a written instrument, or a judgment or decree, land is deemed to have been possessed and occupied in the following cases:

1. Where it has been usually cultivated or improved;
2. Where it has been protected by a substantial enclosure;
3. Where, although not enclosed, it has been used for the supply of fuel, or of fencing-timber for the purposes of husbandry, or for pasturage, or for the ordinary use of the occupant;
4. Where a known farm or single lot has been partly improved, the portion of such farm or lot that may have been left not cleared, or not included according to the usual course and custom of the adjoining country, shall be deemed to have been occupied for the same length of time as the part improved and cultivated.

However, when a person is claiming title, but not under a written document, California Civil Code Section 325 applies:

For the purpose of constituting an adverse possession by a person claiming title, not founded upon a written instrument, judgment, or decree, land is deemed to have been possessed and occupied in the following cases only:

1. Where it has been protected by a substantial enclosure.
2. Where it has been usually cultivated or improved.

Case Example: Mr. Lowe owned a house as his separate property. He married Wyonna in August 1973 and she moved into the house and was repeatedly reminded that it belonged only to him. In 1978, unknown to Mrs. Lowe, Mr. Lowe deeded the house to himself and 3 sons from his first marriage as joint tenants. When Mr. Lowe died in August 1981, the sons demanded and continued to demand that Wyonna move from the property. Wyonna refused, stayed on the property believing she owned it under community property laws and made all mortgage and tax payments.

December 1981, Wyonna sued to set aside Mr. Lowe's gift of community property to the sons and they sued to quiet title and for ejectment. In May 1988, the lawsuit was dismissed for failure to prosecute. In December 1988, the actions were refiled. Wyonna claimed title by adverse possession.

The court of appeal held that Wyonna did not have a community property interest in the house, however all of the elements of adverse possession had been established. 1) She made the tax payments; 2) had actual possession; 3) possession was open and notorious; 4) continuous and uninterrupted for 5 years; 5) hostile and adverse to the three owner's title; and 6) either under claim or right or color of title. The 5 year time period was not tolled (interrupted) by Wyonna's lawsuit to set aside Mr. Lowe's deed to the sons when it was dismissed for failure to prosecute. *First Boston Credit Corp. v. Lowe*, 37 Cal. App. 4th 1798, 44 Cal. Rptr. 2d 784 (1995).

EXCLUSIVE, CONTINUOUS, AND UNINTERRUPTED. An adverse possessor must be the exclusive user of the property; he or she can't share possession with the owner. You can't adversely possess a summer cabin by using it every other weekend if the owner is there on the weekends in between.

The adverse possession must be continuous and uninterrupted for five years. Of course, that doesn't mean the adverse possessor can't ever leave the property during that period. The possession is considered continuous if the property is used as constantly as an owner would ordinarily use that type of property. But the use must be uninterrupted; there can't be a significant break in the period of exclusive possession.

Example: P is adversely possessing a cabin beside a mountain lake. She spends every summer there for five years in a row, but never goes there in the winter. This would probably be considered continuous possession, since the cabin is really only intended for summer use.

On the other hand, suppose P spent three summers at the cabin, didn't come up at all during the fourth summer, but returned the next summer and the summer after that. Over a period of six years she has used the property for a total of five summers. But her adverse possession claim would fail because her use was interrupted during the fourth summer; she wasn't in possession for five summers in a row. She would have to start counting her five years over again beginning the summer she came back.

P's possession would also be considered interrupted if the cabin's record owner turned up one summer. P would have to start counting her five years over again after the owner left.

However, it doesn't necessarily have to be the same person adversely possessing the property during all five years. In some cases, a court will tack together the periods of possession from a series of adverse possessors, so that they add up to five years. This is called **tacking**.

Case Example: In 1901, when Mr. Costa purchased unimproved property in a Benicia subdivision, he was given a deed describing the west half of Lot 7. But when he took possession, he accidentally moved onto the east half of Lot 8 instead of the west half of Lot 7.

No one realized Costa's mistake, and it set up a chain reaction. Mr. Nelson held the deed to the east half of Lot 7, but he moved onto the west half of Lot 7. The person who received a deed for the west half of Lot 6 took possession of the east half of Lot 7, and so on down the street.

The property owned by Nelson changed hands several times over the years. Each time the new owners were given a deed describing the east half of Lot 7, and each time they moved onto the west half of Lot 7.

Meanwhile, Costa (whose deed described the west half of Lot 7) continued to live next door on the east half of Lot 8. In 1940 he bought property described as the east half of Lot 8 at a tax sale. He had a survey done, and discovered that the tax sale deed described the property he'd been living on for almost 40 years. And that meant his neighbors had actually been living on his property all that time.

A dispute arose between Costa and Sorensen, the neighbor living on the west half of Lot 7, over the ownership of that parcel. Sorensen sued to quiet his title to the west half of Lot 7, claiming adverse possession. Sorensen had only purchased his lot and moved in a few months before. But in considering his adverse possession claim, the court treated all the owners who had held the deed to the east half of Lot 7 and lived on the west half of Lot 7 as a series of adverse possessors. Tacked together, their periods of possession added up to more than 40 years. The court confirmed Sorensen's ownership of the west half of Lot 7. (And his neighbor to the east had, in turn, adversely possessed the property described in Sorensen's deed.) *Sorensen v. Costa*, 32 Cal. 2d 453, 196 P.2d 900 (1948).

LOT 8		LOT 7	
W 1/2	E 1/2	W 1/2	E 1/2
	Costa's house	Costa's deed	Sorensen's deed
		Sorensen's house	unimproved property

Chapter 10

PAYMENT OF TAXES. The adverse possessor not only has to occupy the property for five years in a row, he or she has to pay the property taxes during those years. In the Sorensen case, the court found that Sorensen and his predecessors in interest had paid taxes on the west half of Lot 7 rather than the east half, because the tax assessment rolls made the same mistake that everyone living on the street had made. This was easily shown because the east half of Lot 7 was unimproved and the west half of Lot 7 had a house on it. The tax rolls had always treated the unimproved property (the east half of Lot 7) as the west half of Lot 6, and the improved property (the west half of Lot 7) as the east half of Lot 7.

But often the adverse possessor can't prove that he or she has paid the taxes, and many claims fail because of this requirement.

> **Case Example:** Because a survey stake was incorrectly placed, everyone thought the Hallams' property extended 15 feet further than it actually did. The Hallams planted poplar trees and grass on that 15-foot strip and put in a sprinkler system and a sidewalk. More than five years later, the neighbors (the Gilardis) had their property surveyed and discovered that the trees, lawn, and sidewalk were on their lot, not the Hallams'. They sued to quiet title.
>
> The Hallams were able to establish all the necessary elements of an adverse possession claim, except that they couldn't prove that they had paid property taxes for the 15-foot strip of land. The tax assessments were done by lot number; the Hallams had paid for their lot number and the Gilardis had paid for theirs. There was nothing to indicate that the assessor had treated the 15-foot strip with its improvements as part of the Hallams' lot. The court quieted the Gilardis' title to the strip. *Gilardi v. Hallam*, 30 Cal. 3d 317, 636 P.2d 588 (1981).

The court noted that the Hallams might be able to claim a prescriptive easement over the 15-foot strip, even though they hadn't acquired title to it. The requirements for a prescriptive easement are the same as those for adverse possession, except that the easement claimant's use doesn't have to be exclusive (the owner may be using the property at the same time), and it's not necessary to pay the taxes.

CONDEMNATION

Condemnation of private property by the government is another form of involuntary alienation. Under the U.S. Constitution, the government has the power to take private property for public use. This power is called eminent domain. The California state constitution also provides for **eminent domain**. Both constitutions require the government to pay **just compensation** to the owner.

http://www.eminentdomainlaw.net/propertyguide.html
(Property Owners' Guide to Eminent Domain)

Eminent domain can be exercised by the state, cities, counties, school districts, and other government entities. And limited use of the power has been delegated to some private entities by statute. For example, privately owned utility companies are authorized to condemn property for public utility uses. And nonprofit cemetery authorities can use condemnation to expand existing cemeteries. But whether the entity is public or private, its intended use of the property must benefit the public.

In California, the government (or other authorized entity) must first offer to purchase the property it needs. If the owner rejects the offer, then the government files a condemnation lawsuit. The court will consider evidence concerning the fair market value of the property taken, and direct the government to compensate the owner. Then the court will order the property condemned.

When only part of a parcel of property is taken, the owner must also be compensated for any injury to the remainder of the parcel. So if the value of the remainder drops because of the condemnation, the government has to repay the owner for that loss of value. This payment is called severance damages.

Case Example: Mr. Daley owned a large tract of land known as the Rancho Jamul, which he was planning to subdivide. The San Diego Gas & Electric Company filed suit to condemn a 200-foot wide power line easement across part of the ranch.

The fair market value of the 200-foot strip was determined to be $190,000. But in addition to that amount, the jury awarded Daley $1,035,000 to compensate him for damage to the remainder of the property. The power line project was going to make the rest of the ranch much less desirable as a housing subdivision.

The jury considered not only the ugly steel transmission towers and the noise of the power lines, but also public fear of the electromagnetic fields generated by the lines. The utility argued that there was no conclusive scientific evidence that electromagnetic fields were hazardous to human beings. But prospective buyers might be afraid (however unreasonably), and the jury was allowed to take that into account in deciding on the amount of compensation. *San Diego Gas & Electric Co. v. Daley*, 253 Cal. Rptr. 144 (Cal. App. 4 Dist. 1988).

INVERSE CONDEMNATION involves a situation where a private landowner's property is damaged by government conduct but the government takes no condemnation action. This leaves the landowner suing the government for damages for inverse condemnation.

Case Example: In 1987 the City of San Luis Obispo had a severe drought problem. The city decided to draw down its surface water supply instead of using strict water conservation measures. In 1989, looking for more water, the city decided to drill new wells rather than take available agricultural water. The city's water policy caused subsidence and structural damage to LOVA'S shopping mall when the wells pulled water from the ground under the mall. LOVA sued for damages for inverse condemnation.

The Court of Appeal held that removal of the underground support for the mall caused by the city 's water policy constituted a physical taking of property and damages were appropriate. *Los Osos Valley Associates v. City of San Luis Obispo*, 30 Cal. App 4th, 1670, 36 Cal. Rptr. 2d 758 (1994).

Chapter 10

DEDICATION

Dedication is a gift of privately owned land to the public. Dedication can either create an easement or actually transfer title from the private owner to the local government. In some cases, dedication is voluntary, as when a wealthy philanthropist dedicates a portion of his estate to the city for use as a public park.

Usually, however, dedication is more or less involuntary. Cities often require developers to dedicate portions of their property to public use in exchange for permission to subdivide. For example, a developer almost always has to dedicate land within a subdivision for use as public streets and sidewalks. Dedication of recreational areas or open space in the subdivision may also be required.

Another kind of dedication can be completely involuntary: **implied dedication**. If the public makes use of private property for at least five years and the owner neither openly objects nor grants permission, the local government can declare that the owner has dedicated the property to the public by implication.

Implied dedication may result in an public easement, or in a transfer of the property to public ownership. Either way, the government isn't required to pay the owner compensation. When an easement is created by implied dedication it's very similar to a prescriptive easement, but the right created belongs to the public, not to particular individuals.

Unfortunately, the possibility of implied dedication discourages private owners from allowing public use of their property. So the legislature passed a statute that protects owners from implied dedication. Since 1971, a government body can claim implied dedication only if:

1. the property is coastal property (within 1,000 yards of the ocean), or
2. the government has been improving or maintaining the property to such an extent that the owner should be aware of the public use.

And even in these situations, the owner can prevent implied dedication by recording a notice, posting signs, or publishing a notice in the newspaper. The notice or signs must state that the right to use the property is by permission of the owner. As long as the owner has granted permission, implied dedication can't occur. But if the owner doesn't want to permit public use, he or she must take steps to keep the public off the property, or else risk losing control of it through implied dedication.

ACCESSION

When something is added to a parcel of real property, the property owner acquires title to the addition by **accession**. Accession can occur in two ways: by annexation, or by the action of natural forces.

Annexation by People

When someone builds a house or installs a swimming pool or plants a tree, personal property is **annexed** to real property. As a general rule, annexation transforms personal property into a natural attachment or a fixture, part of the real property (see Chapter 2). Then the owner of the real property also owns the annexed property.

Example: The neighbor kids think the big oak tree on the west edge of X's property would be perfect for a tree house. X isn't a very friendly man, so the kids build the tree house without asking his permission.

Although X isn't even aware of the tree house, he owns it—it's part of his real property. If he finds out about it, he can require the neighbors to remove it. Or he can chase the kids away and use it himself.

However, a different rule applies when property is annexed by a **good faith improver**. A good faith improver is someone who annexes personal property to real property in the mistaken belief that he or she owns the real property.

Example: Q thinks the row of sumac trees marks her property boundary, but her lot actually ends seven yards east of the trees. Q builds a gazebo beside the trees, on her neighbor's land. Her mistake isn't discovered for several months— not until the neighbor sells his property and the new owner has a survey done.

A good faith improver has the right to remove the annexed property: Q could have the gazebo moved over onto her own land. But if she chooses to do that, she will have to pay the neighboring landowner for any damages resulting from the annexation or the removal. A good faith improver also may have to pay damages to subsequent lienholders who believed their liens against the real property also covered the annexed property. This might be a lender who says the improvement was on the property and, in good faith, made a secured loan relying on the improvement being part of the property. Or it might be a mechanic's lien of someone who helped construct the improvement.

In special circumstances, a court may order a different remedy. For example, if the landowner would like to keep the improvement, and removal would destroy it, the court could order the landowner to pay the good faith improver the value of the improvement. Or, if it isn't possible to remove the improvement and the landowner doesn't want it, the court could order the improver to pay the landowner the value of the land. Then title to the land and the improvement would be quieted in favor of the improver.

Forces of Nature

The land itself can move or change shape, and sometimes that results in an involuntary transfer of title. Land beside the ocean or a lake or river is increased by **accretion** when waterborne silt is deposited on the shore. These deposits of sand or soil are called **alluvion** or **alluvium**. A key feature of accretion is that the buildup of soil is very gradual, almost imperceptible. When land is added to by accretion, the landowner acquires title to the newly deposited soil.

When a body of water recedes, the adjoining landowner acquires title to the newly exposed land. This is called **reliction** or **dereliction**. Like accretion, reliction must be very gradual. The waterline must retreat little by little.

Avulsion is *not* a gradual process: land is violently torn away by flowing water or waves. Avulsion does not transfer title immediately; the land torn away still legally belongs to the original owner. If it's possible to identify the severed land, the original owner can reclaim it within one year. After one year, however, the severed land becomes part of the property where it ended up.

Avulsion can also refer to a sudden change in a watercourse. Suppose a river has always marked the boundary line between two properties. Then flood waters tear away the land, and when the flood subsides the river flows in a different channel. The boundary between the two properties does not move, even though the river has moved.

Case Example: Mr. Butts owned land to the west of the Russian River in Sonoma County. When the property was first surveyed in 1856, it bordered on the river. But by the 1950s the river had moved 1,500 feet to the east.

Butts claimed that the river had moved very gradually. He sued to quiet title to the 1,500 feet of land between the river and the property line described in his deed. But testimony in the case revealed that the river's position had changed suddenly, not gradually, as a result of flooding. This was avulsion, not accretion or reliction. Consequently, Butts had not acquired title to the 1,500 foot strip. It still belonged to the person who owned the parcel east of the river, even though the strip was now west of the river. *Butts v. Cummings*, 117 Cal. App. 2d 432, 256 P.2d 52 (1953).

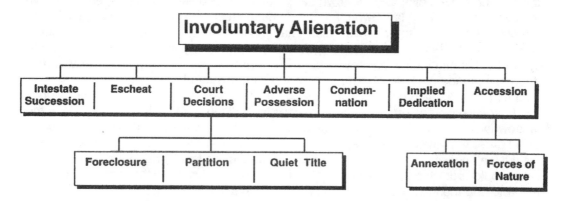

When you consider all the different ways that title to real property can change hands, it's surprising that anyone can keep track of who owns what. That's what makes the recording system and title insurance invaluable for buyers and lenders. They don't take care of all the problems, but they're a big help.

Recording

Just because someone offers to sell real property, that doesn't necessarily mean he or she actually owns it. The seller may be lying, or (much more commonly) there may be some problem with the title that the seller isn't aware of. To limit these risks, every state has recording laws. By making it possible to determine who holds an interest in a piece of property, the recording system protects real estate buyers and lenders against secret conveyances and encumbrances.

 www.zanatec.com/californ.html
(County Recorders' Directory)

After accepting a listing, a real estate agent isn't required to verify a seller's title. That takes place later, when a prospective buyer has been found and a title report is requested. But it's always helpful to know as much as possible about the property you're trying to sell. Through the recording system an agent can find out some useful information about the property, such as:

◆ who is listed as the present owner,
◆ the legal description,
◆ whether there are liens, easements, or restrictions.

Any legal document that transfers or encumbers title to real property can be recorded, and most should be: deeds, easements, restrictive covenants, court orders, long-term leases, trust deeds and reconveyances, land contracts, agreements relating to community or separate property, and so on. Most documents must be acknowledged before they can be recorded.

Certain documents have no legal effect unless they're recorded. These include mechanics' liens, declarations of homestead, attachment liens, execution liens, judgment liens, lis pendens, and powers of attorney for the conveyance of real estate. For other documents, recording is optional—the parties to the document are bound by it even if it's unrecorded. The purpose of recording those documents is to provide notice to others. (The importance of notice is discussed below.)

THE RECORDER'S OFFICE

To have a document recorded, you file it at the county recorder's office in the county where the property is located and pay the recording fee. (If it's a deed, you'll also have to pay the documentary transfer tax.) The document is said to be **filed for record**. The recorder then places the document in the public record. Long ago, this meant that a clerk actually transcribed the document into a record book. Nowadays, the document is photographed onto microfilm.

The documents are microfilmed in the order that they were filed for record—not just according to date, but also according to time of day. This is extremely important, since deed priority or lien priority often depends on when the competing documents were filed. Each document is stamped with a **recording number** so that it can be located in the public record.

After recording, the original document is returned to the person who submitted it. But once a document has been recorded, it generally doesn't matter if the original is lost or destroyed. The public record provides evidence of the document's existence and contents. If a recorded document has a defect in the execution of the instrument or the certificate of acknowledgment or it lacks a certificate, the document does not give constructive notice until one year after it is recorded.

INDEXES. The recorder must keep an index of all the recorded documents. The index is usually divided into two parts: the **grantor/grantee index** (or **direct index**) and the **grantee/grantor index** (or **inverted index**). In the grantor/grantee index, documents are listed in alphabetical order under the last name of the grantor. In the grantee/grantor index, they're listed in alphabetical order under the last name of the grantee.

For the purpose of these indexes, a "grantor" is not just the grantor of a deed, but anyone transferring an interest in property, such as a lessor, or the trustor on a trust deed. And "grantee" refers to anyone receiving an interest in real property: a lessee, a trust deed beneficiary, and so on.

For each document, the index states the names of the grantor and grantee, the type of document, the recording date, and (usually) a brief property description. The index also tells you the recording number of the document, so that you can locate it and request a copy.

These indexes are often divided according to time of recording. For instance, one set of indexes might include all instruments recorded from January 3, 1989, through June 30, 1989. So it's helpful to have some idea of when the property was transferred when searching the record for a deed.

Plat Maps

The recorder also keeps **plat books** containing all the subdivision plat maps for the county. There's an alphabetical index listing each plat by name. (See Chapter 2 for more information about plats.)

NOTICE

When two people have conflicting claims, their rights and liabilities sometimes depend on whether one had notice of the other's claim. You have **actual notice** of something if you actually know about it. You have **constructive notice** of something you ought to know about, even though you don't actually know about it. Constructive notice can come from recordation of documents or being placed on a duty to inquire.

The law holds that everyone has constructive notice of recorded documents. Even if you didn't know about a particular recorded document, you could have found out about it by searching the public record. The law expects a buyer or lender to take that step for his or her own protection. The law won't look after a buyer or lender who doesn't bother.

> **Example:** Summerville grants an easement across his property to Jones and Jones records the easement document. Summerville then sells his property to Kruger. Kruger claims that she doesn't have to honor the easement because she couldn't tell that it existed simply by looking at the property, and Summerville never told her about it.
>
> But the easement is still valid because Kruger is deemed to have constructive notice of it. Even though she didn't have actual notice, she could have found out about it by checking the public record.

However, recorded documents only give a buyer or lender constructive notice if they are within the **chain of title** for the property. The chain of title is the series of recorded deeds transferring title from one owner to the next. The chain can be traced backwards using the grantee/grantor index: the current owner took title from so-and-so, and so-and-so took title from such-and-such, and so forth.

A recorded document is considered to be within the chain of title if the person who executed the document was the **record owner** of the property at the time the document was recorded. In other words, a search of the public record would show that person was the owner during the period when the document was recorded. But if the person who executed the document wasn't the record owner, the document is **wild** (a "wild deed" "wild trust deed," or whatever). A wild document does not give a buyer or lender constructive notice.

> **Example:** Richardson buys a house and records her deed. Later she sells the property to Singer, but Singer doesn't record his deed. Although Singer is now the actual owner, Richardson is still the record owner of the property. Someone searching through the grantor/grantee indexes would find that Richardson was the grantee on the most recently recorded deed, and wouldn't find any sign of Singer's interest.
>
> Singer sells the property to Tanabe, and Tanabe records his deed promptly. Now there's a break in the chain: the record shows only Richardson's deed and Tanabe's deed, and the link between them (Singer's deed) is missing. That makes Tanabe's deed a wild deed.
>
> Richardson is aware that Singer never recorded his deed, and she decides to sell the same property a second time. This time she sells it to Sharif.
>
> Sharif doesn't know about Singer or Tanabe, so he has no reason to look up those names in the grantee/grantor index. He looks up Richardson's name, and as far as he can tell from the record, she is still the owner of the property. So Sharif goes ahead with the purchase.

Sharif doesn't have constructive notice of Singer's deed because it wasn't recorded. And Sharif doesn't have constructive notice of Tanabe's deed—even though it was recorded—because it was outside the chain of title.

A person is held to also have **constructive notice** when there's some indication of a claim or a problem that would lead a reasonable person to inquire further into the condition of the title. If you don't find out about the claim because you fail to investigate any further, you may still be held to have had notice of the claim.

> **Example:** Jarrell is thinking of buying Valencia's house. He visits the property a few times before closing. There's a well-worn path across the front yard that leads to the neighbor's property.
>
> After buying the house, Jarrell learns that the neighbors claim Valencia granted them an easement across the front yard, although it was never recorded. Jarrell sues to prevent the neighbors from using the path. He says he took the property without notice of the easement. But the court holds that Jarrell was on inquiry notice. The path was so apparent that a reasonable person would have inquired about it.

The Race/Notice Rule

What happens when an owner sells property to one person, and then sells the same property to another person? California follows the **race/notice rule**. Figuratively speaking, the two grantees race each other to the recorder's office,

and whoever records a deed first wins. The first to record has title to the property, unless he or she had notice of an earlier conveyance.

> **Example:** Newkirk sells his property to Chang and gives him a deed on June 10. Chang fails to record his deed. Newkirk sells the same property to Murphy on August 15. Murphy has no knowledge of the sale to Chang. Murphy records her deed on August 15.

Murphy has valid title to the property even though Chang purchased it first. Murphy won the race by recording first, and she had no notice of the earlier sale. She didn't have actual notice, and couldn't be deemed to have constructive notice because Chang's deed wasn't recorded.

Murphy is a **bone fide purchaser** for value and without notice—someone who in good faith pays for an interest in land that has already been conveyed to another, without any notice (actual or constructive) of the earlier conveyance. Chang can sue Newkirk for damages, but he has no claim against Murphy or the property.

In the same way, a trust deed lender can be a **good faith encumbrancer without notice**. Once the lender's trust deed is recorded, that lien isn't affected by earlier conveyances or encumbrances, as long as the lender did not have notice of them. The good faith encumbrancer's lien attaches to the property and has priority over the earlier liens.

A subsequent purchaser who has notice of a previous conveyance never has valid title, even if he or she records first. And a subsequent encumbrancer who has notice of a previous trust deed loan doesn't have first lien position, even if he or she records first.

> **Example:** Newkirk sells his property to Chang and gives him a deed, but Chang fails to record the deed. A few weeks later, Newkirk negotiates a sale of the same property to Murphy.
>
> Before Newkirk and Murphy actually close their transaction, Murphy drives by the property to take another look. She sees a man next door out mowing his lawn, so she goes over says, "Hi, I'm going to be your new neighbor." The man looks surprised and asks Murphy what happened to Mr. Chang. Murphy asks him who Mr. Chang is, and the man explains that he thought someone named Chang had bought the property from Newkirk a little while ago. In fact, she sees a sign on the house that says "Chang residence".
>
> Murphy decides to put this conversation out of her mind and go ahead with the purchase. Newkirk gives her a deed and she records it immediately.

The conversation with the neighbor gave Murphy constructive notice of the earlier sale to Chang. She should have investigated further, and her failure to do so was not in good faith. She isn't a good faith purchaser. Even though her deed was recorded before Chang's, she does not have title to the property. However, how will Chang be able to prove what Murphy knew prior to purchase? If Murphy purchased the property "sight unseen", she is still bound by what she should have seen had she inquired.

The recording statutes are primarily intended to protect purchasers and lenders. Someone who inherits property or receives it as a gift is not protected in the way that a good faith purchaser is.

Example: Phillips gives the bank a trust deed on his property, but the bank fails to record it. Phillips later deeds the property to his son as a gift. The son records his deed. The son is not protected against the unrecorded trust deed because he is not a purchaser. The bank can still enforce the trust deed.

However, if the son sells the property to Monroe and Monroe records the deed, Monroe will take title free of the unrecorded trust deed. She is a good faith purchaser without notice.

Recording Problems

A county recorder may be liable for losses resulting from his or her negligence (or an employee's negligence) in recording a document. For instance, the recorder may be liable for failing to record an instrument in the order in which it was filed for record, recording an unacknowledged deed, indexing a document incorrectly, or altering records. Such a failure can seriously effect the parties.

Case Example: In 1993 Stuart and Romero Hochstein were divorced with Stuart receiving the house and an obligation for payments to Romero. Stuart married Portia in October 1986 and deeded the property to himself and Portia as joint tenants. In November 1986 Stuart died owing Romero $19,425. Subsequently, Romero recorded an abstract of judgment for that amount.

However, the abstract of judgment showed Stuart as the debtor and on the reverse side named Portia as an additional debtor. Portia was never named in the lawsuit, served or had any knowledge of it. In March 1988 the Evans purchased the house from Portia. In August, the recorder indexed the abstract under Portia's name. In November, Romero sought to sell the house by reason of her lien.

The Court of Appeal held that the Evans purchased the house without constructive notice of the abstract of judgment because it had not be indexed properly. *Hochstein v. Romero*, 219 Cal. App. 3d 447, 268 Cal. Rptr. 202 (1990).

But the recorder is **not** liable for mistakes made by a person who submits a document for recording. For instance, if a name on the original document is incorrect or misspelled, the county recorder is not liable. The following case shows how important it can be to make sure the names on a document are absolutely correct before recording it.

> **Case Example:** Mr. Orr won a lawsuit and was granted a $50,000 judgment against Mr. Elliott. But on the abstract of judgment that Orr filed for record, Elliott's name was spelled "Elliot" and "Eliot." As a result, the Orange County recorder listed the judgment in the grantor/grantee index only under those two spellings. Elliott later acquired some property in Orange County, and Orr's judgment automatically became a lien against it. Then Elliott sold the property to Mr. Byers. But the title search failed to turn up Orr's judgment because of the misspelled name. As a result, Byers was unaware of the judgment lien and didn't require Elliott to satisfy it out of the sale proceeds.
>
> Orr sued for a declaration of his rights against the Elliott/Byers property. The court held that the judgment lien no longer attached to the property, since Byers acquired title without notice of the lien. *Orr v. Byers*, 198 Cal. App. 3d 666, 244 Cal. Rptr. 13 (1988).

Title Insurance

A title insurance policy is a contract in which the insurance company agrees to **indemnify** the policy holder against losses caused by defects in title. In other words, if there turns out to be something wrong with the title, and the policy holder loses money (or even the property) as a result, the company will compensate or reimburse the policy holder. Different types of title policies cover different types of title problems, and no policy covers every possible risk.

www.caltitle.com/titleins.htm
(What is Title Insurance?)

OBTAINING TITLE INSURANCE

Almost all title insurance policies are taken out when property is about to be transferred or encumbered. The policy holder is usually a buyer or lender.

There are generally two steps in taking out a title insurance policy. The first step is ordering a **title search**.

Most title insurance companies have their own **title plant**, a microfilmed copy of the public record, which is constantly updated. That way the title searchers don't have to spend all their time in the county recorder's office.

Title companies also have **tract indexes** of recorded documents. In a tract index, the recorded documents pertaining to a particular piece of property are listed together. So you can look up Lot 3, Block 9 of the Hindenberg Addition and find a list of all the recorded deeds, trust deeds, easements (and so forth) with that legal description. A tract index is much easier to use than a grantor/grantee index.

The title searcher finds the most recent deeds for the property in question, tracking the chain of title backwards in time. The searcher also looks for other recorded documents that affect the chain of title or create encumbrances. In addition, probate, domestic, and bankruptcy court files may have to be checked, since court orders based on wills, intestate succession, dissolution of marriage, and bankruptcy are often not recorded.

After the title search is completed, a title examiner prepares a **preliminary title report** on the condition of the title. The report lists all the defects and encumbrances of record. These will be listed as exceptions in the insurance policy and excluded from coverage. (At this stage, the property owner may eliminate some of the exceptions by paying off liens.)

The second step in the process is the issuance of the title insurance policy itself. The title company charges a single premium, which covers the entire life of the policy. The policy lasts as long as the policy holder has a legal interest in the property. The amount of the premium depends on the amount of the coverage. A policy with $100,000 worth of coverage would indemnify the policy holder for any losses up to $100,000.

How Title Insurance Works

Sometimes there are latent (hidden) title defects that can't be discovered by a search of the public record. These include forgery or fraud by a grantee, a deed or release of lien executed by a minor or incompetent person, a deed or trust deed that indicates the wrong marital status, and deeds that weren't properly delivered. This kind of hidden defect is usually covered by a title insurance policy; the title company takes on the risk that these defects may exist. (Other problems that don't show up on the public record, such as adverse possession, are often not covered.)

The title company also insures against its own errors. If there's a recorded lien or an easement that the title searcher fails to discover, that encumbrance won't be listed as an exception to the policy. As a result, any losses that result from that encumbrance will be covered. That's also true if the policy lists an encumbrance incorrectly.

Case Example: The J.H. Trisdale Company was buying some property, so it applied for title insurance. The title search revealed that Pacific Gas & Electric had a recorded easement across the property.

The title company's preliminary report and the policy itself listed this easement as an exception from coverage. Unfortunately, the report and policy erroneously stated that the easement holder was Pacific Telephone & Telegraph, not Pacific Gas & Electric. As a result, the report and policy gave the impression that there was an easement for telephone poles and lines, not one for electrical transmission lines.

The Trisdale Company went ahead and bought the property. When the company later discovered the true nature of the easement, it sued the title insurer. Power lines have a much greater impact on the value of property than telephone lines. So the Trisdale Company claimed it would not have paid the same price for the property (or might not have bought it at all) if it had been aware of the power line easement. Since the policy had failed to accurately list the easement as an exception from coverage, the title company was liable for any loss resulting from the easement. *J.H. Trisdale, Inc. v. Shasta County Title Co.*, 146 Cal. App. 2d 331, 304 P.2d 832 (1956).

TYPES OF COVERAGE

A title insurance policy can generally be classified either as a **standard coverage** policy or an **extended coverage** policy. Either type of policy can be an owner's policy (insuring the buyer), a lender's policy (insuring the lender), or a joint protection policy (insuring both the buyer and the lender). Lenders require title insurance to make sure that their trust deed has first lien position (see Chapter 12), and they generally insist on extended coverage. Extended coverage is also becoming a more common choice for owners.

Standard coverage insures against any recorded encumbrances that aren't listed as exceptions in the policy. It also insures against hidden title defects such as forgery, fraud, incompetency, and improperly delivered deeds.

The standard policy doesn't insure against claims and problems that might be disclosed by an inspection or survey of the property, such as unrecorded easements, encroachments, boundary disputes, and adverse possession.

The extended coverage policy insures against all matters covered by the standard policy, plus problems that should be discovered through inspection of the property. In fact, before issuing an extended policy, a title company sends an inspector out to take a look around. The inspector is trained as a surveyor, and in some cases will actually survey the property. If the inspection turns up encroachments, adverse possessors, boundary problems, and so on, these will be listed as exceptions to the coverage. But if any of these problems aren't specifically listed as exceptions, the extended policy covers them. It also insures against unrecorded easements, restrictions, and liens, including mechanics' liens for work begun before the closing date.

A policy holder can obtain coverage for a specific type of problem the policies don't ordinarily cover by paying extra for a special endorsement to cover that problem. However, title insurance companies generally refuse to insure against losses due to government action such as condemnation or changes in zoning. And they won't cover defects and encumbrances created by the policy holder, or unrecorded defects and encumbrances that the policy holder is aware of but doesn't disclose to the title company.

TITLE INSURANCE COVERAGE

Standard Coverage
   Latent title defects
      ◆ forged deeds
      ◆ incompetent grantors
   Recorded encumbrances not listed as exceptions
   Marketable title
   Access to Public street

Extended Coverage
   All of the above, plus:
   Defects that should be apparent from inspection or survey
      ◆ adverse possessors
      ◆ encroachments
      ◆ boundary problems
   Unrecorded encumbrances

Title and Alienation

DUTY TO DEFEND

A title insurance policy obligates the title company to handle the legal defense of the title if someone makes a claim against it.

> **Case Example:** The Jarchows and the Canaviers wanted to buy a three-acre parcel. They took out a title policy with $72,000 worth of coverage. The title search turned up a recorded deed that gave an easement to a neighbor, Mr. Perez. But by an oversight, the Perez easement wasn't disclosed in the preliminary report or the policy.
>
> Shortly after closing, Perez told the Jarchows and Canaviers about his easement. They, in turn, contacted the title company about Perez's claim. But the title company refused to take any action, leaving it up to the Jarchows and the Canaviers to clear their title.
>
> After a successful quiet title suit against Perez (the conveyance of the easement was held to be void), the Jarchows and the Canaviers sued the title company. In the policy, the title company agreed to defend the policy holders' title; by failing to do so the company breached the insurance contract. A judgment was entered against the title company for $7,100 to cover the policy holders' attorney's fees, plus $200,000 for bad faith and negligent infliction of emotional distress. *Jarchow v. Transamerica Title*, 48 Cal. App. 3d 917,122 Cal. Rptr. 470 (1975).

But the title insurance company is not required to initiate a lawsuit for the policyholder.

> **Case Example:** In September 1986, the Mannecks purchased a home for $200,000, and had a policy of title insurance from Lawyers Title Insurance Corporation (Lawyers). In 1988 they had the property surveyed to replace a fence. The survey showed that "virtually everything beyond their back door, including their swimming pool, surrounding deck and appurtenant equipment, was constructed on adjoining property not owned by the plaintiffs." The Mannecks notified Lawyers and demanded an immediate lawsuit for a prescriptive easement. Lawyers stated that they were covered under their policy only in the event they were "forced to remove your existing structure other than a boundary wall or fence" and since there was no impeding removal, there was no coverage for their claim. The Mannecks sued Lawyers for breach of contract for failing to litigate on their behalf and to indemnify them for their losses. Subsequently Mannecks sold the home. The problem was later settled by Lawyers for the benefit of the new owners by getting title to the land under the improvement.
>
> The Court of Appeal held that the language of the policy was clear and Lawyers was not obligated to bring a lawsuit on behalf of Mannecks. Since the Mannecks were not forced to remove their improvements, they were not covered under the title insurance policy. *Manneck v. Lawyers Title Ins., Corp.*, 28 Cal. App. 4th 1294, 33 Cal. Rptr. 2d 771 (1994).

Chapter 10

Abstract and Opinion

Before title insurance was developed, a buyer would obtain an **abstract of title**, a condensed history of the title based on the public record. The buyer would then have the abstract examined by a lawyer, who would give a professional opinion on the condition of the title. But this process did not protect the buyer against latent or undiscovered defects in the title. If the lawyer was negligent, the buyer could sue for malpractice, but that was the only recourse.

It's still possible to get an abstract instead of title insurance, but nowadays virtually all real estate purchase and loan transactions in California are insured.

www.insurance.ca.gov/LGL/Title.htm
(List of Licensed Title Insurance Companies in California)

CHAPTER SUMMARY

1. A deed must be in writing and signed by a competent grantor, include words of conveyance and an adequate property description, and name an identifiable, living grantee. Consideration generally isn't necessary for a valid deed. A deed isn't effective until the grantor delivers it to the grantee with donative intent, and the grantee accepts it.

2. The only types of deeds commonly used in California now are grant deeds and quitclaim deeds. A grant deed carries limited implied warranties and conveys after-acquired title. A quitclaim deed carries no warranties and conveys only the interest that the grantor holds when the deed is executed.

3. A will must be in writing and signed by the testator or testatrix. Ordinarily, at least two witnesses must also sign the will. But a holographic will is valid even without witnesses. A new will revokes an earlier will to the extent that they're inconsistent. A will is also revoked if the testator or testatrix destroys the document with the intent to revoke it.

4. When a person dies without a valid will, the estate passes to the heirs according to the rules of intestate succession. If there are no heirs, the intestate person's property escheats to the state.

5. Property can be involuntarily transferred by court order, as in a foreclosure action, a partition suit, or a quiet title action.

6. An adverse possessor acquires title to another's property through possession and use. The possession must be actual, open, notorious, hostile, and under a claim of right or color of title. It must be exclusive, continuous, and uninterrupted for at least five years. The adverse possessor also has to pay the property taxes for at least five years.

7. Private property is transferred to the government for public use by condemnation or dedication. The government is constitutionally required to pay the property owner just compensation for condemned property. The owner isn't compensated for implied dedication, however.

8. A real property owner acquires title by accession when something is added to the property. Personal property annexed to real property belongs to the real property owner, unless it was annexed by a good faith improver. Title is transferred when natural forces gradually add to a parcel of land (accretion and reliction). Sudden natural changes generally don't transfer title (avulsion).

9. Most documents that affect title to property should be recorded. Each document filed for record is given a recording number, microfilmed, and listed in the grantor/grantee and grantee/grantor indexes.

10. A buyer or lender has constructive notice of all recorded documents in the chain of title. Possession or use of the property by someone other than the record owner puts a prospective buyer on inquiry notice.

California follows the race/notice rule. A subsequent good faith purchaser who records a deed holds title free of earlier unrecorded claims or encumbrances, unless he or she had actual notice of them.

11. A title insurance policy indemnifies a buyer or lender for losses resulting from undiscovered title defects. The title company prepares a preliminary report listing the known defects and encumbrances. Then the company issues a standard or extended coverage policy. A standard policy insures against latent defects and recorded encumbrances that aren't listed as exceptions. An extended coverage policy also insures against unrecorded encumbrances, and against problems that should be discovered by an inspection or survey of the property.

CASE PROBLEM

Far West Savings & Loan v. McLaughlin, 201 Cal. App. 3d 67, 246 Cal. Rptr. 872 (1988)

Mr. Geiger bought some property in Sylmar. His deed was recorded on June 1, 1982. On July 8th, Geiger deeded the property to GTB Properties. But GTB didn't record its deed at that time. On August 3rd, GTB executed a $51,888 trust deed in favor of Ms. McLaughlin. McLaughlin recorded her trust deed on August 10th.

Almost a year later, GTB sold the property to the Stapletons. The Stapletons borrowed $105,300 from Far West Savings, and executed a trust deed in favor of Far West. On July 1, 1983, the deed from GTB to the Stapletons and the Far West trust deed were recorded. On the same date, the old deed from Geiger to GTB was recorded for the first time.

The next year, the Stapletons stopped making loan payments to Far West, and Far West foreclosed. At the foreclosure sale, Far West ended up acquiring title to the property.

Shortly afterwards, McLaughlin (who had loaned money to GTB two years before) notified Far West that she was going to foreclose. GTB had never paid her, and she claimed her trust deed was still a lien against the property.

Far West sued, asking the court for a declaratory judgment to prevent McLaughlin from foreclosing. Far West argued that McLaughlin's trust deed lien could not be enforced because Far West had acquired its trust deed lien without actual or constructive notice of McLaughlin's lien. That gave Far West's lien priority over McLaughlin's, so her lien was extinguished in Far West's foreclosure.

On the other hand, McLaughlin contended that Far West had constructive notice of her lien, since her trust deed was recorded long before Far West acquired its lien against the property.

Did Far West have constructive notice? Or was Far West a subsequent good faith encumbrancer without notice? Was McLaughlin allowed to foreclose?

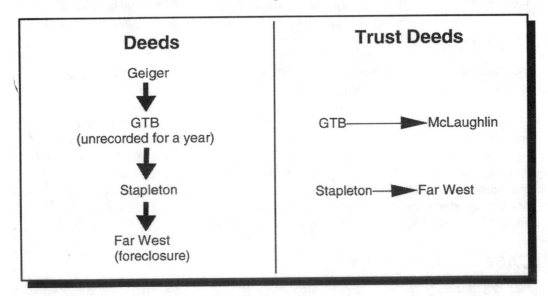

Answer: McLaughlin was not allowed to foreclose. The court held that Far West did not have constructive notice of McLaughlin's trust deed because it wasn't within the chain of title.

At the time McLaughlin's trust deed was recorded, GTB was not the record owner of the property, since it had never recorded its deed from Geiger. So GTB's trust deed in favor of McLaughlin was a "wild trust deed." Someone searching the grantor/grantee indexes is only expected to look for conveyances to and from people the record shows as owners or lienholders during a particular period. Since GTB didn't have a record interest in the property until July 1, 1983, the title searcher didn't look for deeds or encumbrances under GTB's name recorded before that date. McLaughlin's trust deed had been recorded almost a year earlier, so it wasn't discovered.

Even if the person who executes a wild document later becomes the record owner of the property (as GTB did when it finally recorded its deed), the earlier recorded document is still outside the chain of title.

So although McLaughlin's trust deed was recorded, it didn't give constructive notice of her claim because it wasn't within the chain of title for the property. Since Far West didn't have actual or constructive notice of McLaughlin's lien, Far West was a subsequent good faith encumbrancer, and its lien had priority over McLaughlin's. As a result, McLaughlin's lien was extinguished by Far West's foreclosure (see Chapter 10).

To give constructive notice of her interest to subsequent buyers and lenders, McLaughlin would have had to record her trust deed again after GTB's deed was recorded. Then her trust deed would have been in the chain of title. (But that probably wouldn't have helped her in this case, where GTB's deed wasn't recorded until the same day that GTB conveyed the property to someone else. McLaughlin would have had to re-record her trust deed after GTB's deed was recorded, but before Far West's trust deed was recorded, to give Far West constructive notice of her claim.)

CHAPTER 10 KEY TERMS

	conveyance	intestate succession
	dedication	inverse condemnation
	deed	involuntary alienation
abstract of title	devise	issue
acceptance	devisee	legatee
accession	donative intent	probate
accretion	escheat	probate homestead
acknowledgment	executor/executrix	quiet title action
adverse possession	good faith purchaser for	quitclaim deed
after-acquired title	value	race/notice rule
alluvion	good faith improver	recording
annexation	grant deed	reliction (dereliction)
avulsion	grantee	tacking
bequeath	granting clause	testator/testatrix
codicil	grantor	title insurance
color of title	grantor/grantee index	voluntary alienation
condemnation	heir	
constructive notice	holographic will	

Quiz—Chapter 10

1. J conveys her property to M. J is 23 and M is 17. M signs the deed but J does not. The deed doesn't state how much M paid for the property, and M never has the deed recorded. This deed is invalid because:

   a. M is only 17.
   b. J didn't sign it.
   c. it doesn't contain a recital of the consideration.
   d. it wasn't promptly recorded.

2. A homebuyer in California is most likely to take title with a:

   a. grant deed.
   b. special warranty deed.
   c. express warranty deed.
   d. quitclaim deed.

3. A quitclaim deed:

   a. conveys after-acquired title.
   b. carries an implied warranty of marketability.
   c. conveys whatever interest the grantor holds when the deed is executed.
   d. all of the above.

4. R's friend just died, leaving a will giving R her house. R is:

   a. an heir.
   b. a legatee.
   c. a codicil.
   d. a devisee.

5. W died intestate. She is survived by her husband and his daughter, whom W legally adopted several years earlier. What share of W's estate is the daughter entitled to?

   a. Half of the separate property
   b. Half of the entire estate
   c. One-third of the entire estate
   d. None of it, since the daughter wasn't actually related to W

6. When property escheats, the title:

   a. passes to the next of kin.
   b. passes to the heirs.
   c. reverts to the state.
   d. reverts to the remainderman.

7. What's the difference between prescription and adverse possession?

   a. An adverse possessor acquires title to the property, not just an easement
   b. An adverse possessor must pay the property taxes
   c. Adverse possession must be exclusive
   d. All of the above

8. When the government acquires an easement or title to property through public use, it's called:

   a. eminent domain.
   b. implied dedication.
   c. condemnation.
   d. annexation.

9. A trust deed has been recorded, and it's within the chain of title. But the prospective buyer hasn't checked the record. The prospective buyer has:

   a. constructive notice of the trust deed.
   b. actual notice of the trust deed.
   c. inquiry notice of the trust deed.
   d. none of the above.

10. Which type of title insurance policy insures the policy holder against adverse possession claims?

   a. Standard coverage policy
   b. Extended coverage policy
   c. Both a and b
   d. Neither a nor b

ANSWERS: 1. b; 2. a; 3. c; 4. d; 5. a; 6. c; 7. d; 8. c; 9. a; 10. b

SMALL CLAIMS
OFFICE
——————
HUMAN RESOURCES

CHAPTER 11
Escrow and Closing

CHAPTER OVERVIEW

A seller listed property with a broker. The broker found an interested buyer, and the buyer and seller signed a deposit receipt. But there's still a lot to be done before title is actually transferred to the new owner. This stage of the transaction is known as the closing process. An escrow is opened to facilitate the closing.

This chapter describes the closing process. It discusses the role of the escrow agent, the requirements for a valid escrow, and the preparation of settlement statements.

Preparing for Closing

Closing is the consummation of a real estate transaction, when the seller delivers the deed to the buyer and the buyer pays the seller the purchase price. Before closing can take place, all preliminary matters must by taken care of: 1) obtaining title search, 2) clear all liens, 3) performing all inspections, 4) completing required repairs, 5) paying off loans /obtaining new loans and 6) securing title insurance.

When the deposit receipt is signed, the broker usually sets a projected closing date. The closing date is when the documents transferring title from the seller to the buyer will be delivered and recorded.

The most significant factor in estimating a closing date is the state of the finance market. A broker needs to be aware of the current market in order to make an accurate estimate. If many people are seeking financing at the same time, lenders and appraisers may be too busy to act immediately. Then the closing period will be fairly long, perhaps three or four months. If the finance market is not particularly busy, 45 days is a common period estimated for closing. The closing date may be set to take place as soon as reasonably possible, or the buyer and seller may agree to delay it.

Nowadays a real estate buyer seldom just hands the seller the cash when the seller transfers the title. Usually an escrow is opened to handle the details of the closing process. An escrow is not required by law in California, but it is more convenient and safer for both parties.

Escrow

Escrow is an arrangement in which a third party (the escrow agent) holds money and documents on behalf of the principals in a transaction. In the case of a real estate sale, the escrow agent holds the purchase money and the deed for the buyer and seller. The escrow agent distributes the money and delivers the deed according to instructions from the parties.

 **www.ceaescrow.org/**
(California Escrow Association)

In northern California, escrow services are most often provided by **title companies**. In the southern part of the state, **"independent" escrow corporations** are more common. An "independent" escrow corporation is subject to strict regulation. But a number of organizations are allowed to act as escrow agents without a special license: banks, trust companies, savings and loan associations, insurance companies, title insurance companies and California real estate brokers. Attorneys can also perform escrow services for their clients.

Facts About Escrow Organizations

Northern California uses mostly **title insurance companies**.
In **Southern California, independent escrow (agents) corporations** are more common.

Organizations are allowed to act as escrow agents without a special license: **banks, trust companies, savings and loan associations, insurance companies, and title insurance companies**.

Attorneys can also perform escrow services for their clients.

A **California real estate broker** may act as an escrow agent, but only in a transaction where he or she is the buyer or seller, or is the listing or selling broker. A broker can't participate in a transaction only as an escrow agent.

Escrow and Closing

A real estate broker may act as an escrow agent, but only in a transaction where he or she is the buyer or seller, or is the listing or selling broker. A broker can't participate in a transaction only as an escrow agent. A broker also isn't permitted to delegate escrow duties (except for minor clerical tasks) to a salesperson or another broker. The word "escrow" can't be included in the name of a real estate brokerage. And if a broker advertises escrow services, the ad has to state that the escrow services are only provided in connection with brokerage services.

An escrow agent cannot pay, prior to the close of escrow, any compensation to a real estate agent or anyone else when it is contingent upon performance of the escrow. Nor can escrow agents pay a fee or commission to anyone for referring or soliciting escrow customers to them. A real estate developer selling single family homes cannot require the use of a specific escrow company as a condition for the sale if the developer has more than a 5 percent ownerships interest in the escrow company. If the developer does so, the developer is liable for 3 times the amount charged for escrow services but not less than $250 plus reasonable attorney's fees and costs.

GROUNDS FOR DISCIPLINARY ACTION. If a real estate broker is acting as an escrow agent, the following acts by the broker are grounds for disciplinary action under section 2950 of the commissioner's regulations:

(a) Soliciting or accepting an escrow instruction (or amended or supplemental escrow instruction) containing any blank to be filled in after signing or initialing of such escrow instruction (or amended or supplemental escrow instructions).

(b) Permitting any person to make any addition to, deletion from, or alteration of an escrow instruction (or amended or supplemental escrow instruction) received by such licensee, unless such addition, deletion or alteration is signed or initialed by all persons who had signed or initialed such escrow instruction (or amended or supplemental escrow instruction) prior to such addition, deletion or alteration.

(c) Failing to deliver at the time of execution of any escrow instruction (or amended or supplemental escrow instruction) a copy thereof to all persons executing the same.

(d) Failing to maintain books, records and accounts in accordance with accepted principles of accounting and good business practice.

(e) Failing to maintain the office, place of books, records, accounts, safes, files and papers relating to such escrows freely accessible and available for audit, inspection and examination by the commissioner.

(f) Failing to deposit all money received as an escrow agent and as part of an escrow transaction in a bank trust account, or escrow account on or before the close of the next full working day after receipt thereof.

(g) Withdrawing or paying out any money deposited in such trustee account or escrow account without the written instruction of the party or parties paying the money into escrow.

(h) Failing to advise all parties in writing if he has knowledge that any licensee acting as such in the transaction has any interest as a stockholder, officer, partner or owner of the agency holding the escrow.

(i) Failing upon closing of an escrow transaction to render to each principal in the transaction a written statement of all receipts and disbursements together with the name of the person to whom any such disbursement is made.

(j) Delivery or recording any instrument which purportedly transfers a party's title or interest in or to real property without first obtaining the written consent of that party to the delivery or recording.

PURPOSE OF ESCROW

The purpose of escrow is to ensure that the concerns of the buyer, the seller, and the lender will all be met. A buyer is reluctant to make more than an earnest money deposit until it is certain that the seller can convey title as agreed. A seller is reluctant to deliver the deed before receiving the agreed payment from the buyer. The escrow arrangement helps ensure that the seller receives the purchase price, the buyer receives clear title, and the lender's security interest in the property is properly perfected.

Escrow protects each party from the other's change of mind. For example, once the deed is in escrow, the seller can't refuse to deliver it to the buyer just because he or she has had second thoughts about the sale. By turning the deed over to the escrow agent, the seller relinquishes control over it. When the buyer meets all the conditions specified in the escrow instructions, the escrow agent must deliver the deed.

Escrow makes it unnecessary for the buyer and seller to meet during the closing process. This allows them to avoid face-to-face confrontations over any conflicts that crop up. It's also a great convenience when the parties live in different states (or even different countries), travel extensively, or are occupied with other business. Escrow allows closing to go forward even when both parties aren't available.

 http://www.escrowassociation.net/New_Home/new_home.shtml
(The Escrow Association Network)

OPENING ESCROW

Escrow may be opened by any of the people involved in the sale transaction. In many cases, it's opened by the broker or salesperson, who delivers a copy of the purchase contract (deposit receipt) to the escrow agent. In other cases, escrow is opened when the lender delivers a copy of the deposit receipt or loan commitment to its escrow department or escrow subsidiary.

The escrow agent reviews the purchase contract (deposit receipt) or loan commitment to determine whether it can serve as the basis for a valid sale escrow (see below). Then he or she helps prepare the escrow instructions and explains them to the parties. The escrow agent orders a preliminary title report, while the real estate agent orders the structural pest control inspection, and any other necessary tests. If the seller has an outstanding loan, the escrow agent will request a payoff figure from the seller's lender. If the preliminary title report shows encumbrances the buyer won't accept, the escrow agent arranges with the seller to have them cleared. The escrow agent collects and disburses funds required for closing, arranges for all necessary documents to be executed, recorded, and delivered, and finally prepares the settlement statements. In most transactions, the real estate agent works together with the escrow agent to get the sale closed.

REQUIREMENTS FOR A SALE ESCROW

Enforceable Contract

There should be an enforceable contract between the parties before escrow can be opened. In most cases, this requirement is fulfilled by a deposit receipt. But if no deposit receipt (purchase agreement) was prepared, some other mutual agreement is necessary, such as escrow instructions signed by both parties. When there are mutually executed (signed) escrow instructions, a deposit placed in to escrow is irrevocable. Neither party can remove the items they deposit until and unless the escrow terminates. If there are no mutually executed escrow instructions, either of them can revoke their escrow deposits.

Requirements for a Sale Escrow:

- ◆ an enforceable contract,
- ◆ relinquishment of control,
- ◆ a valid deed,
- ◆ an escrow agent, and
- ◆ escrow instructions with conditions.

Relinquishment of Control

In a valid escrow (mutually executed escrow instructions), each party's deposit of funds or documents must be irrevocable. The depositor must give up all right to retrieve or control the deposit for as long as the escrow is in effect.

Case Example: Mr. Wade agreed to sell his walnut grove to Mr. Mosier. They opened an escrow, and Mosier gave the escrow agent a check for $15,000 as earnest money for the purchase. However, Mosier told the escrow agent to hold onto the check until Mosier instructed him to put it into the escrow account. The agent attached a note to the check ("Hold, do not deposit—Mosier will notify us") and kept it in the file.

Mosier retained control over the check, since it was to be processed only under his direction. Because he did not relinquish control, the check was not validly delivered into escrow. (Mosier went bankrupt shortly afterwards, so the check never could be cashed.) *Wade v. Lake County Title Co.*, 6 Cal. App. 3d 824, 86 Cal. Rptr. 182 (1970).

In the event the other party does not execute (sign) the mutually binding escrow instructions, the depositor can withdraw the deposit at any time. But once the depositor has given up control (signed the escrow instructions), he or she cannot regain control unless the escrow is terminated, or the other party agrees to allow the deposit to be withdrawn.

Escrow Progress Chart

	Sch. Date	Actual Date	Escrow Operations
1.			Notice of sale to multiple listing service
2.			Buyer's deposit increased to $
3.			Escrow opened with
4.			Preliminary title searched
5.			Clouds on title eliminated
6.			Credit report ordered from
7.			Credit report received
8.			Report of residential record ordered
9.			Report of residential record received
10.			Pest control inspection ordered
11.			Pest control report received; work—
12.			Pest control report accepted by seller
13.			Pest control work ordered
14.			Pest control work completed
15.			Other inspections ordered
16.			Report received; work—
17.			Report accepted by
18.			Special contingencies eliminated
19.			Payoff or beneficiary statement ordered
20.			Payoff or beneficiary statement received
21.			Payoff or beneficiary statement ordered
22.			Payoff or beneficiary statement received
23.			1st loan commitment ordered from
24.			Received: @ % Fee Pts.
25.			2nd loan commitment ordered from
26.			Received: @ % Fee Pts.
27.			Loan application submitted to
28.			Loan application approved
29.			Loan/assumption papers received by escrow
30.			Hazard insurance placed with
31.			Escrow closing instructions requested
32.			Client called for closing appointment
33.			Closing papers signed
34.			Closing papers to escrow holder
35.			Funds ordered
36.			Deed recorded

Received	Delivered	AFTER CLOSE OF ESCROW	Received	Delivered	AFTER CLOSE OF ESCROW
		Final adjusted closing statement			Seller's loss payee ins. policy
		Check of seller's proceeds			Record deed
		Check of buyer's refund			Title insurance policy
		Commission check			

Valid Deed

A deed can't be the subject of escrow unless it's valid. If the deed is invalid, it can be recalled by the seller. And if an item can be recalled, it isn't adequately delivered into escrow.

> **Example:** Q signs a deed and delivers it to the escrow agent. But the deed doesn't contain a description of the property conveyed, so it's invalid and Q can recall it. Since Q retains the power to recall the deed, the escrow isn't valid. But if Q requested the escrow agent to insert the correct legal description it would be valid.

ESCROW AGENT

In theory, the escrow agent is chosen by mutual agreement between the buyer and seller. In actual practice, the decision is often made by the real estate salesperson handling the sale, or by the buyer's lender.

An escrow agent is a special agent; his or her authority is limited by the escrow instructions (see below). An escrow agent is also a dual agent, with fiduciary duties toward both parties in the closing process.

For that reason, it's a good idea for the escrow agent to be a disinterested third party, independent of the seller and the buyer. But an escrow agent is not legally required to be a completely neutral third party. One party's lawyer or real estate broker can act as the escrow agent, as long as the other party approves and no fiduciary duties are violated. And a lawyer or real estate broker can even act as the escrow agent when he or she is the buyer or seller, if the other party agrees.

 www.ceaescrow.org/consumer.html
(Escrow Consumer Information)

Case Example: A divorce property settlement provided that the ex-wife could buy the ex-husband's community property interest in their Newport Beach home for $70,000. Instead of paying cash, she was to give him a security interest in the property. The ex-husband delivered a quitclaim deed to his ex-wife's lawyer, instructing the lawyer to record it as soon as the ex-wife executed the promissory note and trust deed.

But the quitclaim deed was recorded even though the ex-wife never signed the note and trust deed. The ex-husband sued the lawyer for negligence. The lawyer argued that his only duty was to his client, the ex-wife. The court disagreed. In accepting the quitclaim deed he acted as an escrow agent, and as an escrow agent he owed fiduciary duties to both parties to the transaction. *Wasmann v. Seidenberg*, 202 Cal. App. 3d 752 (1988).

Escrow Instructions

The escrow instructions (also called the escrow agreement) are the escrow agent's written authorization to deliver the deposited funds and documents. They tell the agent exactly what conditions each party must fulfill in order to be entitled to delivery. For example, the buyer's instructions might state that the purchase money can't be turned over to the seller until all encumbrances except the utility easement have been cleared from the title.

Escrow instructions can differ greatly from one transaction to another. Escrow agents and lenders usually provide preprinted forms, but the parties should review the forms carefully. Sometimes a form includes a provision that isn't suitable for a particular transaction. All escrow instructions must contain the license, name and the department issuing the license or the authority under which the person is operating.

Written escrow instructions can serve as the parties' contract of sale if they have no other enforceable contract.

> **Example:** J agreed to sell K his house for $175,000, but they never signed a deposit receipt or put their agreement in writing. When they opened an escrow, however, they both signed written escrow instructions.
>
> J later tries to get out of the sale, and K sues. Without the escrow instructions, K would lose his lawsuit, because the statute of frauds makes an unwritten agreement to sell real property unenforceable. But the escrow instructions are considered a written memorandum of the parties' agreement, and they satisfy the statute of frauds.

However, as long as the parties have some other written contract, the escrow instructions don't have to be in writing to be binding. If the buyer and seller signed a deposit receipt, and then gave an escrow agent oral instructions, the escrow agent would be required to carry out those instructions. Of course, it's always safer to put everything in writing.

The buyer and seller may prepare separate escrow instructions, or use joint escrow instructions. Separate instructions are used frequently in northern California, whereas joint instructions are standard in southern California. In some instances, primarily in northern California, escrow instructions are prepared but not signed until the escrow is ready to close.

Separate instructions allow each party to keep certain information confidential from the other party. (The seller might not want the buyer to know what the broker's commission is, for example.) On the other hand, joint instructions eliminate the risk of conflicting statements or inconsistencies. If separate instructions are prepared and the seller's don't match up with the buyer's in some important respect, the instructions can't be treated as a contract of sale between the parties. (Remember that there can't be a contract without mutual consent to all material terms.)

Once the parties have signed joint instructions or matching separate instructions, they are legally bound to go through with the transaction. If a buyer or seller tries to back out, he or she can be sued for breach of contract, even if no deposit receipt was signed.

On the other hand, what if the buyer and seller did sign a deposit receipt, and that earlier agreement doesn't match the escrow instructions? As a general rule, when two consecutive contracts involve the same subject matter, the two are interpreted together to determine the whole agreement. If the two contracts have material terms that are inconsistent and can't be reconciled, the later contract supersedes the earlier one. So when the escrow instructions conflict with the deposit receipt, the terms of the escrow instructions control.

> **Example:** The deposit receipt states that the seller will pay for the pest inspection. But the escrow instructions provide that the buyer will pay for the pest control inspection.

Since the two contracts are inconsistent, the later contract controls. The buyer will be required to pay for the pest inspection, as agreed in the escrow instructions.

When the buyer is taking out a loan, the escrow instructions must match the lender's loan commitment. If there's a discrepancy between those two documents (such as different loan amounts or interest rates), the lender will require the parties to sign amended escrow instructions. As you can see, it's important to prepare and review the escrow instructions very carefully.

Provisions. The instructions usually state which party is responsible for paying the various transaction costs: inspection fees, escrow fees, the broker's commission, recording charges, appraisal fees, title insurance costs and premiums, and so forth. Later in this chapter, we'll run through a settlement statement, to show how these charges are ordinarily allocated.

The instructions generally include a list of the deposits each party must make (and when they must make them). For the seller, these might be the deed, a bill of sale for any personal property, receipts showing that taxes have been paid, a hazard insurance policy, leases, service contracts, a pest inspection report, and other inspection reports. Depending on how the purchase is financed, the buyer may be required to deposit the full price in cash, or a downpayment and a trust deed in favor of the lender or the seller.

Case Example: The Amens opened an escrow for the purchase of a tavern (bulk sale—personal property) by signing escrow instructions on forms provided by the escrow company (Merced County Title Company). The instructions provided how much the Amens were paying, which included the assumption of $10,000 of certain debts. The instructions also stated that the escrow company would pay any debts over the $10,000 out of the proceeds of the sale. The State Board of Equalization mailed to the Amens, in care of the escrow company, a notice that they should obtain a tax clearance certificate to avoid liability for state sales taxes owed by the seller.

A second warning by telephone was given to the person handling Amen's escrow for the company. The Amens were never advised of this, no certificate was requested and the escrow closed. Several months later the Amens received a notice of unpaid sales taxes of the seller of $4,749.48 and of their liability as seller's successor. The Amens sued the escrow company. The California Supreme Court held that an escrow holder must strictly follow the escrow instructions and a failure to do so makes the escrow holder liable for the loss occasioned thereby. *Amen v. Merced County Title Company*, 58 Cal. 2d 528, 25 Cal. Rptr. 65 (1962).

Escrow Agent's Duty. An escrow agent must follow the instructions to the letter. An agent who acts contrary to the instructions is liable for any resulting damages.

The instructions also set the limit of the escrow agent's obligations. Also, there is a statutory obligation to give a notice to the buyer of the advantages of title insurance if no policy of title insurance is to be issued in the transaction.

Chapter 11

> **Case Example:** A title company provided escrow services for a complicated transaction. The seller was an elderly widow who didn't understand the risk involved in carrying back the trust deed that gave her fourth lien position. Her trust deed became worthless after a senior lienholder foreclosed.
>
> The seller sued most of those involved in the transaction. She sued the title company for negligence and breach of fiduciary duty, because its escrow agent didn't advise her that she was taking a very weak security interest in the property. The court ruled that the company had not acted negligently, since it had followed the seller's escrow instructions exactly. In so doing, the company fulfilled its fiduciary duty to the seller. *Axley v. Transamerica Title Insurance Co.*, 88 Cal. App. 3d 1, 151 Cal Rptr. 570 (1978).

Termination of Escrow

When the parties have performed all the conditions and the escrow agent has delivered the deed and the purchase money, the escrow ends automatically. An escrow is set up for a particular transaction. When that transaction is consummated, the escrow terminates.

But what happens if the escrow conditions are not fulfilled? Then the escrow may be cancelled by mutual agreement, or expire, or be terminated as a result of one party's default.

MUTUAL AGREEMENT

The parties may terminate escrow at any time by mutual agreement. This happens when unforeseen events make both buyer and seller decide they don't want to go through with the transaction.

> **Example:** The sellers plan to retire, sell the house, and spend the next year traveling around Europe. But after escrow is opened, the husband dies. The wife decides she would rather keep the house instead of going on the voyage by herself.
>
> Meanwhile, the buyers have decided to get a divorce, and neither wants to go ahead with the purchase of the new house. After discussing their situations, the seller and buyers agree to cancel the escrow.

When the parties agree to cancel, they notify the escrow agent. The escrow agent will usually send a letter or cancellation agreement to all of the parties, to clarify the situation and resolve any questions. The cancellation agreement should explain which party is responsible for paying any costs (such as title insurance and inspection fees) that have already been incurred. The escrow agent may also charge a cancellation fee. After the parties have signed the cancellation agreement, the escrow agent will return any deposits.

Escrow and Closing

EXPIRATION

Escrow instructions usually state that the conditions must be performed within a certain time limit. As a general rule, when that time expires and the conditions have not been performed, the escrow continues until one of the parties makes a written demand to stop. Once escrow instructions are executed by the seller and buyer, the escrow holder generally will not automatically release funds or return funds until mutually executed cancellation instructions have been provided to the escrow holder.

> **Case Example:** Mr. Pothast agreed to sell some property to Mr. Cly. On April 26, they executed escrow instructions that allowed Cly 90 days to deposit $2,000 into the escrow.
>
> Pothast changed his mind about the sale. On July 16, he sent the escrow agent a letter canceling the escrow and demanding the return of his deed. This was ineffective, because he had relinquished control of the deed, and one party can't cancel escrow unilaterally. Cly still wanted to go through with the purchase, and on August 3 he gave the escrow agent $2,000.
>
> Pothast brought a quiet title action, and the court ruled in his favor. Although Pothast's attempt to cancel the escrow didn't work, Cly failed to make the 90-day deadline stated in the escrow instructions. The escrow expired on July 25, more than a week before Cly deposited the $2,000. After that date, the escrow agent wasn't authorized to deliver Pothast's deed to Cly. Pothast v. Kind, 218 Cal. 192, 24 P.2d 771 (1933).

But as with most contracts, courts don't always strictly enforce time limits in escrow instructions. If the instructions didn't state that time was of the essence, or one party didn't insist that the deadline be met, a court might hold that the time limit was waived. And if one party causes a delay, he or she can't hold the other party to a time limit.

Example: The closing date was set for July 25, but neither party performed on that date. The seller hadn't cleared her title yet, so the buyer didn't deposit the purchase money.

On August 20, the escrow agent finally received the paperwork necessary for clearing title. On October 9, the escrow agent asked the buyer to deposit the purchase money, and he promptly complied.

But the seller had changed her mind, and she refused to complete the transaction by delivering the deed. She believed she was not required to, since the July 25 closing date was long past.

In the ensuing lawsuit, the court awarded the buyer specific performance. The buyer had been ready to go on July 25, and it was the seller's fault that the transaction didn't close then. The buyer was not required to perform until the title had been cleared. The seller couldn't use the missed deadline as an excuse for backing out of the sale. (Based on *Langston v. Huffacker*, 36 Wash. App. 779, 678 P.2d 1265 [1984].)

Chapter 11

DEFAULT

The escrow instructions may provide for cancellation of escrow in the event of default. In that case, it's not necessary to wait for the escrow to expire if one party clearly fails to fulfill a condition. For example, the instructions might provide that if the seller refuses to correct a termite problem as agreed, the buyer may cancel escrow before the scheduled closing date without the seller's consent.

But keep in mind that cancelling escrow doesn't terminate the buyer and seller's underlying agreement.

Case Example: The Shearers agreed to sell their home to the Cohens, and escrow was opened. However, a few months later the escrow agent received a cancellation notice signed by both the buyers and the sellers: "All previous instructions given by Buyer and Seller in the above escrow are hereby cancelled, and this escrow is not to be consummated." The earnest money deposit was returned to the Cohens.

Shortly afterwards, the Cohens filed a specific performance action, asking the court to order the Shearers to go through with the sale. The trial judge dismissed their case. The judge interpreted the escrow cancellation notice as a mutually agreed rescission of the property sale contract.

The appellate court reversed that decision. The notice cancelled only the escrow, not the parties' contract. The Cohens might be entitled to specific performance. *Cohen v. Shearer*, 108 Cal. App. 3d 939, 167 Cal. Rptr. 10 (1980).

Most deposit receipts provide that if the buyer defaults, the seller keeps the earnest money deposit. If the seller defaults, the buyer gets it back. But the escrow agent shouldn't let either one have the deposit without the other's consent.

Whenever there's a dispute over which party is entitled to funds in escrow, it's not up to the escrow agent to resolve the issue. The escrow agent can either hold onto the funds until the parties work it out, or start an **interpleader** action. In an interpleader, the escrow agent turns the funds over to the court. The parties then argue the case to the judge, who decides what to do with the funds.

Case Example: A broker was acting as both real estate broker and escrow agent in a transaction. The parties disagreed about the terms of the sale, and the buyer told the broker the escrow was cancelled. The broker released the earnest money deposit to the buyer without asking the seller about it.

The seller protested that he hadn't authorized cancellation of escrow or the return of the deposit. The broker believed he was allowed to release the deposit because the sale was dead. The Department of Real Estate disciplined the broker for acting without authorization from both parties. The broker appealed, but the appellate court affirmed the DRE's action. *Mullen v. Dept. of Real Estate*, 251 Cal. Rptr. 12 (1988).

A special statutory rule applies to a sale of residential property with one to four units (one of which was to be occupied by the buyer) when the transaction isn't completed by the scheduled closing date. If one party submits a written request for the return of funds in escrow, within 30 days the other party must sign a release allowing the escrow agent to return the funds. Otherwise the party making the request can sue. The court will order the other party to release the funds, and in addition, to pay the plaintiff treble damages and attorney fees. (Treble damages would be three times the amount of the deposited funds. The treble damages award can't be more than $1,000 or less than $100, however.) This rule only applies when the plaintiff is clearly entitled to the funds and the defendant is not holding them in good faith to resolve a dispute.

When Title Passes

When does title to funds or property that one party places in escrow pass to the other party? Unless otherwise agreed, title passes only when all the conditions for delivery have been performed. So the buyer still holds title to the deposited funds, and the seller still holds title to the property. The seller ordinarily stays in possession of the property, collects any rents, and pays the taxes. But when all the conditions have been performed, legal title to the funds or property passes to the other party. In some cases, California courts have held that title passes even before the escrow agent actually delivers the funds or the deed.

The risk of loss as to property or funds in escrow follows legal title or possession of the property. As long as the seller has both title and possession of the property, it's the seller's loss if the property is destroyed. But once legal title or possession has been transferred to the buyer, the risk of loss is the buyer's.

DEPOSIT ....CONDITIONS PERFORMED...DELIVERY

↓

TITLE PASSES
Risk of Loss Shifts

Example: The deed is in escrow, but the seller is still living on the property. The house is destroyed by fire. The buyer doesn't have to go through with the purchase. The seller had both legal title and possession, so the risk of loss was his or hers.

But if the buyer has already taken possession of the property when the fire occurs, it's her loss—even though the deed is still in escrow and the seller holds legal title. The buyer is not relieved of her obligation to pay the seller.

> **Case Example:** Mr. Beck listed his Los Angeles property with the H.B. Eshelman Realty Company. Mr. Hildebrand offered to buy Beck's property for $1,800, and Beck agreed. The broker, Mr. Eshelman, acted as escrow agent for the sale.
>
> Beck deposited a deed in escrow, and Hildebrand deposited $1,800. The escrow instructions authorized Eshelman to deliver the purchase money to Beck as soon as a title insurance policy was issued.
>
> However, a few days after receiving Hildebrand's deposit, Eshelman embezzled all the money he held as an escrow agent for several transactions (totaling more than $40,000). As you might imagine, he left Los Angeles immediately.
>
> Two weeks later, the title company issued a policy for the Beck-Hildebrand transaction. Hildebrand brought a quiet title action to establish that he now owned Beck's property. Hildebrand argued that he had deposited the purchase money as agreed, and all conditions of the sale had been met, so the property was his. But Beck, who never saw a penny of Hildebrand's money, disagreed.
>
> The court ruled in favor of Beck. Hildebrand still held title to the deposited funds when Eshelman ran off with them. Since Beck never took title to the funds, he could not be compelled to complete the sale. *Hildebrand v. Beck*, 196 Cal. 141, 236 P. 301 (1925).

A similar rule applies to funds in escrow. If the escrow agent absconds with deposited funds, the party who holds legal title to the funds suffers the loss.

UNAUTHORIZED DELIVERY

If the escrow agent delivers a deposit before one of the conditions has been performed, title does not pass unless the depositor ratifies the escrow agent's action. The unauthorized transfer or use of another person's money or property is a tort called conversion. The injured party may recover damages from the escrow agent or from the other party, who accepted the wrongful delivery.

RELATION BACK

In special circumstances, there's an exception to the rule that title doesn't pass until all the escrow conditions have been performed. To avoid injustice and carry out the parties' intentions, a court may rule that title passed on the date the deed or funds were deposited in escrow, instead of the date all conditions were performed. This is known as the **doctrine of relation back**: the transfer relates back to the date of deposit in escrow. (This doctrine is also used in connection with option contracts. See Chapter 8.)

The doctrine of relation back is often applied when a seller deposits a deed in escrow, but dies before the deed is delivered to the buyer. Under the ordinary rules governing transfer, the buyer would be out of luck. A deed must be delivered to the grantee while the grantor is alive. However, if the delivery is held to relate back to the date the deed was deposited (when the seller was still alive), the transfer is effective.

Case Example: Mrs. Brunoni was dying of cancer. She asked her lawyer to draw up a will dividing her property equally between her children. But she wanted the will to provide that her son Antonio could buy her ranch for $6,500 (considerably less than its market value).

The lawyer explained that it would be simpler if Mrs. Brunoni sold the ranch to Antonio while she was still living, rather than having him purchase it from her estate. Mrs. Brunoni agreed.

The lawyer wrote up a will leaving Mrs. Brunoni's property to all her children, and also prepared escrow instructions. The instructions required the lawyer to deliver the deed to the ranch to Antonio if he paid $6,500 and agreed to support his mother for the remainder of her life. On June 18, Mrs. Brunoni signed the will and the escrow instructions, and gave the lawyer a deed transferring the ranch to Antonio.

Two days later (June 20), Antonio signed a document in which he agreed to purchase the ranch for $6,500 and fulfill the other conditions in his mother's escrow instructions.

On June 23, Mrs. Brunoni died. Antonio didn't deposit the $6,500 in escrow until July 1. The lawyer delivered the deed to him.

Some of Mrs. Brunoni's other children sued to establish that the deed was invalid, so that Antonio was not the sole owner of the ranch. The court ruled in Antonio's favor, however. In order to carry out Mrs. Brunoni's intentions, the court held that title passed to Antonio when the deed was deposited in escrow—that is, while Mrs. Brunoni was still alive. *Brunoni v. Brunoni*, 93 Cal. App. 2d 215, 208 P.2d 1028 (1949).

The outcome in this case would have been different if Mrs. Brunoni had died on June 19th, the day after she deposited the deed in escrow. Antonio didn't sign a purchase agreement until June 20th. It wasn't until he signed the agreement that a valid escrow was created. Remember that there can't be a valid escrow unless there's a binding agreement between the parties. And without a valid escrow, the doctrine of relation back would not apply.

RESPA

The **Real Estate Settlement Procedures Act (RESPA)** is a federal law passed by Congress in 1974. It requires lenders to disclose information about closing costs to loan applicants. RESPA applies to most federally related loans. A loan is federally related if it meets all of the following criteria:

◆ it will be used to finance the purchase of real property;

◆ it is secured by a first trust deed (or mortgage) on residential property (one to four units); and

◆ the lender is federally regulated, has federally insured accounts, makes loans in connection with a federal program, sells loans to FNMA, GNMA, or FHLMC, or makes more than $1 million per year in real estate loans.

In short, the act applies to almost all institutional lenders and to most residential loans.

Requirements. RESPA has four basic requirements:

1. The lender must give a copy of the booklet "Settlement Procedures and You" (prepared by HUD, the Department of Housing and Urban Development) to each loan applicant within three days of receiving a written loan application.

2. The lender must give the applicant a good faith estimate of settlement costs within three days after receiving the loan application. (An example of the type of form lenders use is shown below.)

3. The lender must itemize all loan settlement charges on a Uniform Settlement Statement. (A uniform statement example is included at the end of this chapter.)

4. The lender may not pay kickbacks or referral fees to anyone for referring customers for any transaction involving a federally related loan.

http://www.hud.gov/offices/hsg/sfh/res/respa_hm.cfm (RESPA)

Settlement Statements

A settlement statement (also called a closing statement) sets out the financial details of a real estate transaction. It itemizes the sums to be paid by each party, and to be paid to each party. It also shows the net amount of cash the buyer will have to pay at closing and the net cash that the seller will receive.

If the transaction is subject to RESPA, a Uniform Settlement Statement form must be used. If RESPA doesn't apply, any one of several different forms may be used. There may be separate statements for buyer and seller, or the statements may be combined.

ALLOCATING EXPENSES

Preparing a settlement statement involves little more than determining the amounts of the charges and credits that apply to the transaction and allocating them to the right parties. The division of expenses is usually determined by the terms of the deposit receipt or other written agreements between the buyer and seller. The way expenses are apportioned may also be influenced by local custom, as long as the custom doesn't conflict with the parties' written agreement.

An Equal Housing Lender

GOOD FAITH ESTIMATE OF SETTLEMENT CHARGES
AND
ITEMIZATION OF AMOUNT FINANCED

Listed below is the Good Faith Estimate of Settlement Charges made pursuant to the requirements of the Real Estate Settlement Procedures Act (RESPA). Loan types ☐ CONV ☐ Fixed Rate ☐ ARM ☐ GEM ☐ FHA ☐ VA ☐ Assumption ☐ Substitution of Liability

This Good Faith Estimate is provided, based upon your application for a loan of $ _____ for _____ years, with a requested interest rate of _____ % (_____ % of Loan to Value). This Loan has a _____ year call option.

Branch _____ Number _____ Purchaser _____
Prepared by _____ Date _____ Prop. Address _____
Application # _____
Mailing Address _____

ESTIMATED SETTLEMENT CHARGES'

Estimate Closing Date _____

		Loan Amount	$ _____
Amount Paid to You Directly	$ _____	Prepaid Finance Charges	
Amount Paid to Your Account	$ _____	Loan Fee	$ _____
Amount Paid to Others on Your Behalf		Loan Discount (Paid by Borrower)	$ _____
Credit Reporting Agency	$ _____	Buy Down Fee (Paid by Borrower)	$ _____
Appraisal	$ _____	Tax registration	$ _____
Title Company _____	$ _____	Private Mtge. Insur. Prem.	$ _____
Reconveyance _____	$ _____	Insurance Reserve PMI/FHA	$ _____
Public Officials	$ _____	Interim Interest $ _____ per Day	$ _____ **
Settlement Fee to Lender	$ _____	Review Fee	$ _____
Inspection Fee _____	$ _____		
Attorney Review Fee _____	$ _____	Total Prepaid Finance Charges	$ _____ (2)
Real Estate Taxes _____	$ _____		
Real Estate Tax Reserve to Lender	$ _____	Total Amount Financed	$ _____
Hazard Insurance Reserve to Lender	$ _____	(Loan Amount-Prepaid Finance	
_____	$ _____	Charges)	

This is a notice to you as required by the Right to Financial Privacy Act of 1978 that the Veterans Administration Loan Guaranty Service or Division/Federal Housing Administration has right of access to financial records held by a financial institution in connection with the consideration or administration of assistance to you. Financial records involving your transaction will be available to the Veterans Administration Loan Guaranty Service or Division/Federal Housing Administration without further notice or authorization but will not be disclosed or released to another Government agency or department without your consent except as required or permitted by law.

Total Amount Paid to Others $ _____ (1)

"THIS FORM DOES NOT COVER ALL ITEMS YOU WILL BE REQUIRED TO PAY IN CASH AT SETTLEMENT. FOR EXAMPLE, DEPOSIT IN ESCROW FOR REAL ESTATE TAXES AND INSURANCE. YOU MAY WISH TO INQUIRE AS TO THE AMOUNTS OF SUCH OTHER ITEMS. YOU MAY BE REQUIRED TO PAY OTHER ADDITIONAL AMOUNTS AT SETTLEMENT." (FOR FURTHER EXPLANATION OF THESE CHARGES CONSULT YOUR BOOKLET ON SETTLE-MENT COSTS.)
++This interest calculation represents the greatest amount of interest you could be required to pay at settlement. The actual amount will be determined by the day of the month on which your settlement is concluded.

Principal & Interest	$ _____ **	Purchase Price	$ _____	Total to Close	$ _____
Mtg. Ins. Prem.	$ _____	Less Loan Amount	$ _____	Less Monies Paid	$ _____
1/12 Annual R/E Taxes	$ _____	Down Payment	$ _____	Est. Funds	
1/12 Hazard Ins.	$ _____	Plus	$ _____	to CLOSE	$ _____
Homeowner's Dues	$ _____	C/C Etc. (1&2 Above)	$ _____	Source of Funds to CLOSE:	
Other	$ _____				
EST. MONTHLY PMT.	$ _____			_____	

**Principal and Interest Amounts for GPM's, GEM's and Buydown (years)
Annual percentage increase in payment _____ %.

1st $ _____	2nd $ _____	3rd $ _____
4th $ _____	5th $ _____	6th $ _____
7th $ _____	8th $ _____	9th $ _____
10th $ _____	11th $ _____	12th $ _____

☐ Adjustable Rate Mortgage: Payment Rate _____ % Index _____ Chg. Rate: Pmt. _____ mos. Int. _____ mos.

The undersigned hereby acknowledges receipt of a photocopy of this page and a HUD Guide to Settlement Costs booklet.

_____ (Borrower)   _____ (Co-Borrower)

PL-040 6-89

Example: It's customary for the buyer to pay for the appraisal. However, in the deposit receipt the seller agreed to pay the appraisal fee. As a result, the custom will be disregarded, and the seller will be charged for the appraisal.

Of course, neither local custom nor the parties' agreement may be contrary to local, state, or federal law. For instance, Veterans Administration regulations (which have the effect of law) prohibit buyers seeking VA guaranteed financing from paying any portion of the loan discount (points).

 www.paterson.com/sfhrestc.html
(Settlement Costs)

TRANSACTION SETTLEMENT GUIDE

A transaction settlement guide shows how the various debits and credits are usually allocated. A **debit** is an amount owed or a charge that must be paid. **Credits** are the opposite of debits: amounts to be received. A transaction settlement guide will help the real estate agent determine what costs will be paid by each party.

Although it generally isn't possible to calculate the exact closing costs in advance, a reasonably accurate estimate can be prepared. Real estate agents are often called upon to make an estimate, since the parties should have a good idea of the closing costs before they sign the deposit receipt. There are standard forms that agents may use in estimating the costs and proceeds, such as the California Association of REALTORS® forms shown below.

BUYER'S COST (Debits)

Obviously, the main cost for the buyer will be the **purchase price**. It appears on the settlement statement as a debit to the buyer and a credit to the seller. In most transactions the purchase price will be offset by some form of **financing**, such as an institutional loan or seller financing. New loans or assumption of existing loans are listed as credits for the buyer. The difference between the price and the financing is the downpayment.

After the purchase price, the buyer's second largest debit at closing is typically the **loan origination fee** (also called the **loan fee** or **loan service fee**). This is a fee charged by the lender to cover the administrative costs of making the loan; it's stated as a percentage of the loan amount. The VA limits loan fees to 1% of the loan amount. Conventional lenders usually charge more (between 1% and 3%). To calculate the loan fee, simply multiply the loan amount (not the purchase price) by the fee percentage.

A lender may charge an **assumption fee** when the buyer assumes an existing loan. FHA and VA fees are minimal, but some conventional lenders' assumption fees are quite substantial—as large as a loan origination fee.

In addition to the origination fee or assumption fee, some lenders charge a **loan processing fee**. This is likely to be between $200 and $300.

For some loans, the lender charges **discount points**. These are a percentage of the loan amount paid up front to increase the lender's yield on the loan. One point is 1% of the loan amount. The VA prohibits borrowers from paying any points (they can only be paid by the seller), but in other transactions the buyer may be responsible for the points. If buyer pays points, they are shown as a debit on the buyer's statement.

Transaction Settlement Guide

	BUYER'S STATEMENT		SELLER'S STATEMENT	
	DEBIT	**CREDIT**	**DEBIT**	**CREDIT**
Purchase Price	X			X
Deposit		X	X	
Documentary Transfer Tax			X	
Sales Commission			X	
Pay-Off Existing Loan			X	
Assume Existing Loan		X	X	
New Loan		X		
Seller Financing		X	X	
Owner's Title Insurance	VARIES ACCORDING TO LOCAL CUSTOM			
Lender's Title Insurance	VARIES ACCORDING TO LOCAL CUSTOM			
Loan Discount (Points)	BY AGREEMENT, EXCEPT VA			
Loan Fee	X			
Property Taxes				
Arrears		X	X	
Current/Not Due		X	X	
Prepaid	X			X
Hazard Insurance				
Assume Policy	X			X
New Policy	X			
Interest				
Pay-off Existing Loan			X	
Assume Existing Loan		X	X	
New Loan (Prepaid Interest)	X			
Impound Accounts				
Pay-off Existing Loan				X
Assumption	X			X
Credit Report	X			
Survey	X			
Pest Inspection	BY AGREEMENT			
Appraisal	X			
Escrow Fee	BY AGREEMENT, EXCEPT VA			
Sale of Chattels (Personal Property)	X			X
Recording Fees	X		X	
Balance Due From Buyer		X		
Balance Due Seller			X	
TOTALS	X	X	X	X

CALIFORNIA
ASSOCIATION
OF REALTORS®

ESTIMATED SELLER'S PROCEEDS

SELLER _____ DATE _____

PROPERTY ADDRESS _____

This estimate is based on costs associated with _____ type of financing.

PROJECTED CLOSING DATE _____ ESTIMATED SELLING PRICE $ _____

ESTIMATED COSTS: **ENCUMBRANCES** (Approximate):

Escrow Fee $ _____   First Trust Deed $ _____

Drawing, Recording, Notary   _____   Second Trust Deed   _____

Title Insurance Policy   _____   Bonds, Liens   _____

Documentary Transfer Tax: Other Encumbrances   _____

   County   _____   **TOTAL:** $ _____

   City   _____   **GROSS EQUITY:** $ _____

Transfer Tax   _____   **APPROXIMATE CREDITS:**

Prepayment Penalty   _____   Prorated Taxes $ _____

Bene/Demand Fee   _____   Prorated Insurance   _____

Prorated Interest (all loans)   _____   Impound Accounts   _____

Reconveyance Deed   _____   Other: _____   _____

Misc. Lender Fees   _____   Other: _____   _____

Appraisal Fee   _____   **TOTAL:** $ _____

VA/FHA Discount _____ Points _____   **RECAP:**

Preparation of Documents   _____   **ESTIMATED SELLING PRICE:** $ _____

Misc. VA/FHA Fees   _____   **LESS:**

Prorated Taxes   _____   Total Encumbrances   - _____

Structural Pest Control Inspection   _____   Estimated Costs   - _____

Structural Pest Control Repairs   _____   Sub-Total $ _____

Other Required Repairs   _____   **PLUS:**

Natural Hazard Disclosure Report   _____   Approximate Credits   + _____

Home Protection Policy   _____   **ESTIMATED SELLER'S PROCEEDS:** $ _____

Brokerage Fee   _____   **LESS:**

Buyer's Closing Costs   _____   Purchase Money Note   - _____

Security Deposits   _____   (If carried by Seller)

Prorated Rents   _____   **PLUS:**

Administrative/Transaction Fee   _____   Proceeds From Sale of

Other Fees/Costs: _____   Purchase Money Note   + _____

_____   _____   **ESTIMATED SELLER'S CASH PROCEEDS:** $ _____

_____   _____

_____   _____

ESTIMATED TOTAL COSTS: $ _____

This estimate, based upon the above projected selling price, type of financing and projected closing date, has been prepared to assist the Seller in computing his/her costs and proceeds. Lenders, title companies and escrow holders will vary in their charges. Expenses will also vary depending upon any required repairs, differences in unpaid loan balances, bond assessments, other liens, impound account, if any, and other items. Therefore, these figures cannot be guaranteed by the Broker or his/her representatives. All estimates and information are from sources believed reliable but not guaranteed.

I have read the above figures and acknowledge receipt of a copy of this form.   Real Estate Broker (Firm) _____

Presented by _____

SELLER _____ Date _____   Address _____

SELLER _____ Date _____   Phone _____

Published and Distributed by:
REAL ESTATE BUSINESS SERVICES, INC.
a subsidiary of the CALIFORNIA ASSOCIATION OF REALTORS®
525 South Virgil Avenue, Los Angeles, California 90020

Reviewed by _____
Broker or Designee _____ Date _____

EQUAL HOUSING
OPPORTUNITY

REVISION DATE 10/2000   Print Date
ESP-11 (PAGE 1 OF 1)

ESTIMATED SELLER'S PROCEEDS (ESP-11 PAGE 1 OF 1)

CALIFORNIA
ASSOCIATION
OF REALTORS®

ESTIMATED BUYER'S COSTS

BUYER _____ DATE _____

PROPERTY ADDRESS _____

This estimate is based on costs associated with _____ type of financing.

LOAN AMOUNT $ _____ INTEREST RATE _____% ☐ FIXED ☐ ADJUSTABLE ☐ OTHER

PROPOSED PURCHASE PRICE $ _____ PROJECTED CLOSING DATE _____

ESTIMATED BUYER'S EXPENSE:

Loan Origination Fee	$ _____
Processing Fee	_____
Funding Fee	_____
Lender's Prepaid Interest: Days _____	_____
Appraisal Fee	_____
Credit Report	_____
PMI/MIP	_____
Other Lender Fees	_____
Tax Service	_____
Tax Impounds	_____
Prorated Taxes	_____
Documentary Transfer Tax:	
County	_____
City	_____
Hazard Insurance	_____
Prorated Insurance	_____
Insurance Impounds	_____
Title Insurance (Owners)	_____
Title Insurance (Lenders)	_____
Escrow Fee	_____
Sub-Escrow Fee	_____
Recording Fees	_____
Notary Fees	_____
Preparation of Documents	_____
Structural Pest Control Inspection	_____
Structural Pest Control Repairs	_____
Physical Inspection Fee	_____
Natural Hazard Disclosure Report	_____
Other Inspection Fees	_____
Home Protection Policy	_____
Homeowners' Association Transfer Fees	_____
Brokerage Fee	_____
Administrative/Transaction Fee	_____
Other: _____	_____
TOTAL ESTIMATED EXPENSES:	$ _____

ESTIMATED CREDITS:

Prorated Taxes	$ _____
Rent	_____
Security Deposits	_____
Other _____	_____
Other _____	_____
Other _____	_____
TOTAL CREDITS:	$ _____

ESTIMATED CASH REQUIRED:

Expenses	$ _____
Down Payment	_____
Less Credits	- _____

**ESTIMATED
TOTAL CASH REQUIRED:** $ _____

ESTIMATED MONTHLY PAYMENTS

Principal & Interest*	$ _____
(at origination)	
Taxes	_____
Insurance	_____
Other _____	_____
Other _____	_____
TOTAL MONTHLY PAYMENTS:	$ _____

*Buyer is aware that with regard to adjustable rate loans, the monthly payment may increase at various times over the life of the loan. Buyer should confirm directly with lender all terms and conditions of said loan.

This estimate, based upon the above proposed purchase price, type of financing and projected closing date, has been prepared to assist Buyer in computing his/her costs. Lender, title companies and escrow holders may vary in their charges. Expenses will also vary according to expenses for required repairs, if any, and other items. Therefore, these figures cannot be guaranteed by the Broker or his/her representatives. All estimates and information are from sources believed reliable but not guaranteed.

I have read the above figures and acknowledge receipt of a copy of this form.

Real Estate Broker (Firm) _____

Presented by _____

BUYER _____ Date _____ Address _____

BUYER _____ Date _____ Phone _____

Published and Distributed by:
REAL ESTATE BUSINESS SERVICES, INC.
a subsidiary of the CALIFORNIA ASSOCIATION OF REALTORS®
525 South Virgil Avenue, Los Angeles, California 90020

Reviewed by _____
Broker or Designee _____ Date _____

REVISION DATE 10/2000   Print Date
EBC-11 (PAGE 1 OF 1)

ESTIMATED BUYER'S COST (EBC-11 PAGE 1 OF 1)

Several other loan costs are customarily charged to the buyer in a real estate sale. These include the appraisal fee, the credit report fee, reserve amounts for taxes and insurance, and prepaid interest.

The **appraisal fee** and **credit report fee** are usually set at a flat rate, which varies depending on the location of the property and the person or firm preparing the report. Residential appraisals usually cost a few hundred dollars and credit reports are generally less than $100.

An **impound account** (or **reserve account**) is a trust account maintained by the lender for paying property taxes and mortgage insurance premiums. The borrower pays a portion of these expenses as a part of each monthly loan payment, and the lender deposits those contributions in the impound account. When the taxes or insurance premiums become due, the lender pays them out of the impound account.

In some cases a lender requires the borrower to make an initial deposit into an impound account at closing. It might be enough to cover six months' or one year's taxes and insurance. In California, a lender can't require an impound account for a conventional loan on an owner-occupied, single-family home, unless the loan amount is more than 80% of the appraised value of the property.

Prepaid interest (also called **interim interest**) is the amount of interest due on the loan during the first (partial) month of the loan term. Interest on real estate loans is generally paid in arrears. In other words, the interest for a given month is paid at the end of that month: the loan payment due on October 1 includes the interest accrued during September. However, when a new loan is made, the interest is paid in advance (at closing) for the month in which closing takes place.

Example: Closing occurs on June 15. Interest for the period from June 15 through June 30 is paid at closing. The first regular payment on the loan is then due on August 1, and it covers the interest due for the month of July.

To calculate the interim interest due, you need to find out the approximate amount of interest owed per day. First multiply the loan amount by the annual interest rate to get an annual interest amount. Divide that amount by 365 to get the amount of interest owed per day. Multiply the daily amount times the number of days between the closing date and the end of the month (in the example above, that's 16 days). That gives you the amount of interim interest that will have to be paid at closing.

Example: Suppose that the buyer's loan in the previous example was for $200,000 with a 12% annual interest rate.

$200,000 x .12 = $24,000 (annual interest)
$24,000 ÷ 365 = $65.75 (daily interest)
$65.75 x 16 days = $1,052 (interim interest)

The buyer will also be required to take out a **hazard insurance** policy (or assume seller's policy). A premiums for at least one year's coverage is usually paid at closing.

Other items typically charged to the buyer include a share of the **escrow fee**, and some of the **notary fees** and **recording fees**. The buyer will also be charged an **attorney's fee** if he or she retained a lawyer. The cost of the **structural pest control inspection** (required by most lenders) may be the buyer's responsibility, depending on the parties' agreement.

The buyer will probably also be charged for **title insurance**. Although the allocation of this expense varies according to local custom, it's common to have the buyer pay for the lender's policy, while the seller pays for the owner's policy. Of course, the parties may agree to any other allocation of the costs, as long as they include that agreement in the deposit receipt or escrow instructions.

Depending on the status of the **property taxes**, the buyer may get a credit or may owe an amount to the seller. If the seller has paid the property taxes for a period after the closing date, the buyer will have to reimburse the seller. If the taxes are in arrears, the seller will owe the buyer. Delinquent taxes (past due) are always owed by seller.

> **Example:** Suppose the closing date is June 15, and the taxes have been paid through the end of June. The buyer owes the seller an amount equal to the tax for the last half of June.
>
> If the closing date were not until July 15, the seller would owe the buyer the amount of tax due from the end of June until July 15.

To calculate the amount of tax payable, you need to know the daily rate of the tax and the number of days for which each party is responsible. The expense can then be **prorated** (allocated) between the parties. Proration is also used to allocate interest on assumed loans, premiums on assumed insurance policies, and rents from income property. (See the proration discussion at the end of this section.)

All California property buyers are required to fill out a transfer statement for the county assessor. A fee is charged to buyers who file a late or incorrect filing. Escrow agents are now suggesting that the buyer file this form as part of closing.

BUYER'S CREDITS

To determine how much the buyer will actually be required to pay at closing, certain credits must be deducted from the buyer's closing costs. The proceeds of a new or assumed loan are a credit for the buyer. If the buyer has already given the lender a deposit to cover initial loan costs such as the appraisal and credit report, that will also be listed as a credit on the settlement statement. And as mentioned above, the buyer may be entitled to credits for some prorations, such as taxes, insurance, or rents.

SELLER'S COST (Debits)

The seller's major cost at closing is usually the **payoff of any existing loans**. The seller may also be charged a **prepayment penalty** in connection with the payoff (see Chapter 12), and will be responsible for a prorated portion of the **interest** due for the month of closing. All of these appear as debits on the seller's settlement statement. If the buyer is assuming or taking subject to the seller's loan, or if the seller is carrying back a trust deed from the buyer, those would also be debits for the seller.

The seller is usually also debited for the **broker's commission**, part of the **escrow fee**, and some **notary fees and recording fees**. And if the seller was represented by a lawyer, he or she will have to pay an **attorney's fee**.

Depending on local custom or the parties' agreement, the seller may be responsible for all or part of the **title insurance premium**, the **pest control inspection** (and any necessary repairs), and **discount points** on the buyer's loan. If the **property taxes** are in arrears, the seller will also owe the tax due up to the date of closing.

The **documentary transfer tax** is ordinarily paid by the seller. This is a tax applied to every transfer of real estate in most California cities and counties. The rate is 55¢ for each $500 of the sales price.

Example: The house is being sold for $100,000.

$100,000 ÷ 500 = 200
200 x $.55 = $110

The seller is required to pay $110 for the documentary transfer tax.

Note that the documentary transfer tax doesn't apply to the amount of any loans the buyer is assuming or taking subject to. If the buyer in the example above had assumed the seller's existing $70,000 trust deed, the tax would only be due on the $30,000 difference between the sales price and the assumed loan. The tax would then be only $33.

If the property is income property, the seller may get a credit for prorated **rents** paid in advance.

SELLER'S CREDITS

The seller's major credit is, of course, the **purchase price**. In addition to this, the seller may be credited for prorated **taxes** and **insurance premiums**. If there was an impound account for an existing loan, any remaining balance in the account will be credited to the seller.

PRORATIONS

The term **prorate** means to divide or distribute proportionately. In a real estate sale there are often expenses that must be prorated so that each party takes care of amounts owed during his or her ownership of the property. Some of the items that may need to be prorated are property taxes, hazard insurance premiums, rents, and interest on loans.

Although prorating may seem complicated, it's really just a process of dividing an expense as of a specific date. The date most commonly used for computing prorations is the date of close of escrow, since that's usually the date when the actual change of ownership occurs. The buyer's responsibility begins on the closing date—that is, the buyer pays the costs for that day.

Example: The seller paid for a one-year hazard insurance policy in advance. The policy runs from January 1 through December 31. The premium was $675. Escrow closes on April 1. The insurance payment must be prorated; the buyer must reimburse the seller for the amount paid for the period from April 1 through December 31.

The first step in prorating this expense is to figure out how much the insurance costs per day. Divide the total cost by the number of days in the year: $675 ÷ 365 days = $1.85 per day.

Since the buyer becomes responsible for the insurance costs as of April 1, the seller is required to pay for the period from January 1 through March 31 (90 days). Multiply the number of days by the cost per day: 90 days x $1.85 = $166.50. That's the seller's portion of the cost.

Subtract the seller's portion from the total amount paid: $675 - $166.50 = $508.50. The buyer must pay the seller $508.50 as the prorated portion of the hazard insurance premium. Of course, the buyer should get an assignment from the hazard insurance company. The assignment will name the new owner as the insured party on the policy.

When figuring prorations, a 360-day year and 30-day months are sometimes used to simplify the calculations. (Thus, although February has 28 days and March has 31, in the proration process both would be treated as having 30 days.) However, now that calculators are available in almost every office, there is a trend toward using a 365-day year (or 366 days for a leap year) and the actual number of days in each month. The method used in a particular transaction depends on the preference of the escrow agent or lender. If the lender is using a 360-day year on a conventional loan, it may tell the escrow agent to use a 360-day year. A 365-day year is used for most new VA and FHA loans.

Some title companies still use preprinted forms that calculate prorations based on a 360-day year and **30-day months**. However, if the client requests it, they will change the form and calculate using the actual number of days. The real estate agent should ask which method is being used; the parties may request one method or the other.

CLOSING

Once the buyer's loan is approved, the lender forwards the loan documents to the escrow agent. Then the buyer is in a position to fulfill his or her obligations by signing the loan documents, which the escrow agent returns to the lender. If all other conditions in the escrow instructions have been met, the transaction is ready to close.

At this point, the buyer may not have seen the property for weeks or even months. It's a good idea for the buyer to inspect the property again personally just before closing. He or she should make sure that the property and the fixtures are in the same condition that they were in when the deposit receipt was signed.

In most transactions, the buyer's lender disburses the loan funds to the title company insuring the transaction. The escrow agent also sends the seller's deed to the title company, with instructions to record it on receipt of the loan funds. A final title search is run to make sure that no new liens have attached to the property. Then the title company has the deed, loan documents, and any other documents recorded. The title company turns the loan funds over to the escrow agent.

The actual closing may take place at the escrow agent's office, or it may be carried out by mail. The deed is delivered to the buyer and the purchase money is delivered to the seller. Each party receives a final settlement statement. The buyer will

also receive copies of the loan documents, insurance policies, and inspection reports. An escrow agent is required by law to issue a settlement statement.

Sometimes there is money left over in an escrow account after closing. This can happen when the actual cost of a particular item (such as the pest inspection) turns out to be less than the amount deposited for that purpose. Often the parties (and the agents) are so concerned with the details of closing that they forget to tie up loose ends. Check to see that there aren't any leftovers in the escrow account.

CHAPTER SUMMARY

1. Escrow is an arrangement in which money and documents are held by a third party on behalf of the buyer and seller. The purpose of escrow is to ensure that the concerns of the buyer, the seller, and the lender are all met before the transaction is final.

2. An escrow agent may be a bank or other financial institution, a title insurance company, an independent escrow firm, a lawyer, or a real estate broker.

3. The requirements for a valid escrow are an enforceable contract between the parties, relinquishment of control, a valid deed, an escrow agent, and escrow instructions with conditions.

4. Escrow instructions are the escrow agent's written authorization to deliver the funds and the deed. They set out the conditions that the buyer and seller must meet before they will be entitled to delivery.

5. Escrow may be terminated when all of the conditions have been met and the transaction concludes; or when the parties agree to cancel the escrow; or when the escrow instructions expire; or when there is a default.

6. Title does not pass to the new owner until all of the conditions specified in the instructions have been performed. However, the relation back doctrine provides that in special circumstances, the date of delivery of the deed to the new owner relates back to the date it was deposited in escrow.

7. The Real Estate Settlement Procedures Act (RESPA) requires lenders to disclose information regarding closing costs to loan applicants. RESPA applies to almost all institutional loans for residential purchases. When RESPA applies, the lender must itemize all loan settlement charges on a Uniform Settlement Statement.

8. A settlement statement sets out the costs each party is to pay and the amounts each is to receive at closing. A transaction settlement guide shows how the various charges and credits are usually allocated, but the buyer and seller may agree to a different allocation.

9. Certain expenses, such as taxes or hazard insurance premiums, may need to be prorated between the parties. Proration is simply the division of an expense so that each party is responsible for the amount owed during his or her ownership of the property.

SETTLEMENT STATEMENT PROBLEM

Using the form on the following page and the information given below, prepare a settlement statement. (You won't have to fill out every line on the form, since some of the items listed don't apply to this transaction.)

This problem is self-contained. Don't add or subtract any expenses to reflect your local customs. Refer to the text or the Transaction Settlement Guide to determine how an expense should be allocated. For computations, use a 365-day year and exact-day months.

Jenny Borden is buying a house in southern California from Manuel Salazar. The purchase price is $175,000, and the closing date is set for December 28, 2051. The seller will pay the broker a 7% commission.

The buyer has made an earnest money deposit of $8,750. She is supposed to make a 20% downpayment (including the deposit), and take out a 30-year conventional loan at an annual interest rate of 10.5% for the remainder of the price. The lender will charge a 1.5% loan origination fee. The buyer will be required to prepay interest from the date of closing until the end of the month (four days, from the 28th through the 31st). The first regular loan payment will be due February 1, 2052.

The appraisal fee is $275, and there's a $40 charge for a credit investigation. The lender's title policy costs $322, and the buyer will pay for it. The buyer's hazard insurance is $260 a year, and that's to be paid in advance at closing.

This year's property taxes were $1,350. The seller has already paid the taxes through June 30, 2052.

The structural pest control inspection turned up some termite damage. The inspection and required repairs came to $500, which will be charged to the seller.

The seller's loan balance at closing is $55,950 and the payments are current; no prepayment penalty will be charged. The seller will have to pay the December interest on the old loan (for December 1 through December 27); the annual interest rate was 9.25%. (This can be calculated in the same way that prepaid interest is calculated.) At closing, the seller has an impound account balance of $286.05.

The documentary transfer tax will be paid at closing. No attorneys were involved in this transaction (which is often true in California residential sales), so there won't be any attorneys' fees. The escrow fees came to $494, and that cost will be split evenly by the buyer and seller. The document preparation fees were $22 for the buyer and $14 for the seller; the notary fees were $10 for the buyer and $5 for the seller; and the recording fees were $18 for the buyer and $6 for the seller. (Lump the document prep and notary fees together with the recording fees on the simplified worksheet on the next page.)

CHAPTER 11 KEY TERMS		
	deposit	prorations
	discount points	relation back doctrine
	documentary transfer tax	RESPA
closing	escrow	settlement statement
conversion	impound account	transaction settlement
credits	interpleader	guide
debits	loan origination fee	
delivery	prepaid (interim) interest	

Escrow and Closing

	BUYER'S STATEMENT		SELLER'S STATEMENT	
	DEBIT	CREDIT	DEBIT	CREDIT
Purchase Price				
Deposit				
Documentary Transfer Tax				
Sales Commission				
Pay-Off Existing Loan				
Assume Existing Loan				
New Loan				
Carryback Loan (Seller Financing)				
Owner's Title Insurance				
Lender's Title Insurance				
Loan Discount (Points)				
Loan Fee				
Property Taxes				
Arrears				
Current/Not Due				
Prepaid				
Hazard Insurance				
Assume Policy				
New Policy				
Interest				
Pay-off Existing Loan				
Assume Existing Loan				
New Loan (Prepaid Interest)				
Impound Accounts				
Pay-off Existing Loan				
Assumption				
Credit Report				
Pest Inspection				
Survey				
Appraisal				
Escrow Fee				
Sale of Chattels (Personal Property)				
Recording Fees				
Balance Due From Buyer				
Balance Due Seller				
TOTALS				

Chapter 11

SETTLEMENT STATEMENT COMPUTATIONS

1. SALES COMMISSION (7%)   .07 x $175,000 = $12,250

2. NEW LOAN AMOUNT (80%)   80 x $175,000 = $140,000

3. LOAN FEE (1.5%)   .015 x $140,000 = $2,100

4. BUYERS INTEREST
$140,000 x .105 = $14,700
    (annual interest)
$14,700 ÷ 365 = $40.27
    (daily interest)
$40.27 x 4 days = $161.08

5. SELLER'S INTEREST
$55,950 x .0925 = $5,175.38
    (annual interest)
$5,175.38 ÷ 365 = $14.18
    (daily interest)
$14.18 x 27 days = $382.86

6. PROPERTY TAX PRORATION
$1,350 ÷ 365 = $3.70 per day
$3.70 x 185 days = $684.50
(buyer owes seller)

7. TRANSFER TAX
$175,000 ÷ 500 = 350
350 x .55 = $192.50

8. DUE FROM BUYER
Total Debits $179,107.58
Total Credits <u>-148.750.00</u>
           $30,357.58

9. DUE TO SELLER
Total Credits $175,970.55
Total Debits   <u>-79.123.36</u>
        $ 96,847.19

Escrow and Closing

	BUYER'S STATEMENT		SELLER'S STATEMENT	
	DEBIT	CREDIT	DEBIT	CREDIT
Purchase Price	$175,000.00			$175,000.00
Deposit		8,750.00	8,750.00	
Documentary Transfer Tax			192.50	
Sales Commission			12,250.00	
Pay-Off Existing Loan			55,950.00	
Assume Existing Loan				
New Loan		140,000.00		
Carryback Loan (Seller Financing)				
Owner's Title Insurance			845.00	
Lender's Title Insurance	322.00			
Loan Discount (Points)				
Loan Fee	2,100.00			
Property Taxes				
Arrears				
Current/Not Due				
Prepaid	684.50			684.50
Hazard Insurance				
Assume Policy				
New Policy	260.00			
Interest				
Pay-off Existing Loan			382.86	
Assume Existing Loan				
New Loan (Prepaid Interest)	161.08			
Impound Accounts				
Pay-off Existing Loan				286.05
Assumption				
Credit Report	40.00			
Pest Inspection			500.00	
Survey				
Appraisal	275.00			
Escrow Fee	247.00		247.00	
Sale of Chattels (Personal Property)				
Recording Fees	18.00		6.00	
Balance Due From Buyer		30,357.58		
Balance Due Seller			96,847.19	
TOTALS	179,107.58	179,107.58	175,970.55	175,970.55

A.	B. TYPE OF LOAN
U.S. DEPARTMENT OF HOUSING AND URBAN DEVELOPMENT	1..[ ] FHA 2. [ ] FmHA 3. [ ] Conv. units
SETTLEMENT STATEMENT	4. [ ] VA 5. [XX] Conv. ins
	6. ESCROW NUMBER: 7. LOAN NUMBER
	10984
	8. MORTGAGE INSURANCE NUMBER:

NOTE: THIS FORM IS FURNISHED TO GIVE YOU A STATEMENT OF THE ACTUAL SETTLEMENT COSTS. AMOUNTS PAID TO AND BY THE SETTLEMENT
ARE SHOWN. ITEMS MARKED "(P.O.C.)" WERE PAID OUTSIDE OF THE CLOSING: THEY ARE SHOWN HERE FOR INFORMATIONAL PURPOSES AND ARE NOT
INCLUDED IN THE TOTALS.

D. NAME OF BORROWER:	E. NAME OF SELLER:	F. NAME OF LENDER:
Jennifer Borden	Manuel Salazar	Miracle Savings, , , CA

G. PROPERTY LOCATION:	H. SETTLEMENT AGENT:	I. SETTLEMENT DATE:
Lot 3, Block 9, Highland Heights , CA	Chicago Title Co. - Laguna Escrow Branch	12/28/51
	PLACE OF SETTLEMENT: 917 Glenneyre Street Laguna Beach, CA 92651	

J. SUMMARY OF BORROWER'S TRANSACTIONS		K. SUMMARY OF SELLER'S TRANSACTIONS	
100. GROSS AMOUNT DUE FROM BORROWER		400. GROSS AMOUNT DUE TO SELLER	
101. Contract sales price	175,000.00	401. Contract sales price	175,000.00
102. Personal property		402. Personal property	
103. Chgs to borrower (fm. 1400)	3,455.08	403.	
104.		404.	
105.		405.	
Adjustments items paid by seller in advance		Adjustments items paid by seller in advance	
106. Taxes-12/28/51 to 01/01/52	684.50	406. Taxes-12/28/51 to 01/01/52	684.50
107.		407.	
108.		408.	
109.		409.	
110.		410.	
111.		411.	
112.		412.	
120. GROSS AMOUNT DUE FROM BORROWER	179,139.58	420. GROSS AMOUNT DUE TO SELLER	175,684.50
200. AMOUNTS PAID BY OR IN BEHALF OF BORROWER		500. REDUCTIONS IN AMOUNT DUE TO SELLER	
201. Principal amt of new loan	140,000.00	501. Excess deposit	
202.		502. Chgs to seller (fm. 1400)	14,059.50
203.		503. Payoff of First mortgage	55,950.00
204.		504. Interest due	382.86
205.		505. Impound account	(286.05)
206.		506.	
207.		507.	
208.		508.	
209. Deposit	8,750.00	509.	
Adjustments items paid by seller in advance		Adjustments items paid by seller in advance	
210.		510.	
211.		511.	
212.		512.	
213.		513.	
214.		514.	
215.		515.	
216.		516.	
217.		517.	
218.		518.	
219.		519.	
220. TOTAL PAID BY/FOR BORROWER	148,750.00	520. TOTAL REDUCTIONS IN AMOUNT DUE SELLER	70,106.31
300. CASH AT SETTLEMENT FROM/TO BORROWER		600. CASH AT SETTLEMENT FROM/TO SELLER	
301. Gross amounts due FROM BORROWER (line 120)	179,139.58	601. Gross amount due to SELLER (line 420)	175,684.50
302. Less amounts due BY/FOR BORROWER (line 220)	(148,750.00)	602. Less reductions in amount due SELLER (line 520)	(70,106.31)
303. CASH FROM BORROWER	30,389.58	603. CASH TO SELLER	105,578.19

L. SETTLEMENT STATEMENT	Escrow: 10984-CR	
700. TOTAL SALES/BROKER'S COMMISSION	PAID FROM BORROWER'S FUNDS AT SETTLEMENT	PAID FROM SELLER'S FUNDS AT SETTLEMENT
Division of Commission (line 700) as follows:		
701.12,250.00 to		
702.		
703.Commission Paid at Settlement		12,250.00
704.		
800. ITEMS PAYABLE IN CONNECTION WITH LOAN		
801.Loan Origination Fee	2,100.00	
802.		
803.Appraisal Fee	275.00	
804.Credit Report	40.00	
805.		
806.		
807.		
808.		
809.		
810.		
811.		
900. ITEMS REQUIRED BY LENDER TO BE PAID IN ADVANCE		
901.Interest at 40.27 from 12/28/51 to 01/01/52	161.08	
902.New Insurance to	260.00	
903.		
904.		
905.		
1000. RESERVES DEPOSITED WITH LENDER		
1001.City Property Taxes		
1002.		
1003.		
1004.		
1005.		
1006.		
1007.		
1008.		
1100. ESCROW AND TITLE CHARGES		
1101.Settlement or closing Fee to Chicago Title Co. - Laguna	247.00	247.00
1102.Document Preparation	22.00	
1103.Other Chgs - See Attch	10.00	19.00
1104.		
1105.		
1106.		
1107.		
1108.Title Insurance Premium	322.00	845.00
1109.Lenders Coverage $199,000.00		
1110.Owner's Coverage $199,800.00		
1111.		
1112.		
1113.		
1200. GOVERNMENT RECORDING AND TRANSFER CHARGES		
1201.Rec. Fees: Deed $6.00 Mortgage $12.00 Releases $6.00	18.00	6.00
1202.City/County tax/Stamps:		
1203.State Tax/Stamps $192.50		192.50
1204.Deed $0.00		
1205.		
1300. ADDITIONAL SETTLEMENT CHARGES		
1301.Pest Inspection to		500.00
1302.		
1303.		
1304.		
1305.		
1306.		
1307.		
1400. TOTAL SETTLEMENT CHARGES (ENTER ON LINES 102 SECTION J AND 501, SECTION K)	3,455.08	14,059.50

Chapter 11

Escrow and Closing

Quiz—Chapter 11

1. After the deposit receipt is signed, the closing date:
a. must be within 30 days.
b. can't be scheduled for at least 90 days.
c. is usually scheduled according to how busy the finance market is.
d. is usually set by the seller.

2. The seller deposits a valid deed into escrow. Two weeks later, he changes his mind about the sale and instructs the escrow agent to return the deed to him. The escrow agent:
a. must return the deed to the seller by the end of the next business day.
b. should cancel the escrow immediately.
c. may not return the deed to the seller without the buyer's consent.
d. may not return the deed to the seller without a court order.

3. While escrow is open, the escrow agent is:
a. a dual agent.
b. the lender's agent.
c. the seller's agent.
d. the buyer's agent.

4. Title to the property passes to the buyer:
a. as soon as the seller deposits the deed in escrow.
b. when an acceptable title report has been issued.
c. on the closing date set in the escrow instructions, unless the seller unilaterally cancels the escrow.
d. when all the conditions specified in the instructions have been fulfilled.

5. If the escrow instructions don't match the loan commitment prepared by the buyer's lender:
a. the escrow agent must follow the instructions anyway.
b. the lender will require the parties to sign amended escrow instructions.
c. the terms of the deposit receipt control.
d. the escrow is invalid.

6. Under RESPA, a loan is considered federally related if:
a. it will be used to finance the purchase of residential property.
b. it is secured by a first trust deed.
c. the lender is federally regulated.
d. it meets all of the criteria listed in a, b, and c.

7. A lender requires the buyer to prepay interest at closing:
a. to increase the lender's yield on the loan.
b. to make sure that the credit report on the buyer was accurate.
c. for the period from the closing date through the last day of the month in which closing takes place.
d. for the first six months of the loan term.

8. A buyer usually pays:
a. the loan fee.
b. the real estate broker's commission.
c. the prepayment penalty.
d. nothing.

9. A seller usually pays:
a. the appraisal fee.
b. the documentary transfer tax.
c. the hazard insurance premium.
d. all of the above.

10. When an expense is prorated it means that it:
a. does not appear on the settlement statement.
b. is paid by the buyer's lender.
c. is not paid until after closing.
d. is divided between the buyer and the seller.

CHAPTER 12
Real Estate Financing

CHAPTER OVERVIEW

It takes a lot more than pocket change to buy real estate. As a result, most real estate purchases involve a loan, and some involve more than one. Buyers, sellers, and real estate agents need to understand the rights and obligations of borrowers and lenders. Buyers, since they'll be borrowers; sellers, since they may be lenders; and agents, since they'll have to help the parties obtain financing.

This chapter explains promissory notes and security agreements, the basic financing documents. It describes the foreclosure process—what happens when a borrower defaults. And it takes a brief look at the land contract, a security device no longer widely used in California. The chapter closes with an overview of some state and federal consumer protection laws that regulate real estate lending.

Promissory Notes

A **promissory note** makes a promise to repay a debt. One person loans another money, and the other signs a promissory note, promising to repay the loan (plus interest, in most cases). The borrower who signs the note is called the **maker**, and the lender is called the **payee**. Today, almost all promissory notes are negotiable instruments. One reason this is true is because of secondary marketing. Unless the promissory note given for a real estate loan is negotiable, it will be very difficult for the lender to sell the loan on the secondary market. The big agencies such as the Federal National Mortgage Association (FNMA) and Federal Home Loan Mortgage Corporation (FHLMC) won't even consider it. A copy of a standard negotiable promissory note is reprinted later.

Relationship between Promissory Note and Security Agreement. A person borrowing money to buy real estate signs a promissory note in favor of the lender. In addition, the borrower signs a **security agreement**, such as a deed of trust or mortgage. The security agreement is a contract that makes the real property collateral for the loan. It creates a lien on the property. If the borrower doesn't repay as agreed in the promissory note, the security agreement gives the lender the right to foreclose. Basically, in foreclosure the property is sold and the proceeds are used to pay off the loan balance.

A promissory note can be enforced whether or not it is accompanied by a security agreement. The payee/lender can file a lawsuit and obtain a judgment if the maker/borrower breaches by failing to repay. But without a security agreement, the judgment may turn out to be uncollectible. For example, the borrower may already have resold the property, so there's nothing left for a judgment lien to attach to.

Note and Security Agreement

Real Estate Financing Documents

1. PROMISSORY NOTE—a promise to repay a loan; states the terms of repayment and gives the lender the right to sue

2. SECURITY AGREEMENT—creates a lien against the property and gives the lender the right to foreclose after default; deed of trust or mortgage

---

By creating a lien on the property at the time of the loan, a security agreement ensures that the lender will be able to get at least some of its money back. Because real estate loans are substantial sums, they are virtually always secured. Security agreements will be discussed in detail in the next section of the chapter. For now, let's look more closely at promissory notes.

BASIC NOTE PROVISIONS

In a real estate loan transaction, the promissory note should state that it is secured. The note should identify the security agreement by date or recording number. The note and the security agreement are signed on the same date, and are linked together. If the lender negotiates the note, the security interest in the property is automatically transferred along with it. And the security agreement can't be assigned unless the right to payment under the note is also transferred too.

The note generally states the loan amount (the **principal**), the amount of the payments, and when and how the payments are to be made. It includes the **maturity date**, when the loan is to be fully paid. The note also lists the interest rate, which may be either fixed or adjustable.

STRAIGHT NOTE

$ California 19

after date, for value received,

I/We promise to pay in lawful money of the United States of America, to

or order, at place designated by payee, the principal sum of

DOLLARS,

with interest in like lawful money from , until paid at the

rate of per cent per annum, payable

Principal and interest payable in lawful money of the United States of America. Should default be made in payment of interest when due the whole sum of principal and interest shall become immediately due at the option of the holder of this note. If action be instituted on this note I promise to pay such sum as the Court may fix as Attorney's fees. This note is secured by a Deed of Trust.

....

....

FTG-3014

387

When a noninstitutional lender (a private individual or business, as opposed to a bank, savings and loan, or similar regulated lending institution) makes an adjustable rate loan secured by residential property with four units or less, California law requires the promissory note to include this warning in large, boldface type: **NOTICE TO BORROWER: THIS DOCUMENT CONTAINS PROVISIONS FOR AN ADJUSTABLE INTEREST RATE.** The law also places a number of restrictions on noninstitutional, residential, adjustable rate loans; for example, the rate can't change more than once every six months.

Promissory notes are classified according to the way the principal and interest are to be paid. With a **straight note**, the periodic payments are interest only, and the full amount of the principal is due in a lump sum when the loan term ends. With an **installment note**, the periodic payments include part of the principal as well as interest. If the installment note is **fully amortized**, the amount of the payments is enough to pay off the entire loan, both principal and interest, by the end of the term. If it is only **partially amortized**, the payments don't cover the full amount of principal and interest, and a balloon payment will be due at the end of the term.

A **balloon payment** is a final payment that is much larger than the earlier payments. Borrowers often find it more difficult than they anticipated to come up with the extra money at the end of the loan. As a result, California law doesn't allow balloon payments on certain loans secured by residential property. (That rule is explained in connection with the Mortgage Loan Broker Law, at the end of this chapter.) And when a residential loan with a term longer than one year calls for a balloon payment, the lender is usually required to send the borrower a reminder notice at least 90 days (but not more than 150 days) before the balloon payment is due.

A promissory note usually contains provisions that explain the consequences of failure to pay as agreed. Real estate lenders often protect themselves with late charges, acceleration clauses, and similar provisions. All of these are recited in the promissory note. We'll discuss these and other optional loan terms later in the chapter, after an overview of security agreements.

Security Agreements

As you've seen, a loan can be secured or unsecured. An unsecured lender has a legal right to be repaid, but there's no assurance that a judgment against the borrower will be collectible. So lenders prefer to obtain a security interest in the borrower's property. Then if the borrower defaults, the lender can recover the money by having the property sold.

Hypothecation. The oldest and simplest security arrangement is the pawnbroker's. To borrow money from a pawnbroker, you have to bring in some property as security for the loan—your great-grandfather's gold watch, for example. If you repay the loan within a specified period, you get the watch back. But if that period expires and you haven't paid the pawnbroker, he or she will sell the watch and keep the proceeds. The legal term for this system is **pledging**; your great-grandfather's watch is the pledge.

In pledging, you're required to turn over possession of the security property to the lender. But the security arrangement for a real estate loan is more sophisticated. You don't have to give up possession of your house to get the loan. You only have to grant the lender the right to sell the house in case you default. This is called **hypothecation**.

According to the original theory behind real estate security agreements, the borrower transferred title to the property to the lender (or a neutral third party) during the loan period. When the loan was paid off, title was transferred back to the borrower. The language in some security agreements still reflects this theory, stating that the borrower "conveys" the property; and after the loan is paid off, a "reconveyance" is recorded. But this is essentially a legal fiction. For all practical purposes, the security agreement merely creates a voluntary lien against the property (see Chapter 3), and no real transfer of title is involved. The lien enables the lender to foreclose if the borrower defaults.

Deeds of trust and mortgages. There are two main types of real property security agreements: **deeds of trust** (also called **trust deeds**) and **mortgages**. Either type must be in writing and must meet the formal requirements for a deed (see Chapter 7). Either creates a lien on everything that would be transferred by a deed—so it includes the fixtures and the appurtenances such as water rights, as well as the land and the improvements (see Chapter 2).

The key difference between the two types is their foreclosure procedures. A mortgage must be foreclosed judicially—that is, by filing a lawsuit. But a deed of trust is usually foreclosed nonjudicially, without going to court. That saves the lender a lot of time, money and effort.

In California, nearly all lenders use deeds of trust instead of mortgages. (A survey of California title insurers indicated that deeds of trust are used in about 98% of all recorded real estate transactions.) For this reason, our discussion will focus on deeds of trust.

 www.catrustee.org/
(California Trustee's Association - CTA)

DEEDS OF TRUST

There are three parties to a deed of trust: the **trustor** (the borrower), the **beneficiary** (the lender), and the **trustee** (a neutral third party). The trustor makes payments to the beneficiary; the trustee steps in to conduct foreclosure proceedings in case of default.

Institutional lenders (that is, banks and savings and loans) almost always use standard forms for their trust deeds. This is necessary if the loan is going to be sold to the FNMA or FHLMC. The secondary marketing agencies require the use of standard forms because they don't have time to review all the terms of a complicated security agreement for each transaction, and because they insist on certain protective provisions. A copy of a deed of trust for single-family residences is reprinted here.

Basic Provisions

A trust deed identifies the parties and almost always includes a full legal description of the security property. A lender doesn't want there to be any doubt about what its lien covers, in case foreclosure is necessary.

SHORT FORM DEED OF TRUST AND ASSIGNMENT OF RENTS

This Deed of Trust, made this _____ day of _____ , between _____ , herein called TRUSTOR,

whose address is _____

(number and street)   (city)   (state)   (zip)

OLD REPUBLIC TITLE COMPANY, a California corporation, herein called TRUSTEE, and

_____ , herein called BENEFICIARY,

Witnesseth: That Trustor IRREVOCABLY GRANTS, TRANSFERS AND ASSIGNS TO TRUSTEE IN TRUST, WITH POWER OF SALE, that property in _____ County, California, described on *"Exhibit A" attached hereto*

In the event the herein described property or any part thereof, or any interest therein is sold, agreed to be sold, conveyed or alienated by the Trustor, or by the operation of law or otherwise, all obligations secured by this instrument, irrespective of the maturity dates expressed therein, at the option of the holder hereof and without demand or notice shall immediately become due and payable.

TOGETHER WITH the rents, issues and profits thereof, SUBJECT, HOWEVER, to the right, power and authority given to and conferred upon Beneficiary by paragraph (10) of the provisions incorporated herein by reference to collect and apply such rents, issues and profits.

For the Purpose of Securing: 1. Performance of each agreement of Trustor incorporated by reference or contained herein. 2. Payment of the indebtedness evidenced by one promissory note of even date herewith, and any extension or renewal thereof, in the principal sum of $ _____ executed by Trustor in favor of Beneficiary or order. 3. Payment of such further sums as the then record owner of said property hereafter may borrow from Beneficiary, when evidenced by another note (or notes) reciting it is so secured.

To Protect the Security of This Deed of Trust, Trustor Agrees: By the execution and delivery of this Deed of Trust and the note secured hereby, that provisions (1) to (14), inclusive, of the fictitious deed of trust recorded in Santa Barbara County and Sonoma County October 18, 1961, and in all other counties October 23, 1961, in the book and at the page of Official Records in the office of the county recorder of the county where said property is located, noted below opposite the name of such county, viz.:

COUNTY	BOOK	PG	COUNTY	BOOK	PG	COUNTY	BOOK	PG	COUNTY	BOOK	PG	COUNTY	BOOK	PG
Alameda	435	684	Imperial	1091	501	Modoc	184	851	San Diego Series 2 Book 1961 Page 183887			Sonoma	1851	689
Alpine	1	250	Inyo	147	598	Mono	52	429	San Francisco	A332	905	Stanislaus	1715	456
Amador	104	348	Kern	3427	60	Monterey	2194	538	San Joaquin	2470	311	Sutter	572	297
Butte	1145	1	Kings	792	833	Napa	639	86	San Luis Obispo	1151	12	Tehama	401	289
Calaveras	145	152	Lake	362	39	Nevada	305	320	San Mateo	4078	420	Trinity	93	366
Colusa	296	617	Lassen	171	471	Orange	5889	611	Santa Barbara	1878	860	Tulare	2294	275
Contra Costa	3978	47	Los Angeles	T2055	899	Placer	895	301	Santa Clara	5336	341	Tuolumne	135	47
Del Norte	78	414	Madera	810	170	Plumas	151	5	Santa Cruz	1431	494	Ventura	2062	386
El Dorado	568	456	Marin	1508	339	Riverside	3005	523	Shasta	684	528	Yolo	653	245
Fresno	4626	572	Mariposa	77	292	Sacramento	4331	62	Sierra	29	335	Yuba	334	486
Glenn	422	184	Mendocino	579	530	San Benito	271	383	Siskiyou	468	181			
Humboldt	657	527	Merced	1547	538	San Bernardino	5567	61	Solano	1105	182			

(which provisions, identical in all counties, are printed on the reverse hereof) hereby are adopted and incorporated herein and made a part hereof as fully as though set forth herein at length; that he will observe and perform said provisions; and that the references to property, obligations, and parties in said provisions shall be construed to refer to the property, obligations, and parties set forth in this Deed of Trust.

The undersigned Trustor requests that a copy of any Notice of Default and of any Notice of Sale hereunder be mailed to him at his address hereinbefore set forth.

STATE OF CALIFORNIA

COUNTY OF _____ } SS.

On_____ before me, the undersigned, a Notary Public in and for said State, personally appeared _____

_____

_____ ,

personally known to me (or proved to me on the basis of satisfactory evidence) to be the person(s) whose name(s) is/are subscribed to the within instrument and acknowledged to me that he/she/they executed the same in his /her /their authorized capacity(ies), and that by his/her/their signature(s) on the instrument the person(s), or the entity upon behalf of which the person(s) acted, executed the instrument.
WITNESS my hand and official seal.

Signature _____

_____
Notary Public in and for said County and State   (Type or Print)   (Seal)

ORT 215 [1/94]

Note: Legal Description Must Be Attached As "Exhibit A" Prior To Recordation

390

The trust deed refers to the underlying debt and the promissory note that it secures. It states the total amount of the debt and the maturity date, but usually doesn't go into more detail. The interest rate and the amount of the payments, late charges, and other charges are generally found only in the note. However, when a noninstitutional loan secured by residential property (one to four units) is subject to a adjustable interest rate, a provision explaining the rate must be included in the trust deed as well as the note.

Deeds of trust do go into considerable detail about the borrower's obligations regarding care of the property and the title. The borrower agrees to insure the property against fire and other hazards. (California law prevents the lender from requiring insurance for more than the replacement value of the improvements, however.) The borrower must not commit waste (something that substantially decreases the value of the property) or allow the property to deteriorate. The trust deed grants the lender the right to inspect the property, to make sure the borrower is maintaining it.

The borrower agrees to keep property taxes, special assessments, and insurance up to date. If the borrower allows any of these bills to become delinquent, the lender has the right (but not the obligation) to pay them. This is important to the lender, since delinquent taxes reduce the value of the security property. If the delinquencies become severe, the taxing authority can foreclose—and the tax liens have higher priority than the trust deed (see Chapter 3). Any amounts the lender pays to prevent the taxes from becoming delinquent or the insurance from lapsing will be added to the borrower's debt and may cause the lender to declare a default and foreclose.

POWER OF SALE. The key provision in a deed of trust—the one that makes it different from a mortgage—is the **power of sale** clause. The borrower grants the trustee the power to sell the property in case of default. That's what enables the lender to foreclose nonjudicially, rather than having to file a judicial foreclosure suit.

A trust deed usually briefly outlines the procedures to be followed if the trustee exercises the power of sale and forecloses. For the most part, however, those procedures are prescribed by law. The foreclosure process is described later in this chapter.

Recording

A lender always records its trust deed, since its lien priority is determined by the recording date. In California, a county recorder cannot accept a trust deed unless the grantor's (borrower's) signature on the document is acknowledged and notarized. The document must also include the grantor's address, along with a request that any notice of default or notice of sale be sent to that address.

Title insurance companies often serve as trustees for deeds of trust, and one company may record hundreds of documents each month. To cut down on recording costs, a title company may record a **fictitious trust deed**. That's a standard trust deed form that hasn't been filled out. Once the company's blank form has been recorded, it's only necessary to record the first page and signature page of any actual trust deed that is executed on that form. The standard provisions on the middle pages are incorporated into the actual trust deed by reference to the recording number of the fictitious trust deed. So if you look up a trust deed in the public record or request a certified copy from the recorder, don't be surprised if the document is incomplete.

Chapter 12

Reconveyance

If the borrower is going to pay off the existing loan, the lender must give the borrower a **beneficiary statement**, if requested by the borrower. This statement shows the borrower the exact amount due on the loan. Once a trust deed borrower has paid off the entire amount of the debt, he or she is entitled to a full reconveyance of the trust deed. That's a document stating that the debt secured by the deed of trust has been discharged.

On receiving the final payment, the lender/beneficiary must send the trustee the original promissory note and trust deed, along with a request for reconveyance. The trustee is then required to execute and record the reconveyance document within 21 days. That makes it a matter of public record that the debt has been paid off and the trust deed is no longer a lien on the property. The borrower may ask the trustee for the original note and trust deed. (The trustee and beneficiary are allowed to charge the borrower a reasonable fee for these reconveyance services.)

The Civil Code outlines steps the borrower can take to clear the title if the beneficiary and trustee don't execute a reconveyance promptly. (And the beneficiary and trustee may be fined.) There are also procedures for clearing the title when the beneficiary cannot be located or refuses to request a reconveyance.

When several parcels of property are the security under a single trust deed, the borrower may be given a **partial reconveyance** after a certain portion of the debt has been repaid. The partial reconveyance removes the trust deed lien from specified parcels; the lien still attaches to the other parcels.

www.fanniemae.com
http://aero.com/lamb/links.htm
(Places of Interest Regarding Deeds of Trust, Mortgages and Financing)

Common Optional Loan Terms

A promissory note is a borrower's promise to repay a loan, and a security agreement gives the lender the power to have the borrower's property sold in case of default. These are the basic terms for every real estate loan. But most real estate loan agreements include additional provisions governing prepayment, default, and transfer or encumbrance of the security property. Some of these provisions appear in the note, some in the trust deed, and some in both documents.

These common additional terms generally provide extra protection for the lender. That's not surprising; when the parties work out the details of their agreement, the lender is ordinarily in a better bargaining position than the borrower. If you apply for a loan at a bank and start haggling about the prepayment clause, the loan officer may wish you good afternoon and turn her attention to the next customer. However, as you'll see, California law places some limits on the protective provisions a lender can impose, especially on a loan secured by residential property.

Most conventional real estate loan agreements provide for:

- ◆ late charges,
- ◆ acceleration on default,
- ◆ acceleration on transfer (due-on-sale),
- ◆ some also provide for prepayment.

PREPAYMENT PROVISIONS

When a contract states a specific time for performance, the law requires it to be performed at the stated time—not after that time, and also not before that time. Suppose our loan agreement obligates me to pay you $789 on the 15th of each month. I don't necessarily have the right to pay more or pay sooner.

However, a loan agreement may expressly give the borrower the right to **prepay**—that is, make a larger payment than required, or pay off the entire loan before its maturity date. And in fact prepayment is permitted by the terms of most promissory notes. The note may simply state that the monthly payment is $789 "or more," or that the payments are due "on or before" the 15th of each month. Or the note may include a provision expressly stating that the borrower has the right to prepay. There may be a prepayment penalty which is an added expense to the borrower if the loan is paid before the due date.

When a loan agreement doesn't give the borrower the option to prepay, the loan is said to be **locked in**. Nowadays it would be extremely unusual for a real estate loan to be completely locked in, but some loan agreements include a lock-in clause that prevents prepayment during a certain period.

Case Example: To develop an office building complex in West Los Angeles, the Trident Center partnership borrowed $56,500,000 from the Connecticut General Life Insurance Company in 1983. The interest rate was 12.25%, and the loan was to be paid off in 15 years. The promissory note stated that the partnership "shall not have the right to prepay the principal amount hereof in whole or in part" during the first 12 years of the loan.

Everything went smoothly for a few years, but interest rates were dropping during that period. By 1987, the 12.25% rate on the Trident Center loan was good for the lender, but bad for the borrower. The partnership wanted to refinance, to take advantage of the lower rates that were available. But refinancing would involve paying off the original loan long before its due date. Connecticut General refused to accept the prepayment, and the partnership sued. The court held that Connecticut General's lock-in clause was enforceable; the partnership could not prepay without the lender's consent during the first 12 years of the loan period. *Trident Center v. Connecticut General Life Ins.*, 847 F.2d 564 (9th Cir. 1988).

RESIDENTIAL PROPERTY. The California legislature enacted a statute that prohibits lock-in clauses in loans on residential property with one to four units. With those loans, the borrower has the right to make a partial prepayment or to pay off the entire loan balance, at any time. But the lender is allowed to impose a **prepayment charge** only if agreed to in writing. Any clause providing for a prepayment charge may be separately initialed by the borrower.

Even prepayment charges are limited if the property is owner-occupied. For owner-occupied property, during the first five years of the loan the borrower must be allowed to prepay up to 20% of the original loan amount in any 12 month period without penalty. But if the borrower prepays more than 20%, the lender can assess a prepayment charge. The charge cannot be more than the equivalent of six months' interest on the amount of prepayment over 20%.

Example: Suppose a bank has loaned you $100,000 at 10% interest so that you can buy a condominium unit. If you prepay $20,000 (20%) in one year, the lender can't require you to pay a prepayment charge.

However, if you prepay more than that in one year—for example, $25,000 (25%)—the lender may add on a prepayment charge. But the charge cannot exceed the equivalent of six months' interest on 5% of the original loan amount (25% - 20% = 5%). One year's interest on $5,000 at a 10% annual rate would be $500, so six months' interest would be $250. The prepayment charge could not be more than $250.

After a loan on owner-occupied property has been in place for five years, the borrower can't be required to pay any further prepayment charges. A different rule applies to loans secured by single-family, owner-occupied homes that are covered by the Mortgage Loan Broker Law, which is discussed at the end of this chapter.

Prepayment

Nonresidential Property

◆ No right to prepay unless agreed
◆ Lock-in clauses allowed
◆ Prepayment penalties allowed (if reasonable)

Residential Property (1-4 units)

◆ Right to prepay at any time (seller financing exception)
◆ Lock-in clauses not allowed
◆ Borrower must initial prepayment provisions
◆ Owner-occupied: limited penalties for first 5 years (unless Mortgage Loan Broker Law applies)

SELLER FINANCING. The statute that establishes the residential borrower's right to prepay makes an exception for seller financing. Under this exception, a home seller who carries back a deed of trust for the purchase price can prevent any prepayment during the year of the sale.

This addresses a seller's concern about income tax liability. When a buyer prepays all or part of a carryback loan in a large lump, the seller may end up owing much higher taxes (because the seller may be in a higher rate tax bracket) on that money than if the payments had been spread out over a few years.

Note, however, that this exception doesn't apply to a seller who carries back four or more residential deeds of trust in one year. In that situation, the seller is required to allow prepayment during that year, just like an institutional lender.

Keep in mind that these rules on lock-in clauses and prepayment charges apply only to loans on residential property where the owner lives in one of the one to four units. There are no statutory restrictions on lock-in clauses and prepayment charges for other real estate loans.

NATURAL DISASTER. No prepayment charge is allowed if the residence cannot be occupied; if damage from a natural disaster for which a state of emergency is declared by the Governor.

www.wellsfargo.com/
www.eloan.com
www.countrywide.com
™ **(Financing — Getting a Loan)**

DEFAULT PROVISIONS

LATE CHARGES AND DEFAULT RATES. Many promissory notes provide for a late payment penalty. The penalty may take the form of a flat fee: for example, $5 per month is added to the debt until the overdue payment is received. Or there may be a **default interest rate:** for example, the interest rate on the loan balance is ordinarily 8%, but 10% is charged on any delinquent amounts.

Late payment charge provisions such as these generally must comply with the rules for liquidated damages (see Chapter 7). That means the amount of the late charge must have been reasonable at the time the loan agreement was made. Thus, if a promissory note provided that a $200 late fee would be added to the $500 monthly payment whenever the payment was overdue, a court would undoubtedly refuse to enforce that provision.

The borrower must be given notice that a late fee or default rate will be charged. The notice must state the amount of the fee and the date it will be charged, and explain how the penalty is calculated.

A default interest rate can be assessed on the delinquent amount until it is paid, but not on the entire loan balance.

> **Example:** The interest rate on my loan is 8.5%, but the note provides for a default rate of 10%. My payments are $500 a month, and the loan balance is currently $59,432. For one reason or another, I miss my October payment. The lender can charge 10% interest on the delinquent $500 until I pay it. However, the lender can't charge 10% on $59,432; the interest rate on the non-delinquent balance must remain at 8.5%.

> **Residential Property.** The California Civil Code has placed special restrictions on late charges for loans on single-family, owner-occupied residences. A late charge can't be imposed until a payment is more than ten days overdue. There is a 10 day advance notice requirement before assessing the first late charge. The late charge on a single delinquent payment cannot exceed $5, or 6% of the payment amount, whichever is greater. Only one charge can be assessed against each delinquent payment. Whatever the borrower does pay must be applied first to the most recent payment due.

ACCELERATION ON DEFAULT. Virtually every real estate loan agreement provides for **acceleration** of the loan in case of default. If the borrower defaults, the lender has the right to declare the entire balance due *immediately*, no matter how many years away the original maturity date might be. This is sometimes referred to as "calling the note"; the provision in the loan agreement is an **acceleration clause** or **call provision**.

A lender does not have the right to accelerate unless that was expressly included in the loan agreement. An acceleration clause in the promissory note allows the lender to accelerate if the borrower fails to make payments on time. An acceleration clause in the trust deed gives the lender the right to accelerate if the borrower breaches any part of the security agreement: for example, by failing to pay the property taxes or keep the property insured.

Acceleration is a lender's option, not an automatic event. The lender decides whether or not to accelerate, and when—after the borrower has missed two payments, or five or six. But the right to accelerate ends as soon as the borrower cures the default by tendering payment of the delinquent amounts, renewing the insurance, or taking whatever other action is necessary. And the borrower can cure the default even after the lender has accelerated the loan. But if the default isn't cured, the lender will foreclose.

Prepayment Charges and Acceleration. When a lender accelerates a loan because of default and has the property sold, the proceeds from the foreclosure sale are used to pay off the debt. This usually occurs long before the loan's original maturity date. So, in effect, acceleration and foreclosure lead to prepayment of the loan. Can the lender assess prepayment charges after a foreclosure? Yes—at least if it says so in the loan agreement.

Case Example: Mr. and Mrs. T borrowed $405,500 from Columbia Savings to buy a home in Rolling Hills. Paragraph 1 of the promissory note provided for acceleration in case of default. The note also stated that a fee would be charged for any prepayment, "whether or not such prepayment is voluntary or involuntary (even if it results from [Columbia's] exercise of its rights under Paragraph 1, above)..."

Two years later, Mr. and Mrs. T defaulted, the loan was accelerated, and the home was sold at a foreclosure sale. Columbia Savings included a prepayment charge of $22,795 in the price.

The foreclosure sale purchaser, Golden Forest Properties, sued for a declaration that it was not required to pay the prepayment charge. The court disagreed, however. The lender and borrowers clearly intended that the prepayment charge would be owed if the lender foreclosed, and this provision of their agreement was enforceable. *Golden Forest Properties v. Columbia Savings & Loan Assn.*, 202 Cal. App. 3d 193, 248 Cal. Rptr. 316 (1988).

As the *Golden Forest* case suggests, the terms of the loan agreement are controlling. If the note hadn't specifically stated that the charge would be due even for involuntary prepayment, Columbia Savings could not have collected it. However, a prepayment penalty can not be collected upon acceleration on residential property containing four units or less.

TRANSFER PROVISIONS

When real property is sold (or otherwise transferred), the new owner takes title **subject to** any existing liens. That means the lienholders still have the power to foreclose on the property, in spite of the transfer. However, the new owner does not necessarily take on personal responsibility for the liens.

Personal responsibility becomes important if the lienholder forecloses and the foreclosure sale proceeds aren't enough to pay off the full amount of the lien. In some cases, the lienholder can sue for the remainder. That's called a **deficiency judgment**—it makes up for the deficiency in the sale proceeds. When a new owner takes property subject to existing liens, he or she may lose the property to foreclosure, but isn't personally liable for a deficiency judgment. The lienholder has to collect the deficiency judgment from the former owner.

It's different if the new owner **assumes** an existing lien, instead of merely taking title subject to it. In an assumption, the new owner agrees to take on personal responsibility for the lien. Then if the lender obtains a deficiency judgment, the new owner will be liable. However, the original borrower (the former owner) remains secondarily liable for a deficiency judgment. If the new owner doesn't pay, the lender can collect from the former owner. The former owner can then go after the new owner for payment, but may be out of luck. Deficiency judgments and anti-deficiency judgment rules are discussed later in the chapter.

Even though the original borrower is still liable, an assumption may increase the lender's risk. The lender wants to be paid as agreed—foreclosure is a last resort. The new owner could be a much worse credit risk than the former owner, or might be more likely to allow the security property to deteriorate.

Because of these concerns, most conventional real property loan agreements contain a due-on-sale clause.

DUE-ON-SALE CLAUSES. A lender can't include a provision in the loan agreement that prevents the borrower from selling or transferring the security property. In the eyes of the law, that would be an **unreasonable restraint on alienation**. Transfer of property from one person to another is generally good for commerce, so the law protects an owner's right to freely transfer property.

However, lenders can use **due-on-sale clauses** to protect their interests. A due-on-sale clause provides that if the borrower sells or transfers any interest in the property without the lender's consent, the lender has the right to accelerate the loan and demand immediate payment in full. (See paragraph 2 on the deed of trust example.)

These provisions are also called **alienation clauses**. Alienation clauses are always acceleration clauses—but don't confuse them with the provisions for acceleration on default that were discussed earlier. Here there's no default; the monthly payments, taxes, and so forth have been paid reliably. The borrower has simply exercised his or her right to sell or transfer the property. If a lender chooses to use the due-on-sale clause to accelerate the loan, the full balance must be paid. If it isn't, the lender can foreclose.

Sometimes (if the new owner is a good credit risk) instead of exercising its due-on-sale rights, the lender is willing to agree to an assumption of the loan. In that case, the new owner is usually required to pay an assumption fee, or a higher interest rate on the assumed loan, or both. The lender and the new owner sign a written assumption agreement, and the former owner has no further liability for the debt.

Residential Property. The California legislature has adopted some rules for due-on-sale clauses in loans on residential property with one to four units.

For loans made since July 1, 1972, if the loan agreement includes a due-on-sale provision, it must appear in full in both the promissory note and the trust deed.

For loans made since January 1, 1976, a due-on-sale clause can't be triggered by certain types of transfers. The lender can't accelerate the loan when:

◆ the borrower's spouse becomes a co-owner of the security property;
◆ the borrowers are a married couple, and one of them dies, making the other sole owner of the property;
◆ married borrowers separate or divorce and one of them becomes the sole owner; or
◆ the borrower transfers the property to a trust in which he or she is a beneficiary.

Prepayment Charges and Due-on-sale Clauses. In general, if a loan agreement contains both a prepayment provision and a due-on-sale clause, the lender can collect prepayment charges after accelerating the loan because the property has been sold. But federal law prohibits prepayment charges on a loan secured by an owner-occupied home, and state law prohibits prepayment charges on a loan on residential property with one to four units, if the due-on-sale clause is exercised.

DUE-ON-SALE CLAUSES

For residential property:

◆ clause must be in both note and security agreement

◆ certain transfers are exempt

◆ prepayment penalties can't be charged after acceleration pursuant to a due-on-sale clause

DUE-ON-ENCUMBRANCE PROVISIONS. Some due-on-sale clauses allow the lender to accelerate the loan not only if ownership is transferred, but even if the borrower encumbers the property with another lien. The borrower can't take out an additional loan using the property as security, even though the first lender's trust deed would have higher priority than the second trust deed. These due-on-encumbrance provisions are generally enforceable. However, federal law prohibits them in loans secured by owner-occupied homes, and California law prohibits them in loans on residential property with one to four units.

SUBORDINATION PROVISIONS

Lien priority is extremely important to every lender. The higher the lender's priority, the more likely that lender is to recover all (or most) of the debt if any lienholder forecloses. As you know, the priority of a trust deed depends on the date it was recorded. A trust deed has lower priority than any voluntary liens on the same property that were recorded earlier, and higher priority than any that were recorded later.

But a lender can agree to accept a lower priority position than the one established by the recording date. The lender may **subordinate** its trust deed to another trust deed that was (or will be) recorded later. The earlier trust deed that takes on a lower priority is called a **subordinated trust deed**. The later trust deed that is given a higher priority is called the **subordinating trust deed**.

Subordination is most common when a seller carries back a trust deed for part of the purchase price. The borrower/buyer intends to improve the security property, but to do so, he or she will have to obtain a construction loan. Construction lenders generally insist on having **first lien position** (the highest priority). As a result, the buyer won't be able to get the construction loan unless the seller is willing to subordinate the purchase loan.

A subordination clause can be included in the earlier trust deed, or a separate subordination agreement may be drawn up. The provision may subordinate the trust deed to a loan that has already been arranged, or to one that the borrower intends to apply for.

Because subordination can have a drastic effect on the strength of a lender's security, any subordination provision must be drafted or carefully reviewed by a competent lawyer. When the other loan hasn't been arranged yet, the provision should establish strict standards for the quality and purpose of the other loan. Otherwise, the borrower can subordinate the earlier trust deed to any kind of loan and do anything he or she wants with the money. That can make the subordinated lender's security worthless.

Case Example: Mr. Handy contracted to buy the 320-acre Gordon Ranch for $1,200,000. The contract provided that Handy would sign a ten-year deed of trust in favor of the Gordons to cover the purchase price. Handy intended to obtain other loans for construction and permanent financing, and the Gordons agreed to subordinate their trust deed to these other loans.

Continued

A few months later, however, the Gordons had changed their minds about selling the property to Handy. Handy sued for specific performance of the contract.

The court stated that a subordination clause "must contain terms that will define and minimize the risk that the subordinating liens will impair or destroy the seller's security." Nothing in the Gordons' subordination provision ensured that Handy would use all of the proceeds from the other loans to improve the security property. As a result, the amount of those loans might be much greater than the amount Handy's improvements added to the value of the property. If he defaulted and the subordinating lenders foreclosed, their claims would probably absorb all the foreclosure sale proceeds. Thus, the contract leaves defendants with nothing but plantiff's good faith and business judgment to insure them that they will ever receive anything for conveying their land. The court ruled that this was not just and reasonable for the Gordons, and refused to make them go through with the contract. *Handy v. Gordon*, 65 Cal. 2d 578, 55 Cal. Rptr. 769 (1967).

In California, to lessen the chances that an unsophisticated lender will subordinate a trust deed without realizing it, certain trust deeds with subordination provisions must have **SUBORDINATED TRUST DEED** printed in large, bold type at the top of the document. The document also has to include certain warnings about the risks involved in subordination. But these rules don't apply when either the subordinated loan or the subordinating loan (the later loan) will be for more than $25,000.

Foreclosure

The purpose of every real estate security agreement is to give the lender the right to foreclose: to have the property sold and the debt paid out of the sale proceeds. The power of sale clause in a deed of trust enables the lender to foreclose nonjudicially, without filing a lawsuit to obtain a judge's decree of foreclosure. The foreclosure must take place within 10 years of maturity date of the note as can be determined from the documents recorded or 60 years after recording the deed of trust.

A power of sale clause can also be included in a mortgage, and that makes the mortgage for all intents and purposes just like a trust deed. But a standard mortgage does not contain a power of sale, and can only be foreclosed through judicial process.

For a trust deed lender, on the other hand, judicial foreclosure is an option. But there is usually no need for it, and rarely any advantage to it; nonjudicial foreclosure is always faster and cheaper. (Nonjudicial foreclosure can be accomplished in less than four months and usually costs less than $500; judicial foreclosure can take years and cost thousands of dollars.) Since most foreclosures in California are nonjudicial, we'll look at the nonjudicial procedure in detail. Later in the chapter, we'll compare the judicial foreclosure process.

www.law.cornell.edu/uscode/12/3710.shtml
(USC Title 12 - Chapter 38 - Section 3710 - Foreclosure Sale)

NONJUDICIAL FORECLOSURE OF A TRUST DEED

There are three main steps in the nonjudicial foreclosure process:

◆ the notice of default;
◆ the notice of sale; and
◆ the trustee's sale.

Notice of Default

When a trust deed beneficiary (the lender) asks the trustee to start the foreclosure process, the first step is to record a **notice of default**. If necessary, a new trustee can be substituted for the former trustee. The notice identifies the trust deed, states that the borrower has breached the terms of the trust deed, and describes the nature of the breach. Remember, default doesn't have to be failure to make monthly payments on time. Failing to maintain the property, pay the taxes, or keep the property insured can also constitute default.

The notice of default is recorded in the county where the property is located. Within ten business days after it is recorded, the trustee must mail a copy to the borrower by certified or registered mail. In addition, a second copy must be sent to the borrower by first class mail, and the sender has to execute an affidavit of mailing.

In that same ten business-day period, the trustee must also send a copy of the notice of default, by certified or registered mail, to everyone who requested notice. Anyone who wants to receive notice of default on a particular trust deed can record a **request for notice of default**. (Sometimes a request for notice of default is included in the trust deed itself.) The request must include an address so that the trustee knows where to send the notice. For example, a commercial tenant might be interested in knowing if the landlord is in default on the building loan.

 www.lawaid.com/forecl.htm
(Foreclosure Law in a Nutshell)

In addition, the trustee has to send a copy of the notice of default to:

◆ the borrower's successors in interest (that's everyone who has acquired an ownership interest in the property—heirs, for example);
◆ the junior trust deed beneficiaries (the lenders with lower lien priority than the foreclosing lender);
◆ the vendee in a land contract with lower priority than the trust deed; and
◆ the lessee in a lease with lower priority than the trust deed.

Like the others, these copies must be sent by certified or registered mail, but they don't have to be sent within ten business days. The trustee has one month after the notice of default is recorded to send copies to these parties. (If any of them want to be notified sooner, they have to record a request for notice.)

Notice of Sale

The trustee's next step is to issue a **notice of sale**. This can't be done until at least three months after the notice of default was recorded, but it must be done at least 20 days before the date set for the trustee's sale.

The notice of sale states the time and place that the trustee's sale will be held. It gives the name, address, and phone number of the trustee conducting the sale; it identifies the borrower and the property to be sold. The notice states the amount of the unpaid loan balance and an estimate of the costs and expenses. It also includes a warning to the borrower:

> "UNLESS YOU TAKE ACTION TO PROTECT YOUR PROPERTY, IT MAY BE SOLD AT A PUBLIC SALE. IF YOU NEED AN EXPLANATION OF THE NATURE OF THE PROCEEDING AGAINST YOU, YOU SHOULD CONTACT A LAWYER."

To issue a notice of sale, the trustee must do all of the following at least 20 days before the sale date:

◆ post a copy of the notice in a public place (such as the courthouse) in the city or judicial district where the property is located;

◆ begin publishing the notice once a week in a newspaper of general circulation in the city or judicial district where the property is located;

◆ post a copy in a conspicuous place on the property to be sold (if it's a single-family residence, the notice should be on the front door, if possible);

◆ send the borrower one copy by registered or certified mail, and another copy by first class mail; and

◆ send a copy to each of the other parties that were sent a notice of default.

In addition, at least 14 days before the sale, the trustee must record a copy of the notice of sale in the county where the property is located.

Preventing a Trustee's Sale

Once the foreclosure process has begun, there are three ways the borrower can cure the default:

◆ curing the default to reinstate the loan,

◆ redeeming the property, or

◆ giving the lender a deed in lieu of foreclosure.

CURE AND REINSTATEMENT. When the borrower has defaulted by failing to make payments, or failing to pay taxes, assessments, or insurance, the default can be cured. (Note that a cure isn't always permitted: not if the borrower has committed waste, or if the loan has been accelerated pursuant to a due-on-sale clause, for example.)

A default can be cured by paying the delinquent taxes or assessments, reinsuring the property, or paying the overdue amounts (including late charges). In addition, the costs incurred because of the default must be paid (the cost of recording and mailing notices, for example). The trustee's fees and any attorneys' fees must also be paid, and these are limited by statute.

Example: Before the notice of sale is mailed. Until the notice of sale is deposited in the mail, if the borrower wishes to reinstate, the trustees' or attorneys' fees that may be recovered may not exceed $240 for an unpaid principal of $50,000 or less, plus 1/2 of 1 percent of the amount from $50,000 to $150,000, plus 1/4 of 1 percent of the unpaid amount from $150,000 through $500,000 plus 1/8 of 1 percent of any portion of the unpaid principal sum exceeding $500,000.

After the notice of sale is mailed. If the borrower wishes to redeem after the notice of sale has been deposited in the mail, the trustee's or attorney's fees are set at an amount which does not exceed $350 on the first $50,000 or unpaid principal plus 1 percent of the unpaid principal exceeding $50,000 through $150,000 plus 1/2 of 1 percent from $150,000 through $500,000, 1/4 of 1 percent of the unpaid principal sum exceeding $500,000.

Trustee's or attorney's fees. Any charge for trustee's or attorney's fees are presumed to be lawful when they do not exceed these authorized amounts.

It's not just the borrower and the borrower's successors in interest who can cure the default. A junior lienholder might pay off the delinquencies, costs, and fees in order to protect its lien.

The default can be cured any time after the notice of default has been recorded, until five business days before the date of the trustee's sale. This is known as the **reinstatement period**. If the sale is postponed, the right to cure the default revives until five business days before the new sale date.

When the default is curable, the notice of default must contain an explanation of the right to reinstate the loan. It must also inform the borrower that the lender may be willing to allow additional time or arrange a payment schedule. The amount necessary for curing the default as of the notice date must be listed, along with a phone number to call for an update of the necessary amount.

Once a default has been cured, the loan is reinstated. Regular payment resumes—the lender can't demand higher payments or a higher interest rate because of the earlier default. The borrower may ask the lender to record a **notice of rescission**. The notice of rescission gives public notice that the notice of default and notice of sale have been rescinded. The lender must record a notice of rescission within 30 days after receiving a written request from the borrower.

REDEMPTION. Five days before the sale date, the borrower (and everyone else such as junior lienholders) loses the right to cure the default. In that five-day period, there's still a chance to prevent the sale and retain control of the property. But now it would be necessary to pay the lender the entire loan balance—not merely the delinquencies—plus costs and fees. If the borrower could come up with that much, he or she would own the property free and clear of the lender's interest. This doesn't happen often. Once the trustee's sale is over, the right to redeem the property is lost.

Chapter 12

DEED IN LIEU OF FORECLOSURE. The only other way for the borrower to prevent a trustee's sale is by giving the lender a deed in lieu of foreclosure. In other words, the borrower simply deeds the property to the lender, surrendering ownership. Why would a borrower do that? Often the borrower is going to lose the property anyway, since he or she can't afford to cure the default, much less pay off the entire loan. By giving the lender a deed in lieu, the borrower can avoid liability for costs and fees, and may be able to protect his or her credit rating.

A lender isn't required to accept a deed in lieu of foreclosure. The lender can decide whether accepting it will be more advantageous than foreclosing. That may not be the case, for example, if the property is encumbered with other liens.

Trustee's Sale

A trustee's sale is a public auction; the foreclosure property is sold to the highest bidder. The sale must be held during ordinary business hours, in the county where the property is located. The trustee's role is to conduct the sale in a fair and open manner, to protect all interested parties (the borrower, the foreclosing lender, and the other lienholders) and obtain a reasonable price for the property.

The trustee can postpone the sale if necessary to protect the interests of the beneficiary or borrower. Remember that when a trustee's sale is postponed, the right to cure the default is revived until five business days before the new sale date.

The foreclosing lender is allowed to **credit bid** at the sale. With credit bidding, the amount owed to the lender is offset against the amount of the bid. No other lienholders are allowed to credit bid.

> **Example:** The amount due to the foreclosing lender is $100,000. (That includes the unpaid balance on the trust deed, plus costs and fees.) The lender bids $100,000, which is the highest bid. The lender gets the property without actually paying anything for it. If the bid had been $120,000, the lender would only pay $20,000.
>
> Suppose there's a junior trust deed on the property with a $15,000 unpaid balance. If the lender on that junior trust deed bid $100,000, he or she would have to pay the full $100,000 (not $85,000).

SALE PROCEEDS. After the property has been sold at the trustee's sale, the proceeds are applied in the following order:

1. First, the costs of the foreclosure are paid (including the costs of publishing, recording, and mailing notices, a title search, and the trustee's and attorney's fees).

2. Next, the trust deed that was foreclosed is paid.

3. Then any junior liens are paid off in order of priority.

4. Finally, anything left over is paid to the borrower.

If there's nothing left after the foreclosed trust deed is paid off, the junior lienholders get nothing. If there is something left, junior lienholders are sent a notice to file a written claim and the trustee determines priority. If there's only enough left to pay the first junior lienholder, the second and third get nothing (and so on). If the trustee can not determine priority, the matter is transferred for determination to the superior court. The foreclosure extinguishes the junior liens: the junior lienholders have lost their security interest in the property—they can't foreclose later on. Not only that, because of the anti-deficiency rules (discussed below), the junior lienholders have no other recourse—they can't sue the borrower for payment.

However, the foreclosure does not extinguish any liens that had higher priority than the foreclosed trust deed (a property tax lien, for example). The purchaser at the trustee's sale takes the property subject to those senior liens.

TRUSTEE'S DEED. The purchaser at a trustee's sale receives title to the property immediately. The borrower has no further right to redeem the property. If the borrower is still in possession of the property, he or she can be evicted.

The purchaser is given a **trustee's deed** (not the same thing as a trust deed!). Like a quitclaim deed, it conveys whatever ownership rights the borrower had, but carries no warranties of title.

NONJUDICIAL FORECLOSURE

Default & Acceleration
Notice of Default
Notice of Trustee's Sale........................ 3 months after notice of default
Cure & Reinstatement........................ until 5 business days before sale
Redemption...until the sale
Trustee's Sale.. 20 days after notice of sale
    trustee's deed.................................... issued immediately after sale
    junior liens extinguished
    no deficiency judgments

Protection for Junior Lienholders

The beneficiary of a junior trust deed (or any other junior lienholder) has the same right to foreclose as the beneficiary of the senior trust deed. But as you've seen, if the senior lender forecloses first, the junior lender's security interest will be wiped out altogether. The junior lender may receive full payment, partial payment, or nothing at all.

The only protection for a junior lender (besides choosing the borrower carefully) is to submit a **request for notice of delinquency** to the senior lender(s). If a junior lender knows that the borrower is having trouble with a senior loan, the junior lender can cure the default and reinstate the senior loan. The amount it costs to cure the default is added to what the borrower already owes the junior lender. With the senior loan reinstated, the junior lender can decide whether to foreclose on its own lien.

A junior lender can only use a request for notice of delinquency if the security property is residential property with one to four units, or if the junior lien is for $300,000 or less. And the junior lender must first obtain written permission from the borrower. Delinquencies of 4 months or more are reported. The notice fee is $40 and is good for 5 years, it can be renewed.

But any junior lender can (and should) record a **request for notice of default**. The borrower's consent is not necessary. The request for notice of default was described earlier in this chapter. When a junior lender has filed a request for notice of default, the trustee has to send a notice of default to the junior lender within ten business days (rather than a month) after recording it. The notice of default doesn't warn the junior lender as early as a notice of delinquency, but it's better than nothing.

JUDICIAL FORECLOSURE OF A MORTGAGE

There are only two parties to a mortgage. The borrower is the **mortgagor**, the lender is the **mortgagee**, and there's no trustee. Up until the point of foreclosure, the mortgagor and mortgagee have the same rights and obligations as a trust deed trustor and beneficiary. A promissory note secured by a mortgage is the same as one secured by a trust deed, usually containing an acceleration clause and providing for late charges. Like a trust deed, a mortgage requires the borrower to maintain the property and keep it insured. And there's usually a due-on-sale clause.

The difference is that a mortgage doesn't ordinarily have a power of sale clause. As a result, nonjudicial foreclosure is not permitted. To foreclose, the mortgagee has to file a complaint in the superior court of the county where the property is located within four years of payment being due. The defendants in a foreclosure lawsuit are the borrower and junior lienholders. If the mortgagee doesn't include one of the junior lienholders as a defendant, that junior lien isn't affected by the foreclosure. But as with nonjudicial foreclosure, all the other junior liens are extinguished.

After filing a foreclosure suit, the mortgagee records a notice called a **lis pendens**. The lis pendens states that a legal action is pending that may affect title to the property. It provides constructive notice of the foreclosure, so anyone who acquires an interest in the property takes it subject to the outcome of the foreclosure suit.

The mortgagor and junior lienholders have the right to cure the default and reinstate the loan, while the lawsuit is pending. But once the court issues a decree of foreclosure, the right to reinstate the loan ends.

The decree of foreclosure establishes the amount that the mortgagor owes the mortgagee. It also states whether or not the mortgagee is entitled to a deficiency judgment if the foreclosure sale proceeds are less than the debt. (That depends on the anti-deficiency rules, discussed below.)

The sale after a judicial foreclosure is called a **sheriff's sale** or an **execution sale** (as opposed to a trustee's sale). The court appoints a receiver to conduct the sale. The receiver records a **notice of levy**.

The rest of the process depends on whether the lender is seeking a deficiency judgment. If not, the receiver must wait at least 120 days after recording the notice of levy before posting, publishing, and mailing out the notice of sale. The foreclosure sale purchaser receives a **sheriff's deed** immediately after the sale. (Like a trustee's deed, it carries no warranties.)

On the other hand, if the mortgagor will be liable for any deficiency, the receiver may issue the notice of sale immediately. But the property will be sold subject to the mortgagor's right of redemption. The foreclosure sale purchaser is given a **certificate of sale** instead of a deed.

The mortgagor can redeem the property by paying the amount that the foreclosure sale purchaser paid for it (plus interest), and whatever the purchaser has spent on taxes, insurance, and maintenance. And if the purchaser was a junior lienholder, the mortgagor must also pay off that junior lien, plus interest. If the purchaser has used the property during the redemption period, the reasonable value of that use can be offset against the redemption price.

If it turns out that no deficiency judgment is necessary, then the redemption period only lasts for three months after the sale. If the mortgagor hasn't redeemed the property by then, the purchaser receives a sheriff s deed.

But when the sale proceeds don't cover the debt, costs, and fees, and a deficiency judgment is entered against the mortgagor, the redemption period lasts one year. That's a long period of uncertainty for the purchaser. As a general rule, the borrower is entitled to remain in possession of the property during the redemption period, paying rent to the purchaser.

California law used to allow junior lienholders to redeem the property after a judicial foreclosure sale. But now the defaulting mortgagor and the mortgagor's successors in interest are the only ones with the right of redemption with in 12 months of the sale.

If they do redeem the property, a **certificate of redemption** is issued and recorded. If a deficiency judgment was entered and they haven't paid it, a judgment lien attaches to the redeemed property. But junior liens that were extinguished by the foreclosure sale aren't revived by the redemption. They're gone for good.

JUDICIAL FORECLOSURE

Default & Acceleration
Lawsuit Filed & Lis Pendens Recorded
Cure & Reinstatement (until decree of foreclosure)
Decree of Foreclosure
Notice of Levy
Notice of Sale
Sheriff's Sale
    junior liens extinguished
    certificate of sale (issued immediately)
Redemption (3 months after sale if no deficiency judgment)
       (1 year after sale if deficiency judgment)
Sheriff's Deed (issued after redemption period ends)

The same procedures are followed when a trust deed beneficiary chooses to foreclose judicially instead of using the power of sale. There are real disadvantages to the judicial foreclosure process, in terms of both time and money. So why would a trust deed beneficiary choose judicial foreclosure? The most common reason is that it's the only way to obtain a deficiency judgment. Let's take a look at the rules that govern when deficiency judgments are available.

Chapter 12

DEFICIENCY JUDGMENTS

During the Great Depression in the 1930s, thousands of families lost their homes to foreclosure. Legislatures in many states, including California, passed laws to grant some relief to borrowers. For example, there was legislation that delayed foreclosure sales, extended redemption periods, and limited lenders' ability to obtain deficiency judgments. Most of these laws were temporary, emergency measures that later lapsed or were repealed. But restrictions on deficiency judgments are still in effect.

When a foreclosing lender is entitled to a deficiency judgment, the lender must apply to the court for the judgment within three months after the property is sold at the foreclosure sale. The court will order an appraisal of the property's fair market value as of the time of the sale. The deficiency judgment will be the difference between the amount owed to the lender (including costs and fees) and either:

- ◆ the fair market value at the time of the sale, or
- ◆ the actual sale proceeds.

The deficiency judgment will always be the smaller of these two amounts. If the fair market value is less than or equal to the sale proceeds, the lender's total recovery (sale proceeds plus deficiency judgment) will equal the full amount owed. But that won't be true if the fair market value is more than the sale proceeds.

Example: The borrower owes the foreclosing lender $100,000, including foreclosure costs and attorney's fees. At the foreclosure sale, the property was purchased for $75,000. The lender applies to the court for a deficiency judgment.

The court orders an appraisal. The appraiser estimates the property's fair market value at the time of the sale was $85,000. Then the deficiency judgment would be for only $15,000, the difference between the appraised value and the debt. The lender's total recovery would be less than the $100,000 owed: $75,000 (sale proceeds) + $15,000 (deficiency judgment) = $90,000.

That rule may seem hard on the lender, but it prevents an abuse that was once widespread. Foreclosing lenders used to purchase the property at the foreclosure sale for much less than its fair market value, and then obtain a deficiency judgment for the difference between the sale proceeds and the debt. As a result, the lender came away from the foreclosure with far more than the borrower had owed.

Beyond that limitation on the amount of a deficiency judgment, there are rules that prohibit deficiency judgments altogether in some cases. A lender cannot obtain a deficiency judgment:

- ◆ after a nonjudicial foreclosure, or
- ◆ after foreclosing on certain purchase money loans.

Real Estate Financing

When a trust deed lender believes that a foreclosure sale is likely to result in a substantial deficiency, it may be worth the extra trouble to start a foreclosure lawsuit and get a deficiency judgment instead of exercising the power of sale. But even after a judicial foreclosure, a deficiency judgment is often prohibited if the loan was a purchase money loan—that is, the loan funds were used to purchase the security property.

No deficiency judgment is allowed for a purchase money trust deed or mortgage carried back by the seller. Suppose you sell me your land, and I give you a $40,000 trust deed as part of the purchase price. If I default and you foreclose, the sale proceeds are all you can get, no matter how severe the deficiency.

There's an important exception, however. If the seller has subordinated the purchase money loan to a non-purchase money loan (such as a construction loan), the anti-deficiency rule doesn't apply. The subordinated seller can obtain a deficiency judgment.

No deficiency judgment is allowed after a third-party lender forecloses on a purchase money loan, if the security was residential property with one to four units, and one of the units was occupied by the borrower/purchaser. Most residential real estate loans fall into that category. This rule has been interpreted to include loans for the construction of a residence on vacant land.

Case Example: The Pruntys used their savings to buy an unimproved lot in Oakland, intending to build a home there. They borrowed $40,000 from Bank of America, giving the bank a trust deed on their lot.

Without improvements, the land was worth $7,500. After the house was built, the property value rose to $96,000. But then a landslide destroyed the house, and the hazard insurance didn't cover landslides.

Foreclosure was inevitable, so the borrowers sued for a declaratory judgment. They contended that the $40,000 loan was a purchase money loan, and asked the court to rule that the bank could not obtain a deficiency judgment. The bank argued that it was a construction loan, not a purchase money loan.

The court agreed with the borrowers. Using the funds to build a home was essentially the same as using them to buy one. The bank wouldn't be allowed to apply for a deficiency judgment. *Prunty v. Bank of America*, 37 Cal. App. 3d 430, 112 Cal. Rptr. 370 (1974).

THE ANTI-DEFICIENCY JUDGMENT RULES

A lender cannot obtain a deficiency judgment after:

- foreclosing nonjudicially;
- foreclosing judicially on a seller-financed purchase money loan (unless it was subordinated to a non-purchase money loan); or
- foreclosing on a residential purchase money loan (one to four units and borrower occupied).

Real Property Sales Contracts

There's another type of security agreement besides trust deeds and mortgages. We'll call them **land contracts**, although they go by various similar names: land sales contracts, installment land contracts, installment sales contracts, or real property sales contracts.

Land contracts were once a popular form of seller financing. They used to have some advantages over a trust deed, from the seller's point of view. But court decisions have trimmed back the seller's rights, and added to the seller's obligations. As a result, land contracts are rarely used in California anymore. (One important exception: the Cal-Vet program uses land contracts to finance purchases by veterans.)

In a land contract purchase, the buyer pays the seller in installments, over a long period of time. Although the buyer usually takes possession of the property immediately, the seller retains title to the property as security for payment of the contract price. The seller doesn't deliver the deed to the buyer until the full price has been paid off, which is often many years later.

The parties to a land contract are called the **vendor** (the seller) and the **vendee** (the buyer). The vendor has **legal title**; the vendee has **equitable title**. The vendor's interest in the property decreases as the contract is paid off, and the vendee's interest increases.

A land contract has to comply with all the requirements for any valid contract: capacity, mutual consent, and consideration. The land contract must be in writing and signed. The Civil Code also requires that a land contract state the number of years it will take to complete payment according to the agreed terms. A vendee buying residential property (with four units or less) must be allowed to prepay, except that the vendor can prohibit prepayment during the first year of the contract. And the vendor, like a trust deed lender, may charge a prepayment penalty.

http://www.intcounselor.com/real-property.html
(Overview of Real Property Laws in the U.S.)

Most of the parties' rights and obligations are set by the terms of the contract. Because the vendor still has legal title to the property, he or she can transfer or encumber it without the vendee's consent. But the vendor is required to deliver clear, marketable title whenever the vendee pays off the contract. The vendor isn't allowed to grant any rights to third parties that would encumber the property after the vendee takes legal title (easements, for example). And if the vendor creates any liens, he or she must pay them off before delivering the deed to the vendee—otherwise, it's a breach of contract.

There are also statutory restrictions on the vendor's right to create liens if the land contract is unrecorded. The vendor must not encumber the property with liens that add up to more than the unpaid contract balance, unless the vendee consents to the liens. The vendor also can't create liens without the vendee's consent if the monthly payments on those liens total more than the vendee's monthly payment on the land contract.

Even if the land contract has been recorded and the vendee has consented to the liens, the vendor must apply the vendee's contract payments to any amounts due on the liens. So if the vendor owes a $400 monthly payment on a trust deed, when the vendee pays $450 on the contract the vendor can't spend it all on scuba diving equipment. If she does, she could face criminal penalties for misuse of the vendee's funds: up to a $10,000 fine and a year in jail. This gives the vendee some protection against the possibility that the vendor will default on the liens and lose the property to foreclosure.

The vendee also has the right to encumber the property. However, few lenders are willing to make loans with the vendee's equitable interest as the only security.

A land contract should be recorded to give constructive notice of the vendee's interest in the property. It's illegal for a vendor to transfer the property without assigning the contract to the new owner. But if the vendor violates that rule, anyone who buys the property with actual or constructive notice of the contract takes title subject to the vendee's interest. When the vendee tenders full payment, the buyer will have to deliver title to the vendee, just as the vendor would have had to.

But if the contract isn't recorded and someone buys the property without notice of the vendee's interest, the buyer can cut off the vendee's rights. (The vendor will be liable to the vendee for breach of contract, but the vendee will lose the property.) However, that can only happen if the vendee isn't in possession of the property, since possession gives constructive notice of an interest (see Chapter 10).

THE VENDOR'S REMEDIES

If a vendee defaults, the vendor can end the contract by sending the vendee a **notice of election to terminate**, and regain possession of the property. It used to be that the vendor wouldn't even reimburse the vendee for the payments already made. The vendee would forfeit the property and everything he or she had put into it.

But the courts no longer permit that harsh result. Now the vendor must reimburse the vendee for the amount paid on the contract. However, the vendee's recovery may be reduced by any damages that the vendor incurred. Or the vendee may be charged the rental value of the property during the period he or she was in possession. For example, suppose the vendee lived on the property for eight months and paid the vendor $4,200 on the contract. If the rental value was $450 a month ($3,600), the vendor would only have to give the vendee $600 back ($4,200 - $3,600 = $600).

A vendee has the right to cure the default and reinstate the contract. Once the vendee has paid a substantial portion of (contract price), the vendee gains a right of redemption.

Case Example: In 1953, Mrs. Walker began buying some forested land from Mr. MacFadden on a land contract. She made her payments regularly and by late 1963 had paid MacFadden $2,500.

But then Walker discovered that timber had been cut from her land without her permission, and she suspected MacFadden. Walker decided to stop making payments on the contract.

Later, MacFadden sent Walker a notice that he was terminating her rights under the contract because of her default. Walker offered to pay off the remaining balance of $1,174. MacFadden rejected her offer and filed a quiet title action.

Because Walker had paid a substantial part of the amount due on the contract, the court ruled that she was entitled to redeem the property by paying off the remainder. MacFadden was required to accept her payment and deliver legal title to her. *MacFadden v. Walker*, 5 Cal. 3d 809, 97 Cal. Rptr. 537 (1971).

As the *MacFadden* case indicates, the vendor often has to file a lawsuit against the defaulting vendee (unless they reach a settlement agreement). Or the vendee may sue the vendor for reimbursement or redemption. So the parties wind up in court, just as if it were a mortgage foreclosure. In fact, the court may decide that foreclosure is the fairest remedy and order the property sold.

Although they don't traditionally include a power of sale, land contracts can include one. Then the vendor can foreclose nonjudicially, as if the land contract were a trust deed. But since there aren't any real advantages to a land contract nowadays. a seller might as well start out with a trust deed instead.

Lending Disclosure Laws

A number of federal and state laws require real estate lenders to fully inform borrowers about the terms of their loans. Here's an overview of the main consumer protection laws affecting California lenders.

THE TRUTH IN LENDING ACT

The Truth in Lending Act is a federal law that requires lenders to disclose the complete cost of credit to consumer loan applicants. The act also regulates advertising of consumer loans. Congress outlined these goals in the act, and delegated the responsibility for carrying them out to the Federal Reserve Board. The Federal Reserve Board's **Regulation Z** implements the Truth in Lending Act. Regulation Z sets out the detailed rules that lenders must comply with.

COVERAGE OF THE ACT. A loan is a consumer loan if it is used for personal, family, or household purposes. A consumer loan is covered by the Truth in Lending Act if it is to be repaid in more than four installments, or is subject to finance charges, and is either:

- ◆ for $25,000 or less, or
- ◆ secured by real property.

Thus, any loan secured by a trust deed is covered by the Truth in Lending Act, as long as the proceeds are used for personal, family, or household purposes (such as buying a home or sending the kids to college). If the loan is used for business, commercial, or agricultural purposes, however, the act wouldn't apply. And a loan for more than $25,000 isn't covered by the act if it isn't secured by real property, regardless of how the proceeds are used.

DISCLOSURE REQUIREMENTS. The Truth in Lending Act's disclosure requirements apply not only to lenders but also to credit arrangers, go-betweens who help would-be borrowers find willing lenders.

The primary disclosures that a lender or credit arranger must make to a loan applicant are the total finance charge and the annual percentage rate. The **total finance charge** is the sum of all fees the lender charges a borrower in exchange for granting the loan. That includes the interest on the loan, plus charges like the origination fee, points, finder's fees, and service fees. Title insurance costs, credit report charges, the appraisal fee, and points paid by the seller are not included.

The **annual percentage rate (APR)** states the relationship of the total finance charge to the amount of the loan, expressed as an annual percentage. A loan's APR is higher than its annual interest rate, since it reflects all the other finance charges in addition to the interest. For example, a loan with an 11% annual interest rate might have an 11.25% APR.

The lender or credit arranger must give the loan applicant a clear, easily understandable disclosure statement. In addition to the total finance charge and the APR, the statement must disclose the total amount financed, the payment schedule, the total number of payments, the total amount of payments, and information regarding any balloon payments, late fees, or prepayment charges. In the case of a real estate loan, it must also state whether the loan may be assumed by someone who buys the security property from the borrower.

Additional disclosures are required for adjustable-rate loans. The lender must give the applicant an informational brochure on ARM loans, the *Consumer Handbook on Adjustable Rate Mortgages*, published jointly by the Federal Reserve and the Federal Housing Finance Board. The lender must also provide specific information regarding the particular ARM loan program being applied for, such as the index, the initial rate, and any rate or payment caps.

The Truth in Lending Act has some special rules for home equity loans. (A home equity loan is a loan secured by the borrower's existing residence, as opposed to a loan financing the purchase or construction of a residence.) When the security property is the borrower's principal residence, the act gives a home equity borrower a right of rescission. The borrower has the right to rescind the loan agreement up until three business days after signing the agreement, receiving the disclosure statement, or receiving notice of the right of rescission, whichever comes latest. If the borrower never receives the statement or notice, the right of rescission does not expire for three years. (Remember that this right only applies to home equity loans. There is no right of rescission for a loan financing the purchase or construction of the borrower's principal residence.) The Truth in Lending Act also requires certain disclosures for home equity plans that involve repeated extensions of credit, versus a single loan.

ADVERTISING. The Truth in Lending Act strictly controls advertising of credit terms. Its advertising rules apply to anyone who advertises consumer credit, not just lenders and credit arrangers. For example, a real estate broker advertising financing terms for a listed home has to comply with Regulation Z.

The cash price for a property and a loan's annual percentage rate can always be advertised. But if any other particular loan terms (the downpayment or the interest rate, for example) are stated in an ad, then all the terms must also be included. For example, if an ad says, "Assume 11% VA loan," it will violate the Truth in Lending Act unless it goes on to reveal the APR and all the terms of repayment. However, general statements such as "low down" or "easy terms" don't trigger the full disclosure requirement.

SELLER FINANCING DISCLOSURE LAW

When a seller carries back a purchase money loan on residential property, California law requires that certain disclosures be made to both buyer and seller if there is an "arranger of credit" involved. For the purposes of the statute, an arranger of credit is anyone (other than the buyer or the seller) who:

- ◆ is involved in negotiating the terms of the loan agreement,
- ◆ participates in preparing the financing documents, or
- ◆ is directly or indirectly compensated for arranging the financing or the sale.

There's an exception for escrow agents, and for lawyers representing either party— these aren't considered arrangers of credit. But if the buyer or seller is a lawyer or real estate agent, he or she is considered an arranger of credit if neither party is represented by a real estate agent.

COVERAGE OF THE LAW. The disclosure law applies when a seller gives the buyer credit for all or part of the purchase price, if:

1. the property is residential with one to four units,
2. the credit arrangements involve a finance charge or provide for four or more payments (not including the downpayment), and
3. an arranger of credit is involved.

However, a transaction is exempt if it's already covered by other disclosure laws, such as the Truth in Lending Act, the Real Estate Settlement Procedures Act (see Chapter 11), or the Mortgage Loan Broker Law.

DISCLOSURE REQUIREMENTS. When the seller financing disclosure law applies to a transaction, the required disclosures must be made before the buyer signs the note or security agreement. The seller must make disclosures to the buyer, and the buyer must make disclosures to the seller. The arranger of credit is responsible for ensuring that each party discloses all required information to the other.

The statute contains a long list of required disclosures. Here are some (but not all) of the things that must be disclosed:

- ◆ the terms of the note and security agreements;
- ◆ the terms and conditions of senior encumbrances (such as a first trust deed that the buyer will be assuming or taking subject to);
- ◆ whether the financing may result in negative amortization;
- ◆ whether the financing will result in a balloon payment (if so, the buyer must be warned that it may be difficult to obtain refinancing to cover the balloon payment); and
- ◆ employment, income, and credit information about the buyer, or a statement that the arranger of credit has made no representation regarding the buyer's creditworthiness.

MORTGAGE LOAN BROKER LAW

Real estate agents often help buyers obtain financing. This assistance may go beyond simply helping the buyer apply to one institutional lender. In some cases, it's necessary to get loans from two or more lenders to raise enough cash to close the transaction.

California's Mortgage Loan Broker Law (also known as the Necessitous Borrowers Act or the Real Property Loan Law) regulates real estate agents who act as loan brokers. The law requires a loan broker to give the borrower a disclosure statement. And for loans secured by residential property, the law places restrictions on the fees and commissions paid by the borrower or received by the loan broker, and regulates other aspects of the loan terms. We'll give only an overview of some of the law's key provisions here.

DISCLOSURE STATEMENT. The disclosure statement required by the Mortgage Loan Broker Law must be on a form approved by the California Real Estate Commissioner. It discloses all the costs involved in obtaining the loan, and the actual amount the borrower will receive after all costs and fees are deducted. The borrower must receive the statement before signing the note and security agreement.

A disclosure statement is required whenever a real estate agent negotiates a loan or performs services for borrowers or lenders in connection with a loan. It's required for loans secured by commercial property as well as for residential loans. But there's an important exception. The disclosure statement is not required if:

◆ the lender is an institutional lender, and
◆ the commission paid by the borrower is 2% of the loan amount or less.

COMMISSIONS AND COSTS. The Mortgage Loan Broker Law limits the commissions and costs that a real estate agent may charge the borrower for arranging a loan secured by residential property with one to four units. But these restrictions only apply when the security agreement is as stated below.

The maximum commissions that an agent can charge are:

First trust deeds, a first trust deed for less than $30,000.
◆ 5% of the principal if the loan term is less than three years, and
◆ 10% of the principal if the term is three years or more;

Junior trust deeds, a second trust deed for less than $20,000.
◆ 5% of the principal if the term is less than two years,
◆ 10% of the principal if the term is at least two years, but less than three years, and
◆ 15% of the principal if the term is three years or more.

And for these loans, the costs of making the loan (such as the appraisal and escrow fees) cannot exceed 5% of the loan amount, or $390, whichever is greater. But the costs charged to the borrower must never exceed $700, and must never exceed the actual costs.

BALLOON PAYMENTS. The Mortgage Loan Broker Law prohibits balloon payments in certain residential loans secured by first trust deeds for less than $30,000 or junior trust deeds for less than $20,000. Balloon payments are prohibited in these loans if the loan is to be paid off in less than three years. And if the security property is an owner-occupied home, balloon payments are prohibited when the loan term is less than six years. (These rules don't apply to seller financing, however.) For the purposes of this law, a balloon payment is one that is more than twice as large as the smallest payment required by the loan agreement.

SPANISH TRANSLATION. When a mortgage loan broker represents a borrower who speaks Spanish and not English, the broker must give the borrower a written Spanish translation of the loan documents before the borrower signs them. This rule only applies to loans used for personal, family, or household purposes (such as the purchase of a home).

PREPAYMENT CHARGES. The borrower can prepay up to 20% of the unpaid balance at the time of payment in any 12 month period during the first seven years of the loan without a prepayment penalty. If more than the 20% is paid, the excess is subject to a maximum of 6 months interest. After seven years there is no prepayment charge.

LATE CHARGES. The late charge provisions are the same as those mentioned earlier in this chapter for residential property except the rate is 10% of the installment or $500, whichever is greater.

HOME EQUITY PURCHASERS OF FORECLOSURE PROPERTY

The California legislature found that homeowners whose residences are in foreclosure have been subjected to fraud and unfair dealings by home equity purchasers. During a foreclosure period, the poor, elderly, and financially unsophisticated are vulnerable to the harassment of equity purchasers who induce the homeowner to sell their home for a small fraction of its fair market value through the use of schemes which often involve misrepresentations, deceit, intimidation and other unfair dealing practices. Consequently, the legislature adopted some rules for home equity purchasers of owner occupied property with 1-4 units after the recording of a notice of default. The contents of the equity purchase contract and the cancellation notice are set by the legislature. The seller may not waive any rights under this law and can cancel the contract within 5 business days after the equity sales contract was entered into or until the foreclosure sale date, whichever occurs first. Taking unconscionable advantage of the equity seller is unlawful and the seller has 2 years from recording the equity sale to rescind the contract. However, there can be no rescission in the event of a subsequent bona fide purchaser or encumbrancer. The equity seller has 4 years to bring a civil action against the equity buyer and may recover damages or equitable relief, attorney's fees and possible exemplary damages. If the equity purchaser fails to comply with the statutory law, the purchaser may be fined not more than $10,000, sentenced to jail for not more than one year, or both. An equity purchaser is one who acquires title to a residence in foreclosure, except one who acquired title:

1. for use as a residence
2. by a deed in lieu of foreclosure
3. by trustee's deed
4. by a statutory sale
5. pursuant to a court order
6. from a spouse, blood relative, or blood relative of a spouse.

MORTGAGE FORECLOSURE CONSULTANTS LAW

The California legislature placed numerous restrictions on foreclosure consultants who were found to use fraud and harassment to obtain a fee from the property owner representing that the consultant could provide beneficial services to save the home from foreclosure. These consultants often charged high fees or secured their fee by a deed of trust on the residence to be saved, or performed worthless services in order to collect a fee. A foreclosure consultant is any person who, for compensation, will:

1. stop or postpone the foreclosure, or
2. obtain any forbearance from the beneficiary or mortgagee, or
3. assist with reinstatement of the loan, or
4. obtain an extension of time to reinstate the loan,
5. obtain waiver of the acceleration clause in the note, or
6. assist the owner with obtaining any loan or other funds, or
7. protect the owner's credit, or
8. save the residence from foreclosure.

There are a number of persons who are not considered foreclosure consultants, for example, attorneys providing legal services, licensed accountants, the person holding the lien being foreclosed, and institutional lenders. The law covers owner-occupied residences of 1-4 units after the recording of the notice of default. The contents of the foreclosure consultant contract are established by the law. No waiver of rights or limitations of liability are allowed in the contract. The property owner can cancel the contract within 3 business days following its signing. Foreclosure consultants may not:

1. receive any compensation until full performance of all terms of the contract,
2. receive a fee of more than 10 percent per year of the loan amount,
3. take any security interest for the consulting fee,
4. receive a fee from a third party without a full disclosure to the property owner,

5. acquire any interest in the property being foreclosed,
6. receive a power of attorney from the property owner except to inspect the documents,
7. induce the property owner to enter into a contract which does not comply with the law.

The property owner has 4 years from a violation of the law to sue for recovery of actual damages, attorney's fees and court costs, plus, it is possible to recover exemplary damages. Any violation of law subjects the financial consultant or representative to a fine of not more than $10,000, a jail term not exceeding 1 year or both. The financial consultant is liable for all actions of any representative, and the representative must provide the owner with proof of a valid sales license and bonding, for twice the fair market value of the residence, in writing prior to any interest being transferred by the owner.

Agricultural Security Interests

Suppose a borrower wants to give the lender a security interest in standing timber or crops growing in a field with the idea that the lender will harvest the collateral if there is a default. How is this accomplished? The parties sign and record a financing statement (Form UCE-1) which describes the collateral and where the real property is located. Once recorded in the grantor-grantee index it becomes constructive notice of the security interest.

CHAPTER SUMMARY

1. A promissory note is the maker's promise to repay a debt. The payee may transfer the note to another person. Almost all promissory notes are negotiable.

2. A promissory note can be a straight note (with interest-only payments) or an installment note (with payments of principal and interest). An installment note may be fully amortized, or partially amortized with a balloon payment required at the end of the loan term.

3. A security agreement makes real property collateral for a loan, creating a lien and giving the lender the right to foreclose if the debt isn't paid. A deed of trust includes a power of sale clause, which enables the lender to foreclose nonjudicially. A mortgage must be foreclosed judicially. Nonjudicial foreclosure is faster and cheaper than a foreclosure lawsuit.

4. Most loan agreements permit the borrower to prepay, but nonresidential loans can be locked in. A residential borrower must be allowed to prepay. If residential property is owner-occupied, only a limited prepayment penalty may be charged, and only during the first five years of the loan term.

5. A lender may impose late fees and charge a default interest rate on delinquent amounts. An acceleration clause gives the lender the right to declare the entire loan balance due if the borrower defaults. The loan agreement may provide that the lender can impose a prepayment penalty after accelerating the loan.

6. A due-on-sale clause gives the lender the right to accelerate the loan if the borrower transfers the security property to a new owner. But the lender may be willing to let the new owner assume the loan at a higher rate of interest, or upon payment of an assumption fee.

7. When a trust deed contains a subordination clause, the lender agrees to subordinate its lien to another trust deed that would otherwise have lower lien priority. The clause should establish strict standards for the subordinating trust deed, to minimize the subordinated lender's risk.

8. To foreclose nonjudicially, the trustee records a notice of default and mails copies to the borrower, all junior lienholders, and other interested parties. At least three months after recording the notice of default, and at least 20 days before the sale, the trustee must record, post, publish, and mail out a notice of sale.

9. A trustee's sale can be prevented by curing the default and reinstating the loan, by paying off the entire loan (plus costs) to redeem the property, or by giving the lender a deed in lieu of foreclosure.

10. Trustee's sale proceeds are first applied to the foreclosure costs, then to the foreclosed trust deed, then to junior liens in order of priority. Anything left over belongs to the borrower. All junior liens are extinguished by the sale. The purchaser is given a trustee's deed.

11. For judicial foreclosure, the lender files a lawsuit against the borrower and junior lienholders. The court issues a decree of foreclosure, and the property is sold at a sheriff's sale. If the lender obtains a deficiency judgment, the sale purchaser is only given a certificate of sale, and the borrower has one year to redeem the property. If the borrower doesn't redeem it, the purchaser is finally given a sheriff's deed.

12. If the foreclosure sale proceeds don't cover the debt and the lender's costs, in a few cases the lender is entitled to a deficiency judgment. But a deficiency judgment is never available after a nonjudicial foreclosure, or if the loan was a residential purchase money loan. A deficiency judgment also isn't available after foreclosure of a seller-financed purchase money loan (on any type of property), unless it was subordinated to a non-purchase money loan.

13. In a land contract purchase, the vendee takes possession of the property immediately, but the vendor retains legal title as security for payment. The vendee has equitable title. The vendor doesn't deliver the deed to the vendee until the contract price has been paid off.

14. The federal Truth in Lending Act and California's seller financing disclosure law and Mortgage Loan Broker Law require lenders and credit arrangers to fully inform residential loan applicants about the cost of financing. The Truth in Lending Act also regulates consumer finance advertising.

15. Because of problems with equity purchasers of foreclosure property and those selling foreclosure consulting services, both practices are regulated in California.

16. Recording a financing statement gives constructive notice of a security interest in growing crops or timber.

CASE PROBLEM

Williams v. Fassler, 110 Cal. App. 3d 7, 167 Cal. Rptr. 545 (1980)

Mr. Fassler owned a 20-acre ranch with a house on it in Stanislaus County. He agreed to sell it to Mr. Williams for $114,000. For income tax reasons, Fassler didn't want to collect the full price at the time of the sale. So Williams executed an $80,940 promissory note and a trust deed in favor of Fassler. Williams was to pay $8,709 (principal and 8.75% annual interest) each year for 20 years. The note provided that if Williams paid anything extra during the first five years of the loan, Fassler would charge a 50% penalty on the extra amounts.

Seven months after buying the property, Williams decided to build a new house there. He couldn't obtain financing for the project unless he paid off Fassler's trust deed. But if Williams did that, Fassler would charge the 50% prepayment penalty on more than $70,000—so the penalty alone would come to more than $35,000.

Williams sued for a declaratory judgment, asking the court to rule that the prepayment penalty was invalid. Could Fassler enforce the penalty provision? Does it make any difference whether the court treated the ranch as residential property? Could Fassler have included a lock-in clause in the loan agreement?

Answer: Treating the ranch as nonresidential property, the court ruled that Fassler could enforce the prepayment penalty provision.

If the property had been residential, Fassler couldn't have charged a 50% penalty on the entire balance. Williams would have had the right to prepay 20% of the original loan amount in one year without penalty. Fassler could only have charged a penalty on the prepayment exceeding 20%. And even that penalty couldn't amount to more than six months' interest on the excess. It probably would have worked out to be in the neighborhood of $2,450.

But since the ranch wasn't residential, none of the statutory limits on prepayment charges applied. Williams argued that the 50% penalty was unreasonably high, but the court disagreed. Fassler presented evidence that if Williams paid him the full price in one year, Fassler would have to pay $16,371 more in taxes. And he'd have to pay taxes on the collected penalty, too. All in all, unless the penalty came to about $33,000, Fassler would be worse off because of the prepayment.

Fassler could have included a lock-in clause in the loan agreement and prevented prepayment altogether, since this wasn't residential property. And even if it were residential, Fassler could have included a provision preventing any prepayment during the year of the sale, because this was seller financing rather than a third-party loan.

BORROWER'S RIGHT TO RECEIVE COPY OF APPRAISAL REPORT

A borrower has the right to a copy of the appraisal report to be obtained in connection with the loan for which he or she is applying, providing he or she is willing to pay for it.

CHAPTER 12 KEY TERMS		
	fictitious trust deed	promissory note
	hypothecation	reconveyance
	judicial/nonjudicial	redemption
acceleration	foreclosure	Regulation Z
amortized	legal/equitable title	reinstatement period
annual percentage rate	lis pendens	security agreement
assumption	lock-in clause	senior/junior lienholder
balloon payment	maker	sheriff's deed
beneficiary statement	maturity date	subject to
beneficiary	mortgage	subordination
call provision	mortgagor/mortgagee	trustee
certificate of sale	negotiable instrument	trustee's deed
credit bid	notice of default	trustor
cure	notice of sale	vendor/vendee
deed in lieu	payee	
deed of trust	pledging	
deficiency judgment	power of sale	
due-on-sale (alienation)	prepayment penalty	
clause	principal	

Credit Scoring

Over the past several years, lenders have increased their use of "credit scores," derived from information in a consumer's credit report, using a mathematical model to develop a 3 digit score and determine whether or not to make a loan, and at what interest rate. California Governor Gray Davis signed SB 1607 (Figueroa), CAR's landmark credit-scoring legislation giving consumers access to their credit scores. In addition to providing consumers with their specific credit score and key reasons why a score was not better, the legislation also gives consumers the right to receive a copy of their credit scores when they request copies of their credit file.

What is credit scoring?

Credit scores are assigned numbers used by lenders to determine whether a consumer will get a loan and at what interest rate. Individual lenders often contract with a credit reporting agency such as Trans Union, Experian, or Equifax who compile consumer credit information. These companies then contract with a credit scoring company, more often than not, Fair, Issacs and Company (www.fairisaac.com), who own the mathematical model used to create the score. They provide the lender with a list of "reason codes" that the lender can choose from when receiving scores for consumers applying for mortgages. The "reason codes" can include things like, "too few bank card accounts", "too many sub-prime accounts," etc. The credit scoring company uses information from a consumer's credit report, together with these "reason codes" and the mathematical formula to create an individual's credit score.

This new law will:

1. require lenders to provide consumers with their specific credit score, what credit information went into making up the score, and an explanation of how credit scores work in the loan approval process;

2. compel credit reporting agencies to correct inaccurate information in a timely manner; and

3. require credit reporting agencies to correct inaccurate information more quickly and provide consumers with additional legal recourse if an agency continues to report inaccurate information once they become aware that a mistake has been made.

TransUnion: www.transunion.com
Experian: www.experian.com/experian us.htmi
Equifax: www.equifax.com

Quiz—Chapter 12

1. L loans B $100,000 to buy a house. B signs a promissory note for the loan, but doesn't sign a security agreement. Which of the following is true?
   a. The note is only enforceable if it's negotiable
   b. The note is unenforceable because it isn't backed up by a security agreement
   c. L can sue B to enforce the note, but L doesn't have a lien against B's house
   d. The note gives L the right to foreclose on B's house if he doesn't pay him back

2. When the borrower desires to pay off a note secured by a deed of trust and wants to known the exact amount. The lender upon request supplies the borrower with:
   a. a beneficiary statement.
   b. a deed of reconveyance.
   c. a reinstatement bill.
   d. a rescission notice.

3. The monthly payments on the promissory note are enough to pay off the entire loan, both principal and interest, by the maturity date. The note is called a:
   a. straight note.
   b. fully amortized note.
   c. partially amortized note.
   d. balloon note.

4. The provision in a deed of trust that makes it different from a mortgage is the:
   a. power of sale clause.
   b. subordination clause.
   c. prepayment provision.
   d. acceleration clause.

5. When the borrower pays off a loan secured by trust deed, the lender must arrange for the trustee to record:
   a. the canceled note.
   b. a notice of rescission.
   c. a payoff certificate.
   d. a full reconveyance.

6. If the borrower defaults, the lender has the right to declare the entire loan balance due immediately. This trust deed must contain:
   a. a due-on-sale clause.
   b. an assumption clause.
   c. an acceleration clause.
   d. a deficiency provision.

7. An alienation clause is the same thing as a:
   a. lock-in clause.
   b. due-on-sale clause.
   c. subordination clause.
   d. default interest provision.

8. The borrower has fallen behind in his payments and the lender has asked the trustee to start the foreclosure process. During the reinstatement period, the borrower can reinstate the loan by:
   a. paying off the loan in full, including the prepayment penalty.
   b. paying all delinquent amounts, plus the costs incurred because of default.
   c. paying all delinquencies, plus the acceleration penalty.
   d. filing a notice of rescission.

9. The Truth in Lending Act:
   a. requires lenders to provide loan applicants with information about charges.
   b. limits the maximum amount of finance charges a leader can impose.
   c. doesn't apply to trust deed loans for more than $25,000.
   d. all of the above.

10. B is buying a house on a land contract, and he has made about half of the required payments. B has:
   a. legal title.
   b. subordinated title.
   c. contract title.
   d. equitable title.

ANSWERS: 1. c; 2. a; 3. b; 4. a; 5. d; 6. c; 7. b; 8. b; 9. a; 10. d

CHAPTER 13
Land Use Controls

CHAPTER OVERVIEW

A prospective buyer considers property with particular plans in mind—remodeling the house, opening a gas station, or planting a lemon grove. To decide whether the property is suitable, the buyer needs to find out what restrictions there are on the use of the property. The real estate agent and the seller are required to tell the buyer about any restrictions they are aware of.

This chapter discusses public restrictions on land use, laws imposed by federal, state, and local governments on private owners. It also explains private restrictions, imposed by a previous owner or the developer.

Public Restrictions

Public restrictions on the use of privately owned land have proliferated in the past few decades. They take the form of zoning ordinances, building codes, subdivision laws, and environmental legislation.

ZONING

In Colonial times, a landowner could do just about anything he wanted with his property. He could build a house or raise pigs or run a blacksmith shop, or even do all three on the same piece of property. But as the country's population grew and cities became crowded, people began to see a pig farm right next to a shopping district as a problem.

Chapter 13

To prevent that kind of conflict, and to gain some control over the problems of overcrowding, U.S. cities began to enact zoning laws. (New York City adopted the first major zoning ordinance in 1916, and the California legislature enacted a statewide zoning law in 1917.) A zoning law divides a city or county into zones, and segregates different types of land use in different zones. The typical ordinance creates residential zones, commercial zones, industrial zones, and agricultural zones. Zoning laws also regulate the size of lots, the size and height of buildings, and the placement of buildings on each lot.

POWER TO REGULATE LAND USE

At first it was argued that zoning laws were an unconstitutional interference with a landowner's property rights. But in 1926, in the landmark case *Village of Euclid v. Ambler Realty Co.* (272 U.S. 365), the U.S. Supreme Court ruled that zoning was a constitutional exercise of the police power.

The **police power** is a state government's power to adopt and enforce laws for the protection of the public health, safety, morals, and general welfare (Article XI, Section 7 of the California Constitution). A state may delegate this power to local governments (county or city). Because zoning ordinances prevent overcrowding and the problems with sanitation, fire protection, and law enforcement that overcrowding creates, they protect the public health, safety, and welfare. So, as a general rule, they are a legitimate use of the police power and are not unconstitutional.

But the constitutionality of a particular zoning law can still be challenged. For example, a plaintiff may argue that an ordinance isn't necessary for the protection of the public. That argument rarely wins a lawsuit, however; courts allow local governments a lot of discretion in deciding what the public good requires.

Case Example: The area in San Diego known as Old Town is the site of the city's original settlement; many of the buildings there were built before 1871. The San Diego City Council adopted an ordinance to regulate the design of buildings in Old Town. The law required property owners in Old Town to apply to an architectural review board before constructing new buildings, altering old buildings, or putting up signs. The goal was to make all the buildings look like those built before 1871.

Mr. Bohannan, who owned a store in Old Town, filed a lawsuit challenging the constitutionality of the law. He argued that because the ordinance regulated only the appearance of buildings, its purpose was merely esthetic. It didn't protect the public health, safety, morals, or welfare.

Ruling that the ordinance was constitutional, the court stated, "The police power extends to measures designed to promote the public convenience and the general prosperity." Preservation of the historical character of Old Town had educational value for the public. It also encouraged tourism, which helped the local economy. *Bohannan v. City of San Diego*, 30 Cal. App. 3d 416 (1973).

A landowner whose property has been severely restricted by a zoning law can challenge the law as unconstitutionally excessive. But to win the lawsuit, the owner has to prove that the zoning law has rendered the property virtually useless, by preventing the only kind of development it was suited for. It isn't enough to show that the value of the property was lowered—even if it was lowered substantially.

Case Example: HFH, a limited partnership, bought a tract of unimproved land in Cerritos for $388,000. At the time of the purchase, the property was zoned for commercial use. But the city adopted a new zoning law a few years later. Now HFH's property was in a low-density residential zone, where very few commercial uses were permitted.

HFH decided to sell its property, and Diversified Associates contracted to buy it for $400,000. The contract was conditional, however: Diversified wouldn't go through with the purchase unless the tract was rezoned for commercial use. HFH applied to the city to have it rezoned, but the request was turned down.

HFH sued the city. The partnership claimed the zoning change had lowered the value of its land from $400,000 to approximately $75,000. But the court dismissed the case. Even though the property's value was sharply reduced as a result of the zoning law, it could be developed for residential use. The law was constitutional, and the city was not required to compensate HFH for its loss. *HFH, Ltd. v. Superior County of Los Angeles County*, 15 Cal. 3d 508, 125 Cal. Rptr. 365 (1975).

---

http://freeadvice.com/law/592us.htm
(Free Advice - Zoning Questions)

Zoning laws can be challenged on a number of other constitutional grounds. Generally, a citizen has 120 days after the zoning ordinance is adopted to challenge it. An ordinance can't be discriminatory—that is, it must be applied in the same manner to all similarly situated property owners. It also can't be **exclusionary**, excluding certain classes of people from a community. (For example, requiring all residences in a town to be large single-family homes would effectively prevent low-income families from living there.) And ordinances regulating signs can't violate the right to freedom of speech.

Also, some zoning laws have been struck down because they invade the property owner's right to privacy. For instance, a Santa Barbara ordinance prohibited more than five unrelated people from sharing a single-family home. It didn't limit the number of people who could share a home as long as they were related by blood, marriage, or adoption. The California Supreme Court ruled that the ordinance's arbitrary distinction between families and groups of unrelated people violated privacy rights. The court stated "In general, zoning ordinances are much less suspect when the focus on the use than when they command inquiry into who are the users." (*City of Santa Barbara v. Adamson*, 27 Cal. 3d 123, 164 Cal. Rptr. 539 [1980].)

Land Use Planning

Zoning activity was fairly limited until the real estate boom following World War II. Returning veterans all seemed to want a home in the suburbs, so developers began snatching up farm land to subdivide and fill with tract houses. Longtime residents fought

Chapter 13

to keep out the developers, and local governments tried to keep up with the growth by adopting more comprehensive zoning laws.

California has many examples of the problems that haphazard, unplanned growth causes. To promote more rational development, the state now requires each city and county to have a planning agency. Most counties and cities have an independent **planning commission**. In smaller communities, however, the city council often acts as the planning agency.

The planning commission is responsible for preparing a comprehensive, long-term **general plan** for all development within the city or county. The general plan outlines the community's development policies and establishes an overall design for the various land uses in the area. It is supposed to address many issues: population density, building intensity, housing, traffic patterns, transportation systems, noise control, open space, safety, hazards such as earthquakes and wildfires, and conservation of natural resources. While developing the plan, the commission must hold public hearings to gather ideas and opinions from citizens, public agencies, and developers.

Once the commission has prepared a general plan, the city council or county board of supervisors holds at least one more public hearing, and then decides whether to adopt the plan. If the plan is adopted, all land use regulations (including zoning ordinances) must be consistent with it. The plan may be amended, but there must be another public hearing on the proposed change, and the property owners who would be affected must be notified.

Several state and regional agencies help coordinate the general plans of neighboring communities. When a city expands (by annexing new land) or two communities merge, the **Local Agency Formation Commission (LAFCO)** supervises the change to make sure it accords with the general plans of the communities involved. The **Metropolitan Transportation Commission (MTC)** oversees transportation planning on a regional basis. And the **Association of Bay Area Governments (ABAG)** works to coordinate the general plans of all cities and counties in the San Francisco Bay area.

www.wld.com
(West's Legal Directory - Zoning)

PLANNING COMMISSION
develops the general plan

COUNTY BOARD OF SUPERVISORS OR CITY COUNCIL
adopts the general plan
implements the general plan through zoning ordinances

BOARD OF ADJUSTMENT
grants variances and other exceptions to zoning laws

(In many smaller communities, the town council performs all these functions.)

Implementing the General Plan

As the name suggests, a general plan sets out the community's land use policies in general terms. To carry out those policies, detailed zoning ordinances must be drafted that conform to the plan. In most cases, these are enacted by the county board of supervisors or city council (usually with the planning commission's advice). Since zoning can have far-reaching effects, the council or board is required to hold a public hearing before adopting a new ordinance or changing a current ordinance.

California's state constitution also permits citizens to bypass the council or board and adopt local land use controls by popular vote, through the initiative process. In the 1970s, the citizens of Livermore enacted an ordinance prohibiting residential construction until a number of problems (overcrowded schools, sewage pollution, and water shortages) were solved. The ordinance led to a lawsuit, and the court upheld both the use of the initiative process and the ordinance. (*Associated Home Builders of the Greater Eastbay, Inc. v. City of Livermore*, 18 Cal. 3d. 582, 135 Cal. Rptr. 41 [1976].)

Typical Zoning Provisions

Early zoning laws usually established only four land use categories: residential, commercial, industrial, and agricultural/rural. Modern zoning regulations tend to be much more complicated. In addition to the four basic categories, numerous subcategories are used.

A Zoning Map

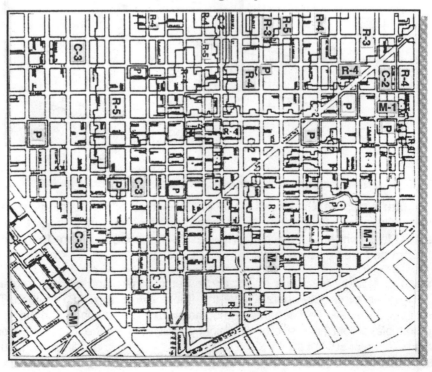

Example: In Nowhere City, there are several types of residential zones. In zones designated R1, only detached single-family houses are allowed; in R2 zones, row houses and duplexes (as well as detached single-family houses) are permitted; R3 zones also have apartments and condominiums; and any kind of housing (including manufactured housing) is allowed in an R4 zone.

An industrial zone might be divided into a section for light industry and a section for heavy industry. And sometimes a mixture of uses is allowed in a single zone: commercial and light industrial in the same zone, or multi-family residential and retail in the same zone.

Each zone generally has its own minimum lot size and building height limits. There are usually **setback** and **side yard** rules, requiring buildings to be at least a specified distance from the property lines. And there may be a limit on how much of a lot can be covered by a building.

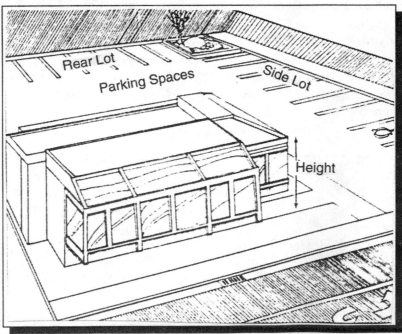

Example: Nowhere City's ordinance provides that office buildings in a C2 commercial zone may not be higher than ten stories and must be set back at least 20 feet from any of the property lines. In that zone, no more than 80% of a lot can be taken up by a building.

Instead of strictly prescribing height and coverage limits and setback requirements, some ordinances allow developers to use the **floor area ratio (FAR)** method. The FAR method controls the ratio between the area of the building's floor space and the area of the lot. For example, a floor area ratio of two might permit 100% of the lot to be covered by a two-story building, or 50% of the lot to be covered by a four-story building. The FAR method gives architects and developers more flexibility in deciding the shape and height of buildings.

Zoning ordinances regulate many other aspects of development in addition to type of use and building size and placement. For instance, an ordinance is likely to include requirements for off-street parking, landscaping, and outdoor lighting.

Even if a proposal satisfied the requirements of the general plan and zoning ordinances, there is no guarantee that a permit will be issued.

Case Example: Dore owned one of four commercial lots in an exclusive 796 residential lot development in Ventura County. Dore sought a planned development permit to construct three commercial buildings on the lot. At the hearing many residents opposed the permit because of a driveway on a blind curve and graphic congestion. Dore's application complied with applicable zoning ordinances and conformed to the general plan. The permit was denied and the denial sustained by the Board of Supervisors. Dore sued to have the permit issued.

The Court of Appeal held that the Board of Supervisors could deny the permit, even though it complied with the zoning laws, because of danger to people on the blind curve, traffic congestion, and resident opposition. *Dore v. County of Ventura*, 23 Cal. App. 4th 320, 28 Cal. Rptr 2d 299 (1994).

Exceptions to Zoning Regulations

As you've seen, zoning can have a big impact on the use and value of property. To be constitutional, a zoning law must be applied in the same manner to all similarly situated property owners. But if zoning regulations are rigidly applied, it can lead to unnecessarily harsh results for a few owners. Zoning laws usually have special provisions for existing uses that conflict with the new rules. They also establish procedures for creating limited exceptions to the regulations.

NONCONFORMING USES. When a new zoning designation is imposed on a neighborhood, some owners find that the way they've been using their property is no longer permitted, even though it was fine under the old law.

> **Example:** B opens a small bakery in an area zoned for mixed residential and commercial use. A few years later, the city council rezones that neighborhood to allow only single-family homes.

B's bakery is now a nonconforming use—it doesn't conform to the new law. If an owner were ordered to discontinue a nonconforming use immediately, that might be considered a taking of the property, and the government would have to pay compensation (see the discussion of eminent domain in Chapter 10). That practice could also create a lot of uncertainty: if I open a business here, will I be ordered to shut it down six months from now?

Chapter 13

So zoning laws usually provide that existing nonconforming uses may continue. However, a nonconforming use is subject to a number of restrictions. These restrictions are intended to gradually phase out the nonconforming use. For instance, as a general rule, a nonconforming use may not be enlarged or expanded.

> **Case Example:** Mr. and Mrs. Rehfeld owned a grocery store on the corner of Filbert and Baker Streets in San Francisco. The neighborhood was not zoned when the store first opened, but many years later it was zoned for residential use. The Rehfelds were allowed to continue operating their grocery store as a nonconforming use.
>
> After the zoning ordinance went into effect, the Rehfelds applied to the planning commission for a permit to expand the store. The lot behind the store was vacant, and the Rehfelds wanted to extend the store 22 feet onto that lot. The permit was denied; the ordinance didn't allow nonconforming uses to be enlarged. *Rehfeld v. San Francisco*, 218 Cal. 83, 21 P.2d 419 (1933).

When the buildings involved in a nonconforming use become obsolete, the owners are usually not allowed to renovate them. Even maintenance and repairs may be restricted: minor repairs are okay, but major repairs that would extend the lifespan of the building aren't permitted. And ordinances generally provide that if a nonconforming building is destroyed by a hazard such as a fire or an earthquake, it may not be rebuilt. Any new structure must comply with the current zoning regulations. If the Rehfelds' store burned down, they could build a house on their property, but would not be allowed to rebuild the store.

Instead of relying on obsolescence or destruction to phase out nonconforming uses, some ordinances simply establish time limits. For example, the zoning authority might have ruled that the Rehfelds could only go on running their store for ten years after the zoning ordinance went into effect. As long as the time limit is reasonable, it will generally be upheld by the courts. One factor in determining whether a time limit is reasonable is the life expectancy of the buildings involved. If at the time the ordinance was passed, the life expectancy of the Rehfelds' building was ten years, that would probably be considered a reasonable time limit for the nonconforming use.

 www.slonet.org/vv/slocity/community_development/zoning_reqs/17_10.html
(City of San Luis Obispo - Zoning Regulations - Nonconforming Uses)

Under most ordinances, if a nonconforming use is discontinued, it can't be resumed later on. If the Rehfelds closed their store for a year or more, they might not be allowed to reopen it. However, a court may require proof of intent to abandon the use. A nonconforming use would usually be allowed to resume after a temporary closure due to events the owner has no control over (a war, for example).

Permission to continue a nonconforming use ordinarily isn't tied to a particular owner. If the Rehfelds sold their property to someone else, the new owner could continue to operate the store as a nonconforming use. But the same restrictions would apply to the new owner. A prospective buyer should find out whether there's a time limit on the existing use of the property, or restrictions on expansion, renovation, or rebuilding.

VARIANCES. Sometimes a zoning ordinance creates special problems for a particular owner because his or her property is unusual in some way. To deal with this, zoning ordinances provide for variances. A **variance** is a permit that lets an owner build a structure or use property in a way that isn't otherwise allowed.

Case Example: The Pasadena zoning ordinance required swimming pools in R1 residential zones to be set back at least 25 feet from the property lines.

Ms. Brown's home was in an R1 zone. She wanted to have a pool installed in her back yard. But her yard was smaller than the other yards in the neighborhood, and there wasn't enough room to place a pool 25 feet from the rear property line.

Ms. Brown was granted a variance permitting her to install a pool only 20 feet from the property line. *Ames v. City of Pasadena*, 167 Cal. App. 2d 510. 334 P.2d 653 (1959).

Variances are a zoning law's safety valve; they provide flexibility when the injury to the property owner would be greater than the public benefit from strict enforcement.

To obtain a variance, a property owner applies to the local zoning authority. That may be a **board of adjustment** or a **zoning administrator**. In some small communities, the town council acts as the zoning authority. Generally, the zoning authority gives public notice of the variance request, and a public hearing is held. If the requested variance is minor and the neighbors don't object, the hearing is perfunctory and the variance is easily granted. (Some ordinances provide that routine variances may even be granted without a public hearing.) But if there are objections, the process takes longer. Expert witnesses may be called to testify about the possible effects of the proposed variance.

The zoning authority's decision can be appealed to the **board of zoning appeals** (or to the county board of supervisors or city council if there is no appeals board). The appeals board's decision may in turn be appealed to a superior court. However, courts usually won't overrule a local authority's zoning decision unless there has clearly been an abuse of discretion.

In most cases, a variance authorizes only a minor deviation from the regulations. If a property owner needs the rules loosened too much, a variance is inappropriate. Ordinances often provide that a variance can't conflict with the general intent of the law, lower the value of surrounding properties, or change the essential character of the neighborhood. Since 1970, California law has prevented local authorities from granting **use variances**—a variance allowing a commercial use in a residential zone, for example.

California law also limits variances to special circumstances. The property in question must have an unusual size, shape, topography, or location, in comparison to the other properties in the zone. The owner has to show that because of the property's unusual characteristics, he or she would be more restricted by strict application of the zoning law than the neighbors are. Thus, a variance is supposed to bring a property owner up to the same level as the neighbors, not grant extra privileges that the neighbors don't have.

 www.ci.san-marino.ca.us
www.cityofla.org/PLN/index.htm
(Department of Planning and Building)

Case Example: An investment company owned 28 acres in Topanga Canyon. The Los Angeles County zoning ordinance permitted only light agricultural and single-family residential use in that area, and set the minimum lot size at one acre. The investment company was granted a variance to establish a 93-space mobile home park on its land. The Topanga Association for a Scenic Community appealed the variance decision.

The investment company defended the variance by pointing out that its property was unusually difficult to develop; it was hilly, and extremely steep in places. Using the property for one-acre homes would generate much lower profits than the proposed mobile home park.

The California Supreme Court ruled that the variance should be denied. The investment company's property was difficult to develop because of its terrain, but the same was true of the surrounding properties affected by the zoning law. The variance would have put the investment company in a better position than its neighbors. *Topanga Association for a Scenic Community v. Los Angeles*, 11 Cal. 3d 506, 113 Cal. Rptr. 836 (1974).

It should be noted that these state variance rules (no use variances, and the unusual circumstances requirement) don't apply to municipalities that were organized as **chartered cities**. San Diego and San Francisco are examples of chartered cities. The zoning ordinances for a chartered city may or may not follow the state zoning laws.

CONDITIONAL USE PERMITS. Most zoning ordinances allow the local zoning authority to issue special permits for certain uses that are inconsistent with a neighborhood's zoning designation, but are necessary or beneficial to the community. These are called **conditional uses** or **special exceptions**. Common examples include schools, hospitals, churches, cemeteries, and public utility structures. The ordinance will usually have a specific list of conditional uses that may be allowed in a particular zone.

The zoning authority controls the number and placement of these uses, and grants permits subject to conditions that limit their possible adverse effects on neighboring property. One church or one hospital on a residential street might be no problem, but if there were two or three the neighborhood would lose its residential character.

Rezoning

Exceptions to Zoning Regulations

◆ NONCONFORMING USES
◆ VARIANCES
◆ CONDITIONAL USES

In many situations, neither a variance nor a conditional use permit is available. There's one other possibility for a property owner who doesn't want to accept the zoning law's restrictions: requesting a **rezone**. A rezone is actually an amendment to the zoning law, not just an authorized exception to the law. For example, a property owner in an R1 zone (detached single-family homes only) might ask to have part of that zone redesignated R3 (multi-family housing allowed).

A rezone must be consistent with the community's general plan, so drastic changes are usually not allowed. (For instance, a rezone from residential to heavy industrial use is very unlikely.) But a property owner may be able to show that circumstances have changed since the original ordinance was passed, and a new zoning designation would be more appropriate.

> **Example:** Q owns a lot on the edge of a residential zone. The next street over is zoned for commercial use. When the zoning ordinance was adopted, there was a row of small, quiet businesses on the commercial street: a book shop, a grocery store, a dry cleaner's, and a doctor's office. The street was widened several years later, and the businesses changed over time. Now there's a car dealership, a seven-screen movie theater, some taverns and fast-food restaurants, and a bowling alley.
>
> As a result of these changes, the value of Q's home and the other houses on her street has dropped sharply. People don't want to buy homes right next to the noisy commercial strip. The properties on Q's street would be worth a lot more if apartment buildings could be built there, since renters aren't as particular as buyers.
>
> So Q petitions the zoning authority for a rezone. There's very little opposition to the proposal at the public hearing, and Q's request is granted. The boundary lines on the zoning map are redrawn to create a multi-family residential zone as a buffer between the single-family zone and the commercial zone.

SPOT ZONING. The rezoning process can be abused. If a zoning authority grants an isolated zoning change that favors a particular property owner without real justification, it's called spot zoning. That's illegal.

> **Case Example:** Mr. Kerr bought a large tract of property in South Lake Tahoe. The maximum building height limit in that area of the city was 50 feet. Kerr wanted to build a high-rise, so he applied to the city planning commission for a variance. But there weren't legal grounds for a variance; Kerr's property didn't have unusual characteristics that made it more difficult to develop than the surrounding lots. So the variance was denied.
>
> However, the city council then passed an ordinance removing the height limit from Kerr's property. Neighboring landowners sued, and the court ruled that the rezoning was invalid. The change violated the community's general plan without justification and gave Kerr special treatment. *Silvera v. City of South Lake Tahoe*, 3 Cal. App. 3d 554, 83 Cal. Rptr. 698 (1970).

In the *Silvera* case, the council probably voted for the rezone because they felt Kerr's development would be economically beneficial for the community. But in some spot zoning cases, the zoning authority has been bribed. For example, in 1979 a developer paid $30,000 to some members of the San Jose City Council in an effort to obtain a rezone. Occasionally, spot zoning is used against a developer. That's illegal too.

Case Example: Mr. Bateson, a builder, was planning a condominium development. When he applied for a construction permit, he was told he'd have to meet certain requirements before the permit would be issued. Bateson complied with all of these requirements. But then the city council rezoned Bateson's site so the project he'd planned couldn't be built there.

Bateson sued. The court found that the city council's action was solely intended to prevent that particular project. It singled out Bateson unfairly, in violation of his constitutional right to due process. *Bateson v. Geisse*, 856 F.2d 1300 (9th Cir. 1988).

Sometimes a legitimate zoning change can look like spot zoning. But as long as there are sound reasons for the rezone and it doesn't conflict with the general plan, it isn't illegal.

Example: Homeowners in a residential area complain that they have to travel too far for groceries, gas, and other basic services. The city council rezones the four corner lots at an intersection in the neighborhood for commercial use. This would be probably be considered a legitimate change.

In deciding whether or not a particular rezone is illegal spot zoning, the courts consider all the circumstances: How large an area was rezoned? Does the new use meet community needs, or does it benefit a few owners without serving the community?

http://ceres.ca.gov/planning/pzd/1998/
(State of California - Planning, Zoning and Development Law)

Enforcement of Zoning Ordinances

A zoning ordinance usually provides that fines and other penalties can be imposed on a property owner who violates its rules. The owner may be required to tear down an illegal structure or stop an illegal use. However, most counties and cities don't have enough personnel to make routine checks on all the land uses in their jurisdiction. So unless someone files a complaint, a property owner may get away with a minor zoning violation.

The building permit system (described below) helps enforce zoning laws. If a permit application proposes a project inconsistent with the zoning, it will be turned down. And construction inspectors sometimes come across zoning violations and report them.

In case you're interested in just how far legislation in California goes regarding the use of property, consider a homeowner who doesn't like it that the neighbor is raising pigeons and thinks that is an activity for rural Californians. What can the homeowner do? The answer is probably not much, because of legislation enacted in 1990 contained in Government Code section 65852.6 which provides:

(a) It is the policy of the state to permit breeding and the maintaining of homing pigeons consistent with the reservation of public health and safety.

(b) For purposes of this section, a "homing pigeon," sometimes referred to as a racing pigeon, is a bird of the order Columbae. It does not fall in the category of "fowl" which includes chickens, turkeys, ducks, geese and other domesticated birds other than pigeons.

BUILDING CODES

Building codes establish minimum standards for construction, requiring builders to use particular methods and materials. There are usually several specialized building codes: a fire code, a plumbing code, an electrical code, and so on. Like zoning laws, they are an exercise of the police power, protecting public health and safety. To establish some uniformity, California has adopted the State Building Standards Code and the State Housing Law. These set minimum standards; some local governments require more.

Building codes are mainly enforced through the permit system. A property owner intending to build or remodel a structure must submit plans to the local building department for approval. A building permit will be issued only if the plans comply with the codes. Once construction begins, an inspector may visit the site at different stages. If there are problems, the inspector can stop work on the project until they're resolved. The completed building is inspected, and a **certificate of occupancy** will be issued only if every aspect of the building is in compliance with the codes.

> **Case Example:** Thompson applied for a building permit to renovate an existing building in August 1986 and obtained the permit in January 1987, having met all building codes and passing a final inspection. Thompson sought a certificate of occupancy. The request was denied until Thompson renovated additional properties owned by Thompson. This demand was refused and Thompson sued the City of Lake Elsinore for failure to promptly issue the building permit and failure to issue the certificate of occupancy.
>
> The Court of Appeal held that the city is required to issue the certificate of occupancy under the uniform building code since the permit had been issued and it passed final inspection. The case was returned for trial on Thompson's claim for damages for the loss of use of the property because of the delay on the theory of inverse condemnation. *Thompson v. City of Lake Elsinore*, 18 Cal. App. 4th 49, 22 Cal. Rptr. 2d 344 (1993).

It isn't just new or remodeled structures that have to comply with building codes. In some cases, when the government imposes a new, stricter standard, a property owner may be required to bring an old building "up to code."

Case Example: The Hotel Padre in Bakersfield was built in 1929. It was constructed in accordance with the laws that applied at that time.

In 1951, Bakersfield adopted a new building code. Many aspects of the Hotel Padre violated the fire safety provisions of the new code: unenclosed stairways and inadequately enclosed elevator shafts, a dangerous boiler room, and unsafe fire escapes, among other things.

The city tried to work with the hotel's owner to correct the violations, but he was extremely uncooperative. The owner claimed he couldn't afford the changes, and couldn't be required to comply with the new law. The city sued, and the court ruled against the hotel owner—he had to bring the hotel up to the new standards. The city wasn't trying to penalize the owner for the construction methods used in 1929; it was trying to eliminate a present danger to public safety. *City of Bakersfield v. Miller*, 64 Cal. 2d 93, 48 Cal. Rptr. 889 (1966).

It's a good idea for a prospective buyer (or the buyer's real estate agent) to check with the building department to verify that all structures on the property have been inspected and approved for occupancy. All sorts of information can be obtained from the building department about the property improvements.

Second Units

The legislature of California has recognized that second units are a valuable and useful form of housing and stated:

> The Legislature finds and declares that second units are a valuable form of housing in California. Second units provide housing for family members, students, the elderly, in-home health care providers, the disabled, and others, at below market price within existing neighborhoods. Homeowners who create second units benefit from added income, and an increased sense of security.
>
> It is the intent of the Legislature that any second-unit ordinances adopted by local agencies have the effect of providing for the creation of second units and that provisions in these ordinances relating to matters including unit size, parking, fees and other requirements, are not so arbitrary, excessive, or burdensome so as to unreasonably restrict the ability of homeowners to create second units in zones in which they are authorized by local ordinance.

To implement this policy, a special use permit or conditional use permit must be granted if the application meets the following maximum requirements:

1. the unit is not intended for sale and may be rented
2. the property is zoned for single-family or multi-family use
3. a single family dwelling is on the property
4. the unit is either attached or detached to the existing dwelling on the same lot
5. an attached unit's floor space does not exceed 30% of the existing living area or a detached unit's floor space does not exceed 1200 square feet
6. unit complies with local requirements and building codes
7. approval has been given for any private sewage disposal system.

Local agencies are given the power to add a requirement that the applicant be an owner-occupant. In the alternative, a local agency may enact its own ordinance that regulates second units, which generally must follow the state requirements. If minimum and maximum sizes are locally established, they cannot prevent at least an efficiency unit from being constructed. Parking regulations cannot normally exceed one parking space per bedroom or unit and such units cannot be considered in any local policy to limit growth. However, local agencies may determine where second units may be located as long as they are not totally excluded. To be excluded there must be a finding that such an ordinance may limit housing opportunities and that specific adverse impacts on the health, safety, and welfare of the area would result from allowing second units. Finally, in addition to an efficiency unit, a second unit may be a manufactured home.

If a local ordinance regulates second unit permits, there is no guarantee that one will be issued. The Desmonds discovered that when their application was denied because of a finding under the Contra Costa County Ordinance Codes that "there was ample evidence of community concern with the impact of a residential second rental unit on the general aesthetic character of the neighborhood, as well as on traffic, safety, and protection of property values." *Desmond v. County of Contra Costa*, 21 Cal. App. 4th 308, at 339, 25 Cal. Rptr. 2d 842, at 848 (1993).

Manufactured Homes

Manufactured homes must be allowed on lots zoned for single-family dwellings provided they are certified under the National Manufactured Housing Construction and Safety Standards Act of 1974 and are installed on a foundation system. The manufactured home is subject to the same standards as conventional housing except for architectural requirements. Architectural requirements are limited to roof overhang, roofing materials and siding materials and cannot exceed those required of conventional housing. If there are no existing requirements for overhangs on both conventional housing and manufactured housing, 16 inches is the maximum. However, an ordinance may be adopted which prevents installation of a manufactured home if it is more than 10 years old.

SUBDIVISION REGULATIONS

Local authorities also control land use by regulating the development of new subdivisions. Subdivision regulations may control the size of the lots and the location of streets, sidewalks, and sewer and water lines. They may also require the developer to provide open spaces and recreational areas within the subdivision.

California has two laws that govern the subdivision of land in the state: the Subdivision Map Act and the Subdivided Lands Act.

http://ceres.ca.gov/planning/pzd/1998/#subd_contents
(The Subdivision Map Act)

The Subdivision Map Act

This law gives cities and counties the power to regulate subdivisions, and sets out rules for the exercise of that power. The purpose of the Map Act is to ensure that new

subdivisions comply with the local general plan for development. It also ensures that adequate utilities (water, sewer, electricity, and so on) are provided for each new subdivision. The act applies to any subdivision of land into two or more parcels, but its most important provisions only affect subdivisions with five or more parcels.

When land is subdivided into five or more parcels, the subdivider must file a **tentative subdivision map** with the local planning agency. The tentative map shows the proposed lot boundaries, the width and location of utility easements and access roads, and provisions for the control of flooding, among other things. The planning agency can approve or reject the tentative map, or approve it on condition that the subdivider takes certain actions. For example, the agency may require the subdivider to dedicate some of the property for public streets.

After the planning agency approves the tentative map, the subdivider has 24 months to file a **final map**, showing the subdivision in its final form. No sale, lease, or contract for sale or lease of a subdivision lot is valid until the final map has been filed.

Instead of tentative and final maps, a **parcel map** can be filed for subdivisions with two to four lots, and for condominiums and cooperatives. A parcel map doesn't have to be as detailed as tentative and final maps. Parcel maps can also be used for subdivisions with lots that are 40 acres or larger, certain subdivisions with access to existing streets, and some subdivisions zoned for commercial or industrial use.

The Subdivided Lands Act

This is actually a consumer protection law rather than a land use control law. The act requires a subdivider to disclose certain information to lot buyers. It applies to most subdivisions with five or more parcels. It applies to any sale that takes place in California, whether or not the property is in the state. The Department of Real Estate must approve advertisements in advance and is given 15 days to do so or the advertisements are deemed approved.

Lots in a subdivision covered by the act cannot be sold, leased, or financed until the Real Estate Commissioner investigates the subdivision and issues a **final subdivision public report**. The report provides information about title to the property, liens that affect the entire subdivision, utilities and improvements, and terms and warranties that will apply to a transaction.

As a general rule, the developer must give a copy of the final report to a prospective buyer, renter, or lender before he or she enters a transaction. But in some cases the Commissioner issues a **preliminary report**. If the developer gives a prospective buyer a copy of the preliminary report, the buyer can reserve a lot in the subdivision. However, until the buyer receives the final report, he or she has the right to back out and have any deposit refunded in full.

The Subdivided Lands Act also applies to manufactured home parks and planned unit developments with five or more lots, to condominiums and cooperatives with five or more units, to some residential timeshare projects, and to rural land projects with fifty vacant lots or more. Leases of apartments, offices, and retail space within a building are generally exempt from the law. Standard subdivisions that are entirely within the limits of an incorporated city may also be exempt if the developer complies with certain rules.

Land Use Controls

www.leginfo.ca.gov/.html/bpc_table_of_contents.html
(Subdivided Lands Act - Business & Professions Code 11000-11200)

Another consumer protection law concerning subdivision sales is the **Interstate Land Sales Full Disclosure Act (ILSFDA)**. This is a federal law that applies when subdivision property in one state is offered for sale in another state. For example, when a subdivision in California is advertised in a magazine that is distributed in other states, the subdivider may have to comply with ILSFDA.

Common Interest Developments (CIDs)

The Davis Stirling Common Interest Development Act (Civil Code sec. 1350-1376) covers the development of:

- condominium projects,*
- community apartment projects,*
- planned developments, and
- stock cooperatives.*

It is very comprehensive and, among other things, requires necessary documentation; provides for management by an association; set up a procedure enforcing assessments, liens, covenants and restrictions; and establishes a procedure to amend existing documentation. In essence, a common interest developments consists of separately owned spaces and additional space owned in common. (*See Chapter 4 for details of these other common interest developments.)

Planned Unit Developments (PUDs)

For example, some communities use planned unit developments (PUDs) to provide flexibility in zoning requirements. A PUD is often larger than a traditional subdivision. In most PUDs the houses are clustered close together on undersized lots, to provide larger open spaces shared by all of the residents.

A PUD developer may be allowed to mix residential and retail uses, single-and multi-family homes, or some other combination that wouldn't ordinarily be permitted in the district. In return, the developer usually must provide more open space, dedicate more land for public use, or take other actions that benefit the public.

To qualify for a PUD, a developer submits detailed plans of the proposed development to the planning authority for approval. The planning authority may require additional concessions to the community before granting approval for the project. Some communities designate specific areas as PUD zones. More often, a floating-zone system is used: a PUD could be put in any area if the developer's proposal is approved.

Development Permit Streamlining

To insure that development projects receive approval or disapproval within a reasonable amount of time, such projects are now deemed approved if the appropriate government agency fails to act within the time deadlines required by the California Government Code.

ENVIRONMENTAL REGULATIONS

When land use controls first developed, not much thought was given to protection of the environment. In recent years, however, this has become an area of great concern. Use of land, air, and water need to be controlled not just for the public health and welfare, but also for the preservation of natural resources. To this end, several federal and state environmental laws have been enacted. Here's a list of the more important ones.

National Environmental Policy Act

The National Environmental Policy Act (NEPA) of 1969 was enacted by Congress:

> Recognizing the profound impact of man's activity on the interrelations of all components of the natural environment, particularly the profound influences of population growth, high-density urbanization, industrial expansion, resource exploitation, and new and expanding technological advances and recognizing further the critical importance of restoring and maintaining environmental quality to the overall welfare and development of man, declares that it is the continuing policy of the Federal Government, in cooperation with State and local governments, and other concerned public and private organizations, to use all practicable means and measures, including financial and technical assistance, in a manner calculated to foster and promote the general welfare, to create and maintain conditions under which man and nature can exist in productive harmony, and fulfill the social, economic, and other requirements of present and future generations of Americans.

In addition to defining our nation's environmental policy, the NEPA establishes The Environmental Protection Agency (EPA), The Council on Environmental Quality (CEQ) and The Environmental Impact Statements (EIS). The CEQ, which consist of 3 members appointed by the President, assists and advises the President on national environmental quality. The EPA is responsible for carrying out environmental policy. An EIS is required on all federal actions which may significantly affect the quality of the human environment.

NEPA applies to all kinds of federal development projects, such as dam and highway construction and waste control plans. NEPA also applies to private action when the use or development requires a license or permit from a federal agency, or even a federal loan. In these cases, the federal agencies may require submission or an EIS before granting approval.

An EIS should examine the impact of the development on energy consumption, sewage systems, school population, drainage, water facilities, and other environmental, economic, and social factors, as well as alternatives including a "no action" alternative.

Clean Air Act

The federal Clean Air Act requires the Environmental Protection Agency (EPA) to regulate emission of air pollutants that are harmful to the public's health. National standards have been issued for certain pollutants. Each state is required to prepare a **state implementation plan (SIP)** for meeting the national standards.

Developers of projects that will involve direct emission of pollutants into the air must obtain permits from state or regional air pollution control authorities. States are given authority to prevent development that would interfere with attainment or maintenance of clean air objectives.

Clean Water Act

The federal Clean Water Act sets water quality standards. A permit is required for discharging pollutants into a lake, stream, or other waterway. Any industrial land use that would discharge an unacceptable level of water pollutants is prohibited.

The Clean Water Act also regulates waste water treatment systems. It encourages local governments to investigate new technology and alternatives to traditional sewage treatment plants. The wastewater facilities available may have a significant effect on the type and amount of new construction permitted.

Resource Conservation and Recovery Act

The Resource Conservation and Recovery Act allows regulation of hazardous waste facilities through the EPA. The Office of Solid Waste issues permits for storage, treatment and disposal of hazardous wastes. Hazardous substances are identified, site inventories are conducted and information is stored as part of the ongoing effort to keep track of hazardous materials.

CERCLA

The Comprehensive Environmental Response, Compensation, and Liability Act (CERCLA), a federal law, concerns liability for environmental cleanup costs. Under the act, the current owner of contaminated property may be required to pay for cleanup, even if the owner did not cause the contamination, and even if someone else owned the property when the contamination occurred.

Endangered Species Act

Enacted in 1973, this very important federal conservation law became one of the most highly publicized and controversial laws. The general purpose, as stated by congress, is as follows:

(a) Findings

(1) various species of fish, wildlife, and plants in the United States have been rendered extinct as a consequence of economic growth and development untempered by inadequate concern and conservation;

(2) other species of fish, wildlife, and plants have been so depleted in numbers that they are in danger of or threatened with extinction;

(3) these species of fish, wildlife, and plants are of esthetic, ecological, educational, historical, recreational, and scientific value to the Nation and its people;

(4) the United States has pledged itself as a sovereign state in the international community to conserve to the extent practicable the various species of fish or wildlife and plants facing extinction...;

(5) encouraging the States and other interested parties, through Federal financial assistance and...incentives, to develop and maintain conservation programs ...is a key to meeting the Nation's international commitments and to better safeguarding, for the benefit of all citizens, the Nation's heritage in fish, wildlife, and plants.

(b) Purpose

The purposes of this chapter are to provide a means whereby the ecosystems upon which endangered species and threatened species depend may be conserved, provide a program for the conservation of such endangered species and threatened species, and to take such steps as may be appropriate to achieve the purposes of (the findings).

California Environment Quality Act (EQA)

This state law is similar to the National Environmental Policy Act. EQA requires state or local agencies to prepare an environmental impact report (EIR) for any project (public or private) that may have a significant impact on the environment. A development can only be excepted from this requirement if the public agency overseeing the project rules that it will not have significant adverse effects.

A public hearing is held for each EIR. Alternatives to the proposed action must be considered, and a developer may be required to make changes in the project to reduce its impact.

California Coastal Act

The Coastal Act established the California Coastal Zone Conservation Commission. The commission researches ways to protect the California coastline and controls development along the coast. It has several regional divisions, and no development is permitted in the coastal zone without a permit from the appropriate regional board. A coastal zone is normally from the highest coastal mountain peak to the outer sea limits, but this distance has been reduced in large urban areas.

Alquist-Priolo Act

Under the Alquist-Priolo Special Studies Zone Act, any application for new residential development or construction in certain areas of the state must include a geologic report.

The report considers the earthquake risks for the property. Additionally a seller must disclose to a potential buyer if the property is in a special studies zone, where there is a recently active or potentially active earthquake fault.

Safe Drinking Water and Toxic Enforcement Act

Proposition 65 generated the Safe Drinking Water and Toxic Enforcement Act of 1986 which is enforced by the Department of Health Services. The purpose of the Act is to warn the public of health hazards and protect drinking water from toxic contamination through discharge into the water or onto the land. Actions for endorsement are brought by public prosecutors or can be brought by any person in the public interest.

Environment Responsibility Acceptance Act

An owner of property who is actually aware of a release of a hazardous material must send notice of potential liability to those identified as potentially responsible parties for the release and to the appropriate government agency. Those receiving the notice of potential responsibility are given an opportunity to assess the magnitude of the release and seek agreement for proportional division of the cleanup task and cost.

Other Regulations

Sometimes federal and state regulations that don't seem to directly apply to real estate may also have an effect on land use.

> **Example:** The school district is anxious to sell a school building that has been closed and unused for several years. A real estate broker has a client who would like to purchase the school and turn it into an office building.
>
> Unfortunately, there is asbestos in the building's insulation. The federal Occupational Safety and Health Act (OSHA) sets standards to protect employees in the workplace. OSHA has specific asbestos limits, and the school building would not be approved for use as office until the asbestos has been removed. The broker should make sure the client realizes that there would probably be substantial expense above and beyond the price of the property before it could be used as an office building.

Private Restrictions

In some cases, private restrictions on the use of property are simply a contract between a seller and a buyer, or between an owner and the neighboring owner.

> **Example:** A and B are neighbors. A is concerned that B might put an addition on her house that would block his view of the mountains. He discusses this with B. B says that if A pays her $500, she will never obstruct his view. A puts this agreement in writing, they both sign it, and A gives B the $500.
>
> This is an enforceable contract between A and B. If B breaks her promise, A can sue her. This kind of agreement is called a **restrictive covenant**.
> But what if B sells her property to X? X is interested in astronomy; she builds an observation tower that blocks A's view of the mountains. A would not have the right to sue X, because X was not a party to the contract between A and B.

However, by following certain statutory rules, A and B could have made their restrictive covenant run with the land, in the same way that an easement can (see Chapter 3). Then the restriction against blocking the view would apply to X (or anyone else who bought B's property). And if A sold his property to someone else, the new owner would have the right to enforce the restrictive covenant and protect the view, just as A did.

COVENANTS RUNNING WITH THE LAND

To make a restrictive covenant run with the land, the original parties must record a document that states the terms of the restriction. This document is often a deed.

Example: Q owns a large lot; he sells part of it to P. Q can include a restrictive covenant in the deed that will prevent P from building within 40 feet of their common property line. By accepting the deed, P agrees to the restriction.

Whether restrictions are included in a deed or take the form of an independent agreement between neighbors, the recorded document must:

◆ describe the property that benefits from the restriction and the property that is burdened by the restriction; and

◆ expressly state that future owners of the burdened property are to be bound by the restriction, for the benefit of the other property.

If the document doesn't fulfill these requirements, the restrictions won't run with the land. The original promisor will have to comply, but a subsequent owner won't have to.

A developer often places restrictions on all the lots in a new subdivision by recording a **declaration of covenants, conditions, and restrictions** (better known as **CC&Rs**). Subdivision restrictions are discussed in more detail below.

RELATED TO THE PROPERTY. A restrictive covenant won't run with land unless it relates to the use, repair, maintenance, or improvement of property, or directly benefits property. A covenant is said to run with the land "if it binds not only the person who entered into it, but also later owners and assigns who did not personally enter into it." A covenant in a deed stating that the grantee must never smoke cigarettes couldn't run with the land, but if the covenant prohibited smoking on the property being transferred, it might run with the land.

Case Example: The Anthonys bought a home in the Glenbrook Hills subdivision in Brea, a community in Orange County. The recorded CC&Rs for the subdivision required all homeowners to belong to the Brea Glenbrook Club. The private club owned and operated a recreational area in the subdivision, with a swimming pool and a clubhouse. Every homeowner had to pay membership dues, which were used to maintain the club's facilities. **Continued**

The Anthonys didn't want to be members of the club or use its facilities. They sued for a declaration that the membership requirement in the CC&Rs was not a covenant running with the land.

The court disagreed. The covenant related to the use, repair, and maintenance of the club's property. It also directly benefited the other properties in the subdivision, since the recreational facilities increased the market value of the homes. *Anthony v. Brea Glenbrook Club*, 58 Cal. App. 3d 506, 130 Cal. Rptr. 32 (1976).

Subdivision Restrictions

Today, most private restrictions are imposed by subdivision developers. As the *Anthony* case suggests, a developer's CC&Rs are generally intended to keep the subdivision attractive and protect the market value of the homes.

By following certain rules, a developer can establish a **common plan** of restrictions for the whole subdivision. When there's a common plan, any homeowner in the subdivision can enforce the CC&Rs against any other homeowner there. The lots are mutually burdened and benefited by the restrictions.

Example: In the Maytag Meadows subdivision, Lot 47 is half a mile away from Lots 18, 19, and 20. The family that lives on Lot 19 hangs its laundry out to dry in the back yard, which violates one of the rules in the CC&Rs. The owners of Lot 18 and Lot 20 don't mind. But the owner of Lot 47 is outraged. Because the developer established a common plan of restrictions for the entire subdivision, the owner of Lot 47 can enforce the restriction against Lot 19, even though she doesn't live next door.

To establish a common plan, the developer must clearly state in the CC&Rs that the restrictions are mutually binding on all the homeowners in the subdivision. And the developer must make sure that the CC&Rs are incorporated by reference in the deed to the first purchaser of each lot. Even if the developer has recorded CC&Rs that state they benefit and burden all the lots, the homeowners won't be bound by the restrictions if the first deeds don't incorporate the CC&Rs by reference. They won't be able to enforce them against other homeowners, either.

Case Example: The subdivision developer recorded CC&Rs. When Mr. Scaringe bought a home with a view, the developer told him the CC&Rs would prevent the neighbors from obstructing his view. But the deed from the developer to Scaringe didn't mention the CC&Rs. Neither did the deed from the developer to Mr. Rice, who bought the lot next door to Scaringe.

Rice began building a two-story house that would block Scaringe's view. Scaringe sued to stop construction. The court ruled that Scaringe couldn't rely on the CC&Rs. Since they weren't incorporated into his deed or any other agreement he'd signed, he wasn't bound by them and couldn't enforce them. *Scaringe v. J.C.C. Enterprises, Inc.*, 206 Cal. App. 3d 1, 253 Cal. Rptr. 344 (1988).

Chapter 13

However, once the CC&Rs have been incorporated in the first deed for a lot and that deed is recorded, the restrictions are binding on subsequent buyers, even if the later deeds don't mention the CC&Rs. Private restrictions work basically the same way easements do: once they're in the recorded chain of title for the burdened property, subsequent purchasers have constructive notice and take title subject to the restrictions.

> **Example:** J was the first person to buy Lot 10, and his deed from the developer states that the property is subject to the recorded CC&Rs. J records his deed. But when J sells Lot 10 to K, he doesn't tell K about the restrictions, and they aren't mentioned in the new deed.
>
> K violates the restrictions by putting a satellite dish in his front yard. One of his neighbors sues. K claims he isn't bound by the CC&Rs because they weren't mentioned in his deed. The court rules against K. The CC&Rs bind all successive owners of Lot 10, since J put them in the chain of title by recording his deed. It doesn't matter that they weren't expressly incorporated into K's deed.

PRIVATE RESTRICTIONS

- ◆ a contract that doesn't run with the land
- ◆ restrictive covenants running with the land in a separate recorded document such as:
    1. a deed, or
    2. CC&Rs that apply to all lots in a subdivision

- ◆ a condition in a deed

ENFORCING PRIVATE RESTRICTIONS

When a court finds that a property owner has violated a restrictive covenant, the owner may be required to pay damages to the person who is asking to have the restriction enforced. In addition (or instead), the court may issue an injunction ordering the owner to comply with the restriction: take down the satellite dish, stop mowing the lawn at midnight, get rid of the chickens. If the owner doesn't do what the court orders, he or she can be fined or even put in jail for contempt of court.

> **Example:** L purchased a home overlooking a lake. All lots in this subdivision were bound by a restrictive covenant stating that no structure should be more than one story high, except that the Architectural Control Committee could grant a special variance if it wouldn't restrict the view from other lots.

L builds a one-story house. Several years later (without a variance) he begins adding a second story that would block the view of the lake for his neighbor N. N brings a lawsuit to enforce the covenant and stop construction.

L argues that N is only entitled to damages. But a view is a special asset, and it would be extremely difficult to place a monetary value on it. N testifies that the view was one of the main reasons he bought that particular house. The court orders L to remove the partially constructed addition to restore N's view.

Covenants vs. Conditions

So far we've discussed only restrictive covenants. But a restriction in a deed can be either a covenant or a condition, and there's a significant difference between them. A **covenant**, as you've seen, is a promise to do or not do something. It may just be a contract between two parties, or it may run with the land. In either case, someone who breaches a covenant will be ordered to comply with the restriction or pay damages.

Breach of a **condition** is a much more serious matter than breach of a covenant. A condition in a deed makes the owner's title provisional. Someone who breaches a condition may forfeit title to the property, so that it reverts to the previous owner (who placed the condition in the deed). In other words, if there's a condition in the deed, the grantee has a fee simple defeasible estate instead of a fee simple absolute (see Chapter 3).

Because forfeiture of title is an extremely harsh result, a court will always try to interpret a deed restriction as a covenant rather than a condition. But if the wording is absolutely clear and leaves no room for interpretation, the restriction will be enforced as a condition.

Case Example: General Petroleum sold some property to Kelley and Clark. The deed included a restriction prohibiting the grantees from opening a service station on the property for 20 years. The deed stated: "Should the property be used for service station purposes...the title should be revested and revert to General Petroleum Corporation."

A few years later, Kelley and Clark sold the property to Mr. Boughton. Boughton sued for a declaration that General Petroleum's restriction was unenforceable. But the court held that Boughton would forfeit his title if he violated the condition. *Boughton v. Socony Mobil Oil Co.*, 231 Cal. App. 2d 188, 41 Cal. Rptr. 714 (1964).

Nearly all private restrictions are covenants rather than conditions, however. Even though "CC&Rs" stands for covenants, *conditions*, and restrictions, they virtually never make a grantee's title subject to forfeiture.

TERMINATING RESTRICTIVE COVENANTS

Many restrictive covenants have no time limit, but others state that they will expire after a certain date. In that case, the covenant becomes unenforceable when time runs out.

Some states impose statutory time limits on restrictive covenants. In New York, for example, private restrictions terminate automatically after 30 years, unless they're formally renewed. But there isn't a statutory time limit in California; if a restrictive covenant doesn't limit itself, it can be enforced indefinitely—unless something happens to terminate it.

One of the ways a restrictive covenant can be terminated is by agreement. The owner of the benefited property agrees to release the burdened property from the restriction. In that case, the parties should be sure to record a release.

A restrictive covenant can also be terminated by **merger**, just like an easement. If the owner of the burdened property acquires title to the benefited property too, the restriction disappears. It won't revive if the two properties are sold separately again later on.

If a restrictive covenant isn't enforced, it may become unenforceable. That's called termination by **abandonment**.

Case Example: The subdivision restrictions required all buildings to be set back at least 20 feet, with side yards at least four feet wide. The Whitneys built their home only three feet eight inches from one of the side boundaries of their lot, and a neighbor sued.

The Whitneys offered evidence that there were many similar violations in the subdivision. For instance, on Lots 21 and 23 the side yards were less than four feet wide, and on Lot 5 the side yards were only one foot wide. There was a house built right on top of the side boundary between Lots 17 and 18.

The court ruled that because there hadn't been uniform enforcement of the restrictions, they should be treated as abandoned. Enforcing the side yard requirements against the Whitneys wouldn't restore the area to its intended design, and failing to enforce them didn't diminish the value of the surrounding properties. *Bryant v. Whitney*, 178 Cal. 640, 174 P. 32 (1918).

Similarly, a restrictive covenant may no longer be enforceable if the character of the restricted neighborhood has changed. This is called termination due to **changed circumstances**.

Case Example: A 24-lot subdivision in Orange County was restricted to single-family residential use. Commercial uses were forbidden. These restrictions were placed on the subdivision in 1940. **Continued**

In 1955, Mr. McCabe bought Lot 1, which fronted on Highway 101. Part of that lot was zoned for commercial use, and part of it was zoned for multi-family residential use. Although McCabe was aware of the subdivision restrictions, he started constructing a commercial building on his lot. Some of the neighbors sued.

McCabe argued that conditions around Lot 1 had changed since the subdivision restrictions were imposed, and it was no longer suitable for single-family residential use. Traffic on that stretch of Highway 101 had increased, and the authorities were considering expanding it to four lanes. The court agreed with McCabe that Lot 1 wasn't suitable for single-family homes, and decided that commercial use of the property wouldn't have adverse effects on the other lots in the subdivision. As a result, the court refused to enforce the restriction. *Key v. McCabe*, 54 Cal. 2d 736, 8 Cal. Rptr. 425 (1960).

However, in other cases the court reaches a different conclusion. As long as the original purpose of the restrictive covenants can still be realized, they are supposed to be enforceable.

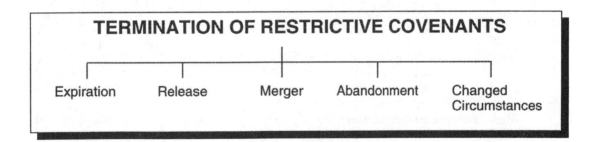

TERMINATION OF RESTRICTIVE COVENANTS

Expiration   Release   Merger   Abandonment   Changed Circumstances

PUBLIC POLICY LIMITS ON PRIVATE RESTRICTIONS

Until just a few decades ago, it was commonplace for CC&Rs to prohibit conveyance of property within a subdivision to blacks, Jews, or other minorities. Now private restrictions forbidding transfer based on race, religion, ancestry, national origin, sex, or physical disability are illegal. You may still run across discriminatory provisions in CC&Rs recorded forty years ago, but those provisions are unenforceable.

In some subdivisions, the CC&Rs prevented homeowners from putting up "For Sale" signs on their property. But the California legislature decided such restrictions were an unreasonable restraint on alienation.

California Civil Code section 712 provides:

(a) Every provision contained in or otherwise affecting a grant of a fee interest in, or purchase money security instrument upon, real property in this state

heretofore or hereafter made, which purports to prohibit or restrict the right of the property owner or his or her agent to display or have displayed on the real property, or on real property owned by others with their consent, or both, signs which are reasonably located, in plain view of the public, are of reasonable dimensions and design, and do not adversely affect public safety, including traffic safety, and which advertise the property for sale, lease or exchange, or advertise directions to the property, by the property owner or his or her agent is void as an unreasonable restraint upon the power of alienation.

(b) This section shall operate retrospectively, as well as prospectively, to the full extent that it may constitutionally operate retrospectively.

(c) A sign that conforms to the ordinance adopted in conformity with Section 713 shall be deemed to be of reasonable dimension and design pursuant to this section.

Section 713 provides:

(a) Notwithstanding any provision of any ordinance, an owner of real property or his or her agent may display or have displayed on the owner's real property, and on real property owned by others with their consent, signs which are reasonably located, in plain view of the public, are of reasonable dimensions and design, and do not adversely affect public safety, including traffic safety, as determined by the city, county, or city and county, advertising the following:

(1) That the property is for sale, lease, or exchange by the owner or his or her agent.
(2) Directions to the property.
(3) The owner's or agent's name.
(4) The owner's or agent's address and telephone number.

(b) Nothing in this section limits any authority which a person or local governmental entity may have to limit or regulate the display or placement of a sign on a private or public right-of-way.

Additionally, any covenant, restriction or condition that effectively prohibits or restricts the installation or use of a solar energy system is void and unenforceable. It is a state policy in California to encourage the use of solar energy systems and remove obstacles to their use, however, reasonable restrictions are allowed.

It's also illegal for private restrictions to forbid an owner from having a manufactured home installed. The manufactured home can be required to comply with the restrictions that apply to all homes in the subdivision—size, building materials, and so on. But it can't be ruled out just because it was constructed in a factory instead of on the property.

Finally, CC&Rs prohibiting a residence from being used as any business or for non-residential purposes does not prohibit a residence being used as a family daycare home under Health & Safety section 1597.40(c) or a group home for the disabled elderly under Government Code section 12955.

CHAPTER SUMMARY

1. The government's power to regulate land use is based on the police power: the power to pass laws for the protection of the public health, safety, morals, and general welfare. Land use regulations are unconstitutional if they are discriminatory or exclusionary, or if they are excessive, preventing the owner from making any use of the property.

2. State law requires every city and county in California to have a planning agency. The agency is responsible for creating a long-range general plan for development. Local authorities adopt detailed zoning ordinances to carry out the general plan.

3. Zoning ordinances segregate different types of land use into different areas. They usually also regulate the size of lots, height of buildings, building setbacks, lighting, signs, and off-street parking. Zoning ordinances provide for certain exceptions to their rules: nonconforming uses, variances, and conditional uses.

4. A nonconforming use is an established use that violates a new zoning ordinance, but is permitted to continue. A nonconforming use generally can't be expanded, renovated, rebuilt after destruction, or resumed after abandonment.

5. A variance allows an owner to build a structure or use property in a way that violates the zoning ordinance. Variances usually only authorize a minor deviation from the rules. Under California law, a variance can only be granted when the zoning regulations have a greater impact on the property (because of its unusual size, shape, or topography) than on neighboring properties. California law also prohibits use variances.

6. A rezone is a revision of the zoning ordinance. Spot zoning—rezoning to benefit or restrict a particular property owner without justification—is illegal.

7. Building codes establish minimum standards for construction methods and materials. Building inspectors issue a certificate of occupancy for new construction that complies with the codes. Existing buildings may also be required to comply with new building codes.

8. The Subdivision Map Act requires a subdivider to file a map with the local planning agency for approval. Under the Subdivided Lands Act, lots in a subdivision can't be sold, leased, or financed until the Real Estate Commissioner issues a public report on the development.

9. The National Environmental Policy Act and the California Environmental Quality Act require government agencies to prepare environmental impact statements before approving major development projects. The developers may be required to modify their plans to reduce the adverse effects on the environment. The federal Clean Air Act and Clean Water Act set standards for air and water quality and regulate pollution.

10. Private restrictions relating to the use, maintenance, or improvement of property, or benefiting property, can run with the land. A recorded document must state that future owners of the burdened property will be bound by the restrictions.

11. If the developer establishes a common plan of restrictions for a subdivision, any lot owner can enforce the restrictions against any other lot owner. To establish a common plan, CC&Rs must be recorded and also incorporated into the first deed for each lot.

12. Restrictive covenants can be terminated by agreement, merger, abandonment, or a change in the character of the neighborhood.

CASE PROBLEM

City of National City v. Wiener, 3 Cal. 4th 832, 12 Cal. Rptr. 2d 701, (1992)

The City of National City, (The City) has 17.9 percent of its land zoned for commercial use, 40.6 percent zoned for residential use, 16.9 percent for industrial use and 24.6 zoned for institutional and military use. The City has an ordinance prohibiting an adult entertainment business within 1500 feet of another adult business, school or public park, or within 1000 feet of a residential zone, unless it is located in an enclosed mall or a mall where the business front is isolated from public off-site view. The ordinance does not limit the number of adult businesses or the hours of operation. Wiener and his sister opened Chuck's Bookstore, an adult bookstore and arcade on National City Boulevard. The City sought an injunction against the bookstore for violating the ordinance by being too close to another adult business and a residential area. Weiner claimed the ordinance was unconstitutional as a violation of his First Amendment rights of free speech, especially since there was only one other adult business in The City, a theater. Additionally, The City is mostly strip zoned and the distance requirements make all locations almost impossible except for a mall.

The City claimed the ordinance was a reasonable regulation designed to serve a substantial government interest and that it provided a reasonable alternative avenue of communication since there are other shopping malls which could accommodate an adult business and plenty of commercial property which could do likewise. Weiner responded that even though there were vacancies in the three shopping malls, no mall would rent space to an adult business. He would, therefore, have to build his own mall.

Is the ordinance unconstitutional?

Land Use Controls

Answer: The superior court agreed with The City. The Court of Appeal reversed finding that the ordinance was constitutional on its face but failed to provide reasonable alternative avenues of communications because the distance requirements allowed too few alternative sites and the opportunity to locate in enclosed malls was illusive. Therefore the ordinance was an impermissible restriction on protected speech.

The Supreme Court noted that the ordinance was not designed to prevent adult entertainment materials from being sold but to limit the secondary effects such business have on the surrounding community. This is done not by banning adult businesses, but by providing that such business may only be located in certain areas. The inward facing store front "decreases the problems of harassment of neighborhood adults and children, littering of sexually explicit reading material and paraphernalia, loitering, and visual blight from bright colors and explicit signage associated with adult businesses." Additionally, malls tend to regulate their own tenants in terms of signs, paint, landscaping, hours of operation, parking and security, thereby reducing the need for city services and protecting a commercial tax base. With regard to reasonable alternatives for communication, the City has zoned 17.9 percent of its area for commercial activities where an adult store can be locate.

The fact it may be difficult to rent in an existing mall does not make the ordinance unconstitutional. "We decline to hold local governments responsible for the business decisions of private individuals who act for their own economic concerns without any reference to the First Amendment. The Constitution does not saddle municipalities with the tax of enduring either the popularity or economic success of adult business." The fact that there is only one other adult store is of no particular significance. "We find no authority that mandates a constitutional ration of adult business to a particular population ratio." The ordinance is constitutional.

CHAPTER 13 KEY TERMS	EQA	police power
	exclusionary zoning	restrictive covenant
	floor area ratio	rezone
board of adjustment	general plan	setback
building code	LAFCO	side yard
CC&Rs	NEPA	special exception
certificate of occupancy	nonconforming use	spot zoning
conditional use	parcel map	tentative subdivision map
environmental impact statement	planned unit development	use variance
	planning commission	variance

Land Use Controls

Quiz—Chapter 13

1. The constitutional basis for governmental regulation of the use of private property is:

   a. the police power.
   b. eminent domain.
   c. the zoning clause.
   d. the National Environmental Policy Act.

2. The planning commission is a:

   a. state agency responsible for enforcement of local zoning laws.
   b. state agency that coordinates land use planning of neighboring communities.
   c. federal agency responsible for enforcement of state zoning laws.
   d. local agency responsible for preparing a comprehensive general plan.

3. A section of the neighborhood has recently been rezoned for commercial use. Z's house is located in this section. He'll be allowed to continue to use his property for residential purposes. This is known as a:

   a. variance.
   b. spot zone.
   c. nonconforming use.
   d. conditional use.

4. Which of these variances is illegal under California law? X was granted a variance so that she could:

   a. put a bakery on residential property.
   b. build house two feet closer to property line than setback rules allowed.
   c. install a TV antenna on the side of her house instead of at the back.
   d. all of these are illegal.

5. J owns a tract of property in an area of the city that's zoned for light industrial use. The city council rezones J's tract for commercial use, although the surrounding properties are zoned industrial. The zoning change enables J to build a very profitable commercial development. This is:

   a. an illegal spot zone.
   b. an illegal variance.
   c. a legitimate zoning modification.
   d. a legitimate special exception.

6. When a buildings construction is complete, the building department inspects and decides whether to issue a:

   a. construction permit.
   b. notice of compliance.
   c. conditional use permit.
   d. certificate of occupancy.

7. When Z divided her land into two lots, she had to comply with California's:

   a. Interstate Land Sales Full Disclosure Act.
   b. Subdivided Lands Act.
   c. Subdivision Map Act.
   d. Subdivision Developer's Act.

8. EQA requires an environmental impact report to be prepared for certain development projects. This only applies to:

   a. public projects.
   b. private projects that may have a significant impact on the environment.
   c. projects that may have a significant impact on the environment.
   d. industrial projects.

9. X and Y are neighbors. Y dislikes Spanish tile roofs, he asks X to promise never to put a tile roof on her house. Y pays X $200 and X signs a binding agreement. Later X sells her house to B. B can put a tile roof on the house because:

   a. Y never recorded the agreement.
   b. restrictive covenants can't run with the land.
   c. tile won't lower value of Ys property.
   d. private restrictions are unenforceable if they control buildings appearance.

10. If there's an ambiguity in the wording of a restriction in a deed, a court usually interprets the restriction as:

   a. a condition rather than a covenant, a condition can result in forfeiture of title.
   b. a condition rather than a covenant, a covenant can result in forfeiture of title.
   c. a covenant rather than a condition, a covenant can result in forfeiture of title.
   d. a covenant rather than a condition, a condition can result in forfeiture of title.

WEST CD·ROM LIBRARIES™

CHAPTER 14
Civil Rights and Fair Housing Laws

CHAPTER OVERVIEW

Numerous federal and state civil rights and fair housing laws prohibit discrimination. The U. S. Congress and the California legislature have made it clear that ensuring fair housing for everyone is an important goal for our society.

A real estate agent needs to be able to recognize conduct that violates anti-discrimination laws in order to avoid liability. A violation could lead to the suspension or revocation of the agent's license, and could result in a civil lawsuit or even criminal prosecution.

An agent can also play a role in combating discrimination by explaining the fair housing laws to clients. Sellers and landlords want to avoid liability, and buyers and tenants want to know their rights.

This chapter discusses the most important federal and California state anti-discrimination laws. It explores how these laws affect the day-to-day relationships between real estate agents and their clients.

Historical Background

In the United States, the first civil rights laws were passed more than 120 years ago. The Thirteenth, Fourteenth, and Fifteenth Amendments to the Constitution were adopted right after the Civil War. They abolished slavery, guaranteed equal protection of the laws, and established that citizens of all races had the right to vote. During the same period, Congress enacted the Civil Rights Act of 1866.

Chapter 14

But early civil rights laws were originally interpreted only to prohibit discrimination that involved **state action**—that is, action by a federal, state, or local governmental body. (See the discussion of the Constitution in Chapter 1.) So it was illegal for a city government to enact discriminatory ordinances, or for the police to enforce the laws in a discriminatory way, favoring one group over another. It wasn't illegal for private citizens to discriminate, however.

The landmark case concerning discrimination in connection with real estate was decided by the U.S. Supreme Court in 1948. At that time, it wasn't unlawful for a deed to include a covenant restricting ownership of the property to members of a particular race or religion. But in *Shelley v. Kraemer*, 334 U.S.1, the Court held that it was unconstitutional for a court to enforce discriminatory restrictions. A court order enforcing the restrictions would be discriminatory state action.

So even though the restrictive covenants (private action) were legal, a court order enforcing them (state action) was illegal. Without enforcement, a restrictive covenant isn't very effective, so Shelley v. Kraemer was an early step toward eliminating housing discrimination by private citizens. The Shelley rule still depended on state action, however.

But in the last few decades, court decisions and legislation have extended laws against discrimination to purely private activities involving no state action. Federal and state laws now make it illegal to include discriminatory covenants in deeds or other documents, or to honor such provisions already in existing documents. It is also now unlawful for county recorders to record documents containing discriminatory covenants.

Federal Legislation

http://home.earthlink.net/~gfeldmeth/chart.civrights.html
(Key Events in the American Civil Rights Movement)

The federal government uses legislation and regulations to carry out a policy of eliminating discrimination in housing and other real estate related areas, such as lending and employment.

As you read the following discussion of federal discrimination laws, it's important to remember that California state law in this area is often stricter than federal law. California law prohibits more types of discrimination in more types of transactions, and with far fewer exceptions.

The stricter law is the one that must be followed. With that in mind, you can treat the material covering exemptions from the Federal Fair Housing Act as general background information, recognizing that for the most part, those exemptions do not exist under California law.

THE CIVIL RIGHTS ACT OF 1866

The Civil Rights Act of 1866 prohibits discrimination based on race or ancestry in any property transaction in the United States. The act states, ". . .all citizens of the United States shall have the same right, in every state and territory as is enjoyed by white citizens thereof to inherit, purchase, lease, sell, hold and convey real and personal property."

Civil Rights and Fair Housing Laws

Unlike the 1968 Fair Housing Act (discussed below), which applies only to housing and certain other particular types of property, the 1866 Civil Rights Act contains no exceptions and applies to all property, whether real or personal, residential or commercial, improved or unimproved.

Civil Rights Act of 1866

1866

◆ Only prohibits discrimination based on race or ancestry

◆ Applies to any real estate transaction

◆ No exceptions

Enforcement

A lawsuit based on the 1866 Act can only be filed in federal district court. The federal law doesn't specify a time limit for filing an action; the lawsuit must be filed within the time limit specified by state law for similar claims. In California, that's three years.

Since the statute itself doesn't specifically mention remedies, the court fashions the remedies it finds necessary. The case law shows that the remedies available to a claimant who proves unlawful discrimination under the 1866 Act include:

◆ injunctions,
◆ compensatory damages, and
◆ punitive damages.

An **injunction** is a court order requiring the defendant to do or refrain from doing a particular act (see Chapter 1). In a discrimination case, a court might order the defendant to sell his or her house to the plaintiff, for example.

An award of **compensatory damages** in a discrimination suit could include out-of-pocket expenses (such as rent or transportation payments) and compensation for emotional distress. In many discrimination cases, awards for compensatory damages total thousands of dollars; in exceptional cases, hundreds of thousands of dollars have been awarded.

Punitive damages are intended to punish the wrongdoer and discourage others from engaging in similar behavior (see Chapter 6). There is no limit on the amount of punitive damages that may be awarded for claims under the 1866 Act. Punitive damage awards have exceeded $100,000 in some cases.

Constitutionality

The constitutionality of the 1866 Act was challenged in a landmark case decided by the U.S. Supreme Court just a few weeks after Congress passed the 1968 Civil Rights Act.

www.withylaw.com/history.htm
(A Short History of American Civil Rights Laws)

Chapter 14

Case Example: Mr. and Mrs. Jones, a black couple, attempted to buy a home in a subdivision being developed near St. Louis by the Mayer Company. When their offer was refused, they brought suit against the Mayer Company based on the 1866 Civil Rights Act. They claimed they were turned down because of their race. The court ruled in favor of the Joneses and held that the 1866 Act was constitutional. *Jones v. Alfred H. Mayer Co.*, 392 U.S. 409 (1968).

The ruling in favor of the Joneses established three important points:

1. The 1866 Act prohibits all racial discrimination in the sale and rental of property—the actions of private parties as well as state action—because the right to buy or lease property can be impaired as effectively by those who place property on the market as by government actions.

2. The 1866 Act is constitutional under the Thirteenth Amendment to the Constitution, which abolished slavery and also gave Congress the power to enforce the amendment through appropriate legislation. The Court held that the 1866 Act was an example of "appropriate legislation." The Thirteenth Amendment was intended to eliminate not only slavery but also the various conditions associated with slavery, often referred to as "badges of slavery." One of these badges was the inability to own or exchange property. Thus, it was proper for Congress to eliminate this incident of slavery through legislation.

3. The provisions of the 1866 Act are independent of and not superseded by the 1968 Civil Rights Act. The Court noted that the 1866 Act is not a comprehensive fair housing law. It doesn't address discrimination on grounds other than race or ancestry; it doesn't deal with discrimination in the provision of services or facilities connected with housing, financing, advertising, or brokerage; and it doesn't provide for any federal agency to assist aggrieved parties, or for intervention by the U.S. attorney general. The 1866 Act is a general statute enforceable only by private parties bringing private lawsuits. By contrast, the Fair Housing Act is a detailed housing law covering a great variety of discriminatory practices and enforceable by federal authorities.

http://webusers.anet-stl.com/~civil/docs-civilrightsact1964.html
(Civil Rights Act of 1964)

THE FEDERAL FAIR HOUSING ACT (1968)

Title VIII of the Civil Rights Act of 1968 is commonly called the Federal Fair Housing Act. The first section of Title VIII states, "It is the policy of the United States to provide, within constitutional limitations, for fair housing throughout the United States." To that end, the act prohibits discrimination based on **race, color, religion, sex, national origin, disability,** or **familial status** in the sale or lease of residential property. It also prohibits discrimination in advertising, lending, brokerage, and other services in residential transactions.

Civil Rights and Fair Housing Laws

Application

The law applies to most sales, rentals, and exchanges of residential property. It covers transactions involving:

1. any building or structure, or portion of a building or structure, that is occupied as (or designed or intended to be occupied as) a residence for one or more persons; and,

2. vacant land offered for sale or lease for the construction of any buildings to be used (entirely or in part) for residential purposes.

Exemptions

Although the act covers the majority of residential transactions in the U.S., there are several specific exemptions. The following transactions are completely exempted from the act:

1. The law doesn't apply to a single-family home sold or rented by a private individual owner, provided that:

    ◆ the owner owns no more than three such homes,
    ◆ no discriminatory advertising is used, and
    ◆ no real estate broker (or anyone else in the business of selling or renting homes) is employed.

    If the owner isn't the occupant or most recent occupant, he or she may use this exemption only once every 24 months.

2. The law doesn't apply to the rental of a room or unit in a dwelling with up to four units, provided that:

    ◆ the owner occupies one unit as his or her residence,
    ◆ no discriminatory advertising is used, and
    ◆ no real estate broker is employed.

    This is often referred to as "the Mrs. Murphy exemption."

3. In dealing with their own property in non-commercial transactions, religious organizations or societies or affiliated nonprofit organizations may limit occupancy to or give preference to their own members, provided that membership isn't restricted on the basis of race, color, or national origin.

4. Private clubs with lodgings that aren't open to the public and that aren't operated for a commercial purpose may limit occupancy to or give preference to their own members.

Even the limited exemptions listed above are available in far fewer situations than it first appears. Remember that under the 1866 Civil Rights Act, discrimination based on race or ancestry is prohibited in any property transaction regardless of any exemptions available under the Fair Housing Act. And no transaction involving a real estate licensee is exempt. Most importantly for California residents, these exemptions don't exist under California law (see below).

Familial Status. As mentioned above, the Fair Housing Act prohibits discrimination on the basis of familial status: it's illegal to discriminate against a person because he or she has custody of a child under 18 years of age. However, that rule does not apply to "housing for older persons." The act defines housing for older persons as any housing that is:

1. provided under a state or federal program designed to assist the elderly; or

2. intended for and solely occupied by persons 62 or older; or

3. designed to meet the physical or social needs of older persons, if the management publishes and follows policies and procedures demonstrating an intent to provide housing for persons 55 or older, and at least 80% of the units are occupied by at least one person 55 or older.

FEDERAL FAIR HOUSING ACT 1968

In residential transactions, prohibits discrimination based on:

Race	Color	Religion	Sex	Disability

National Origin   **Familial Status**

Prohibited Acts

The following acts are unlawful under the Federal Fair Housing Act if they are based on race, color, religion, sex, national origin, disability, or familial status:

1. refusing to rent or sell residential property after receiving a bona fide offer;
2. refusing to negotiate for the sale or rental of residential property;
3. any action that would otherwise make residential property unavailable or deny it to any person (this general clause covers **steering**, **redlining**, and many other discriminatory practices);
4. discriminating in the terms or conditions of any sale or rental of residential property, or in providing any services or facilities in connection with such property;

Equal Housing Lender

We Do Business In Accordance With The Federal Fair Housing Law

(Title VIII of the Civil Rights Act of 1968, as Amended by the Housing and Community Development Act of 1974)

IT IS ILLEGAL TO DISCRIMINATE AGAINST ANY PERSON BECAUSE OF RACE, RELIGION, CREED, COLOR, NATIONAL ORIGIN, ANCESTRY, PHYSICAL HANDICAP, MEDICAL CONDITION, FAMILIA STATUS, SEX, OR AGE TO:

- Deny a loan for the purpose of purchasing, constructing, improving, repairing or maintaining a dwelling or

- Discriminate in fixing of the amount, interest rate, duration, application procedures or other terms or conditions of such a loan.

IF YOU BELIEVE YOU HAVE BEEN DISCRIMINATED AGAINST, YOU MAY SEND A COMPLAINT TO:

U.S. DEPARTMENT OF HOUSING AND URBAN DEVELOPMENT
Assistant Secretary for Fair Housing and Equal Opportunity
Washington, D.C. 20410

or call your local HUD Area or Insuring Office.

5. discriminatory advertising or any other notice that indicates a limitation or preference or intent to make any limitation, preference, or discrimination;

6. making any representation that property is not available for inspection, sale, or rent when it is in fact available;

7. inducing or attempting to induce, for profit, any person to sell or rent property based on representations regarding entry into the neighborhood of persons of a particular race, color, religion, sex, or national origin (**blockbusting**);

8. discrimination by a commercial lender in making a loan for buying, building, repairing, improving, or maintaining a dwelling, or in the terms of such financing;

9. denying access to a multiple listing service or any similar real estate brokers' organization, or discriminating in the terms or conditions for access to the organization; or

10. coercing, intimidating, threatening, or interfering with anyone on account of his or her enjoyment, attempt to enjoy, or encouragement or assistance to others in enjoying the rights granted by the Fair Housing Act.

www.fairhousing.com/legal_research/regs/index.htm
(Discriminatory Conduct Under The Fair Housing Act)

In 1972, the Fair Housing Act was amended to require display of fair housing posters and use of the fair housing logo in advertising. If a real estate broker or other person or business required to display the poster is investigated for alleged discriminatory acts, failure to display the poster and logo may be considered evidence of discrimination.

As you can see, most discriminatory behavior in connection with residential transactions would violate federal law. Three terms mentioned above frequently come up in discussions of fair housing and fair lending laws:

◆ steering,
◆ blockbusting, and
◆ redlining

Steering refers to channeling prospective buyers or renters to specific neighborhoods based on their race (or religion, national origin, or other protected class), in order to maintain or change the character of the neighborhoods. For example, white customers might only be shown homes in white neighborhoods, and black customers only shown homes in black neighborhoods.

Case Example: In the Detroit area it was a widespread practice to code listing agreements with an "X" or some other mark to indicate that the home could be shown to black prospects. One real estate brokerage used a separate phone number in ads for properties located in black neighborhoods. The telephone setup in the office allowed the person answering the phone to see if the call was coming in on the special line. If so, he or she would direct the caller to one of the black sales associates working in the office. *U.S. v. Real Estate One*, 433 F. Supp. 1140 (E.D. Mich. 1977).

Civil Rights and Fair Housing Laws

In most jurisdictions, a real estate agent's good faith answer to a question from a prospective buyer about the composition (racial, ethnic, religious, etc.) of a neighborhood would not be a violation if there was no intent to discriminate. However, it is a violation for an agent, by words or actions, to direct or advise a buyer to buy or not buy based on the racial or ethnic composition of the neighborhood.

Example: "You probably wouldn't be interested in looking at that house, it's in a (black or white, as appropriate) neighborhood."

"You wouldn't want to buy in this neighborhood, it's in transition."

Since discriminatory intent may be difficult to disprove, it's safest for an agent to avoid all statements regarding race or ethnic background. If prospects ask questions about the racial or ethnic composition of the neighborhood surrounding a listed property, offer to show them the property.

Blockbusting (or **panic selling**) refers to the practice of predicting the entry of minorities into a neighborhood, and stating or implying that this will result in lower property values, higher crime rates, or some other undesirable consequence. The purpose is to induce property owners to list their property for sale or sell their property at a reduced price, so the individual making the predictions (often a real estate agent) can profit. A wide variety of blockbusting "techniques"—many of them shocking—appear in the case law. For example:

◆ passing out pamphlets stating that a member of a minority group has purchased a home nearby;

◆ "wrong number" phone calls where the callers indicate that they thought they were calling "the black family that just moved in"; or

◆ purchasing a home in the area and selling it on contract to a minority buyer, then suggesting to white owners that it's time to move.

Redlining is refusal, for discriminatory reasons, to make loans on property located in a particular neighborhood. In the past, many lenders assumed that an integrated or predominantly black neighborhood was automatically a neighborhood where property values were declining. Based on that assumption, they refused to make loans in those neighborhoods. In many cases, this worked as a self-fulfilling prophecy. Since it was almost impossible to obtain purchase or renovation loans, it was extremely difficult to market, maintain, or improve homes in those neighborhoods, and that caused values to decline.

 www.adversity.net/favormor.htm
(News About Racial Preferences, Targets, etc.)

Lenders may still deny loans in neighborhoods where property values are declining. However, that action must be based on objective economic criteria concerning the condition and value of the particular property or the surrounding neighborhood, without regard to the racial or ethnic composition of the neighborhood. A lender may not simply equate an integrated or minority neighborhood with declining values.

Chapter 14

Enforcement

An individual who feels he or she has been discriminated against in violation of the Federal Fair Housing Act may file a complaint with the Office of Equal Opportunity (OEO) of the Department of Housing and Urban Development (HUD). In addition (or instead), he or she may file a lawsuit in federal or state court. HUD may also file a complaint on its own initiative. A complaint must be filed with HUD within one year; a lawsuit must be brought within two years.

When a complaint is filed with HUD, the agency will attempt to obtain voluntary compliance through negotiation and conciliation. If that's unsuccessful, the parties may have the dispute decided by HUD. The agency can award compensatory damages to the plaintiff, issue injunctions against the defendants, and impose civil penalties (fines ranging from a maximum of $10,000 for a first offense, up to $50,000 for a third offense).

In states such as California, where there are state or local fair housing laws substantially equivalent to the federal law, HUD may refer complaints to the state or local agency that has similar responsibilities (for example, the California Department of Fair Employment and Housing).

A complainant may file suit in federal district court or in the state trial court having general jurisdiction (in California, a superior court). The court may grant the relief it deems appropriate, including:

- a temporary or permanent injunction,
- compensatory damages,
- punitive damages, and
- attorney's fees if the court believes the plaintiff is not able to pay the fees.

The defendant may also be ordered to take certain steps to insure that no discrimination occurs in the future.

The U.S. attorney general may also bring a civil suit in federal district court if he or she has reason to believe that anyone is engaged in a pattern of discriminatory activities, or if there is a group of people who have been denied their rights in such a manner that it raises an issue of general public importance. The attorney general may request temporary or permanent injunctions or other orders to insure that all persons are able to exercise the rights granted under the Fair Housing Act. The court may also impose civil penalties of up to $100,000.

FEDERAL FAIR LENDING LAWS

There are several federal laws and regulations designed to eliminate discrimination in lending. They include:

- the Fair Housing Act (discussed above),
- the Equal Credit Opportunity Act, and
- the Home Mortgage Disclosure Act.

Civil Rights and Fair Housing Laws

The Fair Housing Act prohibits discrimination in home loans and other aspects of residential financing. It does not apply to any credit transactions other than residential financing, however.

The **Equal Credit Opportunity Act (ECOA)** applies to all consumer credit, including residential real estate loans. Consumer credit is credit extended to an individual (not a corporation or business) for personal, family, or household purposes. The ECOA prohibits any institution or lender regularly engaged in financing from discriminating on the basis of **race, color, religion, national origin, sex,** or **marital status**. It also prohibits discrimination based on **age**, as long as the applicant is of legal age to contract. And it prohibits discrimination against an applicant because his or her income is derived (partly or entirely) from **public assistance**.

The **Home Mortgage Disclosure Act** is a tool for gathering information on whether lenders are fulfilling their obligation to serve the housing needs of their communities. The act facilitates enforcement of laws against redlining. Large institutional lenders are required to make annual reports on the residential mortgage loans (both purchase money and improvement loans) that were originated or purchased during the fiscal year. Each loan is categorized according to its dollar amount, type (FHA, VA, FMHA, other), and geographic location by census tract (or by county, for small counties with no established census tracts). If analysis of the reports discloses areas where few or no home loans have been made, that alerts investigators to the possibility that those areas are being redlined.

California Legislation

In California, the Unruh Civil Rights Act, the Fair Employment and Housing Act (formerly called the Rumford Act), the Housing Financial Discrimination Act (also called the Holden Act), and the Real Estate Law all include provisions designed to promote fair housing within the state.

The California courts have taken a somewhat different approach to interpreting civil rights legislation than the courts in other states. The result has been that California laws against discrimination often have a far greater impact than is immediately apparent from the language of the statutes themselves.

In most states, discrimination is permitted unless it is expressly prohibited by a particular law. Only discrimination against specified classes of people is unlawful, not all discrimination. For example, if you don't like lawyers, you could refuse to rent or sell to a lawyer unless a state law specifically prohibited discrimination based on profession or occupation.

www.usc.edu/go/hmap/library/rights.html
(Civil rights Handbook - Fair Employment and Housing Act/
Unruh Civil Rights Act)

Unruh Civil Rights Act (California)

It doesn't work that way in California, primarily for historical reasons. The precursor to the current Unruh Act (which prohibits discrimination by business establishments) was a rather broad statute that stated:

Chapter 14

> *All citizens within the jurisdiction of this state shall be entitled to the full and equal accommodations, advantages, facilities, and privileges of inns, restaurants, hotels, eating-houses, barbershops, bathhouses, theaters, skating-rinks, and all other places of public accommodation or amusement, subject only to the conditions and limitations established by law and applicable alike to all citizens.*

So the original California anti-discrimination statute required full and equal treatment for all citizens, rather than specifying certain classes (such as sex, race, national origin, and religion) that were to be protected from discrimination. Additionally, individuals with disabilities are entitled to full and equal access to public facilities, as are other members of the general public.

As a result, California courts have taken the approach that if a state civil rights law includes a list of protected classes, the list is only illustrative, not a complete list of all groups that may not be discriminated against. Thus, the courts could find and did find that arbitrary discrimination against anyone was prohibited, even when it was not directed against a class listed in a statute. For example, California courts have held that it is unlawful to discriminate against the following groups, although it isn't expressly prohibited by any statute: homosexuals, students, welfare recipients, persons of a particular occupation or profession, children, persons who associate with blacks, and unmarried persons.

This doesn't mean that all discrimination is prohibited in California, just arbitrary discrimination. Discrimination is considered arbitrary if it is based solely on the fact that the person belongs to a particular class or group. If there is an objective reason for the discrimination, or if it is based on particular conduct, it is not unlawful.

The Unruh Civil Rights Act states that all persons are entitled to the full use of any services provided by a business establishment. Thus, real estate brokers are required to offer their facilities and services to everyone who wants to make use of them, without arbitrary discrimination. If a broker refuses a listing or turns away a customer, it must not be for discriminatory reasons.

Case Example: Mr. Frantz, a real estate broker, contracted to buy lot 282 in the Pierce Ranch subdivision. But after a disagreement with Frantz, the developer refused to go through with the contract. Frantz sued for specific performance. In an out-of-court settlement, the developer agreed to pay Frantz $35,000 in damages.

Sometime later, Frantz tried to buy another lot in the same subdivision, but the developer refused to sell it to him. Frantz sued again, alleging that the developer had unlawfully discriminated against him. Frantz claimed that the developer refused to sell him the house because he belonged to a particular class: the class of people who had previously sued the developer. The developer answered that he had refused simply because he believed Frantz was operating as an investor or speculator, rather than intending to occupy the property himself. Speculation violated the terms of the sale agreements for the development.

The court ruled that since the discrimination was based on conduct (acting as a speculator), it was not arbitrary or based solely on class and wasn't unlawful. *Frantz v. Blackwell*, 189 Cal. App. 3d 91, 234 Cal. Rptr. 178 (1987).

Civil Rights and Fair Housing Laws

Rental properties, condominiums, and other real estate developments are considered business establishments for the purposes of the Unruh Act. The general terms of the act make it illegal for an apartment complex or condo to have a "no kids" rule. The act was amended to allow developments designed for senior citizens to require that at least one member of each household be 62 or older, and to exclude people younger than 45. Large developments that comply with certain other rules can have a slightly lower age limit, requiring at least one member of each household to be 55 or over.

The California Legislature adopted this amendment to the Unruh Act before Congress amended the Federal Fair Housing Act to prohibit discrimination based on familial status. The state law must be interpreted in conjunction with the federal law's rules concerning "housing for older persons" (see above). The state law may be applied to give more protection against age discrimination than the federal law, but it may not be applied to give less protection.

Enforcement

Someone who has been discriminated against in violation of the Unruh Act may sue for an injunction, compensatory damages, attorney's fees, and punitive damages. (The punitive damages award can't be more than three times the amount of the compensatory damages.) In addition, the victim of discrimination may file a complaint with the California Department of Fair Employment and Housing. The state attorney general also has the right to sue for violations of the Unruh Act.

Unruh Civil Rights Act

◆ Prohibits all arbitrary discrimination by business establishments in California: "All persons within the jurisdiction of the state are free and equal, and no matter what their sex, race, color, religion, ancestry, national origin, familial status or disability are entitled to the full and equal accommodations, advantages, facilities, privileges, or services in all business establishments of every kind whatsoever."

◆ Exception: senior citizens' housing

FAIR EMPLOYMENT AND HOUSING ACT (California)

This act generally prohibits all housing discrimination in California. It declares that it is against public policy to discriminate in housing because of race, color, religion, sex, marital status, national origin, or ancestry.

It is unlawful for any owner, lessor, assignee, managing agent, real estate broker or salesperson, or any business establishment, to discriminate in selling or leasing any housing accommodation. The law specifically prohibits a seller or lessor from asking about the race, color, religion, sex, marital status, national origin, or ancestry of any prospective tenant or buyer. It also prohibits sellers and lessors from making any statement or using advertising that indicates an intent to discriminate.

The act also prohibits discrimination in the financing of housing. Under the act, it is unlawful for any person, bank, mortgage company, or other financial institution to discriminate against any person or group of persons because of the race, color, religion, sex, marital status, national origin, or ancestry of the person or group.

Case Example: A landlord required a black applicant to fill out a credit application and told him no action could be taken regarding rental of an apartment until after the credit investigation was complete. Three hours later, the landlord offered to rent the apartment to a white applicant as soon as the apartment could be cleaned, without requiring any credit investigation. The landlord was found to have violated the California Fair Employment and Housing Act. He was ordered to stop his discriminatory practices and pay damages to the black applicant. *Stearns v. Fair Employment Practices Commission*, 6 Cal. 3d 205, 98 Cal. Rptr. 467, 490 P. 2d 1155 (1971).

Exceptions

The act doesn't apply to rental of a portion of a single-family, owner-occupied home. It also doesn't apply to accommodations operated by nonprofit religious, fraternal, or charitable organizations.

California Fair Employment and Housing Act

◆ Prohibits all arbitrary discrimination

◆ Applies only to residential transactions

Exceptions:

- rental of a portion of a single-family, owner-occupied home;
- accommodations operated by nonprofit religious, fraternal,
- or charitable organizations

Enforcement

A person who has been discriminated against in violation of the Fair Employment and Housing Act may file a complaint with the Department of Fair Employment and Housing within 60 days. The attorney general may also file a complaint for any practices that appear to violate the act. After receiving a complaint, the department may bring an action in superior court to obtain an injunction preventing the alleged violator from renting or selling the property until after the department has completed its investigation.

If the investigation appears to confirm the charges, the department will hold a formal hearing. If the department finds that there has been a violation, the violator will be ordered to stop the discriminatory practices. He or she may also be ordered to sell or rent the property (if it is still available), or similar property, to the complainant, or to provide financial assistance or other services that had been denied. The violator may also be liable for compensatory damages and for punitive damages of up to $1,000.

In addition to the department's actions, the victim of discrimination may bring a civil action in superior or municipal court.

Civil Rights and Fair Housing Laws

HOUSING FINANCIAL DISCRIMINATION ACT (California) (Holden Act)

This law states that it is against public policy to deny mortgage loans or give stricter terms for loans because of neighborhood characteristics unrelated to the creditworthiness of the borrower or the value of the real property. Under the Holden Act, financial institutions in California are prohibited from:

1. discriminating in the provision of financial assistance to purchase, construct, rehabilitate, improve, or refinance housing on the basis of the characteristics of the neighborhood surrounding the property, unless the lender can demonstrate that such consideration is necessary to avoid an unsound business practice;

2. discriminating in the provision of financial assistance for housing, based on race, color, religion, sex, marital status, national origin, or ancestry; and

3. considering the racial, ethnic, religious, or national origin composition of the neighborhood surrounding the property when providing financial assistance.

But the Holden Act doesn't prohibit a financial institution from taking the fair market value of the property into consideration when deciding whether or not to grant a loan.

REAL ESTATE COMMISSIONER'S REGULATIONS

www.dre.ca.gov/relaw_pdf/Regs.pdf
(Real Estate Commissioner's Regulations)

The Business and Professions Code (sec. 125.6) prohibits discrimination by anyone holding a state business license—including real estate brokers and salespersons. This provision of the law is implemented by Commissioner's Regulations 2780, 2781, and 2782, which specifically address the duties of real estate agents with respect to unlawful discrimination based on race, color, sex, religion, ancestry, physical disability, marital status, or national origin.

Regulation 2780 is essentially an explanatory regulation. It gives licensees some guidance as to the types of discriminatory conduct that are prohibited, and also describes some conduct that is permitted even though it may involve discriminatory treatment.

The regulation takes the form of several pages of examples of prohibited conduct. The examples are merely illustrative—they don't cover all prohibited actions. Other conduct by licensees, even though not specifically listed in the regulation, may constitute unlawful discrimination and be the basis for license suspension or revocation.

Here are some of Regulation 2780's examples of conduct that is prohibited when it is based on the prospect's race, color, sex, religion, ancestry, physical disability, marital status, or national origin:

1. refusing or failing to provide information regarding real property;

2. using codes or other means of identifying the applications of minority prospects with a discriminatory intent or effect;

3. processing an application more slowly or otherwise acting to delay or hinder a sale, rental, or financing of real property;

4. soliciting sales, rentals, or listings from one person but not from another in the same area;

5. informing some persons but not others of the existence of waiting lists or other procedures concerning the future availability of property; and

6. providing different information to different persons concerning the desirability of a particular property or neighborhood.

It is also a violation of Regulation 2780 to assist anyone in any way in the sale, rental, or financing of real property when there is reason to believe that person intends to discriminate.

But in addition to the numerous examples of prohibited conduct, Regulation 2780 recites several examples of permissible discriminatory conduct. For example, it is not unlawful discrimination to fail to show, rent, sell, or finance property to a prospect with a physical disability if the property is dangerous or inaccessible to the physically disabled. Advertising directed at the physically disabled (such as an ad that mentions the presence or absence of particular features that are useful to the disabled) is also permissible.

Regulation 2781 concerns panic selling or blockbusting. The regulation states that a licensee may not solicit listings by making any written or oral statement, warning, or threat, or taking any other action, to induce owners to sell or lease property because persons of another race, color, sex, religion, ancestry, marital status, or national origin have moved into the neighborhood, or may be about to move in.

Regulation 2782 addresses the supervisory duties of real estate brokers in connection with civil rights laws. The regulation requires brokers to take reasonable steps to familiarize themselves with state and federal laws relating to discrimination in the sale, rental, and financing of real property. They must also take reasonable steps to familiarize their salespersons with the requirements of those laws.

Case Examples of Discrimination

The overall effect of federal and state legislation and regulations is to outlaw discrimination based on race or ancestry in all property transactions, with no exceptions. Discrimination based on other classes (religion, national origin, sex, familial status, or disability) is also generally prohibited, but there are a few exceptions.

Civil Rights and Fair Housing Laws

So in most cases, discrimination by an owner or real estate agent violates one or more laws. This section of the chapter briefly discusses real estate case examples in which the courts have applied anti-discrimination legislation. These examples cover the sale and rental of real estate, MLS membership, brokers' employment and business practices, advertising, lending, and zoning and other regulatory actions. The cases are drawn from a number of different states, but similar results would probably be reached in California courts.

RENTING AND SELLING

It's unlawful to refuse to sell or rent after receiving a good faith offer if it can be shown that the offeror's race, religion, sex, national origin, or disability was a factor, even if it wasn't the only reason for the refusal. In one case, the landlord claimed that a sub-tenant was unacceptable for several reasons, including a poor credit history. But even though there were some legitimate reasons for rejecting the sub-tenant, a federal court held that the landlord had violated the law if race was one of the reasons for the refusal.

Sometimes discrimination is straightforward. A seller or landlord might tell a potential buyer or renter to get lost. More often, the landlord or seller avoids minority applicants, or pretends that all applicants are being treated equally.

Case Example: The manager's apartment was located so that she could observe the building's main entrance from her own door. When the manager's buzzer rang, she looked down the hall. If the person standing at the main door was black, the manager simply went back inside and refused to answer the door.

This practice was easily discovered, since people ringing the buzzer could see the manager from the main door. A complaint was filed with the state Human Rights Commission.

After the complaint was filed, the building owner installed a peephole in the manager's door. Although the owner maintained this was for the manager's safety, at least one member of the hearing tribunal thought it could also be for the purpose of allowing the manager to continue discriminating without being seen by persons ringing the buzzer. *Skold v. Johnson*, 29 Wash. App. 541, 630 P. 2d 456 (1981).

A property manager might accept an application from a member of a minority and tell the applicant that he or she will be contacted later, or when a vacancy comes up. The manager then takes no further action and never contacts the applicant again. In one case, it was the practice of the owner not to process rental applications that weren't accompanied by a deposit. White applicants were told of this procedure and, accordingly, made a deposit with their applications. Black applicants were not informed, so that few made deposits, and their applications were never processed.

Discrimination in selling property may be relatively simple. For example, the salespersons in a model home may just go out the back door when a potential purchaser drives up. Or a developer might discriminate by making minority purchasers pay higher closing costs. But sometimes discrimination entails an elaborate scheme, as in the following case, which took place near Chicago.

Case Example: A home in an exclusive residential community (with private roads and a security entrance) was listed for sale. The asking price was $850,000, but after some negotiation, the seller and a black couple signed an agreement with a sales price of $675,000. The buyers made an earnest money deposit of $75,000.

News spread that a black couple had bought the home, upsetting a number of the community residents. Restrictive covenants required all sales in the community to be reported to the homeowners' association. The covenants also gave the association a 30-day assignable option to buy the property on the same terms that had been offered. In an unprecedented action, the president of the association called a special meeting to discuss the situation. In 16 or 17 previous sales, the option right had been routinely waived without discussion.

At the meeting, talk centered on the buyers' race and occupation (the husband operated a number of car washes), and on ways to prevent the sale. Although the seller was a member of the board of governors and vice president of the association, he was not told of the meeting.

The association's attorney suggested that it might not be advisable for the association itself to buy the property to frustrate the sale, but perhaps they could form a separate syndicate or find another buyer. Shortly before the 30-day option period expired, the association contacted another buyer (a white woman) who had viewed the home earlier. She agreed to buy the association's option.

The black couple filed a lawsuit, alleging that the homeowners' association and the white buyer had conspired to deny them housing based on their race. The court ruled in favor of the black couple.

While the white buyer claimed she wasn't aware of the race of the other prospective buyers, the court did not believe her. The court also did not believe that the failure to notify the seller of the meeting was an oversight, or the association's claim that its main concern was that the low sales price would lower the value of other properties in the community. The price had not been discussed at all at the meeting (no one there even knew what the price was), and the white buyer had agreed to pay exactly the same price.

The court concluded that the only difference between the second deal and the first was the that the second buyer was a white professional and the first was a black car wash operator.

The court entered judgments in favor of both husband and wife against both the association and the white buyer: $2,675 in compensatory damages for storage expenses and other out-of-pocket expenses occasioned by the delay and additional move; $25,000 for each of them for emotional distress and other compensatory damages; $50,000 for each against each defendant for punitive damages ($200,000 total); $35,000 in attorneys' fees, and $1,016 in costs. The total judgment was $288,691. *Phillips v. Hunter Trails*, 785 F. 2d 184 (7th Cir. 1982).

MULTIPLE LISTING SERVICES

Just as with refusal to sell or rent, denying access to a multiple listing service or other discrimination in brokerage services may involve an outright refusal, or may take a slightly more subtle form.

Civil Rights and Fair Housing Laws

Case Example: In Gary, Indiana in 1973, there was a multiple listing service called Northwest MLS, serving the local Board of Realtors. The Board was made up of 40 white brokers and four black brokers. The MLS had 26 broker members, all of whom were white.

Between January and November 1973, the four black members of the Board applied for membership in the MLS but were denied. Northwest MLS ceased operations in November, but was soon replaced by another multiple listing service. This MLS was made up of 18 white brokers and three black brokers, and it operated in the city.

At about the same time, eight white brokers in the city MLS joined an MLS and local Board in a nearby suburb. All of the members of that suburban MLS and Board were white. The eight white brokers who belonged to both the city MLS and the suburban MLS began directing all their listings to the suburban MLS, even though they continued doing most of their business in the city.

Since the black brokers were not members of the suburban MLS, they were unable to obtain access to those listings. In 1977, the white brokers withdrew from the city MLS altogether and operated solely out of the suburban MLS, although most of their business still involved properties located in the city.

The drastic reduction in the number of brokers and listings in the city MLS caused it to cease operations almost immediately. Seven black brokers then attempted to join the suburban MLS but were unable to do so. In order to qualify for membership, it was necessary to belong to the suburban Board. In order to qualify for membership in the Board, a broker was required to maintain an office in the suburban area.

The black brokers alleged that although they tried to rent office space in that suburb, they were unable to because of discriminatory attitudes prevalent there. As a result, they couldn't gain admission to the only operating MLS in the metropolitan area, and were denied access to most of the real estate listings in the area.

They sued the suburban MLS, the suburban Board, and eight individual white brokers. Through the lawsuit, the black brokers obtained a consent order in which the Board waived the requirement that members maintain an office in the suburban area. *U.S. v. South Suburban MLS*, No. H 77-417 and No. H 80-307 (N. D. Ind. March 12, 1984) (consent order).

EMPLOYMENT BY BROKERS

It is, of course, a violation of anti-discrimination laws and the California Real Estate Law for a broker to discriminate based on race or any other protected class in hiring, compensation, work assignments, or other terms and conditions of employment. Sometimes even apparently well-meaning actions can get a broker in trouble.

Case Example: A large brokerage corporation in Detroit, with over 20 offices and more than 300 salespersons, had a policy of nondiscrimination in hiring. In fact, the brokerage took affirmative steps to recruit, train, and keep black salespersons. Several of its officers were recognized leaders (not only within their own organization but throughout the state) in educating real estate professionals about compliance with fair housing laws. The brokerage was the only one in the state that operated on a large scale both in predominantly white suburban neighborhoods and in predominantly black urban neighborhoods with a biracial sales force.

However, almost all of the brokerage's black salespersons were assigned to offices in predominantly black urban neighborhoods, and almost all of the white salespersons were assigned to offices in predominantly white suburbs.

The brokerage was sued for discrimination. The judge agreed that the brokerage's work assignments had the effect of racial steering because:

1. an all-black office has a tendency to attract black buyers and discourage white buyers;
2. an all-white office has a tendency to attract white buyers and discourage black buyers; and
3. agents tend to sell homes in the area near their offices.

The judge believed that an integrated sales staff would foster an integrated neighborhood. The brokerage was ordered to give all salespersons information about all offices and neighborhoods served by the firm, allowing them to visit other offices and homes listed by other offices. The brokerage was also required to encourage black salespersons to try working out of suburban offices, without losing the right to be reassigned to the offices in the city if they desired. *U.S. v. Real Estate One, Inc.*, 433 F. Supp. 1140 (E.D. Mich. 1977).

ADVERTISING

Both federal law and California law prohibit any advertising that indicates a restriction, preference, or intent to discriminate based on race or other protected classes. Discriminatory advertising or solicitations may be very subtle. Apparently innocent statements may be intended or interpreted as discriminatory.

Example: In some areas of the country an advertisement that describes a home as "near schools and churches" may be taken to mean that it is a gentile neighborhood and that Jews (who attend temple or synagogue, not church) are not welcome.

Under certain circumstances, even the newspapers a broker chooses for advertising may be held to have the effect of racial steering.

www.dre.ca.gov/relaw_pdf/Regs.pdf
(Department of Real Estate Advertising Guidelines)

Civil Rights and Fair Housing Laws

Case Example: A real estate brokerage in Detroit advertised listed properties in two newspapers that were distributed over the entire metropolitan area, a number of smaller newspapers that were circulated primarily in certain neighborhoods, and in a weekly newspaper circulated mainly in black neighborhoods.

The practice that attracted the attention of the attorney general was the company's standard policy of advertising listings in the so-called "changing areas" of the city in the black newspaper and not regularly advertising those homes in the newspapers of general distribution.

The court believed this had an impermissible steering effect because, for the most part, only people who read the black newspaper were made aware of available homes in the "changing" neighborhoods. Because most of these readers were black, this would accelerate the change from a mixed neighborhood to a predominantly black neighborhood, in violation of the government's policy of fostering integrated neighborhoods.

The brokerage was ordered to maintain the same level of advertising in the newspaper circulated primarily in black neighborhoods, but also advertise those same homes in the two newspapers of general distribution, with some advertising in the smaller community papers nearby. *U.S. v. Real Estate One, Inc.*, 433 F. Supp. 1140 (E.D. Mich. 1977).

LENDING

Redlining is the most common discrimination charge against real estate lenders. But financing discrimination may also take the form of differing loan fees and other financing charges, or differing foreclosure practices.

A lender found guilty of discrimination may be ordered to take affirmative steps to increase its lending activities in neighborhoods where few loans have been made. Remedial action might include appointing a bank officer to oversee the affirmative lending program, setting goals for the number of purchase money and improvement loans to be made in particular neighborhoods, consulting with minority marketing experts to implement advertising programs in the target areas, and conducting fair lending seminars for personnel. In one California case, the lender hired two additional loan agents to serve the targeted areas, paid them a guaranteed minimum salary (which agents outside the target areas did not receive), and paid them a higher rate of commission because of the lower average loan amount in the target areas. (Settlement agreement, *United Neighbors in Action v. American Savings*, No. C-78-1799 [N. D. Calif. 1979].)

ZONING AND OTHER MUNICIPAL REGULATIONS

The clause "make otherwise unavailable or deny" in anti-discrimination legislation has been interpreted to include zoning practices that have the effect of denying housing to minorities. This is known as **exclusionary zoning**. Since it's currently unlikely that a municipality would enact an openly racist ordinance, these cases usually involve arguments based on the concept of **disparate impact**.

Chapter 14

A law with disparate impact may be neutral on its face, but it has a discriminatory effect: the law has a much heavier impact on one group than it has on others. For example, in the field of employment discrimination there have been a number of cases alleging that height restrictions for police or fire departments had a discriminatory effect. Women and certain minorities tend to be shorter than white males, and there was no evidence to indicate that the height restrictions were related to job requirements.

Exclusionary zoning cases usually involve ordinances that prohibit or unreasonably restrict multi-family or low-income housing. In comparison to the white population, members of minority groups are much more likely to be low-income. As a result, it has been successfully argued in a number of cases that ordinances limiting low-cost housing have a discriminatory impact on minority groups, excluding them from certain communities.

Case Example: A municipality near Chicago refused to rezone to permit construction of multi-family dwellings within its boundaries. The population of the Chicago metropolitan area was approximately 18% black, but the municipality in question had only 27 black residents out of a population of approximately 65,000 (.04%).

Since a greater percentage of the occupants of multi-family dwellings were black rather than white, the court ruled that the municipality's zoning ordinance had the effect of excluding black people from living there. *Metropolitan Housing Development Corp. v. Arlington Heights*, 517 F. 2d 409 (7th Cir. 1975).

Case Example: Yonkers, New York, had a practice of approving low-income housing in only one section of town, which was predominantly black. The court found this had the discriminatory effect of preventing blacks from moving into predominantly white sections of the city, since there was little or no housing available in those areas for low or middle-income residents. *U.S. v. Yonkers Board of Education*, 624 F. Supp. 1276 (S. D. N. Y. 1985).

The Extent of Liability for Discrimination

In a discrimination lawsuit, compensatory damages are intended to reimburse the plaintiff for expenses caused by the discrimination, such as extra rent or transportation, storage, or moving costs. They're also intended to provide compensation for the mental distress—humiliation and anger—that results from being discriminated against. Punitive damages are added to compensatory damages to punish the wrongdoer and to discourage others from discriminating.

Awards for both compensatory damages and punitive damages have been growing much larger in recent years. The court opinions suggest one possible reason for larger judgments: the more time that passes since the enactment of fair housing laws and other civil rights laws, the more inexcusable any discrimination becomes. Whatever the reasons, the awards can be substantial, as the following case shows.

Civil Rights and Fair Housing Laws

Case Example: Ms. Grayson and Ms. Futrell were black women employed as air traffic controllers by the FAA. They saw a newspaper ad for apartments available in a complex near their jobs at MacArthur Airport on Long Island, and tried to rent apartments there.

Both women were repeatedly told over a period of several months that no apartments were available. Yet the complex continued to advertise apartments in the newspaper, and white "testers" who visited the apartments were shown vacant apartments and were told that space was available. Grayson and Futrell themselves were told that apartments were available when they called on the phone and didn't identify themselves.

Grayson and Futrell sued the realty company that managed the apartment complex. The jury had no trouble finding the realty company guilty of racial discrimination. The company was ordered to pay compensatory damages of $40,000 to Futrell and $25,000 to Grayson, and punitive damages of $250,000 to each plaintiff, for a total judgment of $565,000. *Grayson v. S. Rotundi & Sons Realty Co.,* No. CV 83-0844 (E. D. N. Y. 1984) (order rejecting motion for judgment notwithstanding the verdict).

Like the Grayson case, many discrimination cases involve the use of **testers**. Someone who believes he or she is being lied to about the unavailability of housing complains to a government agency or a community organization. Then the agency or organization sends out testers who pretend they're interested in renting or buying the property. Often a "sandwich test" is used. A white tester is shown available space; then a minority tester is told there are no vacancies; then another white tester is shown available space. This kind of test is very convincing evidence of discrimination.

Of course the original rental applicant (who complained to the fair housing organization) can sue for damages. But in addition, the testers and the fair housing organization may also be able to sue.

Case Example: Mr. Coles, a black man, inquired about renting an apartment in a complex near Richmond, Virginia, and was told there were no vacancies. He complained to a local nonprofit organization whose purpose was to promote equal opportunity in housing.

The organization sent out a black tester and a white tester. On four different occasions the black tester was told there were no vacancies. The white tester was shown vacant apartments.

The realty company and one of its employees were then sued by Mr. Coles (the actual rental applicant), the black tester, the white tester, and the fair housing organization. The defendants challenged the testers' and the organization's rights to sue, and the case went all the way to the U.S. Supreme Court.

The Court held that all of the plaintiffs were entitled to sue. The rental applicant's claim was based on straightforward allegations of denial of housing and racial steering. The black tester's claim was based on a provision of the Fair Housing Act that makes it unlawful for anyone to misrepresent that housing isn't available when in fact it is. To recover under that provision, it isn't necessary to be actually seeking housing. Even testers who expect that they will be lied to still have a right to sue. **Continued**

The white tester's claim was based on a general right to enjoy the benefits of an integrated society. The defendants' discriminatory practices interfered with that right. Finally, the fair housing organization had a right to sue on the theory that the defendants' discriminatory practices interfered with the organization's housing counseling and referral services, with a resulting drain on its financial resources. *Havens Realty v. Coleman*, 455 U.S. 363 (1982).

So just about everyone affected by an act or practice of unlawful discrimination can sue. And just about everyone connected with the violation can be held liable, either because of their own actions, or on the basis of agency responsibility: property managers, real estate brokers, real estate salespersons, and property owners. Remember, too, that if a seller refuses to go through with a transaction because of the prospective buyer's race, religion, ethnic background, or sex, the broker may sue the seller for the commission.

WHO CAN SUE FOR VIOLATIONS OF ANTI—DISCRIMINATION LAWS

Prospective Buyer/Tenant
Tester
Fair Housing Organization
California Department of Fair Employment and Housing

State Attorney General
U.S. Attorney General
HUD

WHO CAN BE HELD LIABLE FOR UNLAWFUL DISCRIMINATION

Seller/Landlord
Homeowners' Association
Real Estate Broker
Real Estate Salesperson
Multiple Listing Service

Property Manager
Resident Manager
Rental Agent
Lender
Loan Officer

One final point: refusing to deal with someone who has sued you for discrimination may be considered unlawful retaliation.

Case Example: After several black brokers brought suit against the MLS and its members for denying them membership, a number of the white brokers refused to split commissions or co-broker any transactions with the plaintiff black brokers. The black brokers then sued those white brokers in a separate lawsuit, alleging that their refusal to cooperate was in retaliation for the discrimination lawsuit.

The white brokers freely admitted that their refusal to cooperate was because of the lawsuit. They didn't choose to work with or share commissions with anyone who was suing them. But the court held that the white brokers' refusal to cooperate interfered with the black brokers' exercise of their rights under the Fair Housing Act. *U.S. v. South Suburban MLS*, No. H 80-307 (N. D. Ind. March 1, 1984) (order granting partial summary judgment).

Civil Rights and Fair Housing Laws

SUMMARY CHART

	Civil Rights Act of 1866	Federal Fair Housing Act	California Housing Act
Race	X	X	X
Color		X	X
Religion		X	X
National origin		X	X
Ancestry	X		X
Sex		X	X
Age			*
Disability		X	X
Familial status		X	*
Marital status			X
All property	X		
Housing only		X	X

*The law doesn't specifically mention this type of discrimination, but it has been interpreted to prohibit all arbitrary discrimination in housing.

EQUAL HOUSING
OPPORTUNITY

CHAPTER SUMMARY

1. The Civil Rights Act of 1866 prohibits discrimination based on race or ancestry in any real estate transaction in the United States. The Supreme Court held that the law applies to private action as well as state action.

2. The Federal Fair Housing Act prohibits discrimination based on race, color, religion, sex, national origin, disability, or familial status in the sale or lease of residential property. It also prohibits discrimination in advertising, lending and real estate brokerage in residential transactions. Steering, channeling, and redlining are among the practices outlawed by the act. The act's limited exceptions never apply to racial discrimination (because of the Civil Rights Act of 1866), and don't matter in California (because of stricter state laws).

3. The Equal Credit Opportunity Act prohibits discrimination in residential lending on the basis of race, color. religion, national origin, sex, marital status, age, or receipt of public assistance. To detect redlining, the Home Mortgage Disclosure Act requires lenders to make annual reports on residential loans.

4. California civil rights laws are interpreted to prohibit all arbitrary discrimination, not just discrimination against the groups expressly listed in the statutes.

5. The Unruh Civil Rights Act prohibits any discrimination by a business establishment in California. An exception to the act allows housing developments designed for senior citizens to impose age limits.

6. The Fair Employment and Housing Act prohibits all housing discrimination in California. The act specifically makes it illegal for a seller or, lessor to ask questions about a prospective buyer or tenant's race, religion, sex, marital status, national origin, or ancestry. It prohibits advertising that indicates an intent to discriminate. There are only two exceptions to the act. It doesn't apply to rental of part of a single-family, owner-occupied home, or to accommodations operated by nonprofit religious, fraternal, or charitable organizations.

7. California's Holden Act prohibits discrimination in residential lending.

8. Commissioner's Regulations 2780, 2781, and 2782 explain the duties of real estate agents in regard to unlawful discrimination.

9. Nearly everyone connected with a discriminatory act can be held liable for it: the owner, homeowners' association, property manager, broker, or salesperson. They may be ordered to pay compensatory and punitive damages, attorney's fees, court costs, and civil penalties. Testers and fair housing organizations may be entitled to damages, as well as the victim. A court can also issue an injunction requiring the defendant to sell or lease property to the plaintiff, or to stop a discriminatory business practice.

CASE PROBLEM

Hankins v. El Torrito, Inc., 63 Cal. App. 4th 510, 74 Cal. Rptr. 2d 684 (1998)

In 1988, Mark Hankins had his right leg amputated several inches below the knee due to an accident. Wearing his prosthesis causes Hankins periodic problems and pain which sometimes requires that he use crutches or a wheel chair. Using crutches, he and his fiancee went to the El Torrito restaurant in Burlingame. There were six steps at the entrance and three steps separating the dining room from the lower bar level.

Additionally, there were eighteen steps from the main level to the second floor of the building where the public restrooms were located. With his fiancee's assistance, Hankins climbed the six stairs leading to the restaurant entrance. During dinner, Hankins had to use the restroom. He explained to the manager that he could not climb the eighteen stairs and asked if he could use the employee restroom on the first floor. The manager refused the request and told him to use the restroom in another restaurant which was located next door. Using his crutches, Hankins made his way out of the restaurant (up the three interior stairs and down the six exterior stairs) and across approximately seventy-five yards of parking lot to the restaurant next door.

Civil Rights and Fair Housing Laws

However, that restaurant was not handicap accessible. Returning to the El Torrito, and unable to wait any longer, Hankins found a bush and relieved himself. He was angered and humiliated by this experience. Hankins sued El Torrito seeking damages and other relief for violation of the Unruh Civil Rights Act (CC§51) and laws providing equal rights to public facilities for individuals with disabilities (CC54-54.1). El Torrito contended, among other things, its policy is not to allow customers access to the employee restroom and the policy was therefore not discriminatory because it applied to all restaurant customers. Did El Torrito unlawfully discriminate against Hankins?

Answer: Yes. The Court of Appeal stated that El Torrito's restroom policy discriminated against Hankins. The restaurant's policy and the physical layout of the restaurant allowed customers who were not physically handicapped to use the restroom (the one on the second floor) but denied the same restroom service to physically handicapped customers even though there was a restroom on the premises (the one behind the kitchen) that a physically handicapped person could otherwise use. Therefore, El Torrito's policy discriminated against disabled customers. El Torrito also argued that kitchen sanitation prohibited customers from the using the kitchen restroom because the customers may stop in the kitchen and sample food going to and from the restroom which would pose a health hazard to other diners. The court found that this allegation was unsubstantiated and totally speculative. Therefore, such a speculative concern that El Torrito would be unable to prevent a customer from sampling food on the way to or from the restroom does not justify denying restroom access to a handicapped customer.
El Torrito also argued that it could not have violated the law regarding access to facilities by handicapped individuals under Civil Code section 54 since the building was in compliance with all state laws regarding disability access at the time of the incident. The issue was whether El Torrito violated the law by maintaining a policy, unrelated to any structural impediment, which resulted in the denial of full and equal access by a disabled customer to a public accommodation. The Court of Appeal held that the law applies to policies as well as structural impediments and was violated by El Torrito's policy which denied disabled individuals full and fair access to public accommodations even though the physical structure did not violate the law. Hankin's trial court award of $80,000 in damages was upheld.

**CHAPTER 14
KEY TERMS**

blockbusting
Department of Housing
 and Urban Development
 (HUD)

Department of Fair
 Employment and
 Housing
disparate impact
exclusionary zoning
Office of Equal
 Opportunity (OEO)

panic selling
redlining
steering
testers

Civil Rights and Fair Housing Laws

Quiz—Chapter 14

1. The Civil Rights Act of 1866 prohibits:
   a. all housing discrimination.
   b. all discrimination in lending.
   c. any arbitrary discrimination in the provision of government services.
   d. racial discrimination in the sale or lease of any property.

2. The Federal Fair Housing Act has a direct impact on:
   a. federally subsidized housing.
   b. federally insured loans on residential property.
   c. non-federal housing.
   d. all of the above.

3. HUD's Office of Equal Opportunity handles complaints based on the:
   a. Federal Fair Housing Act.
   b. Civil Rights Act of 1866.
   c. Unruh Civil Rights Act.
   d. Rumford Act.

4. All of the following have to display a fair housing poster EXCEPT:
   a. an owner selling her own home.
   b. a broker specializes in multi-family dwellings.
   c. a real estate office in new subdivision.
   d. none of the above are required to display the poster.

5. The Home Mortgage Disclosure Act helps to enforce the prohibition against:
   a. steering.
   b. blockbusting.
   c. redlining.
   d. all of the above.

6. Under California law a landlord can legally refuse to rent to a prospective tenant because the tenant:
   a. has a child.
   b. was born in Ireland.
   c. has a poor credit history.
   d. none of the above.

7. Which of the following laws prohibits all age discrimination in housing without exceptions?
   a. Civil Rights Act of 1866
   b. Federal Fair Housing Act
   c. Unruh Civil Rights Act
   d. None of the above

8. Generally the California laws against discrimination:
   a. are broader in application with fewer exemptions than the federal laws.
   b. are narrower in scope than federal legislation.
   c. provide exactly the same coverage as federal legislation because of the principle of federal supremacy.
   d. are enforceable only in so far as they offer the same protection against discrimination that federal laws provide.

9. Blockbusting is an acceptable practice:
   a. under federal law but not under California law.
   b. only when approved by HUD or the California Department of Real Estate.
   c. only if the buyer and seller are notified and agree to participate.
   d. under no circumstances.

10. The term "racial" steering refers to:
   a. giving special preference to minority customers.
   b. directing prospects to different listings based on their race and the racial composition of the neighborhoods.
   c. directing minority customers toward affordable property based on their income and assets.
   d. refusing to represent minority clients.

CHAPTER 15
Landlord/Tenant Law

CHAPTER OVERVIEW

One of the most common of all real estate transactions is renting a place to live or work. This chapter describes the different types of leases, and explains the rights, duties, and liabilities of the landlord and tenant. Real estate agents need a basic knowledge of landlord/tenant law, since they may be asked to act as rental agents. When property is for sale, but no buyer can be immediately found, some sellers rent it with an option to buy (at the right price and terms acceptable to the owner). Many licensees specialize in property management as their specialty. For them, an understanding of landlord/tenant law is essential.

Leases

A lease is both a conveyance and a contract. As a conveyance, it temporarily transfers an interest the right of possession, occupancy, quiet enjoyment, and use of property from the owner (the **landlord** or **lessor**) to another (the **tenant** or **lessee**). Although the landlord still retains the ownership of the estate, the tenant has a leasehold estate. (See Chapter 3.)

As a contract, the lease states the terms of the parties' relationship: what has each agreed to do? Leases are often called **rental agreements**.

A landlord and tenant are free to negotiate the terms of their lease, just as with any contract. But landlords are often in a much better bargaining position than tenants (especially residential tenants). As a result, in the past many leases were slanted in the landlord's favor. To protect tenants against overreaching, the law now prohibits landlords from including certain unfair provisions in a lease. The law also imposes a number of duties on landlords that apply regardless of what terms are express in the lease. Thus, there are several limits on the freedom of contract between landlord and tenant. They will be discussed throughout this chapter.

Lease

Conveyance: transfer leasehold estate to tenant

Leasehold—to—Tenant

Contract: capacity, offer, and acceptance, consideration

— in writing, if term ends more than 1 year from signing —

REQUIREMENTS FOR VALIDITY

Since a lease is a contract, the basic requirements for a valid contract are necessary for a valid lease. The lessor and lessee must have the legal capacity to contract— they can't be incompetent or under age. And a lease has to be supported by consideration. In most cases, the consideration is a sum of money paid as rent.

Under the statute of frauds, a lease must be in writing if it is for more than one year, or if it won't be fully performed within one year from the date it is signed.

Example: M is a college student. In June she signs a lease for the next school year. The lease runs from September 10th through August 30th. It has to be in writing even though the lease term is less than one year, since it won't end until more than a year from June, when it was made (signed).

If the lease has to be in writing under the statute of frauds and it is signed by an agent on behalf of a principal, then the agent's authority from the principal must also be in writing.

A written lease must be signed by the landlord or owner's authorized agent. All landlords must sign, if the property is owned jointly. A tenant usually also signs the lease, but the tenant's signature isn't required. A tenant who takes possession and pays rent is considered to have accepted the terms of the lease.

California law limits the duration of some leases. A lease of land for agricultural purposes can't last more than 51 years; a lease of a town or city lot or the lease of land for oil, gas or mineral production can't last more than 99 years.

BASIC PROVISIONS

Every written lease should include certain basic information: the parties' names, an adequate description of the property (the address may be enough for residential or business property), the amount of the rent, when rent it is due, how payable, and the duration of the lease.

If the lease doesn't specify its duration, the law presumes it is a month-to-month tenancy. But there are two important exceptions to that rule. An agricultural lease is presumed to be for one year unless otherwise stated. And a residential lease is presumed to last as long as the rental period: if rent is due every week, it's presumed to be a week-to-week tenancy; if rent is due every month, it's presumed to be a month-to-month tenancy.

Most leases also contain clauses concerning acceptable uses of the property, the right to assign or sublet, required security deposits, and the responsibility for repairs and maintenance. Other issues that are often addressed in a lease: the landlord's access to the property during the lease term; alterations or damage by the tenant; the consequences of default; extensions or renewals; and each party's duties if the property is destroyed.

TYPES OF LEASES

Fixed Lease

A fixed lease may also be called a **flat**, **gross**, or **straight** lease. Most residential leases are fixed. Under a fixed lease, the rent is set at a fixed amount, and that's all the tenant has to pay the landlord. Operating expenses such as maintenance and repair costs, taxes, special assessments, and insurance are all the landlord's responsibility. However, the tenant under a fixed lease often has to pay for utilities (electricity, heat, and so on) in addition to the rent.

Graduated Lease

A graduated lease may also be called a **"cost of living adjustment"** or **"step-up"** lease and is similar to a fixed lease except that it provides for periodic increases, called "bumps," in the rent. These increases are usually set for specific future events, such as a date, an occupancy rate for the building (or by other tenants), or by attainment of a certain sales volume. The amount of each increase is based on a fixed amount or an index, such as the Consumer Price Index. This is also called a **stepped lease**.

Net Lease

When a tenant pays rent plus all the operating expenses (such as utilities, taxes, insurance, and repairs), it's called a net lease or sometimes a "triple-net" lease. The rent is pure "net" to the landlord. Many commercial leases are net leases.

Percentage Lease

Some commercial leases provide for a percentage rent. The rental amount is based on a percentage of the tenant's monthly or annual gross sales. Percentage leases are common for retail stores, especially in large shopping centers.

There are many types of percentage leases. For instance, under a pure percentage lease, the entire rental amount is a percentage of gross sales. But under the most common type of percentage lease, a fixed minimum rent is required.

ARCO closed its gas station three years before the 20-year lease expired. ARCO contended that it only had to pay the $1,000 monthly minimum rent for the remaining three years of the lease term. The court held that ARCO might be required to pay more than the minimum, even though it was no longer selling gas on the property. A percentage lease tenant is generally expected to continue operating its business for the entire lease term.

Chapter 15

> **Case Example:** Circle K corporation leased property for 20 years from Frank Collins agreeing to pay rent calculated at 2% of "gross sales." Subsequently, state law legalized lotteries and Circle K began selling lottery tickets.
>
> The issue became whether Circle K paid 2% on the commission it received on lottery ticket sales or 2% of the total sale price of lottery tickets. The court held that "Circle K acts more nearly as a tax collector for the state than as a retailer." Circle K is paid for its services by a commission and that commission is considered a "gross receipt" for services performed on the premises.
>
> The 2% is calculated on the commission not the total lottery ticket sales. *In Re Circle K Corp.*, 98 F. 3d 484 (9th Cir. 1996).

GROUND LEASE. In a ground lease, the owner leases vacant land to a tenant who agrees to erect a building on it. The property involved in the College Block case was vacant until ARCO built its gas station there.

To make construction of a building worth the tenant's while, ground leases tend to be long-term. They are popular in large metropolitan areas, where land is particularly valuable. For example, a tenant might lease a block from the landowner, demolish the existing structures, put up a 40-story office building, and lease office space to various businesses. This also creates a **"sandwich lease"**: the tenant who constructed the building is both a tenant (as to the land), and landlord (as to the building).

TRANSFERRING LEASED PROPERTY

A lessor is free to sell the leased property at any time. Occasionally a lease provides that it will terminate if the property is sold. In most cases, however, the new owner takes the property subject to the existing lease and must honor the terms. However what if the lessor sells the leased property but fails to tell the purchaser that it is leased? The purchaser would be on constructive notice if the tenant was in possession or the lease was recorded. How important is recording the lease? The answer is found in California Civil Code Section 1214:

> *If the lease term is for more than one year the tenant cannot force the lease on the new owner unless the lease is recorded. Where the owner fails to notify the buyer or a new lender of the tenancy, the tenant's only recourse is to sue the previous owner.*

Sale

Once the property has been transferred, all of the former owner's rights and duties under the lease are transferred to the new owner. If the tenant gave the former owner a security deposit or paid any rent in advance, the former owner must either turn that money over to the new owner or refund it to the tenant (Civil Code 1950.5-7).

Case Example: In 1971, Ms. Trypucko leased some commercial property in Pasadena from Mr. Clark. The lease term was five years, with an option to renew for an additional five years. Trypucko gave Clark a $2,500 security deposit.

Two years later, Clark sold the property to Security Pictures. He told Trypucko to start sending her rent payments to Security, but didn't tell her he'd sold the property. He also didn't transfer Trypucko's deposit to Security.

In 1976, Trypucko exercised her option and renewed the lease for five more years. When the renewal expired in 1981, Trypucko moved out and demanded her security deposit back from Clark. Clark refused to return the money; he had spent it several years earlier. Trypucko sued.

Clark claimed that Trypucko had violated the terms of the lease in 1980, so she wasn't entitled to the return of her deposit. The court ruled that Clark's rights under the lease ended when he sold the property. Trypucko's conduct after that point had nothing to do with Clark, and certainly didn't excuse his failure to refund the deposit. *Trypucko v. Clark*, 142 Cal. App. 3d Supp. 1, 191 Cal. Rptr. 165 (1983).

Assignment

A tenant has the right to assign the lease to someone else unless the lease expressly states that it can't be assigned without the landlord's consent. (Many leases do require consent.) Assignment transfers the right of occupancy to a new tenant (assignee on the original; tenant /assignor for the entire remainder of the lease term). The statute of frauds requires a lease assignment for more than one year to be in writing.

After assignment, the assignee is responsible for paying the rent to the landlord. But the original tenant also remains liable to the landlord. If the assignee doesn't pay, the landlord can demand the rent from the original tenant (assignor).

If the landlord wants the assignee to be bound by every contractual obligation in the current lease, it is very important for the landlord to get a written assumption of the lease signed by the assignee.

Case Example: The trustees of the Meredith estate leased some commercial property in Los Angeles to Mr. Dardarian. The lease was for five years, from July 1, 1971, to June 30, 1976. It could not be assigned without consent.

In November 1971, Dardarian asked the trustees for permission to assign the lease to DA&W Commercial Corporation. The trustees gave their consent. DA&W took over the lease from November 1971 through June 30, 1976.

All went well for a few years, but DA&W stopped paying rent in April 1975. In May 1976, the trustees finally filed a lawsuit to evict DA&W and collect the rent. They also made Dardarian a defendant in the lawsuit. A judgment for the unpaid rent was entered against Dardarian, the original tenant, as well as against DA&W, the assignee. *Meredith v. Dardarian*, 83 Cal. App. 3d 248, 147 Cal. Rptr. 761 (1978).

Sublease

A sublease is similar to an assignment, except that it is for less than the entire remainder of the lease term: the original tenant intends to resume occupancy at a future date. If the lease forbids assignment without consent, but doesn't mention subleasing, the tenant has the right to sublease. In a sublease, the **subtenant** usually pays the rent to the original tenant rather than to the landlord.

> **Example:** T leases an apartment. His tenancy will last from October through the following September. In March, T's company gives him a four-month assignment in Taiwan. He subleases his apartment to S for the four months he will be gone. S agrees to pay rent to T from April 1st through July 31st. T continues to pay rent to the landlord.
>
> When T returns from Taiwan, S moves out and T moves back in for the final two months of the lease term.

A sublease doesn't alter the legal relationship between the landlord and the original tenant at all. If the landlord doesn't get paid, ordinarily the landlord can sue only the original tenant.

Withholding Consent. Many commercial leases prohibit both assignment and subleasing without the landlord's consent. It's common for those leases to state that consent may not be unreasonably withheld; the landlord must have a good reason for refusing to accept the assignee or sublessee as a tenant.

Case Example: Mr. Schweiso leased some commercial property. The lease stated that it could not be assigned without the lessors' written consent. Sometime later Schweiso wanted to sell his business to the Grofs, so he asked the lessors for permission to assign the lease to the Grofs.

The lessors would not consent unless they were paid $6,000. They said the lease gave them the right to be unreasonable and arbitrary; the consent provision was their "license to steal." After the lessors withheld consent, the Grofs cancelled their conditional contract to buy Schweiso's business.

Schweiso sued the lessors. The court ruled that the lessors did not have the right to arbitrarily withhold consent. They couldn't turn down the tenant's request just on the basis of personal taste or whim, or in order to demand more money. *Schweiso v. Williams*, 150 Cal. App. 3d 883, 198 Cal. Rptr. 238 (1984).

But what if the lease says nothing about the grounds for withholding consent—can the landlord be unreasonable then? The California Supreme Court addressed this issue in a 1985 decision, *Kendall v. Ernest Pestana, Inc.*, 40 Cal. 3d 488, 220 Cal. Rptr. 818. Like the *Schweiso* court, the Supreme Court held that a commercial landlord cannot withhold consent without a commercially reasonable objection, even if the lease doesn't say so. The court listed these examples of commercially reasonable considerations: the assignee's financial instability, proposed use of the property, or need for alterations.

In 1989, the legislature responded to Kendall with a new statute (Civil Code 1995.010-.270) which applies to nonresidential property. The statute modifies the Supreme Court's rule. Now if a commercial lease requires the landlord's consent to assignment or subleasing, but provides no standard for giving or withholding it, consent cannot be unreasonably withheld. If the lease does not restrict a transfer by the tenant, the tenant has an unrestricted right to assign or sublet. However, a lease may expressly state that the landlord can withhold consent on any grounds whatsoever, no matter how unreasonable. Or, a lease may prohibit assignment or subleasing altogether or provide that a transfer is subject to a condition such as payment of the $6,000 transfer fee in *Schweiso*.

The legislature also provided that the *Kendall* rule does not apply to leases executed before September 23, 1983 (the date of the first California appellate court decision dealing with this issue *Cohen v. Ratinoff*, 147 Cal. App. 3d 321, 195 Cal. Rptr. 84). For a lease executed before that date, consent to an assignment or sublease can be unreasonably withheld, unless the consent provision expressly states that it may not be.

Keep in mind that the *Kendall* decision and the 1989 statute do not apply to residential leases. Also, a landlord's acceptance of rent, or a failure to object in a timely manner after a tenant's breach of a transfer restriction clause, may constitute a waiver of the breach and therefore landlord's consent.

Novation

As you've seen, neither an assignment nor a sublease takes the original tenant off the hook. He or she is still liable to the landlord for the rent. To avoid any further liability under the lease, the original tenant has to arrange a **novation** rather than an assignment or sublease.

A novation replaces the lease between the landlord and the original tenant with a new lease between the landlord and the substitute tenant. The original tenant is released. Of course, a novation always requires the landlord's consent.

Rights, Duties of the Landlord and Tenant

In the lease, landlord and tenant each agree to take on certain duties in exchange for certain rights. The law also imposes duties on each party, creating corresponding rights for the other. These duties imposed by law apply even when they aren't expressly stated in the lease, and they override any inconsistent lease provisions. They're sometimes called **implied covenants** or **implied warranties**; the law makes them part of the lease.

There are often different legal rules for residential tenancies and nonresidential tenancies. Commercial tenants are presumed to be more sophisticated than residential tenants, and better able to protect their interests during lease negotiations. As a result, the law imposes duties on residential landlords that don't apply to commercial and other nonresidential landlords. California also has a special landlord/tenant law for mobile home parks, which will be discussed later. For now, we'll look at the general rules.

Delivery of Possession

There's an implied covenant in every lease that the landlord will deliver possession of the property to the tenant on the date the lease term begins. If the tenant is prevented from taking possession, that's a breach of this implied covenant.

> **Example:** The apartment rental agreement says the tenancy will begin on August 1. But when the new tenant shows up on that day ready to move in, she discovers that the previous tenant hasn't moved out yet. It was up to the landlord to make sure the old tenant was out before August 1, and his failure to do so is a breach of the new lease.

When the covenant to deliver possession is breached, the tenant has the option of rescinding the lease: asking the landlord to return any money already paid, and looking for another place to live or set up shop. But if the tenant decides not to rescind and just waits for the landlord to deliver possession, the tenant may only request consequential damages.

Consequential damages are an award of money intended to compensate someone for the consequences or results of a wrongful act. Suppose the apartment in the previous example wasn't ready for the new tenant until August 6. If the new tenant chooses to wait instead of rescinding the lease, she must still pay rent, but may demand that the landlord pay her consequential damages. These may include a six-day hotel bill, cost of storing her furniture for six days, and moving expenses.

RENT

Not surprisingly, the tenant's primary duty is to pay the rent as agreed. Most leases state a specific date when rent is due, usually at the beginning of the rental period. But if the lease doesn't specify when rent is to be paid, it isn't due until the end of the rental period (unless the period is longer than one year).

Many landlords require tenants to pay a late charge if the rent isn't paid within a certain time after the due date. A landlord has the right to terminate a lease or evict a tenant for nonpayment of rent. Some cities have rent control ordinances (discussed later) limiting the amount of and ability to increase rent amounts.

EVICTION

Eviction can be either actual or constructive. There's **actual eviction** if the landlord orders the tenant to leave the leased property, or physically forces the tenant out (by changing the locks, for example). But sometimes the tenant is forced to leave because the property has become uninhabitable or can no longer be used as intended. When that's the landlord's fault, it's called **constructive eviction**.

www.nolo.com/lawcenter/ency/article.cfm/objectID/1DC31D3C-B648-4BA7-9B9179DA80039436
™ **(10 Tips Every Tenant Should Know)**

CONSTRUCTIVE EVICTION
◆ Substantial interference with use of property
◆ Problem must be landlord's responsibility
◆ Tenant must actually move out
◆ Duty to pay rent ends

Case Example: Ms. Buckner rented an apartment in Mr. Azulai's building. Sometime later the building became infested with vermin. Buckner did her best to exterminate them in her own apartment, but it was hopeless—since the whole building was infested, the bugs kept coming back. The landlord didn't take action, so Buckner moved out. In the ensuing lawsuit, the court held that she had been constructively evicted. *Buckner v. Azulai*, 251 Cal. App. 2d Supp. 1013, 59 Cal. Rptr. 806 (1967).

COVENANT OF QUIET ENJOYMENT

The implied covenant of quiet enjoyment provides that the tenant has a right to undisturbed possession of the property during the lease term. The tenant is protected from intrusion by the landlord or by anyone else claiming a right to the property. This covenant is breached if the tenant is wrongfully evicted.

A breach of the covenant of quiet enjoyment (either actual or constructive eviction) relieves the tenant of the duty to pay rent. But to claim constructive eviction the tenant must actually move off the property—Buckner couldn't have stopped paying rent because of the bugs if she were still living in that apartment. And not every problem or disturbance can be the basis for a claim of constructive eviction. The problem must substantially interfere with the tenant's use of the property, and it must be the landlord's responsibility. (Of course, the tenant may stay and sue for damages.)

Case Example: Mr. Brown leased an apartment. The lease stated that the landlord was not liable to the tenant for any damage resulting from the acts of other tenants in the building.

It turned out that the family in the apartment below Brown liked to sing and quarrel loudly at all hours. Brown couldn't get a good night's sleep. He complained to the family and to the landlord, but without effect. So he moved out and stopped paying rent. The landlord sued Brown for the money.

The court ruled in the landlord's favor. Since the lease expressly stated that the landlord wasn't responsible for the acts of other tenants, the neighbors' noise wasn't constructive eviction. Brown was required to pay his rent. *Conterno v. Brown*, 263 Cal. App. 2d 135, 69 Cal. Rptr. 393 (1968).

PRIVACY

Unless otherwise agreed, a landlord doesn't have the right to enter the leased property without the tenant's consent. But if the landlord is supposed to maintain the property, it's understood that he or she may enter to make necessary repairs. Most leases contain a clause stating that the landlord may show the premises to prospective tenant or purchaser after receiving the notice of intent to vacate. California has special rules to protect the privacy of residential tenants. A residential landlord may not enter the property without the tenant's consent to merely "inspect the premises", an exception is for an emergency that threatens to injure someone or damage property—then notice must be given immediately afterwards.

Example: A water pipe bursts and begins flooding a tenant's apartment. The tenant isn't home. This is an emergency—the landlord may enter the apartment without the tenant's consent to stop the flood, then leave notice.

But when there's no emergency, a residential landlord must obtain the tenant's permission or give reasonable notice before entering and can enter for only the following reasons: to make necessary or agreed repairs, or show the property to a prospective new tenant, prospective buyer, lender or workmen. Twenty-four hours' notice is considered reasonable under state law; some local ordinances may require more notice. Except in emergencies or unusual circumstances, the landlord may only enter during ordinary business hours, unless the tenant agrees. Otherwise, in some instances, in may be necessary for the landlord to get a court order to enter.

These rules don't apply when the landlord believes the tenant has abandoned the property. Abandonment is discussed later in this chapter.

MAINTENANCE, REPAIRS, AND HABITABILITY

Tenant's Duties

Unless otherwise agreed, the tenant has a duty to keep the leased property clean and in good condition, dispose of garbage in a clean and sanitary manner, properly use all fixtures and keep them clean and to use each portion of the premises as they are intended to be used. Of course, if the tenant is just renting part of a building, that duty applies only to the tenant's own apartment or office space, not to the hallways and other common areas.

The tenant must not intentionally or negligently damage any part of the property, or permit guests to damage it. The tenant is expected to repair damage caused by unauthorized alterations, failure to exercise ordinary care or use of the property in a way it wasn't intended to be used. If the tenant doesn't make these repairs, he or she is liable to the landlord for their cost. But a tenant isn't liable for the ordinary wear and tear that results from normal use of the property.

www.nolo.com/lawcenter/ency/article.cfm/objectid/2C3DE8C3-C0B5-4BA5-A5E6CEB42242322B/catID/87E807D0-D2A1-451F-BA5489CEE3A90ECA
™ (Landlord Liability for Tenant Injuries FAQ)

Security Deposits. Unfortunately, it's not uncommon for a tenant to move out without paying all the rent that's due, leaving the property in a mess or even badly damaged. To protect themselves, most landlords require a tenant to pay a security deposit before the tenancy begins.

If the tenant pays the rent and keeps the apartment in good condition, the security deposit is refunded when the lease ends. But the landlord can retain as much of the deposit as is reasonably necessary to cover unpaid rent, damage caused by the tenant or cleaning costs. A security deposit cannot be used for ordinary wear and tear, however.

Example: T rents an apartment from L and pays her a $700 security deposit. When T moves in, the living room carpet isn't new, but it's in fairly good shape. T moves out two years later. Now the carpet looks worn and shabby, so L decides to replace it before renting the apartment again. L is not allowed to use T's security deposit to help purchase a new carpet. The deterioration of the old carpet was ordinary wear and tear.

On the other hand, suppose the carpet was new when T moved into the apartment. When she moves out a year later, there are cigarette burns and coffee stains in several places. L wouldn't usually have replaced the carpet this soon, but forced to because of the burns and stains. In this case, L could legitimately apply T's security deposit to the cost of a new carpet.

California law limits the amount a residential landlord can demand as a security deposit. For unfurnished apartments or houses, the deposit can't be more than the equivalent of two months' rent. (So if the rent is $500 a month, the deposit can't be more than $1,000.) For furnished property, the deposit can't be more than three months' rent. The deposit is usually collected in addition to the first month's rent prior to giving possession.

Commercial landlords may charge nonrefundable deposits, but residential landlords are not allowed to. To get around these rules, some residential landlords began making new arrangements and giving new names to special charges. But the law now treats any advance payment as a security deposit, no matter what it is called (key deposits, pet deposit, water bed).

Case Example: The Parkmerced Company owned a huge apartment complex. All tenants had one-year leases, paid rent by the month, and were required to give Parkmerced a refundable security deposit. But the first month's rent was $65 higher than the rent for the remaining 11 months of the year. For example, if the annual rent was $3,665, the tenant would have to pay $365 the first month and $300 each month thereafter.

On behalf of the tenants, the state of California sued Parkmerced for this practice. The court held that the additional $65 was actually an illegal nonrefundable fee, not part of the rent. Even in Parkmerced's internal accounting records, the $65 was noted separately from the rent payments. The court ordered Parkmerced to refund the $65 charges to all the tenants (even former tenants), and also pay $221,700 in punitive damages. People v. Parkmerced Company, 198 Cal. App. 3d 683, 244 Cal. Rptr. 22 (1988).

In most California rental agreements, no interest is due to the tenant on the security deposit, where exceptions occur, the requirements are specific.

Within three weeks after a residential tenant moves out, the landlord must give the tenant an itemized statement with any refund and explanation why all or part of the deposit has been retained. Any residential landlord who keeps a security deposit in bad faith can be ordered to pay $600 in punitive damages in addition to actual damages. In commercial tenancies, if the landlord's only claim against the deposit is for unpaid rent, the remainder of the deposit (if any) and an itemized statement must be sent to the tenant within three weeks. But if deductions are made for cleaning or damage, then he or she has 30 days to send the remainder and the statement. Any commercial landlord who keeps a security deposit in bad faith can be ordered to pay $200 in punitive damages, in addition to having to pay actual damages.

If a tenant caused severe damage and the repair costs are greater than the security deposit, the landlord may bring a lawsuit against the former tenant to collect the additional amount. The security deposit doesn't limit the tenant's liability—it isn't treated as liquidated damages. A lease may include a liquidated damages provision.

Example: In the earlier example involving a burned and stained carpet, the tenant gave the landlord a $700 damage deposit. Suppose it cost the landlord $1,000 to replace the carpet. The landlord could sue the tenant for $300, the amount the deposit didn't cover. The court would consider whether or not it was reasonably necessary to replace the carpet. If so, the landlord would be entitled to the full amount of damages.

On the other hand, if the tenant could prove that it wasn't necessary to replace the carpet, then the landlord wouldn't collect a judgment. Perhaps the carpet could have been restored for only $400. If so, the restoration costs would have been less than the security deposit. The landlord would be ordered to refund the tenant the extra $300.

SECURITY DEPOSITS

- ◆ Unpaid rent, damage, & cleaning—not ordinary wear & tear
- ◆ Not treated as liquidated damages; landlord may sue
- ◆ Full refund and itemized explanation required (residential: 3 weeks, commercial: 3 weeks)
- ◆ Residential property—no more than **two months'** rent (**three months'** rent if furnished)—no nonrefundable deposits.

Landlord's Duties

In California there is a obligation on the part of the landlord to make the premises fit for occupancy or to maintain the premises.

TENANT'S REMEDY FOR UNTENANTABILITY

When a problem develops that makes the property untenantable, the tenant must notify the landlord. If the landlord doesn't fix the problem within a reasonable time, the tenant has the right to hire someone to do the repairs, and then deduct the cost from the rent. The cost can't be more than one month's rent, and the tenant can use this remedy no more than twice in any twelve month period.

How long does the tenant have to wait for the landlord? Thirty days is presumed to be a reasonable time, but in many cases the tenant would be justified in taking action sooner. An example would be a broken hot water heater.

Instead of having the property repaired and deducting the cost, the tenant has the option of terminating the lease if the landlord doesn't make repairs as required by law (or as agreed in the lease). This is constructive eviction, discussed earlier in the chapter. If the tenant moves out, he or she will not owe the landlord any further rent.

If the dwelling is untenantable and the landlord has not, without good cause, corrected the problem within 60 days, the landlord may not demand or collect rent. A landlord who does so is liable to the tenant for actual damages and special damages of not less than $100 or more than $1,000 plus reasonable attorneys' fees, and the court can order the landlord to correct the problem.

The landlord has further obligations to:

- ◆ provide the tenant with and maintain, one telephone jack;
- ◆ disclose to the tenant the lack of separate utility meters, and reach an agreement regarding payment;
- ◆ allow the tenant to install a water bed, provided certain requirements are met;
- ◆ disclose any deaths (except AIDS) on the premises within the last 3 years;
- ◆ disclose any former state or federal ordnance (military explosives) location with in one mile, if the landlord has knowledge of it.

Residential Property. The California Civil Code requires that property rented as a dwelling must meet a basic standard of **tenantability**. This means that the landlord, to make the dwelling tenantable, must provide effective waterproofing and weather protection; plumbing, heating, and electrical wiring that's up to code: hot and cold running water; adequate garbage receptacles; and safe floors, stairs, and railings. At the beginning of a residential lease, the landlord must have made sure that the tenant's unit (or house) is free from trash, garbage, rodents, and insects. In the case of a residential building with more than one tenant, the landlord is always responsible for keeping the common areas uninfested and reasonably clean. The landlord must meet the standards of tenantability before renting the property and throughout the term of the lease.

The only exception is when the tenant agrees to perform repairs or improvements in exchange for lower rent. The landlord should also provide adequate locks and lighting to help prevent crime. In the Hinson case which follows, an implied **"warranty of habitability"** was created by the court for residential property. This is separate and distinct from the Civil Code requirements of tenantability.

If the landlord breaches the implied warranty of habitability, the tenant doesn't have to pay the full amount of rent charged while the landlord's breach continues. Instead, the tenant is required to pay only the reasonable rental value of the property in its substandard condition.

Case Example: Ms. Hinson rented an apartment in Richmond for $90 a month and moved in with her children. The apartment was in adequate condition at that time, but over the next few months several problems developed. Dry rot caused a large hole in the bathroom floor; the toilet leaked badly; and a glass panel in the front door let in a cold draft that made it difficult to keep the main room warm.

Hinson repeatedly asked the landlord to take care of all these problems, but she got no response. There was so little low-income housing in the area that Hinson couldn't find another place to live. Finally, Hinson told the landlord's manager that she wouldn't pay her rent until the apartment was repaired. When the unpaid rent amounted to $200, the landlord sent an eviction notice, stating that Hinson had to pay up within three days or get out.

Hinson sued to prevent the landlord from evicting her. The court held that she wasn't required to pay the full $90 a month as long as the landlord was breaching the implied warranty of habitability. Until the apartment was made habitable, Hinson was only required to pay the reasonable rental value of the property. *Hinson v. Delis*, 26 Cal. App. 3d 62, 102 Cal. Rptr. 661 (1972).

In the *Hinson* case, the appellate court didn't decide what was the reasonable rental value of the non-repaired apartment. (The appellate court remanded the case back to the trial court to determine the reasonable rental value.) Presumably, the reasonable rental value was very low. Note that Hinson could have avoided any further liability for rent if she'd moved out of the apartment and claimed constructive eviction. But she and her family had nowhere else to go.

In addition to using the implied warranty of habitability as a defense against eviction, a residential tenant can also bring a tort suit against the landlord for failing to maintain the property.

Case Example: Ms. Stoiber's apartment had sewage leaking from the bathroom plumbing, dangerous electrical wiring, structurally unsound walls and floors, a leaking roof, broken windows, cockroaches, and a few other problems. Stoiber notified her landlords about all of these conditions. On one occasion they sent out a plumber to fix the toilet, but that was it. Eventually the Kern County Health Department ordered the property vacated and demolished.

Stoiber sued the landlords for breach of the warranty of habitability, asking them to repay the difference between the rent she'd paid and the fair rental value of the property. She also sued them for damage to her personal property (some of it had been destroyed by water leaking into the apartment), and for discomfort, annoyance, and emotional distress. *Stoiber v. Honeychuck*, 101 Cal. App. 3d 903, 162 Cal. Rptr. 194 (1980).

Landlords must repair uninhabitable items (leaking water, lack of heat and dangerous situations—health code violations) immediately. The landlord is not entitled to a reasonable time to fix a defect which makes the dwelling uninhabitable, since the defect exists whether or not the landlord has repair time. Also, a new owner is liable for breach of the warranty of habitability of a previous owner.

13/16 of an inch deadbolt lock on the front door

A residential landlord is required to install and maintain locks on doors and windows in common areas. The bolt on deadbolt locks on each main (swinging) entry door must protrude 13/16 inches into the doorjamb at a minimum.

Liability for Personal Injuries on Leased Property

When someone—a tenant, a tenant's guest, or a meter reader—is injured on leased property, is the landlord liable? Regarding common areas under the landlord's control, the answer is nearly always "yes."

Example: A steep stairway leads up to the main entrance of the apartment building. The steps are covered with moss, and they become quite slick after a rain. A tenant slips on the top step and breaks his arm. He sues the landlord. The landlord is held liable for negligence because the landlord failed to use ordinary care in maintaining the property's common areas. When it happens inside a unit, the answer isn't as simple.

Landlord/Tenant Law

The rule used to be that the landlord usually wasn't liable in those cases. Once the lease term started, the landlord was no longer in control of the single-family home or the office space; the tenant had control. The landlord was only held liable if he or she knew that there was a hidden hazard on the property before the tenant moved in. Then the landlord had a duty to warn the tenant. But the landlord was virtually never liable for injuries resulting from a problem that developed after the lease began.

For a short period, California courts expanded the landlords' liability well beyond those limits. For example, a landlord who was engaged in the business of leasing dwellings was held strictly liable for injuries resulting from a latent defect on the premises when the tenant rented the premises. In *Peterson v. Superior Court*, 10 Cal. 4th 1185, 43 Cal. Rptr. 2d 836 (Cal. 1995) (explained on next page), the California Supreme Count reconsidered whether a landlord should be held strictly liable for injuries to tenants caused by defects in the premises, and determined that the reasons for imposing strict liability on a retailer or manufacturer of a defective product do not apply to landlords. A landlord still may be held libel for negligence if he breaches the applicable standard of care.

Case Example: A real estate broker owned several single-family rental homes in one neighborhood in Modesto. He rented one of these homes to a family with a large German Shepherd. He specifically granted them permission to keep the dog on the leased property.

The dog was vicious. Although it was usually kept chained, it attacked neighbors on two separate occasions. One day it attacked Juliana, a girl who had come over to play with the tenants' children. Juliana was badly injured.

After this, many of the neighbors signed a petition demanding that the tenants get rid of the dog. But the tenants didn't give up the dog until several months later, after it attacked their own daughter.

Juliana's parents sued the dog owners and their landlord, requesting compensation for Juliana's injuries. The trial judge dismissed the case against the landlord, but the appellate court reversed. The tenants had a month-to-month lease, which the landlord could have terminated at any time. Thus, the landlord retained considerable control over the leased property. If the landlord was aware of the dog's vicious character, he was negligent in failing to make the tenants remove the dog from his property. The landlord, as well as the tenants, could be held liable for Juliana's injuries. However, "a landlord is under no duty to inspect the premises for the purpose of discovering the existence of a tenant's dangerous animal; only when the landlord has actual knowledge of the animal, coupled with a right to have it removed from the premises, does a duty of care arise." *Uccello v. Laudenslayer*, 44 Cal. App. 3d 504, 118 Cal. Rptr. 741 (1975).

However, commercial landlords, not small residential landlords, must conduct reasonable inspections to maintain the safety of any premises open to the public. A landlord is not liable for injuries when a reasonable inspection was conducted but the presence of the dangerous condition was not discovered.

Case Example: While delivering beer to a liquor store, Portillo was severely injured by the store owner's guard dog. Portillo sued the store owner and Aiassa who was the landlord. Aiassa had not inspected the premises prior to the tenant's renewal of the lease, but stated he visited the premises several times a year and the dog did not appear vicious. Store customers testified the dog was always there, was dangerous, and had bitten people. The tenant posted a sign which read "Beware of Dog...WE HAVE A GUARD DOG! DO NOT PET OR TEASE!" A newspaper article was also posted concerning the dog's recent attack on a robber in which the dog was described as "a furry juggernaut, replete with iron trap jaws, razor sharp fangs and a rotten disposition."

The jury found for Portillo and awarded damages of $300,000. The Court of Appeal agreed and held that "a landlord has a duty to exercise reasonable care in the inspection of his commercial property and to remove a dangerous condition. A dog, should be removed from the premises, if he knew, or in the exercise of reasonable care would have known, the dog was dangerous and usually on the premises. The risk of harm to the general public clearly outweighs the presence of a particular tenant on the premises." *Portillo v. Aiassa*, 27 Cal. App. 4th 1128, 32 Cal. Rptr. 2d 755 (1994).

The landlord's liabilities in the *Uccello* case and the Portillo case were based on negligence, a failure to use ordinary care. Most cases in which a landlord is held liable for injuries involve negligence: negligently failing to repair the property, or making repairs in a negligent manner. However, in 1985 the California Supreme Court decided *Becker v. IRM Corp.*, 38 Cal. 3d 454, 213 Cal. Rptr. 213 (1985), which involved a tenant injured in a fall through untempered shower doors. The holding was that a landlord should be treated as a "retailer" of rental housing and thus subject to strict products liability for defects in the premises rented. In August 1995, the California Supreme Court, swayed by the Peterson case, overruled Becker concluding that it was a mistake to apply the doctrine of strict product liability to a residential landlord who is not a part of the manufacturing or marketing enterprise of the product that caused the injury.

Case Example: Nadine Peterson claimed that while she was a guest at the Palm Springs Marquis Hotel she slipped and fell in the bathtub while taking a shower, sustaining serious head injuries. She alleged that the bottom surface of the bathtub was extremely slick and slippery and the bathtub had no safety measures like anti-skid surfaces, grab rails or rubber mats. In addition to a cause of action for negligence, she brought a cause of action for strict liability asserting the bathtub was a defective product, relying on Becker. The Court held that landlords and hotel owners should not be held strictly liable in tort for injuries to tenants and guests caused by defects in the premises. Landlords may still be held liable for injuries resulting from defects on the premises if they were negligent in handling the property. The case was sent back for trial on her negligence claim. *Peterson v. Superior Court (Paribas)*, 10 Cal. 4th 1185, 43 Cal. Rptr. 2d 836 (1995).

CRIMINAL ACTS. In the past, landlords weren't held to have a duty to protect tenants against crimes committed by third parties on the leased property. But in recent years, California courts have found landlords liable for failing to protect tenants against foreseeable crimes. A landlord is especially likely to be held liable if the building was advertised as a security building, or if it's in a neighborhood where criminal activity is likely. In other words, should the landlord have anticipated the criminal act and taken precautions to protect the tenant? If the act could not have been anticipated or prevented, there is no landlord liability.

> **Case Example:** Ms. O'Hara rented an apartment in a San Jose complex owned by Western Seven Trees Corporation. She was told that professional guards patrolled the property at night, and the complex was safe. She wasn't told that several of the tenants had been raped in their apartments and the rapist had not yet been arrested.
>
> Three months after moving in, O'Hara was raped in her apartment by the same man who committed the earlier crimes. She sued her landlords for failing to provide adequate security, and for deceit. The trial judge dismissed the case, but the appellate court ruled that the landlords could be held liable. *O'Hara v. Western Seven Trees Corp.*, 75 Cal. App. 3d 798, 142 Cal. Rptr. 487 (1978).

At least one court has held that the landlord's duty to protect tenants from crime only creates liability for personal injuries, not for a loss of property. That case, *Royal Neckware Company, Inc. v. Century City, Inc*, 252 Cal. Rptr. 810 (1988), involved a burglary at a clothing and jewelry store in a shopping mall. The court said it's up to the tenant to insure personal property against theft.

Termination of a Lease

A lease for a set term (an **estate for years**—see Chapter 3) expires on a specified date. Sometimes when a lease is about to expire, the parties decide to renew it. They may renegotiate the terms of the lease at this point; the rent may be raised or lowered.

Expiration, Renewal, and Notice

But a lease can be renewed even if the landlord and tenant don't expressly arrange for renewal. If the tenant remains in possession after the lease term expires, and the landlord continues to accept rent, it's presumed that they've renewed the lease on the same terms. With this type of implied renewal, if the rent is paid monthly the new lease will be month-to-month.

> **Example:** T rented L's house for a one-year term, paying $575 a month in rent. At the end of the year, the lease expired, but T doesn't move out. He continues to pay L $575 a month. This is an implied renewal, and T and L have the same duties as they had under the original lease. But now instead of an estate for years, T has a month-to-month periodic tenancy.

Nothing seems to have changed (T is paying L $575 each month, just as he always has), but the lease term is now only one month long, not one year. Either T or L can terminate the periodic tenancy by giving notice to the other party.

In California, notice of termination must be in writing. For a month-to-month tenancy (or any periodic tenancy with a rental period longer than one month), you must give notice at least 30 days before the end of the period, unless otherwise agreed. If the rental period is less than a month, the notice period must be at least as long as the rental period, unless otherwise agreed. The parties can agree to a longer or shorter notice period in the lease, but it can't be less than seven days. If neither party gives notice, the tenancy is automatically renewed for another rental period.

 www.nolo.com/lawcenter/ency/article.cfm/objectID/66BB4E6B-8A0E-4230-9E0E7AAE42638269/catID/1F6840E5-5262-46EA-9347E71F16315DE3 ™ **(State Laws on Secuirty Deposit Limits)**

Although a periodic lease can be terminated at any time just by giving notice, a lease for a set term doesn't work that way. In that case, both the landlord and tenant are bound by the lease until the term expires. However, a lease for a set term can end before the expiration date in one of five ways:

◆ surrender,
◆ foreclosure of a senior deed of trust,
◆ destruction of the leased property,
◆ eviction, or
◆ abandonment.

SURRENDER

Sometimes both landlord and tenant would like to terminate their lease before its term expires. When they agree to terminate the lease, it's called surrender. Surrender is often preferred, by the tenant and landlord, when a novation is used to begin a new lease with a new tenant.

FORECLOSURE

The title conveyed to a purchaser at a trustee's sale relates back to the date when the trust deed was recorded. A lease is subordinate to the trust deed if it was executed after the trust deed was recorded. Therefore, the lease is terminated by the foreclosure sale.

DESTRUCTION OF THE PREMISES

If a lease is for a part of a building (such as an office or apartment), the entire purpose of the lease is frustrated if the building is destroyed by fire, flood or an earthquake. The tenant is released from the duty to pay rent.

Of course, the landlord and tenant can (and should) include a provision in the lease concerning destruction of the premises. Most leases specify who will maintain insurance on the property, and who is liable for rebuilding if a structure is destroyed. If there is no express stipulation, and the building is destroyed without fault, it's generally the landlord's loss. Most commercial landlord require the landlord to be named as a co-insured on the hazard insurance policies.

EVICTION

Almost every lease provides that, if the tenant doesn't pay the rent, the landlord may terminate the lease and evict the tenant from the property. But that doesn't mean the lease terminates automatically if the tenant fails to pay.

Notice to Quit

First the landlord must give the tenant a written **notice to remedy or quit**. The notice states the amount due and warns that if it isn't paid within three days, the tenant must move out. If the tenant doesn't move out, the landlord may begin legal proceedings to recover the unpaid rent and evict the tenant.

The landlord also has the right to end the tenancy if the tenant violates other terms of the lease or uses the property in an unauthorized manner. Again, before taking legal action, the landlord must give the tenant a written notice to remedy or quit ("If the boa constrictors are not removed from the apartment within three days..."). Sometimes just a notice to quit is enough as the problem can not be remedied.

A landlord who makes a tenant move out without legal justification can be held liable for **wrongful eviction**. The landlord would be required to compensate the tenant for any damages suffered as a result of the eviction.

Unlawful Detainer

The landlord served a notice to quit, but the tenant still hasn't paid the rent or gotten rid of the snakes. At this point, if the tenant stays in possession of the property, he or she is "unlawfully detaining" it. The landlord's next step is to file an **unlawful detainer action**—a lawsuit to recover possession of leased property from a defaulting tenant. (Unlawful detainer can also be used against a holdover tenant—one who stays on without the landlord's permission after the lease expires or when the landlord gives notice of termination.)

An unlawful detainer action is usually filed in municipal court but in some jurisdictions superior court are required, depending on the amount in controversy (see Chapter 1). Because possession of the property is at issue (not just money), unlawful detainer suits are supposed to be resolved as quickly as possible. They take priority on a court's trial schedule, and the procedures are expedited. For example, the tenant has only five days to respond to the summons and complaint, compared to 30 days for defendants in other civil suits.

At the trial, the tenant might argue that the landlord breached the implied warranty of habitability, or a lease provision, or the property was untenantable. If the tenant proves that charge, he or she will not be evicted or held liable for the full amount of unpaid rent. Usually, possession of the premises is given to the landlord along with a judgment for a lesser amount against the tenant.

If the court finds that the tenant has in fact defaulted and the landlord is entitled to possession of the property, a judgment for possession and rent will issue. After that, a writ of possession will issue. The writ requires the tenant to move out within five days or be forcibly removed by the sheriff.

Chapter 15

Self-Help Eviction

Despite expedited procedures, the process of legal eviction often seems slow from the landlord's point of view. But a landlord should never try to force the tenant off the property by other means. It's illegal for a landlord to remove or exclude a tenant from the leased property without a court order.

Sometimes a landlord tries to force a tenant to leave by cutting off utility services to the property. It's hard to stay in an apartment with no electricity or water, or no heat in the middle of January. And some landlords use a variety of ways to get rid of unwanted tenants: changing the apartment's locks when the tenant isn't home (lockout tenants); removing windows or doors; or remove the tenants' personal property from the dwelling. These practices are illegal. The landlord can be ordered to pay $100 in punitive damages with a minimum of $250 for each day of violation. The landlord can also be required to pay any actual damages the tenant suffers, plus the tenant's reasonable attorney's fees.

Retaliatory Eviction

When a landlord raises the rent sharply, decreases services or terminates a lease because the tenant exercises a legal right, such as making a complaint about the condition of the property, requesting repairs, organizing or participating in a tenant's organization, it's called **retaliatory eviction**. The landlord is retaliating against the tenant for asserting a lawful right. Retaliatory eviction is illegal.

Case Example: For four years, Mr. Schweiger had been a month-to-month tenant in an apartment building owned by Mr. Bonds. The rent for Schweiger's apartment was $75 a month, like most of the other apartments in the building. Schweiger sent Bonds a letter on June 16, asking Bonds to repair some long-standing problems in Schweiger's apartment. There were two broken windows, and the back door wouldn't lock.

On July 1, Bonds notified Schweiger that his rent would be raised to $125 a month as of August 1. Bonds didn't raise the rent for any of the other apartments in the building. Sometime in July Bonds had Schweiger's windows fixed, but not the back door.

On August 1, Schweiger paid Bonds only $60. This represented his ordinary rent payment, less $15, the estimated cost of repairing the back door. (When Schweiger actually carried out the repairs, it cost him $35.) Schweiger refused to pay the higher rent, claiming Bonds had raised it in retaliation against his complaint.

Bonds brought an unlawful detainer action to evict Schweiger. The California Supreme Court ruled that if the rent hike and the lawsuit were retaliatory, Bonds was not entitled to evict Schweiger. *Schweiger v. Superior Court of Alameda County*, 3 Cal. 3d 507, 90 Cal. Rptr. 729 (1970).

An unlawful detainer action is retaliatory when it occurs within 180 days after the tenant complains to the landlord about the condition of the property, files a complaint with a housing authority, sues the landlord for breach of the implied warranty of habitability, or is awarded a judgment against the landlord in such a lawsuit. If the landlord raises the rent or evicts the tenant during that 180-day period, the landlord will have to prove that a valid reason (not retaliation) was the cause for the action. The tenant has the overall burden of proving his landlord's retaliatory motive by a preponderance of the evidence.

If retaliatory action is taken within the 180-day period, the landlord will have to compensate the tenant for any damages suffered, and also pay the tenant's attorney's fees. Punitive damages of not less than $100, nor more than $1,000 for each retaliatory act are included if the court finds that the landlord was also guilty of fraud, oppression, or malice. A tenant can only invoke the retaliatory eviction once a year.

Case Example: For four years, Alice Barela rented an apartment from Leonard Valdez on a month-to-month tenancy at $200 per month. She called the police to complain that Valdez had sexually molested her nine year old daughter. Valdez then served her with a 30-day notice terminating her tenancy. She did not move and was sued for unlawful detainer. Barela alleged an affirmative defense that she was being evicted in retaliation for her exercise of constitutionally protected rights.

The California Supreme Court noted that Civil Code Section 1942.5 provides that it is unlawful for a landlord to sue to recover the property "for the purpose of retaliating against the lessee because he or she has... lawfully and peaceably exercised any rights under the law." Reporting a crime is such a right. Public policy is served by reporting crimes. Barela's defense of retaliatory eviction is valid. *Barela v. Superior Court of Orange County*, 30 Cal. 3d 244, 178 Cal. Rptr. 618 (1981).

ABANDONMENT

Sometimes a tenant moves out (or simply disappears) before the lease expires. When a tenant relinquishes possession of the property, it's called **abandonment**. In this situation the landlord usually wants to retake possession of the property and rent it out again as soon as possible, rather than waiting until the lease term runs out.

When the landlord reasonably believes that the property has been abandoned and the rent is at least 14 days overdue, he or she can terminate the lease and sue the tenant for damages. To terminate the lease, the landlord must send a **notice of belief of abandonment** to the tenant's last known address. The notice states that the lease will be terminated unless the tenant responds before a specified date. The termination date (of the notice period) must be at least 18 days after the notice was mailed to the tenant (or, if the notice was served on the tenant in person, at least 15 days after the date of service).

To prevent termination, the tenant must inform the landlord in writing that he or she does not intend to abandon the property. The tenant must also give the landlord an address where he or she can be served if the landlord files an unlawful detainer action.

Chapter 15

If the tenant doesn't respond by the specified date, the lease is terminated. Then the landlord can rent the property to a new tenant, and sue the former tenant for damages (see below). However, when a tenant abandons the rental unit, they often leave behind personal property. The law is specific on the storage tenant's property. The landlord must give a notice of intent to dispose of it, and the tenant must pay reasonable cost of storage to reclaim the property.

Under some leases, the landlord has another option after abandonment. Instead of terminating the lease and suing for damages, the landlord may choose to let the lease continue. The tenant will still have the right of possession of the property (although he or she is not taking advantage of it), and will still owe the landlord the rent as it becomes due. This remedy is only available to the landlord if the lease expressly provides for it, and if the lease allows the tenant to assign or sublease, subject only to reasonable limitations.

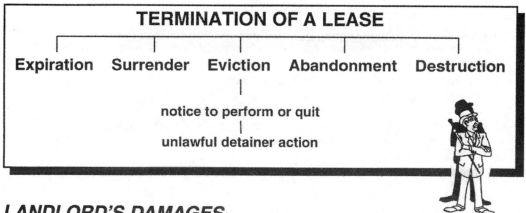

LANDLORD'S DAMAGES

When a lease is terminated after abandonment or by an unlawful detainer action, the landlord is usually entitled to a judgment against the tenant for unpaid rent. In some cases, the award for landlord's damages is only the unpaid rent up to the termination date. But in other cases the tenant will also be charged for rent that would have been owed if the lease had not been terminated.

> **Example:** In January 2019, T signed a two-year lease for L's house, agreeing to pay $1,000 a month. But in June, T lost her job. She couldn't pay the rent due on July 1, and a few days later she moved out and went to stay with her brother.
>
> Near the end of July, L sent T a notice of belief of abandonment stating that the lease would be terminated on August 15. T didn't respond, so the lease terminated on that date.
>
> L cleaned up the house and began advertising it for rent again. However, L didn't find a new tenant until November 1.

If L sues T for damages, she can be required to pay him not just the rent due from July 1 through August 15, but the rent due up until November 1—a total of $4,000, plus interest (and any costs L incurred in trying to find a new tenant). And in some cases there will be additional damages.

Example: Suppose rental rates have fallen, and L can only charge the new tenant $900 a month instead of the $1,000 that T was paying. Then T would owe L the difference for the rest of her original lease term—from November 1, 2019, all the way to December 31, 2020: $100 x 14 months = $1,400.

Depending on when the lawsuit is filed, the landlord may be asking the court to award damages for future losses—losses the landlord has not incurred yet. The court can award damages for future losses only if the lease expressly provides for that, or if the landlord acting reasonably and in good faith to re-rent the property again. An award for future losses will be discounted to represent the present value of the money.

MITIGATION. Keep in mind that the landlord has a duty to mitigate the damages by trying to rent the property to a new tenant as soon as possible. If the former tenant can prove that the landlord could have rented the property again sooner, or for more money, the damages award will be reduced.

Example: Continuing with the previous example, suppose T's friend Joe offered to rent the house from L for $1,000 a month starting on October 1, 2019. Joe has a good credit rating and rental history. But L's niece told him that she wanted to rent the house, so L turned Joe down. L's niece moves in on November 1st and pays only $900 a month.
T would not be required to pay L for the month of October or the $100 difference in the rent. These were damages that L could have avoided by accepting Joe's offer.

TENANT'S PERSONAL PROPERTY

If a tenant leaves personal property behind after vacating the leased property (either by abandonment or at the end of the term), the landlord must either leave it where it is or place it in storage. Within 18 days after moving out, the tenant must request in writing that the landlord surrender the property. The tenant must pay the landlord's reasonable removal and storage expenses. The landlord and tenant mutually agree when the property will be picked up, but not later than 72 hours after payment of the landlord's expenses. A landlord's failure to comply with the tenant's request subjects the landlord to liability for actual damages, not to exceed the value of the personal property, plus up to $250 and reasonable attorney's fees.

If the tenant doesn't contact the landlord about the property, the landlord must send the tenant a **notice of right to reclaim abandoned property**. The notice tells the former tenant where the property can be claimed, and usually sets a deadline for claiming it. The deadline must be at least 15 days after the notice if served on the tenant in person, or at least 18 days after it's mailed. Again, the tenant must pay the landlord's expenses when claiming the property.

If the tenant doesn't claim the property by the deadline, it will be sold at public auction. (But if the value of the property is less than $300, the landlord can keep it for his or her own use, or dispose of it in any way, such as putting it in the trash.) After deducting the costs of storage, advertising, and sale, the proceeds of the public auction are paid into the county treasury. The tenant has one year to claim the sale proceeds from the county.

Mobile Home Residency Law

In a mobile home park, the tenants usually own their mobile homes and rent a space from the park owner. It's much more difficult for a mobile home owner to move than for an ordinary tenant. In many communities, there are few mobile home parks and very few vacancies in those parks. And it can be expensive to move a mobile home, especially a large one. The landlord has the right to require a picture of the unit as part of the application process and to inspect the unit prior to approving the mobile home for the park.

To address these problems, the California legislature adopted the Mobile Home Residency Law (Civil Code Section 798-798.88). It governs the relationship between mobile home owners and park management. The statute applies to manufactured homes, but not to recreational vehicles.

Mobile Home Park Rental Agreements

There are two sections in the law relating to rental agreements. One section sets out the requirements for all agreements. The other describes optional provisions. If these are included in the agreement, it will be exempted from local rent control ordinances.

Requirements

All mobile home park rental agreements must be in writing. They must include:

◆ the length of the lease term, where the park offers one year minimum,
◆ the rent to be charged, and how payable,
◆ a description of the physical improvements to be provided to the homeowner,
◆ a description of the services to be provided and any fees that will be charged for the services with separate billing for those fees, and
◆ the park's rules and regulations with the name, address and phone number of the owner.

The agreement must state that it is the management's responsibility to maintain the common facilities. It also has to explain that the management may charge a fee for maintaining the property on which a home is located if the homeowner fails to do so after being given 14 days' notice. A copy of the Mobile Home Residency Law must be attached and incorporated into the agreement by reference. Management must also post a sign showing the name, address and phone number of the state mobile home ombudsman.

The mobile home owner must be offered at least a one-year lease. A shorter lease term can be arranged only if that's what the homeowner wants. Neither party can have the sole option of automatically extending or reviewing,the lease for a term longer than 12 months.

Of concern for the owners and management of a mobile home park is the risk of paying an amount not to exceed $2,000 to homeowners who are successful in enforcing their legal rights against the park management. The amount is discretionary with the court and is in addition to any other damages awarded.

Rent Control Exemption

A mobile home park rental agreement is exempt from local rent control laws if it meets these criteria:

- the agreement is for longer than one year;
- the agreement is for personal residence by the owner of the mobile home;
- a written notification and receipt that the owner is given at least 30 days from the time the agreement is first offered to decide whether to accept it or reject it; and,
- a written notification and receipt that the owner may rescind the agreement within 72 hours after signing it.

Although the management must offer a lease for one year, the mobile homeowner must have the option of taking a shorter lease. However long or short the lease, the rent and other provisions of the agreement must be the same as those offered for a 12-month lease, at least during the first 12 months of the term. (For example, the management can't charge a higher or lower rent on a six-month lease than it would on a 12-month lease.)

The first sentence of the first paragraph of an exempt rental agreement must be printed in bold type to notify the tenant that the rent control ordinance won't apply.

Any newly constructed spaces in a mobile home park that were initially held out for rent after January 1, 1990, are exempt from rent control, whether or not their rental agreements comply with these rules. Park rules can be amended with homeowner's consent, but they must be reasonable to be enforced.

A security deposit is limited to a maximum of 2 months' rent and the payment of interest is not required. The deposit is refunded after 12 consecutive months of prompt rental payment.

GROUNDS FOR TERMINATION

Because of the high cost of moving mobile homes, the statute severely limits the landlord's right to terminate or refuse to renew a lease. Park management may terminate a lease or refuse to renew it only for one of these reasons:

- the homeowner has failed to comply with park rules and regulations, or with local or state laws regulating mobile homes within a reasonable time after notice;
- the homeowner has engaged in conduct that is a substantial annoyance to other park residents;
- the homeowner (or someone residing in the home) is convicted of prostitution or a drug crime, if the crime was committed in the mobile home park;
- the homeowner hasn't paid rent, utilities, or reasonable service charges after receiving proper notice of nonpayment;
- the park has been condemned; or,
- there is going to be a change in the use of the park.

Management generally must give a mobile home owner 60 days' notice before terminating the tenancy and 90 days before raising the rent. When the management is changing the use of the park and has received governmental approval for the change, it must give the tenants at least six months' notice. If governmental approval isn't necessary, tenants must be given at least one year's notice.

REMOVAL UPON SALE. When a mobile home is sold, the management ordinarily can't require that it be removed from the park. They may require notice of the sale, and the right to approve the buyer as a tenant. But approval can't be withheld unless the buyer isn't financially able to pay the rent, or the buyer's rental history indicates he or she probably won't comply with park rules.

The management can require removal of a home upon sale in order to upgrade the park. Even in that case, they can only require removal if the home is old and doesn't meet construction and safety standards, or if it's dilapidated or in disrepair. When these conditions are met, the management can order the buyer to remove the home even if the seller's lease hasn't expired yet. Management can also sell an abandoned mobile home.

FLOATING HOME RESIDENCY LAW. California has enacted regulations involving the landlord-tenant relationship in a floating home marina. The comprehensive regulations can be found starting with California Civil Code Section 800.

Rent Control

www.cato.org/pubs/pas/pa-274.html
(Analysis - How Rent Control Drivers Out Affordable Housing)

Rent control laws are local ordinances that set maximum limits on the amount of rent a landlord may charge. The intent of these laws is to make rental property available at reasonable rates when there is a housing shortage. Unfortunately, rent control discourages new construction and forces out other lower income people. State law prohibits local governments from imposing rent controls on most commercial property. But some communities in California have adopted residential rent control ordinances.

Some rent control ordinances have exemptions for new construction and other property being offered for rent for the first time. And some ordinances have a **vacancy decontrol** provision: when an apartment becomes vacant, the rent can be raised to the current market rate. In effect, these ordinances only limit rent increases once the tenancy has begun. (When an ordinance doesn't have a vacancy decontrol provision, the rent control limits apply even for new tenants.) Ordinances with vacancy decontrol provisions usually restrict the landlord's right to terminate a tenancy.

State law now prohibits a landlord from evicting a tenant from a rent-controlled unit to make it available to a relative, or for the landlord's own use, unless the relative or the landlord lives there for at least six months. A landlord who fraudulently evicts a tenant or intentionally charges an illegal rent may be ordered to pay treble damages. On the other hand, state law limits the penalties a city may impose on a landlord who has made a good faith effort to comply with the rent control ordinance.

State law also prohibits local governments from compelling property owners to continue offering their property for rent. If an owner doesn't want to rent the property for the amount allowed by the rent control ordinance, he or she may withdraw it from the market. The landlord may have to pay compensatory damages to tenants who are displaced when the property is withdrawn. In some cases, punitive damages (not to exceed six months' rent) may also be charged.

Case Example: Ms. Castillo had been renting a two-bedroom apartment from Mr. Friedman on a month-to-month basis for more than eight years. There had never been any problems between Castillo and Friedman.

The apartment was subject to the Los Angeles Rent Stabilization Ordinance. The ordinance limited the amount of rent Friedman could charge and the grounds on which he could terminate a tenancy. Under the ordinance, Castillo paid $346 per month. The ordinance's vacancy decontrol provision would allow Friedman to raise the rent if Castillo moved out.

In July 1982, Friedman sent Castillo a notice of termination stating that her tenancy would end on August 31st. To comply with the city ordinance, Friedman attached a rent stabilization declaration form to the notice. On the form, he explained that he wanted Castillo's apartment so that his mother could move into it. The ordinance permitted termination of a tenancy if the apartment was going to be occupied by the landlord or the landlord's spouse, children, or parents.

So Castillo and her daughter moved out. Castillo tried to find another two-bedroom apartment in the same neighborhood, but they were being rented for $450 to $500, and Castillo couldn't afford that much. She finally signed a one-year lease on a one-bedroom apartment several miles away. The rent was $350 a month. Because her new apartment was so much smaller, she had to store some of her furniture. The storage cost her $25 a month.

In October Castillo drove by her old building and saw a "For Rent" sign advertising a two-bedroom apartment. Suspicious, she asked her friend Mr. Silva to inquire about the apartment. Friedman showed Silva Castillo's old apartment and told him the rent was $565 a month.

Since Castillo had signed a lease on her new apartment, she wasn't in a position to demand her old apartment back from Friedman. But she sued him for fraud and wrongful eviction. Friedman was ordered to pay Castillo the difference between what it would have cost her to stay in her rent controlled apartment for another two years (at $346 a month) and what a comparable apartment would cost her at current market rates. He also had to pay her storage expenses. *Castillo v. Friedman*, 197 Cal. App. 3d Supp. 6, 243 Cal. Rptr. 206 (1987).

If the withdrawn property is offered for rent again within one year, it may be subject to the controls in effect at the time of withdrawal. If it's put back on the market more than a year after withdrawal, the controls currently in effect may be applied. When property returns to the market any time within ten years after withdrawal, a local ordinance may require the landlord to first offer the units to the displaced tenants.

Unlawful Detainer Assistants

The California legislature has determined that there are numerous unscrupulous individuals and associations who purport to offer protection to tenants from eviction. In fact, these individuals defraud tenants of both their funds and their rights under the law

while filing thousands of frivolous or fraudulent legal pleadings in both state and federal courts. Not only have there been thousands of defrauded tenants, but also severe economic losses to landlords as well as the clogging of both state and federal courts, severally taxing the judicial system. Consequently, the legislature passed a law (Business and Professions Code sections 6400 et. seq.) regulating unlawful detainer assistants. An unlawful detainer assistant is an individual who, for compensation, assists or advises in the prosecution or defense of an unlawful detainer action.

These assistants must register with the county clerk where they reside and where they work. Additionally, the assistant must post a bond of $25,000, or the same amount in cash, with the county clerk. The registration is effective for two years and can be renewed. Once registered, the assistant is given a photo identification card with an assigned number. The registration number and county registration has to appear on any advertisement or work product of the assistant. A written contract containing certain requirements is mandatory along with a 24-hour right of recession. The county clerk retains power to revoke the registration under certain conditions. Additionally, a person who practices as an assistant but has failed to comply with the registration requirements is guilty of a misdemeanor with a fine of not less than a $1,000, no more than $2,000 for each violation or imprisonment for a maximum of one year or both. Exempt from the registration requirements are government employees, attorneys and their employees, employees of non-profit tax exempt corporations who assist clients free of charge, and licensed real estate brokers or salespersons who are parties to the unlawful detainer action or perform certain acts such as the collection of rent.

PROPERTY MANAGEMENT

Many real estate licenses perform **off-site management** services on behalf of the landlord for a fee, on-site, resident managers are not required to hold a real estate license. An **on-site manager** is required for residential buildings containing 16 or more units. The **management contract** (employment contact) must comply with the requirements of a valid contact, and must be in writing if performed by a licensee.

CHAPTER SUMMARY

1. A lease is both a conveyance and a contract, and must meet all the requirements for a valid contract. A lease has to be in writing and signed by the lessor if it will end more than one year after it was made.

2. There are fixed leases, graduated leases, net leases, percentage leases, and ground leases. The differences between them generally concern who pays which expenses and how rent is calculated.

3. Unless the lease expressly forbids assignment and subleasing, the tenant has the right to transfer possession of the property to a third person. Neither assignment nor subleasing relieves the original tenant of liability as does novation. Many leases require the tenant to obtain the landlord's consent before assigning the lease or subleasing.

4. A landlord is required to deliver possession of the property to the tenant on the date the lease begins. If the property isn't ready for possession, the tenant may rescind the lease or demand consequential damages.

5. The implied covenant of quiet enjoyment gives the tenant the right to undisturbed possession of the property. The covenant is breached by actual or constructive eviction. An evicted tenant is no longer required to pay rent. To claim constructive eviction, the tenant must move out.

6. A landlord may not enter the property without the tenant's permission, unless otherwise agreed. Except in an emergency, a residential landlord must obtain the tenant's consent and give reasonable notice (usually 24 hours' notice) before entering.

7. Unless otherwise agreed, the tenant is required to keep the leased property clean and in good repair. But the landlord is responsible for the common areas. The landlord can keep the tenant's security deposit to cover unpaid rent, damage, or cleaning costs, but not for ordinary wear and tear. California law limits the amount a residential landlord can charge as a security deposit, and prevents residential landlords from charging nonrefundable fees.

8. A landlord must make a dwelling fit for human occupancy before leasing it. The landlord must also keep it up to that standard during the lease term. A nonresidential tenant may waive these requirements, however.

9. There's an implied warranty of habitability in every residential lease. The landlord must keep the property habitable. This requirement can't be waived by the tenant. If the landlord breaches the implied warranty, the tenant is only required to pay the reasonable rental value of the non-repaired property.

10. If the landlord fails to make repairs (as agreed or as required by law) within a reasonable time, the tenant may arrange for the repairs and deduct the cost from the rent. If the problems interfere with use of the property, the tenant may move out and claim constructive eviction.

11. A landlord may be held liable for injuries that occur on leased property if the landlord is held to have retained some control over the property. A landlord generally won't be liable unless the injuries resulted from his or her negligence, but the doctrine of strict liability has been applied to large residential landlords.

12. A periodic lease is renewed automatically unless one of the parties gives notice of termination. A lease for a set term expires on the specified date unless the parties agree to renew it. It can be terminated before it expires by surrender, foreclosure, eviction, abandonment, or destruction of the leased property.

13. To evict a tenant, the landlord must send a notice to remedy or quit if that is possible. If the tenant doesn't comply with the notice, the landlord has to file an unlawful detainer action. Self-help eviction is illegal. It's also illegal to evict a tenant in retaliation for making a complaint against the landlord or participating in a tenants' rights group.

14. When a lease is terminated by abandonment or an unlawful detainer action, the landlord may be entitled to a judgment for the unpaid rent and other damages.

15. The Mobile Home Residency Law requires mobile home parks to offer tenants at least one-year leases. It also limits the grounds for termination of leases.

16. Many cities in California have adopted residential rent control ordinances. State law prohibits rent controls on most commercial property. Local governments are also prohibited from compelling a landlord to continue offering a property for rent.

17. Because of problems involving those who offer assistance involving unlawful detainer actions, these activities are regulated in California.

CASE PROBLEM

Evans v. Thomason, 72 Cal. App. 3d 978, 140 Cal. Rptr. 525 (1977)

The Evans family rented an unfurnished one-bedroom apartment in Healdsburg on a month-to-month basis. They plugged their refrigerator and their freezer into a double electrical outlet in the kitchen. In December the lower outlet stopped working. There wasn't another outlet nearby. So the tenants bought a extension cord, plugged it in to the top outlet, and plugged both the refrigerator and freezer into that.

The landlords were renovating the apartment next door at that time. One of the Evanses went over and told the landlords about the problem with the electrical outlet. The landlords said they'd fix it, but they never did. Two of them were experienced electricians, and it would have taken them less than ten minutes to do the repairs. On at least two occasions, one of the landlords was in the Evans's kitchen and saw their extension cord arrangement.

In May, the overloaded extension cord started a fire. Mr. and Mrs. Evans and their children were severely injured and lost most of their possessions. They sued the landlords for damages.

Could the landlords be held liable, when it was the tenants themselves who had created the dangerous extension cord arrangement? Did the landlords have a duty to repair the electrical outlet? If so, was it based on their agreement with the tenants, or imposed by law?

What if the lease had stated that the landlords had no duty to repair any problems that arose after the lease began? What if the lease had provided that the landlords could not be held liable for injuries occurring on the property during the tenancy? Would the answers to these questions be different if this had been a commercial lease?

If this had been a one-year lease instead of a month-to-month lease, would the tenants have had a right to move out and stop paying rent because of the landlords' failure to make the repairs? What could the tenants have done aside from moving out?

Answer: The landlords were liable for the Evans's injuries and loss of property. The court held that if the landlords had fulfilled their duty to repair the outlet, the fire would not have occurred. They were told that repairs were needed, and they knew of the extension cord arrangement. As experienced electricians, they should have realized the extension cord was dangerously overloaded. The fire (and the Evans's injuries) were foreseeable consequences of the arrangement. Under these circumstances, failure to repair the outlet for five months was extremely negligent.

The court's opinion doesn't say what the terms of the lease were. Since it was a residential lease, it probably provided that the landlords would make repairs. Even if the lease didn't discuss responsibility for repairs, the landlords took on that duty when they promised to fix the outlet after the tenants told them about the problem.

But even if the landlords hadn't agreed to fix the problem—even if the lease had expressly stated that they wouldn't repair any problems that arose during the tenancy—the law probably required them to. The court didn't say whether the problem with the electrical outlet amounted to a breach of the implied warranty of habitability. But since the problem (or the makeshift solution to the problem) made the Evans's home unsafe, the court could have held that the apartment wasn't in habitable condition. A tenant can't waive the implied warranty of habitability, so the terms of the lease wouldn't affect this legal duty.

The implied warranty of habitability only applies to residences. If this were a commercial lease, a provision stating that the landlords had no duty to make repairs would be enforceable.

An exculpatory clause (a provision in the lease stating that the landlords weren't liable for any injuries on the property during the tenancy) is always void in a residential lease. But if this were a commercial lease with an exculpatory clause, the landlords probably wouldn't have been liable.

If they'd had a one-year lease, it's hard to say whether the Evanses could have moved out and stopped paying rent on the grounds of constructive eviction. To claim constructive eviction, the tenant must show that the non-repaired problem substantially interfered with use of the property. Before the fire, it would have been difficult to argue that a broken electrical outlet substantially interfered with use of the apartment. Hindsight shows that a broken electrical outlet isn't a trivial problem.

When the landlords failed to repair the outlet within a reasonable time, the Evanses could have hired an electrician to fix it and deducted the cost from their rent. But even though the tenants had the right to take action on their own, that didn't relieve the landlords of liability in this case.

Chapter 15

CHAPTER 15 KEY TERMS	lessor/lessee	security deposit
	lockout	self-help eviction
	mitigation	strict liability
abandonment	Mobile Home Residency	sublease
assignment	Law	surrender
constructive eviction	net lease (triple net)	unlawful detainer
fixed (gross, straight)	notice to remedy or quit	assistants
lease	novation	unlawful detainer
graduated lease (step-up)	percentage lease	untenantable/
ground lease	quiet enjoyment	tenantability
implied warranty of	rent control	writ of possession
habitability	retaliatory eviction	wrongful eviction

Quiz—Chapter 15

1. What lease provides for periodic rental increases based on cost-of-living index?
   a. Periodic lease
   b. Term lease
   c. Graduated lease
   d. Inflation lease

2. L leases her house to T for a two-year term and T moves in. After three months, X makes a very tempting offer to buy the house. Which of the following is true?
   a. L can sell the house, but X will take title subject to the lease
   b. L can't sell without T's consent, since this is a residential lease
   c. L can't sell the property until lease expires, a lease is for a set term
   d. L can't sell the house unless T agrees to surrender the lease

3. T leases an apartment for a one-year term, from November 1 through October 31. In January, T's brother buys a house and asks T to move in. T rents his apartment to X to October 31. This is called:
   a. a novation.
   b. a sublease.
   c. a reconveyance.
   d. an assignment.

4. A new tenant signs a two-year lease. If the previous tenant will not leave apartment, which is true?
   a. New tenant must eviction old tenant
   b. Landlord has duty to get the old tenant out so new tenant can take possession
   c. The new tenant is entitled to damages, she doesn't have right to rescind lease
   d. None of the above

5. L rents out a $750 unfurnished apartment, can she require a security deposit?
   a. Depends if deposit is refundable or not
   b. The law doesn't set a limit on deposit amount, but it must be refundable
   c. $1,500
   d. $375

6. If landlord or tenant wants to terminate a month-to-month lease must give the other party written notice at least:
   a. one week in advance.
   b. 15 days in advance.
   c. 30 days in advance.
   d. two months in advance.

7. Who brings an unlawful detainer action?
   a. Tenant against a landlord when landlord fails to refund security deposit
   b. Landlord against tenant to evict tenant
   c. Tenant against a landlord who wrongfully refuses to renew a lease
   d. Landlord against a tenant who removes fixtures at the end of the lease

8. A tenant moves out before the end of lease term. The landlord sends a notice of belief of abandonment to the tenant's last known address. The landlord has the right to:
   a. keep or sell personal property tenant has left behind without further notice.
   b. assign lease without tenant's consent.
   c. terminate the lease and rent the property to a new tenant.
   d. all of the above.

9. L owns a mobile home park. T has the ugliest mobile home and is rude to L. When T's lease ends, L would rather not renew it. L need not renew the lease if:
   a. T has frequently failed to comply with rules concerning noise after 10:00 PM.
   b. other tenants have complained about the appearance of T's mobile home.
   c. T's mobile home is over 20 years of age.
   d. Any of the above would be legitimate grounds for refusal to renew the lease.

10. California state law prohibits local governments from:
   a. imposing residential rent controls
   b. including a vacancy decontrol provision in a rent control ordinance
   c. requiring damage payments to displaced tenants if rental isn't marketed
   d. compelling owner to market rental

ANSWERS: 1. c; 2. a; 3. d; 4. b; 5. c; 6. c; 7. b; 8. c; 9. a; 10. d

Notes

Notes

The definitions given here explain how the listed terms are used in the real estate field. Some of the terms have additional meanings, which can be found in a standard dictionary.

A

Abandonment—Failure to occupy and use property; may result in a loss of rights.

Abstract of Judgment—A summary of the provisions of a court judgment; when recorded, it creates a lien on all the real property of the debtor in the county where recorded.

Abstract of Title—A brief, chronological summary of the recorded documents affecting the title to a particular parcel of real property. COMPARE: Title Report.

Acceleration Clause—1. A provision in a loan agreement allowing the lender to declare the entire debt due immediately if the borrower defaults. Also known as a call provision. 2. A due-on-sale clause.

Acceptance—1. Agreeing to the terms of an offer to enter into a contract, thereby creating a binding contract. 2. Taking delivery of a deed.

Accession—The acquisition of title to additional property by its annexation to real estate already owned. This can be the result of human actions or natural processes. SEE: Annexation; Accretion; Reliction.

Accord and Satisfaction—An agreement to accept something different than (and usually less than) what the original contract called for.

Accretion—A gradual addition to dry land by the forces of nature, as when the tide deposits waterborne sediment on shoreline property. SEE: Accession: Alluvion.

Accusation—A written statement of rules violated, used in a property right hearing.

Acknowledgment—When a person who has signed a document formally declares to an authorized official (usually a notary public) that he or she signed voluntarily. The official attests that the signature is voluntary and genuine.

Act—A statute.

Actual Notice—SEE: Notice, Actual.

Adjustable-Rate Mortgage (ARM)—A mortgage or deed of trust with a variable interest rate (an interest rate that changes periodically).

Adjudicative Methods—The resolution of a dispute by mirroring the judicial process in that a third party decides the controversy much as a judge does in court.

Administrative Agency—A government agency (federal, state, or local) that administers a complex area of law, adopting and enforcing detailed regulations that have the force of law.

Administrative Law Judge—A law judge that conducts hearings enforcing the detailed regulations that have the force of law, by a government agency (federal, state, local and DRE.) It is a complex area of law.

Administrator—A person appointed by the probate court to manage and distribute the estate of a deceased person when no executor is named in the will or there is no will.

Ad Valorem—A Latin phrase meaning "according to value"; used to refer to taxes assessed on the value of property.

Adverse Possession—Acquiring title to someone else's real property by possession of it. The possession must be actual, open, notorious, hostile, exclusive, continuous, and uninterrupted for ten years. COMPARE: Prescription.

Affiant—One who makes an affidavit.

Affidavit—A sworn statement that has been written down and acknowledged; may be submitted as evidence in a trial.

Affirm—In an appeal, to rule that the lower court's decision was correct, rejecting the appellant's arguments.

After-Acquired Title—SEE:Title, After-Acquired.

Agency—A relationship of trust created when one person (the principal) gives another (the agent) the right to represent the principal in dealings with third parties.

Agency, Apparent—SEE: Agency, Ostensible.

Agency, Dual—When an agent represents both parties in a transaction, as when a broker represents both buyer and seller.

Agency, Exclusive—SEE: Listing, Exclusive Agency.

Agency, Ostensible—1. When someone who has not been authorized to represent another acts as if he or she is that person's agent. 2. When an agent acts beyond the scope of his or her authority, giving a third party the impression that the acts are authorized. Also called apparent agency.

Agency Coupled With an Interest—When the agent has an personal interest in the subject of the agency; as when one co-owner has been authorized by the others to sell their property.

Agent—A person authorized to represent another (the principal) in dealings with third parties.

Agent, Dual—SEE: Agency, Dual.

Agent, General—An agent authorized to handle all of the principal's affairs in one area or in specified areas.

Agent, Special—An agent with limited authority to do a specific thing or conduct a specific transaction .

Agent, Universal—An agent authorized to do everything that can be lawfully delegated to a representative.

Agreement—SEE: Contract.

Air Lot—A parcel of property above the surface of the earth, not containing any land; for example, a condominium unit on the third floor.

Air Rights—The right to undisturbed use and control of the airspace over a parcel of land; may be transferred separately from the land.

Alienation—The transfer of ownership or an interest in property from one person to another, by any means.

Alienation, Involuntary—Transfer of an interest in property against the will of the owner, or without action by the owner, occurring through operation of law, natural processes, or adverse possession.

Alienation, Voluntary—When an owner voluntarily transfers an interest to someone else.

Alienation Clause—SEE: Due-on-sale Clause.

Alternative Dispute Resolution (ADR)—The resolution of disputes by negotiation, mediation, and arbitration.

Alluvion—The solid material deposited along a shore by accretion. Also called alluvium.

Alluvium—SEE: Alluvion.

Amortized—SEE: Note, Installment.

Amount in Controversy—The amount of money at issue in a lawsuit; used as a limitation on the jurisdiction of some courts.

Annexation—Attaching personal property to land so that the law views it as part of the real property (a fixture). Annexation can be actual or constructive.

Annexation, Actual—A physical attachment of personal property to land. SEE: Fixture.

Annexation, Constructive—When personal property is associated with real property in such a way that the law treats it as a fixture, even though it is not physically attached to the real property.

Annual Percentage Rate (ARP)—the charges a borrower pays a lender for a loan (interest, discount points, loan fees, etc.), - expressed as an annual percentage.

Answer—The document a defendant must file with the court in response to the plaintiff's complaint.

Anticipatory Repudiation—When one party to a contract informs the other before the time set for performance that he or she does not intend to perform as agreed. SEE: Tender.

Anti-Deficiency Rules—Laws that prevent a secured lender from suing the borrower for a deficiency judgment after foreclosure, in certain circumstances.

Appeal—The process in which a higher court reviews the decision of a lower court or an administrative tribunal.

Appellant—The party who files an appeal because he or she is dissatisfied with the lower court's decision. Also known as the petitioner.

Appellee—In an appeal, the party who did not file the appeal. Also known as the respondent.

Appraisal—An estimate or opinion of the value of a piece of property as of a certain date. Also called **valuation**.

Appraiser—One who appraises property, especially an expert qualified to do so by education and experience.

Appropriative Right—SEE: Prior Appropriation.

Appurtenance—A right that goes along with ownership of a piece of real property; usually transferred with the property, but may be sold separately.

Appurtenance, Intangible—An appurtenant right that does not involve ownership of physical objects; for example, an easement (as opposed to mineral rights).

Appurtenant Easement—SEE: Easement, Appurtenant.

APR—Annual percentage rate.

Arbitration—A neutral third party who listens to each party's position and makes a final binding decision.

Arbitrator—A neutral third party who receives evidence and resolves the dispute.

ARM—Adjustablerate mortgage.

Artificial Person—A person created by law, as distinguished from a natural person, a human being; usually refers to a corporation.

"As Is" Clause—A provision in a deposit receipt stating that the buyer accepts the property in its present condition.

Assessment—1. A government's valuation of property for tax purposes. 2. A special assessment.

Assessor—An official who determines the value of property for taxation.

Assign—To transfer a right or an interest in property to another.

Assignee—One to whom a right or interest has been assigned.

Assignor—One who assigns a right or interest to another.

Assumption—When a buyer takes on personal responsibility for paying off a mortgage or deed of trust that was originally taken out by the seller.

Assumption Fee—A sum paid to the lender, usually by the buyer, when a mortgage or deed of trust is assumed.

Attachment—Court ordered seizure of property belonging to a defendant in a lawsuit, so that it will be available to satisfy a judgment. In the case of real property, attachment creates a lien.

Attachments, Man-Made—SEE: Fixture.

Attachments, Natural—Things growing on a piece of land, such as trees, shrubs, or crops. SEE: Emblements; Fructus Industriales; Fructus Naturales. COMPARE: Fixture.

Attestation—The act of witnessing the execution of an instrument (such as a deed or will).

Attorney in Fact—Any person authorized to act for another by a power of attorney; not necessarily a lawyer (an attorney at law). Authority, Actual-Authority actually given to an agent by the principal, either expressly or by implication.

Authority, Apparent—SEE: Agency, Apparent.

Authority, Implied—An agent's authority to do everything reasonably necessary to carry out the principal's express orders.

Avulsion—1. When land is suddenly (not gradually) torn away by the action of water, potentially causing a transfer of title. 2. A sudden shift in a watercourse, which doesn't cause a transfer of title.

Award—The decision of the arbitrator.

B

Balloon Payment—A final payment on a loan that is significantly larger than the earlier installment payments. SEE: Note. Installment.

Base Line—In the government survey system, a main east-west line from which township lines are established. Each principal meridian has one base line associated with it.

Base Value—SEE: Value, Base.

Basis—A figure used in calculating gain on the sale of real estate for income tax purposes. Initially, the basis is the amount the owner originally paid for the property, but the figure is adjusted to reflect improvements, cost recovery deductions, and other factors.

BATNA—Best alternative to a negotiated agreement.

Bench Mark—A metal disk set in a stable position at a known elevation, used as a reference point in calculating the elevation of land and other objects in a surveyed area.

Beneficiary—1. One for whom a trust is created and on whose behalf the trustee administers the trust. 2. The lender in a deed of trust transaction. 3. One entitled to receive real or personal property under a will; a legatee or devisee.

Beneficiary Statement—A statement of the amount necessary to pay off a loan.

Bequeath—To transfer personal property to another by a will.

Bequest—Personal property transferred by a will. Also called a legacy.

Bill—A proposed law, formally submitted to a legislature for consideration.

Bill of Sale—A document used to transfer title to personal property from one person to another.

Binding Arbitration—The decision of the arbitrator is final and not reviewable by the courts.

Blanket Trust Deed (Mortgage)—SEE: Deed of Trust, Blanket.

Block—In reference to platted property, a group of lots surrounded by streets or unimproved land.

Blockbusting—The illegal practice of inducing owners to sell their homes (often at a deflated price) by suggesting that the ethnic or racial composition of the neighborhood is changing, with the implication that property values will decline as a result. Also called panic selling.

Bona Fide—In good faith; genuine.

Boot—In an exchange, any property that isn't treated as like-kind for income tax purposes; for example, if a building is traded for vacant land and a yacht, the yacht is boot.

Boundary—The perimeter or border of a parcel of land; the dividing line between one piece of property and another.

Bounds—Boundaries. SEE: Metes and Bounds.

Breach—Violation of an obligation, duty, or law.

Breach, Material—A breach of contract important enough so that it excuses the nonbreaching party from performing his or her contractual obligations.

Breach of Contract—An unexcused failure to perform according to the terms of a contract.

Broker—One who is licensed to represent one or more of the parties in a real estate transaction, for compensation.

Broker, Associate—One who is licensed as a real estate broker but works for another broker.

Brokerage—A broker's business.

Building Code—A set of rules establishing minimum standards for construction methods and materials.

Bump Clause—A provision in a deposit receipt that allows the seller to keep the property on the market until a condition in the contract is fulfilled.

Burden of Proof—SEE: Proof, Burden of.

Business Compulsion—SEE: Duress, Economic.

C

Call Provision—SEE: Acceleration Clause.

Cancellation—Termination of a contract without undoing acts that have already been performed under the contract. COMPARE: Rescission.

Capacity—Legal ability to perform some act, such as enter into a contract or execute a deed or will. SEE: Competence; Minor.

Capital Expenditure—Money expended on improvements and repair or prolong its life; not deductible. COMPARE: Deduction, Repair.

CAR—California Association of Realtors.

Carryback Loan—SEE: Loan, Carryback.

Carryover Clause—SEE: Extender Clause.

Case Law—Rules of law developed in court decisions, as opposed to constitutional law, statutory law, or administrative regulations. Also called decisional law.

Case or Controversy Requirement—A provision in the U.S. Constitution that limits judicial power to deciding actual, active conflict (as opposed to hypothetical questions. Declaratory relief is an exception to this rule.

Caucus—Occurs when the mediator meets with each party individually.

Caveat Emptor—A Latin phrase meaning "let the buyer beware." It expresses the common law rule that a buyer is expected to examine the property carefully, instead of relying on the seller to disclose problems. The rule has lost most of its strength, particularly in residential transactions.

CC&Rs—A declaration of covenants, conditions, and restrictions; usually recorded by a developer to create a common plan of private restrictions for a subdivision.

Certificate of Occupancy—A statement issued by a local government verifying that a newly constructed building is in compliance with all codes and may be occupied.

Certificate of Sale—The document given to the purchaser at a mortgage foreclosure sale, instead of a deed; replaced with a sheriff's deed only after the redemption period expires.

Chain of Title—SEE: Title, Chain of.

Chattel—A piece of personal property.

Chattel Real—Personal property that is closely associated with real property, such as a lease.

Civil Law—The body of law concerned with the rights and liabilities of one individual in relation to another; includes contract, tort, and property law. COMPARE: Criminal Law.

Civil Rights—Fundamental rights guaranteed to all persons by the law. The term is primarily used in reference to constitutional and statutory protections against discrimination based on race, religion, sex, or national origin.

Civil Wrong—SEE: Tort.

Client—One who employs a broker, lawyer, or other professional. A real estate broker's client can be the seller, the buyer, or both, but usually is the seller.

Closing—The final stage in a real estate transaction, when the seller receives the purchase money and the buyer receives the deed.

Closing Costs—Expenses incurred in the transfer of real estate in addition to the purchase price; for example, the appraisal fee, title insurance premiums. broker's commission, transfer tax.

Closing Statement—SEE: Settlement Statement.

Cloud on the Title—A claim, encumbrance, or apparent defect that makes the title to real property unmarketable. SEE: Title, Marketable.

Codicil—An addition to or revision of a will. It must be executed with the same formalities as a will.

Codification—Collection and organization of piecemeal laws into a comprehensive code.

Collateral—Anything of value used as security for a debt or obligation.

Collusion—An agreement between two or more persons to defraud someone.

Color of Title—Title that appears to be good title, but which in fact is not.

Commercial Property—Property zoned and used for business purposes, such as a store, restaurant or office building; as distinguished from residential, industrial, or agricultural property.

Commingling—Illegally mixing personal funds with money held in trust on behalf of a client. SEE: Conversion.

Commission—The compensation paid a broker for services in a real estate transaction; usually a percentage of the sales price, rather than a flat fee.

Common Areas—The land and improvements in a condominium, planned development, or cooperative that are owned and used collectively by all the residents, such as the parking lot, hallways, and recreational facilities; does not include the individual apartment units or homes.

Common Grantor—A person who owned two or more adjacent properties and then sold them to different buyers.

Common Law—1. Early English law. 2. Long-established rules based on English law, followed in many states. 3. Case law.

Common Law Remedy—Money awarded to the plaintiff in a civil lawsuit; damages. COMPARE: Equitable Remedy.

Community Property—Property owned jointly by a married couple in California; any property acquired through the labor or skill of either spouse during marriage. COMPARE: Separate Property.

Competent—1. Of sound mind, for the purposes of entering a contract or executing a will; not suffering from mental illness, retardation, or senility. 2. Of sound mind and having reached the age of majority.

Complaint—The document a plaintiff files with the court to start a lawsuit.

Concurrent Ownership—Any form of ownership in which two or more people share title to a piece of property, holding undivided interests. Also called cotenancy. SEE: Community Property; Tenancy, Joint; Tenancy in Common; Tenancy in Partnership.

Condemnation—1. Taking private property or public use, through the government's power of eminent domain. 2. A declaration that a structure is unfit for occupancy and must be closed or demolished.

Condition—A provision in an agreement or deed that makes the parties' rights and obligations depend on the occurrence (or nonoccurrence) of a particular event. Also called a contingency clause.

Conditional Fee—SEE: Fee, Conditional.

Conditional Use Permit—A permit issued bar a zoning authority that allows property to be used in a manner not ordinarily allowed in the zone where it's located; primarily for uses that benefit the public, such as hospitals, schools, and cemeteries. Also called a special exception permit.

Condominium—Property developed for concurrent ownership, where each co-owner has a separate interest in an individual unit, combined with an undivided interest in the common areas of the property. COMPARE: Cooperative.

Condominium Association—The organization that manages the operation of a condominium, imposing assessments and arranging for the maintenance of the common areas. The association's members are the unit owners, and they usually elect a board of directors.

Condominium Declaration—The document that must be filed for record when property is developed as or converted to a condominium.

Consideration—Anything of value given to induce another to enter into a contract, such as money, services, goods, or a promise. Sometimes called valuable consideration.

Consideration, Adequate—Consideration that is comparable in value to the consideration the other party to the contract is giving. A contract is enforceable even if the consideration is inadequate, but a court can't order specific performance in that case.

Constitution—A fundamental document that establishes a government's structure and sets limits on its power.

Constitutional—1. Pertaining to or based on a constitution. 2. Not in violation of the U.S. Constitution or a state constitution.

Constructive Eviction—SEE: Eviction, Constructive.

Constructive Notice—SEE: Notice, Constructive.

Consummate—To complete.

Contingency Clause—SEE: Condition.

Contract—An agreement between two or more persons to do or not do a certain thing. The requirements for an enforceable contract are capacity, mutual consent, a lawful purpose, and consideration. In addition, many contract must be in writing to be enforceable.

Contract, Bilateral—A contract in which each party promises to do something. COMPARE: Contract, Unilateral.

Contract, Executed—A contract in which both parties have completely performed their contractual obligations.

Contract, Executory—A contract in which one or both parties have not yet completed performance of their obligations.

Contract, Express—A contract that has been put into words, either spoken or written.

Contract, Implied—An agreement that has not been put into words, but is implied by the actions of the parties.

Contract, Installment Land—SEE: Contract, Land.

Contract, Land—A contract for the sale of property in which the buyer pays in installments, taking possession of the property immediately, but not taking title until the purchase price has been paid in full. Also called an installment land contract, installment sales contract, land sales contract, real estate contract, and other names.

Contract, Oral—A spoken agreement, as opposed to a written one.

Contract, Unenforceable—An agreement that a court would refuse to enforce; for example, it may be unenforceable because its contents can't be proven, or because it isn't in writing, or because the statute of limitations has run out.

Contract, Unilateral—When one party promises to do something if the other party performs a certain an, but the other party does not promise to perform it; the contract is formed only if the other party does perform the requested act. COMPARE: Contract, Bilateral.

Contract, Valid—A binding, legally enforceable contract.

Contract, Void—An agreement that isn't an enforceable contract because it lacks a required element or is defensive in some other respect.

Contract, Voidable—A contract that one of the parties can disaffirm without liability, because of lack of capacity or a negative factor such as fraud or duress.

Conversion—1. Misappropriating property or funds belonging to another. 2. Changing an existing rental apartment building into a condominium.

Conveyance—The transfer of title to real property from one person to another by means of a written document, such as a deed.

Cooperative—A building owned by a corporation, where the residents are shareholders in the corporation; each shareholder receives a proprietary lease on an individual unit and the right to use the common areas. COMPARE: Condominium.

Corporation—An association organized according to strict regulations, in which

individuals purchase ownership shares; regarded by the law as an artificial person, separate from the individual shareholders. COMPARE: Partnership.

Corporation, Domestic—A corporation doing business in the state where it was created (incorporated).

Corporation, Foreign—A corporation doing business in one state, but created (incorporated) in another state.

Correction Lines—Adjustment lines used in the government survey system to compensate for the curvature of the earth. They occur at 24-mile intervals (every fourth township line), where the distance between range lines is corrected to 6 miles.

Cotenancy—SEE: Concurrent Ownership.

Co-Tenant—Anyone who shares ownership of a piece of property with another; may be a joint tenant, a tenant in common, a tenant in partnership, or a spouse owning community property.

Counter Offer—A response to an offer to enter into a contract, changing some of the terms of the original offer. A counter offer is a rejection of the offer (not a form of acceptance), and does not create a binding contract unless accepted by the original offeror.

Course—A direction, stated in terms of a compass bearing, in a metes and bounds description of property.

Court-Annexed—A court mandated arbitration.

Covenant—1. A contract. 2. A promise. 3. A guarantee (express or implied) in a document such as a deed or lease. 4. A restrictive covenant.

Covenant, Restrictive—SEE: Restrictive Covenant.

Covenant of Quiet Enjoyment—A promise that a buyer or tenant's possession will not be disturbed by the previous owner, the lessor, or anyone else claiming an interest in the property.

Covenants, Conditions, and Restrictions—SEE: CC&Rs.

Credit—A payment receivable (owed to you), as opposed to a debit, which is a payment due (owed by you).

Credit Bid—When a lienholder purchasing the security property at a foreclosure sale is allowed to apply the amount the borrower owes him or her to the purchase, rather than having to pay the full amount of the bid in cash.

Creditor—One who is owed a debt.

Creditor, Secured—A creditor with a lien on specific property, which enables him or her to foreclose and collect the debt from the sale proceeds if it isn't otherwise paid.

Glossary

Criminal Law—The body of law concerned with crimes, an individual's actions against society. COMPARE: Civil Law.
Cure—To remedy a default, by paying money that's overdue or fulfilling other obligations.
Customer—A prospective property buyer.

D

Damages—An amount of money a defendant is ordered to pay to a plaintiff.
Damages, Actual—Compensatory damages.
Damages, Compensatory—Damages intended to compensate the plaintiff for harm caused by the defendant's an or failure to an, including personal injuries (physical and mental), property damage, and financial losses.
Damages, Consequential—Damages compensating for losses that were not the direct result of the defendant's wrongful act, but which were a foreseeable consequence of it.
Damages, Exemplary—Punitive damages.
Damages, Liquidated—A sum that the parties to a contract agree in advance (at the time of entering into the contract) will serve as compensation in the event of a breach.
Damages, Punitive—An award added to compensatory damages, to punish the defendant for malicious or outrageous conduct and discourage others from similar acts.
Datum—An artificial horizontal plane of elevation, established in reference to sea level, used by surveyors as a reference point in determining elevation.
Dealer—One who regularly buys and sells real estate in the ordinary course of business.
Dealer Property—Property held for sale to customers rather than as a long-term investment; a developer's inventory of subdivision lots, for example.
Debit—A charge or a debt owed to another.
Debtor—One who owes money to another.
Decedent—A person who has died.
Decisional Law—SEE: Case Law.
Declaration of Abandonment—A document recorded by an owner that voluntarily releases a property from homestead protection.
Declaration of Homestead—The recorded document that establishes homestead protection.
Declaration of Restrictions—SEE: CC&Rs.
Declaratory Relief—When a court issues a binding judgment that explains the plaintiff's and defendant's rights and duties in advance, rather than waiting until a breach of contract or other violation has occurred.

SEE: Case or Controversy Requirement.
Dedication—An appropriation or gift of private property for public use; may transfer ownership or simply create a public easement.
Dedication, Implied—Involuntary dedication, resulting from an owner's acquiescence to public use of his or her property for at least five years. Also called common law dedication. COMPARE: Prescription.
Dedication, Statutory—A dedication required by law; for example, dedication of property for streets and sidewalks as a prerequisite to subdivision approval .
Deduction—An amount a taxpayer is allowed to subtract from his or her income before calculating the tax on the income.
Deduction, Cost Recovery—An income tax deduction that allows the taxpayer to recover the cost of depreciable property used for the production of income or used in a trade or business. Formerly called a depreciation deduction.
Deduction, Depreciation—SEE: Deduction, Cost Recovery.
Deduction, Repair—An income tax deduction allowed for expenditure made to keep property in ordinary, efficient operating condition; not allowed for a principal residence or personal use property. COMPARE: Capital Expenditure.
Deed—An instrument that conveys ownership of real property from the grantor to the grantee.
Deed, Correction—A deed used to correct minor mistakes in an earlier deed, such as misspelled names or errors in the legal description.
Deed, General Warranty—A deed in which the grantor warrants the title against defects that might have arisen before or during his or her period of ownership. COMPARE: Deed, Special Warranty.
Deed, Gift—A deed that isn't supported by valuable consideration; often lists "love and affection" as the consideration.
Deed, Grant—Any deed that uses the word "grant" in its words of conveyance; carries two implied warranties and conveys after-acquired title. The most commonly used deed in California. COMPARE: Deed, Quitclaim.
Deed, Quitclaim—A deed that conveys any interest in a piece of real property the grantor has at the time the deed is executed. Often used to clear up a cloud on the title. It contains no-warranties of any kind, and does not convey after-acquired title. COMPARE Deed. Grant.

Deed, Sheriff's—A deed delivered by the sheriff, on court order, to the holder of the certificate of sale when the redemption period after a mortgage foreclosure has expired.

Deed, Special Warranty—A deed in which the grantor warrants title only against defects arising during the time he or she owned the property, and not against defects arising before that time; often used by executors and administrators of estates. COMPARE: Deed, General Warranty.

Deed, Tax—A deed given to a purchaser of property at a tax foreclosure sale.

Deed, Trustee's—A deed given to a purchaser of property at a trustee's sale.

Deed, Warranty—A deed carrying warranties (guarantees) of clear title and the grantor's right to convey. SEE: Deed, General Warranty; Deed, Special Warranty.

Deed, Wild—A deed that won't be discovered using the grantor-grantee indexes, because of a break in the chain of title. A deed of trust or other document can also be wild.

Deed in Lieu of Foreclosure—A deed given by a borrower to the lender to satisfy the debt and avoid foreclosure.

Deed of Trust—An instrument that creates a voluntary lien on real property to secure the repayment of a debt. The parties to a deed of trust are the grantor or trustor (borrower), beneficiary (lender), and trustee (neutral third party). Unlike a mortgage, a deed of trust includes a power of sale, allowing the trustee to foreclose nonjudicially. Also called a trust deed.

Deed of Trust, Blanket—1. A trust deed that covers more than one parcel of real estate. 2. A trust deed that covers an entire building or development, rather than an individual unit or lot.

Deed of Trust, Fictitious—A blank trust deed form filed for record to save recording costs on real deeds of trust. Only the first page and signature page of a real trust deed executed on that form have to be recorded; the other pages are incorporated by reference to the fictitious trust deed.

Deed of Trust, First—The deed of trust that has higher priority than any other on a property. This is usually the one that was recorded first, unless there's a subordination agreement.

Deed of Trust, Junior—A second (or third, etc.) deed of trust, with lower lien priority than the first trust deed.

Deed of Trust, Senior—A deed of trust with higher priority than another deed of trust on a property.

Deed Restriction—A restrictive covenant in a deed.

Default—Failure to fulfill an obligation, duty,

or promise, as when a borrower fails to make payments, or a tenant fails to pay rent.

Defeasible Fee—SEE: Fee Simple Defeasible.

Defendant—1. The person being sued in a civil lawsuit. 2. The accused person in a criminal lawsuit.

Deferment—A right to delay fulfillment of an obligation (such as paying a tax) until a later date.

Deficiency Judgment—A personal judgment entered against a debtor if the proceeds from a foreclosure sale of security property are not enough to pay off the debt.

Delivery—The legal transfer of a deed (or other instrument). A valid deed doesn't convey title until it has been delivered (annually or constructively) to the grantee. SEE: Donative Intent.

Deposit—1. Money offered as an indication of good faith regarding the future performance of a contract to purchase. Also called earnest money. 2. A security deposit.

Deposition—The formal, out-of-court testimony of a witness in a lawsuit, taken before the trial; used as part of the discovery process, to determine the fans of the case, or if the witness won't be able to attend the trial. A transcript of a deposition can be introduced as evidence in the trial.

Deposit Receipt—The document used for a prospective real estate buyer's offer to a seller, which also serves as the buyer's receipt for the deposit. If the seller accepts the. buyer's offer, the deposit receipt becomes their contract; also called an earnest money agreement or purchase and sale agreement.

Depreciable Property—Property that's eligible for depreciation (cost recovery) deduction, because it will wear out and have to be replaced. SEE: Deduction, Cost Recovery.

Depreciate—To decline in value.

Dereliction—SEE: Reliction.

Detrimental Reliance—SEE: Estoppel, Promissory.

Devise—1. (noun) Real property transferred in a will. 2. (verb) To transfer real property by will. COMPARE: Bequest; Bequeath; Legacy.

Devisee—A recipient of real property under a will. COMPARE: Beneficiary; Legatee.

Disaffirm—To ask a court to terminate a voidable contract.

Discount Point—One percent of the principal amount of a loan, paid to the lender at the time the loan is made, to give the lender an additional yield above the interest rate. Because of the points paid at the outset, the lender is willing to make the loan at a lower interest rate.

Discovery, Pretrial—When each of the opposing parties in a lawsuit is required to disclose requested information and evidence to the other party, and each is allowed to examine witnesses who will testify for the other side at trial. Depositions and interrogatories are used during discovery.

Discrimination—Arbitrarily treating people unequally because of their race, religion, sex, national origin, age, or some other characteristic.

Distributive Negotiation—Goals of the parties are interdependent but not compatible, win-lose.

Diversity Jurisdiction—SEE: Jurisdiction, Diversity.

Domicile—The state where a person has his or her permanent home.

Dominant Tenement—SEE: Tenement, Dominant.

Donative Intent—An intent to transfer title immediately and unconditionally.

DRE—California Department of Real Estate.

Dual Agent—SEE: Agency, Dual.

Due-on-Encumbrance Clause—A clause in a loan agreement giving the lender the right to declare the entire amount of the loan due immediately if the borrower places any other liens on the security property.

Due-on-Sale Clause—A clause in a loan agreement giving the lender the right to declare the entire amount of the loan due immediately if the security property is sold. Also called an **alienation clause**.

Due Process—A fair hearing before an impartial judge. Under the U.S. Constitution, no one may be deprived of life, liberty, or property without due process of law.

Duress—Unlawfully confining someone to force him or her to sign a document; or confining the signer's spouse, child, or other close relative. COMPARE: Menace.

Duress, Economic—Threatening to take some action that will be financially harmful to a person, to force him or her to sign a document; for example, threatening to breach a contract. Also called business compulsion.

E

Earnest Money—SEE: Deposit.

Earnest Money Agreement—SEE: Deposit Receipt.

Easement—A right to use some part of another person's real property for a particular purpose; unlike a license, an easement is irrevocable and creates an interest in the property.

Easement, Appurtenant—An easement that benefits a particular piece of property, the dominant tenement. COMPARE: Easement in Gross.

Easement, Implied—SEE: Easement by Implication.

Easement, Negative—An easement that prevents the servient tenant from using his or her own land in a certain way (instead of allowing the dominant tenant to use it). Essentially the same thing as a restrictive covenant.

Easement, Positive—An easement that allows the dominant tenant to use the servient tenement in a particular way.

Easement, Prescriptive—An easement acquired by prescription.

Easement by Express Grant—An easement granted to another in a deed or other document.

Easement by Express Reservation—An easement created in a deed when a landowner is dividing the property, transferring the servient tenement but retaining the dominant tenement.

Easement by Implication—An easement created by law (not by express grant) when a parcel of land is divided, if there is a long-standing, apparent use that is reasonably necessary for the enjoyment of the dominant tenement. Also called an implied easement. COMPARE: Easement by Necessity.

Easement by Necessity—A special type of implied easement; when the dominant tenement would be completely useless without an easement, an easement exists even if it isn't a long-standing, apparent use.

Easement in Gross—An easement that benefits a person instead of a piece of land; there's a dominant tenant, but no dominant tenement. COMPARE: Easement, Appurtenant.

Emblements, Doctrine of—The rule that an agricultural tenant has the right to enter the land to harvest crops after the lease ends.

Eminent Domain—The government's constitutional power to take (condemn) private property for public use, as long as the owner is paid just compensation.

Employee—Someone who works under the direction and control of another. COMPARE: Independent Contractor.

Encroachment—A physical intrusion onto neighboring property, usually due to a mistake regarding the boundary.

Encumbrance—A nonpossessory interest in property; a lien, easement, or restrictive covenant burdening the property owner's title.

Endorsement—When the payee on a negotiable instrument (such as a check or promissory note) assigns the right to payment to another, by signing the back of the instrument.

Enjoin—To prohibit an act, or command performance of an act, by court order; to issue an injunction.

EQA—The California Environmental Quality Act.

Equal Protection Requirement—Under the U.S. Constitution, all citizens are entitled to equal protection of the laws; no law may arbitrarily discriminate between different groups, or be applied to different groups in a discriminatory manner.

Equitable Remedy—A judgment granted to a plaintiff that is something other than an award of money (damages); an injunction, quiet title, rescission, and specific performance are examples. COMPARE: Common Law Remedy.

Equitable Title—SEE: Title, Equitable.

Equity—1. An owner's unencumbered interest in his or her property; the difference between the value of the property and the liens against it. 2. A judge's power to soften or set aside strict legal rules, to bring about a fair and just result in a particular case.

Erosion—A gradual loss of soil due to the action of water or wind.

Error, Harmless—A mistake by a trial judge that did not affect the final judgment in the case.

Error, Prejudicial—A mistake by a trial judge that may have affected the final judgment in the case. Also called reversible error (because it's grounds for reversing the trial court's decision).

Escheat—When property reverts to the state after a person dies and the heirs (or the beneficiaries of the will) cannot be located.

Escrow—The system in which things of value (such as money or documents) are held on behalf of the parties to a transition by a disinterested third party (an escrow agent), until specified conditions have been complied with.

Escrow Instructions—The document that authorizes an escrow agent to deliver items deposited in escrow once the parties have complied with specified conditions.

Estate—1. A possessory interest in real property; either a freehold or a leasehold. 2. The property left by someone who has died.

Estate for Life—SEE: Life Estate.

Estate for Years—A leasehold estate set to last for a definite period (one week, three years, etc.), after which it terminates automatically. Also called a term tenancy.

Estate in Fee Simple—SEE: Fee Simple.

Estate in Remainder—SEE: Remainder.

Estate in Reversion—SEE: Reversion.

Estate of Inheritance—An estate that can be willed or descend to heirs, such as a fee simple estate.

Estoppel—A legal doctrine that prevents a person from asserting rights or fans that are inconsistent with his or her earlier actions or statements.

Estoppel, Promissory—A doctrine applied when someone has made a technically unenforceable promise to another, and the other person has acted in reasonable reliance on the promise. If the person who relied on the promise will suffer harm unless it is enforced, a court may enforce it. Also called the doctrine of detrimental reliance.

Ethics—A system of accepted principles or standards of moral conduct.

Eviction—Dispossessing or expelling someone from real property. SEE: Unlawful Detainer.

Eviction, Actual—Physically forcing someone off of property (or preventing them from reentering), or using the legal process to make someone leave. COMPARE: Eviction, Constructive.

Eviction, Constructive—When a landlord's an (or failure to an) interferes with the tenant's quiet enjoyment of the property, or makes the property unfit for its intended use, to such an extent that the tenant is forced to move out.

Eviction, Retaliatory—When a landlord evicts a tenant in retaliation for requesting repairs, filing a complaint against the landlord, or organizing or participating in a tenants' rights group.

Eviction, Self-Help—When a landlord uses physical force, a lockout, or a utility shutoff to get rid of a tenant, instead of using the legal process.

Eviction, Wrongful—When a landlord evicts a tenant in violation of the tenant's rights.

Evidence—Testimony, documents, and objects used in a lawsuit as proof of a fan.

Exclusive Agency—SEE: Listing, Exclusive Agency.

Exclusive Right to Sell—SEE: Listing, Exclusive Right to Sell.

Execute—1. To sign. 2. To perform or complete. SEE: Contract, Executed.

Execution—The legal process in which a court orders an official (such as a sheriff) to seize and sell the property of a judgment debtor to satisfy a judgment lien.

Executive—The head of a government, such as president, governor, or mayor.

Executor/Executrix—A person named in a will to carry out its provisions. If it's a man, he's an executor; if it's a woman, she's an executrix. COMPARE: Administrator.

Exemption—A provision holding that a law or rule doesn't apply to a particular person or group. For example, a person entitled to a property tax exemption is not required to pay property taxes. An exemption can be full or partial.

Exhibit—1. Documentary or physical evidence submitted in a trial. 2. An attachment to a document.

Express—Stated in words, spoken or written. COMPARE: Implied.

Extender Clause—A clause in a listing agreement providing that for a specified period after the listing expires, the broker will still be entitled to a commission if the property is sold to someone the broker dealt with during the listing term. Also called a carryover clause or safety clause.

F

Failure of Purpose—When the intended purpose of an agreement or arrangement can no longer be achieved; in most cases, this releases the parties from their obligations.

Fair Market Value—SEE: Value, Fair Market. Fannie Mae-The FNMA.

FAR—Floor area ratio.

Federal Question—A legal issue involving the U.S. Constitution, a treaty, or a federal statute. Federal courts have jurisdiction to hear federal question cases, but they may also be decided in state court.

Fee—An estate of inheritance; title to real property that can be willed or descend to heirs.

Fee, Conditional—Title that may be terminated by a former owner if conditions stated in the deed are not met. The only type of defeasible fee that's recognized in California now. Also called fee simple subject to a condition subsequent. SEE: Power of Termination.

Fee Simple Absolute—The greatest estate one can have in real property; freely transferable and inheritable, and of indefinite duration, with no conditions on the title. Often called fee simple or fee title.

Fee Simple Defeasible—A fee estate in real property that may be defeated or undone if certain events occur or certain conditions are not met. SEE: Fee, Conditional; Fee Simple Determinable.

Fee Simple Determinable—A defeasible fee that is terminated automatically if certain conditions occur. No longer recognized in California; now treated as a conditional fee.

Fee Simple Subject to a Condition Subsequent—SEE: Fee, Conditional.

FHA—Federal Housing Administration.

FHLMC—Federal Home Loan Mortgage Corporation; also known as "Freddie Mac." SEE: Secondary Marketing.

Fiduciary Relationship—A relationship of trust and confidence, where one party owes the other (or both parties owe each other) loyalty and a higher standard of good faith than they owe to third parties. For example, an agent is a fiduciary in relation to the principal; husband and wife are fiduciaries in relation to each other.

Finance Charge—Any charge a borrower is assessed, directly or indirectly, in connection with the loan.

Financing Statement—A brief document that, when recorded, gives constructive notice of a creditor's security interest in an item of personal property.

Finder's Fee—A referral fee paid to someone for directing a buyer or seller to a real estate agent.

First Lien Position—The spot held by the deed of trust with highest lien priority, when there's more than one deed of trust on the property. SEE: Deed of Trust, First.

Fixed Term—A period of time with a definite ending date.

Fixture—An item of personal property that has been attached to or closely associated with real property in such a way that it has legally become part of the real property. SEE: Annexation, Actual; Annexation, Constructive.

Floor Area Ratio Method—A flexible method of limiting the size of a building in relation to the size of a lot; used in some zoning ordinances as an alternative to strict size and coverage limits.

FNMA—Federal National Mortgage Association; also known as "Fannie Mae." SEE: Secondary Marketing.

Foreclosure—When a lienholder causes property to be sold, so that the unpaid lien can be satisfied from the sale proceeds.

Foreclosure, Judicial—A lawsuit filed by a mortgagee or deed of trust beneficiary to foreclose on the security property when the borrower has defaulted.

Foreclosure, Nonjudicial—Foreclosure by a trustee under the power of sale clause in a deed of trust.

Forfeiture—Loss of a right or something else of value as a result of failure to perform an obligation or condition.

Four Unities—SEE: Unities, Four.

Fraud—An intentional or negligent misrepresentation or concealment of a material fact.

Fraud, Actionable—Fraud that meets certain criteria, so that the victim can successfully sue. The victim/plaintiff usually must prove that the defendant concealed a material fan or made a false statement (intentionally or negligently) with the intent to induce the victim to enter a transaction, and that the victim was harmed because he or she relied on the misrepresentation.

Fraud, Actual—Intentional misrepresentation or concealment, or negligent misrepresentation, which is making a false statement without reasonable grounds for believing it is true.

Fraud, Constructive—A breach of duty that misleads the person the duty was owed to, without an intention to deceive.

Freddie Mac—The FHLMC.

Freehold—An ownership estate in real property; either a fee simple or a life estate. The holder of a freehold estate has title, whereas the holder of a less-than-freehold estate (leasehold estate) is merely a tenant, having a temporary right to possession, but no title.

Frontage—The distance a piece of property extends along a street or a body of water. Fructus Industriales-Plants planted and cultivated by people, such as crops ("fruits of industry").

Fructus Naturales—Naturally occurring plants ("fruits of nature").

Full Cash Value—SEE: Value, Full Cash.

Future Interest—SEE: Interest, Future.

G

Gain—The portion of the proceeds from the sale of an asset that the IRS recognizes as taxable profit.

Gain, Capital—A gain realized on the sale of a capital asset. Real estate is considered a capital asset if it is income property, investment property, or property used in a trade or business.

Garnishment—A legal process by which a creditor gains access to the funds or personal property of a debtor that are in the hands of a third party. For example, if the debtor's wages are garnished, the employer is required to turn over part of each paycheck to the creditor.

General Lien—SEE: Lien, General.

General Plan—A long-term, comprehensive plan for the development of a city or county, used as a guide in preparing zoning ordinances.

Ginnie Mae—The GNMA.

GNMA—Government National Mortgage Association. SEE: Secondary Marketing. Good Faith Improver-Someone who makes an improvement on land in the mistaken belief that he or she owns the land. Also called an innocent improver.

Government Lot—A parcel of land that can't be divided into a regular section in the government survey, because of the convergence of range lines, or because of a body of water or some other obstacle or irregularity.

Government Survey—A system of land description that divides the land into squares called townships (each approximately six miles square, containing 36 square miles), which are divided into 36 sections (each approximately one mile square and containing approximately 640 acres). Also called the rectangular survey or the section, township, and range system.

Grant—To transfer or convey an interest in real property by means of a written instrument.

Grantee—One who receives a grant of real property.

Granting Clause—Words in a deed that indicate the grantor's intent to transfer an interest in property.

Grantor—One who grants an interest in real property to another.

Grantor/Grantee Indexes—Indexes of recorded documents, with each document listed in alphabetical order according to the last name of the grantor (in the grantor/grantee index) and grantee (in the grantee/grantor index). The recording number of each document is given, so that they can be located in the public record. COMPARE: Tract Index.

Guardian—A person appointed by a court to administer the affairs of a minor or an incompetent person .

Guide Meridians—SEE: Meridians, Guide.

H-I

Habendum Clause—A clause included after the granting clause in many deeds; it begins "to have and to hold," and describes the type of estate the grantee will hold.

Heir—Someone entitled to inherit another's property under the laws of intestate succession.

Holder in Due Course—A person who obtains a negotiable instrument for value, in good faith, without notice that it is overdue or notice of any defenses against it.

Holdover Tenant—A tenant who fails to surrender possession of the premises at the end of a tenancy.

Homeowner's Association—A nonprofit association made up of homeowners in a subdivision, responsible for enforcing the subdivision's CC&Rs and managing other community affairs.

Homestead Protection—Limited protection against the claims of judgment creditors, for property used as the debtor's residence. SEE: Declaration of Homestead; Declaration of Abandonment.

HUD—The Department of Housing and Urban Development.

Hypothecate—To make property security for a loan without giving up possession of it. COMPARE: Pledge.

Implied—Not expressed in words, but understood from actions or circumstances. COMPARE: Express.

Implied by Law—Required by law to be part of an agreement; read into an agreement even if it contradicts the express terms the parties agreed to.

Implied Warranty—SEE: Warranty, Implied.

Implied Warranty of Habitability—A warranty implied by law in every residential lease, that the property is safe and fit for habitation.

Impound Account—A bank account maintained by a lender for paying property taxes and insurance premiums on the security property; the lender requires the borrower to make regular deposits, and pays the expenses out of the account. Also called a reserve account.

Improvements—Man-made additions to real property.

Income Property—Property that generates rent (or other income) for the owner, such as an apartment building.

Incompetent—Not legally competent; not of sound mind; mentally ill, senile, or feebleminded.

Independent Contractor—A person who contracts to do a job for another but maintains control over how he or she will carry out the task, rather than following detailed instructions. COMPARE: Employee.

Ingress and Egress—Entering and exiting; usually refers to a road or other means of access to a piece of property. An easement for ingress and egress is one that gives the dominant tenant access to the dominant tenement.

Inherit—In strict legal usage, to acquire property by intestate succession, but commonly used to mean acquiring property either by intestate succession or by will.

Injunction—A court order prohibiting anact or compelling anact to be done. SEE: Enjoin; Equitable Remedy.

Innocent Improver—SEE: Good Faith Improver.

Inquiry Notice—SEE: Notice, Inquiry.

Installment Sale—A sale in which less than 100% of the sales price is received in the year the sale occurs.

Instrument—A document that transfers title, creates a lien, or gives a right to payment, such as a deed, deed of trust, or contract. SEE: Negotiable Instrument.

Insurance Hazard—Insurance against damage to real property caused by fire, flood, or other disasters.

Insurance, Homeowner's—Insurance against damage to the real property and the homeowner's personal property.

Insurance, Mortgage—Insurance that protects a lender against losses resulting from the borrower's default.

Insurance, Title—Insurance that protects against losses resulting from undiscovered title defects.

Insurance, Title, Extended Coverage—Title insurance that covers problems that should be discovered by an inspection of the property (such as encroachments and adverse possession) in addition to the problems covered by standard coverage policies.

Insurance, Title, Standard Coverage—Title insurance that protects against latent title defects (such as forged deeds) and undiscovered recorded encumbrances, but does not protect against problems that would only be discovered by an inspection of the property.

Integration Clause—A provision in a contract document stating that the document contains the entire agreement between the parties.

Integrative Negotiation—Goals of the parties are mutual gain, win-win.

Intent, Objective—A person's manifested intention; what he or she appears to intend, whether or not that is what he or she actually intends.

Intent, Subjective—What a person actually intends, whether or not that is apparent to others.

Interest—1. A right or share in something (such as a piece of real estate). 2. A charge a borrower pays to a lender for the use of the lender's money. COMPARE: Principal.

Interest, Future—An interest in property that will or may become possessory at some point in the future. SEE: Remainder; Reversion.

Interest, Prepaid—Interest on a new loan that must be paid at the time of closing; covers the interest due for the first month of the loan term. Also called interim interest.

Interest, Undivided—A co-tenant's interest, giving him or her the right to possession of the whole property, rather than to a particular section of it. SEE: Unity of Possession.

Interpleader—A court action filed by someone who is holding funds that two or more people are claiming. The holder turns the funds over to the court; the court resolves the dispute and delivers the money to the party who's entitled to it.

Interrogatories—Written questions submitted to the opposing party in a lawsuit during discovery, which he or she is required to answer in writing and under oath.

Intestate—Dying without leaving a will.

Intestate Succession—Distribution of the property of a person who died intestate to his or her heirs.

Invalid—Not legally binding or legally effective; not valid.

Inverse Condemnation Action—A court action by a private landowner against the government, seeking compensation for damage to property that resulted from government action.

Inverted Pyramid—A way of visualizing ownership of real property; theoretically, a property owner owns all the earth, water, and air enclosed by a pyramid that has its tip at the center of the earth and extends up through the property boundaries out into the sky.

Investment Property—Unimproved property held as an investment because it is appreciating in value.

IRS—Internal Revenue Service.

Issue—A person's direct descendants: children, grandchildren, great-grandchildren, and so on.

J

Joinder Requirements—The rules requiring both husband and wife to consent to and sign agreements and conveyances concerning community property.

Joint Tenancy—SEE: Tenancy, Joint.

Joint Venture—Two or more individuals or companies joining together for one projects or a related series of projects, but not as an ongoing business. COMPARE: Partnership.

Judgment—1. A court's binding determination of the rights and duties of the parties in a lawsuit. 2. A court order requiring one party to pay the other damages.

Judgment Creditor—A person who is owed money as a result of a judgment in a lawsuit.

Judgment Debtor—A person who owes money as a result of a judgment in a lawsuit.

Judgment Lien—SEE: Lien, Judgment.

Judicial Foreclosure—SEE: Foreclosure, Judicial.

Judicial Review—When a court considers whether or not a statute or regulation is constitutional.

Jurisdiction—The extent of a particular court's authority; a court can't hear a case that's outside its jurisdiction.

Jurisdiction, Appellate—The authority to hear an appeal (as opposed to conducting a trial). COMPARE: Jurisdiction, Original.

Jurisdiction, Diversity—The federal courts' power to hear cases in which a citizen of one state sues a citizen of another state (or country).

Jurisdiction, General—When a court's jurisdiction is not limited to specific types of cases.

Jurisdiction, Original—The authority to conduct a trial (as opposed to hearing an appeal). COMPARE: Jurisdiction, Appellate.

Jurisdiction, Personal—A court's authority over a particular individual; usually obtained by service of process.

Jurisdiction, Subject Matter—The types of cases a particular court has authority to hear. COMPARE: Jurisdiction, General.

Just Compensation—SEE: Eminent Domain.

L

LAFCO—Local Agency Formation Commission.

Land Contract—SEE: Contract, Land.

Landlocked Property—A parcel of land without access to a road or highway.

Landlord—A landowner who has leased his or her property to another. Also called a lessor.

Latent Defects—Defects that are not visible or apparent; hidden defects.

Lateral Support—SEE: Support, Lateral.

Lawful Object—A legal purpose.

Lease—A conveyance of a leasehold estate from the fee owner to a tenant; a contract in which one party pays the other rent in exchange for the possession of real estate.

Lease, Fixed—A lease in which the rent is set at a fixed amount, and the landlord pays most or all of the operating expenses (such as taxes, insurance, and repair costs). Also called a flat lease, gross lease, or straight lease.

Lease, Graduated—A lease in which it is agreed that the rental payments will increase at intervals by an agreed amount or according to an agreed formula.

Lease, Ground—A lease of the land only, usually for a long term, to a tenant who intends to construct a building on the property.

Lease, Net—A lease requiring the tenant to pay all the costs of maintaining the property (such as taxes, insurance, and repairs), in addition to the rent paid to the landlord.

Lease, Percentage—A lease in which the rent is based on a percentage of the tenant's monthly or annual gross sales.

Leasehold Estate—An estate that gives the holder (the tenant) only a temporary right to possession, without title. Also called a less-than-freehold estate.

Legacy—A gift of personal property by will. Also called a bequest. SEE: Legatee.

Legal Description—A precise description of a piece of property; may be a lot and block description, a metes and bounds description, or a government surrey description.

Legatee—Someone who receives personal property (a legacy) under a will.

Legislature—The arm of a government that has primary responsibility for making new laws.

Lender, Institutional—A bank, savings and loan, or similar regulated lending institution; as opposed to an individual or private business that loans money.

Lessee—One who leases property from another; a tenant.

Lessor—One who leases property to another; a landlord.

Less-Than-Freehold Estate—A leasehold estate.

Levy—To impose a tax.

Liable—Legally responsible.

License—1. Official permission to do a particular thing that the law doesn't allow everyone to do. 2. Revocable, nonassignable permission to enter another person's land for a particular purpose. COMPARE: Easement.

License, Restricted—A real estate broker's or salesperson's license that includes limitations on the licensee's right to do business; usually issued after a suspended or revoked license has been reinstated.

Lien—A nonpossessory interest in property, giving the lienholder the right to foreclose if the owner doesn't pay a debt owed to the lienholder; a financial encumbrance on the owner's title.

Lien, Attachment—A lien intended to prevent transfer of the property pending the outcome of litigation.

Lien, Equitable—A lien arising as a matter of fairness, rather than by agreement or by operation of law.

Lien, General—A lien against all the property of a debtor, rather than a particular piece of his or her property.

Lien, Involuntary—A lien that arises by operation of law, without the consent of the property owner. Also called a statutory lien.

Lien, Judgment—A general lien against a judgment debtor's property, which the judgment creditor creates by recording an abstract of judgment in the county where the property is located.

Lien, Materialman's—Similar to a mechanic's lien, but based on a debt owed to someone who supplied materials (as opposed to labor) for a project.

Lien, Mechanic's—A specific lien claimed by someone who performed work on the property (construction, repairs, or improvements) and has not been paid. This term is often used in a general sense, referring to materialmen's liens as well as actual mechanics' liens.

Lien, Property Tax—A specific lien on property to secure payment of the property taxes.

Lien, Specific—A lien that attaches only to a particular piece of property (as opposed to a general lien, which attaches to all of the debtor's property).

Lien, Statutory—SEE: Lien, Involuntary.

Lien, Tax—A lien on property to secure the payment of taxes.

Lien, Voluntary—A lien placed against property with the consent of the owner; a deed of trust or a mortgage.

Lienholder, Junior—A secured creditor whose lien is lower in priority than another's lien.

Lien Priority—The order in which liens are paid off out of the proceeds of a foreclosure sale.

Life Estate—A freehold estate that lasts only as long as a specified person lives. That person is referred to as the measuring life.

Life-Estate Pur Autre Vie—A life estate "for the life of another," where the measuring life is someone other than the life tenant.

Life Tenant—Someone who owns a life estate; the person entitled to possession of the property during the measuring life.

Limited Liability Company—A business entity where each owner has the limited liability of a corporate shareholder and the tax advantages of a partner.

Limited Partnerships—SEE: Partnership, Limited.

Liquidated Damages—SEE: Damages, Liquidated.

Lis Pendens—A recorded notice stating that there is a lawsuit pending that may affect title to the defendant's real estate.

Listing—A written agency contract between a seller and a real estate broker, stipulating that the broker will be paid a commission for finding (or attempting to find) a buyer for the seller's property.

Listing, Exclusive Agency—A listing agreement that entitles the broker to a commission if anyone other than the seller finds a buyer for the property during the listing term.

Listing, Exclusive Right to Sell—A listing agreement that entitles the broker to a commission if anyone—including the seller—finds a buyer for the property during the listing term.

Listing, Net—A listing agreement in which the seller sets a net amount he or she is willing to accept for the property; if the actual selling price exceeds that amount, the broker is entitled to keep the excess as his or her commission.

Listing, Open—A non-exclusive listing, given by a seller to as many brokers as he or she chooses. If the property is sold, a broker is only entitled to a commission if he or she is the procuring cause of the sale.

Litigant—A party to a lawsuit; a plaintiff or defendant.

Litigation—A lawsuit (or lawsuits).

Loan, Carryback—When a seller extends credit to a buyer to finance the purchase of the property, accepting a deed of trust or mortgage instead of cash. Sometimes called a purchase money loan. SEE: Seller Financing.

Loan, Construction—A loan made to cover the cost of construction of a building, usually arranged so that the money is advanced in installments as the work progresses.

Loan, Conventional—Loan with only the property as security, without the government insuring (FHA) or guaranteeing (VA) the loan.

Loan, Guaranteed—A loan in which someone (the VA, for example) guarantees repayment; so that if the borrower defaults, the guarantor reimburses the lender for some or all of the loss.

Loan, Purchase Money—1. A loan the borrower uses to buy the security property (as opposed to a loan secured by property the borrower already owns). 2. A carryback loan.

Loan Assumption Fee—A fee a lender charges a buyer in return for granting the buyer permission to assume an existing loan.

Loan Fee—A loan origination fee.

Loan Origination Fee—A fee a lender charges a borrower in exchange for issuing a loan; also called a loan fee.

Lock-in Clause—A clause in a promissory note or land contract that prohibits prepayment before a specified date, or prohibits it altogether.

Loss, Capital—A loss taken on the sale of a capital asset. Real estate is considered a capital asset if it's income property, investment property, or property used in a trade or business.

Loss, Passive—A loss taken in connection with income property. SEE: Passive Income.

Lot—A parcel of land; especially, a parcel in subdivision.

Lot and Block Description—The type of legal description used for platted property. The description states only the property's lot number and block number in a particular subdivision. To find out the exact location of the property's boundaries you consult the plat map for that subdivision at the county recorder's office.

M

Mailbox Rule—An acceptance of a contract offer is effective as of the moment it is mailed, even though the other party hasn't received it yet.

Majority, Age of—The age at which a person gains legal capacity; in California, 18 years old. COMPARE: Minor.

Maker—A person who signs a promissory note; the borrower who promises to repay the debt.

Marketable Title—SEE: Title, Marketable Market Price-The price actually paid for property. Not the same as market value.

Market Value—SEE: Value, Fair Market.

Material Breach—SEE: Breach, Material.

Material Fact—An important fan; one that is likely to influence a decision.

Materialman—Someone who supplies materials for a construction project. SEE: Lien, Materialman's. COMPARE: Mechanic.

Maturity Date—The date by which a loan is supposed to be paid off in full.

Measuring Life—SEE: Life Estate.

Mechanic—Someone who performs work (construction, improvement, or repairs) on real property. SEE: Lien, Mechanic's. COMPARE: Materialman.

Mediation Clause—A clause in a contract requiring mediation in the even of a dispute.

Mediator—A person who helps the parties reach a voluntary agreement.

Meeting of Minds—SEE: Mutual Consent.

Menace—Threatening physical harm to a person, or threatening harm to a person's reputation, to force someone to sign a document. COMPARE: Duress; Duress, Economic.

Merger—Uniting two or more separate properties by transferring ownership of all of them to one person.

Meridian, Principal—In the government survey system, the main north-south line in a particular grid, used as the starting point in numbering the ranges. California has the Humboldt Meridian, the Mt. Diablo Meridian, and the San Bernardino Meridian.

Meridians, Guide—In the government survey system, lines running north-south (parallel to the principal meridian) at 24-mile intervals.

Metes—Measurements.

Metes and Bounds Description—A legal description that starts at an easily identifiable point of beginning, then describes the property's boundaries in terms of courses compass directions) and distances, ultimately returning to the point of beginning.

Mineral Rights—Rights to the minerals located beneath the surface of a piece of property.

Minor—A person who has not yet reached the age of majority; in California, a person under 18.

Minor, Emancipated—A minor who is or has been married, is on active duty in the armed forces, or has a declaration of emancipation from a court. An emancipated minor has legal capacity to contract.

Misrepresentation—A false or misleading statement. SEE: Fraud.

Mistake, Mutual—When both parties to a contract were mistaken about a fan or a law.

Mistake, Unilateral—When only one of the parties to a contract was mistaken about a fan or a law.

Mitigation—When the nonbreaching party takes action to minimize the losses resulting from a breach of contract.

MLS—Multiple Listing Service.

Monument—A visible marker (natural or artificial) used in a survey or a metes and bounds description to establish the boundaries of a piece of property.

Mortgage—An instrument that creates a voluntary lien on real property to secure repayment of a debt. The parties to a mortgage are the mortgagor (borrower) and mortgagee (lender). Unlike a deed of trust, a mortgage does not include a power of sale, so it can only be foreclosed judicially.

Mortgage, Satisfaction of—The document a mortgagee gives the mortgagor when the mortgage debt has been paid in full, acknowledging that the debt has been paid and the mortgage is no longer a lien against the property. COMPARE: Reconveyance.

Mortgagee—A lender who accepts a mortgage as security for repayment of the loan.

Mortgagor—A person who borrows money and gives a mortgage to the lender as security.

Multiple Listing Service—An organization of brokers who share their exclusive listings.

Mutual Consent—When all parties freely agree to the terms of a contract, without fraud, undue influence, duress, menace, or mistake. Mutual consent is achieved through offer and acceptance; it can be referred to as a "meeting of the minds."

Mutual Mistake—SEE: Mistake, Mutual.

N

NAR—National Association of Realtors.

Natural Person—A human being, an individual (as opposed to an artificial person, such as a corporation).

Negligence—Conduct that falls below the standard of care that a reasonable person would exercise under the circumstances; carelessness or recklessness. Negligence that causes harm is a tort. COMPARE: Strict Liability.

Negotiable Instrument—An instrument containing an unconditional promise to pay a certain sum of money, to order or to bearer, on demand or at a particular time. It can be a check, promissory note, bond, draft, or stock. SEE: Note, Promissory.

NEPA—National Environmental Policy Act.

Nonbinding Arbitration—The decision of the arbitrator is reviewable by the court.

Nonconforming Use—A property use that doesn't conform to current zoning requirements, but is allowed because the property was being used in that way before the present zoning ordinance was enacted.

Nonpossessory Interest—An interest in property that does not include the right to possess and occupy the property; an encumbrance, such as a lien or an easement.

Nonrecognition Provision—A provision in the income tax law that allows a taxpayer to defer recognition and taxation of a gain until a later time or later transaction.

Notary Public—An official whose primary function is to witness and certify the acknowledgment made by someone signing a legal document.

Note—SEE: Note, Promissory.

Note, Demand—A promissory note that is due when-ever the holder of the note demands payment.

Note, Installment—A promissory note that calls for regular payments of principal and interest until the debt is fully paid. The note is fully amortized if the regular payments are enough to pay it off in full by the maturity date. The note is partially amortized if the payments won't pay it off, so that a balloon payment is due at the end of the term.

Note, Promissory—A written promise to repay a debt; may or may not be negotiable.

Note, Straight—A promissory note that calls for regular payments of interest only, so that the entire principal amount is due in one lump sum at the end of the loan term.

Notice, Actual—Actual knowledge of a fact, as opposed to knowledge imputed by law.

Notice, Constructive—Knowledge of a fact imputed to a person by law. A person is held to have constructive notice of something when he or she should have known it, even if he or she didn't know it. Everyone has constructive notice of the contents of recorded documents, since everyone is expected to protect his or her interests by searching the public record.

Notice, Inquiry—When there were circumstances that should have alerted someone to a possible problem and caused him or her to investigate further, he or she may be held to have had notice of the problem.

Notice of Cessation—A notice recorded by a property owner when construction on the property has ceased, although the project hasn't been completed; it limits the period in which laborers and suppliers can file mechanics' liens.

Notice of Completion—A recorded notice that announces the completion of a construction project and limits the period in which mechanics' liens can be filed.

Notice of Default—A notice issued by a trustee, stating that the deed of trust borrower has breached the loan agreement.

Notice of Levy—A notice recorded by the receiver after a court has issued a decree of foreclosure.

Notice of Sale—A notice issued by a trustee (or by the receiver after a decree of foreclosure) setting the date for the foreclosure sale.

Notice to Quit—A notice to a tenant, demanding that he or she vacate the leased property.

Novation—1. When one party to a contract withdraws and a new party is substituted, relieving the withdrawing party of liability. 2. The substitution of a new obligation for an old one.

O

Objective Intent—SEE: Intent, Objective.

Offer—When one person proposes a contract to another; if the other person accepts the offer, a binding contract is formed. SEE: Acceptance.

Offeree—One to whom an offer is made.

Offeror—One who makes an offer.

Opinion, Judicial—A judge's written statement of a decision m a court case, outlining the fans of the case and explaining the legal basis for the decision.

Option—A contract giving one party the right to do something, without obligating him or her to do it.

Optionee—The person to whom an option is given.

Optionor—The person who gives an option.

Option to Purchase—An option giving the optionee the right to buy property owned by the optionor at an agreed price during a specified period.

Ordinance—A law passed by a local legislative body, such as a county board of supervisors or city council.

Ouster—One co-tenant refuses to allow occupancy by the other co-tenant.

Ownership—Title to property, dominion over property; the rights of possession and control.

Ownership in Severalty—Ownership by a single individual. COMPARE: Concurrent Ownership.

P

Panic Selling—SEE: Blockbusting.

Parcel—A lot or piece of real estate, particularly a specified part of a larger tract.

Parol Evidence—Evidence concerning negotiations or oral agreements that were not included in a written contract, often altering or contradicting the terms of the written contract.

Partition, Judicial—A court action to divide up a property among its co-owners, so that each owns part of it m severalty, or (if it's not practical to divide the property physically) each gets a share of the sale proceeds.

Partition, Voluntary—When co-owners agree to terminate their co-ownership, dividing up the property so that each owns a piece of it in severalty.

Partner, General—A partner who has the authority to manage and contract for a general or limited partnership, and who is personally liable for the partnership's debts.

Partner, Limited—A partner in a limited partnership who is primarily an investor and does not participate in the management of the business, and who is not personally liable for the partnership's debts.

Partnership—An association of two or more persons to carry on a business for profit. The law regards a partnership as a group of individuals, not as an entity separate from its owners. COMPARE: Corporation.

Partnership, General—A partnership in which each member has an equal right to manage the business and share in the profits, as well as an equal responsibility for the partnership's debts. All of the partners are general partners.

Partnership, Limited—A partnership made up of one or more general partners and one or more limited partners.

Partnership Property—All property that partners bring into their business at the outset or later acquire for their business; property owned as tenants in partnership. SEE: Tenancy in Partnership.

Passive Income—Income (rents) received from income property, as opposed to wages, salaries, interest, dividends, or royalties. An IRS term.

Patent—The instrument used to convey government land to a private individual.

Payee—The person entitled to payment under a promissory note.

Personal Property—Any property that is not real property; movable property not affixed to land. Also called chattels or personalty.

Personalty—Personal property.

Personal Use Property—Property that a taxpayer owns for his or her own use (or family use), as opposed to income property, investment property, dealer property, or property used in a trade or business.

Petition to Confirm—Filed with the court when a party refuses to comply with the arbitration award.

Petitioner—1. An appellant. 2. A plaintiff (in some actions, such as a dissolution of marriage).

Plaintiff—The party who starts a civil lawsuit; the one who sues.

Planned Unit Development (PUD)—A development (usually residential) with small, clustered lots designed to leave more open space than traditional subdivisions have.

Planning Commission—A local government agency responsible for preparing the community's general plan for development. SEE: General Plan.

Plat—A detailed survey map of a subdivision, recorded in the county where the land is located. Subdivided property is often called platted property.

Plat Book—A large book containing subdivision plats, kept at the county recorder's office.

Pledge—When a debtor transfers possession of property to the creditor as security for repayment of the debt. COMPARE: Hypothecate.

Point of Beginning (POB)—The starting point in a metes and bounds description; described by reference to a monument.

Points—SEE: Discount Point.

Police Power—The constitutional power of state and local governments to enact and enforce laws that protect the public's health, safety, morals, and general welfare.

Possession—1. The holding and enjoyment of property. 2. Actual physical occupation of real property.

Possessory Interest—An interest in property that includes the right to possess and occupy the property; not necessarily ownership.

Power of Attorney—An instrument authorizing one person (the attorney in fact) to an as another's agent, to the extent stated in the instrument.

Power of Sale Clause—A clause in a deed of trust giving the trustee the right to foreclose nonjudicially (sell the debtor's property without a court action) if the borrower defaults.

Power of Termination—The right to terminate a conditional fee estate if the state holder fails to meet the required conditions. Also called a right of reentry. SEE: Fee, Conditional.

Precedent—A published judicial opinion that serves as authority for determining a similar issue in a later case. SEE: Stare Decisis.

Precedent, Binding—A precedent that a particular court is required to follow.

Preemption—SEE: Right of Preemption.

Prepayment—Paying off part or all of a loan before payment is due.

Prepayment Penalty—A penalty charged to a borrower who prepays.

Prepayment Privilege—A provision in a promissory note allowing the borrower to prepay. COMPARE: Lock-in Clause.

Prescription—Acquiring an interest in real property (an easement) by using it openly and without the owner's permission for at least five years. In contrast to adverse possession, a prescriptive use does not have to be exclusive (the owner may be using the property, too), and the user does not acquire title to the property.

Principal—1. One who grants another person (an agent) authority to represent him or her in dealings with third parties. 2. One of the parties to a transaction (such as a buyer or seller), as opposed to those who are involved as agents or employees (such as a broker or escrow agent). 3. In regard to a loan, the amount originally borrowed, as opposed to the interest.

Principal Meridian—SEE: Meridian, Principal.

Principal Residence Property—Real property that is the owner's home, his or her main dwelling. A person can only have one principal residence at a time. The term is most often used in connection with the income tax laws.

Prior Appropriation—A system of allocating water rights. Under this system, a person who wants to use water from a particular lake or river is required to apply for an appropriation permit. It is not necessary to own property beside the body of water in order to acquire an appropriative right. COMPARE: Riparian Rights.

Probate—A judicial proceeding in which the validity of a will is established and the executor is authorized to distribute the estate property; or, when there is no valid will, in which an administrator is appointed to distribute the estate to the heirs.

Probate Court—A court that oversees the distribution of property under a will or by intestate succession.

Procedural Law—A law that establishes a legal procedure for enforcing a right. COMPARE: Substantive Law.

Procuring Cause—The real estate agent who is primarily responsible for bringing about a sale; for example, by introducing the buyer to the property, or by negotiating the agreement between the buyer and seller. SEE: Listing, Open.

Promisee—Someone who has been promised something; someone who is supposed to receive the benefit of a contractual promise.

Promisor—Someone who has made a contractual promise to another.

Promissory Estoppel—SEE: Estoppel, Promissory.

Proof, Burden of—The responsibility for proving or disproving a particular issue in a lawsuit. In most cases, the plaintiff has the burden of proof.

Proof, Standard of—The extent to which the plaintiff or prosecutor must have convinced the jury or judge in order to win the case. In most civil suits, a preponderance of the evidence must support the plaintiff's case. In a criminal action, the prosecutor's case must be proven beyond a reasonable doubt.

Property—1. The rights of ownership in a thing, such as the right to use, possess, transfer, or encumber the thing. 2. Something that is owned.

Property Held for Production of Income—SEE: Income Property.

Property Manager—A person hired by a property owner to administer, market, and maintain property, especially rental property.

Property Tax—SEE: Tax, Property.

Property Used in a Trade or Business—Property such as business sites and factories used in one's trade or business.

Proposition 13—The initiative measure passed in 1978 that led to major revisions in California's property tax laws.

Proration—The process of dividing something (especially a sum of money or an expense) proportionately.

Public Record—The official collection of legal documents that individuals have filed with the county recorder in order to make the information contained in them public. SEE: Constructive Notice; Recording.

Puffing—Superlative statements about a property that shouldn't be considered assertions of fact. "The best buy in town," or "It's a fabulous location" are examples of puffing.

Punitive Damages—SEE: Damages, Punitive.

Pur Autre Vie—SEE: Life Estate Pur Autre Vie.

Purchase and Sale Agreement—A contract in which a seller promises to convey title to real property to a buyer in exchange for the purchase price. Usually called a deposit receipt in California. SEE: Deposit Receipt.

Q

Question of Fact—in a lawsuit, a question about what actually occurred, as opposed to a question about the legal consequences of what occurred (a question of law).

Question of law—In a lawsuit, a question about what the law is on a particular point; what the legal rights and duties of the parties were.

Quiet Enjoyment—Use and possession of real property without interference from the previous owner, the lessor, or anyone else claiming title. SEE: Covenant of Quiet Enjoyment.

Quiet Title Action—A lawsuit to establish who has title to a piece of property, or to remove a cloud on the title.

Quitclaim Deed—SEE: Deed, Quitclaim.

R

Race/Notice Rule—When the same property has been sold to two different buyers, if the second buyer records his or her deed before the first buyer, the second buyer has good title to the property-as long as he or she did not have notice of the first buyer's interest.

Range—In the government survey system, a strip of land six miles wide, running north and south.

Range Lines—In the government surrey system, the north-south lines located six miles apart.

Ratification—The later confirmation or approval of anact that was not authorized when it was performed.

Ready, Willing, and Able—Making an offer to purchase on terms acceptable to the seller, and having the financial ability to complete the purchase.

Real Estate Contract—1. A purchase and sale agreement. 2. A land contract. 3. Any contract having to do with real property.

Real Estate Investment Trust (REIT)—A real estate investment business with at least 100 investors, organized as a trust.

Realization—The point at which a gain or profit is actually obtained; for example, the value of a piece of property has been increasing steadily, but the owner's profit won't be realized until she sells the property.

Real Property—Land and everything attached to or appurtenant to it. COMPARE: Personal Property.

Realtor—A broker or salesperson who is an active member of a state or local real estate board that is affiliated with the National Association of Realtors®.

Realty—Real property.

Receiver—A person appointed by a court to manage and look after property or funds involved in litigation.

Recognition—The point at which a gain is taxed (which is ordinarily in the year it was realized, but may be later if a nonrecognition provision applies).

Reconsideration—A request by The Department of Real Estate or the respondent made before the effective day of the hearing decision.

Reconveyance—An instrument that releases the security property from the lien created by a deed of trust; a trustee is required to record one when the borrower has paid off the debt.

Reconveyance, Partial—A reconveyance that releases some parcels from the lien of a blanket deed of trust, usually recorded when the borrower has paid off a certain amount of the debt.

Recording—Filing a document at the county recorder's office, so that it will be placed in the public record.

Recording Number—The numbers stamped on documents when they're recorded, used to identify and locate the documents in the public record. (Each page is stamped with a consecutive number, but an entire document is often referred to by the number on the first page.)

Rectangular Survey—SEE: Government Survey.

Redemption—1. When a defaulting borrower prevents foreclosure by paying the full amount of the debt, plus costs. 2. When a mortgagor regains the property after foreclosure by paying whatever the foreclosure sale purchaser paid for it, plus interest and expenses. COMPARE: Reinstatement.

Redemption, Equitable Right of—The right of a borrower to redeem property prior to the foreclosure sale.

Redemption, Statutory Right of—The right of a mortgagor to redeem property after a foreclosure sale.

Redlining—When a lender refuses to make loans secured by property in a certain neighborhood because of the racial or ethnic composition of the neighborhood.

Reformation—A legal action to correct a mistake, such as a typographical error, in a deed or other document. The court will order the execution of a correction deed.

Regulation—1. A rule adopted by an administrative agency. 2. Any governmental order having the force of law.

Regulation Z—The Federal Reserve Board's regulation that implements the Truth in Lending Act.

Reinstatement—Preventing foreclosure by curing the default. COMPARE: Redemption.

Relation Back—A legal doctrine that allows a court to rule that a party acquired title at some point before he or she actually received the deed. Applied in cases involving escrow or the exercise of an option to purchase.

Release—1. To give up a legal right. 2. A document in which a legal right is given up.

Relation—When a body of water gradually recedes, exposing land that was previously under water. Also called dereliction.

Remainder—A future interest that becomes possessory when a life estate terminates, and that is held by someone other than the grantor of the life estate; as opposed to a reversion, which is a future interest held by the grantor.

Remainderman—The person who has an estate in remainder.

Remand—When an appellate court orders further trial proceedings in a case, sending the case back to the court that originally tried it, or to a different trial court.

Rent—Compensation paid by a tenant to the landlord in exchange for the possession and use of the property.

Rent Control—Government restrictions on how much rent a landlord can charge.

Renunciation—When someone who has been granted something or has accepted something later gives it up or rejects it; as when an agent withdraws from the agency relationship. COMPARE: Revocation.

Rescission—When a contract is terminated and each party gives anything acquired under the contract back to the other party. The verb form is rescind.) COMPARE: Cancellation.

Reservation—A right retained by a grantor when conveying property; for example, mineral rights, an easement, or a life estate can be reserved in the deed.

Reserve Account—SEE: Impound Account.

Res Judicata—The legal doctrine holding that once a lawsuit between two parties has been tried and a final judgment has been issued, neither one can sue the other over the same dispute again.

RESPA—Real Estate Settlement Procedures Act.

Respondent—1. An appellee. 2. In a DRE disciplinary hearing, the licensee accused of misconduct. 3. In a dissolution of marriage, the party who did not file the action.

Restitution—Restoring something to a person that he or she was unjustly deprived of.

Restriction—A limitation on the use of real property.

Restriction, Deed—A restrictive covenant in a deed.

Restriction, Private—A restriction imposed on property by a previous owner, or the subdivision developer; a restriction covenant or a condition in a deed.

Restriction, Public—A law or regulation limiting or regulating the use of real property.

Restrictive Covenant—A promise to do or not do an act relating to real property; usually an owner's promise to not use property in a particular way. May or may not run with the land.

Restricted License—A license with restrictions attached.

Revenue Stamps—SEE: Tax, Documentary Transfer.

Reverse—To overturn a lower court's decision on appeal, ruling in favor of the appellant. COMPARE: Affirm.

Reversion—A future interest that becomes possessory when a temporary estate (such as a life estate) terminates, and that is held by the grantor (or his or her successors in interest). COMPARE: Remainder.

Revocation—When someone who granted or offered something withdraws it; as when a principal withdraws the authority granted to the agent, an offeror withdraws the offer, or the Real Estate Commissioner cancels a real estate agent's license. COMPARE: Renunciation.

Rezone—An amendment to a zoning ordinance, usually changing the uses allowed in a particular zone. Requires the approval of the local legislative body. Also called a zoning amendment. COMPARE: Zoning, Spot.

Right of First Refusal—A right of reemption.

Right of Preemption—A right to have the first chance to buy or lease property if the owner decides to put it up for sale or make it available. Also called a right of first refusal. COMPARE: Option.

Right of Survivorship—A characteristic of joint tenancy; surviving joint tenants automatically acquire a deceased joint tenant's interest in the property.

Right of Way—An easement that gives the holder the right to cross another person's land.

Riparian Rights—The water rights of a landowner whose property is adjacent to or crossed by a body of water. COMPARE: Prior Appropriation.

Rollover—When a taxpayer sells his or her principal residence and reinvests the sale proceeds in another home, deferring recognition of the gain on the sale.

Rule of Capture—A legal principle that grants a landowner the right to all oil and gas produced from wells on his or her land, even if it migrated from underneath land belonging to someone else.

Running with the Land—Binding or benefiting the successive owners of a piece of property, rather than terminating when a particular owner transfers his or her interest. Usually said in reference to an easement or a restrictive covenant.

S

Safety Clause—SEE: Extender Clause.

Satisfaction of Mortgage—SEE: Mortgage, Satisfaction of.

Secondary Marketing—Buying and selling existing mortgage and trust deed loans. The primary market is the one in which lenders loan money to borrowers; the secondary market is the one in which the lenders sell their loans to the large secondary marketing agencies (FNMA, FHLMC, and GNMA) or to other investors.

Secret Profit—A financial benefit that an agent takes from a transaction without informing the principal; usually the result of self-dealing.

Section—In the government survey system, a section is one mile square and contains 640 acres. There are 36 sections in a township.

Security Agreement—An instrument that creates a voluntary lien on property to secure repayment of a loan. For debts secured by real property, a security agreement is either a deed of trust or a mortgage.

Security Deposit—Money a tenant gives a landlord at the beginning of the tenancy to ensure that the tenant will comply with the terms of the lease. The landlord may retain all or part of the deposit to cover unpaid rent or repair costs at the end of the tenancy.

Security Interest—The interest a creditor may acquire in the debtor's property to ensure that the debt will be paid.

Seisin—The possession of a freehold estate; ownership. Also spelled seizen or seizin.

Self-Dealing—When a real estate agent buys the principal's property him or herself (or sells it to a relative, friend, or associate, or to a business he or she has an interest in), without disclosing that fan to the principal, and in violation of his or her fiduciary duties to the principal.

Self-Executing Arbitration Clause—The parties do not need to use the court to compel arbitration.

Seller Financing—When a seller extends credit to a buyer to finance the purchase of the property; as opposed to having the buyer obtain a loan from a third party, such as an institutional lender. SEE: Loan, Carryback.

Separate Property—Property owned by a married person that is not community property; includes property acquired before marriage, or by gift or inheritance after marriage.

Service of Process—Delivery of a legal document (especially a summons) to a person in accordance with the rules prescribed by statute, so that he or she is held to have received it (whether or not he or she actually did).

Setback Requirements—Provisions in a zoning ordinance that do not allow structures to be built within a certain distance of the property line.

Settlement—1. An agreement between the parties to a civil lawsuit, in which the plaintiff agrees to drop the suit in exchange for money or the defendant's promise to do or refrain from doing something. 2. Closing.

Settlement Statement—A document that presents a final, detailed accounting for a real estate transaction, listing each party's debits and credits and the amount each will receive or be required to pay at closing. Also called a closing statement.

Severable—When one provision in a law or a contract can be held unenforceable, without making the entire law or contract unenforceable.

Severalty—SEE: Ownership in Severalty.

Severance—Termination of a joint tenancy, turning it into a tenancy in common.

Sheriff's Sale—A foreclosure sale held after a judicial foreclosure. Sometimes called an execution sale.

Short Platting—Subdividing a parcel of land into two, three, or four lots.

Side Yard—The area between a building and one of the side boundaries of the lot on which it's located.

Special Assessment—A tax levied only against the properties that have benefited from a public improvement (such as a sewer or a street light), to cover the cost of the improvement; creates a special assessment lien.

Special Exception Permit—SEE: Conditional Use Permit.

Specific Performance—A legal remedy for breach of contract in which a court orders the breaching party to actually perform the contract as agreed, rather than simply paying money damages.

Spot Zoning—SEE: Zoning, Spot.

Standard of Proof—SEE: Proof, Standard of.

Stare Decisis—The legal doctrine holding that in resolving a lawsuit, a court should try to follow precedents decided in the same jurisdiction, to make the law evenhanded and predictable.

State Action—In constitutional law, action by a government (federal, state, or local) rather than by a private party.

Statement of Issues—A written allegation by the commissioner identifying the issues and listing the rules violated, used in a non-property right hearing.

Statute—A law enacted by a state legislature or the U.S. Congress. SEE: Statutory Law. COMPARE: Ordinance.

Statute of Frauds—A law that requires certain types of contracts to be in writing and signed in order to be enforceable.

Statute of Limitations—A law requiring a particular type of lawsuit to be filed within a specified time after the event giving rise to the suit occurred.

Statutory Construction—When a judge interprets and applies a statute in the course of resolving a lawsuit.

Statutory Law—Laws adopted by a legislative body (Congress, a state legislature, or a county or city council), as opposed to constitutional law, case law, or administrative regulations.

Steering—Channeling prospective buyers or tenants to particular neighborhoods based on their race, religion, national origin, or ancestry.

Stock Cooperative—SEE: Cooperative.

Strict Liability—When someone is held legally responsible for an injury to another, even though he or she did not an negligently. COMPARE: Negligence.

Strike List—An arbitration service sends a list of arbitrators to each party and the parties strike the names that are unacceptable.

Subagent—A person that an agent has delegated authority to, so that the subagent can assist in carrying out the principal's orders.

Subdivision—1. A piece of land divided into two or more parcels. 2. A residential development.

Subdivision Plat—SEE: Plat.

Subdivision Regulations—State and local laws that must be complied with before land can be subdivided.

Subjacent Support—SEE: Support, Subjacent.

Subject to—When a purchaser takes property subject to a trust deed or ortgage, he or she is not personally liable for paying off the loan; in case of default, however, the property can still be foreclosed on. COMPARE: Assumption.

Sublease—When a tenant grants someone else the right to possession of the leased property for part of the remainder of the lease term; as opposed to an assignment, where the tenant gives up possession for the entire remainder of the lease term.

Subordination Clause—A provision in a mortgage or deed of trust that permits a later mortgage or deed of trust to have higher lien priority than the one containing the clause.

Submission Agreement—An agreement by the parties to submit a dispute to arbitration.

Subpoena—A document ordering a person to appear at a deposition or court proceeding to testify or produce documentary or physical evidence. An order requiring a witness to attend.

Subpoena Duces Tecum—An order to produce books, records or other document.

Substantial Performance—When a promisor doesn't perform all of his or her contractual obligations, but does enough so that the promisee is required to fulfill his or her side of the bargain. COMPARE: Breach, Material.

Substantive Law—A law that establishes a right or a duty. COMPARE: Procedural Law.

Successor in Interest—A person who has acquired property previously held by someone else; for example, a buyer or an heir.

Summons—A document informing a defendant that a lawsuit has been filed against him or her, and ordering the defendant to file an answer to the plaintiff's complaint with the court.

Support, Lateral—The support that a piece of land receives from the land adjacent to it.

Support, Subjacent—The support that the surface of a piece of land receives from the land beneath it.

Support Rights—The right to have one's and supported by the land adjacent to it and beneath it.

Surrender—Giving up an estate (such as a life estate or leasehold) before it has expired.

Survey—The process of precisely measuring the boundaries and determining the area of a parcel of land.

Survivorship—SEE: Right of Survivorship.

Suspension—When a real estate agent's license is temporarily withdrawn.

Suspension, Summary—License suspension before a hearing has been held.

Syndicate—An association formed to operate an investment business. A syndicate is not a recognized legal entity; it can be organized as a corporation, partnership, or trust.

T

Tacking—When successive periods of use or possession by more than one person are added together to make up the five years required for prescription or adverse possession.

Taking—When the government acquires private property for public use by condemnation, it's called "a taking." The term is also used in inverse condemnation lawsuits, when a government action has made private property useless.

Tax, Documentary Transfer—A tax on the transfer of real property; revenue stamps,

indicating the tax has been paid, usually must be attached to a deed before it can be recorded.

Tax, General Real Estate—Property taxes.

Tax, Property—An annual ad valorem tax levied on real and personal property.

Tax Deed—SEE: Deed, Tax.

Tax Sale—Sale of property after foreclosure of a tax lien.

Tenancy—Lawful possession of realproperty; an estate.

Tenancy, Joint—A form of concurrent ownership in which the co-owners have equal undivided interests and the right of survivorship. The right of survivorship means that when one joint tenant dies, the surviving tenants automatically acquire his or her interest in the property. SEE: Unities, Four. COMPARE: Tenancy in Common.

Tenancy, Periodic—A leasehold estate that continues for successive periods of equal length (such as from week to week or month to month), until terminated by proper notice from either party. Also called a month-to-month (or week-to-week, etc.) tenancy. COMPARE: Estate for Years.

Tenancy, Term—SEE: Estate for Years.

Tenancy at Will—When a tenant is in possession with the owner's permission, but there's no definite lease term; as when a landlord allows a holdover tenant to remain on the premises until another tenant is found.

Tenancy by the Entirety—A form of co-ownership of property by husband and wife (in states that don't use a community property system).

Tenancy in Common—A form of concurrent ownership in which two or more persons each have an undivided interest in the entire property (unity of possession), but no right of survivorship. COMPARE: Tenancy, Joint.

Tenancy in Partnership—The form of concurrent ownership in which general partners own partnership property, whether or not title to the property is in the partnership's name. Each partner has an equal undivided interest, but no right to transfer the interest to someone outside the partnership.

Tenant—Someone in lawful possession of real property; especially, someone who has leased property from the owner.

Tenant at Sufferance—A tenant who holds over beyond the expiration of the tenancy without the permission of the landlord.

Tenant, Dominant—A person who has easement rights on another's property; either the owner of a dominant tenement, or someone who has an easement in gross.

Tenant, Holdover—A lessee who remains in possession of the property after the lease term has expired.

Tenant, Life—Someone who owns a life estate.

Tenant, Servient—The owner of a servient tenement—that is, someone whose property is burdened by an easement.

Tender—An unconditional offer by one of parties to a contract to perform his or her part of the agreement; made when the offeror believes the other party is breaching, it establishes the offeror's right to sue if the other party doesn't accept it. Also called a tender offer.

Tenement, Dominant—Property that receives the benefit of an appurtenant easement.

Tenement, Servient—Property burdened by an easement. In other words, the owner of the servient tenement (the servient tenant) must allow someone who has an easement (the dominant tenant) to use the property.

Tenements—Everything of a permanent nature associated with a piece of land and ordinarily transferred with the land. Tenements are both tangible (buildings, for example) and intangible (air rights, for example).

Term—A prescribed period of time; especially, the length of time a borrower has in which to pay off a loan, or the duration of a lease.

Testament—SEE: Will.

Testate—Refers to someone who has died and left a will. COMPARE: Intestate.

Testator—A man who makes a will.

Testatrix—A woman who makes a will.

Tester—A person working with a fair housing organization, who pretends to be interested in buying or renting property from someone suspected of unlawful discrimination.

Time is of the Essence—A clause in a contract that means performance on the exact dates specified is an essential element of the contract; failure to perform on time is a material breach.

Timeshare Estate—An ownership interest that gives the owner a right to possession of the property only for a specific, limited period each year.

Timeshare Use—A license that entitles the holder to possession of the property only for a specific, limited period each year.

Title—Lawful ownership of real property. Also, the deed or other document that is evidence of that ownership.

Title, After-Acquired—Title acquired by a grantor after he or she attempted to convey property he or she didn't own.

Title, Chain of—The chain of deeds (and other documents) transferring title to a piece of property from one owner to the next, as disclosed in the public record.

Title, Clear—Title that is free of encumbrances or defects: marketable title.

Title, Equitable—The vendee's interest in property under a land contract. Also called an equitable interest. COMPARE: Title, Legal.

Title, Legal—The vendor's interest in property under a land contract. COMPARE: Title, Equitable.

Title, Marketable—Title free and clear of objectionable liens, encumbrances, or defects, so that a reasonably prudent person with full knowledge of the facts would not hesitate to purchase the property.

Title Company—A title insurance company.

Title Insurance—SEE: Insurance, Title

Title Plant—A duplicate (usually microfilmed) of a county's public record, maintained by a title company at its offices for use in title searches.

Title Report—A report issued by a title company, disclosing the condition of the title to a specific piece of property. A preliminary title report is one issued early on in a transaction, before the actual title insurance policy is issued.

Title Search—An inspection of the public record to determine all rights and encumbrances affecting title to a piece of property.

Tort—A breach of a duty imposed by law (as opposed to a duty voluntarily taken on in a contract) that causes harm to another person, giving the injured person the right to sue the one who breached the duty. Also called a civil wrong (in contrast to a criminal wrong, a crime). SEE: Negligence; Strict Liability.

Township—In the government survey system, a parcel of land 6 miles square, containing 36 sections; the intersection of a range and a township tier.

Township Lines—Lines running east-west, spaced six miles apart, in the government survey system.

Township Tier—In the government survey system, a strip of land running east-west, six miles wide and bounded on the north and south by township lines.

Tract—1. A piece of land of undefined size. 2. In the government survey system, an area made up of 16 townships; 24 miles on each side.

Tract Index—An index of the public record, grouping together all recorded documents that carry a particular legal description. COMPARE: Grantor/grantee Indexes.

Trade Fixtures—Articles of personal property annexed to real property by a tenant for use in his or her trade or business.

Transmutation Agreement—A contract in which co-owners agree to change their form of ownership; usually one in which husband and wife agree to change community property to separate property.

Trespass—An unlawful physical invasion of property owned by another.

Trial—The fundamental court proceeding in a lawsuit, in which a judge (and in some cases, a jury) hears evidence presented by both parties and issues a judgment. COMPARE: Appeal.

Trier of Fact—The one who decides questions of fact in a lawsuit. In a jury trial, it's the jury; in a non-jury trial, it's the judge. (Questions of law are always decided by the judge.)

Trust—A legal arrangement in which title to property (or funds) is vested in one or more trustees, who manage the property on behalf of the trust's beneficiaries, in accordance with instructions set forth in the document establishing the trust.

Trust Account—A bank account, separate from a real estate broker's personal and business accounts, used to segregate trust funds from the broker's own funds.

Trust Deed—SEE: Deed of Trust.

Trustee—1. A person appointed to manage a trust on behalf of the beneficiaries. 2. A neutral third party appointed in a deed of trust to handle the non-judicial foreclosure process in case of default.

Trustee's Sale—A non-judicial foreclosure sale under a deed of trust.

Trust Funds—Money or things of value received by an agent, not belonging to the agent but being held for the benefit of others.

Trustor—The borrower on a deed of trust. Also called the grantor.

U

Unconstitutional—Violating a provision of the U.S. Constitution or a state constitution.

Undivided Interest—SEE: Interest, Undivided.

Undue Influence—Exerting excessive pressure on someone so as to overpower the person's free will and prevent him or her from making a rational or prudent decision; often involves abusing a relationship of trust.

Uniform Settlement Statement—A closing statement required for any transaction involving a loan that's subject to the Real Estate Settlement Procedures An (RESPA).

Unilateral Contract—SEE: Contract, Unilateral.

Unilateral Mistake—SEE: Mistake, Unilateral.

Unincorporated Association—The legal designation for an organization that has recorded a statement listing the names of those who are authorized to execute conveyances on its behalf, which makes it possible for title to be held in the association's name.

Unities, Four—The unities of time, title, interest, and possession, required for a joint tenancy.

Unity of Interest—When each co-owner has an equal interest (equal share of ownership) in a piece of property.

Unity of Possession—When each co-owner is equally entitled to possession of the entire property, because the ownership interests are undivided.

Unity of Time—When each co-owner acquired title at the same time.

Unity of Title—When each co-owner acquired title through the same instrument (deed, will, or court order).

Unjust Enrichment—An undeserved benefit.

Unlawful Detainer—A summary legal action to regain possession of real property; especially, a suit filed by a landlord to evict a defaulting tenant.

Untenantable—Not fit for occupancy.

Use Variance—SEE: Variance, Use.

Usury—Charging an interest rate that exceeds legal limits.

V

VA—Veteran's Administration.

Valid—The legal classification of a contract that is binding and enforceable in a court of law.

Valuable Consideration—SEE: Consideration.

Valuation—SEE: Appraisal.

Value—The amount of goods or services offered in the marketplace in exchange for a given thing.

Value, Assessed—The value placed on property by the taxing authority (the county assessor, for example) for the purposes of taxation.

Value, Base—Under Proposition 13, the initial assessed value of a piece of property, used in calculating a particular owner's property taxes; this figure is later adjusted to reflect inflation and improvements.

Value, Fair Market—The amount of money that a piece of property would bring if placed on the open market for a reasonable period of time, with a buyer willing (but not forced) to buy, and a seller willing (but not forced) to sell, if both buyer and seller were fully informed as to the possible use of the property. Also called market value.

Value, Full Cash—Under Proposition 13, the assessed value of newly transferred property; it's the purchase price of the property, unless it can be shown that the property wouldn't have been sold at that price on the open market.

Variable Interest Rate—An interest rate on a mortgage or deed of trust that is adjusted periodically, usually to reflect changes in a particular economic index. A loan with a variable interest rate is often called an adjustable-rate mortgage or ARM.

Variance—A permit obtained from the local zoning authority allowing the holder to use property or build a structure in a way that violates the zoning ordinance. COMPARE: Nonconforming Use, Conditional Use Permit.

Variance, Use—A variance that permits an owner to use the property in a way that isn't ordinarily allowed in that zone; for example, a commercial use in a residential zone.

Vendee—A buyer or purchaser; particularly, someone buying property under a land contract.

Vendor—A seller; particularly, someone selling property by means of a land contract.

Vested—When a person has a present, fixed right or interest in property, even though he or she may not have the right to possession until sometime in the future. For example, a remainderman's interest in property vests when it is granted, not when the life estate ends.

Veto—When the president or governor formally rejects a bill that Congress or the legislature has passed. The bill won't become law unless the legislative body votes to override the veto.

Void—Having no legal force or effect.

Voidable—SEE: Contract, Voidable.

W

Waiver—The voluntary relinquishment or surrender of a right.

Warranty, Implied—In the sale of property, a guarantee created by operation of law, whether or not the seller intended to offer it.

Warranty of Habitability—SEE: Implied Warranty of Habitability.

Waste—Destruction, damage, or material alteration of property by someone in possession who holds less than a fee estate (such as a life tenant or lessee), or by a co-tenant.

Water Rights—SEE: Prior Appropriation; Riparian Rights

Wild Document—SEE: Deed, Wild.

Will—A person's stipulation regarding how his or her estate should be disposed of after he or she dies. Also called a testament.

Will, Formal—A written, witnessed will.

Will, Holographic—A will written entirely in the testator or testatrix's handwriting, which may be valid even if it was not witnessed.

Will, Nuncupative-An oral will made on the testator or testatrix's deathbed. No longer recognized in California.

Will, Statutory—A formal will prepared on the statutory will form provided in California's Probate Code.

Writ of Execution—A court order directing a public officer (usually the sheriff) to seize and sell property to satisfy a debt.

Writ of Possession—A court order issued after an unlawful detainer action, informing a tenant that he or she must vacate the landlord's property within a specified period or be forcibly removed by the sheriff.

Z

Zoning—Government regulation of the uses of property within specified areas. SEE: Conditional Use Permit; Nonconforming Use; Rezone; Variance.

Zoning, Exclusionary—A zoning law that has the effect of preventing certain groups (such as minorities or poor people) from living in a community.

Zoning, Spot—An illegal rezone that favors (or restricts) a particular property owner (or a small group of owners) without ustification.

Zoning Amendment—SEE: Rezone.

Index

Index

Unity of interest, 117
Unity of possession, 113-114, 117
Unity of time, 117
Unity of title, 117
Universal agent, 151
Unlawful detainer, 507
  assistants, 515-516
Unreasonable restraint on alienation, 397
Unreasonable searches and seizures, 10
Unruh Civil Rights Act, 469-471
Untenantable property, 500
U.S. Constitution, 9
Use variances. 433

V

Valid contracts, 209
Value, duty to inform seller of, 180
Variable interest rates, 387
Variances, 433-434
Vendee/vendor, 410
Void and voidable contracts, 208-209

W

Waiver of a condition, 230
Warranty deeds, 312
Warranty of habitability, 501
Waste, 77,114, 391
Water rights, 63-65
  appropriative, 63
  navigable, 63
  non-navigable, 65
  riparian, 63
Wild documents, 335
Wills, 314-318
  and community property, 129-131,317
  no will-see Intestate succession
Witnesses, expert or fact, 36
Witnesses to a will, 315, 316
Words of conveyance, 306

Writ of possession, 507
Writing requirement. See Statute of frauds
Written listing agreement, 151

Z

Zoning, 425-437, 479-480
  by citizens' initiative, 429
  conditional use permit, 434
  constitutionality of, 426-427
  disparate impact, 479-480
  enforcement of, 436-437
  exclusionary, 437, 479-480
  general plan, 428
  historical background, 425-426
  land use planning, 427-428
  nonconforming uses, 431-432
  planning commission, 428
  police power, 426
  and planned unit developments, 441
  rezoning and spot zoning, 434-436
  variances, 433-434

Order Department

SOMETIMES OUR TEXTBOOKS ARE HARD TO FIND!

If your bookstore does not carry our textbooks, send us a check or money order and we'll mail them to you with our 30-day money back guarantee.

Other great books from Educational Textbook Company:

California Real Estate Principles, 9th ed., by Huber......................... $50.00 _____
How To Pass The Real Estate Exam (850 Exam Questions), by Huber... $50.00 _____
California Real Estate Law, by Huber & Pivar .... $50.00 _____
Financing California Real Estate, by Huber................................... $50.00 _____
Real Estate Economics, by Huber & Pivar................................... $50.00 _____
Real Estate Appraisal, by Huber & Pivar..................................... $50.00 _____
Mortgage Loan Brokering, by Huber & Pivar................................ $50.00 _____
Property Management, by Huber & Pivar..................................... $50.00 _____
Escrow I: An Introduction, by Huber.. $50.00 _____
California Real Estate Practice, by Huber & Bond......................... $50.00 _____
California Business Law, by Huber, Owens, & Tyler....................... $65.00 _____
Six-Hour Survey, Continuing Education, by Huber........................ $15.00 _____

Subtotal _____
Add shipping and handling @ $5.00 per book _____
Add California sales tax @ 8.25% _____
TOTAL _____

Allow 2-3 weeks for delivery

Name: _____
Address: _____
City, State, Zip: _____
Phone: _____

Check or money order:
Educational Textbook Company, P.O. Box 3597, Covina, CA 91722

For cheaper prices and faster results, order by credit card direct from
Glendale Community College:
1-818-240-1000 ext. 3024